Fourth Edition

ESSENTIALS OF MANAGEMENT

ANDREW J. DuBRIN
Professor of Management
College of Business
Rochester Institute of Technology

SOUTH-WESTERN College Publishing

An International Thomson Publishing Company

Editor-in-Chief:	Valerie A. Ashton
Acquisitions Editor:	Randy G. Haubner
Developmental Editor:	Alice C. Denny
Production Editor:	Judith O'Neill
Production:	WordCrafters Editorial Services, Inc.
Cover and Internal Designer:	Craig LaGesse Ramsdell
Cover Illustration:	Copyright 1996 by John Weber
Photo Editor:	Jennifer Mayhall
Photo Research:	Alix Roughen
Manufacturing Coordinator:	Sue Disselkamp
Marketing Manager:	Stephen E. Momper

1 2 3 4 5 6 7 C5 2 1 0 9 8 7 6

Printed in the United States of America

Library of Congress Cataloging-in-Publication Data

DuBrin, Andrew J.
    Essentials of management / Andrew J. DuBrin. — 4th ed.
      p.   cm.
    Includes bibliographical references and index.
    ISBN 0–538–85546–0
    1. Management.   I. Title.
    HD31.D793   1996   96–18537
    658—dc20   CIP

I(T)P
International Thomson Publishing

South-Western College Publishing is an ITP Company. The ITP trademark is used under license.

Today's present and future managers and professionals place heavy demands on their schools and instructors to provide usable knowledge. These demands will grow as the business environment becomes increasingly competitive. The skill and knowledge requirements of managerial work continue to increase as organizations become more selective about who is chosen for managerial positions. Higher levels of knowledge and skills are also required to retain one's managerial position. *Essentials of Management* is an attempt to meet this demand for usable knowledge. The text provides comprehensive coverage of a select number of relevant topics relating to the practice of management.

Essentials of Management is a blend of current and traditional topics organized around the functional, or process, approach to

PREFACE

the study of management. Although other approaches have been developed, the functional approach remains a general framework, flexible enough to incorporate many viewpoints about management.

This book is written for newcomers to the field of management and for experienced managers seeking updated information and a review of the fundamentals. The book is also written for the many professionals and technical persons who work closely with managers and who take their turn at performing some management work. An example would be the member of a cross-functional team who is expected to have the perspective of a general manager.

Based on extensive research about curriculum needs, *Essentials of Management* is designed to be used in introductory management courses and supervision courses offered in educational and work settings. Earlier editions of the text were used in the study of management in colleges and universities, as well as in career schools in such diverse programs as hospitality and tourism management. The book can also be used as a basic resource for management courses that rely more heavily on lecture notes, handouts, and videos rather than an encyclopedia-like text.

ASSUMPTIONS UNDERLYING THE BOOK

The approach to synthesizing knowledge for this book is based on the following five assumptions:

1. A strong demand exists for practical and valid information about solutions to managerial problems. The information found in this text reflects the author's orientation toward translating research findings, theory, and experience into a form useful to both the student and the practitioner.
2. Managers and professionals need both interpersonal and analytical skills to meet their day-to-day responsibilities. Although this book concentrates on the management of people, it also provides ample information about such topics as decision making, job design, organization structure, and effective inventory management.
3. The study of management should emphasize a diversity of work settings including large, medium, and small as well as profit and not-for-profit organizations. Many students of management, for example, intend to become small-

business owners. Examples and cases in this book therefore reflect diverse work settings, including retail and service firms.

4. Effective managers and professionals are heavily concerned with productivity, quality, and teamwork. These three factors are therefore noted frequently throughout the text. In addition, separate chapters on total quality and teamwork are included.

5. Introductory management textbooks have become unrealistically comprehensive. Many introductory texts today are over 800 pages long. Such texts overwhelm the student who attempts to assimilate this knowledge in a single quarter or semester. Although the information may be valuable, students learn more when they approach a surmountable task. Toward this end, I have developed a text that I think represents the basis for a realistically sized introduction to the study of management.

FRAMEWORK OF THE BOOK

The new edition of *Essentials of Management* is published in both a full textbook and a modular format. Each chapter is available as a separate module, which allows for ultimate flexibility in course content. Modules may be ordered through your bookstore in any combination and taught in your preferred sequence. Modules taken from *Essentials of Management* may be also combined with modules from *Organizational Behavior: An Applied Perspective* by Andrew DuBrin to allow a completely customized approach to the introductory course.

The first four chapters present an introduction to management. Chapter 1, "The Manager's Job," explains the nature of managerial work with a particular emphasis on managerial roles and tasks. Chapter 2, "The Manager's Domestic and International Environment," describes the major forces inside and outside the firm influencing the managerial worker, including organizational culture. Chapter 3, "Ethics and Social Responsibility," examines the moral aspects of management. Chapter 4, "Managing for Quality," summarizes information managerial workers need to achieve quality and customer satisfaction.

The next three chapters address the subject of planning. Chapter 5, "Essentials of Planning," presents a general framework for planning—the activity underlying almost any purposeful action taken by a manager. Chapter 6, "Problem Solving and Decision Making," explains the basics of decision making, with an emphasis on creativity and other behavioral aspects. Chapter 7, "Specialized Techniques for Planning and Decision Making," describes several adjuncts to planning and decision making such as break-even analysis, PERT, and production scheduling methods used for both manufacturing and services.

The next three chapters focus on organizing. Chapter 8, "Job Design and Work Schedules," explains how jobs are laid out and work schedules arranged to enhance productivity and satisfaction. Chapter 9, "Organization Structure, Reengineering, and Culture," explains how work is organized from the standpoint of the organization, including the use of reengineering to organize for maximum efficiency. Chapter 10, "Staffing and Human Resource Management," explains the methods by which people are brought into the organization, trained, and evaluated.

The following three chapters, on leading, deal directly with the manager's role in influencing group members. Chapter 11, "Leadership," focuses on different approaches to leadership available to a manager and on the personal characteristics associated with leadership effectiveness. Chapter 12, "Motivation," describes what managers can do to increase or sustain employee effort toward achieving work goals. Chapter 13, "Communication," deals with the complex problems of accurately sending and receiving messages. Chapter 14, "Teams, Groups, and Teamwork," explains the nature of teams and how managers can foster group members working together cooperatively.

The next two chapters, on controlling, each deal with an important aspect of keeping performance in line with expectations. Chapter 15, "Control and Information Technology," presents an overview of measuring and controlling performance. Also described is how information technology has influenced the control function and other aspects of the managerial role. Chapter 16, "Managing Ineffective Performers," describes current approaches to dealing with substandard performers with an emphasis on elevating performance.

The final chapter in the text, Chapter 17, "Managing Change, Personal Productivity, and Stress" describes how managerial workers can enhance their productivity and satisfaction by coping with and capitalizing on change. It also shows how personal effectiveness can be increased by keeping stress under control and developing better work habits and time management skills.

PEDAGOGICAL FEATURES OF THE BOOK

Essentials of Management is designed to aid both student and instructor in expanding interest in and knowledge of management. The book contains the following features:

- Learning objectives coordinate the contents of each chapter. They preview the major topics to be covered. The same objectives are integrated into the text by indicating which major topics relate to the objectives. The end-of-chapter Summary of Key Points, based on the chapter learning objectives, pulls together the central ideas in each chapter.

- An opening case example illustrates a major topic to be covered in the chapter.

- Manager in Action, Organization in Action, and similar features present a portrait of how specific individuals or organizations practice an aspect of management covered in the chapter.

- Concrete, real-world examples, with which the reader can readily identify, are found throughout the text. Many of the examples are original, while others are researched from information published in magazines, newspapers, and journals.

- Exhibits, which include figures, tables, and self-assessment quizzes, aid in the comprehension of information in the text. The self-assessment exercises also help in skill building and application.

- Key terms and phrases highlight the management vocabulary introduced in each chapter. Their definitions are also highlighted in notes that appear in the margin.

- Questions at the end of each chapter assist learning by encouraging the reader to review and reflect on the chapter objectives.

- Skill-building exercises appear at the end of each chapter; many of them relate to the SCANS requirements followed by many schools. A special icon designates exercises that involve teams or collaborative activity.

- Each chapter also has several discussion questions that may be used with the CNBC examples video that accompanies the text. Chapters 4, 5, and 14 also contain an introduction for the BusinessLink videos that accompany those topics.

• Case problems also located at the end of each chapter can be used to synthesize the chapter concepts and simulate the practice of management.

CHANGES IN THE FOURTH EDITION

Several changes and additions have been incorporated into this edition, based on my own research and the suggestions of adopters, reviewers, and students.

Chapter 3, "Ethics and Social Responsibility," gives expanded coverage to this topic, which was previously contained in Chapter 2. Chapter 9, "Organization Structure, Reengineering, and Culture," now includes extensive information about reengineering because of the expansion of activity and interest in this topic. Chapter 14, "Teams, Groups, and Teamwork," pulls together and greatly expands on information on this topic provided in the previous edition.

All chapters have been thoroughly updated. Added topics include reengineering, the learning organization, the virtual corporation, more information about managing change, and expanded coverage of how information technology is affecting and shaping the manager's job. Information is also presented about valuing differences and developing cultural fluency.

Textual materials have been selectively pruned to reduce excessive detail and to make room for new developments in the last several years. Chapter 1, "The Manager's Job," has been shortened by reducing content that has become less relevant today.

Skill building receives additional emphasis by placing such exercises at the end of each chapter. Many of these exercises are related to the SCANS requirements. SCANS coverage is described in the next section of this preface.

Almost all the Manager in Action and Organization in Action features are new, and a majority of the cases are new. Approximately half of the cases and the case vignettes are from small businesses, reflecting the continuing growth of this segment of the economy.

MEETING THE SCANS REQUIREMENTS

In 1992, the U.S. Department of Labor published the report of The Secretary's Commission on Achieving Necessary Skills (SCANS). The commission was formed to encourage a high-performance economy characterized by high-skills, high-wage employment. To help achieve this goal, the commission report identifies five workplace competencies and a three-part foundation of skills and personal qualities needed for job performance. These eight requirements are essential preparation for all students, both those going directly to work and those planning further education. The competencies identified by the SCANS study are applicable from the shop floor to the executive suite, in large and small organizations, and in service and goods-producing environments.

According to SCANS, the competencies and the foundation skills should be taught and understood in an integrated fashion that reflects the workplace contexts in which they are applied. *Essentials of Management* fosters that integrated approach and provides information and exercises aimed at satisfying, directly or indirectly, all eight of the stated requirements.

WORKPLACE COMPETENCIES

Effective workers can productively use:

- *Resources: allocating time, money, materials, space, and staff.* Chapter 5, about planning, provides basic concepts for making use of all resources mentioned: time, money, materials, space, and staff. Chapter 10, about staffing, deals directly with allocating staff for jobs and assignments. Chapter 17, about personal productivity, helps with time allocation.
- *Interpersonal Skills: working on teams, teaching others, serving others, serving customers, leading, negotiating, and working well with people from culturally diverse backgrounds.* Chapter 14, about teams and teamwork, provides direct information about working on teams. Chapter 10 includes a section on training that provides information about teaching others. Chapter 4, about managing for quality, includes a section on total customer satisfaction. Chapter 11, about leadership, provides information and skills for leading, and the information about conflict management supports negotiation. Chapter 3, about ethics and social responsibility, deals directly with developing diversity skills and taking diversity initiatives. Chapter 13, about communication, includes a section on overcoming cross-cultural communication barriers.
- *Information: acquiring and evaluating data, organizing and maintaining files, interpreting and communicating, and using computers to process information.* Chapter 13, about communication, provides insights useful in communicating information to others, including overcoming communication barriers. Chapter 15, about control and information technology, describes how software can be used to help make decisions, thus processing information.
- *Systems: understanding social, organizational, and technological systems, monitoring and correcting performance, and designing or improving systems.* Chapter 9, about organizational structure and reengineering, provides information to help understand organizational and technological systems. Chapter 15, about control and information technology, is directly relevant to monitoring and correcting performance. Chapter 16, about managing ineffective performers, provides guidelines and techniques for correcting performance.
- *Technology: selecting equipment and tools, applying technology to specific tasks, and maintaining and troubleshooting technologies.* Chapter 7, about specialized techniques for planning and decision making, describes specific techniques for making good use of technology (such as the technique of economic order quantity). Chapter 15, about control and information technology, provides information about using information technology to assist with specific tasks.

FOUNDATION SKILLS

Competent workers in a high-performance workplace need:

- *Basic Skills: reading, writing, arithmetic and mathematics, speaking and listening.* Chapter 13 includes a component on improving speaking and listening skills.
- *Thinking Skills: thinking creatively, making decisions, solving problems, seeing things in the mind's eye, knowing how to learn, and reasoning.* Chapter 6, about problem solving and decision making, provides concrete information about improving creativity, making decisions, and solving problems. Chapter 11, about leadership, contains a section about using visualization (the mind's eye) to improve performance. All of the end-of-chapter cases provide opportunities for critical thinking and analysis.

- *Personal Qualities: individual responsibility, self-esteem, sociability, self-management, and integrity.* Chapter 11, about leadership, includes information about personal qualities such as individual responsibility, self-esteem, and sociability. The section about personal productivity in Chapter 17 is directly aimed at improving self-management. Chapter 3, about ethics and social responsibility, deals directly with integrity.

INSTRUCTIONAL RESOURCES

Essentials of Management is accompanied by comprehensive instructional support materials.

- *Instructor's Manual.* The instructor's manual (ISBN: 0538-85549-5) provides resources to increase the teaching and learning value of *Essentials of Management.* The *Manual* contains "Chapter Outline and Lecture Notes," of particular value to instructors whose time budget does not allow for extensive class preparation.

  For each text chapter, the *Manual* provides a statement of purpose and scope, outline and lecture notes, lecture topics, comments on the end-of-chapter questions and activities, responses to case questions, an experiential activity, and an examination. The examination contains twenty-five multiple choice questions, twenty-five true/false questions, and three essay questions.

  The *Manual* contains two comprehensive cases that will be useful for those instructors who wish to integrate the topics covered within the course. In addition, instructions are provided for the use of Computer-Aided Scenario Analysis (CASA). CASA is a user-friendly technique that can be used with any word-processing software. It allows the student to insert a new scenario into the case and to then re-answer the questions based on the new scenario. CASA helps to develop creative thinking and an awareness of contingencies or situational factors in making managerial decisions. The use of CASA has spread, and a description of the technique appears in the *The Journal of Management Education* (August 1992): 385–390.

  A set of transparency masters that duplicates key figures in the text is included in the manual.
- *Computerized Test Package.* The examinations presented in the Manual are also available on disk with the test generator program, MicroExam 4.0 (ISBN: 0538-85550-9). This versatile software package allows instructors to create new questions and edit and delete existing questions from the test bank.
- *Videos.* There are two videos that accompany the new edition of the text. One video (ISBN: 0538-85551-7) contains segments taken from CNBC, the cable business news network, broadcasts that will provide examples to accompany lectures and textual materials. Each text chapter contains discussion questions that will allow the instructor to incorporate the CNBC video examples in classroom discussions.

  The second video (ISBN: 0538-86753-1) contains three BusinessLink video case studies. The videos involve real companies and contain critical thinking questions that will provide an excellent forum for classroom analysis. Written cases will accompany the videos; they can be ordered as a supplement to the text.
- *Study Guide.* The study guide (ISBN: 0538-85547-9) that accompanies the fourth edition of *Essentials of Management* will be a real asset for your students. For each

text chapter, the *Study Guide* includes an overview; the objectives and key terms; an expanded study outline; and review questions—matching, multiple choice, true/false, and fill-in. Thought Stoppers, short essay questions, encourage critical thinking. Each chapter also contains an application exercise that requires use of the concepts presented in the text chapter.

A NOTE TO THE STUDENT . . .

The information in the general preface is important for students as well as instructors. Here, I offer additional comments that will enable you to increase the personal payoffs from studying management. My message can be organized around several key points.

- Management is not simply common sense. The number one trap for students in studying management is to assume that the material is easy to master because many of the terms and ideas are familiar. For example, just because you have heard the word *teamwork* many times, it does not automatically follow that you are familiar with specific field-tested ideas for enhancing teamwork.
- Managerial skills are vital. The information in the course for which you are studying this text is vital in today's world. People with formal managerial job titles such as supervisor, department head, or vice president are obviously expected to possess managerial skills. But many other people in jobs without managerial titles are also supposed to have managerial skills. Among them are administrative assistant, customer-service representative, and inventory-control specialist.
- The combination of managerial, interpersonal, and technical skills leads to outstanding career success. A recurring myth is that it is better to study "technical" or "hard" subjects than management because the pay is better. In reality, the people in business making the megabucks are those who combine technical skills with managerial and interpersonal skills. Executives and business owners, for example, can earn incomes rivaled only by leading professional athletes and show-business personalities.
- Studying management, however, has its biggest payoff in the long run. Entry-level management positions are in short supply. Management is a basic life process. To run a major corporation, manage a restaurant or a hair salon, organize a company picnic, plan a wedding, or run a good household, management skills are an asset. We all have some knowledge of management, but formally studying management can multiply one's effectiveness.

Take advantage of the many study aids in this text and the *Study Guide*. You will enhance your learning of management by concentrating on such learning assists as the chapter objectives, summaries, discussion questions, self-quizzes, skill-development exercises, and the glossary. Carefully studying a glossary is an effective way of building a vocabulary in a new field. Studying the glossary will also serve as a reminder of important topics. Activities such as the cases, discussion questions, and skill-development exercises facilitate learning by creating the opportunity to think through the information. Thinking through information, in turn, leads to better comprehension and long-term retention of information. The *Study Guide* will provide excellent review and preparation for examinations.

ACKNOWLEDGMENTS

Any project as complex as this text requires a team of dedicated and talented people to see that it gets completed effectively. Many reviewers made valuable comments during the development of this new edition as well as the previous three editions of the text. I appreciate the helpful suggestions of the following colleagues:

Thelma Anderson
Montana State University – Northern

Tom Birkenhead
Lane Community College

Brenda Britt
Fayetteville Technical Community College

Michael Cardinale
Palomar College

Gary Clark
North Harris College

Jose L. Curzet
Florida National College

Rex Cutshall
Vincennes University

Robert Desman
Kennesaw State College

Ben Dunn
York Technical College

Thomas Fiock
Southern Illinois University at Carbondale

Philip C. Grant
Hussen College

Randall Greenwell
John Wood Community College

David R. Grimmett
Austin Peay State University

Robert Halliman
Austin Peay State University

Paul Hegele
Elgin Community College

Thomas Heslin
Indiana University

Peter Hess
Western New England College

Nathan Himelstein
Essex County College

Judith A. Horrath
Lehigh Corbon Community College

B. R. Kirkland
Tarleton State University

Patricia Manninen
North Shore Community College

Noel Matthews
Front Range Community College

Christopher J. Morris
Adirondack Community College

Ilona Motsiff
Trinity College of Vermont

David W. Murphy
University of Kentucky

Ronald W. Olive
New Hampshire Technical College

J. E. Pearson
Dabney S. Lancaster Community College

Joseph Platts
Miami-Dade Community College

Thomas Quirk
Webster University

Jean Rada
Western Wisconsin Technical College

James Riley
Oklahoma Junior College

William Searle
Asnuntuck Community Technical College

William Shepard
New Hampshire Technical College

Lynn Suksdorf
Salt Lake Community College

Gary Tilley
Surry Community College

Bernard Weinrich
St. Louis Community College,

Alex Wittig
North Metro Technical College

Thanks also to members of South-Western Marketing and Management Team who worked with me on this edition: developmental editor Alice Denny, production editor Judy O'Neill, designer Craig Ramsdell, and photo editor Jennifer Mayhall. Writing without loved ones would be a lonely task. My thanks therefore go to my family, Drew, Douglas, Melanie, Rosemary, and Clare.

Andrew J. DuBrin

ABOUT THE AUTHOR

Andrew J. DuBrin is a Professor of Management in the College of Business at the Rochester Institute of Technology, where he teaches courses and conducts research in management, organizational behavior, leadership, and career management. He has also served as department chairman and team leader in previous years. He received his Ph.D. in Industrial Psychology from Michigan State University. DuBrin has business experience in human resource management and consults with organizations and individuals. His specialties include career management and management development. DuBrin is an established author of both textbooks and trade books, and also contributes to professional journals, magazines, and newspapers. He has written textbooks in management, leadership, organizational behavior, and human relations. His trade books cover many current issues, including reengineering, team play, office politics, coping with adversity, and overcoming career self-sabotage.

BRIEF CONTENTS

CONTENTS

CHAPTER 1

The Manager's Job

LEARNING OBJECTIVES

After studying this chapter and doing the exercises, you should be able to:

1
Explain what the term *manager* means, and identify different types of managers.

2
Describe the process of management, including the functions of management.

3
Describe the various managerial roles, along with those currently emphasized.

4
Identify the basic managerial skills and understand how they can be developed.

5
Identify the major developments in management thought.

© PhotoDisc

When Jim McCann bought 1-800-FLOWERS, the company was in serious trouble. Its order volume had dwindled, advertising had disappeared, and the company was top-heavy with staff. McCann knew intuitively that spending millions to own a name and a lot of fancy telephone equipment could have a big payoff if he brought the business back to life. • Starting with a 12-person telemarketing staff, McCann began aggressively reviving the business. He created promotional programs, initiated reminder and discount campaigns, and cemented advertising deals. He riveted his attention on customer service. Toward that end, telemarketers' calls were regularly monitored to ensure that customers were properly serviced without high-pressure sales tactics. Unlike most telemarketing operations, the employees at 1-800-FLOWERS had upbeat and supportive work surroundings plus advancement opportunities. At the same time, McCann carefully controlled costs. • 1-800-FLOWERS has become a sensational success. The combined influences of word-of-mouth from satisfied customers, creative advertising campaigns, and dozens of magazine articles have pushed the company to the top. In analyzing the success of his business, McCann says, "My single greatest skill is recognizing talent and tapping into other people's skills. I've always been able to bring out the best in people."[1]

Whether or not you send flowers to loved ones, the case history just presented sets the stage for a serious study of management. An effective manager combines business skills, such as knowledge about marketing and cost controls, with people skills to achieve important results. Management is the force that makes things happen. It pulls together resources to get important things accomplished. A manager's job is therefore inherently exciting. A good manager, like Jim McCann, makes things happen through other people.

The alternative to placing effective managers in charge of an operation is chaos. Poor management is one of the major reasons so many businesses of various sizes fail. These firms lack people who can get important things accomplished and tie together loose ends. When business firms fail because of competitive pressures or a dwindling economy, it is often the case that astute management could have overcome the problem. For example, when faced with intense competition, Chrysler Corporation bought the Jeep and Eagle vehicles to diversify and strengthen its product line.

WHO IS A MANAGER?

LEARNING OBJECTIVE

Explain what the term *manager* means, and identify different types of managers.

---

manager
A person responsible for the work performance of group members.

---

management
The process of using organizational resources to achieve organizational objectives through planning, organizing and staffing, leading, and controlling.

---

top-level managers
Managers at the top one or two levels in the organization.

A **manager** is a person responsible for the work performance of group members. (Because organizations have become more democratic, the term *group member* or *team member* is now frequently used as a substitute for *subordinate*.) A manager has the formal authority to commit organizational resources, even if the approval of others is required. For instance, the manager of an H & R Block income-tax service outlet has the authority to order the repainting of the reception area. The income-tax specialists reporting to that manager, however, do not have the authority to have the area repainted.

The concepts of manager and managing are intertwined. From the viewpoint of Peter Drucker, a noted management authority, management is the specific practice that converts a mob into an effective, goal-directed, and productive group.[2] The term **management** in this book refers to the process of using organizational resources to achieve organizational objectives through the functions of planning, organizing and staffing, leading, and controlling. These functions represent the broad framework for this book and will be described later. In addition to being a process, the term *management* is also used as a label for a specific discipline, for the people who manage, and for a career choice.

LEVELS OF MANAGEMENT

Another way of understanding the nature of a manager's job is to examine the three levels of management which Exhibit 1-1 illustrates. The pyramid in this figure indicates that there are progressively fewer employees at each higher managerial level. The largest number of people is at the bottom organizational level. (Note that the term *organizational level* is sometimes more precise than the term *managerial level*, particularly at the bottom organizational level, which has no managers.)

TOP-LEVEL MANAGERS. Most people who enter the field of management aspire to become **top-level managers**—managers at the top one or two levels in an organization. Top-level managers are empowered to make major decisions affecting the

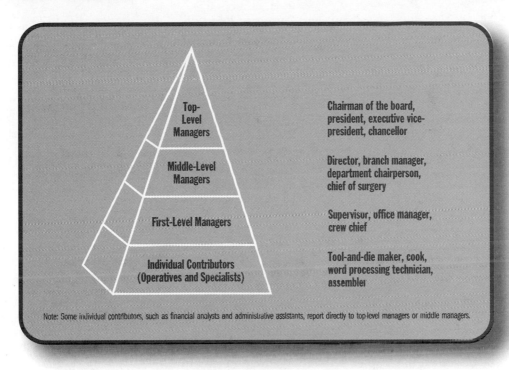

Exhibit 1-1
Managerial Levels
and Sample Job Titles

present and future of the firm. Only a top-level manager, for example, would have the authority to purchase another company, initiate a new product line, or hire hundreds of employees. Top-level managers are the people who give the organization its general direction; they decide where it is going and how it will get there. The terms *executive* and *top-level manager* can be used interchangeably.

MIDDLE-LEVEL MANAGERS. **Middle-level managers** are managers who are neither executives nor first-level supervisors, but who serve as a link between the two groups. Middle-level managers conduct most of the coordination activities within the firm, and they disseminate information to upper and lower levels. The jobs of middle-level managers vary substantially in terms of responsibility and income. A branch manager in a large firm might be responsible for over 100 workers. In contrast, a general supervisor in a small manufacturing firm might have 20 people reporting to him or her.

A traditional task of the middle-level manager is to process and disseminate information. For instance, the middle-level manager might speak to supervisors and specialists about inventory problems, prepare a report, and then pass this information up to top-level management. The widespread use of information technology has lessened the need for middle-level managers to perform this type of task. As a result, the number of middle-level management positions has decreased. Among the new tasks seen for middle-level managers is helping organizations undertake profitable new ventures and finding creative ways to reach goals.

FIRST-LEVEL MANAGERS. Managers who supervise operatives are referred to as **first-level managers,** first-line managers, or supervisors. Historically, first-level managers were promoted from production or clerical positions into supervisory positions. Rarely did they have formal education beyond high school. A dramatic shift has

middle-level managers
Managers who are neither executives nor first-level supervisors, but who serve as a link between the two groups.

first-level managers
Managers who supervise operatives (also known as first-line managers or supervisors).

taken place in recent years, however. Many of today's first-level managers are career school graduates who are familiar with modern management techniques. The current emphasis on productivity and quality has elevated the status of many supervisors.

To understand the work performed by first-level managers, reflect back on your first job. Like most employees in entry-level positions, you probably reported to a first-level manager. Such a manager might be supervisor of newspaper carriers, dining room manager, service station manager, maintenance supervisor, or department manager in a retail store. Supervisors help shape the attitudes of new employees toward the firm. Newcomers who like and respect their first-level manager tend to stay with the firm longer. Conversely, new workers who dislike and disrespect their first supervisor tend to leave the firm early.

TYPES OF MANAGERS

The functions performed by managers can also be understood by describing different types of management jobs. The management jobs discussed here are functional and general managers, administrators, entrepreneurs and small-business owners, and team leaders. (The distinction between line and staff managers will be described in Chapter 9 about organization structure.)

FUNCTIONAL AND GENERAL MANAGERS

Another way of classifying managers is to distinguish between those who manage people who do one type of specialized work and those who manage people who engage in different specialties. *Functional managers* supervise the work of employees engaged in specialized activities, such as accounting, engineering, quality control, food preparation, marketing, sales, and telephone installation. A functional manager is a manager of specialists and of their support team, such as office assistants.

General managers are responsible for the work of several different groups that perform a variety of functions. The job title plant general manager offers insight into the meaning of general management. Reporting to the plant general manager are a number of departments engaged in both specialized and generalized work, such as plant manufacturing, plant engineering, labor relations, quality control, safety, and warehousing. Company presidents are general managers. Branch managers also are general managers if employees from different disciplines report to them.

Six key tasks form the foundation of every general manager's job. These tasks are:[3]

1. Shaping the work environment—setting up performance standards, for example
2. Crafting a strategic vision—describing where the organization is headed
3. Allocating resources—deciding who gets how much money, people, material, and access to the manager
4. Developing managers—helping prepare people for managerial jobs
5. Building the organization—helping solve important problems so the organization can move forward
6. Overseeing operations—running the business, spotting problems, and helping solve them

**Exhibit 1-2
A Partial Organiza-
tion Chart for a
Large Hotel**

The six tasks of a general manager highlight many of the topics contained in the study of management. These tasks will therefore be reintroduced at various places in this book.

Exhibit 1-2 presents a segment of the organization chart of a typical large hotel. The management positions are classified by whether they are functional or general. The banquets manager and the guest rooms manager are classified as general managers because both operatives and specialists report to them. The banquet manager's team, for example, includes chefs, dishwashers, waiters, bartenders, and sales representatives.

ADMINISTRATORS

An *administrator* is typically a manager who works in a public (government) or nonprofit organization rather than in a business firm. Among these managerial positions are hospital administrator and housing administrator. Managers in all types of educational institutions are referred to as administrators. The fact that individual contributors in nonprofit organizations are sometimes referred to as administrators often causes confusion. An employee is not an administrator in the managerial sense unless he or she supervises others.

ENTREPRENEURS AND SMALL-BUSINESS OWNERS

Many students and employees dream of turning an exciting idea into a successful business. Many people think, "If Tom Monaghan started Domino's Pizza from scratch and he is a multimillionaire today, why can't I do something similar?" Success stories such as Monaghan's kindle the entrepreneurial spirit. An **entrepreneur** is a person who founds and operates an innovative business. Most successful entrepreneurs are highly enthusiastic people who take sensible risks and devote extraordinary energy to launching and managing their enterprise. After the entrepreneur develops the business into something bigger than he or she can handle alone, that person becomes a general manager.

Similar to an entrepreneur, the owner and operator of a small business becomes a manager when the firm grows to include several employees. **Small-business owners** typically invest considerable emotional and physical energy into their firms. Note that entrepreneurs are (or start as) small-business owners, but that the reverse is

entrepreneur
A person who founds and operates an innovative business.

small-business owner
An individual who owns and operates a small business.

MANAGER IN ACTION: BETH STEWART OF DENVER TRANSIT ADVERTISING

Denver Transit Advertising, founded in 1986, places ads on the outside of public buses. "You should see the latest one for Burger King," says Beth Stewart, whose company sells ad space measuring the entire surface area of a street bus. "It's a huge hamburger with a beautiful design."

A former real estate agent, Stewart found her ticket to success when a friend mentioned that Denver's Regional Transit District was opening bids to sell ad space on its buses. In just a day and a half, Stewart put together a presentation. She landed a six-month contract, and her business is still cruising. Her clients include Arby's, US West, and Re/Max. The start-up costs for the business were negligible, and gross annual sales are running close to $2.4 million.

Source: Adapted from "Entrepreneurs Across America," *Entrepreneur* (June 1995): 98.

not necessarily true. You need an innovative idea to be an entrepreneur. Simply running a franchise that sells submarine sandwiches does not make a person an entrepreneur.

The accompanying Manager-in-Action features a small-business owner. As you read her story, decide for yourself whether she classifies as an entrepreneur according to a strict interpretation the term.

TEAM LEADERS

> **team leader**
> *A manager who co-ordinates the work of a small group of people, while acting as a facilitator and catalyst.*

A major new development in types of managerial positions is the emergence of the **team leader.** A manager in such a position coordinates the work of a small group of people, while acting as a facilitator and catalyst. Team leaders are found at many organizational levels, and are also referred to as project managers, process managers, and task-force leaders. A team leadership assignment can be full time or part time. You will be reading about team leaders throughout this text.

THE PROCESS OF MANAGEMENT

LEARNING OBJECTIVE 2

Describe the process of management, including the functions of management.

A helpful approach to understanding what managers do is to regard their work as a process. A process is a series of actions that achieves something—making a profit or providing a service, for example. To achieve an objective, the manager uses resources and carries out four major managerial functions. These functions are planning, organizing and staffing, leading, and controlling. Exhibit 1-3 illustrates the process of management.

RESOURCES USED BY MANAGERS

Managers use resources to accomplish their purposes, just as a carpenter uses resources to build a porch. A manager's resources can be divided into four types: human, financial, physical, and informational.

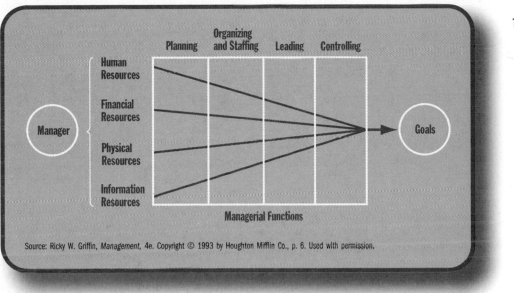

Source: Ricky W. Griffin, *Management*, 4e. Copyright © 1993 by Houghton Mifflin Co., p. 6. Used with permission.

**Exhibit 1-3
The Process of
Management**

Human resources are the people needed to get the job done. Managers' goals influence which employees they choose. Jim McCann has the goal of delivering quality flowers to a nationwide network of customers. Among the human resources he chooses are telemarketers, accountants, information technology specialists, and the network of local florists.

Financial resources are the money the manager and the organization use to reach organizational goals. The financial resources of a business organization are profits and investments from stockholders. A business must occasionally borrow cash to meet payroll or to pay for supplies. The financial resources of community agencies come from tax revenues, charitable contributions, and government grants.

Physical resources are a firm's tangible goods and real estate, including raw materials, office space, production facilities, office equipment, and vehicles. Vendors supply many of the physical resources needed to achieve organizational goals.

Information resources are the data that the manager and the organization use to get the job done. For example, to supply leads to the firm's sales representatives, the sales manager of an office-supply company reads local business newspapers to learn about new firms in town. These newspapers are information resources.

THE FOUR MANAGERIAL FUNCTIONS

Exhibit 1-3 showed the four major resources in the context of the management process. To accomplish goals, the manager performs four managerial functions. These functions are planning, organizing and staffing, leading, and controlling.

PLANNING. Planning involves setting goals and figuring out ways of reaching them. Planning is considered the central function of management, and it pervades everything a manager does. In planning, a manager looks to the future, saying, "Here is what we want to achieve, and here is how we are going to do it." Decision making is usually a component of planning, because choices have to be made in the process of finalizing plans. Planning multiplies in importance because it contributes heavily to performing the other management functions.

Exhibit 1-4
Time Spent on
Supervising Individuals
at the Three Levels of
Management*

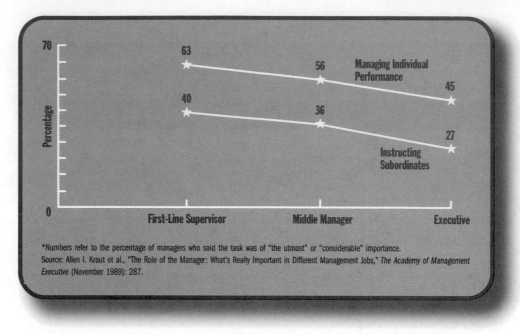

*Numbers refer to the percentage of managers who said the task was of "the utmost" or "considerable" importance.
Source: Allen I. Kraut et al., "The Role of the Manager: What's Really Important in Different Management Jobs," *The Academy of Management Executive* (November 1989): 287.

For example, managers must make plans to do an effective job of staffing the organization. Jim McCann of 1-800-FLOWERS formulated plans to revitalize his company.

ORGANIZING AND STAFFING. Organizing is the process of making sure the necessary human and physical resources are available to carry out a plan and achieve organizational goals. Organizing also involves assigning activities, dividing work into specific jobs and tasks, and specifying who has the authority to accomplish certain tasks. Another major aspect of organizing is grouping activities into departments or some other logical subdivision. Staffing involves making sure there are the necessary human resources to achieve organizational goals. Hiring people for jobs is a typical staffing activity. Staffing is such a major activity that it is sometimes classified as a function separate from organizing.

LEADING. Leading is influencing others to achieve organizational objectives. As a consequence, it involves energizing, directing, activating, and persuading others. Leadership involves dozens of interpersonal processes: motivating, communicating, coaching, and showing group members how they can reach their goals. Leadership is such a key component of managerial work that management is sometimes defined as accomplishing results through people. Beth Stewart provided leadership to her team at Denver Transit Advertising. Without her vision there would not have been such a company!

CONTROLLING. Controlling is ensuring that performance conforms to plans. It is comparing actual performance to a predetermined standard. If there is a significant difference between actual and desired performance, the manager must take corrective action. He or she might, for example, increase advertising to boost lower-than-anticipated sales.

A secondary aspect of controlling is determining whether the original plan needs revision, given the realities of the day. The controlling function sometimes

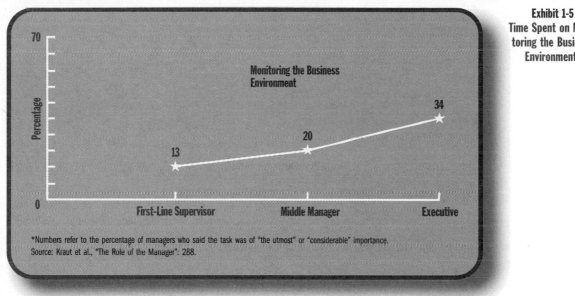

Exhibit 1-5
Time Spent on Moni-
toring the Business
Environment*

Monitoring the Business Environment

Percentage

70

0

13   20   34

First-Line Supervisor   Middle Manager   Executive

*Numbers refer to the percentage of managers who said the task was of "the utmost" or "considerable" importance.
Source: Kraut et al., "The Role of the Manager": 288.

causes a manager to return to the planning function temporarily to fine-tune the original plan. In the early 1990s, for example, paper mills decreased their capacity based on predictions of the paperless office. The paperless office has not yet materialized, despite the explosion of information technology. By the mid-1990s, paper mills could not meet the demand for paper. Company executives then had to plan how to upgrade paper-making capacity quickly.

THE FUNCTIONS EMPHASIZED AT DIFFERENT LEVELS OF MANAGEMENT

One important way in which the jobs of managers differ is in the relative amounts of time spent on planning, organizing and staffing, leading, and controlling. Executives ordinarily spend much more time on strategic (high-level and long-range) planning than do middle- or first-level managers.[4] Lower-level managers are more involved with day-by-day and other short-range planning.

One notable difference in time allocation is that, compared to middle managers and executives, first-level managers spend more time in face-to-face leadership of employees, as Exhibit 1-4 shows. Exhibit 1-5 reveals that executives spend most of their time monitoring the business environment. Such monitoring is a form of controlling. By analyzing what is going on in the outside world, the manager can help the firm compete effectively.

THE SEVENTEEN MANAGERIAL ROLES

To further understand the manager's job, it is worthwhile to examine the various roles managers play. A **role,** in the business context, is an expected set of activities or behaviors stemming from a job. Henry Mintzberg conducted several landmark studies of managerial roles.[5] Other researchers extended his findings.[6] In the sections that follow, the roles delineated by these researchers appear under the major managerial functions they pertain to most closely. (Roles and functions

LEARNING OBJECTIVE

Describe the various managerial roles, along with those currently emphasized.

---

role
An expected set of activities or behaviors stemming from a job.

are quite closely related. They are both activities carried out by people.) The descriptions of these 17 roles should help you appreciate the richness and complexity of managerial work.

PLANNING

Two managerial roles, strategic planner and operational planner, relate to the planning function.

1. *Strategic Planner.* Top-level managers engage in strategic planning. Specific activities in this role include (a) developing long-range plans and priorities for a department, (b) contributing to long-range plans for the total organization, and (c) helping develop corporate policies.
2. *Operational Planner.* Operational plans relate to the day-to-day operation of a company or unit. Two such activities are (a) formulating operating budgets and (b) developing work schedules for the unit supervised. Middle-level managers are heavily involved in operational planning; first-level managers are involved to a lesser extent.

ORGANIZING AND STAFFING

Five roles that relate to the organizing and staffing function are organizer, liaison, staffing coordinator, resource allocator, and task delegator.

3. *Organizer.* As a pure organizer, the manager engages in activities such as (a) designing the jobs of subordinates; (b) clarifying subordinates' assignments; (c) explaining organizational policies, rules, and procedures; and (d) establishing policies, rules, and procedures to coordinate the flow of work and information within the unit.
4. *Liaison.* The purpose of the liaison role is to develop and maintain a network of work-related contacts with people. To achieve this end, the manager (a) cultivates relationships with clients or customers; (b) maintains relationships with suppliers, customers, and other persons or groups important to the unit or organization; (c) joins boards, organizations, or public-service clubs that might provide useful, work-related contacts; and (d) cultivates and maintains a personal network of in-house contacts through visits, telephone calls, and participation in company-sponsored events.
5. *Staffing Coordinator.* In the staffing role, the manager tries to make sure that competent people fill positions. Its specific activities include (a) recruiting and hiring staff; (b) explaining to subordinates how their work performance will be evaluated; (c) formally evaluating subordinates' overall job performance; (d) compensating subordinates within the limits of organizational policy; (e) ensuring that subordinates are properly trained; (f) promoting subordinates or recommending them for promotion; and (g) terminating or demoting subordinates.
6. *Resource Allocator.* An important part of a manager's job is to divide resources in the manner that best helps the organization. Specific activities to this end include (a) authorizing the use of physical resources (facilities, furnishings, and equipment); (b) authorizing the expenditure of financial resources; and (c) discontinuing the use of unnecessary, inappropriate, or ineffective equipment or services.

7. *Task Delegator.* A standard part of any manager's job is assigning tasks to group members. Among these task-delegation activities are (a) assigning projects or tasks to subordinates; (b) clarifying priorities and performance standards for task completion; and (c) ensuring that group members are properly committed to effective task performance. (The role of task delegator could be considered a part of the role of organizer.)

LEADING

Eight roles have been identified that relate to the leadership function. These roles are figurehead, spokesperson, negotiator, coach, team builder, team player, technical problem solver, and entrepreneur.

8. *Figurehead.* Figurehead managers, particularly high-ranking ones, spend some of their time engaging in ceremonial activities, or acting as a figurehead. Such activities are (a) entertaining clients or customers as an official representative of the organization, (b) being available to outsiders as a representative of the organization, (c) serving as an official representative of the organization at gatherings outside the organization, and (d) escorting official visitors.

9. *Spokesperson.* When a manager acts as a spokesperson, the emphasis is on answering letters or inquiries and formally reporting to individuals and groups outside the manager's organizational unit. As a spokesperson, the manager keeps five groups of people informed about the unit's activities, plans, and capabilities. These groups are (a) upper-level management, (b) clients and customers, (c) other important outsiders (such as labor unions), (d) professional colleagues, and (e) the general public. Usually, top-level managers take responsibility for keeping outside groups informed.

10. *Negotiator.* Part of almost any manager's job is trying to make deals with others for needed resources. Three specific negotiating activities are (a) bargaining with superiors for funds, facilities, equipment, or other forms of support, (b) bargaining with other units in the organization for the use of staff, facilities, equipment, or other forms of support; and (c) bargaining with suppliers and vendors about services, schedules, and delivery times.

11. *Coach.* An effective manager takes the time to coach subordinates. Specific behaviors in this role include (a) informally recognizing subordinates' achievements, (b) providing subordinates with feedback about ineffective performance, and (c) ensuring that subordinates know about steps to take to improve their performance.

12. *Team Builder.* A key aspect of a manager's role is to build an effective team. Activities contributing to this role include (a) ensuring that subordinates are recognized for their accomplishments (by issuing letters of appreciation, for example); (b) initiating activities that contribute to group morale, such as giving parties and sponsoring sports teams; and (c) holding periodic staff meetings to encourage subordinates to talk about their accomplishments, problems, and concerns.

13. *Team Player.* Three behaviors of the team player are (a) displaying appropriate personal conduct, (b) cooperating with other units in the organization, and (c) displaying loyalty to superiors by fully supporting their plans and decisions.

14. *Technical Problem Solver.* It is particularly important for first- and middle-level managers to help subordinates solve technical problems. Two such specific activities related to problem solving are (a) serving as a technical expert or ad-

visor and (b) performing individual contributor tasks, such as making sales calls or repairing machinery on a regular basis. The managers most in demand today are those who combine a technical specialty with knowledge of other areas. Such managers are referred to as *totalists*.[7]

15. *Entrepreneur.* Managers who work in large organizations have some responsibility for suggesting innovative ideas or furthering the business aspects of the firm. Three entrepreneurial role activities are (a) reading trade publications and professional journals to keep up-to-date; (b) talking with customers or others in the organization to keep aware of changing needs and requirements; and (c) getting involved in situations outside the unit that could suggest ways of improving the performance of the manager's unit. This could consist of visiting other firms, attending professional meetings or trade shows, and participating in educational programs.

CONTROLLING

One role, that of monitor, fits the controlling function precisely, because the term *monitoring* is often used as a synonym for *controlling*. The role of disturbance handler is categorized under controlling because it involves changing an unacceptable condition to an acceptable stable condition.

16. *Monitor.* The activities of a monitor are (a) developing systems that measure or monitor the unit's overall performance, (b) using management information systems to measure productivity and cost, (c) talking with group members about progress on assigned tasks, and (d) overseeing the use of equipment and facilities (for example, telephones and office space) to ensure that they are properly used and maintained.

17. *Disturbance Handler.* Four typical activities of a disturbance handler are (a) participating in grievance resolution within the unit (working out a problem with a labor union, for example); (b) resolving complaints from customers, other units, subordinates, and superiors; (c) resolving conflicts among group members; and (d) resolving problems about work flow and information exchange with other units. Disturbance handling might also be considered a leadership role.

MANAGERIAL ROLES CURRENTLY EMPHASIZED

Managerial work has shifted substantially away from the controller and director role to that of coach, facilitator, and supporter. As reflected in the position of team leader, many managers today deemphasize formal authority and rank. Instead, they work as partners with team members to jointly achieve results. Managers today emphasize horizontal relations and deemphasize vertical (top-down) relationships.[8] Exhibit 1-6 presents a stereotype of the difference between the role of the modern and the traditional manager. We encourage you not to think that traditional (old) managers are evil, while new managers are good.

THE INFLUENCE OF MANAGEMENT LEVEL ON MANAGERIAL ROLES

A manager's level of responsibility influences which roles he or she is likely to engage in most frequently. Exhibits 1-4 and 1-5 showed this by indicating how managers' levels of responsibility influence which functions they emphasize. (Recall that roles are really subsets of functions.)

Exhibit 1-6
Traditional versus
Modern Managerial
Roles

Old Manager	New Manager
Thinks of self as manager or boss	Thinks of self as sponsor, team leader, or internal consultant
Follows the chain of command	Deals with anyone necessary to get the job done
Works within a set organizational structure	Changes organizational structures in response to market change
Makes most decisions alone	Invites others to join in decision making
Hoards information	Shares information
Tries to master one major discipline, such as marketing or finance	Tries to master a broad array of managerial disciplines
Demands long hours	Demands results

Source: Adapted from Brian Dumaine, "The New Non-Managers, Managers," *Fortune* (22 February 1993): 81.

Information about the influence of level on roles comes from research conducted with 228 managers in a wide variety of private-sector service firms (such as banks and insurance companies) and manufacturing firms. The roles studied were basically those described in this chapter. One clear-cut finding was that, at the higher levels of management, four roles were the most important: liaison, spokesperson, figurehead, and strategic planner. Another finding was that the role of leader is very important at the first level of management.[9]

THE FIVE MANAGERIAL SKILLS

To be effective, managers need to possess technical, interpersonal, conceptual, diagnostic, and political skills. The sections that follow will first define these skills and then comment on how they are developed. Whatever the level of management, a manager needs a combination of all five skills.

LEARNING OBJECTIVE

Identify the basic managerial skills and understand how they can be developed.

TECHNICAL SKILL

Technical skill involves an understanding of and proficiency in a specific activity that involves methods, processes, procedures, or techniques. Technical skills include the ability to prepare a budget, lay out a production schedule, program a computer, or demonstrate a piece of electronic equipment. A well-developed technical skill can facilitate the rise into management. For example, Bill Gates of Microsoft Corp. launched his career by being a competent programmer.

INTERPERSONAL SKILL

Interpersonal (or human relations) skill is a manager's ability to work effectively as a team member and to build cooperative effort in the unit. Interpersonal skills are more important than technical skills in getting to the top.

Communication skills are an important component of interpersonal skills. They form the basis for sending and receiving messages on the job.

An important subset of interpersonal skills for managers is **multiculturalism,** or the ability to work effectively and conduct business with people from different cultures. Closely related is the importance of bilingualism for managers as well as other workers. Being able to converse in a second language has become an important asset in today's global and multicultural work environment.

multiculturalism

The ability to work effectively and conduct business with people from different cultures.

CONCEPTUAL SKILL

Conceptual skill is the ability to see the organization as a total entity. It includes recognizing how the various units of the organization depend on one another and how changes in any one part affect all the others. It also includes visualizing the relationship of the individual business to the industry; the community; and the political, social, and economic forces of the nation as a whole. For top-level management, conceptual skill is a priority because executive managers have the most contact with the outside world.

Conceptual skill has increased in importance for managers because many of them have to rethink substantially how work is performed. One such mind-bender is that many organizations are shifting away from departments and toward processes. Instead of a group of specialists performing work under the direction of an authoritative manager, people work together in teams as generalists. We will return to this theme at several places in the text.

DIAGNOSTIC SKILL

Managers are frequently called on to investigate a problem and then to decide on and implement a remedy. Diagnostic skill often requires other skills, because managers need to use technical, human, conceptual, or political skills to solve the problems they diagnose. Much of the potential excitement in a manager's job centers on getting to the root of problems and recommending solutions.

POLITICAL SKILL

An important part of being effective is being able to get your share of power and prevent others from taking power away from you. Political skill is the ability to acquire the power necessary to reach objectives. Other political skills include establishing the right connections and impressing the right people.

Political skill should be regarded as a supplement to job competence and the other basic skills. Managers who overemphasize political skill at the expense of doing work of substance have been labeled *cosmetic managers.* Such managers are very concerned about self-interest and career advancement, often to the exclusion of reaching organizational goals.[10]

DEVELOPMENT OF MANAGERIAL SKILLS

This text is based on the assumption that managerial skills can be learned. Education for management begins in school and continues in the form of training and development programs throughout a career. Examples of such a program are a seminar about how to be an effective leader and a workshop about using the Internet to expand business.

Developing most managerial skills is more complex than developing structured skills such as computing a return on investment ratio or retrieving E-mail messages. Nevertheless, you can develop managerial skills by studying this text and doing the exercises, which follows a general learning model:

1. *Conceptual knowledge and behavioral guidelines.* Each chapter in this text presents useful information about the practice of management, including step-by-step procedures for a method of group decision making called the nominal group technique.
2. *Conceptual information demonstrated by examples.* Brief descriptions of managers and professionals in action, including small-business owners, are presented throughout the text.
3. *Skill-development exercises.* The text provides an opportunity for practice and personalization through cases and self-assessment exercises. Self-quizzes are included because they are an effective method of helping you personalize the information.
4. *Feedback on skill utilization, or performance, from others.* Feedback exercises appear at several places in the text. Implementing some of these managerial skills outside of the classroom will provide additional opportunities for feedback.

Experience is as important as formal education in forming effective managers. The issue is not whether education or experience is the best teacher. The question is what combination of the two is the most beneficial for a particular individual in a particular situation. People who climb the organizational ladder usually have both education and experience in management techniques.

MAJOR DEVELOPMENTS IN MANAGEMENT THOUGHT

Management is such a complex subject that it can be approached from different perspectives or major developments in thought. Although these developments, or schools of thought, are different, they do not compete with each other as statements of truth about management. Instead, they complement and support each other. Well-trained managers select the management ideas that seem to fit the problem at hand. Correspondingly, this text borrows ideas from the major developments in management thought.

The classical, behavioral, and management-science schools are the major developments in management thought. They are supplemented by the contingency and systems approaches, both of which attempt to integrate these three major developments.

LEARNING OBJECTIVE

Identify the major developments in management thought.

THE CLASSICAL SCHOOL

The **classical school of management** is the original formal approach to studying management. Its followers search for solid principles and concepts that can be used to manage work and people productively. The core of management knowledge is based on the classical school. One of its key contributions has been to study management from the framework of planning, organizing, directing, and controlling. The term *leading* is now often used to replace *directing*, which sounds harsher.

The major strength of the classical school is that it provides a systematic way of managing people and work that has proved useful over time. Its major limitation is that it sometimes ignores differences among people and situations. For example, some of the classical principles for designing an organization are not well suited to fast-changing situations.

classical school of management
The original formal approach to studying management. This school of thought searches for solid principles and concepts that can be used to manage people and work productively.

THE BEHAVIORAL SCHOOL

behavioral school of management
The approach to studying management that emphasizes improving management through understanding the psychological makeup of people.

Concerns that the classical school did not pay enough attention to the human element led to the **behavioral school of management.** Its primary emphasis is on improving management through understanding the psychological makeup of people. The behavioral school has had a profound influence on management, and much of this book is based on behavioral theory. Typical behavioral school topics include leadership, motivation, communication, group decision making, and conflict. Through its insistence that effective leadership depends on understanding the situation, the behavioral school initiated the contingency approach to management.

Much of the behavioral school is rooted in the work of psychologists who applied their insights and research findings to the workplace. Pioneering management thinkers such as Abraham Maslow, Douglas McGregor, and Frederick Herzberg are (or were) psychologists.

The primary strength of the behavioral school is that it encourages managers to take into account the human element. Many valuable methods of motivating employees are based on behavioral research. The primary weakness of the behavioral approach is that it sometimes leads to an oversimplified view of managing people. Managers sometimes adopt one simple behavioral theory and ignore other relevant information. For example, several psychological theories of motivation pay too little attention to the importance of money in peoples' thinking.

THE MANAGEMENT-SCIENCE SCHOOL

management-science school
The school of management thought that concentrates on providing management with a scientific basis for solving problems and making decisions.

The **management-science school** provides managers with a scientific basis for solving problems and making decisions. It uses a wide array of mathematical and statistical techniques. To many people, the use of computers in management is synonymous with management science. Many quantitative techniques for quality improvement stem from the management-science school. Chapter 7, "Specialized Techniques for Planning and Decision Making," describes several important applications of management science.

The primary strength of management science is that it enables managers to solve problems that are so complex they cannot be solved by common sense alone. For example, management-science techniques are used to make forecasts that take into account hundreds of factors simultaneously. A weakness of management science is that the answers it produces are often less precise than they appear. Although management science uses precise methods, much of the data are based on human estimates, which can be unreliable.

THE SYSTEMS APPROACH

systems approach
A perspective on management problems based on the concept that the organization is a system, or an entity of interrelated parts.

The **systems approach** to management is more a perspective for viewing problems than a school of thought. It is based on the concept that an organization is a system, or an entity of interrelated parts. If you adjust one part of the system, other parts will be affected automatically. For example, suppose you offer low compensation to job candidates. According to the systems approach, your action will influence product quality. The "low-quality" employees who are willing to accept low wages will produce low-quality goods. Exhibit 1-3, which showed the process of management, reflected a systems viewpoint.

Another aspect of systems theory is to regard the organization as an open system, one that interacts with the environment. As illustrated in Exhibit 1-7, the or-

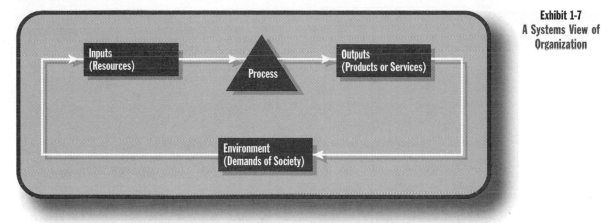

Exhibit 1-7
A Systems View of
Organization

ganization transforms inputs into outputs and supplies them to the outside world. If these outputs are perceived as valuable, the organization will survive and prosper. The feedback loop indicates that acceptance of the outputs by society gives the organization new inputs for revitalization and expansion. Managers can benefit from this diagram by recognizing that whatever work they undertake should contribute something of value to external people (such as customers and clients).

THE CONTINGENCY APPROACH

The **contingency approach to management** emphasizes that there is no one best way to manage people or work. A method that leads to high productivity or morale in one situation may not achieve the same results in another. The contingency approach is derived from the leadership aspects of the behavioral school. Specifically, psychologists developed detailed explanations of which style of leadership would work best in which situation. An example would be for the manager to give more leeway to competent group members. Common sense also contributes heavily to the contingency approach. Experienced managers know that not all people and situations respond identically to identical situations. The contingency approach is emphasized throughout this book.

    The strength of the contingency approach is that it encourages managers to examine individual and situational differences before deciding on a course of action. Its major problem is that it is often used as an excuse for not acquiring formal knowledge about management. If management depends on the situation, why study management theory? The answer is because a formal study of management helps a manager decide which factors are relevant in particular situations.

    The practicing manager can use all five major developments in management thought. An astute manager selects information from the various schools of thought to achieve good results in a given situation. Visualize Beth Stewart establishing her transit sign business. At one point she relied on the management-science school to quantify how many signs she would have to paint to cover her costs. At another point, she relied on the behavioral school to select effective methods for motivating her team.

contingency approach to management
A perspective on management that emphasizes that there is no one best way to manage people or work. It encourages managers to study individual and situational differences before deciding on a course of action.

SUMMARY OF KEY POINTS

To facilitate your study and review of this and the remaining chapters, the summaries are organized around the learning objectives.

1

Explain what the term *manager* means, and identify different types of managers.

A manager is a person responsible for work performance of other people. Management is the process of using organizational resources to achieve specific objectives through the functions of planning, organizing and staffing, leading, and controlling. Organizational levels consist of top-level managers, middle-level managers, first-level managers, and individual contributors. Categories of managers include functional managers (who deal with specialties within the firm) and general managers, administrators (typically managers in nonprofit firms), entrepreneurs (those who start innovative businesses), small-business owners, and team leaders.

2

Describe the process of management, including the functions of management.

To accomplish organizational goals, managers use resources and carry out the basic management functions. Resources are divided into four categories: human, financial, physical, and informational. Top-level managers emphasize high-level planning, whereas first-level managers concentrate on person-to-person leadership. Executives place more emphasis on monitoring the environment than do managers in the other two levels.

3

Describe the various managerial roles, along with those currently emphasized.

The work of a manager can be divided into 17 roles that relate to the four major functions. Planning roles include strategic planner and operational planner. Organizing and staffing calls for the organizer, liaison, staffing-coordinator, resource-allocator, and task-delegator roles. Leading roles include figurehead, spokesperson, negotiator, coach, team builder, team player, technical problem solver, and entrepreneur. Controlling involves the monitor and disturbance-handling roles. Managerial work has shifted substantially away from the controller and director role to that of coach, facilitator, and supporter. Top-level managers occupy more external roles than do lower-ranking managers.

4

Identify the basic managerial skills and understand how they can be developed.

Managers need interpersonal, conceptual, diagnostic, and political skills to accomplish their jobs. An effective way of developing managerial skills is to follow a general learning model. The model involves conceptual knowledge, behavioral guidelines, following examples, skill-development exercises, and feedback. Management skills are also acquired through a combination of education and experience.

5

Identify the major developments in management thought.

The three major developments in management thought are the classical, behavioral, and management-science schools. Each complements and supports the others. They are supplemented by the systems and contingency approaches to management, which attempt to integrate the three schools.

KEY TERMS AND PHRASES

Manager *pg. 2*
Management *pg. 2*
Top-Level Managers *pg. 2*
Middle-Level Managers *pg. 3*
First-Level Managers *pg. 3*
Entrepreneur *pg. 5*
Small-Business Owner *pg. 5*
Team Leader *pg. 6*

Role *pg. 9*
Multiculturalism *pg. 14*
Classical School of Management *pg. 15*
Behavioral School of Management *pg. 16*
Management-Science School *pg. 16*
Systems Approach *pg. 16*
Contingency Approach to Management
    pg. 17

QUESTIONS

Here, as in other chapters, the questions and cases can be analyzed by groups or individually. We strongly recommend small-group discussions to enhance learning.

1. Define the term *manager* in your own words.
2. If you have to be licensed to be a lawyer, plumber, massage specialist, and so forth, why not license executives?
3. Many people in good-paying technical jobs actively seek to become managers. What do you suspect are their reasons?
4. Why might the role of the "new" manager require a higher level of interpersonal skill than required by the "old" manager?
5. Why is being an entrepreneur or small-business owner so attractive to so many people?
6. Why should executives place more emphasis on monitoring the external environment than do first-level managers?
7. How do students use the four management functions to accomplish their goal of graduating?

SKILL-BUILDING EXERCISE 1-A: IDENTIFYING MANAGERIAL ROLES

Interview a manager at any level in any organization, including a retail store or restaurant. Determine which of the 17 managerial roles the manager you interview thinks apply to his or her job. Find out which one or two roles the manager thinks are the most important. Be ready to discuss your findings in class.

SKILL-BUILDING EXERCISE 1-B: MANAGERIAL SKILLS FOR CONDUCTING A PROJECT

GROUP ACTIVITY Form a group of about six students. Your task is to plan a substantial project such as developing a business that can be conducted over the Internet, or creating a fund-raising campaign. Include both general and specific tasks that will have to be accomplished to achieve your goals. As you formulate your plans, identify the managerial skills you will need to get the work accomplished. For each skill you mention, provide a specific example of why the skill is necessary. For instance, in developing an Internet business you will need the technical competence to work your way through the system. You will also need interpersonal skills to attract the right employees and motivate them.

VIDEO DISCUSSION QUESTIONS

1. What are the major managerial roles carried out by Bossidy, the CEO of Allied Signal? **[Allied Signal]**
2. What leadership roles are emphasized by McCall, of Glaxo? **[Glaxo]**
3. Does the founder of How Sweet It Is classify as a true entrepreneur? **[Entrepreneurial Spirit]**

CASE PROBLEM 1-A: KEEPING HORIZON FOOD IN ORBIT

Steven Krane, age 29, is the president of Horizon Meats and Seafood of Virginia, Inc. His company delivers restaurant-quality filet mignon, shrimp, and lobster tails directly to people's homes for about $4 per entree. Annual sales volume is about $32 million.

Krane learned to become an entrepreneur by necessity. When he was 16, his father lost his job as a manufacturer's representative selling men's clothing to department stores in Canada. The reason is that department stores began dealing directly with the manufacturers. If young Steven wanted money, he had to earn it on his own. Within one year, Krane took $1,000 he had saved to purchase a few coffee machines to lease to local businesses. He borrowed money from his mother to buy a delivery car. The company Krane founded, Pronto Coffee Service, became the central activity in his life. He scheduled classes to give him sufficient time to manage his business.

When the coffee-machine service became routine, Krane upgraded his company to get it ready for sale. Armed with impressive figures about the business, he sold it for $100,000. Krane then needed a new source of income. He placed ads in *The Los Angeles Times, The Chicago Times,* and *The New York Times*. He announced, "If you have a product or service you want distributed in Canada, I have the time and money needed to make it a success." (Krane is Canadian.)

Krane received more than 100 inquiries, including one from Horizon Meats and Seafood. Within four years, Krane became a partner and president of the company. At age 29, Krane faces the future wondering if he has found his niche in life. He also has given thought to whether his business is too narrowly focused.

CASE QUESTIONS

1. What managerial skills does Krane appear to possess?
2. What are the key managerial roles Krane occupies?
3. What can Krane do to expand Horizon Meats and Seafood?

Source: Facts as reported in Richard Poe, "Generation E," *Success* (November 1993): 24.

CASE PROBLEM 1-B: MANAGING THE GAP

The Gap, Inc., has earned the reputation as the most popular and profitable specialty clothing chain in America today. Sales at The Gap and its affiliates, GapKids, Banana Republic, and Old Navy, are currently running at $3.7 billion annually. Earnings were $320 million in one year. Predictions have been made that the company will soon surpass 2,000 stores with combined sales of almost $5 billion. The two top executives at The Gap are President Millard (Mickey) S. Drexler and the founder, Chairman Donald G. Fisher.

The formula behind The Gap's extraordinary success is "good style, good quality, good value." Store sites are carefully selected by Fisher, and each Gap store is clean and well lit. Gap stores make it possible for consumers to shop easily and quickly. The atmosphere at the stores leads employees to fuss over details such as cleaning floors and, at GapKids, rounding the corners of the fixtures to prevent puncture wounds. The company boasts a high-tech distribution system that keeps the 1,200 Gap outlets stocked with fresh merchandise.

Fisher, regarded as low-key and conservative in personal style, enjoys working on the details of site selection, store construction, and clothing manufacturing. Drexler, in contrast, makes most of the major merchandising decisions.

Several years ago Drexler simplified the way The Gap did business. He replaced executives who relied too heavily on complicated quantitative research. He preferred executives who relied quickly on intuition in selecting merchandise and deciding when to pull slow sellers from the shelves.

Both Drexler and Fisher have pushed heavily for quality. The company has placed its own quality inspectors in many of the manufacturing sites around the world that make clothing for The Gap label. The company designs its own clothing, chooses its own materials, and monitors manufacturing carefully.

At one time Drexler supervised every major design decision, and he still keeps close tabs on design. He characteristically roams around the stores, dropping in unexpectedly on employees to praise or criticize projects in design, advertising, and merchandising. For reasons such as these, Drexler has been described as a hands-on president.

CASE QUESTIONS

1. Identify the managerial skills of Drexler and Fisher as revealed in the preceding case.
2. Which approaches to management thought are illustrated in the management techniques of the two Gap executives?
3. Which management functions can be identified in the preceding case?
4. What suggestions can you offer The Gap to help ensure its future success?

Source: Facts as reported in Russell Mitchell, "The Gap," *Business Week* (9 March 1992): 58–64; "The *Fortune* 500 Largest U.S. Corporations," *Fortune* (15 May 1995): F-13.

CASE PROBLEM 1-C: LEAPFROG INTO MANAGEMENT

Chrysler President Robert A. Lutz recently wanted to obtain a showroom-level viewpoint on the auto market. He telephoned one of his favorite dealers, Louis P. Patane, owner of two small Chrysler dealerships in Avondale, Arizona. Patane and Lutz stayed on the phone for 30 minutes discussing marketing strategy, customer satisfaction, and the Chrysler selection of models.

President Lutz was so impressed that he casually suggested that Patane come work for him at company headquarters. A week later, Patane surprised Lutz with his plans to sell his thriving dealerships and accept the offer. Many automobile businesspersons were astonished by Patane's leap from small-town dealer to the high-level position of executive director of brand marketing. Large dealers also were surprised by Patane's appointment. A Detroit area megadealer said, "This guy only sold 30 cars a month. What does he know?"

Patane's formal education includes a diploma in computer programming from the Rochester Business Institute, where he also studied management. While at RBI, he worked at auto-body and machine shops. Later he owned a car wash and service station. Next he managed a machining company specializing in race-car engines. Patane bought a Dodge dealership in Arizona in 1986, followed by a Chrysler dealership eight years later. He is known as a "car guy" who races dragsters for fun.

Patane's biggest challenge is to help position Plymouths and Eagles for greater success. Lutz contends that an outsider such as a small-town dealer might have the fresh perspective to better shape marketing. Chrysler Corporation executives believe that the company must find ways to distinguish its several brands and models from one another. Patane has some experience in dealing with brand identity problems. As a member of the National Dodge Dealer Council, he influenced local advertising to emphasize specific brands such as the Ram pickup truck.

As Patane sizes up his qualifications, "I came into this business though the back end, which gives me a strong customer viewpoint."

CASE QUESTIONS

1. In your opinion, is Louis Patane qualified to be Chrysler's executive vice-president of brand marketing?
2. Which several managerial roles will Patane most likely emphasize in his new position?
3. What can Lutz do to silence critics of his decision to promote Patane to his newly created position?

Source: Based on facts reported in Bill Vlasic, "Who's That Guy in Chrysler's Front Seat?" *Business Week* (30 October 1995): 40.

CASE PROBLEM 1-D: THE FAMILY COPY AND PRINT SHOP

After four years of night courses, Kathy Lundquist received an associate's degree in business administration. Shortly thereafter, top management at the bank where she worked promoted her to head teller. Lundquist expressed her appreciation for the promotion and inquired about prospects for future advancement. She was told that, due to the closing of so many branches in the bank, future promotions would be scarce.

Six months after her appointment to head teller, Kathy's uncle on her father's side died. Two weeks after the funeral, Kathy's aunt, Lisa Lundquist, invited Kathy for dinner to discuss some urgent family business. "Now that your uncle has died, I want to phase out of the copy and print shop that he and I have owned for 15 years. You can start right away as the manager, and I'll help you run the business. Within one year, I'll retire, and retain a twenty-five percent interest in the business. With luck, you should be earning much more than you are at the bank."

After discussing details of the deal for several weeks, Kathy decided to accept the position as manager of Lundquist Copy and Print. Aunt Lisa had painted a rosy picture of the business. After one month into the business, Kathy uncovered several disturbing problems. "What do you expect me to do about the following problems I've uncovered?" she asked her aunt. In checklist fashion, Kathy reviewed her findings:

"1. A new Sir Speedy (a national chain specializing in photocopying, printing, and desktop publishing) opened two blocks away. It looks like twenty percent of our customers have jumped ship to Sir Speedy."

"2. My analysis is that our business has not earned a profit in six months, after you take into account a decent salary for the owners."

"3. Many of our customers are more than 90 days overdue on their accounts, suggesting that we will never be paid."

"4. We have nobody on the staff who knows anything about desktop publishing, making it difficult for us to modernize the business."

Lisa Lundquist smiled, and said, "Kathy, I offered you this job because you have the background and the smarts to fix little problems like that. Just think of how much money you will make, and all the fun you will have if you take care of those problems."

CASE QUESTIONS

1. What managerial functions and roles must Kathy Lundquist emphasize to fix the problems she uncovered?
2. How realistic is it for Kathy to solve the problems she has identified?
3. If you were Kathy, would you quit? Or would you stay to work on the problems?

REFERENCES

1. Bob Weinstein, "Flower Power," *Entrepreneur* (June 1995): 146–152.
2. Peter F. Drucker, *The Frontiers of Management* (New York: Truman Talley Books, Dutton, 1986), 1.
3. Andrall E. Pearson, "Six Basics for General Managers," *Harvard Business Review* (July–August 1989): 94–101.
4. Allen I. Kraut et al., "The Role of the Manager: What's Really Important in Different Management Jobs," *The Academy of Management Executive* (November 1989): 286–293.
5. This research is reported in Henry Mintzberg, *The Nature of Managerial Work* (New York: Harper & Row, 1973).
6. J. Kenneth Graham Jr. and William L. Mihal, *The CMD Managerial Job Analysis Inventory* (Rochester, NY: Rochester Institute of Technology, 1987): 2–6; Jeffrey S. Shippmann, Erich Prien, and Garry L. Hughes, "The Content of Management Work: Formation of Task and Job Skill Composite Classifications," *Journal of Business and Psychology* (Spring 1991): 325–354.
7. "Specialist v. Generalist: A Dual Role," *Executive Strategies* (June 1995): 10.
8. Sumantra Ghosal and Christopher A. Bartlett, "Changing the Role of Top Management: Beyond Structure and Process," *Harvard Business Review* (January–February 1995): 86–96.
9. Cynthia M. Pavett and Alan W. Lau, "Managerial Work: The Influence of Hierarchical Level and Functional Speciality," *Academy of Management Journal* (March 1983): 170–177.
10. Jan English and Carol M. Ondeck, "The Cosmetic Manager," *Executive Management Forum* (November 1990): 1.

CHAPTER 2

The Manager's Domestic and International Environment

© Richard Younker

For over 100 years, Bicknell Manufacturing Company has produced industrial drill bits for construction equipment at its facility in Rockland, Maine. The family-owned business thrived during most of its history, but then suffered during the 1990 recession. The company struggled for new business at home before deciding to explore the global marketplace. Unfortunately, none of the 65 employees at the $4 million company had any foreign experience. Yet construction booms were taking place in Brazil, Columbia, and Mexico. • Company general manager John Purcell found a distributor while visiting Mexico on a trade mission sponsored by the Small Business Administration. In 1993 Bicknell began exporting to Latin America, with exceptional results. Purcell recently closed a deal to sell in China and Vietnam. International sales now comprise 20 percent of Bicknell's revenues.[1]

The Bicknell Manufacturing Co. incident illustrates the comprehensiveness of the globalization of business—even small firms have customers outside their own country. In this chapter we describe major aspects of the manager's national and international environments. Understanding these twin forces better equips a managerial worker to deal with today's challenges.

THE DOMESTIC ENVIRONMENT

LEARNING OBJECTIVE

Identify the general and specific environmental forces facing managers and organizations.

A large number of factors in the outside world can and do influence the work of managers. Particularly challenging is that the list of influential factors keeps changing. At one time, for example, only a small proportion of the work force needed to be skilled in information technology. Today, up to 80 percent of employees at some firms must be computer literate. In this first major section of the chapter, we describe the components of the external environment affecting the manager. In addition, we take a brief look at several major challenges facing organizations, such as downsizing and the polarized work force.

COMPONENTS OF THE EXTERNAL ENVIRONMENT

general environmental force

A force that influences the organization's goals, strategies, and tasks in a general way.

The firm's external environment is divided into general and specific environmental forces. Both types of environmental forces are outside the firm's control. A **general environmental force** influences the organization's goals, strategies, and tasks in a general way. A **specific environmental force** influences the firm in a regular and specific way. Recognize, however, that the distinction between general and specific forces is not absolute. Exhibit 2-1 summarizes general and specific environmental forces.

specific environmental force

A force that influences the firm in a regular and specific way.

GENERAL ENVIRONMENTAL FORCES. The five types of general environmental forces organizations and their managers face are described next.

1. *Economic forces.* Private and public organizations are profoundly influenced by general economic conditions, as was Bicknell Manufacturing Co. During prosperous times, for example, managers have more latitude in spending money and hiring personnel. In today's competitive work environment, even the forecast of a business downturn influences some managers to reduce expenses or postpone a new program.

2. *Social/cultural forces.* Changes in social values and demographics can exert important influences on management practices. Today many workers desire to participate in decisions about their work. In response, many managers now solicit the input of group members before making important decisions. An important demographic change influencing firms is the decrease in the number of young people and the increase in the number of older people. Many service businesses such as fast-food restaurants and supermarkets now actively recruit senior citizens to fill jobs traditionally held by young adults.

3. *Political/legal forces.* Many executives believe that the party in power and the officials elected to office can influence business conditions. Consequently, many executives are willing to engage in business expansion when the party of their choice retains or gains power. Legislation exerts a major influence

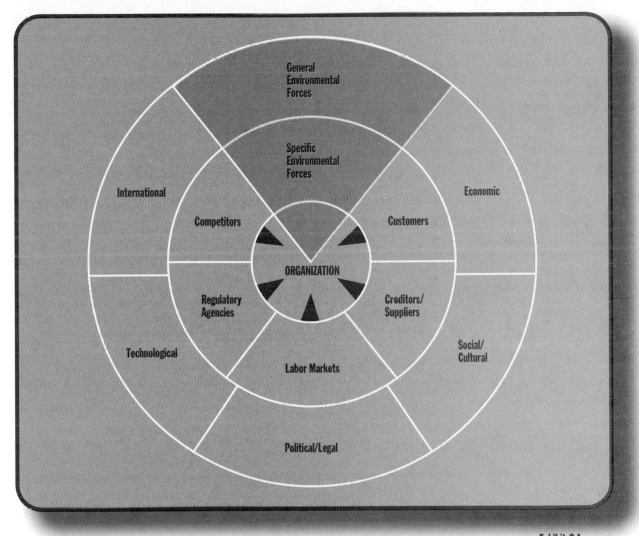

Exhibit 2-1
Major Forces in an
Organization's External
Environment

on the work activities of managers. Laws and executive orders influence count-less activities. Among them are hiring practices, investment practices, and ac-commodating buildings to meet the demands of the physically handicapped. Chapter 10, "Staffing and Human Resource Management," describes some of this legislation.

4. *Technological forces.* Organizations and their managers are forced to adapt to existing technology to remain competitive. Changing technology is one of the most critical issues facing executives, particularly in high-technology industries. **Technology,** in this context, is the systematic application of scientific or other organized knowledge to practical tasks. This means that technology includes ideas and new knowledge, in addition to equipment.

5. *International forces.* As described later in this chapter, business has become in-ternational. All major corporations and most smaller ones engage in some trade with other countries. Managers must now compete with foreign firms in terms of the cost and quality of goods. Many managers now must visit opera-tions and customers in other countries and often must converse in another

technology
*The systematic ap-
plication of scien-
tific or other orga-
nized knowledge to
practical tasks.*

language. Furthermore, many managers work for foreign-owned businesses with operating offices in the United States and Canada. As a result, it is important for these managers to understand cultural differences of the parent corporation.

SPECIFIC ENVIRONMENTAL FORCES. The five types of specific environmental forces organizations and their managers face are described next.

1. *Customers.* As most business owners, marketing specialists, and quality enthusiasts contend, "The real boss is the customer." Changes in customer or client preferences exert direct pressure on companies to satisfy these preferences. Changing demands often create a flurry of activity for firms and managers, such as the surge in demand worldwide for recreational vehicles and pickup trucks. (Forty percent of vehicles used for private transportation in the United States and Canada in 1995 fell into these categories.) Demands for certain products can also decline sharply. Do you remember how quickly the Barney (the friendly dinosaur) craze cooled down?
2. *Creditors/suppliers.* Business firms are also influenced by the people to whom they owe money (creditors) and the firms that provide them with the goods and services they need to operate (suppliers). It is common practice for the officer of a company's bank to serve on the company's board of directors.
3. *Labor markets.* The term *labor market* refers to the supply of workers available to a firm. The labor market influences a firm because, without the right mix of workers, the firm cannot prosper. One of the selling points of many communities in attracting companies is its pool of potential employees.
4. *Regulatory agencies.* Government agencies regulate the activities and firms and managers in five principal areas: consumer protection, investor protection, environmental law, preservation of competition, and labor-management relations. One of hundreds of possible examples is the Environmental Protection Agency (EPA), which attempts to prevent the environment from being damaged by organizations of various types.
5. *Competitors.* Competition exerts a major influence on the actions of organizations and their managers. For-profit and nonprofit firms must respond to the competition. Colleges and career schools compete for students, and health-maintenance organizations (HMOs) compete for patients. At its best, competition forces firms to be more innovative and productive. At its worst, competition encourages firms to overwork their employees and make untrue negative statements about rivals.

CURRENT CHALLENGES FACING MANAGEMENT

LEARNING OBJECTIVE

Describe many of the current challenges facing managers.

Every topic in this text might rightfully be described as a current challenge facing management, because few challenges disappear. Nevertheless, here we mention seven challenges and trends that constitute a demanding part of the manager's domestic environment. Most of these challenges will be presented in more detail at appropriate places in the text.

The first seven challenges are emphasis on total quality, team-based organizations, corporate downsizings, reengineering, the polarized workplace, integration of work and family demands, and an ethics emphasis. An eighth challenge, dealing with labor unions, is also mentioned because labor-management relations are profoundly affected by the other challenges, such as teams, downsizing, and reengineering.

EMPHASIS ON TOTAL QUALITY. Total quality management is a management system for improving performance throughout a firm by maximizing customer satisfaction and making continuous improvements. Successful firms have always emphasized quality. (Do you recall the lonely Maytag repair technician?) The total quality movement, however, heavily emphasizes the team approach and statistical analysis to making suggestions for improvement. A challenge to managers is to maintain high quality, but at the same time make sure that the improvement adds value for the customer.

TEAM-BASED ORGANIZATIONS. The emphasis on total quality is but one manifestation of how organizations are relying more on tightly knit, highly focused groups of people to accomplish important work. Teams are also used for such diverse purposes as product development, selling, and carrying out a project. Teams are granted substantial authority, or *empowered*, to accomplish their tasks. The various teams and team-like structures include top-management teams, self-managing work teams, task forces, committees, project teams (such as for launching a new product), and quality-improvement teams. Add to the list the *virtual team*, in which the members interact by computer, drop in and out as needed, and take turns being a leader. A challenge to the manager is to provide direction to teams yet not detract from empowerment.

DOWNSIZING. A dominating trend shaping the manager's environment is the movement toward streamlined, efficient firms. To remain competitive and provide shareholders with a suitable return on investment, about 80 percent of large organizations have undergone **downsizing.** Downsizing is the slimming down of operations to focus resources and boost profits or decrease expenses. Downsizing is also referred to as *rightsizing*, because the intent is to ensure that the organization is the right size to achieve maximum efficiency.

Downsizings are incessant, with many of them taking place after a merger. In 1995, the newly created Lockheed Martin Corp., the largest defense contractor in the United States, attempted to save $1.8 billion. To accomplish this goal, they laid off 7,000 workers. The company also planned to eliminate 16,000 more jobs and close 12 plants and laboratories.

A major managerial challenge in a downsized environment is to maintain morale and motivation while so many workers become anxious and fearful about losing their jobs. In addition, they may resent a company that laid off so many former coworkers. Many workers feel overworked because the company becomes thinly staffed.

REENGINEERING. One of the most popular new business concepts of the 1990s deals with organization by process rather than by tasks. Called **reengineering,** it is the radical redesign of business processes to achieve substantial improvements in performance. A representative example would be the redesign of the home-mortgage application process to drastically reduce processing time. Time savers would include requiring fewer approvals and fewer hand-offs from one department to another. Reengineering is closely associated with downsizing, because many positions are declared unnecessary after the reengineering process is completed. Managers and professionals must be innovative to contribute to reengineering. They must shake obsolete business processes and create new ones.

---

total quality management
A management system for improving performance throughout a firm by maximizing customer satisfaction and making continuous improvements.

downsizing
The slimming down of operations to focus resources and boost profits or decrease expenses.

reengineering
The radical redesign of business processes to achieve substantial improvements in performance.

THE POLARIZED WORKPLACE. As high technology continues to envelope the workplace, the separation increases between high-skilled and low-skilled workers. In a **polarized workplace,** high-skilled, high-paying jobs and low-skilled, low-paying jobs increase, whereas moderately skilled, moderate-paying jobs decrease. As a consequence, it becomes more difficult to find a good-paying job unless a person is highly skilled. High-wage occupations, such as professional, managerial, and technical jobs, continue to grow, creating more opportunities for people with high-level skills and education. At the same time low-paying service jobs are readily available.[2] A managerial challenge in the polarized workplace is to maintain the motivation of people in low-paying, dead-end jobs.

> **polarized workplace**
> *A workplace in which there are more high-paying and low-paying than moderate-paying jobs.*

INTEGRATION OF WORK AND FAMILY DEMANDS. In recent years employers have invested heavily in developing programs to help employees meet family obligations despite full-time employment. Key factors prompting these programs include more women entering the labor force, and more single parents having heavy family responsibilities yet still working full-time. Another factor is that more working adults have responsibility for elder care.[3] Child care, elder care, modified work schedules, and parental leave are the leading work-family programs. Some top-level managers regard these programs as productivity boosters. William Lee, chairman and president of Duke Power, says, "No worker can be productive if he or she is worrying about a sick baby at home."[4]

The managerial challenge is to satisfy the special needs of employees with heavy family obligations, yet still maintain high productivity and hold everybody accountable for results. The manager may have to deal with the resentment of some workers without heavy family obligations who consider work-family programs to be a form of favoritism.

HEIGHTENED EMPHASIS ON ETHICS. In reality, a small proportion of business executives are unethical, yet their misdeeds create negative publicity and morale problems. To upgrade the ethical conduct of present and future managers, many business firms offer training in ethics. Widespread problems such as *inventory shrinkage* and taking home office supplies for personal use suggest that workers at all levels require ethical training. The managerial challenge is to encourage others to behave ethically when it appears that so many unethical people achieve high incomes and exciting jobs.

DEALING WITH LABOR UNIONS. Labor unions can exert a substantial influence on a manager's job if the company is unionized or if a union drive is in process. Approximately 15.5 percent of the nonagricultural U.S. work force (including both manufacturing and service workers) is unionized. The comparable figure was about 34 percent in 1960, and 25 percent in 1980. Downsizing and sending manufacturing overseas have slowed the growth of organized labor. Nevertheless, in 1994, unions grew by 150,000 members, the second year of growth following 14 years of decline. One-half of the growth of unions is from employee affiliations of public-sector workers. The other half is from low-wage workers such as janitors, clerical, and health-care workers. Combined, these groups are a fast-growing segment of the workforce.[5]

Union leaders, particularly those affiliated with manufacturing employees, are strongly concerned about job security for their members. A challenge facing management is to find ways of offering job security in a volatile environment in which

Exhibit 2-2
The Leading U.S.
Markets and
Suppliers, 1994

Top 25 U.S. Markets		Leading U.S. Suppliers	
	$ Billions		$ Billions
1. Canada	114.4	1. Canada	128.9
2. Japan	53.5	2. Japan	119.1
3. Mexico	50.8	3. Mexico	49.5
4. United Kingdom	26.8	4. China	38.8
5. Germany	19.2	5. Germany	31.7
6. South Korea	18.0	6. Taiwan	26.7
7. Taiwan	17.1	7. United Kingdom	25.1
8. France	13.6	8. South Korea	19.7
9. Netherlands	13.6	9. France	16.8
10. Singapore	13.0	10. Singapore	15.4
11. Hong Kong	11.4	11. Italy	14.7
12. Belgium-Luxembourg	11.2	12. Malaysia	14.0
13. Australia	9.8	13. Thailand	10.3
14. China	9.3	14. Hong Kong	9.7
15. Brazil	8.1	15. Brazil	8.7
16. Italy	7.2	16. Venezuela	8.4
17. Malaysia	7.0	17. Saudi Arabia	7.7
18. Saudi Arabia	6.0	18. Belgium-Luxembourg	6.6
19. Switzerland	5.6	19. Indonesia	6.5
20. Israel	5.0	20. Switzerland	6.4
21. Thailand	4.9	21. Netherlands	6.0
22. Spain	4.6	22. Philippines	5.7
23. Argentina	4.5	23. India	5.3
24. Colombia	4.1	24. Israel	5.2
25. Venezuela	4.0	25. Sweden	5.0

Source: *Business America*, U.S. Department of Commerce (May 1995): 18.

downsizing and reengineering are so popular. Another is to create such positive working conditions for employees that workers do not find it necessary to have outside representation. A third challenge is to make sure that new practices such as employee-involvement groups do not violate provisions of the labor-management agreement.

THE INTERNATIONAL ENVIRONMENT

An important environmental influence on the manager's job is the internationalization of business and management. Approximately 10 to 15 percent of all jobs in the United States and Canada are dependent upon trade with other countries. Exhibit 2-2 provides details about the magnitude of U.S. exports and imports with its biggest trading partners. In general, as business has become more global, the manager must adapt to the challenges of working with organizations and people from other countries. Even keeping time-zone differences

LEARNING OBJECTIVE

Appreciate the importance
of multinational
corporations and emerging
markets in international
business.

MANAGERS IN ACTION: MOTOROLA MOTIVATES ITS MALAYSIAN WORKERS

Members of the Motorola management team have developed a blueprint for creating a well-trained, motivated, and highly productive workforce. The particular focus is on emerging markets such as Malaysia, China, and Vietnam. The walkie-talkie plant in Penang, Malaysia, has become a laboratory for developing motivational techniques that can be applied to Motorola plants everywhere. The spotless plant is decorated with performance charts, trophies for quality performance, and slogans. Yet the core of the motivational program is empowering workers to improve quality and productivity.

The plant's quality-control department relies in part on the thousands of recommendations submitted by workers as part of the "I Recommend" program. In a recent year, employees submitted 41,000 suggestions for improving operations. The net savings from these suggestions was $2 million. The reward for such performance is recognition rather than money.

Source: Facts as reported in "Importing Enthusiasm," *Business Week* (special 1994 issue, *21st Century Capitalism*): 122–123.

clearly in mind challenges many people. Here we present information about some of the key sets of knowledge necessary for becoming an international managerial worker.

MULTINATIONAL CORPORATIONS AND EMERGING MARKETS

multinational corporation (MNC)
A firm with units in two or more countries in addition to its own.

The heart of international trade is the **multinational corporation (MNC),** a firm with units in two or more countries in addition to its own. Today's MNC has headquarters in one country and subsidiaries in others. However, it is more than a collection of subsidiaries that carry out decisions made at headquarters. A multinational corporation develops new products in several countries and promotes key executives regardless of nationality. A multinational corporation sometimes hires people from its country of origin (expatriates) for key positions in overseas facilities. At other times, the MNC will hire citizens of the country in which the division is located (host-country nationals) for key positions.

The continued growth of multinational corporations has been facilitated in recent years by three agreements, as described next.

The North American Free Trade Agreement (NAFTA) establishes liberal trading relationships among the United States, Canada, and Mexico. The agreement creates a giant trading zone extending from the Arctic Ocean to the Gulf of Mexico. Many companies have benefited from NAFTA because they now have better access to the two other countries. Many U.S. companies, for example, have increased exports to Mexico. Furthermore, trade between the United States and Canada surged to $260 billion in 1994. Many Canadians, however, believe that NAFTA makes it too easy for Canadians to purchase U.S. goods. As a result, retail trade has suffered in Canadian stores near the U.S. border.

The European Community (EC) is a 19-nation alliance that virtually turns member countries into a single marketplace for ideas, goods, services, and investment strategies. The EC trades with member nations, the United States and Canada, and other countries throughout the world. In addition, Japanese firms are now investing rapidly in Europe.

The General Agreement on Tariffs & Trade (GATT) liberalizes trade among many nations throughout the world. The idea is to lower trade barriers, therefore facilitating international trade. At the same time, consumers do not pay artificially high prices for imported goods. A concern, however, is that global trade liberalization leads to continuous job cuts and downward pressures on wages in industrialized countries.[6] This occurs because companies from low-wage countries can export more readily into high-wage countries. (The counter-argument is that free trade—in the long run—creates more job opportunities.)

A major contributor to the globalization of business is that new markets emerge, partly as a result of the above agreements. The growing trade with Eastern European countries including Czechoslovakia, Hungary, and Poland has fostered imports and exports. For example, Suzuki of Japan now manufactures automobiles in Hungary. China has become the tenth largest trading partner with the United States. Countries of the Pacific Rim are in the midst of industrial expansion. Among them are Australia, Malaysia, New Zealand, and Thailand. The accompanying insert illustrates the potential significance of a Pacific Rim operation.

SENSITIVITY TO CULTURAL DIFFERENCES

The guiding principle for people involved in international enterprise is sensitivity to cultural differences. **Cultural sensitivity** is awareness of local and national customs and their importance in effective interpersonal relationships. Ignoring the customs of other people creates a communications block that can impede business and create ill will. For example, Americans tend to be impatient to close a deal while businesspeople in many other cultures prefer to build a relationship slowly before consummating an agreement. Exhibit 2-3 presents a sampling of cultural differences that can affect business.

Candidates for foreign assignments generally receive training in the language and customs of the country they will work in. Intercultural training exercises include playing the roles of businesspeople from a different culture. The aircraft-engine unit of General Electric Co. is one of many companies preparing people for the international work environment. Groups of midlevel engineers and managers receive cross-cultural training, including training in foreign-language skills. Although not all of these managers are scheduled to live abroad, the training is designed to help them work effectively with people from another culture.[7] The importance of such training was revealed by a study that found that 30 percent of placements in foreign countries were unsuccessful. These mistakes were due primarily to the employees' failures to adjust properly to a new culture.[8]

Another approach to developing cross-cultural sensitivity is to recognize cross-cultural differences in managerial styles. These differences are cultural stereotypes applicable to many managers from the same country. As in all aspects of human behavior, considerable individual differences can be observed among managers from the same culture. National stereotypes of management styles, as revealed by the research of Geert Hofstede and his collaborators, are as follows:[9]

Germany: German managers are expected to be primarily technical experts, or *meisters,* who assign tasks and help solve difficult problems.

Japan: Japanese managers rely on group consensus before making a decision, and the group controls individual behavior to a large extent. Japanese managers are perceived as more formal and businesslike, and less talkative and emotional, than their American counterparts.

LEARNING OBJECTIVE

Recognize the importance of sensitivity to cultural differences in international enterprise.

cultural sensitivity
Awareness of local and national customs and their importance in effective interpersonal relationships.

**Exhibit 2-3
Cultural Mistakes to
Avoid with Selected
Cultural Groups**

- Insisting on getting down to business quickly in most countries outside the United States. Building a social relationship precedes closing a deal in most countries.
- Shaking hands with or hugging Asians in public. Asians consider these practices offensive.
- Not interpreting "We'll consider it" as a "no" when spoken by a Japanese businessperson. Japanese negotiators mean "no" when they say, "We'll consider it."
- Not giving small gifts to Japanese when conducting business. Japanese are offended by not receiving these gifts.
- Giving small gifts to Chinese when conducting business. Chinese people are offended by these gifts.
- Pressuring an Asian job applicant or employee to brag about personal accomplishments. Boasting about their professional achievements makes Asians feel self-conscious. They prefer to let the record speak for itself.
- Being overly rank-conscious in Scandinavia. Scandinavians pay relatively little attention to a person's place in the hierarchy.
- Greeting a French customer or other business contact for the first time in a French-speaking country and saying, "Glad to meet you." French is a polite language. It is preferable to say, "Glad to meet you, sir [or monsieur, madame, or ms.]."
- Referring to the Queen of England as "Elizabeth" or "Liz" rather than "Queen Elizabeth" when dealing with a person from England or English Canada. English and Canadian people expect outsiders to treat their royalty with respect even if they joke among themselves about royalty.
- Appearing annoyed when someone shows up late for a meeting in most countries outside the United States.

The above suggestions will lead to cross-cultural skill development if practiced in the right setting. Search for an opportunity to relate to a person from a given culture in the way described in the above suggestions. Observe the reaction of the other person to provide feedback on your cross-cultural effectiveness.

France: French managers, particularly in major corporations, are part of an elite class, and they behave in a superior, authoritarian manner.

Holland: Dutch managers emphasize equality and consensus and do not expect to impress group members with their status. Dutch managers give group members ample opportunity to participate in problem solving.

The Overseas Chinese: Many managers from China work in Pacific Rim countries such as Taiwan, Hong Kong, Singapore, Malaysia, and the Philippines. In companies managed by Chinese, major decisions are made by one dominant person, quite often of advanced years. The Chinese manager maintains a low profile.

LEARNING OBJECTIVE 5

Identify major challenges
facing the global
managerial worker.

balance of trade
The difference between exports and imports in both goods and services.

CHALLENGES FACING THE GLOBAL MANAGERIAL WORKER

Managerial workers on assignment in other countries, as well as domestic managers working on international dealings, face a variety of challenges. Rising to these challenges can be the difference between success and failure. A concern at the broadest level is a country's **balance of trade,** the difference between exports and imports in both goods and services. Many people believe that it is to a coun-

Exhibit 2-4
U.S. Trade Balances,
1994

U.S. Surplus		U.S. Deficit	
Positions	$ Billions	Positions	$ Billions
1. Netherlands	+7.6	1. Japan	−65.7
2. Australia	+6.6	2. China	−29.5
3. Belgium-Luxembourg	+4.5	3. Canada	−14.5
4. Argentina	+2.7	4. Germany	−12.5
5. Egypt	+2.3	5. Taiwan	−9.6
6. United Kingdom	+1.8	6. Italy	−7.5
7. Hong Kong	+1.7	7. Malaysia	−7.0
8. Mexico	+1.3	8. Thailand	5.4
9. Turkey	+1.2	9. Venezuela	−4.3
10. United Arab Emirates	+1.1	10. Nigeria	−3.9
11. Spain	+1.1	11. Indonesia	−3.7
12. Panama	+1.0	12. France	−3.2
13. Chile	+1.0	13. India	−3.0
14. Colombia	+0.9	14. Sweden	−2.5
15. Paraguay	+0.7	15. Singapore	−2.3
16. Peru	+0.6	16. Angola	−1.9
17. Ireland	+0.5	17. Philippines	−1.8
18. Bahamas	+0.5	18. Saudi Arabia	−1.7
19. Lebanon	+0.4	19. South Korea	−1.6
20. Greece	+0.4	20. Gabon	−1.1
21. Brunei	+0.3	21. Norway	−1.1
22. Iran	+0.3	22. Denmark	−0.9
23. El Salvador	+0.3	23. Sri Lanka	−0.9
24. Jamaica	+0.3	24. Bangladesh	−0.8
25. Bermuda	+0.3	25. Macao	−0.8

Source: *Business America*, U.S. Department of Commerce (May 1995): 19.

try's advantage to export more than it imports. Yet in 1995 the U.S. trade deficit was $170 billion. The country doing more selling than buying can be considered wealthier. An individual manager might want to contribute to the national economy by exporting more than importing. Exhibit 2-4 lists the U.S. trade balances with various countries. Would you have guessed that the U.S. had its largest trade surplus with the Netherlands?

International business can be challenging because *inflation and currency devaluation* can have a severely negative impact on costs and profits. Also, if the currency of a country suddenly gains in value, it may be difficult to export products made in that country. The reason is that the products become more expensive in the importing countries based solely on exchange rates. When the value of a country's currency falls, a company can profit. It becomes cheaper for other countries to purchase one's products. In 1994, for example, Apple Computer Company benefited from a falling U.S. dollar because it was easier for overseas countries to purchase Apple products.

A more specific financial problem facing the international manager can be *collecting money* from overseas customers. The most common way to get paid is through a letter of credit, a document issued by a bank. It guarantees a company will get paid as soon as it can provide documents showing that the goods or services were delivered as promised. Even with a letter of credit there can be serious delays in getting paid. Eastern Europe, China, and Russia are areas in which getting money out of a country can be difficult.

International managers face a fundamental problem because of the *liability of foreignness.* When doing business abroad, a company faces costs arising from such factors as an unfamiliar environment, and from cultural, political, and economic differences. It is also difficult to coordinate activities across geographic boundaries. A study of Western and Japanese banks suggested that an effective way of overcoming the problem of being foreign is simply to use a firm's best business and managerial practices abroad.[10]

International managers can face ethical problems because their customers and suppliers might reside in countries where *human rights are violated.* Should a U.S. rug distributor purchase carpets from a supplier that employs 10-year-old children who work 11 hours a day for the equivalent of three American dollars? Should a U.S. shoe manufacturer buy components from a country that uses political prisoners as free labor? Ethical issues require careful thought.

A problem faced by many managers and professionals on overseas assignments is **culture shock.** The condition refers to a group of physical and psychological symptoms that can develop when a person is abruptly placed in a foreign culture. Among them are excessive hand washing and concern for sanitation, fear of physical contact with others, fear of being mugged, and strong feelings of homesickness.[11] The type of training program referred to earlier can help minimize culture shock.

A recurring challenge in other countries is that the international managerial worker may have to use a different negotiation style. A do-or-die attitude is often self-defeating. American negotiators, for example, often find that they must be more patient, use a team approach, and avoid being too informal. Patience is a major factor in negotiating outside the United States. Asian negotiators are willing to spend many days negotiating a deal. Much of their negotiating activity seems to be ceremonial (including elaborate dining) and unrelated to the task. A "strictly business" American can be frustrated by this agonizing process.

> **culture shock**
>
> *A group of physical and psychological symptoms that can develop when a person is abruptly placed in a foreign culture.*

METHODS OF ENTRY INTO WORLD MARKETS

LEARNING OBJECTIVE

Explain various methods of entry into world markets.

Firms enter the global market in several different ways. You will recall that Bicknell Manufacturing Company, like many small businesses, found a distributor to gain entry. Here we first look at stages of entering international business (or the stages can be regarded simply as methods of entry). We then describe how a new breed of small businesses is going global from the outset.

STAGE 1: EXPORTING. Goods produced in one country are then sold for direct use or resale to one or more companies in foreign countries. Many small firms specialize in helping companies gain entry to foreign markets through exporting. An overseas distributor can be quite helpful, but one must be chosen carefully. Recent research suggests than an in-person visit to a prospective overseas distributor eliminates many problems.[12]

STAGE 2: LICENSING. Companies operating in foreign countries are authorized to produce and market products or services with specific territories on a fee basis.

STAGE 3: LOCAL WAREHOUSING AND SELLING. Goods that are produced in one country are shipped directly to storage and marketing facilities of the parent company or subsidiary in one or more foreign countries.

STAGE 4: LOCAL ASSEMBLY AND PACKAGING. In this arrangement, components rather than finished products are shipped to company-owned facilities in other countries. There assembly is completed and the goods are marketed. Trade regulations sometimes require that a large product, such as a mainframe computer, be assembled locally rather than shipped from the exporting country as a finished product.

An example of local assembly and packaging by U.S. companies is the use of maquiladoras. A **maquiladora,** a manufacturing plant close to the U.S. border, is a plant established specifically to assemble American products. The U.S. owners of maquiladoras pay no import tax on components. When maquiladora products are exported to the United States, they are taxed only on the value added in Mexico.

The maquiladora industry was established for two main purposes. First, it gave U.S. businesses the opportunity to use high-quality, inexpensive labor. (The average pay of a maquiladora worker is $2.50 per hour.) Second, it gave many economically disadvantaged northern Mexicans an opportunity for a relatively high-paying job and good working conditions. General Motors is one American company that is making extensive use of maquiladoras.

> **maquiladora**
> *A manufacturing plant close to the U.S. border that is established specifically to assemble American products.*

STAGE 5: JOINT VENTURE (OR STRATEGIC ALLIANCE). Instead of merging formally with a firm of mutual interest, a company in one country pools resources with those of one or more foreign companies. Jointly they produce, warehouse, transport, and market products. Profits or losses from these operations are shared in some predetermined proportion. The strategic alliance of Japan's Toshiba Corporation, Germany's Siemens A.G., and IBM Corp. is a joint venture to work on advanced computer chips.

STAGE 6: DIRECT FOREIGN INVESTMENT. The most advanced stage of multinational business activity takes place when a company in one country produces and markets products through wholly owned facilities in foreign countries. Toyota Motor Co. and Ford Motor Co. are two well-known MNCs that conduct business in this manner. Exhibit 2-5 illustrates how an MNC contributes to the economy of the country in which it has a large operation.

Stage 1 offers the least protection for the company doing business in another country. Each successive stage offers more protection against political and economic risks. One major risk is that the firm in the other country may drop its affiliation with the multinational firm and sell the product on its own. The affiliate thus becomes a competitor. To avoid this risk, direct foreign investment is recommended as the best way to protect the company's competitive advantage. The advantage is protected because the manager of the foreign subsidiary can control its operation.

Exhibit 2-5
Multinational Firms
Often Use Domestic
Components

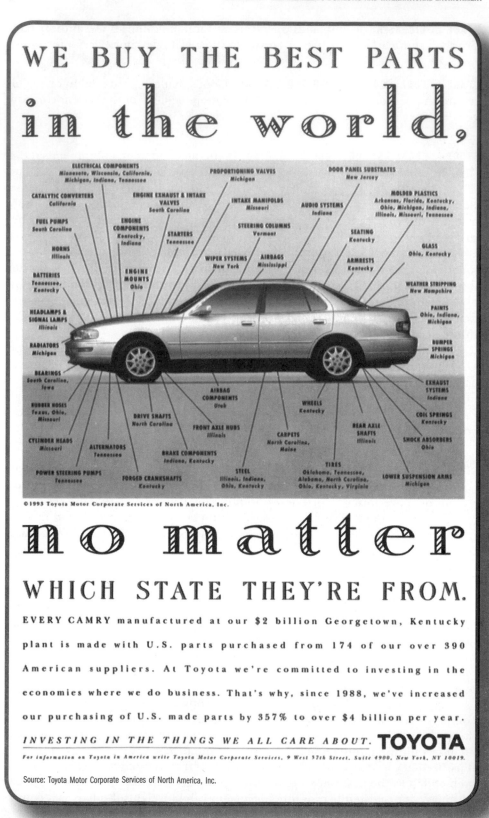

Source: Toyota Motor Corporate Services of North America, Inc.

A **global startup** is a small firm that comes into existence by serving an international market. By so doing, the firm circumvents the stages described above. Logitech Inc., the leading manufacturer of the computer mouse, is one of the most successful global startups. The company was founded in 1982 by a Swiss and two Italians who wanted to be an international company from the start. Logitech began with headquarters, manufacturing, and engineering in California and Switzerland and then established facilities in Taiwan and Ireland. Founders of global startups have one key characteristic in common: some international experience before going global.[13]

> **global startup**
> *A small firm that comes into existence by serving an international market.*

SUCCESS FACTORS IN THE GLOBAL MARKETPLACE

Success in international business stems from the same factors that lead to success at home. The ultimate reason for the success of any product or service is that it satisfies customer needs. Additional strategies and tactics, however, are required for success in the global marketplace. It is important to recognize this, because internationalization of business is not always successful. Most of these strategies and tactics are a logical extension of topics discussed previously in this chapter.

LEARNING OBJECTIVE 7

Pinpoint success factors in the global marketplace.

THINK GLOBALLY, ACT LOCALLY. A competitive enterprise combines global scale and world-class technology with deep roots in local markets.[14] Local representatives of the firm behave as though their primary mission is to serve the local customer.

DIVERSIFY INTO SIMILAR PRODUCT MARKETS. Diversification into product markets similar to markets currently served may result in several competitive advantages. First, managers understand their customer. Second, the structural characteristics of the new industry are likely to be familiar, which facilitates responding to competitive challenges. Third, some of the firm's current skills may be transferred to the new product or market. A fast-food chain might diversify into a fast-food item that is popular in another culture.[15] For instance, Burger King might sell tacos in its restaurants in Mexico.

BE FAMILIAR WITH LOCAL BUSINESS CONCEPTS, LAWS, AND CUSTOMS. Success in foreign markets is contingent upon close familiarity with the local scene. U.S. companies that have established maquiladoras have discovered the importance of this principle. For example, a unique aspect of Mexican law comes into play when an officially recognized labor union declares a strike. All employees, including managers, must leave the building, and red and black flags are hung at entrances to the plant. Furthermore, employees receive full pay for all the time they are out on a legal strike.

RECRUIT TALENTED NATIONALS. A major success factor in building a business in another country is to hire talented citizens of that country to fill important positions. Western firms have the best chance of penetrating the perplexing Japanese market if they hire top Japanese talent. After the host-company nationals are hired, they must be taught the culture of the parent company. By teaching the overseas managers the values and traditions of the firm, those managers can better achieve corporate objectives. At times the prevailing management style in the host country may not fit the parent company culture. Teaching the culture then becomes even more important. An example follows:

Chicago-based Tellabs Inc., a manufacturer of telecommunications products, opened a branch in Munich, Germany. Tellabs had an informal and flexible culture in which all employees had access to senior management. The German culture was much more formal. Laura Bozich, the regional director for Central Europe, was sent to Munich to explain the corporate culture to the newly hired manager.[16]

RESEARCH AND ASSESS POTENTIAL MARKETS. Another basic success strategy in international markets is to acquire valid information on the firm's target market. Trade statistics are usually a good starting point. If the company manufactures long-lasting light bulbs, it must find out where such bulbs sell the best. Basic trade data are often available at foreign embassies, banks with international operations, and departments of commerce.

ENCOURAGE KEY PEOPLE TO DEVELOP FOREIGN LANGUAGE SKILLS. Even though English has become the official language of business and technology, overseas employees should develop skill in the language of the host country. Being able to listen to and understand foreign customers speaking in their native language about their requirements may reveal nuances that would be missed by having them speak in English. Showing that one has made an effort to learn the native language can earn big dividends with employees, customers, prospective customers, bankers, and government officials. To be impressive, however, it is important to go beyond the most basic skill level.

UNDERSTAND YOUR COMPETITORS, POTENTIAL PARTNERS, AND THE DIVERSE MEMBERS OF THE MANAGEMENT TEAM. The most comprehensive strategy for success in international business is to thoroughly analyze and understand the people upon whom your success depends. Understanding your competitors includes such information as their managerial values and strategy, and predicting the types of products and services they will offer in the future. Understanding partners in an overseas alliance includes figuring out what they expect to gain from the relationship. Understanding the diverse members of your management team refers to factors such as knowing their culture and work experiences.[17]

SUMMARY OF KEY POINTS

1

Identify the general and specific environmental forces facing managers and organizations.

The firm's external environment is divided into general and specific environmental forces. The general environmental forces are economic, social/cultural, political/legal, technological, and international. The specific environmental forces are customers, creditors/suppliers, labor markets, regulatory agencies, and competitors.

2

Describe many of the current challenges facing managers.

Major challenges facing managers include the following: emphasis on total quality, team-based organizations, corporate downsizings, reengineering, the polarized workplace (high-skilled versus low-skilled jobs), integration of work and family demands, and an ethics emphasis. Another challenge is dealing with labor unions, because they are affected by the other challenges.

3

Appreciate the importance of multinational corporations and emerging markets in international business.

Multinational corporations (MNCs) are at the heart of international business. The growth of MNCs has been facilitated by the North American Free Trade Agreement, the European Community, and the General Agreement on Trades and Tariffs. Also, the emergence of new markets, such as Eastern European and Pacific Rim countries, facilitates global commerce.

4

Recognize the importance of sensitivity to cultural differences in international enterprise.

The guiding principle for people involved in international enterprise is sensitivity to cultural differences. Candidates for foreign assignments generally receive training in the language and customs of the country in which they will work. Another approach to developing cross-cultural sensitivity is to recognize national differences in managerial styles.

5

Identify major challenges facing the global managerial worker.

Challenges facing global managerial workers include contributing to a healthy balance of trade, inflation and currency devaluation, collecting money, and the liability of foreignness. Other challenges are trading with countries that violate human rights, culture shock, and adapting one's negotiation style.

6

Explain various methods of entry into world markets.

Firms enter the global market via the following methods (or stages): exporting, licensing, local warehousing and selling, local assembly and packaging, joint ventures, direct foreign investment, and global startups.

7

Pinpoint success factors in the global marketplace.

Success factors for the global marketplace include (a) think globally, act locally, (b) diversify into similar products, (c) be familiar with the local business environment, (d) recruit talented nationals, (e) research potential markets, (f) learn the foreign language, and (g) understand competitors, partners, and the diverse management team.

KEY TERMS AND PHRASES

General Environmental Force *pg. 26*
Specific Environmental Force *pg. 26*
Technology *pg. 27*
Total Quality Management *pg. 29*
Downsizing *pg. 29*
Reengineering *pg. 29*
Polarized Workplace *pg. 30*

Multinational Corporation (MNC) *pg. 32*
Cultural Sensitivity *pg. 33*
Balance of Trade *pg. 34*
Culture Shock *pg. 36*
Maquiladora *pg. 37*
Global Startup *pg. 39*

QUESTIONS

1. What technological forces are affecting a manager's job these days?
2. What is your interpretation of the adage "The real boss is the customer"?
3. Describe an example of a high-quality feature of a product that might not add value for a customer.
4. Many full-time job holders today are also collecting public assistance including food stamps. How is this fact related to the polarized workplace?
5. Why do so many business firms go through the trouble of expanding into overseas markets?
6. Assume an American manager is sent abroad to manage a division in another country. Explain whether that manager should change styles to fit the preferred management style in that country.
7. Assume you are interviewing a candidate for an assignment abroad. What characteristics would you look for to minimize the chances of that person suffering from culture shock?

SKILL-BUILDING EXERCISE 2-A: TOP 10 CULTURAL BLOOPERS

GROUP ACTIVITY   To increase student sensitivity to cultural differences, the class will compose two Top 10 Cultural Bloopers lists. Each student will contribute input. The first list will be the top ten cultural bloopers committed by Americans in dealing with foreigners. The second list will be the top ten cultural bloopers committed by foreigners in dealing with Americans. One-half the class searches for bloopers by Americans, and the other half searches for bloopers by foreigners. Speak to other class members, or people with international experience outside of class. Your own experiences and observations are another potential source of input.

Students can submit their entries on 3 × 5 cards, and one or two students do the compiling for each list. The number one blooper is the one most frequently mentioned, and so forth. A class discussion follows, with the goal of enhancing insights into cross-cultural relations.

SKILL-BUILDING EXERCISE 2-B: GOING INTERNATIONAL

GROUP ACTIVITY The class organizes into groups of about five members who assume the role of the members of the management team of a company that produces videos of rap music and country music. Annual sales volume in North America is now about $4 million. The company president says she want to expand overseas and puts the team in charge of the project. Sketch out your plans for going international. Identify the strengths and weaknesses of your plans. The various teams will then compare plans, including specific tactics.

VIDEO DISCUSSION QUESTIONS

1. What are the major challenges in doing business with the Chinese? **[Business in China]**
2. What environmental forces dictated a change in the marketing strategy at Sears? **[Sears]**
3. What is the major concern of the labor union representing the airline workers? **[American Airlines]**

CASE PROBLEM 2-A: COST CONTAINMENT IN CHINESE EXPORTS

A Hong-Kong-based agent who sold to U.S. shoe companies received a telephone call from a Chinese manager who worked at a shoe factory in Guangdong province. The factory needed additional labor to fill the agent's sandal order, and the manager needed quick approval of a subcontractor. After a two-hour road trip, the American shoe-company agent was escorted to a site of about 20 workshops producing shoes, flashlights, and hardware.

Inside, the agent saw 150 men, all shaved bald and wearing blue cotton uniforms with numbers across the chest. "This isn't a factory," the American thought. "It's a prison."

According to a *Business Week* investigation, the use of prison labor is widespread in China. Trade officials in China have crafted a secret policy to use laborers from its camps and prisons. These laborers work up to 15 hours per day and are paid nothing or close to nothing. Most of the output of these prison factories is shipped to the United States, Germany, and Japan.

Many international companies are unknowing partners with prison camps. In other situations, however, Chinese firms are open about their labor source. Officials from U.S. and European companies have been given tours of prison factories. In addition, some Japanese and Taiwanese firms are placing machinery and capital into prison production. The low price of prison goods has contributed immensely to profit margins for retailers.

A U.S. State Department document estimated the prison exports to be worth $100 million per year. Chinese officials deny using prison labor for exports and declined to discuss the matter with reporters.

Prison exports contribute to China's $29.5 billion trade surplus with the United States, the second largest after Japan. U.S. law forbids importing prison goods from abroad, although the practice is legal in other countries. Many of the prison workers are political dissidents who are being detained to be "rehabilitated."

CASECASECASECASECASECASECASECASECASECASE

Prison exports are frequently sold to U.S. firms with the knowledge of the American managers. For example, a U.S. firm places an order with a Hong Kong buying agent for goods made in China. The agent, in turn, makes a deal with a Chinese shipper, who then contacts a Chinese supplier. The supplier gives part of the deal to a subcontractor, who searches for the lowest bid. Often the lowest bidder uses the labor of Chinese prisoners.

CASE QUESTIONS

1. What should the American shoe-company agent do after discovering that prison labor would be used to fill his sandal order?
2. Aside from being illegal, what harm is done by buying goods made with prison labor?
3. How can a firm guard against unknowingly purchasing goods made with prison labor?
4. In the United States, license plates are made with prison labor. Also, a hotel chain hires prison inmates as reservation agents who work from terminals set up in the prisons. Do these facts influence your thinking about the use of imported goods made with prison labor?

Source: Facts reported in Paul Magnusson, "China's Ugly Export Secret: Prison Labor," *Business Week* (22 April 1991): 42–46; "China and the U.S.: A Dangerous Misunderstanding," *Business Week* (21 March 1994): 57; U.S. Department of Commerce, 1995.

CASE PROBLEM 2-B: HEALTH WORKERS, UNITE

Denise Young's office is littered with computer printouts, training materials, and all the paraphernalia of a 70-hour work week. Life is hectic these days for Young, an organizer at Local 1199, Hospital and Health Care Employees Union. The union has been in the throes of an aggressive organizing campaign for six months. "It's very intense at times," says Young. "But it's also very exhilarating. This work provides a vision of how workers' lives can be different."

The local, part of the Service Employees International Union, is campaigning to organize more than 600 home health-care aides at the Visiting Nurse Service, a nonprofit agency. It is a tough campaign, waged with countless meetings, allegations flying back and forth, and behind-the-scenes strategy sessions. Young predicts it will be a long haul.

Young says that, like any organizing drive, the challenge for District 1129 is to help home health aides overcome fear and vote for a collective voice that the union believes will give them some control over their work lives. "The workers have major concerns over the way they're treated. They have a profound sense of not being treated with dignity and respect," she says.

Management at the Visiting Nurse Service, established in 1919, strongly believes that a union is unnecessary and would limit the agency's ability to make changes in wages and benefits to remain competitive. "We don't feel we need a third-party intermediary between us and our employees. We've always had an open and honest relationship with our workers," says spokesperson Karen Rohr.

"If we were saddled with a contract, it would limit our ability to be flexible," she says. Local 1199 contends, however, that the aides, who work out of people's homes, have trouble making ends meet. They also have problems with their irregular schedules and the lack of safety on the job. Some aides are on public assistance even though they have jobs, according to Young.

But Rohr insists that the agency remains competitive in its wages and also offers health benefits, tuition assistance, and opportunities for career advancement. Several years ago the Visiting Nurse Service hired an outside firm to provide advice on human resources issues. Today, its work includes giving the agency advice and reviewing communications to make sure the agency follows the law in response to the organizing.

Local 1194 members say that such consulting firms or "union busters" intimidate workers by producing a constant flow of anti-union information through a variety of techniques. These include one-on-one meetings and newsletters. By doing that, management succeeds in creating a climate of such intense fear that workers stay away from the union, contend the members.

"There's a much greater sophistication today about how the anti-union campaign is conducted," Young says. "It's done so thoroughly and with such surgical precision."

CASE QUESTIONS

1. As a member of management of the Visiting Nurse Service, what steps would you take to prevent your workers from becoming organized?
2. As a union official, what steps would you take to increase the probability that the health-care workers will organize?
3. How fair is it for the agency to hire an outside firm to help deal with human resource issues that could affect unionization?

Source: Adapted with permission from Kathleen Driscoll, "Rochester's Rebirth of Labor," *Inc* (6 March 1995): 1–2.

CASE PROBLEM 2-C: IT'S TOO SOON TO SAY AU REVOIR TO QUÉBEC

Amy Perry had been interested in the medical field since adolescence, but she did not wish to work directly with patients. During high school, Amy decided that a practical career choice would be to enter a health-care-related business. Her plan was to first obtain a degree in business administration and then find a position in a medical products company.

During her last year of business school in Vermont, Amy conducted a thorough job search. The most exciting offer she received was from a medical-products company based in Massachusetts. Amy's job would be to sell a blood analyzer to hospitals, clinics, and wholesalers of medical equipment in Vermont, New Hampshire, Maine, northern New York State, and Québec province. However, she would be required to concentrate on Québec because the company had barely explored that market.

Amy quickly decided to accept the offer as a medical products representative. The base pay was satisfactory, the commission structure was excellent, and she valued the freedom she would have with so much travel. Amy had studied four terms of French in high school. To further prepare herself for working in Québec, she would take an intensive two-month course in conversational French.

Amy's job proceeded generally well during the first six months. Much of her work involved speaking to existing accounts about additional business. Existing accounts readily accepted her as their new representative. Amy also had moderate success in creating new business with some medical clinics and hospitals.

Amy worked the hardest to generate new business in Québec. During her first swing through the territory, the potential buyers Amy called on reacted coolly to her presentation. Amy decided to modify her person-to-person approach on her next trip to Montréal, Quebec. She would begin her conversation in French, hoping to establish rapport between herself and her prospects.

Amy's new opening line was "Bonjour, madame (or monsieur). Je m'appelle Amy Perry. Comment allez-vous? Enchanté de faire votre connaissance. Je voudrais discuter les produits medical." ["Good day, Sir (or Miss, or Ms.). My name is Amy Perry. How are you? It's a pleasure to meet you. I would like to discuss medical products."] Two people who Amy approached with this greeting immediately began to speak English. Two others smiled half-heartedly, and then spoke English. The fifth person replied, "Excusez moi, je suis très occupé. Mais, visitez-nous encore." ["Excuse me, I am very busy. But visit us again."] and terminated the conversation.

Discouraged by her reception in Montréal, Amy reviewed her experiences with her manager. His analysis was this: "It sounds to me as if you're making the right moves to establish rapport in Québec. But maybe we should find a Québecois distributor to represent us up there. Maybe someone who isn't a native of Québec is a poor fit for the job. On the other hand, hiring a distributor would be a big problem. Our profit margins would be awfully thin.

"Your performance in the rest of your territory is fine. Maybe we could drop you from Québec, but assign you more of New York State."

"I'm not willing to say au revoir (goodbye) to Québec quite yet. Give me more time to prove myself," Amy said.

CASE QUESTIONS

1. If you were the manager, would you replace Amy in Québec?
2. How should Amy overcome the problems she is facing with her customers from Québec?
3. What does this case tell you about international business?

CASE PROBLEM 2-D: STOP EXPORTING OUR JOBS

In late October 1995, many labor union members felt better than they had in a long time. John Sweeney had just been elected president of the AFL-CIO in a tough campaign battle against incumbent Thomas Donahue. Sweeney counted on, and received the support of, a spectrum of unions: steelworkers, autoworkers, government employees, teamsters, machinists, and farm workers. Union membership was actually growing, as an increasing number of service-sector employees (such as health-care workers) elected to join unions.

Employers in general were noticing a new militancy among workers. After a decade of downsizing and outsourcing jobs to lower-wage areas and countries, many workers were angry. U.S. Secretary of Labor Robert Reich told a conference on the economy that he repeatedly heard around the country from unorganized workers "I never thought about joining a union, but for the first time I'm now thinking about it, because I need somebody to protect me."

The labor-management climate was particularly strained at Boeing where employees were hoping to achieve major concessions from management. More than 32,000 members of the machinists union walked off jobs in Kansas, Oregon, and Washington state in one day after negotiations on a new contract stalled. A particular sore point was Boeing's increasing practice of moving skilled production work from U.S. plants to China. Many union members believed the jobs were being outsourced so Boeing could increase its sales to China.

George Kouprias, president of the International Association of Machinists and Aerospace Workers, said, "I'm running the Boeing strike, and there's an excitement in the rank and file I haven't seen in years."

Management members of the Boeing negotiation team were pondering what to do next. One team member commented that he never thought the machinists and aerospace workers would actually call a strike when domestic manufacturing jobs were getting scarcer. Another member commented that this is precisely why the union members went on strike—they wanted U.S. managers to stop exporting precious jobs.

"Now we have to figure what to do next," said a senior member of the Boeing negotiating team.

CASE QUESTIONS

1. Do you think the machinists and aerospace workers have a right to prevent management from outsourcing assembly-worker jobs to China in order to boost sales?
2. What tactic should the Boeing negotiation team use to get the union to end the strike?

Source: Some of the facts in this case are based on "The Battle to Revive the Unions," *Time* (30 October 1995): 64–66; "Outsourced and Out of Luck," *Business Week* (17 July 1995): 60–61.

REFERENCES

1. "It's a Small (Business) World," *Business Week* (17 April 1995): 96.
2. "Rethinking Work," *Business Week* (17 October 1994): 81.
3. Bonnie Michaels, "A Global Glance at Work and Family," *Personnel Journal* (April 1995): 85.
4. Kathy Cramer and John Pearce, "Work and Family Policies Become Productivity Tools," *Management Review* (November 1990): 42.
5. Aaron Bernstein, "Can A New Leader Bring Labor Back to Life?" *Business Week* (3 July 1995): 87.
6. Douglas Harbrecht, "GATT: Tales from the Dark Side," *Business Week* (19 December 1994): 52.
7. Joann S. Lublin, "Younger Managers Learn Global Skills," *The Wall Street Journal* (31 March 1992): B1.
8. Marvina Shilling, "Avoid Expatriate Culture Shock," *HRMagazine* (July 1993): 58.
9. Geert Hofstede, "Cultural Constraints in Management Theories," *The Academy of Management Executive* (February 1993): 81–94; David C. Thomas and Elizabeth C. Ravlin, "Responses of Employees to Cultural Adaptation by a Foreign Manager," *Journal of Applied Psychology* (February 1995) 138.
10. Srilata Zaheer, "Overcoming the Liability of Foreignness," *Academy of Management Journal* (April 1995): 341–363.
11. Harry C. Triandis, *Culture and Social Behavior* (New York: McGraw-Hill, 1994), 263.
12. Eugene H. Fram and Riad A. Ajami, "International Distributors and the Role of US Top Management: A Requirement for Export Competitiveness?" *Journal of Business and Industrial Marketing* (9:4): 33–44.
13. Benjamin M. Oviatt and Patricia Phillips McDougall, "Global Start-Ups: Entrepreneurs on a Worldwide Stage," *The Academy of Management Executive* (May 1995): 30.
14. William Taylor, "The Logic of Global Business: An Interview with ABB's Percy Barnevik," *Harvard Business Review* (March–April 1991): 91.
15. Michael A. Hitt and R. Duane Ireland, "Building Competitive Strength in International Markets," *Long Range Planning* (February 1987) 115–122.
16. Charlene Marmer Solomon, "Learning to Manage Host-country Nationals," *Personnel Journal* (March 1995): 61.
17. Michael A. Hitt, Beverly B. Tyler, Camilla Hardee, and Daewoo Park, "Understanding Strategic Intent in the Global Marketplace," *The Academy of Management Executive* (May 1995): 18.

CHAPTER 3

Ethics and Social Responsibility

LEARNING OBJECTIVES

After studying this chapter and doing the exercises, you should be able to:

1

Identify the philosophical principles behind business ethics.

2

Explain how values relate to ethics.

3

Identify factors contributing to lax ethics, and common ethical temptations and violations.

4

Apply a guide to ethical decision making.

5

Describe the stakeholder viewpoint of social responsibility, and corporate social performance.

6

Present an overview of diversity programs and other social-responsibility initiatives.

7

Summarize the benefits of ethical and socially responsible behavior, and how managers can create an environment that fosters such behavior.

The Maguire Group Inc., Foxborough, Massachusetts, is an architecture, engineering, and planning firm. Until a few years ago, the firm did not consider a corporate-wide ethics policy necessary. This was true because most of the 350 employees have codes of ethics in their respective professions. However, in 1992 the president/majority owner of Maguire was forced to resign for making improper payments to city officials in exchange for work (the *kickback* system). The entire company was shocked and disappointed. • Company management then decided to create a code of ethics and guidelines for business conduct and to involve a wide range of employees in formulating the code. Twenty-seven employees from varying organizational levels and different departments volunteered to serve on the Ethics Task Force. The employees were divided into five teams, all of whom were assigned to research and write a policy statement on four issues: gifts and gratuities; political contributions; entertainment/business development; and bribes and kickbacks. • The ethics policy and an accompanying follow-through program have reinforced the message that the "new" company accepts only the highest ethical behavior from all employees.[1]

The experience of the Maguire Group illustrates the importance a firm can attach to ethical behavior, especially after encountering an ethical violation that could damage future business. The purpose of this chapter is to explain the importance of ethics and social responsibility. To accomplish this purpose we present various aspects of ethics and social responsibility. We also present guidelines to help managerial workers to make ethical decisions and conduct socially responsible acts.

BUSINESS ETHICS

> **ethics**
> *The study of moral obligation, or separating right from wrong.*

Understanding and practicing good business ethics is an important part of a manager's job. One of many reasons ethics are important is that customers and suppliers prefer to deal with ethical companies. **Ethics** is the study of moral obligation, or separating right from wrong. Although many unethical acts are illegal, others are legal. An example of an illegal unethical act is giving a government official a kickback for placing a contract with a specific firm. An example of a legal, yet unethical, practice is hiring an employee away from a competitor, "picking her brains" for competitive ideas, and then eliminating her job.

> **moral intensity**
> *The magnitude of an unethical act.*

A useful perspective in understanding business ethics emphasizes **moral intensity,** or the magnitude of an unethical act.[2] When an unethical act is not of large consequence, a person might behave unethically without much thought. However, if the act is of large consequence, the person might refrain from unethical or illegal behavior. For example, a manager might make a photocopy of an entire book or copy someone else's software (both unethical and illegal acts). The same manager, however, might hesitate to dump toxins into a river.

Business ethics will be mentioned at various places in this text. Here we approach the subject from several perspectives: philosophical principles, values, contributing factors to ethical problems, common ethical problems, and a guide to ethical decision making.

PHILOSOPHICAL PRINCIPLES UNDERLYING BUSINESS ETHICS

LEARNING OBJECTIVE

Identify the philosophical principles behind business ethics.

A standard way of understanding ethical decision making is to know the philosophical basis for making these decisions. When attempting to decide what is right and wrong, managerial workers can focus on (1) consequences; (2) duties, obligations, and principles; or (3) integrity.[3]

FOCUS ON CONSEQUENCES. When attempting to decide what is right or wrong, people can sometimes focus on the consequences of their decision or action. According to this criterion, if no one gets hurt, the decision is ethical. Focusing on consequences is often referred to as *utilitarianism.* The decision maker is concerned with the utility of the decision. What really counts is the net balance of good consequences over bad. An automotive body shop manager, for example, might decide that using low-quality replacement fenders is ethically wrong because the fender will rust quickly. To focus on consequences, the decision maker would have to be aware of all the good and bad consequences of a given decision. The body-shop manager would have to estimate such factors as how angry customers would be whose cars were repaired with inferior parts, and how much negative publicity would result.

FOCUS ON DUTIES, OBLIGATIONS, AND PRINCIPLES. Another approach to making an ethical decision is to examine one's duties in making the decision. The theories underlying this approach are referred to as *deontological,* from the Greek word *deon,* or duty. The deontological approach is based on universal principles such as honesty, fairness, justice, and respect for persons and property.

Rights, such as the right for privacy and safety, are also important. From a deontologial perspective, the principles are more important than the consequences. If a given decision violates one of these universal principles, it is automatically unethical even if nobody gets hurt. An ethical body-shop manager might think, "It just isn't right to use replacement fenders that are not authorized by the automobile manufacturer. Whether or not these parts rust quickly is a secondary consideration."

FOCUS ON INTEGRITY (VIRTUE ETHICS). The third criterion for determining the ethics of behavior focuses on the character of the person involved in the decision or action. If the person in question has good character, and genuine motivation and intentions, he or she is behaving ethically. The ingredients making up character will often include the two other ethical criteria. One might judge a person to have good character if she or he follows the right principles and respects the rights of others.

The decision maker's environment, or community, helps define what integrity means. You might have more lenient ethical standards for a person selling you a speculative investment than you would for a bank vice-president who accepted your cash deposit.

The virtue ethics of managers and professionals who belong to professional societies can be judged readily. Business-related professions having codes of ethics include accountants, purchasing managers, and certified financial planners. To the extent that the person abides by the tenets of the stated code, he or she is behaving ethically. An example of such a tenet would be for a financial planner to be explicit about any commissions gained from a client accepting the advice.

When faced with a complex ethical decision, a manager would be best advised to incorporate all three philosophical approaches. The manager might think through the consequences of a decision, along with an analysis of duties, obligations, principles, and intentions. A case in point took place in 1995. A deranged person, labeled the Unabomber, had threatened to set off an explosion in the Los Angeles airport (LAX). He then said he was not serious. Many managers had to decide whether to send subordinates on business trips that went through LAX. Should business be conducted as usual despite the remote possibility of harm? To reach a decision, managers had to think through all three philosophical principles related to ethics.

VALUES AND ETHICS

As incorporated into virtue ethics, values are closely related to ethics. A firm's moral standards and values help guide ethics in decision making. Many firms contend that they "put people before profits" (a value). If this were true, a manager would avoid actions such as delaying payments to a vendor just to hold on to money longer, or firing a group member for having negotiated a deal that lost money.

LEARNING OBJECTIVE

Explain how values relate to ethics.

A person's values also influence which kind of behaviors he or she believes are ethical. An executive who strongly values profits might not find it unethical to raise prices more than are needed to cover additional costs. Another executive who strongly values family life might suggest that the company invest money in an on-premises child-care center.

The concept of **ethically centered management** helps put some teeth into an abstract discussion of how values relate to ethics. Ethically centered management emphasizes that the high quality of an end product takes precedence over its scheduled completion. At the same time, it sets high quality standards for dealing with employees and managing production.[4] Robert Elliott Allinson believes that many work-related catastrophes can be attributed to a management team that is not ethically centered. One such example was the failure of the Hubbell telescope to function properly in outer space because of a flaw in a mirror. (The problem was later corrected.)

According to Allinson, management acted irresponsibly by not emphasizing the importance of quality control and clearly designating officials to be in charge of quality. Also, top management at NASA disowned responsibility for finding out and ensuring that the end product was problem-free and of highest quality.[5]

ethically centered management
An approach to management that emphasizes that the high quality of an end product takes precedence over its scheduled completion.

CONTRIBUTING FACTORS TO ETHICAL PROBLEMS

LEARNING OBJECTIVE

Identify factors contributing to lax ethics, and common ethical temptations and violations.

Individuals, organizations, and society itself must share some of the blame for the prevalence of unethical behavior in the workplace. Major contributors to unethical behavior are an individual's greed and gluttony, or the desire to maximize self-gain at the expenses of others.

Another major contributor to unethical behavior is an organizational atmosphere that condones such behavior. According to one study, even employees with high ethical standards may stray in a climate that rewards unethical behavior. A firm's official code of ethics may not coincide with its actual culture. It is the firm's top executives who set the company's moral tone.[6]

A more recent study on unethical employees found similar results. One-third of employees admitted to having stolen from their employer. The most frequent forms of theft were misuse of the employee-discount privilege and theft of company merchandise or property. The researchers concluded that a perceived management climate more lenient than the norm for management is accompanied by employee attitudes that are more pro-theft. The opposite was also true: a management climate strongly opposed to theft leads to stronger anti-theft attitudes by employees.[7]

A third cause of unethical behavior is **moral laxity,** a slippage in moral behavior because other issues seem more important at the time. The implication is that the businessperson who behaves unethically has not carefully planned the immoral behavior but lets it occur by not exercising good judgment. Many workplace deaths fit into this category. Over 300 people were killed and about 900 injured when a shopping mall collapsed in Seoul, South Korea. Officials blamed the disaster on shoddy construction and negligence by executives of the shopping complex. Police said that the executives knew the floor was crumbling hours before the disaster. Nevertheless, they decided not to close and left the premises without warning anyone.[8]

moral laxity
A slippage in moral behavior because other issues seem more important at the time.

A fourth cause of unethical behavior in the workplace is that time can be easy to steal. As Alan Weiss explained, many white-collar workers steal time from their employers because they are not closely supervised. He notes that moonlighting continues to plague businesses. Managers with spare time run private businesses, such as catalog sales and consulting firms, right from their employers' offices.[9]

A fifth cause of unethical behavior is questionable rationalizations. As described by Saul W. Gellerman, these rationalizations are cited in the following list.[10]

- A belief that the unethical activity is within ethical and legal limits. An example: offering an employee a small bribe for not reporting a workplace accident.
- A belief that, because the activity is in the individual's or firm's best interest, the individual should undertake it. An example would be accepting a substantial gift from a vendor because the buyer felt underpaid and regarded the gift as compensation.
- A belief that the activity is "safe" because it will never be uncovered. Several years ago management at a food processing plant substituted sugar-water for apple juice in baby food, reasoning that the infant consumers would never complain.
- A belief that, because the unethical activity helps the company, the company will condone it and protect the perpetrator. For example, the managers in the counterfeit apple-juice incident believed that saving the company money would exempt them from punishment.

ETHICAL TEMPTATIONS AND VIOLATIONS

Certain ethical mistakes, including illegal actions, recur in the workplace. Familiarizing oneself with these behaviors can be helpful in managing the ethical behavior of others as well as monitoring one's own behavior. A list of commonly found ethical temptations and violations, including criminal acts, follows:[11]

1. *Stealing from employers and customers.* Employee theft costs U.S. and Canadian companies about $40 billion annually. Retail employees often steal goods from their employers, and financial service employees often steal money. Theft from customers includes airport baggage handlers who steal from passenger suitcases, and bank employees, stockbrokers, and attorneys who siphon money from customer accounts.
2. *Illegally copying software.* A rampant problem in the workplace is making unauthorized copies of software for either company or personal use. Similarly, many employees make illegal copies of videos, books, and magazine articles instead of purchasing these products.
3. *Treating people unfairly.* Being fair to people means equity, reciprocity, and impartiality. Fairness revolves around the issue of giving people equal rewards for accomplishing the same amount of work. The goal of human resource legislation is to make decisions about people based on their qualifications and performance—not on the basis of demographic factors like sex, race, or age. A fair working environment is where performance is the only factor that counts (equity). Employer-employee expectations must be understood and met (reciprocity). Prejudice and bias must be eliminated (impartiality).

4. *Sexual harassment.* Sexual harassment involves making compliance with sexual favors a condition of employment, or creating a hostile, intimidating environment related to sexual topics. Harassment violates the law and is also an ethical issue because it is morally wrong and unfair.

5. *Conflict of interest.* Part of being ethical is making business judgments only on the basis of the merits in a situation. Imagine that you are a supervisor who is romantically involved with a worker within the group. When it came time to assigning raises, it would be difficult for you to be objective. A **conflict of interest** occurs when your judgment or objectivity is compromised.

6. *Divulging confidential information.* An ethical person can be trusted by others not to divulge confidential information unless the welfare of others is at stake. The challenge of dealing with confidential information arises in many areas of business, including information about performance-appraisal results, compensation, personal problems of employees, disease status of employees, and coworker bankruptcies.

7. *Misuse of corporate resources.* A corporate resource is anything the company owns, including its name and reputation. Assume that a man named Jason Hedgeworth worked for Microsoft Corporation. It would be unethical for him to establish a software consulting company and put on his letterhead "Jason Hedgeworth, software designer, Microsoft Corporation." Using corporate resources can fall into the gray area, such as whether to borrow a laptop computer to prepare income taxes for a fee.

conflict of interest
A situation that occurs when one's judgment or objectivity is compromised.

A GUIDE TO ETHICAL DECISION MAKING

LEARNING OBJECTIVE

Apply a guide to ethical decision making.

A practical way of improving ethical decision making is to run contemplated decisions through an ethics test when any doubt exists. The ethics test presented next was used at the Center for Business Ethics at Bentley College as part of corporate training programs. Decision makers are taught to ask themselves:[12]

1. *Is it right?* This question is based on the deontological theory of ethics that there are certain universally accepted guiding principles of rightness and wrongness, such as "thou shall not steal."

2. *Is it fair?* This question is based on the deontological theory of justice, implying that certain actions are inherently just or unjust. For example, it is unjust to fire a high-performing employee to make room for a less competent person who is a personal friend.

3. *Who gets hurt?* This question is based on the utilitarian notion of attempting to do the greatest good for the greatest number of people.

4. *Would you be comfortable if the details of your decision were reported on the front page of your local newspaper or through your company's electronic messaging system?* This question is based on the universalist principle of disclosure.

5. *Would you tell your child (or young relative) to do it?* This question is based on the deontological principle of reversibility, referring to reversing who carries out the decision.

6. *How does it smell?* This question is based on a person's intuition and common sense. For example, underpaying many accounts payable by a few dollars to save money would "smell" bad to a sensible person.

A decision that was obviously ethical, such as donating some managerial time for charitable organizations, would not need to be run through the six-question test. Neither would a blatantly illegal act, such as not paying employees for work performed. But the test is useful for decisions that are neither obviously ethical nor obviously unethical. Among such gray areas would be charging clients based on their ability to pay and developing a clone of a successful competitive product.

SOCIAL RESPONSIBILITY

Many people believe that firms have an obligation to be concerned about outside groups affected by an organization. **Social responsibility** is the idea that firms have obligations to society beyond their economic obligations to owners or stockholders and also beyond those prescribed by law or contract. Both ethics and social responsibility relate to the goodness or morality of organizations. However, business ethics is a narrower concept that applies to the morality of an individual's decisions and behaviors. Social responsibility is a broader concept that relates to an organization's impact on society, beyond doing what is ethical.[13] To behave in a socially responsible way, managers must be aware of how their actions influence the environment.

An important perspective is that many socially responsible actions are the by-products of sensible business decisions. For instance, it is both socially responsible and profitable for a company to improve the language and math skills of entry-level workers. Literate and numerate entry-level workers for some jobs may be in short supply, and employees who cannot follow written instructions or do basic math may be unproductive.

This section will examine four aspects of social responsibility: the two viewpoints of social responsibility, corporate social performance, diversity programs, and other social responsibility initiatives.

STOCKHOLDER VERSUS STAKEHOLDER VIEWPOINTS

The **stockholder viewpoint** of social responsibility is the traditional perspective. It holds that business firms are responsible only to their owners and stockholders. The job of managers is therefore to satisfy the financial interests of the stockholders. By so doing, says the stockholder view, the interests of society will be served in the long run. Socially irresponsible acts ultimately result in poor sales. According to the stockholder viewpoint, corporate social responsibility is therefore a by-product of profit seeking. The accompanying Organization in Action feature illustrates how social responsibility might improve business results.

The **stakeholder viewpoint** of social responsibility contends that firms must hold themselves responsible for the quality of life of the many groups affected by the firm's actions. These interested parties, or stakeholders, include those groups composing the firm's general environment. Two categories of stakeholders exist. Internal stakeholders include owners, employees, and stockholders; external stakeholders include customers, labor unions, consumer groups, and financial institutions. Exhibit 3-1 depicts the stakeholder viewpoint of social responsibility.

social responsibility
The idea that firms have obligations to society beyond their obligations to owners or stockholders and also beyond those prescribed by law or contract.

stockholder viewpoint
The traditional perspective on social responsibility that a business organization is responsible only to its owners and stockholders.

stakeholder viewpoint
The viewpoint on social responsibility contending that firms must hold themselves responsible for the quality of life of the many groups affected by the firm's actions.

ORGANIZATION IN ACTION: STRATEGIC GIVING BY WEYERHAUSER

Weyerhauser Co. was one of the first companies to realize the potential for profit in charitable giving. After reviewing a study conducted in 1978, management of the lumber company decided to focus corporate giving "at the crossroads where company and public interest intersect." Mary Hall, Vice-President of Corporate Giving, said that Weyerhauser developed the point of view that it should focus on issues that were relevant to the long-term success of its business.

Weyerhauser for many years sponsored the popular PBS series "This Old House." The show reached many viewers who were either customers or potential customers. The company also donates money to environmental conservation groups. Asked if this practice is cynical, Hall replied, "I wouldn't call it cynical; I would call it an investment. It's not a right of society to have corporations giving away money.

"We're very straightforward," Hall continued. "We let people know we see enlightened self-interest down the pike, as well as the chance to be a good partner with the community. We think it's cynical only if you try to fool people."

Source: Minda Zetlin, "Companies Find Profit in Corporate Giving," *Management Review* (December 1990): 10.

CORPORATE SOCIAL PERFORMANCE

corporate social performance
The extent to which a firm responds to the demands of its stakeholders for behaving in a socially responsible manner.

Corporate social performance is the extent to which a firm responds to the demands of its stakeholders for behaving in a socially responsible manner. After stakeholders have been satisfied with the reporting of financial information, they may turn their attention to the behavior of the corporation as a good citizen in the community. One way of measuring social performance is to analyze the company's annual report in search of relevant statistical information.

Two accounting professors interested in social responsibility scanned the annual reports of the top 100 corporations on the *Fortune* 500 list. The corporations were involved in a variety of industries including chemicals, health, petroleum, manufacturing, foods, electronics, aerospace, and information technology.[14] The analysis most closely tied to social performance was the disclosure of environmental measures, with the following rates of activity being reported:

- Pollution measures, 74%
- Contributions to crime prevention, 0%
- Contribution to the homeless, 10%
- Contribution to AIDS treatment and substance abuse programs, 10%
- Contributions to the arts, 17%
- Contributions to education, 44%

The authors were encouraged that the rate of disclosure in this and other categories had improved over the past. Another approach to measuring corporate social performance is to observe how a company responds to social issues by examining programs in more detail. The next two sections describe corporate activity in relation to a variety of social issues.

Exhibit 3-1
The Stakeholder
Viewpoint of Social
Responsibility

Internal Stakeholders
- Owners
- Stockholders
- Employees
- Board of Directors

The Organization

External Stakeholders
- Customers
- Suppliers
- Creditors
- Labor Unions
- Competitors
- Special Interest Groups
- Consumer Groups
- Government Agencies
- Financial Institutions

DIVERSITY INITIATIVES AND SOCIAL RESPONSIBILITY

A major thrust in organizations is to welcome cultural diversity by ensuring that people from a wide variety of backgrounds have equal access to advancement and opportunity. Equality also means that employees can make full use of their talents. Instead of merely avoiding job discrimination, these organizations are being socially responsible by creating more opportunities for diverse groups. The accompanying Management in Action describes a diversity program.

LEARNING OBJECTIVE

Present an overview of diversity programs and other social-responsibility initiatives.

Diversity initiatives may be socially responsible, but they are also a natural response to population trends. By the year 2000, only 15 percent of entry-level workers in the United States will be native-born male Caucasians. As recently as 1985, the comparable figure was 47 percent.[15] The data presented in Exhibit 3-2 indicate a trend for an increasing number of minority-group members to be promoted into management.

Training programs in valuing differences, or appreciating cultural diversity, are another component of diversity programs. **Valuing-differences training** attempts to bring about workplace harmony by teaching people how to get along better with diverse work associates. Quite often the program is aimed at minimizing open expressions of racism and sexism. All forms of training in valuing differences center around increasing people's awareness of and empathy for people who are different from oneself. At times the difference is immediately visible, such as race or physical status. At other times, the difference is not immediately visible, such as religious beliefs or sexual orientation.

The training sessions focus on the ways that men and women, or people of different races, reflect different values, attitudes, and cultural backgrounds. Some-

valuing-differences training
A form of training that attempts to bring about workplace harmony by teaching people how to get along better with diverse work associates.

MANAGEMENT IN ACTION: WORK-FORCE DIVERSITY AT THE BANK OF MONTREAL

Executives at the Bank of Montreal explored ways to get an edge on the competition. Having a work force that reflected its diverse customer base rose to the top. The new corporate strategy links business success to work-place equality and diversity. A diverse work force brings multiple solutions to problems based on employees' varied knowledge, backgrounds, and experiences.

Johanne M. Totta, vice-president of employee programs and workplace equality, says that making the most of employee potential is how you get ahead of the competition. The bank targeted four segments of the work force for development—women, people with disabilities, aboriginal people (native Canadians), and visible minorities. Four task forces, one for each employee group, were formed to develop action plans for developing a diverse workplace.

The Task Force on Advancement of Women has made the most progress to date. The group surveyed 15,000 women and men employees. The key finding was that women were not advancing because of stereotyped attitudes, myths, and conventional wisdom. A major task-force activity was to provide data to examine these myths. One such myth debunked was that women have babies and quit. The reality discovered was that although women have babies, they also have longer service records than men at every level except senior management. Being a woman *does not* mean reduced commitment.

After examining all the data about women employees, the task force made 26 recommendations for advancing women at the bank. Among them were training programs to make managers aware of the barriers to women, and establishing goals for placing women in higher management positions.

Source: Based on facts reported in Michelle Neely Martinez, "Equality Effort Sharpens Bank's Edge," *HRMagazine* (January 1995): 38–43.

times the programs are confrontational; sometimes not. As described by diversity consultant R. Roosevelt Thomas, Jr., the objectives of valuing differences include one or more of the following:[16]

- Fostering awareness and acceptance of individual differences
- Helping participants understand their own feelings and attitudes about people who are "different"
- Exploring how differences might be tapped as assets in the workplace
- Enhancing work relations between people who are different from each other

An essential part of relating more effectively to diverse groups is to empathize with their point of view. To help training participants develop empathy, representatives of various groups explain their feelings related to workplace issues. Yet companies have found that when employees are too blunt during these sessions, it may be difficult to patch up interpersonal relations in the work group later on. As a result, the diversity training backfires.

OTHER SOCIAL RESPONSIBILITY INITIATIVES

Creating opportunities for a diverse work force is an important social responsibility initiative. Here we describe positive corporate responses to other important social issues. A firm that takes initiatives in these areas can be considered socially respon-

Exhibit 3-2
Minorities as a Percent-
age of Management

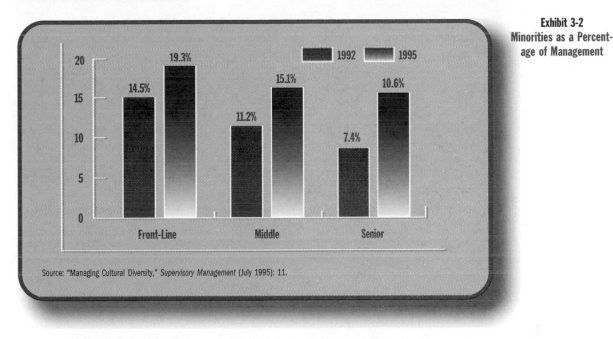

Source: "Managing Cultural Diversity," *Supervisory Management* (July 1995): 11.

sible. Social responsibility initiatives include social leaves of absence, acceptance of whistle blowing, community redevelopment projects, and elder-care programs.

SOCIAL LEAVES OF ABSENCE. Some companies offer employees paid leaves of absence, of anywhere from several weeks to six months, to help them prevent burnout. A **social leave of absence,** however, gives select employees time away from the job to perform a significant public service. For example, American Express Travel-Related Services allows employees with 10 or more years of service to take up to six months to contribute to the community. Obtaining a leave of absence is competitive. Candidates for the leave fill out an application that describes the employee's plans and qualifications for performing the community work. As with other firms offering social leaves, the community work must be integrated into the department's work plans.

The social good performed by the person on leave often takes the form of lending business expertise to a nonprofit agency. An example would be a corporate controller developing a financial plan for a youth agency. At other times the social leave is to perform work indirectly related to one's professional expertise, such as a human resources professional volunteering as a high-school drug counselor for six months.[17]

social leave of absence
An employee benefit that gives select employees time away from the job to perform a significant public service.

ACCEPTANCE OF WHISTLE BLOWERS. A **whistle blower** is an employee who discloses organizational wrongdoing to parties who can take action. Whistle blowers are often ostracized and humiliated by the companies they hope to improve, by such means as no further promotions or poor performance evaluations. More than half the time, the pleas of whistle blowers are ignored. A classic example of whistle blowing took place at Morton Thiokol Inc. in relation to the 1986 Challenger shuttle disaster. Two engineers testified to an outside commission that there had been ongoing problems with the rocket's O-rings. Furthermore, they had urged their managers and NASA officials to postpone the fatal launch. After testifying, the engineers were demoted to menial jobs. Later the investigating commission intervened to get the engineers reinstated.[18]

whistle blower
An employee who discloses organizational wrongdoing to parties who can take action.

Only an organization with a strong social conscience would embrace employees who inform the public about its misdeeds. Yet some companies are becoming more tolerant of employees who help keep the firm socially responsible by exposing actions that could harm society.

COMMUNITY-REDEVELOPMENT PROJECTS. A large-scale social responsibility initiative is for business firms to invest resources in helping rebuild distressed communities. Investment could mean constructing offices or factories in an impoverished section of town, or offering job training for residents from these areas. The Prudential Insurance Company helps rebuild inner cities by investing money in ventures such as grocery stores, housing, and entertainment. The New Jersey Performing Arts Center is one of their investment projects.

Peter Goldberg, president of the Prudential Foundation, explains the rationale for community-redevelopment projects: "The future well-being of this company, this industry and of corporate America is very much intertwined with the health and well-being of American society."[19]

Substantial corporate investment in community redevelopment took place in Los Angeles following the 1992 riots. Southern California Edison, the utility firm, established a $6.5 million job-training center in one of the most devastated areas. The firm is also hiring disadvantaged youths for a variety of community development projects. Another example is that Hyundai Motors of America trains about three dozen minority youths each year to be certified mechanics, at a cost of $10,000 per student. A company representative explains, "We desperately need trained mechanics, and people need jobs. This program trains them for a career."[20]

ELDER-CARE PROGRAMS. A burgeoning challenge facing employees and employers is that about 10 percent of workers have some responsibility for an older relative. An estimated one in three will have such responsibility by 2020. Three demographic trends are behind the predicted surge: The number of old people is increasing rapidly; people with chronic illnesses are living longer; and more women are in the work force than previously. (About three-fourths of caregivers for older people are women.)[21]

A Work and Families Institute study of 305 workers caring for elderly relatives documents the problem. Thirty-nine percent reported that taking care of their responsibilities distracted them from work, and 25 percent changed jobs because of the problem. Other studies have found that work interruptions and absences related to elder care are costly.

Many companies are taking a social-responsibility initiative in response to the growing need for elder care. About 25 percent of large companies (companies with more than 1,000 employees) offer some programs and services that provide assistance with elder care. The various forms of help include resource-and-referral services, seminars, support groups, and long-term care (nursing-home) insurance. About 15 percent of medium-size companies (those with 80 to 999 employees) also provide some assistance. Flexible work policies in general, such as flexible working hours and family leaves under the Family and Medical Leave Act, also help with elder care.[22]

BENEFITS DERIVED FROM ETHICS AND SOCIAL RESPONSIBILITY

Highly ethical behavior and socially responsible acts are not always free. Investing in diversity programs, granting social leaves of absence, and telling customers the absolute truth about potential product problems may not have an immediate return on investment. When social-responsibility initiatives lose money, these costs are eventually passed along to citizens, who pay higher taxes, and to stockholders, who receive lower dividends. Another cost relates to the issue of competitive disadvantage. A company may stay even with its competitors if all the companies invest in social projects. A company that supports such projects alone, however, may lose business if its competitors invest surplus cash into strengthening their competitive positions.[23]

LEARNING OBJECTIVE 7

Summarize the benefits of ethical and socially responsible behavior, and how managers can create an environment that fosters such behavior.

Despite the potential costs just mentioned, ethical and socially responsible behavior appears to be cost-effective, or at least cost-neutral. And behavior of this type also helps achieve important nonfinancial objectives, such as doing social good. The case for developing ethics codes is convincing. The greater the number of ethical workers, the more good an organization will do. There are also financial rewards for being ethical. Unethical behavior, such as employee theft or fraud, is costly. Theft costs U.S. and Canadian businesses about $50 billion annually. Companies can also receive substantial fines for unethical behavior. For example, Sunstrand was fined $227 million after pleading guilty to five counts of defrauding the Pentagon.

A big payoff from socially responsible acts is that they often attract and retain socially responsible employees and customers. To accommodate the interests of socially responsible business people, a trade group has been formed called Businesses for Social Responsibility (BSR). Its charter is to make social, environmental, and worker-friendly practices a key part of business and government policy making. A spokesperson for BSR points to a compelling benefit derived from social responsibility:

This way of doing business is inevitable. The growth in green marketing and socially screened investing shows that consumers and investors are becoming increasingly sensitive to both the quality of products they purchase and the business practices of the company they buy from.[24]

CREATING AN ETHICAL AND SOCIALLY RESPONSIBLE WORKPLACE

Establishing an ethical and socially responsible workplace is not simply a matter of luck and common sense. Top managers, assisted by other managers and professionals, can develop strategies and programs to enhance ethical and socially responsible attitudes. We turn now to a description of several of these initiatives.[25]

FORMAL MECHANISMS FOR MONITORING ETHICS. Large organizations frequently set up ethics committees to help ensure ethical and socially responsible behavior. Committee members include a top-management representative plus other managers throughout the organization. An ethics and social-responsibility specialist from the human resources department might also join the group. The commit-tee helps establish policies about ethics and social responsibility, and might con-duct an ethical audit of the firm's activities. In addition, committee members might review complaints about ethical violations. Many of the ethical violations involve charges of sexual harassment by managers.

A hard-hitting formal mechanism is the appointment of an ethics officer, an action taken by many large firms. Sometimes the ethics officer is the general coun-sel, and at other times he or she is a full-time specialist. A representative job title for this position is "corporate vice-president, ethics and business conduct." The ethics officer is supposed to provide leadership and guidance about fair business conduct and socially responsible acts.

WRITTEN ORGANIZATIONAL CODES OF CONDUCT. Many organizations use written ethi-cal codes of conduct to serve as guidelines for ethical and socially responsible be-havior. Such guidelines have increased in importance because workers placed in self-managing teams have less supervision than previously. Some aspects of these codes are general, such as requiring people to conduct themselves with integrity and candor. Here is a statement of this type from the Johnson & Johnson (med-ical and health supplies) code of ethics:

We believe our first responsibility is to the doctors, nurses, and patients, to mothers and fathers and all others who use our products and services. In meeting these needs everything we do must be of high quality.

Other aspects of the codes might be specific, such as indicating the maximum gift that can be accepted from a vendor. In many organizations, known code vio-lators are disciplined.

WIDESPREAD COMMUNICATION ABOUT ETHICS AND SOCIAL RESPONSIBILITY. Extensive communication about the topic reinforces ethical and socially responsible behav-ior. Top management can speak widely about the competitive advantage of being ethical and socially responsible. Another effective method is to discuss ethical and social responsibility issues in small groups. In this way the issues stay fresh in the minds of workers. A few minutes of a team meeting might be invested in a topic such as "What can we do to help the homeless people who live in the streets sur-rounding our office?"

LEADERSHIP BY EXAMPLE. A high-powered approach to enhancing ethics and social responsibility is for members of top management to behave in such a manner themselves. If people throughout the firm believe that behaving ethically is "in" and behaving unethically is "out," ethical behavior will prevail. Visualize a scenario in which a group of key people in an investment banking firm vote themselves a $3 million year-end bonus. Yet to save money, entry-level clerical workers earning $8.00 an hour are denied raises. Many employees might feel that top management has a low sense of ethics, and therefore that being ethical and socially responsi-ble is not important.

ENCOURAGE CONFRONTATION ABOUT ETHICAL DEVIATIONS. Unethical behavior may be minimized if every employee confronts anyone seen behaving unethically. For ex-ample, if you spotted someone making an unauthorized copy of software, you would ask the software pirate, "How would you like it if other people stole from *our* company?" The same approach encourages workers to play devil's advocate by asking about the ethical implications of decisions.

TRAINING PROGRAMS IN ETHICS AND SOCIAL RESPONSIBILITY. Many companies now train managerial workers about ethics. Forms of training include messages about ethics from executives, classes on ethics at colleges, and exercises in ethics. These training programs reinforce the idea that ethically and socially responsible behavior is both morally right and good for business. Much of the content of this chapter reflects the type of information communicated in such programs. In addition, Skill-Building Exercise 3-B represents the type of activity included in ethical training programs such as those given at CitiCorp.

SUMMARY OF KEY POINTS

1
Identify the philosophical principles behind business ethics.
When deciding on what is right and wrong, people can focus on consequences; duties, obligations, and principles; or integrity. Focusing on consequences is called utilitarianism, because the decision maker is concerned with the utility of the decision. Examining one's duties in making a decision is the deontological approach, and is based on universal principles such as honesty and fairness. According to the virtue approach, if the decision maker has good character, and genuine motivation and intentions, he or she is behaving ethically.

2
Explain how values relate to ethics.
A firm's moral standards and values help guide ethics in decision making. A person's values also influence which kind of behaviors he or she believes are ethical. According to ethically centered management, the high quality of an end product takes precedence over meeting a delivery schedule. Catastrophes can result when management is not ethically centered.

3
Identify factors contributing to lax ethics, and common ethical temptations and violations.
Major contributors to unethical behavior are greed and gluttony, and an organizational atmosphere that condones unethical behavior. Other contributors are moral laxity (other issues seem more important at the time) and the fact that time is easy to steal. Questionable rationalizations also contribute to poor ethics—for example, the notion that if unethical behavior helps the company, it will be condoned.

Recurring ethical temptations and violations, including criminal acts, include the following: stealing from employers and customers, illegally copying software, treating people unfairly, sexual harassment, conflict of interest, divulging confidential information, and misusing corporate resources.

4

Apply a guide to ethical decision making.

When faced with an ethical dilemma, ask yourself: Is it right? Is it fair? Who gets hurt? Would you be comfortable with the deed exposed? Would you tell your child to do it? How does it smell?

5

Describe the stakeholder viewpoint of social responsibility, and corporate social performance.

The stakeholder viewpoint of social responsibility contends that firms must hold themselves accountable for the quality of life of the many groups affected by the firm's actions. Corporate social performance is the extent to which a firm responds to the demands of its stakeholders for behaving in a socially responsible way.

6

Present an overview of diversity programs and other social-responsibility initiatives.

Many firms today are being socially responsible by creating more opportunities for diverse groups. Training programs related to valuing differences, or appreciating cultural diversity, are a component of diversity programs. Other social-responsibility initiatives include social leaves of absence; acceptance of whistle blowers; community-redevelopment projects; and elder-care programs.

7

Summarize the benefits of ethical and socially responsible behavior, and how managers can create an environment that fosters such behavior.

Ethical and socially responsible behavior appears to be cost-effective or at least cost-neutral, and also results in social good. Such behavior can also attract and retain valuable employees and customers.

KEY TERMS AND PHRASES

Ethics *pg. 50*

Moral Intensity *pg. 50*

Ethically Centered Management *pg. 52*

Moral Laxity *pg. 52*

Conflict of Interest *pg. 54*

Social Responsibility *pg. 55*

Stockholder Viewpoint *pg. 55*

Stakeholder Viewpoint *pg. 55*

Corporate Social Performance *pg. 56*

Valuing-Differences Training *pg. 57*

Social Leave of Absence *pg. 59*

Whistle Blower *pg. 59*

QUESTIONS

1. Give examples of several rights that you think every employee is entitled to.
2. Why is ethically centered management supposedly helpful in preventing industrial disasters?
3. What have you observed or read about that is the most frequent ethical violation committed by managers?

4. Why should organizations be so concerned about their stakeholders?
5. Ask an experienced manager to give you an example of an issue he or she faced that is neither clearly ethical nor clearly unethical. Be prepared to report your findings to class.
6. An analysis of company annual reports described in this chapter indicated that none of the companies were making contributions to crime prevention. Are such contributions an important part of social performance?
7. If you were the owner or CEO of a company, would you require ethics training for your managerial workers? Explain your reasoning.

SKILL-BUILDING EXERCISE 3-A: THE ETHICAL REASONING INVENTORY

Describe how much you agree with each of the following statements, using the following scale: disagree strongly (DS); disagree (D); neutral (N); agree (A); agree strongly (AS). Circle the answer that best fits your level of agreement.

	DS	D	N	A	AS
1. When applying for a job, I would cover up the fact that I had been fired from my most recent job.	5	4	3	2	1
2. Cheating just a few dollars in one's favor on an expense account is OK if the person needed the money.	5	4	3	2	1
3. Employees should inform on each other for wrongdoing.	1	2	3	4	5
4. It is acceptable to give approximate figures for expense account items when one does not have all the receipts.	5	4	3	2	1
5. I see no problem with conducting a little personal business on company time.	5	4	3	2	1
6. I would fix up a purchasing agent with a date just to close a sale.	5	4	3	2	1
7. To make a sale, I would stretch the truth about a delivery date.	5	4	3	2	1
8. I would flirt with my boss just to get a bigger salary increase.	5	4	3	2	1
9. If I received $100 for doing some odd jobs, I would report it on my income tax returns.	1	2	3	4	5
10. I see no harm in taking home a few office supplies.	5	4	3	2	1
11. It is acceptable to read the E-mail and fax messages of other co-workers even when not invited to do so.	5	4	3	2	1
12. It is unacceptable to call in sick to take a day off, even if only done once or twice a year.	1	2	3	4	5
13. I would accept a permanent, full-time job even if I knew I wanted the job for only six months.	5	4	3	2	1
14. I would check company policy before accepting an expensive gift from a supplier.	1	2	3	4	5
15. To be successful in business, a person usually has to ignore ethics.	5	4	3	2	1
16. If I were physically attracted toward a job candidate, I would hire him or her over another candidate.	5	4	3	2	1
17. I tell the truth all the time on the job.	1	2	3	4	5
18. Software should never be copied, except as authorized by the publisher.	1	2	3	4	5
19. I would authorize accepting an office machine on a 30-day trial period, even if I knew I had no intention of making a purchase.	5	4	3	2	1
20. I would never accept credit for a coworker's ideas.	1	2	3	4	5

Scoring and interpretation: Add the numbers you have circled to obtain your score.

90–100   You are a strongly ethical person who may take a little ribbing from coworkers for being too straight-laced.

60–89   You show an average degree of ethical awareness, and therefore should become more sensitive to ethical issues.

41–59   Your ethics are underdeveloped, but you have at least some awareness of ethical issues. You need to raise your level of awareness about ethical issues.

20–40   Your ethical values are far below contemporary standards in business. Begin a serious study of business ethics.

SKILL-BUILDING EXERCISE 3-B: ETHICAL DECISION MAKING

GROUP ACTIVITY Working in small groups, take the following two ethical dilemmas through the six steps for screening contemplated decisions. You might also want to use various ethical principles in helping you reach a decision.

SCENARIO 1: TO RECYCLE OR NOT.

Your group is the top-management team at a large insurance company. Despite information technology making paper less necessary, your firm still generates tons of paper each month. Customer payments alone account for truckloads of envelops each year. The paper recyclers in your area contend that they can hardly find a market any longer for used paper, so they will be charging you just to accept your paper for recycling. Your group is wondering whether to continue to recycle paper.

SCENARIO 2: JOB APPLICANTS WITH A PAST.

A state (or provincial) government official approaches your bank asking you to hire three people soon to be released from prison. All were found guilty of fraudulently altering computer records for personal gain in a bank. The official says these people have paid their debt to society and that they need jobs. Your company has three openings for computer specialists. All three people obviously have good computer skills. Your group is wondering whether to hire them.

VIDEO DISCUSSION QUESTIONS

1. What ethical concerns might an American or Canadian company have about doing business with the Chinese? [**Business with China**]
2. Did Union Carbide commit any ethical violations surrounding the Bhopal incident? [**Bhopal**]
3. Should Union Carbide be absolved of responsibility for the Bhopal incident? [**Bhopal**]

CASE PROBLEM 3-A: THE BLUNT PROBLEM

The managers at Havatampa Inc. claim not to know much about fads in the inner city. So they were surprised when the sales of their $1-per-five-pack Phillies Blunts cigars surged. The trend driving the sales increase was that Blunts became a status symbol among inner-city youths. A Latino rap group, Cypress Hill, had publicized the little cigars. A Havatampa vice-president, Ruth Bruzel, said that the company didn't even know rap groups were singing songs about them.

The sales surge of Blunts has become a damage-control problem for the company, because Blunts have become part of the paraphernalia for urban marijuana smokers. In the city, to "get blunt" means to slice open a blunt cigar and restuff it with marijuana. The output is a super-size joint disguised by the odor of cigar smoke. Sales of Phillies Blunts are also improving in suburbia among members of Generation X.

Havatampa management has found it cannot do much to decrease demand among drug users for its product. Instead, the path it has selected is to protect its brand's image. The Phillies Blunts red and white logo has been showing up, mostly in pirated versions, on T-shirts and caps all over North America. Most people who see the logo associate it with pot smoking.

To resolve the problem, Havatampa approached a small company, Not From Concentrate, in New York City, and fashioned a deal. Not From Concentrate was requested to maintain quality control, and avoid any direct association with marijuana. In return, the company was granted exclusive rights to reproduce the Phillies Blunt logo on shirts, caps, and sweatshirts. Although clothing with Blunt logos has become the company's best seller, many T-shirts are still being bootlegged.

To avoid the charge of profiteering from the clothing, Havatampa is donating the $24,000 it has earned in royalties to urban charities. In the meantime, company executives are hoping that the association between Phillies Blunts and marijuana fades away. Several executives have said they don't know what else they can do.

CASE QUESTIONS

1. How would you rate the social performance of Havatampa on the issue of Phillies Blunts being used in conjunction with marijuana?
2. What should the company do to behave in a socially responsible way? Or is Havatampa already being socially responsible?
3. What ethical issues can you identify in this case?

Source: Based on facts in Julie Tilsner, "Reefer Madness at Havatampa," *Business Week* (24 January 1994): 42.

CASE PROBLEM 3-B: THE TRUTH STRETCHERS

Bonita Chavez was excited about her new position as assistant to the vice-president of administration at Long Haul Express, an interstate trucking firm. Chavez's responsibilities included preparing financial statements for her boss, investigating customer complaints, and writing speeches and presentations for company executives. In addition, she was assigned the task of updating the company policies and procedures manual.

Before updating the manual, Chavez read it carefully. A paragraph on the first page stated the company's philosophy: "The cornerstone of our business is total honesty in dealing with customers, employees, and regulatory agencies. Nothing less than complete candor will be tolerated." Chavez thought to herself, "If this philosophy is meant to be followed, Long Haul is in trouble."

Several days later Chavez was still disturbed by what she perceived as a discrepancy between company philosophy and company practice. Unable to concentrate on revamping the manual, she requested a meeting with her boss, Roy Coleman.

"How can I help you, Bonita?" asked Coleman.

"I need to talk to you about a big gap between the written philosophy of Long Haul and the reality of what we do," said Chavez.

"What aspect of the philosophy are you talking about? I'm not familiar with every little detail contained in the manual," said Coleman.

"I'm referring to the statement that says Long Haul believes in total honesty in dealing with customers, employees, and government regulators. I've been working here thirteen months and, quite frankly, I think dishonesty is widely practiced by our managers."

"What specifically are you talking about? Can you give me some examples of dishonesty?" asked Coleman.

"Yes, Roy, I can. I came prepared for this meeting. I wrote down four outright lies that I recall our managers making, you excluded."

"Go ahead, I'm interested," said Coleman.

"Okay, here's my list. Last December management told the drivers and office workers that Long Haul would have to skip the employee bonus this year because profits were so slim. Yet, managers received an average bonus of $6,000 each.

"One of our customers was told that a shipment of china was damaged because a boulder rolled down onto the highway. In reality the driver in question was speeding and lost control on a slippery pavement.

"A state inspector was told that we purchased only top-quality, premium tires for our trucks. Yet I know for a fact that we almost always purchase the lowest-priced tires that meet specifications.

"We tell many customers that we have given them our 'preferred customer rate' when all customers receive the same rate."

With a smile, Coleman said to Bonita, "The examples you have given me all fit into sensible business practice. You have to color the truth a little to stay in business. I think the corporate philosophy refers to lies that actually harm people. I'll go over these so-called lies one by one.

"It's true we didn't have enough profits to pay everybody a bonus. Because our managers have a bigger stake in the company, we give them bonuses first.

"How can you expect us to tell a customer that one of our drivers lost control because of speeding? That would be a sure way to lose a customer in the competitive world of trucking.

"Of course we tell the regulators we purchase top-quality tires only. When we do buy low-priced tires, we make sure they are top quality despite the low price. I see no problem there.

"You're right that we tell each customer they are receiving a preferred rate. It makes them happy, and they are not paying a *higher* rate. The number one principle in this or any other business is to keep the customer happy."

"I understand what you are saying, Roy, but I'm still perplexed. I am being asked to update a manual with a philosophy that isn't being taken seriously."

CASE QUESTIONS

1. What is your opinion of Roy Coleman's position that you have to bend the truth a little to stay in business?
2. Is Chavez acting appropriately in bringing her concern about lying to her boss?
3. What should Chavez do next?

CASE PROBLEM 3-C: THE GREAT AMERICAN SWEATSHOPS

Based on a tipoff in August 1995, U.S. federal agents raided an El Monte, California, garment manufacturer. Evidence was found that the company held 75 Thai immigrants behind barbed wire and paid them $1.00 per hour. The names of several larger retailers were found on the boxes in the grimy, poorly lit shop. Among the names were Sears, Montgomery Ward, and Dayton Hudson. Company representatives agreed to meet with Labor Secretary Robert B. Reich to discuss ways to combat the use of sweatshops.

The representatives explained that they had no idea of the deplorable conditions at the El Monte manufacturer. Furthermore, they promised to adopt a statement of principles requesting that their suppliers adhere to federal labor laws.

The Department of Labor estimates that 20,000 small U.S. garment makers supply the one-half of the country's clothing that is not imported. Many of these firms require their employees to work under cramped, poorly ventilated, and unsafe conditions. A Labor Department spot check of 69 garment-making firms in Southern California uncovered health and safety violations in all but seven of them. The workers are mostly female immigrants from Latin America and Asia who earn an average of $7.34 an hour. Wages are just over the federal poverty level. However, they are comparable to pay for many jobs in the service industry, and well above the minimum wage.

Labor Secretary Reich wants the retail industry to play a major role in enforcing restrictions against sweatshops. He urges retailers to use their enormous purchasing power to ensure that subcontractors comply with labor laws. Part of the plan is for large retailers to hire inspectors to visit shops randomly and without warning. Most retailers say such demands are unfair and that they would create a hardship and inflate the price of clothing. Sears alone has 10,000 direct suppliers. The suppliers in turn subcontract work to smaller firms. It is also difficult for civilian inspectors to detect violations of the complex wage and hour laws.

Robert L. Mettler, the president of apparel at Sears, wants fellow retailers to find ways to combat the problem of suppliers who are sweatshops or who subcontract to sweatshops. The executive vice-president of a giant retailer on the verge of insolvency looks at the problem from a different perspective: "We simply cannot afford to hire inspectors. We won't knowingly do business with a supplier that hires slave labor. Yet if you close down all these alleged sweatshops, a lot of families will go hungry. A $7.00 per hour steady job is decent extra money for a low-income family. A lot of people are lined up looking for these jobs.

"Yet with the pressure the Department of Labor is putting on us, we'll have to think of some official position on the issue."

CASE QUESTIONS

1. Explain whether retailers have a social responsibility to inspect vendors for possible violation of wage and safety laws.
2. What advice can you offer the large retailer who claims his company cannot afford inspectors?
3. What is your position about a $7.00 per hour job being a good opportunity for many workers?

Source: Facts in this case are based on Susan Chandler, "Look Who's Sweating Now," *Business Week* (16 October 1995): 96–98.

CASE PROBLEM 3-D: SAVE THE TIGER

Ever since the 1989 *Exxon Valdez* oil spill, the company has been investing extra resources into demonstrating its social responsibility to the world. In 1995 the company was planning to invest about $5 million to help save the tiger from possible extinction. (As is well known, the tiger is also the Exxon corporate symbol.) The money was to be invested in supporting breeding efforts and information displays in zoos and tiger-care projects in Siberia and Sumatra.

Despite Exxon's efforts, some conservationist groups are dissatisfied. They believe that Exxon's spending fails to deal with the real threats to tigers: poaching, illegal trade in tiger parts, and destruction of the tiger's prey by hunters. (Poaching refers to trespassing on tiger preserves and illegally hunting them.) The concern is that Exxon plans to allocate two-thirds of its first donation to zoos for captive breeding and education. Sources contend that Exxon management will avoid antipoaching programs that could be politically sensitive in Asia. The company also plans no initial effort in India and Nepal, where most of the world's remaining tigers live.

Ullas Karanath, a Wildlife Conservation Society ecologist in India, says, "If Exxon's not addressing the crucial factors that are causing the decline in the wild, the money is probably not doing to do much good."

Exxon intends to have all their save-the-tiger projects approved by a group of tiger experts. The National Fish & Wildlife Foundation will administer the fund. The foundation executive director, Amos S. Eno, points out that "We've been wary of the overemphasis on zoos from day one."

Several Exxon executives were perplexed over which course of action to take. One concern expressed is that attempting to do something beneficial for society has backfired.

CASE QUESTIONS

1. Which stakeholders have been identified in the above description of Exxon's attempt to help save the tiger?
2. What course of action should Exxon take? Should it continue with its original plan, or submit to the demands of the conservationists? Or should it choose a third alternative?

Source: Facts in this case are based on John Carey, "Help or Hype from Exxon: It's $5 million to Save Tigers May Not Stop Poaching," *Business Week* (26 August 1995): 36.

REFERENCES

1. Mary G. Rendini, "Team Effort at Maguire Group Leads to Ethics Policy," *HRMagazine* (April 1995): 63–66.
2. Thomas M. Jones, "Ethical Decision Making by Individuals in Organizations," *Academy of Management Review* (April 1991): 391.
3. Linda K. Trevino and Katherine A. Nelson, *Managing Business Ethics: Straight Talk About How To Do It Right* (New York: Wiley, 1995), 66–70; Larue Tone Hosmer, "Trust: The Connecting Link Between Organizational Theory and Philosophical Ethics," *Academy of Management Review* (April 1995): 396–397.
4. Robert Elliott Allinson, "A Call for Ethically-Centered Management," *The Academy of Management Executive* (February 1995): 73.
5. *Ibid.,* 73–74.
6. "Lax Moral Climate Breeds White-Collar Crime Wave," *Personnel* (January 1988): 7.
7. John Kamp and Paul Brooks, "Perceived Organizational Climate and Employee Counterproductivity," *Journal of Business and Psychology* (Summer 1991): 455.
8. "24 Extracted from Mall Ruins After 4 Days," Associated Press (2 July 1995).
9. Allan Weiss, "Seven Reasons to Examine Workplace Ethics," *HRMagazine* (March 1991): 69.
10. Saul W. Gellerman, "Why 'Good' Managers Make Bad Ethical Choices," *Harvard Business Review* (July–August 1986): 88.
11. Trevino and Nelson, *Managing Business Ethics,* 47–57; Samuel Greengard, "Theft Control Starts with HR Strategies," *Personnel Journal* (April 1993): 81–91.
12. James L. Bowditch and Anthony F. Buono, *A Primer on Organizational Behavior* (New York: Wiley, 1994), 4.
13. Gregory M. Bounds, Gregory H. Dobbins, and Oscar S. Fowler, *Management: A Total Quality Perspective* (Cincinnati, OH: South-Western College Publishing, 1995), 150.
14. Jane Park and Adnan Abdeen, "Are Corporations Improving Efforts at Social Responsibility?" *Business Forum* (Summer/Fall 1994): 26–30.
15. "Managing Cultural Diversity," *Supervisory Management* (July 1995): 11.
16. R. Roosevelt Thomas, Jr., *Beyond Race and Gender: Unleashing the Power of Your Total Work Force by Managing Diversity* (New York: AMACOM, 1991), 25.

17. "Time for a Sabbatical?" *HRfocus* (July 1995): 10.
18. Barbara Ettorre, "Whistleblowers: Who's the Real Bad Guy?" *Management Review* (May 1994): 19.
19. Samuel Greengard and Charlene Marmer Solomon, "The Fire This Time," *Personnel Journal* (February 1994): 60.
20. *Ibid.*, 60–61.
21. Study cited in Julie Lawlor, "Parental Guidance: Why Companies Should Care," *Working Woman* (June 1995): 38–39.
22. *Ibid.*, 41.
23. Ramon J. Aldag and Timothy M. Stearns, *Management*, 2/e (Cincinnati, OH: South-Western College Publishing, 1991), 123.
24. Larry Reynolds, "A New Social Agenda For the New Age," *Management Review* (January 1993), 40.
25. Susan J. Harrington, "What Corporate America Is Teaching About Ethics," *The Academy of Management Executive* (February 1991): 21; Linda Klebe Trevino and Bart Victor, "Peer Reporting of Unethical Behavior: A Social Context Perspective," *Academy of Management Journal* (March 1992): 38; Karen Ireland, "The Ethics Game," *Personnel Journal* (March 1991): 74.

CHAPTER 4

Managing for Quality

LEARNING OBJECTIVES
After studying this chapter and doing the exercises, you should be able to:

LEARNING OBJECTIVES
After studying this chapter and doing the exercises, you should be able to:

1
Fully understand the meaning of quality.

2
Describe principles and practices of total quality management related to attitudes and people.

3
Describe principles and practices of total quality management related to work processes and technology.

4
Summarize principles and techniques of total customer satisfaction for managers as well as customer-service workers.

5
Explain various specialized techniques for quality improvement.

6
Recognize the relevance of the Baldrige Award to quality.

© Claudio Edinger/
Gamma Liaison

Merrill Lynch Insurance Group Services knew that processing annuities was a problem. Staff members were working 60-hour weeks and had to cancel many of their vacation plans to handle the backlog. An upcoming mountain of work threatened to double their workload. The problem was assigned to an employee team, composed mostly of people in their 20s and 30s. Merrill's internal quality coaches trained the team in effective teamwork and problem-solving techniques. Management then granted the team autonomy to tackle the problem. • The team achieved the following results: Errors were cut by two-thirds, annual staff and overtime costs by $313,000, the percentage of contracts issued late was reduced to 5 percent from 50 percent, the cost of delays to $26,000 from $445,000, and the average time required to process annuities to 3 days from 16 days. Also, the quality of life for team members increased because they could now spend more time with their families.[1]

The dramatic results achieved by the team at the Merrill Lynch annuity department illustrate managing for quality at its best. Relying on the basics of total quality management—involving teams of people in solving quality problems—customer service attained a new level. At the same time, the company saved money.

The purpose of this chapter is to help the reader achieve an understanding of major aspects of managing for quality. Toward this end, we discuss the meaning of quality and key principles of total quality management and total customer satisfaction. We also describe several widely used techniques for improving quality, such as quality circles and cause-and-effect analysis. In addition, we mention how the Deming principles and the Baldrige Award contribute to quality.

THE MEANING OF QUALITY

LEARNING OBJECTIVE

Fully understand the meaning of quality.

---

quality
The totality of features and characteristics of a product or service that bears on its ability to satisfy given needs.

Although the term *quality* has an important meaning to every reader, it lacks a universally acceptable definition. The definition developed by the American Society for Quality Control is informative and useful: **Quality** is the totality of features and characteristics of a product or service that bears on its ability to satisfy given needs. Because need satisfaction is an individual matter, what constitutes quality for a specific product or service will vary among people. Quality has been defined in the following major ways:

- Conformance to expectations
- Conformance to requirements
- Loss avoidance
- Meeting and/or exceeding customers' expectations
- Excellence and value[2]

In general, if a product or service does what it is supposed to do, it is said to be of high quality. If the product or service fails in its mission, it is said to be of low quality. The requirements can be objective or subjective. A high-quality automobile might contain certain parts that deviate less than 0.0005 from standard. With such a small deviation, the parts meet objective requirements. The same automobile might also generate a high-quality image, thus meeting a subjective requirement of quality. Exhibit 4-1 presents an advertisement for an automobile that many believe meets objective and subjective quality requirements.

Given the many nuances to the meaning of quality, be cautious when instructing others to achieve high-quality results. Make sure that you and the other person have a similar perception. For example, can a high-quality pair of jeans cost $35, or must the price be $95 to achieve quality?

PRINCIPLES AND PRACTICES OF TOTAL QUALITY MANAGEMENT

A major strategy for achieving high quality is total quality management. As referred to in Chapter 2, total quality management (TQM) was defined as a management system for improving performance throughout a firm by maximizing customer satisfaction, making continuous improvements, and relying heavily on employee involvement. To develop a more complete understanding of the scope and intent of TQM, think through the following definition:

A system of management that involves all people in an organization delivering products or services that meet or exceed customer requirements. It is a preventive, proactive approach to

Exhibit 4-1
An Advertisement
That Projects a
Quality Image

YOU HAVE NO WATER OR COOLANT. YOU HAVE
50 MILES OF DESERT TO CROSS.
YOU HAVE 2 CHOICES. YOU CAN RIDE OR DRIVE.

*A camel's system is so adaptive, it can travel 50 miles in desert heat
without taking fluid…making him one of the world's most dependable animals.
The Seville STS with the Northstar System by Cadillac is so adaptive that,
if necessary for your safety, it is engineered to travel 50 miles in desert heat without a single
drop of coolant…which might also tell you something about its dependability.*

SEVILLE STS.
CHANGING THE WAY YOU THINK ABOUT AMERICAN AUTOMOBILES.

NORTHSTAR SYSTEM: 32-VALVE, 295-HP V8 • ROAD-SENSING SUSPENSION • TRACTION CONTROL
• ABS • SPEED-SENSITIVE STEERING • PLUS DUAL AIR BAGS • PLEASE CALL 1-800-333-4CAD

Source: Courtesy of Cadillac Motor Division, General Motors Corporation.

*doing business. As such it reflects strategic leadership, common sense, data-driven approaches
to problem solving and decision making, employee involvement, and sound management
practice. Its basic philosophy is the customer is the driver of the business, suppliers are joint
partners, and leaders exist to ensure that the entire organization and all its people are po-
sitioned and empowered to meet competitive demand.[3]*

If the definition just presented seems like a short course rather than a definition, your perception is accurate. Proponents of total quality management tend to consider a wide range of good management practices as part of TQM. To achieve better focus, this section approaches TQM by dividing its principles and practices into two categories: those that apply to attitudes and managing people and those that primarily relate to work processes and technology. All aspects of total quality management are geared toward satisfying internal and external customers. A separate section will focus on the vital topic of total customer satisfaction.

DEALING WITH ATTITUDES AND PEOPLE

LEARNING OBJECTIVE 2

Describe principles and practices of total quality management related to attitudes and people.

A system of total quality management directs the effort of an entire firm toward higher customer satisfaction, continuous improvement, and employee involvement. Many quality-management principles are, therefore, expressed in terms of changing individuals' attitudes and the organization culture. It has been suggested that total quality management is 90 percent attitude, specifically the attitude of listening to customers.[4] Such a profound attitude change results in a culture change.

BEGIN WITH TOP-LEVEL COMMITMENT. As a starting point in achieving total quality management, executives must give top priority to quality. They must allocate resources to prevent as well as to repair quality problems. Quality must be included in the organizational strategy, and every organizational unit must be responsible for quality. Workers throughout the firm must perceive the quest for quality as a top management commitment. High-level managers must, therefore, make frequent references to quality and reward quality performance. The top-level commitment goes a long way toward creating a culture of quality.

CLOSE THE QUALITY CREDIBILITY GAP. Most firms talk about quality but few follow through with rigorously enforced plans to achieve it. An important top-level management technique is to close the *credibility gap*—the difference between the message employees hear and the actual follow-through. A survey conducted by the American Society for Quality Control revealed an average credibility gap of almost 20 percent.[5] To close the gap, top-level managers can provide a clear example, such as to accept a late penalty rather than ship a defective product.

MAINTAIN CUSTOMER SENSITIVITY THROUGHOUT THE ORGANIZATION. The essence of quality is to satisfy the needs of internal and external customers. An *internal customer* is someone in the firm who uses the output of another or interacts with someone else for work purposes. If you prepare monthly statistics for the head of another department, that manager is your customer. An *external customer* is a person outside the firm who pays for its goods or services. A person who obtains a home mortgage is thus a bank customer. Workers throughout the firm must get the message that the true purpose of their jobs is to satisfy customer requirements. Every action they take should be linked to customer satisfaction. A telemarketer might say, for example, "Is putting my caller on hold and playing music over the phone in the best interests of the customer?"

COMMUNICATE WIDELY ABOUT QUALITY. Top management in companies that won Baldrige quality awards systematically communicated the quality message throughout the firm. Federal Express, Cadillac, and IBM Rochester use their internal television networks to broadcast quality issues to employees. Most high-quality companies regularly send messages about quality over E-mail. In addition to print and electronic messages, top management conducts face-to-face meetings with employees to share quality victories and future quality objectives. Motorola management conducts quarterly town meetings at company sites. These meetings are supplemented by rap sessions between high-level managers and employee groups, with quality topics often discussed.[6]

MAKE CONTINUOUS IMPROVEMENT A WAY OF LIFE. Just as the team must focus on continuous improvement, so must the individual employee. An employee who is committed to the TQM culture searches daily for ways of improving his or her work process and output. This approach embodies the spirit of *kaizen,* a philosophy of continuing gradual improvement in one's personal and work life. The kaizen philosophy is important because quality improvement is usually a gradual process.

EMPOWER AND INVOLVE EMPLOYEES. To achieve total quality management, managers must empower employees to fix and prevent problems. Equally important, workers have to accept the authority and become involved in the improvement process. Empowerment is valuable because it may release creative energy. For example, at Advance Circuits of Hopkins, Minnesota, an empowered team eliminated pinhole-sized defects in circuit-board film. Team members discovered that by using a smaller darkroom they could eliminate many airborne particles that caused the defects.[7] The accompanying Management in Action presents more details about employee involvement and quality management.

LISTEN TO EMPLOYEES. A successful quality-improvement effort creates an atmosphere in which the manager listens to employees. Management by walking around is there-

MANAGEMENT IN ACTION: QUALITY IMPROVEMENT AT A MACHINE PARTS COMPANY

Associated Company Inc., of Wichita, Kansas, supplies machine parts to aviation companies. At one time the company was suffering from high quality costs due to high scrap and rework rates, along with parts failures in the hands of customers. To help reduce these costs, management initiated a Work Smarter program. To begin quality improvement, management set the product failure rate at 0.5 percent. The company wanted a realistic target for employees, and they also believed that the cost of achieving zero defects might exceed the benefits. Employees were encouraged to be innovative and take more risks.

The work force of 100 production employees was divided into eight groups who, along with their supervisors, met with the quality manager. The quality manager then placed orange tags on defective parts and broken equipment, showing their cost.

At the next round of meetings, workers paid more attention to the cost of quality. Quality-improvement goals were set, and employees were rewarded for reaching goals. Rewards included dinners at local restaurants, movie tickets, and $50 gift certificates. With the success of these initial rewards, Associated management expanded the program, and employees gradually accepted more authority and responsibility for quality.

As a result of Work Smarter, the scrap and rework rate bottomed out at a 0.25 percent rate. Employee turnover decreased from a high of 200 percent to 25 percent. The more stable work force engaged in decision making and quality improvement produced major gains for Associated. The company encouraged employee involvement through suggestions and specific work changes. By so doing, management now treated its employees as human resources to be valued instead of labor costs to be minimized.

Source: Mark L. Lengnick-Hall, George Heinrick, and Earl Middleton, "Employee Involvement Makes TQM Work," *Personnel Journal* (October 1993): 108.

fore standard practice in a TQM organization. Managers should listen for suggestions about even minor aspects of quality. Weyerhauser Mortgage of Woodland Hills, California, was experiencing delays in receiving reimbursement checks from FHA-insured home loans. Team members contended that company mistakes in completing forms were the culprit—not the government. The company listened and eliminated the mistakes. The checks now arrive in one-sixth the time, resulting in substantial savings.[8]

EMPHASIZE THE HUMAN SIDE OF QUALITY. Statistical and decision-making techniques contribute heavily to quality improvement. Yet the real thrust of quality management is for all employees to have positive attitudes toward quality. They must pay attention to detail, take pride in their work, and believe that high quality improves profits. Not paying enough attention to the human side of quality cost Chrysler Corporation a temporary drop in customer satisfaction ratings in 1995. Part of the problem was that large doses of overtime resulted in stressed workers who could not perform up to the high quality standards typical of Chrysler vehicles.[9]

REWARD HIGH-QUALITY PERFORMANCE. The best quality results are likely to be achieved when employees receive financial as well as nonfinancial rewards for achieving quality. Several key figures of the quality movement in the United States have downplayed the importance of financial incentives in achieving quality. Often these experts point to the outstanding quality of Japanese manufactured goods. Nevertheless, the Japanese approach to quality improvement has always emphasized financial bonuses for good performance. PQ Corp., a chemical manufacturer in Pennsylvania, implemented a program of giving financial rewards for achieving high quality. Company management observed that the rewards had a positive impact on maintaining continuous improvements.[10] In their quest for high quality, many other companies are replacing cash awards with such rewards as plaques, banquets, and certificates for quality achievement.[11]

Whether the rewards are cash or noncash, the principle remains the same. Some workers may be motivated by the joy of doing quality work, yet most workers would also like other rewards in addition.

DEALING WITH WORK PROCESSES AND TECHNOLOGY

LEARNING OBJECTIVE

Describe the principles and practices of total quality management related to work processes and technology.

Total quality management began in manufacturing. As a result, many total quality management ideas are aimed at improving work processes and making effective use of technology. The paragraphs that follow describe major principles of this aspect of TQM. More of these ideas will be presented later, in the section about specialized techniques for quality improvement. Before proceeding, let's clarify the widely used term *process*. As already described, a process is a set of activities designed to achieve a goal such as the process of refinishing a table. The accompanying Manager in Action explains a work process in more depth.

IMPLEMENT A FORMAL QUALITY PROGRAM TO SUPPORT THE QUALITY PROCESS. Sponsoring a quality program helps establish a total quality culture and supports the process of quality management. Some employers hold an event such as Quality Week or Quality Day. Ford Motor Company has achieved success with the program Quality Is Job One. Motorola has developed Sigma Six, which is both a program and an incredibly tight goal. The name refers to a quality standard in which errors occur only once in 3.4 million opportunities. Under the normal distribution curve, six sigma is the area found six standard deviations beyond the mean (a very small area indeed). Six-sigma quality means that work is 99.999997 per-

MANAGER IN ACTION: JIM RILEY EXPLAINS A WORK PROCESS

James F. Riley, Jr., is senior vice-president of the Juran Institute Inc., a firm that offers training and consulting about total quality management. When asked to give an example of a work process, he replied: "Take product development. New products begin in the research department with a concept. This progresses to the engineering department for the development of a prototype, which they make ready for manufacturing. The manufacturing function designs a way to produce the product affordably, quickly, and within production schedules. The product then must become ready to enter the marketplace, which involves the marketing, sales, and delivery functions.

"To achieve quality, you have to improve work performance at each stage of this process so that you can make a product that's free of defects, meets customer needs, and is manufactured in the least possible time, at the least possible cost. By necessity, TQM emphasizes teamwork for these reasons: Processes cut through an organization; and no one function, employee, or manager owns the entire process."

Source: "Just Exactly What Is Total Quality Management?" *Personnel Journal* (February 1993): 32.

cent error-free. For example, this standard allows only one input error in an 800-page document. Other organization-wide quality programs at Motorola include training programs and a specific day on which quality is celebrated.

ENGAGE IN BENCHMARKING. A basic total quality principle is to compare the firm's performance to an industry standard or world-class performance. **Benchmarking** is comparing a firm's quality performance to that achieved by competing firms, or some aspect of performance from a firm in another field. The firm in the other field might have achieved outstanding success in some aspect of the business that is relevant even if different. A classic example is that Xerox Corp. compared its shipping capabilities to those of mail-order merchant L.L. Bean.

> **benchmarking**
> *The process of comparing a firm's quality performance to that achieved by a competing firm.*

Several telemarketing firms have recently achieved good success by benchmarking the multilingual services offered by the customer service department of public utilities. Specifically, the telemarketers make their pitch in the mother tongue of the person from whom they want an order. The telemarketer knows in advance which language prevails in a particular neighborhood.

SELECT HIGH-QUALITY SUPPLIERS AND TRAIN THEM PROPERLY. A company needs high-quality components and materials to produce high-quality products. Careful selection of suppliers (or vendors) is, therefore, a major aspect of ensuring reliable and defect-free production. Once the right suppliers are selected, they must be clearly informed about the company's quality requirements. Sharp Electronics Corp. exemplifies this approach. The company teaches many of its suppliers how to produce high-quality components.

BUILD QUALITY INTO THE PROCESS. A basic method for improving quality at the team level is to manufacture quality into the product. In other words, inspecting for defects is not good enough—errors should be prevented through superior design. For example, Velcro USA Inc. was at one time throwing away about 7 percent of the tape it made for General Motors. Velcro then applied appropriate statistical techniques and better manufacturing design. The company was able to trim waste 50 percent in the first year and 45 percent more in the second year.[12] The discussion of robust design later in the chapter provides more details about built-in quality.

ENSURE THE EXCELLENCE OF INCOMING RAW MATERIALS AND SUPPLIES. To achieve TQM, a work group must accept only high-quality raw materials and supplies. The premise is that a high-quality product cannot be made with low-quality materials. Many companies have vendor certification programs to ensure excellent supplies and materials.

DECREASE CYCLE TIME. An important goal of quality management is a short **cycle time,** the interval between the ordering and delivery of a product or service. Receiving goods promptly contributes to a customer's perception of quality. In addition, working toward shorter and shorter cycle times also can expose areas of weakness that adversely affect quality. A small firm that produced videotapes for product demonstrations set out to reduce its cycle time. In the process, managers discovered a bottleneck: a cumbersome procedure for estimating production costs.

PAY PAINSTAKING ATTENTION TO DETAIL. The quality of goods and services is greatly enhanced if everybody pays careful attention to detail. Paying attention to detail enables a worker to satisfy a major tenet of total quality management: do work right the first time. A national ZIP code directory provides an example of the consequences of doing work wrong the first time. The directory contained several errors that were incorporated into hundreds of mailing lists whose compilers were not aware of the inaccuracies. The results have been many delayed shipments and demands from dozens of irate customers insisting that their ZIP codes be corrected. Despite their pleas, the computer traces codes back to the source document and repeats the errors. The errors were finally corrected in a revision of the directory, but many of the incorrect ZIP codes remain stored in computer memories.

INSTITUTE STRINGENT WORK STANDARDS FOR EVERY INDIVIDUAL. Recall the earlier discussion of how Motorola Inc. instituted a six-sigma work standard. For a TQM program to take hold, individuals have to fully accept such standards. Another stringent performance standard used in some TQM programs is **zero defects,** the absence of any detectable quality flaws in a product or service. Quality consultant Philip B. Crosby claimed that if people are truly committed to error-free work, they will accomplish it.[13] Others believe, however, that error-free work is virtually unattainable. A human problem associated with virtually unattainable goals such as zero defects is that it results in needless frustration and stress for employees. It might be possible to achieve zero defects in producing a physical product such as brake linings. But picture yourself as a tax accountant who is told that not even one mistake in preparing a season's worth of tax forms will be tolerated.

CALCULATE THE RETURN ON QUALITY. For some aspects of goods and services, achieving the highest quality is a poor investment. The guiding principle is that a quality improvement is a poor investment if the customer does not care about the improvement or it leads to customer neglect. A vacuum-equipment unit of Varin Associates Inc. became obsessed with meeting schedules in their quest for total quality. In their race to meet deadlines, however, the staff did not return customer telephone calls, and the operation lost money. At Johnson & Johnson, quality-improvement teams for several product lines crisscrossed the country to conduct benchmarking. Unfortunately, costs skyrocketed beyond the value of the information obtained from benchmarking.[14]

Today, many corporate managers are carefully calculating whether quality management is a good investment. Properly implemented, the answer is quite frequently yes.

TRAIN INDIVIDUALS IN QUALITY. As part of total quality management, almost every employee receives quality-related training. Each individual must learn the basic concepts of TQM, including problem-solving, decision-making, and interpersonal skills. Manufacturing operatives learn about statistical techniques useful for quality control, such as sampling and measuring variation.

PROBLEMS ASSOCIATED WITH SYSTEMS AND TQM PROGRAMS

Any mention of the limitations of total quality management systems and programs does not mean that quality is unimportant. Instead, the argument is that there are less time-consuming and cumbersome ways of achieving quality than through TQM. A problem in measuring the contribution of total quality systems and programs is that total quality management has lost its focus. As mentioned previously, TQM advocates appear to include virtually every useful management technique under the quality framework.

Many companies have found that some quality standards are arbitrary and not cost-effective. UPS, for example, has backed off on rapid delivery at any cost. Gradually company officials discovered that many customers enjoyed interacting with the neatly groomed UPS drivers and did not want them rushing off to the next delivery. Drivers now have more time to converse with customers, which has improved customer relations and improved sales.[15]

According to a study conducted with 584 companies in four countries, many total quality programs fail because they attempt too much. The programs attempt to make hundreds of changes instead of focusing on a small number of decisive changes. A consultant noted that many companies are not seeing significant positive results from quality-improvement programs because they isolate these programs from day-to-day operations. Instead, companies should regard total quality management as a way of meeting business objectives.[16]

Another reason cited for the failure of TQM programs is lack of commitment from top-level managers. Organizations rarely measure the performance of top-level managers in terms of the quality of goods and services produced by the firm.[17]

TQM programs work best when managers follow the principles and practices described so far. Although commitment of top-level managers is essential, they cannot become so obsessed with TQM that they neglect other aspects of management.

PRINCIPLES AND TECHNIQUES
OF TOTAL CUSTOMER SATISFACTION

Satisfying customer needs is the major strategy of total quality management. Achieving total customer satisfaction is also part of the strategy of many successful firms that do not have a total quality program. The ultimate goal in achieving customer satisfaction is to achieve **zero defections**—that is, to keep every customer the company can profitably serve. Notice that *zero defections* is a takeoff on the term *zero defects,* but it does not mean the same thing. Zero defections is an important goal to work toward because customer retention has a major impact on profits. Companies can almost double profits by retaining only 5 percent more of their customers.[18]

This section describes key principles and techniques for building constructive customer relationships and achieving total customer satisfaction.[19] The examples focus on the external customer in a retail setting. The principles and techniques for achieving customer satisfaction can be categorized according to whether they

LEARNING OBJECTIVE

Summarize principles and techniques of total customer satisfaction for managers as well as customer-service workers.

zero defections
Keeping every customer a company can profitably serve.

require managerial input or whether front-line customer-service workers alone can implement them.

PRINCIPLES AND TECHNIQUES FOR MANAGERS

Managers must assume responsibility for implementing many of the principles, techniques, and methods that lead toward total customer satisfaction. The following list describes a number of these approaches:

1. *Establish customer-satisfaction goals.* Managers must decide how much help to give to customers. They need to raise questions such as, Will employees attempt to satisfy every customer within 10 minutes of his or her request? Is the company striving to provide the finest customer service in its field? Is our goal zero customer defections to competitors? The answers will dictate how much effort and the type of effort the manager and the team members must put into pleasing customers.

2. *Give decision-making authority to customer-service workers.* Customer service is enhanced when front-line workers are empowered to deal with customer problems without seeking several levels of approval. Such authority includes the ability to grant refunds, exchanges, concessions, and preferred delivery dates. The accompanying Manager in Action illustrates how empowerment can be a good return on investment.

3. *Thoroughly screen applicants for customer-service positions.* High-quality customer service can best be achieved by hiring high-quality people. Companies noted for their good service seek candidates who have good communication skills, project a professional image, display empathy, and who appear happy. Screening for conscientiousness and extroversion is also important. As retail management professor Charles E. Cox observes, "Attract good people, and innovative marketing techniques will follow."[20]

4. *Hire full-time, permanent store associates.* To reduce costs, a growing number of retailers hire many part-time or temporary store associates. These workers frequently lack the commitment and product knowledge of full-time, permanent store (or sales) associates. David Fagiano, president of the American Management Association, believes this practice is wrong. He says that to handle difficult customer transactions requires a representative who is highly skilled in the job functions. Also, the representative must be motivated to provide superior service. Such service requires a degree of company loyalty not typically found in a temporary worker.[21]

5. *Invest in training.* As with quality management, achieving total customer satisfaction requires a substantial investment in training. One study showed that top service companies spend between $750 and $10,000 on training for each employee during the first year of employment. Areas of training include problem solving, listening, communication, and stress management.[22] Workers must also receive enough training to have thorough product knowledge. Many instances of customer dissatisfaction are linked to a sales associate's insufficient knowledge of the merchandise.

6. *Solicit customer feedback regularly.* To stay attuned to customer needs, management needs to solicit regular feedback from customers. Many top-level managers regularly visit company facilities that serve customers, such as stores, restaurants, and hotels. A creative approach to soliciting feedback is to use a store for market evaluation. Belinda Rush, president and owner of V'tae Care, which makes all-natural scents based on aromatherapy, notes, "Our store has become the place where I try new products and test the market. I don't have to rely on what everyone else is saying about what's going on in the world. I can try things out and get instant gratification or instant rejection."[23]

An advanced principle of obtaining customer feedback is not to rely strictly on what they say. Instead, observe customers' actions to obtain insights into their preferences for present and future products. For example, market research indicated that consumers wanted low-fat, nutritious fast foods such as McDonald's McLean, KFC's skinless fried chicken, and Pizza Hut's low-cal pizza. Yet all products failed to meet expectations. In reality, when it comes to diet, there is a big disparity between what people intend to eat (extra healthy foods) and what they actually eat (fat, tasty foods). One way of learning what consumers really do is to observe them directly or through video cameras.[24] A caution is that video-camera recordings for this purpose are considered unethical by many people.

7. *Communicate the fact that everyone contributes to the customer's perception of service.* Customers evaluate the quality of service on the basis of their total perception of how they are treated by all people with whom they interact. For example, shabby treatment by a parking lot attendant can detract from high-quality service received within the store.

8. *Recognize the demands of family and personal life.* Work schedules that interfere with family and personal life cause stress and can make employees grumpy toward customers. Facing customers until 10:00 at night and starting again at 10:00 the next morning creates resentment.

9. *Find ways to buy from your customer.* A powerful tactic for building customer relationships is to buy as many products or services as possible from the customer's firm. This tactic generally applies to industrial customers. A store manager, however, might be able to buy from customers who are themselves store owners or managers. Ask customers for a full listing of the products and services their firms offer. Key managers in the company should have access to this list; perhaps they can find a way to make a purchase.

10. *Develop efficient systems of order fulfillment.* A potential barrier to excellent customer service is a mediocre order-fulfillment process. No matter how courteous and friendly the sales representative, a customer will be upset when orders are filled slowly or inaccurately. The discussion of reengineering in Chapter 9 highlights how business firms strive to improve basic business processes such as order fulfillment.

11. *Take ethical actions.* Ethical violations receive so much publicity that customers may be impressed by conspicuous displays of ethical behavior. Treat customers the same way you would treat family members or valued friends or want to be

treated yourself. James Cash Penney recognized the value of this principle when, in 1902, he called his first store The Golden Rule.

PRINCIPLES AND TECHNIQUES FOR CUSTOMER-SERVICE WORKERS

Customer-service workers, especially sales associates, play a major role in moving an organization toward total customer satisfaction. The list that follows describes a number of techniques that customer-service workers can use:

1. *Understand customer needs.* The most basic principle of selling is to identify and satisfy customer needs. One challenge in applying the principle is that many customers may not be able to express their needs clearly. To help identify customer needs, you may have to probe for information. For example, an associate in a camera and video store might ask, "What uses do you have in mind for your video camera?" Knowing this information will help the associate identify the camcorder that will satisfy the customer's needs.
2. *Put customer needs first.* After customer needs have been identified, the focus must be on satisfying them rather than oneself or the firm. Assume the customer says, "The only convenient time for me to receive delivery this week would be Thursday or Friday afternoon." The sales associate should not respond, "On Thursdays and Fridays our truckers prefer to make morning deliveries." Instead, the associate should respond, "I'll do whatever is possible to accommodate your request."
3. *Respond positively to moments of truth.* An effective customer-contact worker performs well during situations in which a customer comes in contact with the company and forms an impression of its service. Such situations are referred to as **moments of truth.** If the customer experiences satisfaction or delight during a moment of truth, the customer is likely to return. A person who is frustrated during a moment of truth will often not be a repeat customer.
4. *Show care and concern.* During contacts with customers, show concern for their welfare. Ask questions such as, "How have you enjoyed the CD player you bought here a while back?" or "How are you feeling today?" After asking the question, project a genuine interest in the answer.
5. *Communicate a positive attitude.* A positive attitude is conveyed by such attributes as pleasing appearance, friendly gestures, a warm voice tone, and good telephone communication skills. When a customer seems apologetic about making a demand, a possible response might be: "No need to apologize. My job is to please you. Without you, we wouldn't be in business."
6. *Smile at every customer.* Smiling is a natural relationship builder and can help build bonds with customers. Sales associates should smile several times during each customer contact, even if the customer is angry with the product or service.

Few retail or industrial firms can achieve all of the above principles and techniques for total customer satisfaction. Furthermore, according to one market research firm, you can please only about 80 percent of your customers no matter what you do. Few firms can avoid customers who either are chronic complainers or have unrealistic expectations.[25] Nevertheless, as with total quality management, principles of customer satisfaction represent ideals to strive toward.

moment of truth
A situation in which a customer comes in contact with the company and forms an impression of its service.

LEARNING OBJECTIVE

Explain various specialized techniques for quality improvement.

SPECIALIZED TECHNIQUES FOR QUALITY IMPROVEMENT

So far this chapter has described techniques and attitudes that contribute to enhanced quality. Technical methods form another important part of assuring quality. These specialized techniques originated in manufacturing but are also used to improve the quality of services. Among the techniques are quality circles, cause-and-effect analysis, quality control, statistical process control, and robust quality.

QUALITY CIRCLES

An important part of the quality movement is the application of quality circles to improve both quality and productivity. A **quality circle** is a small group of employees that meets regularly and voluntarily to identify, solve, and sometimes implement solutions to work-related problems. A circle usually consists of 8 to 10 members who meet once a week for about one hour during normal working hours.

The quality circle concept was brought to Japan in 1950 by W. Edwards Deming, a noted American quality expert. Quality circles received widespread attention in the United States during the late 1970s and early 1980s, because many people believed they had made a major contribution to Japan's growth in productivity. In recent years, much of the enthusiasm for quality circles has waned, but they are still used as a vehicle for employee involvement.

Quality circles preceded the total quality management movement. The quality circle approach to quality improvement is a *bottom-up approach,* while TQM is a *top-down approach.* Quality circle members initiate improvement by making suggestions to management—thus the ideas originate at the bottom and move up. TQM is a total management system that starts at the top and then involves other employees.

> **quality circle**
> *A small group of employees who perform similar work and who meet regularly to identify, solve, and sometimes implement solutions to work-related problems.*

QUALITY CONTROL

Long before total quality management, manufacturers attempted to ensure product quality. A standard technique to ensure quality is **quality control**—determining the extent to which goods or services match a specified quality standard. There are two primary ways to control quality. One way is to inspect all units of output (100-percent inspection). Another is to inspect samples of the total output, such as checking every 200th can of tuna fish produced. Similarly, a random sample can be used instead of inspecting predetermined units of the product.

> **quality control**
> *Any method of determining the extent to which goods or services match some specified quality standard.*

THE 100-PERCENT INSPECTION. Under the *100-percent inspection technique,* all units are inspected. Those that do not meet quality standards are rejected. A 100-percent inspection is impossible when the process of inspection ruins the product. After a can of tuna is inspected, for instance, it cannot be sold. In contrast, visually inspecting a hair dryer does no harm to the unit.

A 100-percent inspection technique is necessary when the cost of poor quality is enormous. The cost could be measured in terms of money, human lives, or human suffering. Suffering or loss of life would result if there were defects in products such as contact lenses, automobile brakes, airplane controls, and heart pacemakers. The cost of lawsuits would be significant also.

Inspecting every unit is quite expensive when humans perform the inspection. To decrease inspection costs, robots are now used for some forms of inspection. An even more recent development in quality control are machine-vision systems. Such systems have a sensing device that can, for example, check the size of holes in parts going along a conveyor belt. The system can reject parts with holes too big or too small.

Even a 100-percent inspection technique will not catch every defective product. The inspection device—whether human or electronic—is not perfect. The person or machine may have quality problems too.

INSPECTION BY SAMPLING. When a sample is used for quality control, managers must decide how many units to inspect and what to inspect. One strategy is *acceptance inspection,* or checking completed products. The completed products may be finished goods for sale to consumers or they may be intermediate goods that will be used in further production.

Another strategy is *in-process inspection,* in which products are checked during production. If flaws are detected, changes can be made before the product is assembled. Tearing down finished products is expensive and may result in considerable scrap. It is much better to find pieces of fish tail in a batch of tuna meat before it is canned than afterward.

Another strategy for quality control combines acceptance and in-process inspection. Goods and services of the highest quality generally receive both types of inspection. Waterman Ideal, a manufacturer of pens and pencils, uses both types of inspection to ensure the quality of their writing instruments. Because of this, all Waterman Ideal products are guaranteed for three years from the date of purchase. Quality control can also be applied to services. One frequent practice is for a customer-service representative to telephone a customer and inquire about the quality of service (such as repairs made on an automobile).

In a sampling procedure, a small number of items (the *sample*) are drawn from the *lot,* or the total number of units. Characteristics of the lot are inferred from those of the sample. Assume that a lot of 10,000 plastic containers of tennis balls are being manufactured. A quality control inspector selects 20 of these containers at random. If one of these containers lacks the required air pressure, the inspector can assume that 5 percent of the lot is defective. In other words, approximately 500 cans in the lot have unacceptably low pressure.

In practice, sampling is much more complicated than the example just given. The inspector would have to pick a representative sample and specify the probability of making errors in prediction. Using a sampling technique is less expensive and time-consuming than inspecting every unit. The technique also has disadvantages. In any sampling technique, some defective parts will go undetected, so there is the risk that consumers will purchase low-quality products. There is, therefore, increased probability that customer goodwill may decline. Any method of quality control requires managers to determine an acceptable number of defects or poor-quality products. The accompanying Organization in Action feature describes a sampling procedure that has worked very well.

STATISTICAL PROCESS CONTROL

Early attempts to improve the quality of products focused primarily on the inspection of outgoing products. In effect, producers tried to inspect quality into their products. The production process itself and work in process went unmonitored. As thinking about quality became more advanced, many firms shifted the focus of their quality-improvement efforts to in-process inspection.

Process management is the monitoring, controlling, and improving of a production process for the purpose of improving the quality of the output of the process. Deming developed a refinement of in-process inspection, referred to as **statistical process control.** This method uses graphical displays for analyzing deviations in production processes during manufacturing rather than after the completion of a part or product. Similar to other methods of quality control, the goal of statistical process control is to reduce variation in the finished product.

In many cases, variation is inherent in the process; it cannot be predicted or easily eliminated. The causes of such variation are called common causes, and only

statistical process control

A technique for spotting defects during production that utilizes graphical displays for analyzing deviations.

ORGANIZATION IN ACTION: PEPSI ACCEPTS THE QUALITY CHALLENGE

Pepsi USA evaluates each Pepsi bottler's quality by taking samples of cola from production facilities and from various stores within each franchise area. Those with the highest quality receive the Caleb Bradham Award, an award named after the inventor of Pepsi Cola. Of 200 Pepsi bottlers in the United States, the Springfield, Missouri, facility of Pepsi Cola General Bottlers, Inc. produces the best quality.

The Springfield bottling plant received a 100-percent quality rating from Pepsi USA—the first 100-percent rating ever given. The rating means that, when samples were taken at the production plant and at local retail outlets, inspectors found no deviation from the standards. The Springfield plant had achieved a state of perfection, or zero defects.

One of the major reasons for the success of the Springfield facility is adherence to quality standards that exceed national standards. The company performs the same tests that all Pepsi bottlers perform, but more frequently and more strictly. If tests are necessary, they are conducted—no matter how much time they take. The production manager notes: "Most plants run tests on the production line every hour. We run them every fifteen minutes, all day long, on both shifts. We want to know instantly if anything goes wrong." If any production employee notices something suspicious, production is halted until management is satisfied that the problem has been corrected.

Source: As reported in D. Keith Denton, "Quality Is Pepsi's Challenge," *Personnel Journal* (June 1988): 143. In 1995, the Springfield bottling plant was still noted for its superior quality.

improved process technology can eliminate them. In other cases, variation is due to assignable (identifiable) causes, such as worn tools or worker error. Assignable causes can be corrected, so even a superior production process needs a method for controlling quality. A process whose output variance is due only to common causes is said to be in a state of *statistical control*. When assignable causes are present, the process is *out of control* and needs to be corrected.

Statistical process control gauges the effectiveness of the manufacturing process by carefully monitoring changes in whatever is being produced. Potential problems are detected before they result in poor-quality products. Experts can diagnose the reasons for the deviation and modify the process as necessary. Part of the turnaround of Harley-Davidson Motor Co. Inc. has been attributed to the application of statistical process control. Reducing output variation is so important that the U.S. Air Force specifies that suppliers must use statistical process control in the manufacture of parts and armaments.

SOLUTIONS TO QUALITY PROBLEMS

To gain continuous improvement in quality, problems must be identified and corrected. Quality circle members as well as other quality-improvement groups frequently attempt to diagnose the cause of a quality problem. One problem-identification technique involves using a **Pareto diagram,** a bar graph that ranks types of output variation by frequency of occurrence. Managers and workers use Pareto diagrams to identify the most important problems or causes of problems that affect output quality. Identification of the "vital few" allows management or quality circle teams to focus on the major cause or causes of a quality problem.

An example might be an investigation of laser printer failures. As Exhibit 4-2 shows, the causes of a problem are plotted on the *x*-axis (horizontal). The cumulative effects are plotted on the *y*-axis (vertical). In a Pareto diagram, the bars are arranged in descending order of height—that is, frequency of occurrence—from left

> **Pareto diagram**
> *A bar graph that ranks types of output variations by frequency of occurrence.*

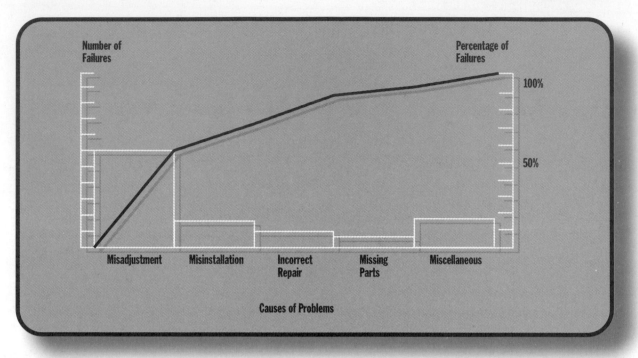

Exhibit 4-2
A Pareto Analysis of
Laser Printer Failures

cause-and-effect
analysis
A graphical tech-
nique for analyz-
ing the factors
that contribute to
a problem. It relies
on a Ishikawa, or
fishbone, diagram.

to right across the *x*-axis. Thus, the most important causes are at the left of the chart. Priorities are then established for taking action on the few causes that account for most of the effect. According to the Pareto principle, generally 20 percent or fewer of the causes contribute to 80 percent or more of the effects.

Cause-and-effect analysis is another graphical technique for analyzing the factors that contribute to a problem. The diagram used in cause-and-effect analysis is known as an *Ishikawa diagram* (after its originator, Karou Ishikawa) or a *fishbone diagram* (because of its shape). According to cause-and-effect analysis, any work process can be divided into major categories or causes, as Exhibit 4-3 illustrates. The main line of the chart represents the process, and the first branches are the immediate causes of the problem shown. Four causes often used are people, machines and equipment, methods, and materials.

Cause-and-effect diagrams are often developed through brainstorming, and the general causes are usually subdivided further into specific contributors to the causes. For example, the people category might be divided into employee selection, education, training, motivation, and job satisfaction. Digging further, a quality defect might be traced to low job satisfaction of employees who are disgruntled about physical working conditions. The job of the quality-improvement team is to investigate the possibility.

Once the team identifies the quality problem and its causes, they can develop possible solutions. Each suggested solution is analyzed in terms of costs, time, barriers to implementation, effects on workers and managers, and expected results. After a solution is chosen, an implementation plan must be determined.

ROBUST QUALITY (THE TAGUCHI METHOD)

The specialized techniques described so far deal with quality control. Quality improvement also involves the prevention of quality problems. One of the most widely used principles of quality-problem solving is that of robust quality, developed by

Exhibit 4-3
A Basic Cause-and-
Effect Diagram

Person

Machine

Quality
Characteristic

Material

Method

Causes   Effect

Source: Courtesy of American Society for Quality Control.

Genichi Taguchi as part of a method that bears his name. **Robust quality** means that engineers must design the part or process so well that it can withstand fluctuations on the production line without a loss of quality. A major goal of robust quality is to prevent products from failing while they are being used by customers. For example, if an automobile tire is not designed properly, it might pass 100-percent inspection but still develop a slow leak after 30,000 miles.

The principle of robust quality is said to surpass in-process inspection methods that concentrate on keeping the production lines stable through constant monitoring. It is vastly superior to traditional acceptance inspection quality control, which relies on inspection, rejection, and rework.

The *Taguchi method* is based on the concept that in any process there are a number of factors that can be combined in an almost infinite number of ways. Finding the best way to run the process by experimenting with all the possible combinations could take years. Robust quality provides statistical methods to define a specific sample that reveals the trends toward the best conditions for the process. As a result, engineers can specify an optimal process by running just a small number of experiments.

A major thrust of robust quality is to consistently meet quality targets rather than tolerate acceptable deviations. A case several years ago involving Ford Motor Co. and Mazda Motor Corp. illustrates this difference. Ford, which owns about 25 percent of Mazda, requested that Mazda manufacture some of the transmissions for a car sold in the United States. Both companies were supposed to build the transmissions with identical specifications. Ford used the zero defects standard of quality, while Mazda adhered to robust quality.

After the cars had been in the hands of consumers for a while, the Ford transmissions had generated more warranty claims and more complaints about noise. Ford engineers disassembled and carefully measured samples of transmissions made by itself and Mazda. Ford parts met specifications—in other words, there

robust quality
The concept of designing a part or process so well that it can withstand fluctuations on the production line without a loss of quality.

were no detectable defects. The Mazda gearboxes, however, showed no variability at all from targets. Many of the Ford-built transmissions were close to the outer limit of specified tolerances. Minor variations in one part were creating a domino effect on other parts. Because of these slight variations, parts interacted with each other. The effect was more friction than the parts could endure. The key point of this example is the critical difference in managers' approaches to quality control. Mazda managers assumed that robustness began with meeting targets consistently. Ford managers, in contrast, assumed that staying within tolerance would prevent quality problems.[26]

The principle of robust quality sends two important messages to the manager: Work hard to achieve designs that can be produced consistently, and demand consistency from the factory. Domino-effect problems tend to occur from scattered deviations within specifications, not from consistent deviation outside specifications. Where deviation from a target is consistent—such as a printer ribbon that is always too light—adjustment is possible.

ISO 9000 QUALITY STANDARDS

ISO 9000

A series of management and quality-assurance standards developed for firms competing in international markets.

Another approach to achieving high quality is to adhere to an internationally recognized standard. **ISO 9000** is a series of management and quality-assurance standards developed for firms competing in international markets. The standards were originally developed by the International Standards Organization for manufacturing firms, but are now also used by service firms. Although referred to as ISO 9000, the set of standards is divided into five subsets:

ISO 9000   The general guidelines for use of the set of standards

ISO 9001   A model for assuring quality in design, development, production, installation, and service of the product

ISO 9002   A complementary model for production and installation

ISO 9003   Specifications for final inspection and testing

ISO 9004   Principal concepts and a guide for overall quality management

To obtain ISO accreditation, the organization must follow 20 steps covering such steps as identifying business processes and writing a quality manual. Writing procedures and work instructions are also required.

THE DEMING PRINCIPLES

Much of the quality movement, including specialized techniques for quality improvement, have been influenced by W. Edwards Deming. Yet, paradoxically, Deming disliked total quality management. Shortly before his death he said, "The trouble with Total Quality Management—failure of TQM, you call it—is that there is no such thing. It's a buzzword. I have never used the term, as it carries no meaning."[27] Deming formulated 14 steps that managers should take to lead firms toward a quality goal. Exhibit 4-4 lists the steps. Some top-level managers post these steps in their offices to remind them of the importance of managing for quality.

Many of the ideas in this chapter stem from and support Deming's steps. However, many managers would rightfully resist doing away with mass inspections and numerical quotas. Would you take medicine to cure a serious illness if you knew the medicine was inspected by sampling alone? If you were running a business, would you do away with numerical production and sales quotas?

1. *Continually improve products and services to enhance the firm's competitive position.*
2. *Adopt the new philosophy of quality without delay.*
3. *Do not rely on mass inspections to detect defects. Instead, use statistical controls to ensure that quality is built into the product.*
4. *Do not select suppliers based on price alone. Reduce the number of suppliers and establish long-term, trusting, single-source partnerships in which both buyer and seller can pursue quality improvements.*
5. *Identify problems—whether caused by faulty systems or by operatives—and correct them.*
6. *Use modern methods of on-the-job training.*
7. *Improve and modernize methods of supervision.*
8. *Drive out fear from the workplace so that everyone can work productively.*
9. *Open up communications and break down barriers among departments.*
10. *Eliminate numerical goals, slogans, and posters as a way to motivate workers without giving them the methods to achieve these goals.*
11. *Eliminate work standards that assign numerical quotas.*
12. *Remove barriers that deprive employees of pride in their work.*
13. *Establish a dynamic program of education and training.*
14. *Create an executive structure that will emphasize the above 13 points every day.*

Sources: Laura B. Forker, "Quality: American, Japanese, and Soviet Perspectives," *Academy of Management Executive* (November 1991): 65; Andrea Gabor, *The Man Who Discovered Quality: How W. Edwards Deming Brought the Quality Revolution to America–The Stories of Ford, Xerox, and GM* (New York: Times Books, 1990).

Exhibit 4-4
Deming's 14 Steps to Quality

THE BALDRIGE AWARD AND QUALITY

LEARNING OBJECTIVE

Recognize the relevance of the Baldrige Award to quality.

The quality movement in the United States is often associated with the Malcolm Baldrige National Quality Award. The award originated from the Malcolm Baldrige Quality Improvement Act of 1987. One objective of the award was to raise the consciousness of American business leaders about quality. The other was to provide a comprehensive framework for measuring the quality efforts undertaken by U.S. businesses.

Awards are given annually in three categories: manufacturing, service, and small business. Baldrige award winners are chosen according to performance in seven major criteria, totaling 1,000 points, as follows:

Leadership, 90 points

Information and analysis, 80 points

Strategic quality planning, 60 points

Human resource development and management, 150 points

Management of process quality, 140 points

Quality and operational results, 180 points

Customer focus and satisfaction, 300 points

Among the well-known recipients of the Baldrige Award have been Xerox Corp., Corning, Inc., the Cadillac Division of General Motors, and Miliken & Co. (a textile manufacturer). The Baldrige Award has been praised for having succeeded in encouraging U.S. business leaders to approach quality from a number of important perspectives. The award criteria in each of the categories serve as a framework for designing and implementing quality programs throughout the nation.

The Baldrige Award has also been criticized sharply. One concern is that the award places too much emphasis on managing for quality and not enough on achieving a high-quality product or service. Another is that the companies nominate themselves. Perhaps customers should be making the nominations. A third criticism is that some companies spend an enormous amount of time and money trying to win the award. For example, one major company established a department of 10 people who worked for 18 months attempting to win. Spending for all this activity took place during a period of downsizing.

Despite these important criticisms, the Baldrige Award has been another force sensitizing firms to the importance of quality. According to consultant Earl Naumann, the real benefit of the Baldrige Award is that applying for it requires a comprehensive, critical analysis of an organization's processes. The analysis begins with top management and also includes the rest of the organization. The rigorous self-examination rapidly identifies a firm's strengths and weaknesses.[28]

SUMMARY OF KEY POINTS

1
Fully understand the meaning of quality.

Quality is the totality of features and characteristics of a product or service that bears on its ability to satisfy given needs. If a product or service does what it is supposed to do, it is said to be of high quality.

2
Describe principles and practices of total quality management related to attitudes and people.

Nine total quality management principles relate primarily to attitudes and people: (1) begin with top-level commitment, (2) close the quality credibility gap, (3) maintain customer sensitivity throughout the organization, (4) communicate widely about quality, (5) make continuous improvements a way of life, (6) empower and involve employees, (7) listen to employees, (8) emphasize the human side of quality, and (9) reward high quality performance

3
Describe principles and practices of total quality management related to work processes and technology.

Ten total quality principles relate primarily to work processes and technology: (1) implement a formal quality program to support the quality process, (2) engage in benchmarking, (3) select high-quality suppliers and train them, (4) build quality into the process, (5) ensure the excellence of incoming raw materials and supplies, (6) decrease cycle time, (7) pay painstaking attention to detail, (8) institute stringent quality work standards for every individual, (9) calculate the return on quality, and (10) train individuals in quality.

4
Summarize principles and techniques of total customer satisfaction for managers as well as customer-service workers.

The ultimate goal in terms of customer satisfaction is zero defections—keeping every customer a company can profitably serve. The customer-satisfaction principles calling for managerial action include: (1) establish customer-satisfaction goals, (2) give decision-making authority to customer-service workers, (3) thoroughly screen applicants for customer-service positions, (4) hire full-time, permanent store associates, (5) invest in training, (6) solicit customer feedback regularly, (7) communicate the fact that everyone contributes to the customer's perception of service, (8) recognize the demands of family and personal life, (9) find ways to buy from your customer, (10) develop efficient systems of order fulfillment, and (11) take ethical actions.

Several customer-service techniques can contribute to total customer satisfaction: (1) understand customer needs, (2) put customer needs first, (3) respond positively to moments of truth, (4) show care and concern, (5) communicate a positive attitude, (6) make the buyer feel good, and (7) smile at every customer.

5
Explain various specialized techniques for quality improvement.

Quality circles are one part of the quality movement. Quality control involves determining the extent to which goods or services match some specified quality standard. A 100-percent inspection involves checking every unit. Statistical quality control involves making inspections by using a sampling method. Acceptance inspection is the checking of completed products. Another strategy is in-process inspection, in which products are checked during production. A third strategy combines acceptance and in-process techniques.

A refinement of in-process inspection is statistical process control, a technique for detecting potential problems before they result in poor-quality products. One tool used to identify quality problems is a Pareto diagram, a bar graph that ranks causes of process variation by frequency of occurrence. Cause-and-effect analysis is a graphical technique for analyzing the contributing factors to a problem. The result is referred to as an Ishikawa diagram, or fishbone diagram. Cause-and-effect analysis divides work processes into major areas such as person, machine, method, and material. The causes can then be further subdivided.

A widely used principle of quality assurance is robust quality, the concept of designing of a part or process so well that it can withstand fluctuations on the production line without a loss of quality. One major goal of robust quality is to prevent products from failing while they are being used by customers. To achieve this, robust quality tries to consistently hit quality targets, rather than just tolerate acceptable deviations. Another way of achieving high quality is to adhere to the ISO 9000 standards. Following these standards helps firms compete in international markets.

W. Edwards Deming formulated 14 steps to help managers improve quality. These principles have been incorporated into managing for quality.

6

Recognize the relevance of the Baldrige Award to quality.

The Malcolm Baldrige National Quality Award was created to help U.S. businesses improve quality through two means. One was to raise the consciousness of business leaders about quality. The other was to provide a framework for quality improvement.

KEY TERMS AND PHRASES

Quality *pg. 74*
Benchmarking *pg. 79*
Cycle Time *pg. 80*
Zero Defects *pg. 80*
Zero Defections *pg. 81*
Moment of Truth *pg. 84*
Quality Circle *pg. 85*

Quality Control *pg. 85*
Statistical Process Control *pg. 86*
Pareto Diagram *pg. 87*
Cause-and-Effect Analysis *pg. 88*
Robust Quality *pg. 89*
ISO 9000 *pg. 90*

QUESTIONS

1. Why would a well-managed firm need a program of total quality management?
2. A business strategy of McDonald's restaurants has been to provide the public high-quality food. In what way might McDonald's be defining *quality*?
3. Why is employee empowerment such an important part of achieving total quality?
4. Why is cycle time related to quality?

5. What ethical issues do you think might be associated with benchmarking?
6. What is your evaluation of the effectiveness of the customer-feedback cards used by restaurants, hotels, car dealers, and other retailers?
7. Explain how a Pareto diagram could be used to increase customer satisfaction.

SKILL-BUILDING EXERCISE 4-A: THE QUALITY AUDIT

GROUP ACTIVITY Each student in the class is asked to think of one product or service he or she personally knows to have a quality problem. Students then (1) write down the product or service, (2) describe the quality problem, and (3) indicate how this quality problem could have been prevented or detected by us-

ing concepts found in the chapter. After the students finish this task, they come up in front of the room one by one to present their findings. After all presentations have been made, a class discussion is held to reach some generalizations and conclusions.

SKILL-BUILDING EXERCISE 4-B: EVALUATING CUSTOMER SERVICE

GROUP ACTIVITY Teams of three or four students arrange to meet outside of class to visit

a retail establishment such as a franchise restaurant, a sports bar, or a retail outlet. During the visit, students should make mental and physical notes of the quality of customer service as related to ideas in this chapter. To provide structure to the assignment, students might make up a checklist of customer-satisfaction principles listed in this chapter. Students report their findings back to the class, including recommendations to managers of the establishments visited.

VIDEO DISCUSSION QUESTIONS

1. According to General Tire management, what features of a tire are associated with quality? [General Tire]
2. How would you rate the effectiveness of the General Tire sales representative in assessing customer needs? [General Tire]
3. In an attempt to satisfy customer needs, how has Interactive Network gone beyond simply asking consumers what they want? [Technology]

CASE PROBLEM 4-A: THE TROUBLESOME DEMO MODE

Early in the basketball season, Billy Appletree, an ardent UCLA Bruins fan, decided that he and his family had suffered enough. After all, their 13″ television set was 12 years old. Billy, a credit manager at a furniture company, conferred with his wife, Maria, a dietitian, and their 11-year-old daughter, Jennifer. All agreed that a big-screen television would contribute greatly to family entertainment.

Friday night the Appletree family shopped for a television set at Consumer Electronics. Maria spotted a 32″ TV set that seemed ideal. A store associate confirmed her judgment by explaining that the set had the highest quality in its class. The cost, including a three-year complete service warranty, was $1,157.

The television set was delivered Monday evening as scheduled. For several days the Appletree family enjoyed watching programs on their big-screen set. Friday evening, however, the family was mystified by an image that appeared on the screen. Shortly after Jennifer punched the menu button, an advertisement appeared on the screen touting the features of the set.

Billy laughed and explained that the demonstration mode was somehow triggered. He said that the solution would be to punch the right buttons. Maria and he punched every button on the television receiver and the TV remote, but the demonstration mode remained. Billy then pulled the plug and reinserted it, but the demonstration mode reappeared. The family scanned the owner's manual but found no information relating to the problem.

Billy telephoned the dealer. He got through to the service department after being placed on hold for six minutes. The service representative said that he knew nothing about the problem, but that Billy should speak to the sales department. After Billy explained his problem to the sales associate, he was told to speak to the service department.

Billy called back the service department and explained the problem again. A customer-service specialist said that the store relied on an outside TV and appliance repair firm to handle such problems. The specialist said she would telephone the repair firm on Monday, and the firm would contact the Appletree family. By Tuesday morning, there was still no word from the repair firm.

Exasperated, Billy scanned a customer-information booklet that came with the television set. He found a list of 10 authorized service centers throughout the U.S. and Canada that repaired his brand of television. Billy telephoned a service center in California to take advantage of the time-zone difference.

A woman with a cheerful voice answered the phone and listened to Billy's problems. With a sympathetic laugh, she said, "We get lots of calls like this. No problem. Just push the volume-up and volume-down buttons at the same time. The demo mode will disappear. The mode was activated when somebody pressed the menu-up and menu-down buttons at the same time. Anybody in your family have arthritis?" Billy raced into the living room and triumphantly restored the TV set to normal functioning.

A representative from the local television service store telephoned on Friday. She said, "This is Modern TV and Appliance. Do you still need service on your set?" With anger in her voice, Maria explained how the problem was finally resolved.

Later that night, as the family gathered to watch the Bruins, Billy said, "I guess we all love our new large-screen TV, but I wouldn't go back to Consumer Electronics even to buy a videotape."

CASE QUESTIONS

1. Trace the quality and customer service mistakes made in this case by all parties involved.

2. How can the demonstration mode problem be fixed so it will not occur again with other customers?

3. What work process and methodology problems relating to quality are revealed in this case?

CASE PROBLEM 4-B: RETURN ON QUALITY AT MINUTEMAN PRESS

Arden Gustafson has owned and operated a six-employee Minuteman Press franchise in Greshman, Oregon, for three and one-half years. Typical of a Minuteman franchise, the workplace is sparkling clean, with supplies neatly arranged on steel shelves. Gustafson wears a white shirt and tie, resembling a corporate manager. The printing, copying, and computer equipment looks showroom fresh.

He doesn't have to look far to improve quality in his operation. A starting point is the 1,000 dots-per-inch (dpi) laser printer he uses for desktop publishing. It could easily be upgraded to a newer model with a 2,500 dpi resolution.

The upgrade would represent a 150 percent improvement—the kind of quality boost most advocates of total quality management think is extraordinary. Yet Gustafson thinks the improvement would be a waste of money. He contends, "My customers' demand for quality is more than satisfied with a thousand dots per inch. I can tell the difference under a magnifying

loupe, and I could say my quality is higher than my competitors. Why should I bother to upgrade if my customers really can't tell the difference between the two resolutions?"

Gustafson also explains that he wants to make sure he gives customers the quality they expect and more. He adds, however, "At the same time, we want to stay away from the idea of quality at all costs."

CASE QUESTIONS

1. What advice can you offer Gustafson about purchasing an upgraded laser printer?
2. What principle, or principles, of total quality management is Gustafson violating?
3. What principle of total quality management is Gustafson following?

Source: Based on facts reported in Mark Hendricks, "ROQ and Roll," *Entrepreneur* (June 1995): 64.

CASE PROBLEM 4-C: THE MARRIOTT MIRACLE

Since J. Willard Marriott, Sr., opened his first curbside restaurant in 1927, the company he founded has stayed with one unifying goal: to deliver exceptional service to every Marriott customer. Bill Marriott, Jr., has followed through with his father's legacy to create a $9 billion lodging and food-service organization with a strong emphasis on customer satisfaction.

While the senior Marriott emphasized perfection in company kitchens and dining rooms, Bill Marriott has placed his stamp on the hotel side of the business. The service organization he has created is driven primarily by customer needs. As suburban business centers developed in the 1960s and 1970s, Marriott built hotels offering easy access to airports, office complexes, and highways.

In the 1980s, the Marriott chain moved forward by taking the results of market research seriously. For example, based on research results, the company concentrated on competing with mid-priced hotels such as the Holiday Inn and Quality Inn. A competitive thrust was the Courtyard by Marriott, which provided travelers with consistently high-quality rooms at below-average prices.

Market research also assists Marriott in satisfying customer needs in specific locations. To attract local

clientele, Marriott hotel and resort restaurants offer menus featuring regional cuisines as well as low-priced value meals and "early bird" specials. Another finding was that seafood could draw locals as well as hotel guests. The moderately priced Sea Grill restaurants were established to satisfy this need.

A major thrust of Marriott management is to find the most effective ways to deliver an outstanding end-product. "We have an awful lot of ways to determine exactly what a Marriott customer values," explains Marriott. "One way is through focus groups that actively seek out customers and talk to them. To make these focus groups as diverse as possible, we target input from all Marriott customers, including business transients, men and women who travel just on business, associations—as many different demographics as we can reach.

"We also recently did a tracking study where we interviewed 700 different customers for 30 minutes each about their lodging experiences. We asked them everything from what they thought specifically about Marriott in terms of our strengths versus what needs improving, to what their experiences had been with other chains. We like to do this kind of customer research regularly because we want to know exactly where we stand with the customer. The more you know about the customer, the better job you can do."

Chairman Bill Marriott travels about 200,000 miles per year visiting from 150 to 200 Marriotts, inspecting operations and talking to associates. He talks to a variety of hotel associates and inspects the kitchen, dining room, and laundry room. He wants to let associates know that they are important to him.

An assistant manager at a Marriott commented about the corporate strategy, "I have the world of faith in top management at the Marriott including Bill Marriott himself. Yet there are a lot of other fine hotels that

are rapidly gaining market share. I wish I knew how our chain could do even better."

CASE QUESTIONS

1. What principles of total customer satisfaction are demonstrated in this case?
2. If you or a classmate can visit a Marriott hotel (or recently visited one), suggest how the Marriott chain can do even better.

Source: Adapted from Malcolm Fleschner with Gerhard Gschwandtner, "The Marriott Miracle," *Selling Power* (September 1994): 17–26.

VIDEO WAINWRIGHT: A STUDY IN QUALITY

Wainwright Industries, a family-owned supplier to the automotive and aerospace industries, decided to upgrade its quality to remain competitive. To move the company forward, top management used the Baldrige Award criteria as guides to quality improvement. Based on employee input and involvement, Waitwright emphasized training and empowering employees, customer satisfaction, and continuous improvement. Team rewards replaced individual rewards. The company first focused on employee satisfaction. Satisfied employees would then be better able to respond to customer needs. Key results from quality improvement included lower costs, better safety, and higher profits. Through its efforts, Wainwright won the Baldrige Quality Award in the Small Business classification.

REFERENCES

1. Facts as reported in Janet L. Fix, "Merrill Lynch Insurance Finds Power in Youth," *USA Today* (5 May 1995): 1B.
2. Carol A. Reeves and David A. Bednar, "Defining Quality: Alternatives and Implications," *The Academy of Management Review* (July 1994): 419–421.
3. Carla C. Carter, *Human Resource Management and the Total Quality Imperative* (New York: AMACOM, 1993), 1.
4. George Labovitz, Y.S. Chang, and Victor Rosansky, *Making Quality Work: A Leadership Guide for the Results-Driven Manager* (New York: Harper Collins, 1993).
5. "Quality Is as Quality Does," *Personnel* (January 1991): 16.
6. Richard Blackburn and Benson Rosen, "Total Quality and Human Resources Management: Lessons Learned from Baldrige Award-winning Companies," *The Academy of Management Executive* (August 1993): 52.
7. Del Jones, "1992 Quality Cup Finalists," *USA Today* (10 April 1992): 2B.
8. Jones, "1992 Quality Cup Finalists," 2B.
9. David Woodruff, "An Embarassment of Glitches Galvanizes Chrylser," *Business Week* (17 April 1995): 76.
10. Jeanne C. Poole, William F. Rathgeber III, and Stanley W. Silverman, "Paying for Performance in a TQM Environment," *HRMagazine* (October 1993): 68.
11. Kathryn Troy, "Recognize Quality Achievement with Noncash Awards," *Personnel Journal* (October 1993): 111–117.
12. K. Theodore Krantz, "How Velcro Got Hooked on Quality," *Harvard Business Review* (September–October 1989): 35.
13. Philip B. Crosby, *Quality Without Tears: The Art of Hassle-Free Management* (New York: McGraw-Hill, 1984), 84.
14. David Greising, "Quality: How to Make It Pay," *Business Week* (8 August 1994): 55.
15. "How Companies Are Rethinking Quality," *Business Week* (8 August 1994): 57.
16. Gilbert Fuchsberg, "Quality Programs Show Shoddy Results," *The Wall Street Journal* (14 May 1992): B1.
17. Jerry Bowles, "Is American Management Really Committed to QUALITY?" *Management Review* (April 1992): 42–46.
18. Frederick F. Reichheld and W. Earl Sasser, Jr., "Zero Defections: Quality Comes to Services," *Harvard Business Review* (September–October 1990): 106.
19. William B. Martin, *Quality Customer Service: A Positive Guide to Superior Service*, rev. ed. (Los Altos, CA: Crisp Publications, 1989); Andrew J. DuBrin, *Stand Out! 330 Ways to Gain the Edge with Bosses, Co-workers, Superiors, Subordinates, and Customers* (Englewood Cliffs, NJ: Prentice Hall, 1993).
20. Charles E. Cox, "18 Ways to Improve Customer Service," *HRMagazine* (March 1992): 72.
21. David Fagiano, "Service in a Temporary World," *Management Review* (February 1994): 4.
22. "Three Steps to Better Customer Service," *Personnel* (September 1991): 19.
23. Minda Zetlin, "Off the Beaten Path," *Management Review* (December 1994): 29.
24. Justin Martin, "Ignore Your Customer," *Fortune* (1 May 1995): 126.
25. "Good Service Is Good Enough," *Working Smart* (July 1993): 1.
26. Genichi Taguchi and Don Clausing, "Robust Quality," *Harvard Business Review* (January–February 1990): 67.
27. Quoted in Catherine Romano, "Report Card on TQM," *Management Review* (January 1994): 22.
28. Earl Naumann, *Creating Customer Value: The Path to Sustainable Competitive Advantage* (Cincinnati, OH: Thomson Executive Press, 1995), 219.

CHAPTER 5
Essentials of Planning

1
Document how plan-
ning contributes to
business success.

2
Summarize a gener-
alized model for
planning, and apply
it to enhance your
planning skills.

3
Summarize the ba-
sics of strategic
planning and busi-
ness strategy.

4
Explain the use of
operating plans, poli-
cies, procedures, and
rules.

5
Present an overview of management by
objectives.

6
Pinpoint how Hoshin planning helps implement strategic objectives.

Photo Courtesy of Georgia-
Pacific Group

Bill Kimpton, a former Wall Street investment banker, is now
in the hotel and restaurant business. His strategy is to transform run-down historic properties into European-style small
hotels and posh restaurants. He calls his
strategy the "junk to antiques theorem."
Among his hotels are the Prescott in San
Francisco and the Alexis in Seattle. •
Kimpton succeeds by following a planning rule of thumb for the hospitality industry: If a hotel has an occupancy rate
of 70 percent, the average nightly room
rate must equal one-thousandth of the
hotel's per-room cost to acquire and re-
furbish the property. The nightly room
rate at a Kimpton hotel ranges from $90
to $160, while his investment per room
is usually below $70,000.[1]

The glimpse just presented of a hotel and restaurant and executive illustrates how knowledge of planning contributes to business success. Planning is one of the major management functions. To review, it is the process of establishing goals and objectives and figuring out how to reach them. By virtue of planning, we manage the future instead of being guided by fate.

The purpose of this chapter is to describe the planning function in such a way that you can use what you learn to plan more effectively as a manager or individual contributor. First the chapter will look at the value of planning and a framework for its application. You will learn the major types of plans, including the planning to develop business strategy. We will then describe two key methods for getting large numbers of people involved in implementing plans: management by objectives and the emerging technique of Hoshin planning.

THE CONTRIBUTION OF PLANNING

LEARNING OBJECTIVE 1

Document how planning contributes to business success.

Planning is important because it contributes heavily to success and gives you some control over the future. According to one analysis, the value of planning is in the process itself. By planning, you set aside your daily tasks and deadlines so you can enlarge your mental focus and see the bigger picture.[2] More specifically, planning often leads to improvement in productivity, quality, and financial results.

Extensive research evidence supports the value of planning, as revealed by an analysis of 26 studies. Companies that engaged in strategic (high-level and long-range) planning achieved better financial results. They also did a better job of fitting into their environment, such as an automotive company adapting to changing preferences for vehicles. Planning was also found to contribute to corporate growth.[3]

Despite the many advantages of planning, it can interfere with the spontaneity necessary for success. Astute businesspeople often seize opportunities as they occur, even if they are not part of any plan. For example, a report cited the contribution of red wine to lowering cholesterol among French people. Several wineries in the United States seized this marketing opportunity by rapidly increasing the production of red wine. Another problem is that planning can create blinders designed to focus direction and block out peripheral vision. As management theorist Henry Mintzberg says, "Setting oneself on a predetermined course in uncharted waters is the perfect way to sail straight into an iceberg."[4]

An effective antidote to the disadvantages of planning is to allow some slack in your plan for capitalizing on the unexpected. For example, in planning a job search, leave room to explore opportunities you did not envision in your plan.

A GENERAL FRAMEWORK FOR PLANNING

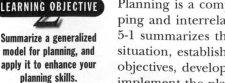

LEARNING OBJECTIVE 2

Summarize a generalized model for planning, and apply it to enhance your planning skills.

Planning is a complex and comprehensive process involving a series of overlapping and interrelated elements, or stages. The framework presented in Exhibit 5-1 summarizes the elements of planning. A planner must define the present situation, establish goals and objectives, forecast aids and barriers to goals and objectives, develop action plans to reach goals and objectives, develop budgets, implement the plans, and control the plans.

Exhibit 5-1
A Framework for
Planning

Evaluation and Feedback

1. Define the present situation

2. Establish goals and objectives

3. Forecast aids and barriers to goals and objectives

4. Develop action plans to reach goals and objectives

5. Develop budgets

6. Implement the plans

7. Control the plans

This chapter will examine each element separately. In practice, however, several of these stages often overlap. For example, a manager might be implementing and controlling the same plan simultaneously.

The planning steps are not always followed in the order presented in Exhibit 5-1. Planners frequently start in the middle of the process, proceed forward, and then return to an earlier step. This change of sequence frequently happens because the planner discovers new information or because objectives change. Also, many managers set goals before first examining their current position.

To illustrate the general framework for planning, we return to Bill Kimpton, the hotel and restaurant developer. His firm, the Kimpton Group, is contemplating purchasing and rebuilding the Bellevue Hotel in San Francisco. Built in the French Renaissance style, it was originally constructed in 1910. To carry out such a comprehensive activity, Kimpton develops a plan as presented next.

DEFINE THE PRESENT SITUATION

Knowing where you are is critical to establishing goals for change. Kimpton has already given some serious thought to the present—to enlarge his business he needs to acquire another valuable property. To define the present situation more clearly, Kimpton works with his chief accountant to see if there are sufficient funds available for expansion now. The answer is affirmative: Move ahead and acquire this nineteenth hotel in the chain.

Defining the present situation includes measuring success and examining internal capabilities and external threats. Kimpton must therefore engage in two more activities to complete this first step. *Success* in this situation would mean that a new hotel would contribute a positive cash flow to his enterprise. *Internal capabilities* refers to the strengths and weaknesses of the firm, or organizational unit, engaging in planning. The capabilities of the Kimpton Group include a solid staff of reliable hotel and restaurant managers and workers. The company also has an extraordinary track record of accomplishment in renovating old properties and converting them into successful hotels and restaurants.

External threats and opportunities include competition, business conditions, customer loyalty, and government regulations. Kimpton recognizes that San Francisco has many attractive European-style hotels along with other types of hotels. On the other hand, Kimpton can visualize how majestic the Bellevue will appear upon restoration. He thinks to himself, "If we build it, people will come."

ESTABLISH GOALS AND OBJECTIVES

The second step in planning is to establish goals and to identify objectives that contribute to the attainment of goals. (Goals are broader than objectives; whereas objectives function as smaller goals.) Being a carefully planned enterprise, the Kimpton Group has precise goals and objectives. Kimpton knows how much he can pay for a hotel and restoration and still return a profit, assuming an occupancy rate of 70 percent and a room rate around $120 per night. Kimpton has the goal of a 15 percent return on investment. To achieve that goal, an objective will be an occupancy rate of 72 percent. Another objective is to build a profitable restaurant in the Bellevue.

FORECAST AIDS AND BARRIERS TO GOALS AND OBJECTIVES

As an extension to defining the present situation, the manager attempts to predict which internal and external factors will foster or hinder attainment of the desired ends. Kimpton relies on intuition and that of other business associates about the future demand for a "B+" hotel in San Francisco created from an ancient property. One of his associates says, "I see a growing trend for people to want an attractive alternative to the giant hotels in San Francisco."

One potential barrier is the shrinking middle-class wages in the United States and other countries. Another barrier is that, as many downsized people shift to lower-paying jobs, travel could decrease enough to lower the occupancy rate. Furthermore, is San Francisco due for another earthquake? Even a small quake that does no damage can hurt tourist trade.

action plan
The specific steps necessary to achieve a goal or objective.

DEVELOP ACTION PLANS TO REACH GOALS AND OBJECTIVES

Goals and objectives are only wishful thinking until **action plans** are drawn. An action plan is the specific steps necessary to achieve a goal or objective. Kimpton and his staff have to figure out specifically how they are going to acquire and renovate the Bellevue property. The action plan includes such items as:

- Secure $29 million to consummate the deal, including $5 million for the property and $24 million for renovation. Use some company cash and some borrowed funds.
- Consult with construction companies to determine if they can accomplish the work needed to be done, when we need it done, and at the price we are willing to pay.

DEVELOP BUDGETS

Planning usually results in action plans that require money to implement. For instance, the Kimpton Group must spend $29 million for the entire purchase and renovation. Money would also be needed for promotion, such as contacting travel agents around the world about the new Bellevue. A formal budget would indicate how much money a manager can afford to spend on each action plan. Some action plans require almost no cash outlay, such as speaking to present hotel guests and restaurant patrons about their preferences. Other items in the budget will include such expenditures as stationery for the new hotel, uniforms, linens, and stocking a new wine cellar.

IMPLEMENT THE PLANS

If the plans developed in the previous five steps are to benefit the firm, they must be put to use. A frequent criticism of planners is that they develop elaborate plans and then abandon them in favor of conducting business as usual. The Kimpton Group has committed itself to the Bellevue project. Implementation has already begun, including Bill Kimpton wearing a hard hat as he checks on construction progress.

CONTROL THE PLANS

Planning does not end with implementation, because plans may not always proceed as conceived. The purpose of the control process is to measure progress toward goal attainment and to take corrective action if too much deviation is detected. The deviation from expected performance can be negative or positive. Construction and renovation expenditures could run over budget or under budget. When the Bellevue is open for business, the occupancy rate could be higher or lower than anticipated.

In Exhibit 5-1, note the phrase "Evaluation and Feedback" on the left. The phrase indicates that the control process allows for the fine tuning of plans after their implementation. One common example of the need for fine tuning is a budget that has been set too high or too low in the first attempt at implementing a plan. A manager controls by making the right adjustment.

MAKE CONTINGENCY PLANS

Many planners develop a set of backup plans to be used in case things do not proceed as hoped. A **contingency plan** is an alternative plan to be used if the original plan cannot be implemented or a crisis develops. If the Bellevue falls behind schedule in construction, the Kimpton Group can work to increase the occupancy rates in its other 18 hotels to compensate for the revenue shortfall. Or, if the construction cost goes over budget, the group can raise the anticipated average room rate for the new hotel.

contingency plan
An alternative plan to be used if the original plan cannot be implemented or a crisis develops.

Contingency plans are often developed from objectives in earlier steps in planning. The plans are triggered into action when the planner detects, however early in the planning process, deviations from objectives. Construction projects are particularly prone to deviations from completion dates because so many different contractors and subcontractors are involved.

STRATEGIC PLANNING AND BUSINESS STRATEGY

LEARNING OBJECTIVE

Summarize the basics of strategic planning and business strategy.

---

strategic planning

Establishing master plans that shape the destiny of the firm.

---

operational planning

Establishing plans that relate to running the firm on a day-to-day, short-term basis.

---

strategy

The organization's plan, or comprehensive program, for achieving its mission and goals in its environment.

The framework for planning can be used to develop and implement both strategic and operational plans. **Strategic planning** is establishing master plans that shape the destiny of the firm. The output of strategic planning by the Kimpton Group was a strategy of restoring ancient hotels into comfortable, European-style hotels and accompanying restaurants. The emphasis of strategic planning in recent years is to help the firm move into emerging markets, or to invent the future. Examples are Nike and Reebok, who have fundamentally reinvented their industry. They brought to the industry high technology, new materials, advertising, and global brands. None of these factors previously existed in the athletic shoe industry.[5] Strategic planning should also result in managerial workers throughout the organization thinking strategically. This would include wondering about how the firm adapts to its environment and how it will cope with the future.

Operational planning is establishing plans that relate to running the firm on a day-to-day, short-term basis. This section concentrates on strategic planning and business strategy. The next section will describe operational planning.

THE NATURE OF STRATEGY

A **strategy** is the organization's plan, or comprehensive program, for achieving its mission and goals in its environment. Simply stated, a strategy is an overall plan of what a firm wants to be. The strategy of Converse (the low-budget athletic shoe supplier) differs from the strategies of Nike and Reebok. A strategy gives an organization a strong purpose as it pursues its daily activities. A planner selects organization strategy from among alternatives. He or she pays serious attention to the relative capabilities, major functions, policies, and resources available. Dozens of different business strategies have been developed. To help you appreciate what strategy means in practice, let us look at a sampling of current business strategies.[6]

COST LEADERSHIP. Produce a product or service at a low price in order to lower price and gain market share. Wal-Mart is a master at cost leadership because the company's massive buying power enables it to receive huge price concessions from suppliers. A dental lab in New York City sells crowns and dentures to dentists throughout New York State and New Jersey because it beats most local labs on price. The lab buys low-priced raw materials from the Pacific Rim and hires part-time student workers.

IMITATION. If you cannot be imaginative, why not imitate the best? The entire industry of PC clones is based on an imitation strategy. The Macintosh clone industry began in 1995 with a personal computer built by Power Computer Corp. The imitation strategy consists of two key components, strategic followership and learning by watching. The company waits for the right time to introduce a lower-priced competitor. Benchmarking is a form of learning by watching.

PRODUCT DIFFERENTIATION. A differentiation strategy attempts to offer a product or service that is perceived by the customer as different from available alternatives. The incredible success of Swatch watches was launched on a strategy of producing a watch that had a dramatically different face, at a competitive price. What differentiates one of your favorite products?

FORMING STRATEGIC ALLIANCES. An increasingly popular business strategy is to form alliances, or share resources, with other companies to exploit a market opportunity. A strategic alliance is also known as a virtual corporation. A groundbreaking strategic alliance in the service industry is the cooperative working relationship between KLM Royal Dutch Airlines and Northwest Airlines Inc. The two carriers have melded their operations to fly into each other's markets. By marketing their services jointly, they are gaining market share at a lower cost than previously.

HIGH SPEED. High-speed managers focus on speed in all of their business activities, including speed in product development, sales response, and customer service. Knowing that "time is money," they choose to use time as a competitive resource. It is important to get products to market quickly because the competition might get there first. By the mid-1990s, IBM began to develop a high-speed strategy to make up for time slippage in the past. For example, in 1994 the IBM PC company missed every deadline, which resulted in some lost opportunities.

GLOBAL DIVERSIFICATION. A widely practiced business strategy is to diversify globally in order to expand business. United Technologies Corp., faced with a declining defense business, decided on a dual strategy of looking for more international business and more commercial business. Nike Inc. decided on a global strategy in 1995 to help cope with flattening sales in the U.S. Chairman Phil Knight said a few years ago, "There's a pretty strong recognition that we'll be bigger in a couple of years outside the U.S. than inside."[7]

STICKING TO CORE COMPETENCIES. Many firms of all sizes believe they will prosper if they confine their efforts to business activities they perform best—their core competencies. Thomas C. McDermott, the president of Goulds Pumps, said his company was going to expand overseas by strategic acquisitions. Nevertheless, he insisted on companies that are either in or related to the pump business. He said, "We're going to stick to our knitting."

PUTTING "WOW" BACK IN THE BUSINESS. Business sage Tom Peters contends that a key success strategy is for managers to provide products or services that they find exciting. He says that if you can't remember the last time your business really turned you on, you are in big trouble. The underlying psychology is that if the manager is not passionate about the company product or services, it will be difficult to convince others. In turn, this will lead customers toward other firms offering more exciting products and services. Oldsmobile and Buick lost some market share in the 1980s and 1990s because these models did not excite a large enough number of consumers—especially younger ones. What is your opinion?

The various business strategies just described are not mutually exclusive. A firm might implement one or more of these strategies simultaneously. For example, a firm might get to market rapidly with a differentiated product in a global envi-

Exhibit 5-2
The Strategic Planning
Process

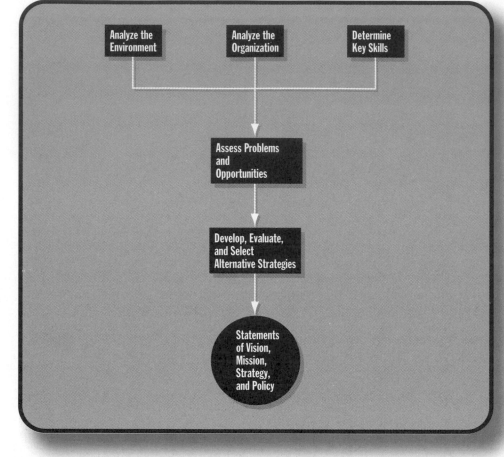

ronment while forming a strategic alliance! Whichever combination of strategies is chosen, current thinking is that the firm should adopt an ambitious strategy that stretches its capability.

THE STRATEGIC PLANNING MODEL

Strategic planning encompasses those activities that lead to the statement of goals and objectives and the choice of strategies to achieve them. Under ideal circumstances, a firm arrives at its strategy after completing strategic planning. In practice, many firms choose a strategy prior to strategic planning. Once the firm has the strategy, a plan is developed to implement it.

Although a general planning model can be applied to strategic planning, it is more beneficial to use one designed exclusively for strategic planning. Do not interpret the five steps in Exhibit 5-2 as a rigid sequence. In reality, several of the steps might be taken simultaneously. A manager using the planning model must:

1. Analyze the environment to understand such factors as the characteristics of the industry, product demand, prevailing technology, and government regulations. This analysis requires substantial time and effort. Some of the information needed is available in computer databases.

Exhibit 5-3
How to Conduct a
SWOT Analysis

In both strategic planning and other situations, managers must conduct a **SWOT** analysis—that is, they must consider the Strengths, Weaknesses, Opportunities, and Threats in a given situation.

Strengths. What are good points about a particular alternative? Use your judgment and intuition; ask knowledgeable people.

Weaknesses. Consider the risks of pursuing a particular course of action, such as subcontracting work (outsourcing) to a low-wage country. Again, use your judgment and ask knowledgeable people.

Opportunities. Think of the opportunities that welcome you if you choose a promising strategic alternative, such as creating a work force as culturally diverse as your customer base. Use your imagination and visualize the possibilities.

Threats. There's a downside to every alternative, so think ahead to allow for contingency planning. Ask people who may have tried in the past what you are attempting now. But don't be easily dissuaded by the naysayers, heel draggers, and pessimists. To quote Nike, "Just do it."

2. Analyze the organization to understand its position in the market, financial status, technical skills, structure, and work force. A well-managed company has much of this information on hand.

3. Determine the key skills necessary for success, such as the ability to reach customers readily or understand what customers really want. Kimpton knew that many upscale people really wanted to pay for a comfortable place to sleep, not an elaborate hotel designed primarily for conventions.

4. Assess the problems and opportunities that could influence the strategic decision. Part of Phil Knight's reason for going global with Nike shoes was that many North Americans were turning to low-priced, non-hyped sneakers. Many consumers were demanding old-fashioned-style athletic shoes. A SWOT analysis, as described in Exhibit 5-3, is widely used to assess problems and opportunities.

5. Develop, evaluate, and select alternative strategies to take advantage of opportunities. Because firms have limited resources, they are forced to select one or two strategies to implement. Sometimes managers choose the wrong alternative. Stanley C. Gault, the chairman at Goodyear Tire & Rubber Co., decided several years ago on a new marketing strategy for tires. Goodyear tires were pushed into new distribution channels, which antagonized independent dealers and did not produce an increase in market share.[8]

> **SWOT analysis**
> *A method of considering the strengths, weaknesses, opportunities, and threats in a given situation.*

The final outcome of strategic planning are statements of mission and vision, strategy, and policy. The **mission** identifies the firm's purpose and where it fits into the world. A vision is similar to a mission except that it projects the firm further into the future and is more general in tone. Exhibit 5-4 presents a sampling of mission and vision statements.

Specifying a mission answers the question "What business are we really in?" A firm's mission may not be apparent to the casual observer. For example, Packard Bell is the leading manufacturer of personal computers in the United States, selling almost entirely through retail stores. Yet, according to one business analyst, "Packard Bell is not a PC company, it's a consumer-electronics company."[9]

> **mission**
> *A statement of the firm's purpose and where it fits into the world.*

Exhibit 5-4
Sample Vision and
Mission Statements

Chrysler Corporation: "Chrysler Corporation is committed to providing our customers with the world's highest level of satisfaction with our products and service."

McDonald's: "To satisfy the world's appetite for good food, well-served, at a price people can afford."

McCormick & Company Inc.: "The primary mission of McCormick & Company Inc. is to expand its worldwide leadership position in the spice, seasoning, and flavoring markets."

Perk Development Corp.: "We are and will continue to be the largest Perkins Family Restaurant franchisee in the United States. We will diversify into other restaurants to satisfy a wide demand for high-quality, family-style restaurants."

Fico's Automotive Repair & Refinish Collision: "We intend to be the premier body shop for high-quality auto or small-truck restoration, refinishing, or body repair. We will be highly respected by auto buffs and insurance companies."

Visions and missions may sound lofty and idealistic, but successful companies take them seriously. The accompanying Organization in Action explains how a consumer-products giant uses a vision statement to guide the company's operations.

Strategic planning is primarily a top-management activity, assisted by planning specialists. Nevertheless, middle- and first-level management can make an important contribution. Compared to top-level managers, lower-level managers are usually closer to available information about forces affecting the direction of the firm. Middle- and first-level managers can provide strategically useful information about product performance, customer reactions, competitive actions, and delivery problems.

Now that you have examined the general framework for planning and the complicated subject of business strategy, this chapter will describe ways in which strategic plans are translated into practice.

OPERATING PLANS, POLICIES, PROCEDURES, AND RULES

LEARNING OBJECTIVE

Explain the use of operating plans, policies, procedures, and rules.

Strategic plans are formulated at the top of the organization. Four of the vehicles through which strategic plans are converted into action are operating plans, policies, procedures, and rules.

OPERATING PLANS

operating plans
The means through which strategic plans alter the destiny of the firm.

Operating plans are the means through which strategic plans alter the destiny of the firm. Operating plans involve organizational efficiency (doing things right), whereas strategic plans involve effectiveness (doing the right things). Both strategic and operational plans involve such things as exploring alternatives and evaluating the effectiveness of the plan. In a well-planned organization, all managers are responsible for making operating plans that mesh with the strategic plans of the business. Operational plans (a term used synonymously with *operating plans*) provide the details of how strategic plans will be accom-

ORGANIZATION IN ACTION: VISION IMPLEMENTATION AT RJR NABISCO

RJR Nabisco faces a critical external environment with consumer activism directed against its key products such as cigarettes. The company has formulated a new mission to deal with these challenges. Its mission statement is "to increase the wealth of all RJR Nabisco shareholders through stock price appreciation, dividend payments, or a combination of the two. We can only accomplish this by producing strong growth over time in earnings."

The mission is translated into the following set of principles to guide company employees and day-to-day business processes at RJR Nabisco:

1. The marketplace is the driving force behind everything we do.
2. We will operate in an entrepreneurial, decentralized organization with a minimum of bureaucracy.
3. We will think and act with a sense of urgency.
4. We will seek quality as a way of life.
5. We will have a sense of ownership that demands resources be used wisely and prudently.
6. We will cherish teamwork.
7. We will act in an ethical manner with each other, our customers and the general public.
8. We will be sensitive to the needs of our employees.

These eight principles are interpreted as a set of organizational values stating the company must serve the following stakeholders: consumers and our customers; employees, suppliers, the financial community; local communities; and our nation and other countries where we do business.

By following these principles and achieving these values, top management at RJR Nabisco believes it will deliver the earnings necessary to create market recognition and increased shareholder value.

Source: Researched and prepared by Ramesh Gehani, Rochester Institute of Technology, 1995.

plished. In many firms, suggestions to be incorporated into operating plans stem from employees at lower levels. As president David Glass of Wal-Mart Stores, Inc. says, "Most of the good ideas come from the bottom up. We keep changing a thousand little things.[10]

Operating plans focus more on the firm than on the external environment. To illustrate, the strategic plan of a local government might be to encourage the private sector to take over government functions. One operating unit within the local government might then formulate a plan for subcontracting refuse removal to private contractors and phasing out positions for civil-service sanitation workers.

Operating plans tend to be drawn for a shorter period than strategic plans. The plan for increasing the private sector's involvement in activities conducted by the local government might be a 10-year plan. In contrast, the phasing out of government sanitation workers might take two years.

Operational planning often translates into planning your week. For skill development in weekly planning, see Exhibit 5-5.

Exhibit 5-5
A Basic Planning Tool

Time-management specialists contend you need only 30 minutes to plan your entire week, if you apply the OATS formula, as follows:

O: Objectives. What results do you want to accomplish by the end of the week? Write them down and rank them in order of importance.

A: Activities. What do you have to do to achieve your goals and objectives? Write down the necessary activities, and put them in sequence.

T: Time. How much time will you need for each activity? To make planning realistic, allot yourself more time than you think you will probably need. You will then have slack time to manage unexpected problems.

S: Schedule. Scrutinize your calendar to decide when you can do each activity. Most people underestimate the contribution of a schedule, but you will accomplish little if you do not schedule time to get things done.

POLICIES

policies
General guidelines to follow in making decisions and taking action.

Policies are general guidelines to follow in making decisions and taking action; as such, they are plans. Many policies are written; some are unwritten, or implied. Policies are designed to be consistent with strategic plans and yet allow room for interpretation by the individual manager. One important managerial role is interpreting policies for employees. Here is an example of a policy and an analysis of how it might require interpretation.

Policy: When hiring employees from the outside, consider only those candidates who are technically competent or show promise of becoming technically competent and who show good personal character and motivation.

A manager attempting to implement this policy with respect to a given job candidate would have to ask the following questions:

- What do we mean by "technical competence"?
- How do I measure technical competence?
- What do we mean by "show promise of becoming technically competent"?
- How do I rate the promise of technical competence?
- What do we mean by "good personal character and motivation"?
- How do I assess good personal character and motivation?

Policies are developed to support strategic plans in every area of the firm. Many firms have strict policies against employees accepting gifts and favors from vendors or potential vendors. For example, many schools endorse the Code of Ethics and Principles advocated by the National Association of Educational Buyers. One of the specific policies states that buyers should "decline personal gifts or gratuities which might in any way influence the purchase of materials."

PROCEDURES

procedures
A customary method for handling an activity. It guides action rather than thinking.

Procedures are considered plans because they establish a customary method of handling future activities. They guide *action* rather than *thinking*, in that they state the specific manner in which a certain activity must be accomplished. Procedures exist at every level in the organization, but they tend to be more complex and specific at lower levels. For instance, strict procedures may apply to the handling of checks by salesclerks. The procedures for check handling by managers may be much less strict.

RULES

A **rule** is a specific course of action or conduct that must be followed; it is the simplest type of plan. Ideally, each rule fits a strategic plan. In practice, however, many rules are not related to organizational strategy. When rules are violated, corrective action should be taken. Two examples of rules follow:

> **rule**
> *A specific course of action or conduct that must be followed. It is the simplest type of plan.*

- Any employee engaged in an accident while in a company vehicle must report that accident immediately to his or her supervisor.
- No employee is authorized to use company photocopying machines for personal use, even if he or she reimburses the company for the cost of the copies.

The next section describes a program that thousands of organizations use to apply the principles and techniques of planning and goal setting.

MANAGEMENT BY OBJECTIVES: A SYSTEM OF PLANNING AND REVIEW

Management by objectives (MBO) is a systematic application of goal setting and planning to help individuals and firms be more productive. An MBO program typically involves people setting many objectives for themselves. However, management frequently imposes key organizational objectives upon people. An MBO program usually involves sequential steps, which are cited in the following list. (Note that these steps are related to those in the basic planning model shown in Exhibit 5-1.)

> **LEARNING OBJECTIVE 5**
> Present an overview of management by objectives.

> **management by objectives (MBO)**
> *A systematic application of goal setting and planning to help individuals and firms be more productive.*

1. *Establishing organizational goals.* Top levels of management set organizational goals to begin the entire MBO process. Quite often these goals are strategic. A group of hospital administrators, for example, might decide upon the strategic goal of improving health care to poor people in the community. After these broad goals are established, managers determine what the organizational units must accomplish to meet these goals.
2. *Establishing unit objectives.* Unit heads then establish objectives for their units. A cascading of objectives takes place as the process moves down the line. Objectives set at lower levels of the firm must be designed to meet the general goals established by top management. Lower-level managers and operatives provide input because a general goal usually leaves considerable latitude for setting individual objectives to meet that goal. The head of inpatient admissions might decide that working more closely with the county welfare department must be accomplished if the health-care goal cited earlier in this list is to be met. Exhibit 5-6 suggests ways to set effective goals.
3. *Reviewing subordinates' proposals.* At this point, subordinates make proposals about how they will contribute to unit objectives. The assistant to the manager of inpatient admissions might agree to set up a task force to work with the welfare department, for example. Each team member is also given the opportunity to set objectives in addition to those that meet the strategic goals.

Exhibit 5-6
Guide to Establishing
Goals and Objectives

Effective goals and objectives have certain characteristics in common. Effective goals and objectives

Are clear, concise, and unambiguous. An example of such an objective is "Reduce damaged boxes of photocopying paper from April 27 to April 30 of this year."

Are accurate in terms of the true end state or condition sought. An accurate objective might state, "The factory will be as neat and organized as the front office after the cleanup is completed."

Are achievable by competent workers. Goals and objectives should not be so high or rigid that the majority of competent team members become frustrated and stressed by attempting to achieve them.

Include three difficulty levels: routine, challenging, and innovative. Most objectives deal with routine aspects of a job, but they should also challenge workers to loftier goals.

Are achieved through team-member participation. Subordinates should participate actively in setting objectives.

Relate to small chunks of accomplishment. Many objectives should concern small, achievable activities, such as uncluttering a work area. Accomplishing small objectives is the building block for achieving larger goals.

Specify what is going to be accomplished, who is going to accomplish it, when it is going to be accomplished, and how it is going to be accomplished. Answering the "who, what, when, and how" questions reduces the chance for misinterpretation.

4. *Negotiating or agreeing.* Managers and team members confer together at this stage to either agree on the objectives set by the team members or negotiate further. In the hospital example, one department head might state that he or she wants to reserve 10 beds on the ward for the exclusive use of indigent people. The supervisor might welcome the suggestion but point out that only five beds could be spared for such a purpose. They might settle for setting aside seven beds for the needy poor.

5. *Creating action plans to achieve objectives.* After the manager and team members agree upon objectives, action plans must be defined. Sometimes the action plan is self-evident. For example, if your objective as a sales manager is to hire three new telemarketers this year, you would begin by consulting with the human resources department.

6. *Reviewing performance.* Performance reviews are conducted at agreed-upon intervals (a semiannual or annual review is typical). Persons receive good performance reviews to the extent that they attain most of their major objectives. When objectives are not attained, the manager and the team member mutually analyze what went wrong. Equally important, they discuss corrective actions. New objectives are then set for the next review period. A new objective for one hospital manager, for example, is to establish a task force to investigate the feasibility of establishing satellite health-care facilities in poor sections of town. Because establishing new objectives is part of an MBO program, management by objectives is a process that can continue for the life of an organization.

Following up on progress and reviewing performance are vital parts of an MBO program. Without appropriate feedback (including encouragement or reprimand) from managers, an MBO program is unlikely to be successful. Instead, objectives will be soon forgotten.

Regular reviewing of progress and performance—including maintaining adequate documentation thereof—is critical to the success of an MBO program. In organizations whose top-level managers are highly committed to the process, productivity gains can soar.

EVIDENCE OF MBO EFFECTIVENESS

The contribution management by objectives makes to improving organizational productivity varies considerably. Two researchers, Rodgers and Hunter, combined the results of 70 studies that evaluated the contribution of MBO programs to organizational productivity.[11] Sixty-eight of the 70 studies showed productivity gains; only two studies showed losses. The mean productivity gain was 44.6 percent. In studies where costs were used to measure the effectiveness of MBO, costs decreased an average of 26 percent. In organizations with high commitment from top management, the average productivity gain was 56.5 percent. In firms with moderate commitment, the average gain was 32.9 percent. In firms with low commitment, the average gain was 6.1 percent.

HOSHIN PLANNING: LINKING DAILY ACTIVITIES WITH STRATEGIC OBJECTIVES

A new approach to linking daily activities with strategic objectives is derived from total quality management. Referred to as **Hoshin planning,** it was initially developed in Japan. Hewlett-Packard, Intel, Zytec, and Proctor & Gamble are among the multinational companies now using Hoshin planning.[12] It provides a disciplined management system to accomplish strategic priorities. Hoshin planning advocates believe it is especially suited to achieving breakthroughs. Six key principles of Hoshin planning are outlined in Exhibit 5-7, and described as follows:

1. *Align the organization's goals with changes in the environment.* People throughout the organization are briefed on exactly what the organization must do to be outstanding. Among the many possibilities are improving market share, developing a product to meet a need, or improving customer satisfaction.

LEARNING OBJECTIVE

Pinpoint how Hoshin planning helps implement strategic objectives.

Hoshin planning
A disciplined management system to accomplish strategic priorities.

Exhibit 5-7
Six Principles That
Support Hoshin Planning

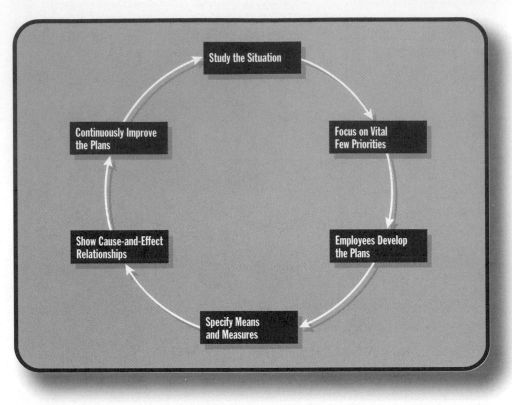

2. *Focus on the vital few priorities.* A key principle is to deploy and track only a few priorities at each level of the organization. Individuals must be able to focus quickly on those activities that offer the greatest advantage to the organization. An example would be the Buick division of General Motors finding that a hot new model would capture the fancy of young drivers.

3. *Ask employees to develop the plans to close the gaps.* Teams throughout the organization help close the gaps that would result in breakthroughs for the firm. They design their own plans, review their own programs, and coordinate their efforts with other teams. Strategic information is widely shared to get everybody involved with the key organizational challenges.

4. *Specify the means and measures to close the gaps.* Every high-level objective is translated into one or more means, such as improving customer service to meet the objective of total customer satisfaction. Every means is assigned a measure or indicator, such as customer-satisfaction surveys.

5. *Make the cause-and-effect relationships visible.* Hoshin planning requires that managers understand the cause-and-effect relationships that drive their business. In a mail-order business, for example, managers would attempt to analyze why some customers continue to order and why others order only once.

6. *Continuously improve the planning process.* At the heart of Hoshin management in the plan-do-study-act (PLAN) principle. A PLAN is used to test an idea. DO adhere to the plan. STUDY discrepancies to identify the root causes of obstacles. Finally, take appropriate ACTion. If the plan works, use it again. If not, revise the plan.

Whether or not Hoshin planning achieves more extraordinary results than MBO, it illustrates an important fact. Managerial workers continue to refine planning and implementation because these processes are the lifeblood of an organization.

SUMMARY OF KEY POINTS

1
Document how planning contributes to business success.

One value of planning is the process itself of self-examination. Extensive research shows that planning contributes to financial success and corporate growth.

2
Summarize a generalized model for planning, and apply it to enhance your planning skills.

A general planning model consists of seven related and sometimes overlapping elements: defining the present situation; establishing goals and objectives; developing action plans; developing budgets; implementing the plan; and controlling the plan. Contingency plans should also be developed.

3
Summarize the basics of strategic planning and business strategy.

Strategic planning is establishing master plans that shape the destiny of the firm. Two of its purposes are to help the firm invent the future and to encourage strategic thinking among managers. A strategy is a comprehensive program for achieving the mission. Current business strategies include cost leadership, imitation, product differentiation, forming strategic alliances, high speed, global diversification, sticking to core competencies, and putting "wow" back in the business.

Strategic planning is composed of activities that lead to the statement of objectives for the organization and the choice of appropriate strategies for achieving those objectives. The outcomes of strategic planning are statements of vision, mission, strategy, and policy.

4
Explain the use of operating plans, policies, procedures, and rules.

Operating plans provide the details of how strategic plans will be accomplished or implemented. They deal with a shorter time span than do strategic plans. Policies are plans set in the form of general statements that guide thinking and action in decision making. Procedures are plans that establish a customary method of handling future activities. A rule sets a specific course of action or conduct and is the simplest type of plan.

5
Present an overview of management by objectives.

Management by objectives (MBO) is the most widely used formal system of goal setting, planning, and review. In general, it has six elements: establishing organizational goals, establishing unit objectives, obtaining proposals from subordinates about their objectives, negotiating or agreeing to proposals, developing action plans, and reviewing performance. After objectives are set, the manager must give feedback to team members on their progress toward reaching the objectives.

6
Pinpoint how Hoshin planning helps implement strategic objectives.

Hoshin planning provides a disciplined management system to accomplish strategic priorities. A key aspect of the method is to get teams at all levels involved in working on breakthrough tasks (vital few priorities). Employees also develop plans to close gaps that would result in breakthroughs for the firm.

KEY TERMS AND PHRASES

Action Plan *pg. 100*

Contingency Plan *pg. 101*

Strategic Planning *pg. 102*

Operational Planning *pg. 102*

Strategy *pg. 102*

SWOT Analysis *pg. 105*

Mission *pg. 105*

Operating Plans *pg. 106*

Policies *pg. 108*

Procedures *pg. 108*

Rule *pg. 109*

Management by Objectives (MBO) *pg. 109*

Hoshin Planning *pg. 111*

QUESTIONS

1. How does planning control the future?
2. Which step in the framework for planning do you think gives management the most trouble? Explain your reasoning.
3. Why do managers whose work involves strategic planning typically receive much higher pay than those involved with operational planning?
4. How can you use strategic planning in planning your career?
5. Write a policy statement about cultural diversity for any organization you choose.
6. How is a rule related to a strategic plan?
7. In what way does Hoshin planning require a high level of employee involvement?

SKILL-BUILDING ACTIVITY 5-A: IMPLEMENTING BUSINESS STRATEGY

GROUP ACTIVITY The class assembles into small groups of business strategy implementation teams. Each team begins with a vision or mission statement from one of the firms mentioned in the section in this chapter about the strategic planning model. (For example, the McDonald's mission statement is "To satisfy the world's appetite for good food, well-served, at a price people can afford.") Or the teams can select a vision or mission statement from another source.

After selecting the vision or mission statement, develop an action plan for implementing the strategy implied by the statement. Implement the strategy by sketching several objectives, operating plans, policies, procedures, and rules to support the strategy. Make note of any particular trouble spots you anticipate in implementing the strategy, and how you would deal with the problem.

SKILL-BUILDING ACTIVITY 5-B: OVERCOMING RESISTANCE TO GOALS

To become an effective planner, a person must set and pursue goals. Yet many people resist the idea of goals. The problem does not seem to lie in setting them, but in *pursuing* goals. Think through the reasons described below for not diligently pursuing work or personal goals. Check the ones that apply to you.

_____ 1. If I achieve my goals, people will expect me to attain many more goals.

_____ 2. It's burdensome to me to think that I will have to spend the rest of my life pursuing goals.

_____ 3. I really hate to try and then fail.

_____ 4. I would be embarrassed if friends knew I was pursuing something and then flopped.

_____ 5. What most people consider to be goals are really cultural standards imposed on us.

_____ 6. I dislike my life being programmed by goals.

_____ 7. I think I'm too talented to bother with having to set goals.

_____ 8. I enjoy my freedom too much to be constrained by goals.

_____ 9. It's hard to believe that goals are really that good.

_____ 10. I've gotten along fine up to this point in my life without paying much attention to goals.

DECREASING YOUR RESISTANCE TO GOALS

The more statements that apply to you, the bigger your problem with resisting goals. But with self-awareness often comes change. Keeping your problem in the back of your mind will serve as a daily reminder to take some constructive action each day about pursuing your goals. Another path to improvement is to review the goals you have set for yourself and those imposed by others. Pursue the most meaningful ones first if priorities allow. If your goal does not appear so relevant, see if it can be modified to make it more relevant. The key to success is to pursue goals to which you are truly committed.

VIDEO DISCUSSION QUESTIONS

1. What business strategies might a North American company implement to capture Chinese people as both customers and suppliers? **[Business with China]**

2. What are the key elements in Bossidy's business strategy for Allied Signal? **[Allied Signal]**

3. What is the major business strategy revealed by Frank Popoff of Dow Chemical? **[Dow Chemical]**

CASE PROBLEM 5-A: THE SEARS CATALOG CHALLENGE

Sears, Roebuck & Co. began its general catalog business in 1893. Over the next 100 years, countless millions of customers ordered something at least once from the Sears "Big Book." For generations, the Sears catalog was the dominant player in an increasingly competitive business. During its last year of operation, customers ordered $3 billion worth of goods through the general-purpose catalog. The purchases included those made by shoppers at home and those made by customers visiting Sears catalog stores. Using the neatly organized Big Book, customers could order such far-ranging items as room air conditioners, golf clubs, and fancy lingerie.

By 1993, top management at Sears decided to cease publication and distribution of its general-purpose catalog. Yet, at the same time, Sears managers knew they had some incredible assets that were difficult to discard. Among them were the well-established Sears name, millions of loyal customers, and access to 24 million credit-card customers. Sears managers held a series of meetings to determine whether they should walk away from the past or figure out some way to squeeze profits out of the catalog business.

CASE QUESTIONS

(Suspend researching what actions Sears chose until you have applied your own strategic thinking to this problem.)

1. Explain how Sears can apply the strategic planning model to the dilemma of what to do about the catalog business.
2. What plans can Sears make to compete against the dozens of other catalog retailers in the present era?
3. Ask other people, or conduct library research, to learn what actually happened to the Sears catalog business.

Source: Some of the facts in this case are based on Susan Chandler, "Strategies for the New Mail Order," *Business Week* (19 December 1994): 82–84.

CASE PROBLEM 5-B: GOAL SETTING AT TAYLOR FOODS

Several years ago Taylor Foods was a meat distributor only. After intensive planning, Taylor Foods became a distributor of a variety of foods, including poultry, fish, and groceries. As the owner, Ralph Taylor, explained to the career school instructor who introduced him to planning, "I'm very impressed with what planning did for us at Taylor. There we were, an old company faced with a declining market. A few strategies and bang—we're now a multiproduct firm in an expanding market."

"Are you experiencing any problems with planning?" asked the management professor. Taylor replied, "I sure am. We are having problems in getting our people to personalize the planning process. They tend to regard planning as something that the owner should be doing rather than something they should be doing. Here are some notes I took from my planning meeting with Max Bloom, the sales manager for meats. He told me something to this effect: 'My plans are to beat out the competition and beat them good and to sell all the meat I can. Beyond that I have no plans. Each day I try to do my job the best I can. If I tell you anything else, I'm really stretching things.' "

Fascinated by what he heard, the professor asked for more evidence about planning problems within Taylor Meats. Taylor responded, "Okay, here are my notes from my planning conference with Georgia Anderson, my sales manager for nonmeat products. She said something of this nature: 'My goals are for my department to become the best it can be. But most of the things I would have to do to accomplish this are beyond my control. It's your job, Ralph, as the owner, to provide the budget so we can be tops in our area. Goal setting and planning in a small company are really the owner's responsibilities.' "

Taylor asked the professor, "Do you get my point about my sales managers not taking personal responsibility for planning?" The professor replied, "Maybe the situation isn't as hopeless as you think."

CASE QUESTIONS

1. Evaluate the effectiveness of the goal statements made by Bloom and Anderson, using the information in Exhibit 5-6.
2. What might Ralph Taylor be doing wrong in his attempts to involve the sales managers in planning and goal setting?

CASE PROBLEM 5-C: HOW DO YOU PUT "WOW" IN A SHOE-REPAIR SHOP?

Derek Johnson owns and operates three shoe-repair shops in suburban Atlanta, Georgia. In addition to repairing and restoring shoes, Johnson's shops also repair and renovate leather handbags and leather jackets. Johnson has been moderately satisfied with the success of his business. He squeezes out an acceptable living from the salary he draws from the business. Johnson is thinking of opening a fourth store, providing he can find a good location at an affordable price.

Johnson thought to himself, however, that before planning for expansion he should first improve his existing business. He is concerned that profits are too thin to fund an expansion that might not be immediately profitable. In search of good business ideas, Johnson enrolled in a seminar given by business consultant Tom Peters. The subject of the seminar was achieving long-term competitiveness, with a special emphasis on small- and medium-size businesses. Johnson was concerned that he might be the owner of the smallest business of anybody in the seminar.

The seminar room was packed, and Johnson was warmly greeted by the other serious-minded participants. The people in attendance included business owners, corporate managers, consultants, and business professors. By the end of the day, ideas were swimming around in Johnson's head. To focus his thinking, he circled several key ideas in his seminar notebook:

- Get to know at least one person who revels in telling you that you are full of hooey. A person of this type would not be afraid to challenge your thinking. Johnson thought that his girlfriend Shawna could fit this requirement.

- Hire rebels who will challenge your preconceptions of how your business should be run. Johnson reasoned that he can barely meet his payroll right now, so he might rely on people in his network to perform this function for free.

- Come up with a good next act. For Johnson's stores, this might mean offering a new service he is not offering now. He had tentatively thought of promoting an attaché-case repair and restoration service. Yet he was concerned about the cost of promotion.

- Put "wow" back in your business. Somehow your business should be different and interesting. The owner should be getting an emotional charge when he or she walks through the store, franchise, or factory. Johnson thought to himself, "Somedays I'm not as charged up as I should be. Maybe I should find a way to put more "wow" back in Derek's Shoe Repair."

CASE QUESTIONS

1. What action steps, if any, should Johnson take to improve his business based on the first three points circled in his notebook?
2. What do you recommend that Johnson do to put more "wow" back in Derek's Shoe Repair?

Source: Some of the facts in this case are based on Robert McGarvey, "The Big Thrill: Top Management Guru Says Put the Wow Back In Your Business," *Entrepreneur* (July 1995): 86–91.

CASE PROBLEM 5-D: THE WORLD LEAGUE OF AMERICAN FOOTBALL TRIES AGAIN

Marc G. Lory, a 44-year-old Frenchman with an MBA from the University of Chicago, has been hired to revive the World League of American Football. The league is a joint venture of the National Football League and Fox Inc., with a $40 million startup investment. The previous effort of the league ended in 1992, after two seasons of play and $50 million in losses. Nevertheless, Europe has a strong interest in American football. In 1995 alone, the NFL sold $250 million of merchandise in Europe. Also, hundreds of amateur football leagues have been established across the European continent.

The World League will operate with a salary cap of $15,000 for all positions except for quarterbacks, who will receive $20,000. Total annual expenditures for all players will be less than $4 million. (In the NFL, many individual players receive $4 million for the season.) Each team roster of 40 will have seven local players—typically soccer or rugby standouts— and 33 American football players who failed to make the NFL. The six teams are the Amsterdam Admirals, the Barcelona Dragons, the Dusseldorf Rhein Fire, the Frankfurt Galaxy, the London Monarchs, and the Scottish Claymores.

Lory, a marketing whiz, anticipates that the games will receive good television coverage. He plans to make football an entertainment extravaganza with rock bands at half time, fireworks, and cheerleaders. Lory says, "People will pay for American culture and entertainment. We'll be part of the globalization of sport." A major part of his strategy is to sell football as a safe alternative to the fan violence of soccer.

An executive vice-president of Fox Sports says, "Our goal is to introduce a sport that's safe and fun. You can bring the family and have a wonderful night out." Part of the plan is to make football equipment available to grade schools to stimulate interest in and sponsoring of flag football contests for youth clubs.

Lory believes strongly that the European market is ready for American football. He contends that the sport is like a tidal wave building up. Yet skeptics wonder if his marketing strategy will work.

CASE QUESTIONS

1. Evaluate the soundness of Marc Lory's marketing strategy for creating interest in the World League of American Football.
2. Assume you are a consultant to the WLAF. What else do you recommend the organization do to ensure the success of its revival?
3. What type or types of strategy are being used by this joint venture of the NFL and Fox?

Source: Based on facts reported in Paula Dwyer, "The Long, Muddy Field Ahead of Marc Lory," *Business Week* (6 March 1995): 97.

KROPF FRUIT COMPANY: A STUDY IN PLANNING

A family-owned fruit processor, Kropf Fruit Company, faced the problem of massive consolidation among its potential customers. To survive, Kropf needed a strategic plan. Two possibilities were to remain a medium-sized regional packer or to grow to a major packing and processing company. Kropf chose to use SWOT as a planning tool. Top management analyzed its Strengths, Weaknesses, Opportunities, and Threats. A major weakness was limited temperature-controlled storage space. A major opportunity was building greater storage space; a major threat was the new types of fruit imported from overseas.

Using SWOT, the company developed a strategic plan to double in size by doubling its acreage and expanding its storage and packing facilities. Kropf's ten-year plan was supported by many short-range plans.

REFERENCES

1. Ingrid Abramovitch, "Mongoose: Bill Kimpton Picks His Moment to Strike—And Wins," *Success* (April 1995): 38–42. The other references to Kimpton in this chapter are from the same source.
2. "The Real Value of Planning," *Working Smart* (January 1995): 1.
3. C. Chet Miller and Laura B. Cardinal, "Strategic Planning and Firm Performance: A Synthesis of More than Two Decades of Research," *The Academy of Management Journal* (December 1994): 1649–1665.
4. Henry Mintzberg, "The Strategy Concept II: Another Look at Why Organizations Need Strategies," *California Management Review* (January 1987): 26.
5. "A Strategy Session With C. K. Prahalad," *Management Review* (April 1995): 50; Gary Hamel and C. K. Prahalad, "Competing for the Future," *Harvard Business Review* (July–August 1994): 122–128.
6. Some of these strategies are primarily from John W. Jones, *High-Speed Management: Time-Based Strategies for Managers and Organizations* (San Francisco: Jossey-Bass, 1993); Praveen R. Nayar, "On the Measurement of Competitive Strategy: Evidence from a Large Multiproduct U.S. Firm," *The Academy of Management Journal* (December 1993): 1652–1669; Michele Kremen Bolton, "Imitation Versus Innovation: Lessons to Be Learned from the Japanese," *Organizational Dynamics* (Winter 1993): 30–45; Kathy Rebello, "Will the Apple Clones Bear Fruit?" *Business Week* (24 April 1995): 132–134; Robert McGarvey, "The Big Thrill: Top Management Guru Says Put the Wow Back in Your Business," *Entrepreneur* (July 1995): 86.
7. "Can Nike Just Do It?" *Business Week* (18 April 1994): 87.
8. Zachary Schiller, "And Fix that Flat Before You Go, Stanley," *Business Week* (16 January 1995): 35.
9. Larry Armstrong, "More Red Meat, Please," *Business Week* (22 May 1995): 134.
10. "Make that Sale, Mr. Sam," *Time* (18 May 1987): 55.
11. Robert Rodgers and John E. Hunter, "Impact of Management by Objectives on Organizational Productivity," *Journal of Applied Psychology* (April 1991): 329.
12. This section is based on Michele L. Bechtell, *The Management Compass: Steering the Corporation Using Hoshin Planning* (New York: American Management Association, 1995).

CHAPTER 6

Problem Solving and Decision Making

LEARNING OBJECTIVES
After studying this chapter and doing the exercises, you should be able to:

1
Differentiate between programmed and nonprogrammed decisions.

2
Explain the steps involved in making a nonprogrammed decision.

3
Understand the major factors influencing decision making in organizations.

4
Understand the nature of creativity and how it contributes to managerial work.

5
Describe organizational programs for improving creativity.

6
Implement several suggestions for becoming a more creative problem solver.

7
Appreciate the value and potential limitations of group decision making.

© George Rose/
Gamma Liaison

The Ritz Carlton chain, with Horst Schulze as president, had received an award as the best hotel in the world. Yet complaints by guests were not eliminated. At one hotel, guests complained for three years that room service was late. To solve the problem, Schulze dispatched a team composed of a room-service order taker, a waiter, and a cook. Everything seemed fine except that the service elevator took a long time. Neither the engineering department nor an elevator company specialist could find a technical problem with the elevator. • Next, team members took turns riding the elevators at all hours for a week. Finally, one of them observed that everytime the elevator made its trip from the first floor to the twenty-fourth, it stopped four or five times. At each stop, housemen (who assisted the maids) got on the elevator to go to different floors. The housemen were stealing towels from other floors to bring them to housekeepers on their own floors who were short of towels. Foraging for towels was slowing down the elevators. • The Ritz Carlton didn't really have a room service problem, it had a towel shortage. After buying more towels, room service complaints dropped 50 percent.[1]

A s illustrated by the Ritz Carlton incident, solving difficult problems is a key part of a manager's job. Often the solution requires perceptive investigation. This chapter explores how managerial workers solve problems and make decisions individually and in groups. A **problem** is a discrepancy between ideal and actual conditions. The ideal situation in the hotel example would be no complaints, while the actual situation was the presence of complaints about slow room service. A **decision** is choosing among alternatives, such as buying more towels rather than adding more elevators!

Problem solving and decision making are important components of planning, and they are also required to carry out the other management functions. For example, while managers are controlling, they must make a series of decisions about how to solve the problem of getting performance back to standard. Understanding decision making is also important because decision making contributes to job satisfaction. Jobs allowing for more decision-making authority are generally more satisfying.

problem
A discrepancy between ideal and actual conditions.

decision
A choice among alternatives.

NONPROGRAMMED VERSUS PROGRAMMED DECISIONS

Differentiate between nonprogrammed and programmed decisions.

Some decisions that managerial workers face are difficult because they occur infrequently. These unique decisions are **nonprogrammed decisions** (or nonroutine decisions). In contrast, a **programmed decision** is repetitive, or routine, and made according to a specific procedure.

NONPROGRAMMED DECISIONS

nonprogrammed decision
A decision that is difficult because of its complexity and the fact that the person faces it infrequently.

When a problem has not taken the same form in the past or is extremely complex or significant, it calls for a nonprogrammed decision. A complex problem is one that contains many elements. Significant problems affect an important aspect of an organization. The room service problem at a Ritz Carlton hotel was complex because there were several potential causes. It was significant because it affected customer satisfaction. Virtually all strategic decisions are nonprogrammed.

A well-planned and highly structured organization reduces the number of nonprogrammed decisions. It does so by formulating hundreds of policies to help managers know what to do when faced with a given problem. In contrast, many small firms do not offer much guidance about decision making. An exception is that many small-business owners make most of the nonprogrammed decisions themselves.

programmed decision
A decision that is repetitive, or routine, and made according to a specific procedure.

Handling a nonprogrammed problem properly requires original thinking. The skill required for decision making varies inversely with the extent to which it is programmed. Highly routine decisions require minimum decision-making skill; highly nonroutine decisions require maximum skill.

Managers and nonmanagers also make many small, uncomplicated decisions involving alternatives that are specified in advance. Procedures specify how to handle these routine, programmed decisions. Here is an example: A person who earns $24,000 per year applies to rent a two-bedroom apartment. The manager makes the decision to refuse the application because there is a rule that families with annual incomes of $28,000 or less may not rent in the building.

DECISION MAKING AT DIFFERENT LEVELS OF MANAGEMENT

Under ideal circumstances, top-level management concerns itself almost exclusively with nonroutine decisions and lower-level management handles all routine ones. In

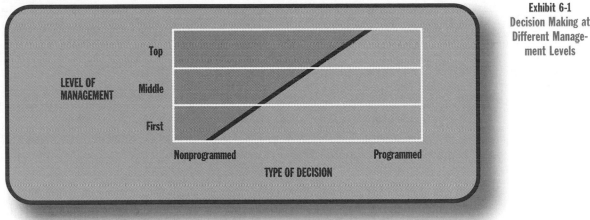

Exhibit 6-1
Decision Making at
Different Manage-
ment Levels

reality, executives do make many small, programmed decisions in addition to non-programmed ones. Some top executives sign expense-account vouchers and answer routine correspondence, for example. Middle managers and first-level managers generally make both routine and nonroutine decisions, with first-level managers making a higher proportion of routine decisions. A well-managed organization encourages all managers to delegate as many nonprogrammed decisions as possible.

Exhibit 6-1 shows the typical relationship between management level and type of decision. The philosophy of top-level managers significantly influences the extent to which lower-ranking managers make nonprogrammed decisions. A firm that has a policy of passing much decision-making authority down the line encourages first-level managers to make nonroutine decisions. In contrast, a firm whose policy restricts authority to top-level managers restricts nonroutine decision making to top-level managers.

THE TIME FACTOR IN MAKING NONPROGRAMMED DECISIONS

Nonprogrammed decisions are complex and therefore may require extensive analysis. Nevertheless, you will recall from the discussions of cycle time and time-based competition that decision-making speed is an asset. Research evidence suggests that making strategic decisions with speed is associated with a firm achieving superior performance. Decision-making speed is particularly important for firms in a quickly changing environment, such as the microcomputer industry. One study drew on information collected in 151 firms to help understand which characteristics of executives were associated with speedy decision making.

A major finding was that executives varied considerably in how quickly they made strategic decisions. Executives who were more adept at making rapid strategic decisions tended to be intuitive, have good problem-solving ability, a toleration for risk, and an action orientation. (More will be said about personal characteristics and decision making later in this chapter.) Another finding was that executives in centralized firms made speedier strategic decisions.[2] In a centralized firm, top executives make most of the major decisions.

STEPS IN PROBLEM SOLVING AND DECISION MAKING

Problem solving and decision making can be regarded as an orderly process, similar to the planning model described in Chapter 5. Yet not every effective solution

LEARNING OBJECTIVE

2

Explain the steps involved
in making a nonpro-
grammed decision.

or decision is the product of an orderly process. The key principle is that managers find better solutions to complex problems—and therefore make better major, or nonprogrammed, decisions—when they follow an orderly process. Drawing a consistent distinction between problem solving and decision making is difficult because they are part of the same process. The basic purpose of making a decision is to solve a problem, but you must analyze the problem prior to making the decision. A broader and grander purpose of decision making is to move the organization forward, to seize opportunities, and to avoid problems.

As shown in Exhibit 6-2, and described next, problem solving and decision making can be divided into steps.

IDENTIFY AND DIAGNOSE THE PROBLEM

Problem solving and decision making begin with the awareness that a problem exists. In other words, the first step in problem solving and decision making is identifying a gap between desired and actual conditions. At times, a problem is imposed on a manager, such as when customer complaints increase. At other times, he or she has to search actively for a worthwhile problem or opportunity. For example, a sales manager actively pursued a problem by conducting an audit to find out why former customers stopped buying from the company.

INDICATORS OF PROBLEMS. Identifying problems requires considerable skill. Managers may become aware of a problem by noticing one of four typical indicators.[3]

1. *Deviation from past performance.* If performance figures are down, a problem almost surely exists. Common problem indicators are declining sales, increased employee turnover, higher scrap rates, increased customer complaints, and an increased number of bad checks cashed.
2. *Deviations from the plan.* When the results you hoped to attain with a plan are not forthcoming, you have a problem. This type of problem identification requires you to see a deviation from anticipated *future* performance. The possibility exists that the established plan was unduly optimistic.
3. *Criticism from outsiders.* Managers sometimes become aware of problems by hearing complaints from individuals and groups who are not employees of the firm. These sources of criticism include customers, goverment regulatory agencies, and stockholders.
4. *Competitive threats.* The presence of competition can create problems for an organization. Apple Computer, for example, has slashed its prices in recent years to compete with lower-priced brands.

DIAGNOSIS. A thorough diagnosis of the problem is important because the real problem may be different from the one that a first look suggests. To diagnose a problem properly, you must clarify its true nature. The Ritz Carlton team invested considerable time and energy into uncovering why room service was slow at one of the hotels.

DEVELOP CREATIVE ALTERNATIVE SOLUTIONS

The second step in decision making is to generate alternative solutions. This is the intellectually freewheeling aspect of decision making. All kinds of possibilities are explored in this step, even if they seem unrealistic. Often the difference between good and mediocre decision makers is that the former do not accept the first alternative they think of. Instead, they keep digging until they find the best solution.

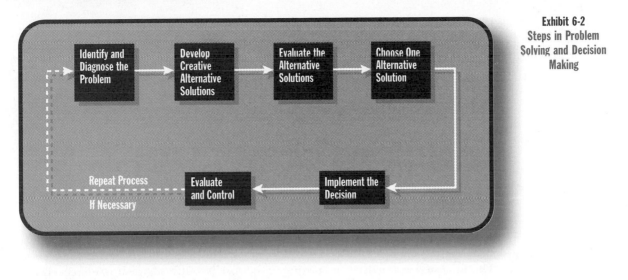

Exhibit 6-2
Steps in Problem
Solving and Decision
Making

EVALUATE ALTERNATIVE SOLUTIONS

The next step involves comparing the relative value of the alternatives. The problem solver examines the pros and cons of each one and considers the feasibility of each. Some alternatives may appear attractive, but implementing them would be impossible or counterproductive. Adding a service elevator to speed up room service is an extreme example of this idea.

Comparing relative value often means performing a cost and savings analysis of each alternative. Alternatives that cost much more than they save are infeasible. The possible outcome of an alternative should be part of the analysis. If an unsatisfactory outcome is almost a certainty, the alternative should be rejected. For example, if a firm is faced with low profits, one alternative would be to cut pay by 20 percent. The outcome of this alternative would be to lower morale drastically and create high turnover, so a firm should not implement that alternative. High employee turnover is so expensive that it would override the cost savings.

One approach to examining the pros and cons of each alternative is to list them on a worksheet. This approach assumes that virtually all alternatives have both positive and negative consequences.

CHOOSE ONE ALTERNATIVE SOLUTION

The process of weighing each alternative must stop at some point. You cannot solve a problem unless you choose one of the alternatives—that is, make a decision. Several factors influence the choice. A major factor is the goal the decision should achieve. The alternative chosen should be the one that appears to come closest to achieving it.

Despite a careful evaluation of alterantives, ambiguity remains in most decisions. The decisions faced by managers are often complex, and the factors involved in them are often unclear. Even when quantitative evidence strongly supports a particular alternative, the decision maker may be uncertain. Human resource decisions are often the most ambiguous because making precise predictions about human behavior is so difficult. Deciding which person to hire from a list of several strong candidates is always a challenge.

IMPLEMENT THE DECISION

Converting the decision into action is the next major step. Until a decision is implemented, it is not really a decision at all. Many strategic decisions represent wasted effort because nobody is held responsible for implementing them. Much of a manager's job involves helping subordinates implement decisions.

A fruitful way of evaluating the merit of a decision is to observe its implementation. A decision is seldom a good one if people resist its implementation or if it is too cumbersome to implement. Suppose a firm tries to boost productivity by decreasing the time allotted for lunch or coffee breaks. If employees resist the decision by eating while working and then taking the allotted lunch break, productivity will decrease. Implementation problems indicate that the decision to boost productivity by decreasing break time would be a poor one.

EVALUATE AND CONTROL

The final step in the decision-making framework is to investigate how effectively the chosen alternative solved the problem. Controlling means ensuring that the results the decision obtained are the ones set forth during the problem identification step.

After gathering feedback, characterize the quality of the decision as optimum, satisficing, or suboptimum. Optimum decisions lead to favorable outcomes. **Satisficing decisions** provide a minimum standard of satisfaction. Such decisions are adequate, acceptable, or passable. Many decision makers stop their search for alternatives when they find a satisficing one. Accepting the first reasonable alternative may only postpone the need to implement a decision that really solves the problem. For example, slashing the price of a personal computer to match the competition's price can be regarded as the result of a satisficing decision. A longer-range decision might call for a firm to demonstrate to potential buyers that the difference in quality is worth the higher price.

Suboptimum decisions lead to negative outcomes. Their consequences are disruptive to the employees and to the firm. When you obtain suboptimum results, you must repeat the problem-solving and decision-making process.

Evaluating and controlling your decisions will help you improve your decision-making skills. You can learn important lessons by comparing what actually happened with what you thought would happen. You can learn what you could have improved or done differently and use this information the next time you face a similar decision.

The accompanying Manager in Action illustrates the magnitude of decisions sometimes made by a key executive. As you read the insert, ponder the consequences of his decisions.

CRITICISM OF THE RATIONAL DECISION-MAKING MODEL. So far, this chapter has presented the classical model of problem solving and decision making. The model regards the activities as an orderly and rational process. In reality, decision making is seldom logical and systematic. Ronald Zarrella at GM, for example, did not require a study to decide that a Cadillac sports vehicle would have limited consumer appeal. Instead, he used his marketing intuition to arrive at that decision.

Awareness that decision making is not always so orderly stems from the research of psychologist and economist Herbert A. Simon. He proposed that bounds (or limits) to rationality are present in decision making. These bounds are the limitations of the human organism, particularly related to the processing and recall of information.[4] **Bounded rationality** means that people's limited mental abilities, combined with external influences over which they have little or no control,

satisficing decision
A decision that meets the minimum standards of satisfaction.

bounded rationality
The observation that people's limited mental abilities, combined with external influences over which they have little or no control, prevent them from making entirely rational decisions.

MANAGER IN ACTION: RON ZARRELLA, GM MARKETING HONCHO

Ronald L. Zarrella was selected from the outside to become the top automotive marketing executive at General Motors Corp. Insiders were concerned that his background in underwear manufacturing and contact lens sales was not appropriate for making automotive marketing decisions. Yet the 45-year-old's marketing savvy and extroverted personality quickly created allies with top GM executives.

Zarella has felt secure enough to make several tough decisions. One of his major decisions was to reject Cadillac's plans to sell a luxury sports vehicle by attaching a Cadillac crest to one of GM's big sports utility trucks. Instead, he has helped formulate plans to introduce a Cadillac Catera, a styl-

ish vehicle based on a European model. He has selected brand managers to help focus marketing efforts. Zarella is also in the process of reducing the number of too-similar cars and trucks from the GM line-up. He claims, "We think we can do more volume with fewer entries."

Zarella's experience with brands such as Ray-Ban sunglasses has shaped his marketing decisions about automobiles. He is pushing GM to spread advertising budgets over the life span of a car model rather than spending most of the money during introduction. He has also decided to rehabilitate familiar product names, such as Cutlass, rather than replace them with new names.

Source: Based on facts reported in "GM Learns to Love an Outsider," *Business Week* (3 July 1995): 32.

prevent them from making entirely rational decisions. Satisficing decisions result from bounded rationality.

You should strive to follow the orderly steps of problem solving and decision making. However, there is usually more than one problem in need of attention, and you may not have the time to carefully evaluate each alternative. The next section will discuss the factors that influence the decision-making process and how they affect the quality of decisions.

INFLUENCES ON DECISION MAKING

Although most people can follow the decision-making steps described, not everybody can arrive at the same quality of decision. Decision-making ability varies from person to person, and other forces can hamper anyone from finding optimum solutions. Exhibit 6-3 shows the factors that influence decision making.

LEARNING OBJECTIVE

Understand the major factors influencing decision making in organizations.

CRISIS CONDITIONS

In a crisis, many decision makers panic. They become less rational and more emotional than they would in a calm environment. Decision makers who are adversely affected by crisis cannot concentrate, use poor judgment, and think impulsively. Under crisis conditions, some managers are prone to ignore differences of opinion. They may be aware of conflicting views but feel too pressured to reach a solution to explore differing views and incorporate them into their choices.[5]

New evidence suggests, however, that groups can make good use of the opposing opinions of team members during a crisis. A group decision-making experiment was conducted with personnel enrolled in a Navy technical school. The fabricated crisis was the threat of tear gas being released in the room unless the problem was solved promptly. Group members with high status were able to seek input from group members and quickly bring the situation under control.[6]

Exhibit 6-3
Factors Influencing
Decision Making

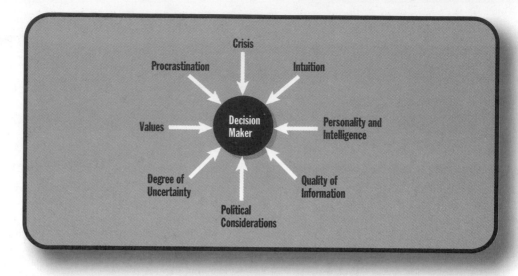

During a business crisis, such as a pending bankruptcy or employee walkout, some managers rise to peak mental alertness. Others are completely paralyzed. The ability to make decisions under pressure is a personal characteristic, but everyone can improve their decision-making skill through education and practice.

INTUITION

> **intuition**
> *An experience-based way of knowing or reasoning in which weighing and balancing evidence are done unconsciously and automatically.*

Intuition is another personal characteristic that influences decision making. Effective decision makers do not rely on analytical and methodological techniques alone. They also use their hunches and intuition. **Intuition** is as an experience-based way of knowing or reasoning in which weighing and balancing evidence are done unconsciously and automatically. Intuition is also a way of arriving at a conclusion without using the step-by-step logical process. (Yet the intuitive person might be racing through the steps in his or her mind without realizing it.) The fact that experience contributes to intuition means that decision makers can become more intuitive by solving many difficult problems.

The distinction between analytical and intuitive thinking is often traced to which half of the brain is dominant. The left half of the brain controls analytical thinking; the right half controls creative and intuitive thinking. Effective problem solvers achieve a balance between analytical and intuitive, or left-brain and right-brain thinking. Rather than operating independently of each other, the analytical and intuitive approaches should be complementary components of decision making.

PERSONALITY AND INTELLIGENCE

> **decisiveness**
> *The extent to which a person makes up his or her mind promptly and prudently.*

The personality and intelligence of the decision maker influence his or her ability to find effective solutions. One relevant personality dimension is a person's degree of cautiousness and conservatism. A cautious, conservative person typically opts for a low-risk solution. If a person is extremely cautious, he or she may avoid making major decisions for fear of being wrong. Cautiousness and conservatism are related to **decisiveness**, the extent to which a person makes up his or her mind promptly and prudently. Take the quiz presented at the end of the chapter to examine your degree of decisiveness.

Perfectionism has a notable impact on decision making. People who seek the perfect solution to a problem are usually indecisive because they are hesitant to accept the fact that a particular alternative is good enough. Self-efficacy, the feeling of being an effective and competent person on a specific task also has an influence. Researchers note, for example, that having the right amount of gall contributes to innovative thinking.[7]

Rigid people have difficult identifying problems and gathering alternative solutions. People who are mentally flexible perform well in these areas. Optimism versus pessimism is another relevant personality dimension. Optimists are more likely to find solutions than pessimists are. Pessimists are more likely to give up searching, because they perceive situations as being hopeless.

Intelligence has a profound influence on the effectiveness of decision making. In general, intelligent and well-educated people are more likely to identify problems and make sound decisions than are those who have less intelligence and education. A notable exception applies, however. Some intelligent, well-educated people have such a fondness for collecting facts and analyzing them that they suffer from "analysis paralysis." One plant manager put it this way: "I'll never hire a genius again. They dazzle you with facts, figures, and computer graphics. But when they get through with their analysis, they still haven't solved the problem." A manager has to make it clear to team members that decision making is more important than data collection. One way for the manager to get this message across is to act as a good model.[8]

QUALITY AND ACCESSIBILITY OF INFORMATION

Reaching an effective decision usually requires high-quality, valid information. One of the most important purposes of information systems is to supply managers with high-quality information. Accessibility may be even more important than quality in determining whether or not information is used. Sometimes it takes so much time and effort to search for quality information that the manager relies on lower-quality information that is close at hand.[9] Think of the decision-making process involved in purchasing a new automobile. Many people are more likely to rely on the opinion of friends than to search through references sources for more systematic information.

POLITICAL CONSIDERATIONS

Under ideal circumstances, organizational decisions are made on the basis of the objective merits of competing alternatives. In reality, many decisions are based on political considerations, such as favoritism, alliances, or the desire of the decision maker to stay in favor with people who wield power.

Political factors sometimes influence which data are given serious consideration in evaluating alternatives. The decision maker may select data that support the position of an influential person whom he or she is trying to please. For instance, one financial analyst was asked to investigate the cost-effectiveness of the firm owning a corporate jet. She knew the president wanted the status of having a private jet, so she gave considerable weight to the "facts" supplied by a manufacturer of corporate jets. This allowed her to justify the expense of purchasing the plane.

A person with professional integrity arrives at what he or she thinks is the best decision and then makes a diligent attempt to convince management of the objective merits of that solution.

DEGREE OF UNCERTAINTY

The more certain a decision maker is of the outcome of a decision, the more calmly and confidently the person will make the decision. Degree of certainty is divided into three categories: certainty, risk, and uncertainty. A condition of certainty exists when the facts are well known and the outcome can be predicted accurately. A retail store manager might predict with certainty that more hours of operation will lead to more sales. It might be uncertain, however, whether the increased sales would cover the increased expenses.

A condition of risk exists when a decision must be made based on incomplete, but accurate, factual information. Managers frequently use quantitative techniques to make decisions under conditions of risk. Suppose a promoter schedules a tour for a popular singing group. Some statistical information about costs and past ticket sales would be available. The promoter can, to an extent, calculate the risk by studying factual information from the past.

Outstanding managers often accept a condition of risk. A calculated risk is where the potential return is well worth the cost that will be incurred if the effort fails. The GM marketing executive, Zarrella, was willing to take the risk of launching a sporty new Cadillac to appeal to a hipper consumer group.

A condition of uncertainty occurs when a decision must be based on limited or not factual information. When faced with a condition of uncertainty, managers rely on intuition.

VALUES OF THE DECISION MAKER

Values influence decision making at every step. Ultimately, all decisions are based on values. A manager who places a high value on the personal welfare of employees tries to avoid alternatives that create hardship for workers and implements decisions in ways that lessen turmoil. Another value that significantly influences decision making is the pursuit of excellence. A manager who embraces the pursuit of excellence will search for the high-quality alternative solution.

PROCRASTINATION

procrastinate
To delay in taking action without a valid reason.

Many people are poor decision makers because they **procrastinate,** or delay taking action without a valid reason. Procrastination results in indecisiveness and inaction and is a major cause of self-defeating behavior. Procrastination is a deeply ingrained behavior pattern. Yet recent research suggests it can be overcome by learning how to become self-disciplined.[10] Part of the process involves setting goals for overcoming procrastination and conquering the problem in small steps. For example, a person might first practice making a deadline for a decision over a minor activity such as ordering a box of copier paper.

creativity
The process of developing novel ideas that can be put into action.

CREATIVITY IN MANAGERIAL WORK

Understand the nature of creativity and how it contributes to managerial work.

Creativity is an essential part of problem solving and decision making. To be creative is to see new relationships and produce imaginative solutions. **Creativity** can be defined simply as the process of developing novel ideas that can be put into action. By emphasizing the application of ideas, creativity is closely linked to innovation. To be innovative, a person must produce a new product, service, process, or procedure.

Without some creativity a manager cannot solve complex problems or contribute to any types of organizational breakthroughs. A new perspective on creativity helps illustrate the point that it is not a rarified talent of the privileged few.

MANAGER IN ACTION: GEORGE LOIS, ADVERTISING EXECUTIVE

Back in the 1960s, advertising executive George Lois was marketing Aunt Jemima pancake mix. Yet there was no Aunt Jemima syrup at the time to accompany the mix. Nobody at Quaker Oats, the manufacturer of Aunt Jemima, was convinced of the importance of the syrup. Lois made the first move by using consumer research. He asked consumers to check the syrup brand they had used most recently. He included Aunt Jemima on the list even though it did not exist. Lois found that a large number of people polled said they had recently used Aunt Jemima.

At his next meeting with the Quaker Oats managers, Lois reviewed his research results. He argued that the new product could not miss because so many people thought they already purchased it. The Quaker Oats executives were stunned and moved quickly into producing Aunt Jemima pancake syrup. Lois was given the opportunity to advertise it, with the slogan "Aunt Jemima . . . what took you so long?"

Source: George Lois and Bill Pitts, *What's the Big Idea?* (New York: Doubleday, 1991).

Psychology professor Ellen Langer believes that learning to be *mindful* is more important than attempting to be creative. Mindfulness is paying attention to what you are doing and what's going on around you, instead of mindlessly cruising through life on automatic.[11] A mindful person can recognize an opportunity or see a problem that needs to be fixed.

Our discussion of managerial creativity focuses on the creative personality, the necessary conditions for creativity, the creative organization, creativity programs, and suggestions for becoming more creative.

CREATIVE ASPECTS OF A MANAGER'S JOB

A manager's workday is a miscellany of activities, from holding scheduled meetings to engaging in impromptu conversations. The day also involves writing memos, making presentations, dealing with emergencies and crises, and entertaining visitors. Managers jump from task to task and from person to person. To fashion order from this potential chaos requires creative problem solving. Managers can display creativity in the way they arrange and rearrange, juggle schedules, collect and disseminate information and ideas, make assignments, and lead people.

One critical job of a high-level manager is to create a network of people who will lend support by carrying out the manager's mission. To do this, a manager must think of creative ways to return favors. One manager, for example, needed the other managers throughout the firm to support his total quality management program. To enlist their support, he told them that he would inform top-level managers when he discovered outstanding examples of quality improvement.

An important point about creativity in managerial work is that many successful new business ideas are straightforward and uncomplicated. A classic example is the experience of the mindful advertising executive described in the accompanying Manager in Action. Can you think of another simple, breakthrough idea in business?

THE CREATIVE PERSONALITY

Creative people are more emotionally open and flexible than their less-creative counterparts. People who rarely exhibit creative behavior tend to be closed-minded and rigid. They suffer from "hardening of the categories"; they cannot overcome the traditional way of looking at things. In business jargon, creative people can *think outside the box,* or get beyond the usual constraints when solving problems.

Creative people are also described as those who can make a paradigm shift. A **paradigm** consists of the perspectives and ways of doing things that are typical of a given context. For example, top management at Toys 'Я' Us was able to shift away from the paradigm that only Japanese-made toys can be sold in Japan.

Closely related to making paradigm shifts is the ability to think laterally. **Lateral thinking** spreads out to find many different solutions to a problem. **Vertical thinking,** in contrast, is an analytical, logical process that results in few answers. A problem requiring lateral thinking would be to specify a variety of ways in which a small-business owner could increase income. A vertical thinking problem would be to calculate how much more money the small-business owner needs each month to earn a 10 percent profit.

Lateral thinking is thus divergent, while vertical thinking is convergent. Creative people are able to think divergently. They can expand the number of alternatives to a problem, thus moving away from a single solution. Yet the creative thinker also knows when it is time to think convergently. For example, the divergent thinker might generate 25 ways to reduce costs. Yet at some point he or she will have to converge toward choosing the best of several cost-cutting procedures. A lateral thinking problem is presented next. Compare your solution to the one given at the end of the chapter.[12]

A truck approached a low overpass on the highway. It was just about the same height as the arch, and managed to get itself in, but not out. Halfway through, the truck became wedged in. It could not move forward or back out without severely damaging its roof. No one could figure a way to get it out, until a small girl suggested a solution. What was it?

CONDITIONS NECESSARY FOR CREATIVITY

Creativity is not just a random occurrence. For creativity to occur, ability, enjoyment of the task itself, and certain mental activities are needed. *Ability* is knowledge in the area in which a person works, combined with the skills to process information to produce a useful, novel solution. A mind disciplined through study is therefore a major contributor to creativity.

Enjoyment or fascination with a task is an important aspect of creative potential. Even if someone has the potential, that person is unlikely to be creative unless he or she is basically excited about the task. To be creative, the person must also engage in certain mental, or *cognitive,* activities. Most of these mental tasks are included in the decision-making stages outlined in Exhibit 6-2. For example, to be creative the individual must diagnose a problem, gather and analyze data, and select an alternative. Another cognitive activity is subconscious thinking about the problem.[13]

In addition to the internal conditions that affect creativity, two factors outside the person have significant effect. An environmental need must stimulate the setting of a goal.[14] This is another way of saying "Necessity is the mother of invention." For example, suppose an information systems specialist is confronted with the problem of linking personal computers. No standard solution is available. The specialist then sets the goal of making the links, and uses creativity to reach that goal.

THE CREATIVE ORGANIZATION

Another perspective on the conditions necessary for creativity is to recognize that certain managerial and organizational practices foster creativity.[15] The most im-

paradigm

The perspectives and ways of doing things that are typical of a given context.

lateral thinking

A thinking process that spreads out to find many different alternative solutions to a problem.

vertical thinking

An analytical, logical process that results in few answers.

portant characteristic of the creative organization is an atmosphere that encourages creative expression. A manager who encourages imaginative and original thinking and does not punish people for making honest mistakes is likely to receive creative ideas from group members.

Research supports the importance of permissiveness for fostering creativity and innovation. Teresa M. Amabile and S.S. Gryskiewicz interviewed 120 research and development scientists in order to gather critical incidents. One incident was to illustrate high creativity, and one low creativity. In describing incidents of high creativity, about 74 percent of the scientists mentioned the following conditions:

- Freedom to decide what to do and how to do one's work
- Freedom from constraints such as tight financial controls
- An open atmosphere[16]

Collectively, these findings suggest that a permissive atmosphere is appropriate for nurturing innovation. The same conclusion applies outside a research and development environment. For example, to foster innovation the leader of a quality-improvement team should grant members as much freedom as organizational policy permits. "Freedom" might mean such things as discretion to switch budget lines or to bring another member onto the team who might add a creative spark.

An organization can enhance innovation by giving positive feedback when an innovation succeeds. Feedback should be supplemented with financial rewards. The financial reward is important in itself and also reflects recognition of outstanding performance. Many large firms have systematic programs for rewarding innovative suggestions with cash payments. At Zytic Corporation, a manufacturer of power supplies, employees receive modest cash awards for *implemented suggestions.* In addition, every idea submitted goes into a hat. A peer review team draws out a submitter's name each month, and that person gets a day off with pay. The winner also has the right to ask anybody in the company—including the president—to take over his or her job during the day off.[17]

Another key aspect of a creative organization is that managers minimize practices that stifle creativity. Seven such creativity dampeners for managers to avoid include:[18]

1. Expressing attitudes that preserve the status quo by using such clichés as "Don't rock the boat"; "Don't make waves"; and "If it ain't broke, don't fix it."
2. Policing employees by every device imaginable.
3. Saying yes to new ideas but not doing anything about them.
4. Being the exclusive spokesperson for everything in the area of responsibility.
5. Putting every idea through formal channels.
6. Responding to most suggestions for change with a pained look and saying, "But that will cost *money.*"
7. Promoting the "not-invented-here" syndrome (if the manager did not invent it, the manager will not consider it).

ORGANIZATIONAL PROGRAMS FOR IMPROVING CREATIVITY

Another aspect of the creative organization is formal programs or mechanisms for creativity improvement. Three such mechanisms are creativity training, widespread use of brainstorming, and suggestion programs.

CREATIVITY TRAINING. About 30 percent of medium- and large-sized American firms provide some sort of creativity training. An outstanding example is the Center for Creativity and Innovation at DuPont. A typical event at the center is a seminar on

LEARNING OBJECTIVE 5

Describe organizational programs for improving creativity.

creative thinking techniques. A representative training exercise used in many firms is the **pet-peeve technique.** The group thinks up as many complaints as possible about every facet of the department. The group is encouraged to take the views of external and internal customers, competitors, and suppliers. The group is also encouraged to throw in some imaginary complaints. "No holds barred" is the rule. A complaint might be "We set up a work schedule to suit our own convenience, not that of the customer." In addition, participants can solicit feedback on themselves from coworkers or from the people they serve. Diplomacy is required for giving constructive feedback, and the technique works best in an atmosphere of trust.

As with many creativity-training exercises, the pet-peeve technique loosens people up and provides information for improving operations. Participants can laugh at their own weaknesses in a friendly setting. Laughter is important because humor facilitates creativity. The pet-peeve technique can also be used outside the training program, as a method for improving productivity, quality, and service.

pet-peeve technique
A creativity-training (or problem-solving) exercise in which the group thinks up as many complaints as possible about every facet of the department.

BRAINSTORMING. The best-known method of improving creativity is **brainstorming.** This technique is a method of problem solving carried out by a group. Group members spontaneously generate numerous solutions to a problem, without being discouraged or controlled. Brainstorming produces many ideas; it is not a technique for working out details. People typically use brainstorming when looking for tentative solutions to nontechnical problems. In recent years, however, many information systems specialists have used brainstorming to improve computer programs and systems. By brainstorming, people improve their ability to think creatively. To achieve the potential advantages of brainstorming, the session must be conducted properly. Exhibit 6-4 presents the rules for conducting a brainstorming session.

Some types of business problems are well suited to brainstorming. These include coming up with a name for a new sports car, developing an idea for a corporate logo, identifying ways to attract new customers, and making concrete suggestions for cost cutting.

Brainstorming can be conducted electronically. In electronic brainstorming, group members simultaneously enter their suggestions into a computer. The ideas are distributed to the screens of other group members. Although the group members do not talk to each other, they are still able to build on each other's ideas and combine ideas.

Electronic brainstorming helps overcome certain problems encountered in traditional brainstorming. Shyness, domination by one or two members, and participants who loaf tend to to be less troublesome than in face-to-face sessions. Several experiments have shown that electronic brainstorming produces more useful ideas than the (usual) oral type. Furthermore, electronic brainstorming was found to be superior to individual brainstorming. This is significant because individual brainstorming usually results in more useful ideas than does the group type.[19]

brainstorming
A group method of solving problems, gathering information, and stimulating creative thinking. The basic technique is to generate numerous ideas through unrestrained and spontaneous participation by group members.

SUGGESTION PROGRAMS. To encourage creative thinking, companies throughout the world use **suggestion programs.** They are a formal method for collecting and analyzing employee's suggestions about processes, policies, products, and services. Typically, the employee who makes a suggestion that is implemented receives a percentage of the savings resulting from it. Useful suggestions save money, earn money, or increase safety or quality. A group of American Airlines mechanics received a $37,500 award for developing a tamper-proof airport security door. Other awards have run as high as $50,000.

suggestion program
A formal method for collecting and analyzing employees' suggestions about processes, policies, products, and services.

RULE 1	Enroll five to eight participants. If you have too few people, you lose the flood of ideas; if you have too many, members feel that their ideas are not important, and there can be too much chatter.	RULE 4	Encourage freewheeling. Welcome bizarre ideas. It is easier to tone down an idea than it is to think one up.
RULE 2	Give everybody the opportunity to generate alternative solutions to the problem. Have them call out these alternatives spontaneously. One useful modification of this procedure is for people to express their ideas one after another, to decrease possible confusion.	RULE 5	Strive for quantity rather than quality. The probability of discovering really good ideas increases in proportion to the number of ideas generated.
		RULE 6	Encourage members to piggyback, or build, on the ideas of others.
RULE 3	Do not allow criticism or value judgments during the brainstorming session. Make all suggestions welcome. Above all, members should not laugh derisively or make sarcastic comments about other people's ideas.	RULE 7	Record each idea or tape-record the session. Written notes should not identify the author of an idea because participants may worry about saying something foolish.
		RULE 8	After the brainstorming session, edit and refine the list of ideas and choose one or two for implementation.

Exhibit 6-4
Rules for Conducting a
Brainstorming Session

Committees evaluate submissions and make awards in suggestion programs. These programs foster creativity by offering financial rewards and by conferring prestige on employees whose ideas are implemented. In addition, suggestion programs help get employees involved in the success of their organization.

Suggestion programs are sometimes criticized because they collect loads of trivial suggestions and pay small awards just to humor employees. One employee, for example, was paid $50 for suggesting that the firm dust light bulbs more frequently to increase illumination.

SELF-HELP TECHNIQUES FOR IMPROVING CREATIVITY

In addition to participating in organizational programs for creativity improvement, you can help yourself become more creative. Becoming a more creative problem solver and decision maker requires that you increase the flexibility of your thinking. Reading about creativity improvement or attending one or two brainstorming sessions is insufficient. You must also practice the methods described in the following sections. As with any serious effort at self-improvement, you must exercise the self-discipline to implement these suggestions regulary. Creative people must also be self-disciplined to carefully concentrate on going beyond the obvious in solving problems.

LEARNING OBJECTIVE

Implement several suggestions for becoming a more creative problem solver.

TEN SPECIFIC CREATIVITY-BUILDING SUGGESTIONS. To develop habits of creative thinking, you must regularly practice the suggestions described in the list that follows.[20]

1. Keep track of your original ideas by maintaining an idea notebook. Few people have such uncluttered minds that they can recall all their past flashes of insight when they need them.
2. Stay current in your field. Having current facts at hand gives you the raw material to link information creatively. (In practice, creativity usually takes the form of associating ideas that are unassociated, such as associating the idea of selling movie tickets with the idea of selling through vending machines.)
3. Try to overcome approaches to problems that lock you into one way of doing things. Avoid becoming a prisoner of familiarity, someone who cannot think

BUSINESS OWNER IN ACTION: NAPOLEON BARRAGAN OF DIAL-A-MATTRESS

In 1978 Napoleon Barragan read an ad in the *New York Post* for "Dial-A-Steak." He thought to himself, If you can sell T-bones by telephone because it's easier and faster, why not do the same with mattresses? Skeptics told Barragan that people like to test out a mattress before they buy it, so his business idea was a loser. In reality, many people are willing to exchange testing for convenience when buying a mattress. Today Dial-A-Mattress is the largest direct marketer of mattresses, with annual sales volume of over $40 million. The company's marketing is facilitated by their telephone order number: 1-800-MATTRES.

Barragan's business strategy is explicit: Attract potential buyers with television and radio ads, then have knowledgeable sales representatives guide them through the purchase of a name-brand mattress. About 500 of the 5,000 calls that come in each day to the Queens, New York, headquarters result in sales. Many competitors have followed this basic marketing strategy, but Dial-A-Mattress still leads the pack.

Source: Based on facts reported in Jenny C. McCune, "A Perfect Sleeper," *Management Review* (August 1994): 19–24.

about doing things more than one way. The accompanying Business Owner in Action feature illustrates how a useful idea stemmed from thinking of marketing a product in a new way.

4. Participate in creative hobbies, such as doing puzzles and exercises or pursuing arts and crafts.

5. Improve your sense of humor, including your ability to laugh at your own mistakes. Humor helps reduce stress and tensions, and you will be more creative when you are relaxed.

6. Adopt a risk-taking attitude when you try to find creative solutions. You will inevitably fail a few times.

7. Develop a creative mental set; allow the foolish side of you to emerge. Creativity requires a degree of intellectual playfulness and immaturity. Many creative people are accomplished practical jokers.

8. Continually hunt for new ideas. A creativity expert says "I've worked with creative people in many industries, disciplines, and professions, and the really good ones are hunters. These people look outside their areas for ideas, and when they find an idea, they bring it back to their own area and apply it."[21]

9. Identify the times when you are most creative and attempt to accomplish most of your creative work during that period. Most people are at their peak of creative productivity after ample rest, so try to work on your most vexing problems at the start of the workday. Schedule routine decision making and paperwork for times when your energy level is lower than average.

10. Be curious about your environment. The person who routinely questions how things work (or why they do not work) is most likely to have an idea for improvement.

PLAY THE ROLES OF EXPLORER, ARTIST, JUDGE, AND LAWYER. One method for improving creativity incorporates many of the suggestions discussed so far. It requires you to adopt four roles in your thinking. First, you must be an explorer. Speak to people in different fields to get ideas you can use. Second, be an artist by stretching your imagination. Strive to spend about 5 percent of your day asking "what if?" questions. For example, an executive in a swimsuit company might ask, "What if the surgeon general decides that since sunbathing causes skin cancer, we have to put warning labels on bathing suits?" Third, know when to be a judge. After developing some wild ideas, evaluate them. Fourth, achieve results with your creative thinking by playing the role of a lawyer. Negotiate and find ways to implement your ideas within your field or place of work. You may spend months or years getting your best ideas implemented.[22]

Despite all the positive things that have been said about creativity, when an organization does not want to disturb the status quo, being creative can work to a person's disadvantage. Also, creativity for its own sake can result in discarding traditional, but useful, ideas.

GROUP PROBLEM SOLVING AND DECISION MAKING

LEARNING OBJECTIVE 7

Appreciate the value and potential limitations of group decision making.

We have described how individuals go about solving problems and making decisions. However, most major, nonroutine decisions in organizations are made by groups. **Group decisions** result when several people contribute to a final decision. Since participative management has become popular, an increasing number of decisions have been made by groups rather than individuals.

The group problem-solving and decision-making process is similar to the individual model in one important respect. Groups often work on problems by following the decision-making steps shown in Exhibit 6-2. Many groups, however, tend to ignore formal sequencing.

We will examine the advantages and disadvantages of group decision making, when it is useful, and present a general problem-solving method for groups. (In the following chapter we describe specialized techniques for group problem solving.)

> **group decision**
> *The process of several people contributing to a final decision.*

ADVANTAGES AND DISADVANTAGES OF GROUP DECISION MAKING

Because many people contribute, group decision making often results in high-quality solutions. It also makes people feel committed to the decision. However, the group approach consumes considerable time and may result in compromises that do not really solve the problem. Two stale jokes about group decision making reflect these disadvantages: "A camel is a horse designed by a committee," and "In a group meeting, minutes are taken and hours are lost."

The explosion of the space shuttle Challenger presents a serious example of the disadvantages of group decision making. According to several analyses of this incident, NASA managers were so committed to reaching space program objectives that they ignored safety warnings from people both inside and outside the agency. An internal NASA brief reported that astronauts and engineers were concerned about agency management's groupthink mentality. (This term will be explained later.) Furthermore, the brief characterized NASA managers as having the tendency not to reverse decisions or heed the advice of people outside management. (The analysis of the style was made several years before the Challenger explosion.)[23]

Seriously flawed group decisions have occurred so frequently in government and business that they have been extensively analyzed and researched. Well-publicized flawed group decisions include the arms-for-hostage deal (an illegal arms sale to Iran to fund Contras in Nicaragua) and the decision by Chrysler Corporation executives

Advantages	Disadvantages
1. Groups provide a larger sum of knowledge than would be accessible to individual members, thus leading to informed decisions.	1. Groups create pressures toward conformity in thinking and mediocrity in decision making. Group members sometimes engage in groupthink.
2. Group members can help each other overcome blocks in their thinking, which leads to creative solutions. Also, groups are less likely than individuals to get into ruts in their thinking.	2. A group cannot be held responsible. Group decision making may therefore result in buck passing.
3. Participation in problem solving and decision making increases the acceptance of decisions, which improves the motivation to implement the decision.	3. When people make decisions in a group, there is a pronounced tendency to accept the first satisficing decision that comes along.
4. Groups are willing to take greater risks than individuals, which leads to aggressive solutions to problems. (This illustrates the point that some of the advantages to group decision making can readily become disadvantages.)	4. Dominant members of the group sometimes make the major decision in a group setting. What appears to be a group decision may really be an individual decision.
5. Group members evaluate each other's thinking, so major errors are likely to be avoided.	5. Group decision making is time-consuming. Time may be wasted as the group deliberates or even as the leader tries to get the group together.
6. Groups are more effective than individuals in establishing objectives, generating alternatives, and evaluating alternatives, because the knowledge and viewpoints of all members are available to them.	6. Group decision making and problem solving may discourage highly intelligent and intuitive individuals who are too impatient to sit through meetings to deliberate over a problem they have already solved.

Exhibit 6-5
Advantages and Disadvantages of Group Problem Solving and Decision Making

groupthink
A psychological drive for consensus at any cost.

to sell as new cars, cars they had personally "sampled." The illusion of newness was created by cleaning up the cars and turning back the odometers.

Flawed decisions of the type just described have generally been attributed to **groupthink,** a psychological drive for consensus at any cost. Groupthink makes group members lose their ability to evaluate bad ideas critically. Glen Whyte believes that many instances of groupthink are caused by decision makers who see themselves as choosing between inevitable losses. The group believes that a sure loss will occur unless action is taken. Caught up in the turmoil of trying to make the best of a bad situation, the group takes a bigger risk than any individual member would.

The arms-for-hostages decision was perceived by those who made it as a choice between losses. The continued captivity of American citizens held hostage by terrorist groups was a certain loss. Making an arms deal with Iran created some hope of averting that loss, although the deal would most likely fail and create more humiliation.[24]

Groupthink can often be avoided if the team leader encourages group members to express doubts and criticisms of proposed solutions. It is also helpful to show by example that you are willing to accept criticism. Exhibit 6-5 summarizes the key advantages and disadvantages of group problem solving and decision making.

WHEN TO USE GROUP DECISION MAKING

Because group decision making takes more time and people than individual decision making, it should not be used indiscriminately. Group decision making should be reserved for nonroutine decisions of reasonable importance. Too many managers use the group method for solving such minor questions as "What should be on the menu at the company picnic?"

1. **Identify the problem.** Describe specifically what the problem is and how it manifests itself.
2. **Clarify the problem.** If group members do not perceive the problem in the same way, they will offer divergent solutions. Make sure everyone shares the same definition of the problem.
3. **Analyze the cause.** To convert "what is" into "what we want," the group must understand the causes of the specific problem and find ways to overcome them.
4. **Search for alternative solutions.** Remember that multiple alternative solutions can be found to most problems.
5. **Select alternatives.** Identify the criteria that solutions must meet, and then discuss the pros and cons of the proposed alternatives. No solution should be laughed at or scorned.
6. **Plan for implementation.** Decide what actions are necessary to carry out the chosen solution.
7. **Clarify the contract.** The contract is a restatement of what group members have agreed to do, and it includes deadlines for accomplishment.
8. **Develop an action plan.** Specify who does what and when to carry out the contract.
9. **Provide evaluation and accountability.** After the plan is implemented, reconvene to discuss its progress and hold people accountable for results that have not been achieved.

Source: Derived from Andrew E. Schwartz and Joy Levin, "Better Group Decision Making," *Supervisory Management* (June 1990):4.

Exhibit 6-6
Steps for Effective Group Decision Making

Aside from being used to enhance the quality of decisions, group decision making is often used to gain acceptance for a decision. If people contribute to a decision, they are more likely to be committed to its implementation.

A GENERAL METHOD OF GROUP PROBLEM SOLVING

When a group of workers at any level gather to solve a problem, they typically hold a discussion rather than rely on a formal decision-making technique. These general meetings are likely to produce the best results when they follow the decision-making steps. Exhibit 6-6 recommends steps for conducting group decision making. These steps are quite similar to the decision-making steps presented in Exhibit 6-2.

In addition, a problem-solving group should also follow suggestions for conducting an effective meeting. Four of these suggestions particularly related to problem solving are:

1. *Have a specific agenda and adhere to it.* Meetings are more productive when an agenda is planned and followed carefully. People should see the agenda in advance so they can prepare for the session.
2. *Rely on qualified members.* Groups often arrive at poor solutions because the contributors do not have the necessary knowledge and interest. An uninformed person is typically a poor decision maker. Also, a person who attends a meeting reluctantly will sometimes agree to any decision just to bring the meeting to a close.
3. *Have the leader share decision-making authority.* A key attribute of an effective problem-solving meeting is a leader who shares authority. Unless authority is shared, the members are likely to believe that the hidden agenda of the meeting is to seek approval for the meeting leader's decision.
4. *Provide summaries for each major point.* Decision-making quality improves when members clearly understand the arguments that have been advanced for and against each alternative. Summarizing major points can help. Summaries also keep the meeting focused on major issues, because minor issues are excluded from the summary.

SUMMARY OF KEY POINTS

1
Differentiate between programmed and nonprogrammed decisions.
Unique decisions are nonprogrammed decisions, whereas programmed decisions are repetitive or routine, and made according to a specific procedure.

2
Explain the steps involved in making a nonprogrammed decision.
The recommended steps for solving problems and making nonprogrammed decisions call for a problem solver to identify and diagnose the problem, develop creative alternative solutions, evaluate the alternatives, choose an alternative, implement the decision, evaluate and control, and repeat the process if necessary. Making strategic decisions with speed is associated with a firm achieving superior performance.

3
Understand the major factors influencing decision making in organizations.
People vary in their decision-making ability, and the situation can influence the quality of decisions. Factors that influence the quality of decisions are crisis conditions; intuition; personality and intelligence; the quality and accessibility of information; political considerations; degree of uncertainty; values of the decision maker; and procrastination.

4
Understand the nature of creativity and how it contributes to managerial work.
Creativity is the process of developing novel ideas that can be put into action. Many aspects of managerial work, including problem solving and establishing effective work groups, require creativity. Creative people are generally more open and flexible than their less creative counterparts. They are also better able to make paradigm shifts and think laterally (divergently).

Creativity requires ability, enjoyment of the task itself, and certain mental activities. An environmental need should be present to stimulate a creativity goal. Certain managerial and organizational practices foster creativity. The most important characteristic of the creative organization is an atmosphere that encourages creative expression. The organization should give positive feedback for innovation and offer financial rewards.

5
Describe organizational programs for improving creativity.
One organizational strategy for improving creativity is to conduct creativity training, such as a session that uses the pet-peeve technique. Brainstorming is the best-known method of improving creativity. The method can also be conducted electronically by people simultaneously sharing ideas by computer. Suggestion programs are another method of encouraging employee creativity.

6
Implement several suggestions for becoming a more creative problem solver.
You can improve your own creativity by engaging in creative hobbies, taking risks, and hunting for new ideas. One approach for improving creativity is to take the roles of an explorer, artist, judge, and lawyer. Each role relates to a different aspect of creative thinking.

7
Appreciate the value and potential limitations of group decision making.
Group decision making often results in high-quality solutions, because many people contribute. It also helps people feel more committed to the decision. However, the group approach consumes considerable time, may result in compromise solutions that do not really solve the problem, and may encourage groupthink. Groupthink occurs when consensus becomes so important that group members lose their ability to evaluate ideas. It is likely to occur when decision makers have to choose between inevitable losses.

General problem-solving groups are likely to produce the best results when the decision-making steps are followed closely. Other steps for conducting an effective meeting include (1) adhering to an agenda, (2) relying on qualified members, (3) sharing decision-making authority, and (4) providing summaries of major points.

KEY TERMS AND PHRASES

Problem *pg. 122*
Decision *pg. 122*

Nonprogrammed Decision *pg. 122*
Programmed Decision *pg. 122*

QUESTIONS

1. Describe a problem a manager might face, and point out the actual and ideal conditions in relation to this problem.
2. Give two examples of decisions you have faced or will be facing that warrant completing the problem-solving and decision-making steps.
3. How does total quality management and empowerment influence the proportion of nonprogrammed decisions made by lower-ranking workers?
4. Explain the term *bounded rationality* in your own words, and illustrate how it might apply to your job or life.
5. Why is the idea of having a Cadillac sports utility vehicle a paradigm shift?
6. In what way are suggestion programs similar to the employee-involvement groups used in total quality management?
7. Why does solving problems in a group often produce higher-quality decisions than independent problem solving?

SKILL-BUILDING EXERCISE 6-A: BRAINSTORMING

GROUP ACTIVITY After studying the rules for brainstorming described on page 135 of this chapter organize into groups to brainstorm one of the following problems:

1. How can a person get noticed by upper management?
2. How can a manager cut costs yet still maintain a productive and satisfied group?
3. How can a company cut down on water consumption?
4. How can we get more people to buy stepladders?

SKILL-BUILDING EXERCISE 6-B: THE FORCED-ASSOCIATION TECHNIQUE

A widely used method for releasing creativity is to make forced associations between the properties of two objects to solve a problem. Apply the method by working in small groups. One group member selects a word at random from a dictionary, textbook, or newspaper. Next, the group lists all the properties and attributes of this word. Assume you randomly chose the word *rock*. Among its attributes are "durable," "low-priced," "abundant in supply," "decorative," and "expensive to ship."

You then force-fit these properties to the problem you are facing. Your team might be attempting to improve the quality of an office desk chair. Reviewing the properties of the rock might give you the idea to make the seat covering more durable because this is a quality hot point.

Think of a problem of your own, or perhaps the instructor will assign you one. Another possibility is to use as your problem the question how to expand the market for snow tires. The groups might work for about 15 minutes. To make the technique proceed smoothly, keep up the random search until you hit a noun or adjective. Prepositions usually do not work well in the forced-association technique. Group leaders share their findings with the rest of the class.

VIDEO DISCUSSION QUESTIONS

1. What evidence does Martinez of Sears give of using decision making based on facts? **[Sears]**
2. Which influences on decision making might interfere with a thorough analysis of the poisonous gas leak? **[Bhopal]**
3. What were the major decisions facing Gerstner when he was appointed as CEO of IBM? **[Gerstner]**

CASE PROBLEM 6-A: COPING WITH THE CLEAN AIR ACT

The Clean Air Act of 1990 requires states that have areas with unacceptable ozone and carbon monoxide levels to reduce air pollution. Eleven states are considered to have unacceptable levels of these two pollutants, including parts of California, Connecticut, Delaware, Illinois, Indiana, Maryland, New Jersey, New York, Pennsylvania, Texas, and Wisconsin. Various state officials have said that the Clean Air Act could affect approximately 5,000 employers and 3.5 million employees.

Given that automobiles are responsible for 90 percent of carbon monoxide pollution, the act requires employers with more than 100 employees at a worksite to reduce the number of autos (and trucks used as autos) arriving between 6:00 A.M. and 10:00 A.M. Companies with fewer than 33 employees arriving during that time are excluded.

The goal of the Clean Air Act is to increase the average passenger occupancy (APO) by 25 percent in states that are exceeding the undesirable levels of pollutants. The APO is calculated by dividing the number of employees by the number of vehicles driven to work. Each company covered by the law must file a compliance plan with the state, clearly indicating how they will meet their average vehicle occupancy target. The states will then enforce these vehicle reduction plans.

One method tried so far to comply with standards is to charge employees for parking. The city of Bellevue, Washington, began charging for parking in 1989, when the city had only 200 parking spaces for 360 employees. The coordinator of the parking program at Bellevue said that charging was painful, but effective.

Tom Hanlon is the marketing and sales director for the Transit Center, a New York-based public-private alliance to promote mass transit. He says, "Companies will look like the bad guys. They will have to govern how employees live outside the office."

CASE QUESTIONS

1. What alternatives can you suggest for increasing the average passenger occupancy?
2. What alternatives can you suggest for monitoring the fact that employees are really lowering the APO?
3. What other ways for reducing vehicle-created pollutants can you suggest other than lowering the APO?

Source: Catherine Romano, "Business Copes with the Clean Air Conundrum," *Management Review* (February 1994): 34–37.

CASE PROBLEM 6-B: THE CORPORATE INNOVATORS

AMI is a $3-billion conglomerate. Its primary businesses involve entertainment, cosmetics and beauty aids, and educational services. The executive vice president, Brett Flagstone, is the manager most directly responsible for investigating new business opportunities for AMI. Typically, these are thriving business organizations that AMI takes over on a friendly basis. AMI begins by buying up much of the stock available for a firm AMI management wants to acquire. Soon thereafter, AMI makes a formal bid to purchase a controlling interest in the firm.

Recently, top managers of AMI observed that sales in many of their existing firms had begun to stabilize or decline. For example, one of their most recent acquisitions, a large pharmaceutical firm, lost $1 million in one year.

To generate new ideas for business expansion, Brett Flagstone assembled the Tiger Team. Members of this select group of eight employees were told they would have considerable latitude in investigating new business opportunities. Nina Morales was appointed project leader of the Tiger Team. She and her teammates were told they should not restrict their thinking to any one type of business expansion. Furthermore, they were encouraged to let their minds wander and to overcome traditional ideas about how a conglomerate (a large firm that is really a collection of smaller firms) should conduct business.

Morales and the other team members were ecstatic about being part of such an elite corporate group. Much to their delight, they were assigned a small office 10 miles away from corporate headquarters. They were given the authority to hire two full-time assistants and assigned a lavish budget for entertainment and any office equipment they needed.

Two months after the Tiger Team was launched, team members made their first presentation to management. They recommended that AMI enter the boating business by acquiring a nationwide boat-rental firm. The Tiger Team noted that leisure time was becoming increasingly important and that interest in boating had become a permanent part of the culture. Brett Flagstone delivered the corporate verdict on the team's first idea: "Your boat proposal has sunk. We think AMI would take a bath on this one. Back to dry land, and good luck."

Morales told the group not to be discouraged, that no new venture group can get all its ideas accepted. After a two-day brainstorming session, the Tiger Team developed a new idea. It proposed the formation of a company called Second Chance, whose work force would be composed of former prisoners. The firm would manufacture basic low-technology household furniture, such as kitchen tables, bookcases, and umbrella stands. Its advertising would focus on the idea that AMI was helping society with one of its thorniest problems by providing former prisoners an opportunity to learn new skills and hold useful jobs.

Fifteen minutes into the presentation about Second Chance, Flagstone stopped the Tiger Team. "Enough's enough," he said emphatically. "Our stockholders are neither social workers nor criminologists. They will not tolerate an idea this farfetched. I assume you would also have these ex-cons keeping the books of the firm. I, in no way, want to discourage your creativity, but please get back to your think tank."

Morales said to the group, "Only two of our ideas have been shot down so far. I still think Second Chance had good possibilities, but there's not much we can do. Top management has the final say."

Three weeks later, the Tiger Team received the following memo from Flagstone:

TO: Nina Morales and the Tiger Team
FROM: Brett Flagstone, Executive Vice President
DATE: May 10, 19—
SUBJECT: Accountability for results

Soon you will be approaching the completion of the first quarter of your existence. As you know, your charter is to develop innovative ideas for expanding the business of AMI. By the time you have been in operation for six months, we would like to see a comprehensive report of your activities. We are giving you substantial advance notice to guide you in data collection for your status report. Please include the following items in your report:

1. How will the corporation benefit from your continued existence?
2. What will be the likely return on investment from the Tiger Team?
3. What are all the ideas you have developed? (Include those you have rejected.)

I will be in touch with you in person to discuss this matter.

Several days later, Flagstone did get in touch with Morales. He told her, "Don't worry at all about the report. It's just a formality. The executive group and I just want to know what we're getting for our money. By the way, I'll be meeting with you every two weeks to discuss how the Tiger Team is progressing. We all have so much faith in you that we're eager to hear how you are doing."

Later that day, Morales relayed the substance of her meeting with Flagstone to the rest of the Tiger Team. Stan Golden, one of the team members, was the first to respond. Scratching his head, he said: "Now I know why they call us the Tiger Team. Brett Flagstone cracks his whip and we're supposed to stand up on our hind legs and perform stunts. Each week, I'm beginning to feel our team is a little less elite."

Clair Benson had a different reaction. "Brett Flagstone is just doing what has to be done. AMI works under a goals philosophy. Why should we be exempt just because we're a creative group?"

CASE QUESTIONS

1. What is your evaluation of the Tiger Team concept as a way of encouraging corporate innovation?
2. How effective do you think Flagstone is in encouraging creativity?
3. How should Morales respond to Flagstone's memorandum and request for biweekly meetings?
4. What problems does the Tiger Team face, and what decisions must its members make?
5. Do you think the Tiger Team was given too many luxuries? What effect do you think the privileges had on the team members?

CASE PROBLEM 6-C: WHERE TO PUT MY NEXT MAIL BOXES ETC.?

Mail Boxes Etc. is a nationwide franchise offering a variety of services to individuals and small businesses. Your local Mail Boxes Etc. can wrap and ship packages, make photocopies, and collect your mail. Some Mail Boxes

Etc. locations offer concierge services such as picking up flowers, arranging limousines, and collecting dry cleaning. Concierge services are offered primarily at Mail Box sites in office buildings.

Many Mail Boxes Etc. franchisees own multiple locations of these profitable, efficient units. One such multiple franchise owner is Audrey Ritt, a Michigan resident. She was recently contemplating opening another franchise. She knew that any location she chose would have to meet with the approval of the franchisor. Ritt also knew that the market for the types of services Mail Boxes Etc. offers has become highly competitive.

Ritt believes strongly that the amount of consumer traffic surrounding a Mail Box Etc. store is more important than the size of the unit. She believes that a cubbyhole in Chicago's O'Hare Airport would beat a spacious location in an infrequently visited mall. She therefore is giving careful thought to suggesting a new location for her next Mail Boxes Etc.

CASE QUESTIONS

1. What problem-solving process should Ritt use to choose her next location?
2. Working in a group, or by yourself, take a stand and recommend a new Mail Boxes Etc. location for Ritt.

Source: As reported in Carol Steinberg, "Break All the Rules," *Success* (October 1995): 83.

ANSWER TO THE LATERAL THINKING PROBLEM

She suggested that the driver let some air out of the truck's tires. He let out enough air to lower the truck by the small amount required to let it pass under the bridge. This problem requires lateral thinking because presumably other alternative solutions might be found.

REFERENCES

1. "Hidden Forces," *Success* (April 1995): 12.
2. Stefan Wally and J. Robert Baum, "Personal and Structural Determinants of the Pace of Strategic Decision Making," *Academy of Management Journal* (August 1994): 932–956.
3. John M. Ivancevich, James H. Donnelly, Jr., and James L. Gibson, *Managing for Performance: An Introduction to the Process of Managing*, Revised Edition (Burr Ridge, IL: Irwin, 1983), 83–84.
4. Herbert A. Simon, "Rational Choice and the Structure of the Environment," *Psychological Review*, 63, 1956, pp. 129–138; John W. Payne, James R. Bettman, and Eric J. Johnson, *The Adaptive Decision Maker* (New York: Cambridge University Press, 1993).
5. Dean Tjosovold, "Effect of Crisis Orientation on Managers' Approach to Controversy in Decision Making," *Academy of Management Journal* (March 1984): 137.
6. James E. Driskell and Eduardo Salas, "Group Decision Making Under Stress," *Journal of Applied Psychology* (June 1991): 473–478.
7. Michael A. West and James L. Farr (ed.), *Innovation and Creativity at Work: Psychological and Organizational Strategies* (New York: John Wiley, 1990).
8. Richard Sharwood Gates, "The Gordian Knot: A Parable for Decision Makers," *Management Review* (December 1990): 47.
9. Charles A. O'Reilly III, "Variations in Decision Makers' Use of Information Sources: The Impact of Quality and Accessibility of Information," *Academy of Management Journal* (December 1982): 769.
10. Andrew J. DuBrin, *Getting It Done: The Transforming Power of Self-Discipline* (Princeton, NJ: Peterson's/Pacesetter Books, 1995): 49–71.
11. Research cited in Nancy Ross-Flanigan, "Pro-Creative: Free the Original Thinker Inside Yourself and Life Will Be More Fulfilling, Experts Say," Knight-Ridder News Service (8 May 1995).
12. Paul Sloane, *Lateral Thinking Puzzlers* (New York, Sterling Publishing, 1992).
13. Christana E. Shalley, "Effects of Productivity Goals, Creativity Goals, and Personal Discretion on Individual Creativity," *Journal of Applied Psychology* (April 1991): 179–180.
14. Daniel G. Tear as quoted in *Issues & Observations* (February 1981): 5.
15. Richard W. Woodman, John E. Sawyer, and Ricky W. Griffin, "Toward a Theory of Organizational Creativity," *Academy of Management Review* (April 1993): 306–308.
16. Teresa M. Amabile and S. S. Gryskiewicz, *Creativity in the R & D Laboratory* (Greesboro, NC: Center for Creative Leadership, 1987).
17. *Award Winning Quality: Strategies from the Winners of the Malcom Baldrige National Quality Award* (Waterford, CT: Bureau of Business Practices, Prentice Hall, 1992).
18. Gareth Morgan, *Creative Organizational Theory: A Resourcebook* (Newbury Park, CA: Sage, 1990).
19. Alan R. Dennis and Joseph S. Valacich, "Computer Brainstorms: More Heads Are Better than One," *Journal of Applied Psychology* (August 1993): 531–537; R. Brent Gallupe, William H. Cooper, Mary-Liz Grise, and Lana M. Bastianutti, "Blocking Electronic Brainstorms," *Journal of Applied Psychology* (February 1994): 77–86.
20. Eugene Raudsepp, "Exercises for Creative Growth," *Success* (February 1981): 46–47; Andrew J. DuBrin, *Reengineering Survival Guide: Managing and Succeeding in the Changing Workplace* (Cincinnati, OH: Thomson Executive Press, 1996), 57–69.
21. Robert S. Wieder, "How to Get Great Ideas," *Success* (November 1983): 30.
22. "Be A Creative Problem Solver," *Executive Strategies* (6 June 1989): 1–2.
23. Kenneth A. Kovach and Barry Render, "NASA Managers and Challenger: A Profile of Possible Explanation," *Personnel* (April 1987): 40.
24. Glen Whyte, "Decision Failures: Why They Occur and How to Prevent Them," *Academy of Management Executive* (August 1991): 25.

CHAPTER 7

Specialized Techniques for Planning and Decision Making

LEARNING OBJECTIVES

After studying this chapter and doing the exercises, you should be able to:

1
Explain the use of forecasting techniques in planning.

2
Describe how to use Gantt charts, milestone charts, and PERT planning techniques.

3
Describe how to use break-even analysis, payoff matrices, and decision trees for problem solving and decision making.

4
Describe how to manage inventory by using materials requirement planning (MRP), the economic-order quantity (EOQ), and just-in-time (JIT) techniques.

5
Describe how to use the nominal-group technique.

Greg Booth, Dallas

A few fashion seasons ago, Bloomingdale executive Kalman Ruttenstein telephoned Allen Schwartz, the CEO of ABS USA. His company manufactures classic fashions for working women. Ruttenstein had spotted a revival of a hot item—flared-bottom pants. He knew that ABS USA was one of the few manufacturers with the resources to rapidly process the order Bloomingdale's had in mind. Within eight working days, the company had 300 bell-bottom pants on Bloomingdale's floor. • ABS USA went on to sell more than 10,000 pairs of the flare pants. Inspired by the company's success in responding so quickly to customer needs and selling high-fashion clothing, Schwartz now specializes in cutting-edge trends. Featuring new fashions has also increased traffic in the 11 retail stores owned by ABS. • Schwartz's astonishingly short cycle times are possible because of the $2 million fabric collection he keeps at his finger tips. "I can get my hands on fabric in five minutes," says Schwartz. Part of the company's rapid cycle times are attributed to long-term relationships with domestic contractors, who are kept working year-round. ABS manufactures everything domestically to save time. "It may be more expensive for me to manufacture everything here," Schwartz admits. "But I'm selling service. ABS is always first with the items."[1]

The women's clothing executive just described has the creative talent to spot trends that will capture the interest of consumers. Yet part of Schwartz's success is also attributable to managing inventory carefully. He and his manufacturing team keep a big enough inventory on hand to capitalize on sudden opportunities. Effective inventory management is but one of several specialized techniques for planning and decision making described in this chapter.

To make planning and decision making more accurate, a variety of techniques based on the scientific method, mathematics, and statistics have been developed. **Management science** (or **decision sciences**) is the field of study dealing with quantified planning and decision making. The major purpose of management science is to provide managers with a scientific basis for solving problems and making planning and operating decisions.

This chapter will provide sufficient information for you to acquire basic skills in several popular techniques for planning and decision making. (You can find more detail about these techniques in courses and books about production and operations management and managerial accounting.) In addition, this chapter will describe a decision-making technique usually associated with the behavioral approach rather than the management science approach: the nominal-group technique.

Managers often rely on quantitative tools for valuable assistance in making decisions. Despite their scientific appearance, however, specialized planning and decision-making techniques cannot replace managerial judgment. The numbers fed into the equations used in these methods are usually subjective estimates made by people. If the subjective estimates are incorrect, no amount of quantitative analysis will yield a valid guide for decision making.

management science (decision sciences)
The field of study dealing with quantified planning and decision making.

FORECASTING METHODS

LEARNING OBJECTIVE 1

Explain the use of forecasting techniques in planning.

All planning includes making forecasts, or predicting future events. The forecasts used in strategic planning are especially difficult to make because they involve long-range trends. Unknown factors might crop up between the time the forecast is made and the time about which predictions are made. This section will describe approaches to and types of forecasting.

QUALITATIVE AND QUANTITATIVE APPROACHES

Forecasts can be based on both qualitative and quantitative information. Most of the forecasting done for strategic planning relies on a combination of both. *Qualitative* methods of forecasting consist mainly of subjective hunches. For example, an experienced executive might predict that the high cost of housing will create a demand for small, less expensive homes, even though this trend cannot be quantified. One qualitative method is a **judgmental forecast,** a prediction based on a collection of subjective opinions. It relies on analysis of subjective inputs from a variety of sources, including consumer surveys, sales representatives, managers, and panels of experts. For instance, a group of potential home buyers might be asked how they would react to the possibility of purchasing a compact, less expensive home.

Quantitative forecasting methods involve either the extension of historical data or the development of models to identify the cause of a particular outcome. A widely used historical approach is **time-series analysis.** This technique is simply an analysis of a sequence of observations that have taken place at regular intervals

judgmental forecast
A qualitative forecasting method based on a collection of subjective opinions.

time-series analysis
An analysis of a sequence of observations that have taken place at regular intervals over a period of time (hourly, weekly, monthly, and so forth).

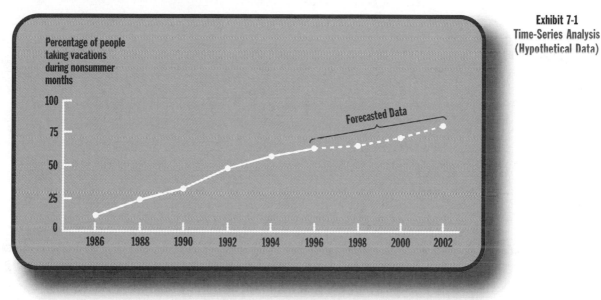

Exhibit 7-1
Time-Series Analysis
(Hypothetical Data)

over a period of time (hourly, weekly, monthly, and so forth). The underlying assumption of this approach is that the future will be much like the past. Exhibit 7-1 shows a basic example of a time-series analysis chart. This information might be used to make forecasts about when people would be willing to take vacations. Such forecasts would be important for the resort and travel industry.

Linear regression is a quantitative method of predicting the relationship of changes in one variable to changes in another. For example, suppose a resort-industry economist wants to predict the influence of age on the number of vacations people take. Because the median age of the North American population is increasing, this prediction could be useful for business planning.

Many firms use quantitative and qualitative approaches to forecasting. Forecasting begins with a quantitative prediction, which provides basic data about a future trend. An example of a quantitative prediction is the forecast of a surge in demand for handheld digital assistants. Next the qualitative forecast is added to the quantitative forecast, somewhat as a validity check. For example, a quantitative forecast might predict that, if the current growth trend continues, every household in North America will contain two handheld digital assistants by 2004. The quantitative forecast is then adjusted according to the subjective data supplied by the qualitative forecast. In this case, it could be reasoned that the growth trend was extrapolated too aggressively.

> **linear regression**
> *A quantitative method of predicting the relationship of changes in one variable to changes in another.*

TYPES OF FORECASTS

Three types of forecasts are used most widely: economic, sales, and technological. Each of these forecasts can be made by using both qualitative and quantitative methods.

ECONOMIC FORECASTING. No single factor is more important in managerial planning than predicting the level of future business activity. Strategic planners in large organizations rely often on economic forecasts made by specialists they hire. Planners in smaller firms are more likely to rely on government forecasts. However, forecasts about the general economy do not necessarily correspond to business activity related to a particular product or service.

MANAGER IN ACTION: TOM CORCORAN, SKI MOGUL

Tom Corcoran runs one of New England's largest ski resorts, Waterville Valley, in New Hampshire. Outside his office, a visitor can hear the roar of compressed air and water showering human-made snow onto downhill trails, building a base for the new ski season. A sign over Corcoran's desk reads: "The ski business is an odd little segment of the industry that is better left to people who deeply care about it, and who are willing to have a less predictable bottom line than most big corporations will tolerate."

The Waterville Valley management team was contacted as they prepared for the 1995–96 ski season. They were still enjoying the excitement of hoping that the economic and atmospheric climates would be favorable for skiing. The ski industry in the United States and Canada suffered from one of the mildest winters in history during the 1994–95 season.

"I read that in *Fortune* magazine about twenty years ago and had it framed," said Corcoran, a Harvard MBA who was once on the U.S. Olympic ski team. "I can't say that the ski industry has changed much since. It's a business for entrepreneurs. Large corporations have tended not to do well in it."

Among the companies that have tried the ski business and then exited are Twentieth Century-Fox Film Corp. (Aspen and Breckenridge, Colorado), the Chrysler Corp. (Big Sky, Montana), and Scott Paper Co. (Squaw Mountain, Maine). An exception to this trend is the Keystone-Arapahoe resort owned by Ralston Purina Co., located in Colorado near the Continental Divide.

"A ski area is not going to produce a stream of uninterrupted earnings that you can rely on for dividends," Corcoran said. "The business is seasonal. It's a weather-sensitive business, perhaps more so than farming. And it attracts managers who are individualistic and independent, not the kind of people who fit the corporate mold."

Source: As reported in John Fry, "Ski Business Works Best for Entrepreneurs," *The New York Times* (20 December 1987); updated with interview, July 26, 1995.

A major factor in the accuracy of forecasts is time span: Short-range predictions are more accurate than long-range predictions. Strategic planning is long-range planning, and many strategic plans have to be revised frequently to accommodate changes in business activity. For example, a sudden recession may abort plans for diversification into new products and services.

SALES FORECASTING. The sales forecast is usually the primary planning document for a business. Even if the general economy is robust, an organization needs a promising sales forecast before it can be aggressive about capitalizing on new opportunities. Strategic planners themselves may not be involved in making sales forecasts, but to develop master plans they rely on forecasts that the marketing unit makes. For instance, the major tobacco companies have embarked on strategic plans to diversify into a number of nontobacco businesses, such as soft drinks. An important factor in the decision to implement this strategic plan was a forecast of decreased demand for tobacco products in the domestic market. The cause for decreased demand will be health concerns of the public.

Sales forecasting is a risky business, even when conducted by the most astute planners. Marketing executives in large corporations generally prefer markets in which forecasts can be made accurately. Entrepreneurs in smaller businesses, however, are often willing to conduct business in markets where sales forecasts are less accurate, as the accompanying Manager in Action feature illustrates.

TECHNOLOGICAL FORECASTING. A technological forecast predicts what types of technological changes will take place. Technological forecasts allow a firm to adapt to new technologies and thus stay competitive. For example, forecasts made in the

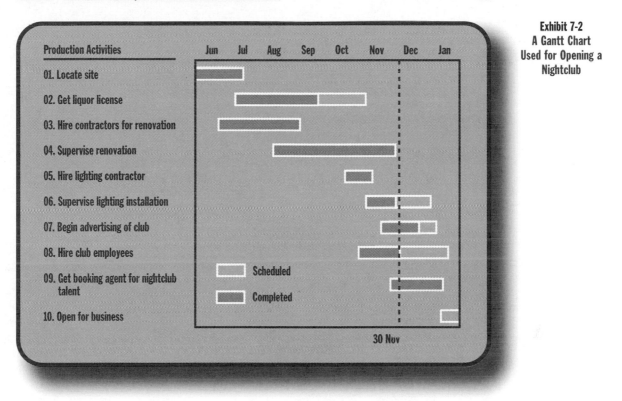

Exhibit 7-2
A Gantt Chart
Used for Opening a
Nightclub

late 1970s about the growth of robotics prompted many manufacturing firms to purchase robots to control manufacturing costs. The actual growth of robotics proved to be slower than predicted, because robots did not inevitably lead to productivity gains. In some cases, however, a firm that delays shifting to a new technology until competitors have tried it loses in the marketplace.

GANTT CHARTS AND MILESTONE CHARTS

Two basic tools for monitoring the progress of scheduled projects are Gantt charts and milestone charts. Closely related to each other, they both help a manager keep track of whether activities are completed on time.

GANTT CHARTS

A **Gantt chart** graphically depicts the planned and actual progress of work over the period of time encompassed by a project. Gantt charts are especially useful for scheduling one-time projects such as constructing buildings, making films, and launching satellites. Charts of this type are also called time-and-activity charts, because time and activity are the two key variables they consider. Time is plotted on the horizontal axis; activities are listed on the vertical axis.

Despite its simplicity, the Gantt chart is a valuable and widely used control technique. It is also the foundation of more sophisticated types of time-related charts, such as the PERT chart, which will be described later.

Exhibit 7-2 shows a Gantt chart used to schedule the opening of a nightclub. Gantt charts used for most other purposes would have a similar format. At the

LEARNING OBJECTIVE

Describe how to use Gantt charts, milestone charts, and PERT planning techniques.

Gantt chart
A chart that depicts the planned and actual progress of working during the life of a project.

Exhibit 7-3
A Milestone Chart Used
for Opening a Nightclub

Production Activities	Jun	Jul	Aug	Sep	Oct	Nov	Dec	Jan
01. Locate site	1 2 3							
02. Get liquor license		4	5 5	6	7	8 9		10
03. Hire contractors for renovation			11	12	13			
04. Supervise renovation		14	15	16	17	18	19	
05. Hire lighting contractor					20	21		
06. Supervise lighting installation						22	23 24	
07. Begin advertising of club						25	26	
08. Hire club employees						27 28	29	30
09. Get booking agent for nightclub talent							31	32
10. Open for business								33

Milestones to be Accomplished

-
-
-

27. Speak to friends and acquaintances about job openings
28. Put ad in local newspapers
29. Conduct interviews with applicants and check references of best candidates
30. Make job offers to best candidates

-
-
-

33. Have grand-opening celebration 5 January

planning phase of the project, the manager lays out the schedule by using rectangular boxes. As each activity is completed, the appropriate box is shaded. At any given time, the manager can see which activities have been completed on time. For example, if the club does not have a liquor license by 30 November, the activity would be declared behind schedule.

The Gantt chart presented here is quite basic. On most Gantt charts, the bars are movable strips of plastic. Different colors indicate scheduled and actual progress. Mechanical boards with pegs to indicate scheduled dates and actual progress can also be used. Some managers and specialists are now using computer graphics to prepare their own high-tech Gantt charts.

Because Gantt charts are used to monitor progress, they are also control devices. When the chart shows that the liquor license activity has fallen behind schedule, the manager can investigate the problem and solve it. The Gantt chart gives a convenient overall view of the progress made against the schedule. However, its disadvantage is that it does not furnish enough details about the subactivities that need to be performed to accomplish each general item.

MILESTONE CHARTS

A **milestone chart** is an extension of the Gantt chart. It provides a listing of the subactivities that must be completed to accomplish the major activities listed on the vertical axis. A milestone is the completion of one phase of an activity. The inclusion of milestones adds to the value of a Gantt chart as a scheduling and control technique. Each milestone serves as another checkpoint on progress. In Exhibit 7-3, the Gantt chart for opening a nightclub has been expanded into a milestone chart. The numbers in each rectangle represent milestones. A complete chart would list each of the 33 milestones. In Exhibit 7-3 only the milestones for hiring employees and the opening date are listed.

> **milestone chart**
> *An extension of the Gantt chart that provides a listing of the subactivities that must be completed to accomplish the major activities listed on the vertical axis.*

PROGRAM EVALUATION AND REVIEW TECHNIQUE

Gantt and milestone charts are basic scheduling tools, exceeded in simplicity only by a "to do" list. A more complicated method of scheduling activities and events uses a network model. The model depicts all the interrelated events that must take place for a project to be completed. The most widely used network-modeling tool is the **program evaluation and review technique** (PERT). It is used to track the planning activities required to complete a large-scale, nonrepetitive project.

A scheduling technique such as PERT is useful when certain tasks have to be completed before others if the total project is to be completed on time. In the nightclub example, the site of the club must be specified and a lease drawn up before the owner can apply for a liquor license. (The liquor commission will grant a license only after approving a specific location.) The PERT diagram indicates such a necessary sequence of events.

PERT is used most often in engineering and construction projects. It has also been applied to such business problems as marketing campaigns, company relocations, and convention planning.

> **program evaluation and review technique (PERT)**
> *A network model used to track the planning activities required to complete a large-scale, nonrepetitive project. It depicts all of the interrelated events that must take place.*

KEY PERT CONCEPTS

Two concepts lie at the core of PERT: event and activity. An **event** is a point of decision or the accomplishment of a task. Events are also called milestones. The events involved in the merger of two companies would include sending out announcements to shareholders, changing the company name, and letting customers know of the merger.

An **activity** is the physical and mental effort required to complete an event. One activity in the merger example is working with a public-relations firm to arrive at a suitable name for the new company. Activities that have to be accomplished in the nightclub example include supervising contractors and interviewing job applicants.

> **event**
> *In the PERT method, a point of decision or the accomplishment of a task.*

> **activity**
> *In the PERT method, the physical and mental effort required to complete an event.*

STEPS INVOLVED IN PREPARING A PERT NETWORK. The events and activities included in a PERT network are laid out graphically, as shown in Exhibit 7-4. Preparing a PERT network consists of four steps:

1. Prepare a list of all the activities necessary to complete the project. In the nightclub example, these would include locating the site, getting the liquor license, and so forth. Many more activities and subactivities could be added to this example.

Exhibit 7-4
A PERT Network for
Opening a Nightclub

Information for Preparing the PERT Diagram

Event	Activity	Estimated Time in Weeks	Preceding Event
A	Locate site	6	None
B	Get liquor license	30	A
C	Hire renovation contractors	13	A
D	Supervise renovation	30	C
E	Hire lighting contractor	6	D
F	Supervise lighting install	13	E
G	Begin advertising club	8	B, F
H	Hire club employees	14	G
I	Get booking agent	8	G, H
J	Open club for business	1	I

→ = Critical Path (thick arrow)

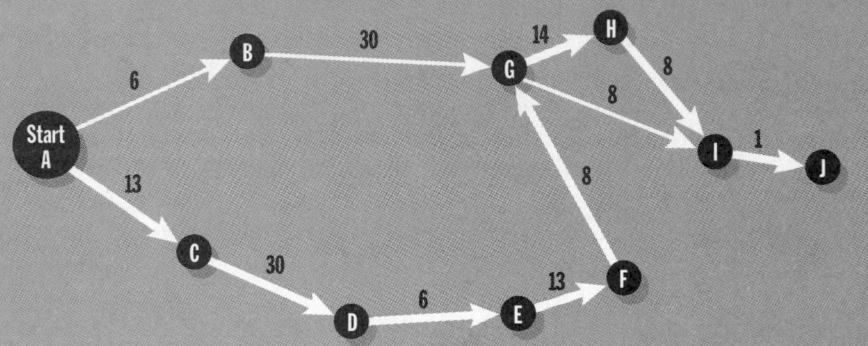

2. Design the actual PERT network, relating all the activities to each other in the proper sequence. Anticipating all the activities in a major project requires considerable skill and judgment. In addition, activities must be sequenced—the planner must decide which activity must precede another. In the nightclub example, the owner would want to hire employees before booking talent.

3. Estimate the time required to complete each activity. This must be done carefully because the major output of the PERT method is a statement of the total time required by the project. Because the time estimate is critical, several people should be asked to make three different estimates: optimistic time, pessimistic time, and probable time.

Optimistic time (O) is the shortest time an activity will take if everything goes well. In the construction industry, the optimistic time is rarely achieved.

Pessimistic time (P) is the amount of time an activity will take if everything goes wrong (as it sometimes does with complicated projects such as installing a new subway system).

Most probable time (M) is the most realistic estimate of how much time an activity will take. The probable time for an activity can be an estimate of the time taken for similar activities on other projects. For instance, the time needed to build a cockpit for one aircraft might be based on the average time it took to build cockpits for comparable aircraft in the past.

After the planner has collected all the estimates, he or she uses a formula to calculate the **expected time.** The expected time is the time that will be used on the PERT diagram as the needed period for the completion of an activity. As the following formula shows, expected time is an "average" in which most probable time is given more weight than optimistic time and pessimistic time.

$$\text{Expected time} = \frac{O + 4M + P}{6}$$

> **expected time**
> *The time that will be used on the PERT diagram as the needed period for the completion of an activity.*

(The denominator is 6 because O counts for 1, M for 4, and P for 1.)

Suppose the time estimates for choosing a site location for the nightclub are as follows: optimistic time (O) is 2 weeks; most probable time (M) is 5 weeks; and pessimistic time (P) is 8 weeks. Therefore,

$$\text{Expected time} = \frac{2 + (4 \times 5) + 8}{6} = \frac{30}{6} = 5 \text{ weeks}$$

4. Calculate the **critical path,** the path through the PERT network that includes the most time-consuming sequence of events and activities. The length of the entire project is determined by the path with the longest elapsed time. The logic behind the critical path is this: A given project cannot be considered completed until its lengthiest component is completed. For example, if it takes one year to get the liquor permit, the nightclub project cannot be completed in less than one year, even if all other events are completed earlier than scheduled.

> **critical path**
> *The path through the PERT network that includes the most time-consuming sequence of events and activities.*

Exhibit 7-4 shows a critical path that requires a total elapsed time of 93 weeks. This total is calculated by adding the numerals that appear beside each thick line segment. Each numeral represents the number of weeks scheduled to complete the activities between each lettered label. Notice that activity completion must occur in the sequence of steps indicated by the direction of the arrows. In this case, if 93 weeks appeared to be an excessive length of time, the nightclub owners would have to search for ways to shorten the process. For example, the owner might be spending too much time supervising the renovation.

When it comes to implementing the activities listed on the PERT diagram, control measures play a crucial role. The project manager must ensure that all critical events are completed on time. If activities in the critical path take too long to complete, the project will not be completed on time. If necessary, the manager must take corrective action to move the activity along. Such action might include hiring additional help, dismissing substandard help, or purchasing more productive equipment.

Delaying the start of activities that are not on the critical path is another means of control. Delays may even be advisable from the financial standpoint if they allow the manager to delay payment for the activities. Delaying payments could save interest on loans or allow an organization to invest available cash in short-term securities.

In practice, PERT networks often specify hundreds of events and activities. Each small event can have its own PERT diagram. Many computer programs are available to help perform the mechanics of computing paths. Furthermore, software has been developed to help planners use advanced scheduling techniques that are based on PERT. Despite increasingly sophisticated approaches to scheduling, however, computerized versions of PERT diagrams remain standard tools in such high-tech organizations as Xerox Corp.

BREAK-EVEN ANALYSIS

break-even analysis
A method of determining the relationship between total costs and total revenues at various levels of production or sales activity.

"What do we have to do to break even?" This question is asked frequently in business. Managers often find the answer through **break-even analysis,** a method of determining the relationship between total costs and total revenues at various levels of production or sales activity. Managers use break-even analysis because—before adding new products, equipment, or personnel—they want to be sure that the changes will pay off. Break-even analysis tells managers the point at which it is profitable to go ahead with a new venture.

Exhibit 7-5 illustrates a typical break-even chart. It deals with a proposal to add a new product to an existing line. The point at which the Total Costs line and the Revenue line interesect is the break-even point. Sales shown to the right of the break-even point represent profit. Sales to the left of this point represent a loss.

BREAK-EVEN FORMULA

The break-even point (*BE*) is the situation in which total revenues equal fixed costs plus variable costs. It can be calculated with several algebraic formulas. One standard formula is:

$$BE = \frac{TFC}{P - AVC}$$

where

P = selling price per unit
AVC = average variable cost per unit, the cost that varies with the amount produced
TFC = total fixed cost, the cost that remains constant no matter how many units are produced

Another version of the preceding formula uses variable cost instead of average variable cost, and fixed cost instead of total fixed cost. Professor Ron Olive, however, believes that using *AVC* and *TFC* is more accurate from the standpoint of economics.[2]

The chart in Exhibit 7-5 is based on the following data: the selling price (*P*) is $10 per unit, the average variable cost (*AVC*) is $5 per unit, and total fixed costs (*TFC*) are $300,000. According to the formula, then, the break-even point is computed as follows:

$$BE = \frac{\$300,000}{\$10 - \$5} = \frac{\$300,000}{\$5} = 60,000 \text{ units}$$

Under the conditions assumed and for the period of time in which these cost and revenue figures are valid, a sales volume of 60,000 units would be required for the company to break even. Anything above that would be a profit and anything below that would result in a loss. If the sales forecast for this new product is above the 60,000 units, it would be a good decision to add it to the line. If the sales forecast is less than 60,000 units, the company would do well to abandon the plan.

ADVANTAGES AND LIMITATIONS OF BREAK-EVEN ANALYSIS

Break-even analysis helps managers keep their thinking focused on the volume of activity that will be necessary to justify a new expense. The technique is also use-

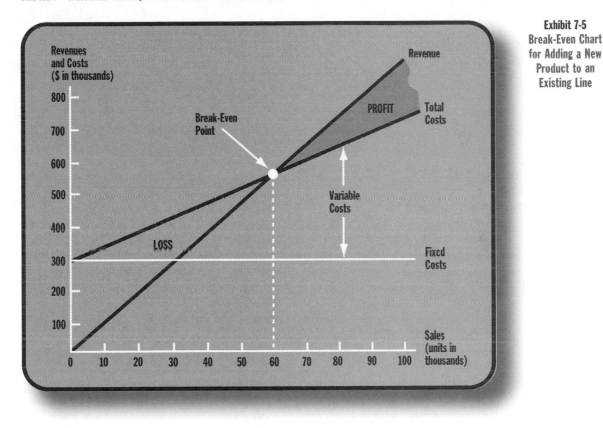

Exhibit 7-5
Break-Even Chart
for Adding a New
Product to an
Existing Line

ful because it can be applied to a number of operations problems. Break-even analysis can help a manager decide whether to drop an existing product from the line, to replace equipment, or to buy rather than make a part.

Break-even analysis has some drawbacks. First, a break-even analysis is only as valid as the estimates of costs and revenues that managers use to create it. Second, a break-even analysis is static in that it assumes there will be no changes in other variables. The dynamic nature of business makes this a questionable assumption. The third limitation of break-even analysis is potentially more serious. Exhibit 7-5 indicates that variable costs and sales increase together in a direct relationship. In reality, unit costs may decrease with increased volume. It is also possible that costs may increase with volume. Suppose, for example, that increased production leads to higher turnover because employees prefer not to work overtime.

Break-even analysis relates to decisions about whether to proceed or not to proceed. The next section will examine a more complicated decision-making technique that relates to the desirability of several alternative solutions.

THE PAYOFF MATRIX. The **payoff matrix** is a technique for indicating possible payoffs, or returns, from pursuing different alternative solutions. These alternatives can be considered as possible courses of action. Each alternative is pursued under different **states of nature,** or circumstances beyond the control of the decision maker. Examples of states of nature that affect business decisions include the demand for a product, availability of qualified job applicants, and weather conditions.

To illustrate the use of a payoff matrix, assume that Funtime Products decides to manufacture and market a line of above-ground swimming pools. Jeff Rogers, the president, cannot really predict the demand for the swimming pools because he is uncertain about such critical factors as competitive products, the weather,

payoff matrix
*A technique for in-
dicating possible
payoffs, or returns,
from pursuing dif-
ferent alternatives.*

states of nature
*Circumstances be-
yond the control of
the decision maker.*

Exhibit 7-6
Payoff Matrix Showing
Conditional Values

Alternatives (Quantity of Pools Produced)	States of Nature (Demand for Pools)		
	Low	Medium	High
Low	$2,000,000	$2,000,000	$2,000,000
Medium	$2,000,000	$4,000,000	$4,000,000
High	$2,000,000	$4,000,000	$5,000,000

Exhibit 7-6
Payoff Matrix Showing
Conditional Values

interest rates, and the general state of the economy. Based on past experience with introducing expensive leisure-time products, he assigns dollar-volume-of-sales values to the three general levels of demand: low, medium, and high.

In deciding how many pools to manufacture, Rogers can only guess at the best number. The true level of demand is uncertain. Each quantity level—a low, medium, or high number of pools—represents a different alternative. A payoff matrix can help a manager reach the best decision in a problem like this. The matrix can show the possible revenue to be realized by pursuing each of the three alternatives under each of the three states of nature.

Exhibit 7-6 shows the possible payoffs to Funtime from pursuing each alternative under the three levels of demand. The possible payoffs are often called **conditional values,** because each depends on a particular condition. As indicated in the payoff matrix, if Funtime produces a low quantity of pools under low demand, anticipated revenues will be $2,000,000. A medium number of pools produced under medium demand will yield $4,000,000; a high number of pools under high demand will yield $5,000,000. Note that, if Funtime produces only a low number of pools, its revenues will not exceed $2,000,000 under any of the demand conditions—Funtime will have only the low quantity to sell.

To make a payoff matrix more accurate, managers assign probabilities to each of the various states of nature. The probabilities indicate the likelihood of each condition occurring. The sum of the probabilities must equal 1.0. As Exhibit 7-7 shows, the probability of each state of nature is multiplied by each conditional value to arrive at an expected value. An **expected value** is the average value incurred if a particular decision is made a large number of times. It is the average return in the long run. The sum of the expected values for all states of nature is the total expected value for each alternative.

Exhibit 7-8 presents the expected values for the three alternative quantities based on probabilities of 0.20 for low demand, 0.50 for medium demand, and

conditional value
In a payoff matrix, the possible payoff of pursuing an alternative solution to a problem under a particular level of demand.

expected value
The average value incurred if a particular decision is made a large number of times.

Exhibit 7-7
Calculating the Expected
Value When a Low
Quantity Is Produced

Demand Level	Probability	×	Conditional Value	=	Expected Value
Low	0.20		$2,000,000		$ 400,000
Medium	0.50		$2,000,000		$1,000,000
High	0.30		$2,000,000		$ 600,000

Exhibit 7-7
Calculating the Expected
Value When a Low
Quantity Is Produced

Alternatives (Pool Production)	Probabilities of Each Demand Level			Total Expected Values
	Low (0.20)	Medium (0.50)	High (0.30)	
Low	$400,000	$1,000,000	$ 600,000	$2,000,000
Medium	$400,000	$2,000,000	$1,200,000	$3,600,000
High	$400,000	$2,000,000	$1,500,000	$3,900,000

0.30 for high demand. The total expected value for the low alternative is $2,000,000. For the medium alternative it is $3,600,000, and for the high alternative it is $3,900,000. Assuming that the various estimates used in developing the payoff matrix are correct, manufacturing a large number of pools will have the biggest payoff. If Rogers believes the payoff matrix is accurate, he will manufacture a large quantity of above-ground pools—and hope for a warm, early summer.

DECISION TREES

Another useful planning tool is called a **decision tree,** a graphic illustration of the alternative solutions available to solve a problem. Decisions trees are like a payoff matrix, except they are designed to estimate the outcome of a series of decisions. As the sequences of the major decision are drawn, the resulting diagram resembles a tree with branches.

> **decision tree**
> *A graphic illustration of the alternative solutions available to solve a problem.*

To illustrate the essentials of using a decision tree for making financial decisions, return to the nightclub owner who used the Gantt and milestone charts. One major decision facing the owner is whether to open a nightclub only or to open a nightclub and dinner restaurant. According to data from a restaurant industry association, the probability of having a good first year is 0.6 and the probability of having a poor one is 0.4.

Discussion with an accountant indicates that the payout, or net cash flow, from a good season with the nightclub only would be $100,000. The payout from a poor first year with the same alternative would be a loss of $10,000. Both these figures are conditional values because they depend on business conditions. The owner and accountant predict that a good first year with the alternative of a nightclub and dinner restaurant would be $150,000. A poor first year would result in a loss of $30,000.

Using this information, the manager computes the expected values and adds them for the two alternatives:

Expected value: Nightclub only   = 0.6 × $100,000   = $60,000
                                    0.4 × −10,000   =   −4,000
                                                           $56,000

Expected value: Nightclub and
     dinner restaurant   = 0.6 × $150,000   = $90,000
                                       0.4 × −30,000   =   −12,000
                                                           $78,000

Exhibit 7-9
First-Year Decision Tree
for Nightclub Owner

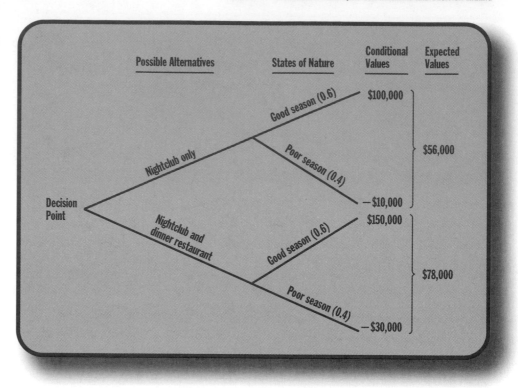

As Exhibit 7-9 graphically portrays, the decision tree suggests that the nightclub-restaurant will probably turn a first-year profit of $78,000. The nightclub-only alternative is likely to show a profit of $56,000. Over one year, running a nightclub and dinner restaurant would be $22,000 more profitable.

The advantage of a decision tree is that it can be used to help make sequences of decisions. After having one year of experience in running a nightclub and dinner restaurant, the owner may think of expanding. One logical possibility for expansion would be to open the restaurant for lunch as well as dinner. The owner would add a new branch to the decision tree to compare the conditional values for the nightclub and dinner restaurant with those of the nightclub and dinner-lunch restaurant.

The new branch of the decision tree might take the form shown in Exhibit 7-10, which focuses on the decision of whether to add luncheon service. The nightclub owner would now have more accurate information about the conditional values for a nightclub and dinner restaurant—the choice the owner made when opening the establishment. With one year of success with the nightclub and dinner restaurant, the probability of having a second good season might be raised to 0.8. With each successive year, the owner would have increasingly accurate information about the conditional values.

Following is an explanation of how the expected values are calculated for the new branch of the decision tree in question, shown in Exhibit 7-10:

Expected value: Nightclub and dinner restaurant	$= 0.8 \times \$180,000$	$=$	$\$144,000$
	$0.2 \times -30,000$	$=$	$- 6,000$
			$\$138,000$
Expected value: Nightclub and dinner-lunch restaurant	$= 0.6 \times \$200,000$	$=$	$\$120,000$
	$0.4 \times -50,000$	$=$	$-20,000$
			$\$100,000$

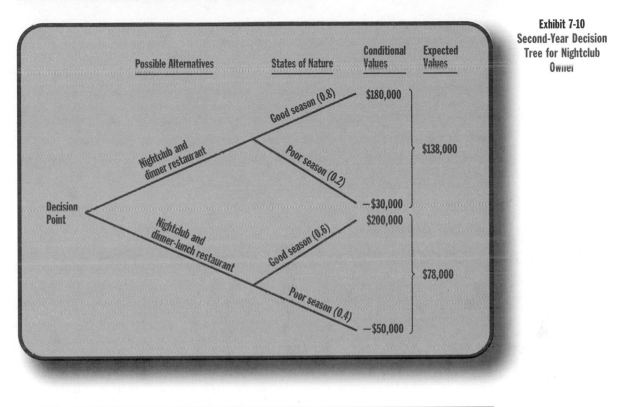

Exhibit 7-10
Second-Year Decision
Tree for Nightclub
Owner

INVENTORY-CONTROL TECHNIQUES

A problem faced by managers of manufacturing and sales organizations is how much inventory to keep on hand. If an organization maintains a large inventory, goods can be made quickly or orders can be shipped rapidly. You will recall that part of the success of clothing manufacturer ABS USA is attributed to the large inventory of fabric it maintains. However, stocking inventory is expensive. The goods themselves are costly, and money tied up in inventory cannot be invested elsewhere. This section will describe three decision-making techniques used to manage inventory and control production: materials-requirement planning (MRQ), economic-order quantity (EOQ), and just-in-time (JIT) inventory control.

LEARNING OBJECTIVE

Describe how to manage inventory by using the materials-requirement planning (MRQ), economic-order quantity (EOQ), and just-in-time (JIT) inventory control.

MATERIALS-REQUIREMENT PLANNING

Manufacturing a finished product is complicated. It involves various production functions, including scheduling, purchasing, and inventory control. Many firms use a master plan to coordinate these production functions. **Materials-requirement planning (MRP)** is a computerized manufacturing and inventory-control system designed to ensure that materials handling and inventory control are efficient. The system is designed to manage inventories that come from components or raw materials to support scheduled production of finished goods. A manufacturer of dishwashers such as Maytag Corporation uses MRP because a dishwasher has many components, including electric motors, rubber belts, and sheet metal.

Materials-requirement planning is important because the parts used in building a product such as dishwashers are needed at exact times in the production cycle. MRP helps smooth the parts-ordering cycle and provides immediate information about the inventory levels of critical parts.

materials-requirement planning (MRP) *A computerized manufacturing and inventory-control system designed to ensure that materials handling and inventory control are efficient.*

Materials-requirement planning has three major components. The *master production schedule* is the overall production plan for the completed products, such as dishwashers. This schedule is expressed in terms of timing and quantity of production. The *inventory record file* consists of information about the status of each item held in inventory. The *bill of materials* is a list of the components needed for each completed item. A bill of materials, for example, might list the many parts of a dishwasher. Materials-requirement planning coordinates all this data and provides information to ensure that materials are available when needed.

Materials-requirement planning makes an important contribution by reducing inventory levels and direct labor costs. The next sections will discuss two other approaches to reducing inventory levels.

ECONOMIC-ORDER QUANTITY

economic-order quantity (EOQ)
The inventory level that minimizes both administrative costs and carrying costs.

Economic-order quantity (EOQ) is the inventory level that minimizes both administrative costs and carrying costs. The EOQ represents the reorder quantity of the least cost. Carrying costs include the cost of loans, the interest foregone because money is tied up in inventory, and the cost of handling the inventory. EOQ is expressed mathematically as

$$EOQ = \sqrt{\frac{2DO}{C}}$$

where

D = annual demand in units for the product
O = fixed cost of placing and receiving an order
C = annual carrying cost per unit (taxes, insurance, and other expenses)

Assume that the annual demand for Funtime Products swimming pools is 100 units and that it costs $1,000 to order each unit. Furthermore, suppose the carrying cost per unit is $200. The equation to calculate the most economic number of pools to keep in inventory is:

$$EOQ = \sqrt{\frac{2 \times 100 \times \$1,000}{\$200}}$$

$$= \sqrt{\frac{\$200,000}{\$200}}$$

$$= \sqrt{1,000}$$

$$= 32 \text{ pools (rounded figure)}$$

Therefore, the president of Funtime concludes that the most economical number of pools to keep in inventory during the selling season is 32. (The assumption is that Funtime has a large storage area.) If the figures entered into the EOQ formula are accurate, EOQ calculations can vastly improve inventory management.

just-in-time (JIT) inventory control
A system to minimize inventory and move it into the plan exactly when needed.

JUST-IN-TIME INVENTORY CONTROL

The Japanese have developed a system, **just-in-time (JIT) inventory control,** to minimize inventory and move it into the plant exactly when needed. The key principle of the system is to eliminate excess inventory by producing or purchasing parts, subassemblies, and final products only when—and in the exact amounts—needed.

JIT is generally used in a repetitive, single-product, manufacturing environment. However, the system is now also used to improve operations in sales and service organizations.

PHILOSOPHIES. Three basic philosophies underlie the specific manufacturing techniques of JIT.[3] *First, setup time for assembly and cost must be reduced.* The goal of JIT is to make setup time and cost so low that small batch sizes are economical, even to the point of manufacturing just one finished product. *Second, safety stock is undesirable.* Stock held in reserve is expensive and hides problems, such as inefficient production methods. "Just in time" should replace "just in case." *Third, productivity and quality are inseparable.* JIT is only possible when high-quality components are delivered and produced. The goal of the JIT system is 100 percent good items at each manufacturing step.

PROCEDURES AND TECHNIQUES. Just-in-time inventory control is part of a system of manufacturing control. Therefore, it involves many different techniques and procedures. Seven of the major techniques and procedures are described in the list that follows. Knowing them provides insight into the system of manufacturing used by many successful Japanese companies.

1. *Kanbans.* The JIT system of inventory control relies on *kanbans,* or cards, to communicate production requirements from the final point of assembly to the manufacturing operations that precede it. When an order is received for a product, a *kanban* is issued that directs employees to finish the product. The finishing department selects components and assembles the product. The *kanban* is then passed back to earlier stations. This *kanban* tells workers to resupply the components. *Kanban* communication continues all the way back to the material suppliers. In many JIT systems, suppliers locate their companies so they can be close to major customers. Proximity allows suppliers to make shipments promptly. At each stage, parts and other materials are delivered just in time for use.

2. *Demand-driven pull system.* The just-in-time technique requires producing exactly what is needed to match the demand created by customer orders. Demand drives final assembly schedules, and assembly drives subassembly timetables. The result is a pull system—that is, customer demand pulls along activities to meet that demand.

3. *Short production lead times.* A JIT system minimizes the time between the arrival of raw material or components in the plant and the shipment of a finished product to a customer.

4. *High inventory turnover (with the goal of zero inventory and stockless production).* The levels of finished goods, work in process, and raw materials are purposely reduced. Raw material in a warehouse is regarded as waste, and so is idle work in process. (A person who applied JIT to the household would regard backup supplies of ketchup or motor oil as shameful!)

5. *Designated areas for receiving materials.* Certain areas on the shop floor or in the receiving and shipping department are designated for receiving specific items from suppliers. At a Toyota plant in Japan, the receiving area is about half the size of a football field. The designated spaces for specific items are marked with yellow paint.

6. *Designated containers.* Specifying where to store items allows for easy access to parts, and it eliminates counting. For example, at Toyota the bed of a truck has metal frame mounts for exactly eight engines. A truckload of engines means eight engines—no more, no less. No one has to count them.

7. *Neatness.* A JIT plant that follows Japanese tradition is immaculate. All unnecessary materials, tools, rags, and files are discarded. The factory floor is as neat and clean as the showroom.

ADVANTAGES AND DISADVANTAGES OF THE JIT INVENTORY SYSTEM. Manufacturing companies have realized several benefits from adopting JIT. Just-in-time controls can lead to organizational commitment to quality in design, materials, parts, employee-management and supplier-user relations, and finished goods. With minimum levels of inventory on hand, finished products are more visible and defects are more readily detected. Quality problems can therefore be attacked before they escalate to an insurmountable degree. Low levels of inventory also shorten cycle times.

Being able to support a customer's JIT system can provide a competitive advantage. A case in point is Wausau Paper Mills Co., a company that has recently achieved outstanding success based on its speed of product delivery. Wausau uses an inventory and production system called time-based competition. The system depends on having large supplies of product on hand so that an order can be delivered quickly. Wausau then holds inventory for customers until it is needed, thus supporting their customers' quest for just-in-time deliveries. In some cases, the company reduced delivery time from four weeks to overnight.[4]

Despite the advantages just-in-time management can offer large manufacturers, it has some striking disadvantages. Above all, a just-in-time system must be placed in a supportive or compatible environment. JIT is applicable only to highly repetitive manufacturing operations such as car or residential furnace manufacturing. Small companies with short runs of a variety of products often may suffer financial losses from just-in-time practices. One problem they have is that suppliers are often unwilling to promptly shift small batches to meet the weekly needs of a small customer.[5]

Product demand must be predictable for JIT to work well. If customer demand creates a surge of orders, a tight inventory policy will not be able to handle this windfall. The savings from just-in-time management can be deceptive. Several manufacturers who used JIT discovered that their suppliers were simply building up inventories in their own plants and adding that cost to their prices.[6] Just-in-time inventory practices also leave a company vulnerable to work stoppages, such as a strike. With a large inventory of finished products or parts, the company can continue to meet customer demand while the work stoppage is being settled.

Just-in-time inventory control also presents ethical problems. The big company saves money by forcing the supplier to maintain expensive inventories, so it (the big company) can be served promptly. Another ethical concern about JIT occurs when a manufacturer ceases dealing with a supplier. The supplier will usually have to close the facility it built just to be in proximity to the manufacturer.

LEARNING OBJECTIVE 5

Describe how to use the nominal-group technique.

> **nominal-group technique (NGT)**
> *A group decision-making technique that follows a highly structured format.*

NOMINAL-GROUP TECHNIQUE

A manager who must make a decision about an important issue sometimes needs to know what alternatives are available and how people would react to them. An approach called the **nominal-group technique** (**NGT**) has been developed to fit this situation. NGT is a group decision-making technique that follows a highly structured format. The term *nominal* means that, for much of the activity, the participants are a group in name only; they do not interact.

A problem that is an appropriate candidate for NGT is the decision about which plants of a multiplant firm should be closed because of declining demand for a product. A decision of this type is highly sensitive and will elicit many different opinions. Suppose Sherry McDivott, the company president, faces the plant-closing problem. A six-step decision process is followed that uses the nominal-group technique.[7]

1. Group members (called the target group) are selected and assembled. McDivott includes her five top managers, each representing a key function of the business, and informs them in advance of the topic.

2. The group leader presents a specific question. McDivott tells the group, "Our board of directors says we have to consolidate our operations. Our output isn't high enough to justify keeping five plants open. Whatever we do, we must cut operating expenses by about 20 percent.

   "Your assignment is to develop criteria for choosing which plant to close. However, if the group can think of another way of cutting operating costs by 20 percent, I'll give it some consideration. I also need to know how you feel about the alternative you choose and how our employees might feel."

3. Individual members write down their ideas independently, without speaking to other members. Using notepads, the five managers write down their ideas about reducing operating costs by 20 percent.

4. Each participant, in turn, presents one idea to the group. The group does not discuss the ideas. The administrative assistant summarizes each idea by writing it on a flip chart. Here are some of the group's ideas:

   Alternative A. Close the plant with the most obsolete equipment and facilities. We all know that the Harrisburg plant is running with equipment built at the turn of the century. Close the plant in 60 days. Give employees six months of severance pay and assist them to find new jobs. Transfer the most outstanding staff to our other plants.

   Alternative B. Close the plant with the least flexible, most unproductive work force. A lot of employees are likely to complain about this type of closing. But the rest of the work force will get the message that we value productive employees.

   Alternative C. Forget about closing a plant. Instead, take our least productive plant and transfer all its manufacturing to our other four plants. Then, work like fury to get subcontracting business for the emptied-out plant. I think our employees and stockholders will be pleased if we take such a brave stance.

   Alternative D. We need a careful financial analysis of which plant is producing the lowest return on investment of capital, all factors considered. We simply close that plant. Employees will accept this decision because they all know that business is based on financial considerations.

   Alternative E. Closing one plant would be too much of a hardship on one group of people. Let's share the hardship evenly. Cut everybody's pay by 25 percent, eliminate dividends to stockholders, do not replace anybody who quits or retires for the next year, and ask all our suppliers to give us a 15 percent discount. These measures would be the starting point. We could then appoint a committee to look for other savings. If everybody pulls together, morale will be saved.

5. After each group member has presented his or her idea, the group clarifies and evaluates the suggestions. The length of the discussion for each of the ideas varies substantially. For example, the discussion about cutting salaries 25 percent and eliminating dividends lasted only 3 minutes.

6. The meeting ends with a silent, independent rating of the alternatives. The final group decision is the pooled outcome of the individual votes. The target group is instructed to rate each alternative on a 1-to-10 scale, with 10 being the most favorable rating. The ratings that follow are the pooled ratings (the sum of the individual ratings) received for each alternative. (50 represents the maximum score):

Alternative A, close obsolete plant: 35
Alternative B, close plant with unproductive work force: 41
Alternative C, make one plant a subcontractor: 19
Alternative D, close plant with poorest return on investment: 26
Alternative E, cut everybody's pay by 25 percent: 4

McDivott agrees with the group's preference for closing the plant with the least productive, most inflexible work force. Ultimately, the board accepts Alternative B. The best employees in the factory chosen for closing are offered an opportunity to relocate to another company plant.

Since its development about 35 years ago, NGT has gained substantial acceptance and recognition. It has been widely applied in many organizations. The nominal-group technique has gained in popularity because it can be computerized. Suggestions are entered on a computer screen and seen by other group members simultaneously. The NGT is effective at helping group members generate alternatives, keep bloopers to a minimum, and satisfy group members.[8]

NGT is effective because it follows the logic of the problem-solving and decision-making method and allows for group participation. It also provides a discipline and rigor that are often missing in brainstorming.

SUMMARY OF KEY POINTS

1
Explain the use of forecasting techniques in planning.
All planning includes making forecasts, both qualitative and quantitative. A judgmental forecast makes predictions based on subjective opinions. Quantitative forecasting methods include time-series analysis and linear regression. Three widely used forecasts are economic, sales, and technological.

2
Describe how to use Gantt charts, milestone charts, and PERT planning techniques.
Gantt and milestone charts are simple methods of monitoring schedules, and are particularly useful for one-time projects. Gantt charts graphically depict the planned and actual progress of work over the period of time encompassed by a project. A milestone chart lists the subactivities that must be completed to accomplish the major activities.

Managers use PERT networks to track complicated projects when sequences of events must be planned carefully. In a PERT network, an event is a point of decision or accomplishment. An activity is the physical and mental effort required to complete an event. To complete a PERT diagram, a manager must sequence all the events and estimate the time required for each activity. The expected time for each activity takes into account optimistic, pessimistic, and probable estimates of time. The critical path is the most time-consuming sequence of activities and events that must be followed to implement the project. The duration of the project is determined by the longest critical path.

3
Describe how to use break-even analysis, payoff matrices, and decision trees for problem solving and decision making.
Managers use break-even analysis to estimate the point at which it is profitable to go ahead with a new venture.

It is a method of determining the relationship between total costs and total revenues at various levels of sales activity or operation. Break-even analysis determines the ratio of total fixed costs to the difference between the selling price and the average variable cost for each unit. The results of break-even analysis are often depicted on a graph. Break-even analysis is based on an assumption of static costs.

A payoff matrix is used to determine the returns or payoffs from pursuing different alternatives. The matrix is expressed in financial terms. Each alternative is pursued in terms of a different state of nature, or circumstance beyond the control of the decision maker. Possible payoffs are referred to as conditional values because each depends on a particular condition. To make the payoff matrix more accurate, probabilities are assigned to each state of nature. The probability of each state of nature is multiplied by each conditional value to arrive at the expected values—the estimated payoffs.

A decision tree provides a quantitative estimate of the best alternative. It is a tool for estimating the outcome of a series of decisions. When the sequences of the major decisions are drawn, they resemble a tree with branches.

4

Describe how to manage inventory by using the materials-requirement planning (MRP), economic-order quantity (EOQ) and just-in-time (JIT) inventory control.

Materials-requirement planning (MRP) is a computerized manufacturing and inventory-control system designed to make materials handling and inventory control efficient. Economic-order quantity (EOQ) is a decision-support technique widely used to manage in-

ventory. The EOQ is the inventory level that minimizes both ordering and carrying costs. The EOQ technique helps managers in a manufacturing or sales organization decide how much inventory to keep on hand.

Just-in-time (JIT) inventory management minimizes stock on hand. Instead, stock is moved into the plant exactly when needed. Although not specifically a decision-making technique, JIT helps shape decisions about inventory. The key principle underlying JIT systems is the elimination of excess inventory by producing or purchasing items only when and in the exact amounts they are needed.

Just-in-time processes involve (1) *hanbans,* or cards for communicating production requirements to the previous operation, (2) a customer demand-driven system, (3) short production lead times, (4) high inventory turnover, (5) designated areas for receiving materials, (6) designated containers, and (7) neatness throughout the factory.

JIT inventory management is best suited for repetitive manufacturing processes. One drawback of JIT is that it places heavy pressures on suppliers to build up their inventories to satisfy sudden demands of their customers who use the system.

5

Describe how to use the nominal-group technique.

The nominal-group technique (NGT) is recommended for a situation in which a manager needs to know what alternatives are available and how people will react to them. Using the technique, a small group of people contribute written thoughts about the problem. Other members respond to their ideas later. Members rate each other's ideas numerically, and the final group decision is the value of the pooled individual votes.

KEY TERMS AND PHRASES

QUESTIONS

1. How could the information presented in this chapter help you become a better manager?
2. Give two examples of work projects you think would benefit from the use of a milestone chart.
3. How could a project manager make use of any of the information in this chapter to improve the chances of completing projects on time?
4. Describe at least one possible job application for a PERT network.
5. Think back to the hotel and restaurant developer described in Chapter 5 about planning. In what way does he make use of break-even analysis?
6. A criticism of just-in-time inventory management is that it simply transfers inventory problems from the manufacturer to the supplier. What does this criticism mean, and how valid is it?

SKILL-BUILDING EXERCISE 7-A: DEVELOPING A PERT NETWORK

Use the following information about a quality improvement project to construct a PERT diagram. Be sure to indicate the critical path with a dark arrow. Work individually or in small groups.

Event	Description	Time Required (units)	Preceding Event
A	Complete quality audit	6	none
B	Benchmark	15	A
C	Collect internal information	6	A
D	Identify performance problems	3	B, C
E	Identify improvement practices	7	D
F	Elicit employee participation	20	A
G	Implement quality program	6	E, F
H	Measure results	8	G

Source: Reprinted with permission from Raymond L. Hilgert and Edwin C. Leonard, Jr., *Supervision: Concepts and Practices of Management*, 6th ed. (Cincinnati, OH: South-Western College Publishing, 1995), 191.

SKILL-BUILDING EXERCISE 7-B: BREAK-EVEN ANALYSIS

On recent vacation trips to Juarez, Mexico, you noticed small stores and street vendors selling original art. The prices ranged from $2 to $20 (U.S.). A flash of inspiration hit you. Why not sell Mexican art back home to Americans, using a van as your store? Every three months, you would drive the 350 miles to Mexico and load up on art. You anticipate receiving generous large-quantity discounts.

You would park your van on busy streets and nearby parks, wherever you could obtain a permit. Typically you would display the art outside the van, but on a rainy day people could step inside. Your intention is to operate your traveling art sale about 12 hours per week. If you could make enough money from your business, you could attend classes full-time during the day. You intend to sell the original paintings at an average of $12 a unit.

Based on preliminary analysis, you have discovered that your primary fixed costs per month would be: $450 for payments on a van, $75 for gas and maintenance, $50 for insurance, and $45 for a street vendor's permit. You will also be driving down to Mexico every three months at $300 per trip, resulting in a $100 per month travel cost. Your variable costs would be an average of $3 per painting and 25¢ for wrapping each painting in brown paper.

1. How many paintings will you have to sell each month before you start to make a profit?
2. If the average cost of your paintings rises to $5, how many pieces of art will you have to sell each month if you hold your price to $12 per unit?

SKILL-BUILDING EXERCISE 7-C: PAYOFF MATRIX

As the sales manager of Funtime Products, you have helped introduce a new line of pool tables. Compute the expected values for low, medium, and high quantities of pool-table production. (The probability of low demand is 0.25; medium demand, 0.50, and high demand,

0.25.) Then decide which production volume represents the best bet for your firm. The following table presents a payoff matrix showing the conditional values you need for your computations. (Refer back to Exhibits 7-7 and 7-8 for assistance with the computations.)

Alternatives (Pool Table Production)	States of Nature (Demand for Pool Tables)		
	Low	Medium	High
Low	$300,000	$300,000	$300,000
Medium	$300,000	$500,000	$500,000
High	$300,000	$500,000	$600,000

SKILL-BUILDING EXERCISE 7-D: ECONOMIC-ORDER QUANTITY

You are the materials-handling manager in a consumer manufacturing plant. Assume that the annual demand for personal digital assistants is 5,000 units and it costs

$575 to order the components for each unit. The carrying cost per unit is $25. How many component units should your plant maintain in inventory?

VIDEO DISCUSSION QUESTIONS

1. Which financial ratio is Popoff using to evaluate the performance of his firm? **[Dow Chemical]**
2. In what ways does a General Tire commercial sales representative use quantitative decision making? **[General Tire]**

3. In what ways does the CEO of Interactive Network make use of forecasting techniques? **[Technology]**

CASE PROBLEM EXERCISE 7-A: INVENTORY BUILD-UP AT MOTOROLA

In February of 1995, Motorola Inc. concluded that its earnings estimates for the previous year presented an overly optimistic picture of its financial position. Motorola had reported record fourth-quarter earnings of $515 million on sales of $6.45 billion. The high earnings estimates stemmed from overenthusiastic ordering of cellular telephones by retail distributors. The spurt in sales during the holiday season may have come at the expense of its sales for the first half of the next year (1995). New orders for cellular phones declined during that period.

According to industry sources, several distributors, including U S West and BellSouth, overordered by a wide margin. Part of the problem was that distributors were reacting defensively. During the previous two holiday seasons, Motorola could not meet consumer demands for handsets, forcing the Bells and other distributors to turn away business. Hoping not to repeat the mistake, the Bell cellular units placed orders early and often. The distributors failed to warn Motorola to cut back on production until it was too late.

CASECASECASECASECAS

The distributors were shocked when the phone orders kept pouring in. Working under a total quality system, Motorola had eliminated practically all bottlenecks and was therefore able to meet holiday demand. An electronics company analyst contends that Motorola did not properly monitor incoming orders. The analyst adds, "Motorola should have known that orders were going beyond demand."

Motorola Inc. is not faced with serious financial problems because of the overshipments, but top management prefers that dealers do not face inventory problems. A problem for some stockholders, however, is that the stock went down 10 percent because of the inventory accumulation.

CASE QUESTIONS

1. How much responsibility should Motorola take for the problem of excess inventory?
2. What forecasting method can Motorola use to prevent inflated orders from happening again?
3. What advice on inventory management can you give the Motorola dealers?

CASE PROBLEM 7-B: SELLING SNOW BOARDS JUST IN TIME

Sharon Prell is the general manager of three Sports Vancouver stores located in shopping malls around Vancouver, British Columbia. About 75 percent of their business stems from the sales of equipment and clothing for ice hockey, figure skating, and snow skiing. The other 25 percent of their business is derived mostly from swimming gear, and golf and tennis equipment.

Prell believes strongly that an important success factor in her business is maintaining the right inventory levels. She notes that she wants her stores to be stocked fully enough so as to excite and entice consumers. Yet she has data to prove that inventory piling up on the showroom floor or in the back room is costly.

Prell says, "If a customer asks for an item in his or her size or color that is not available in one store, we can often get that item in a hurry from one of our other stores. You might say I'm kind of a just-in-time inventory nut."

Two months after making that statement, the Sports Vancouver stores experienced a glorious winter season. Skates, skis, hockey sticks, pucks, and related clothing were being rung up at the cash registers at a heart-warming clip. Sales of snow boards, however, boomed. Fifteen days before Christmas, the stores had sold out every snow board in stock. Frantic pleas to the snow board manufacturers brought in only an extra 25 snow boards. All were sold out in two more days. Prell then asked two competitors to lend them their inventory of snow boards. The competition, however, wanted to hold on to their dwindling stocks to satisfy their own customers.

The ski-department manager kept a log of all the demand for snow boards that Sports Vancouver could not satisfy. By January 5, the figure was 250 boards. In discussing the problem with Prell, the ski-department manager said, "Sharon, I think our just-in-time policy was implemented just in time to choke off what could have been a record season."

Prell responded, "I catch your dig, but this problem warrants further study. Losing money on unsold inventory is the problem on the other side of the ditch."

CASE QUESTIONS

1. How might Prell prevent the snow board-shortage problem (or a similar problem) in the future?
2. How might Prell make more effective use of just-in-time inventory management?
3. How applicable would the economic-order quantity be to the snow board problem?

REFERENCES

1. Facts as reported in "Turn-On-A-Dime Style," *Success* (January/February 1994): 26.
2. Personal communication from Ron Olive, New Hamshire Technical College (17 May 1992).
3. Discussion of JIT is based on Ramon L. Aldag and Timothy M. Stearns, *Management*, 2e (Cincinnati: South-Western College Publishing, 1991), 645–646.
4. "Masters of the Game," *Business Week* (12 October 1992): 117–118.
5. Barbara Marsh, "Allen-Edmonds Shoe Tries 'Just-in-Time' Production," *The Wall Street Journal* (4 March 1993).
6. Doron P. Levin, "Is Auto Plant of the Future Almost Here?" *The New York Times* (14 June 1993): D8.
7. Andrew H. Van de Ven and Andrew L. Delbecq, "The Effectiveness of Nominal, Delphi, and Interacting Group Decision Making Processes," *Academy of Management Journal* (December 1972): 606.
8. D. Scott Sink, "Using the Nominal Group Technique Effectively," *National Productivity Review* (Spring 1983): 181.

CHAPTER 8

Job Design and Work Schedules

1

Identify the major dimensions and different types of job design.

2

Describe job enrichment, including the job characteristics model.

3

Describe job involvement, enlargement, and rotation.

4

Recognize how work teams are related to job design.

5

Illustrate how ergonomic factors can be part of job design.

6

Summarize the various modified work schedules.

Most employees take a break to have a beverage, a snack, or go for a stroll, but Sue Berry uses her breaks to catch up on household chores. As a medical transcriptionist who works from her home, Berry uses the time she used to spend on the road to do housework and just relax. Before she began working at her home in Marietta (an Atlanta suburb) a year ago, Berry used to spend two hours a day commuting to TransQuick in College Park. She's still an employee for the same company, but now it's only a short walk down the hall to get to the office. • Berry is a telecommuter, one of more than 37 million Americans who work either part-time or full-time at home instead of going into the office.[1]

The fact that the medical transcriptionist just described works mostly from her home is not unusual. Employers today use a variety of work schedules and arrangements to increase productivity and job satisfaction. Modifying work schedules is but one aspect of the major thrust of this chapter—job design. To accomplish large tasks—such as building ships or operating a hotel—you must divide work among individuals and groups.

There are two primary ways of subdividing the overall tasks of an enterprise. One way is to design specific jobs for individuals and groups to accomplish. The shipbuilding company must design jobs for welders, metal workers, engineers, puchasing agents, and contract administrators. In addition, many workers may be assigned to teams that assume considerable responsibility for productivity and quality. The other primary way of subdividing work is to assign tasks to different units within the organization—units such as departments and divisions.

This chapter will explain basic concepts relating to job design, such as the reasons why jobs are purposely made easy or complex, departures from traditional work schedules, work teams, and the characteristics of effective work groups. The next chapter will describe how work is divided throughout an organization.

BASIC CONCEPTS OF JOB DESIGN

LEARNING OBJECTIVE 1

Identify the major dimensions and different types of job design.

job design
The process of laying out job responsibilities and duties and describing how they are to be performed.

Understanding how tasks are subdivided begins with **job design.** It is the process of laying out job responsibilities and duties and describing how they are to be performed. The purpose of job design is to achieve an organization's goals. Each position in the organization is supposed to serve an important purpose. Job design is also important because of its potential for motivating workers.[2] The following sections will describe several major aspects of job design: different types of job design, task specialization, automation, job enrichment, and the job characteristics model.

FOUR DIFFERENT TYPES OF JOB DESIGN

Michael Campion and his associates have conducted extensive research into job design. Based on their results, they have identified four approaches to job design: motivational, mechanistic, biological, and perceptual/motor.[3]

1. *The motivational approach.* A motivational approach to job design makes the job so challenging and the worker so responsible that the worker is motivated just by performing the job. The job enrichment and job characteristics model, described later, are examples of this approach.

2. *The mechanistic approach.* The mechanistic approach to job design emphasizes total efficiency in performing a job. It assumes that work should be broken down into highly specialized and simplified tasks that involve frequent repetition of assignments. The mechanistic approach is described later in this chapter in the section called "Job Specialization." The mechanistic approach to job design has its roots in scientific management and the work of Frederick W. Taylor (see Chapter 1).

3. *The biological approach.* The biological approach to job design is based on ergonomics. Its goal is to reduce the physical demands of work and the dis-

comforts and injuries casued by these demands. The biological approach focuses on minimizing physical strain on the workers. It does so by reducing strength and endurance requirements and making improvements to upsetting noise and climate conditions. The biological approach results in less discomfort, fatigue, and illness for workers. The ergonomic workstation shown later in this chapter is based primarily on the biological approach to job design.

4. *The perceptual/motor approach.* The biological approach to job design just described concentrates mostly on the physical demands of a job. In contrast, the perceptual/motor approach concentrates more on mental capabilities and limitations. The perceptual/motor approach aims to ensure that the attention and concentration required by a job are within the capability of the least competent worker. For example, the instruction manual for a piece of equipment should not exceed the information-processing abilities of its least intelligent user. The perceptual/motor approach aims to reduce mental stress and fatigue, along with training time and chances for error.

Exhibit 8-1 summarizes research about the four types of job design. This table merits careful attention because it provides an overview of job design and lists the benefits and costs of each approach. The characteristics of the motivational approach will be discussed later in this chapter, in the sections about job enrichment and the job characteristics model.

In practice, managers may blend these four approaches to job design to create a productive and satisfying job. For example, the job of information systems specialist might be primarily designed along motivational lines. Yet it might also take into account the perceptual/motor demands of working with a computer frequently.

Before choosing a job design, managers and human resource professionals develop a job description. The **job description** is a written statement of the key features of a job, along with the activities required to perform it effectively. Sometimes a description must be modified to fit basic principles of job design. For example, the job description of a customer-service representative might call for an excessive amount of listening to complaints, thus creating too much stress.

job description
A written statement of the key features of a job, along with the activities required to perform it effectively.

JOB SPECIALIZATION

A major consideration in job design is how specialized the job holder must be. **Job specialization** is the degree to which a job holder performs only a limited number of tasks. The mechanistic approach favors job specialization. Specialists are supposed to be able to handle a narrow range of tasks very well. High occupational level specialists include the stock analyst who researches companies in one or two industries and the surgeon who concentrates on liver transplants. Specialists at the first occupational level are usually referred to as *operatives*. An assembly-line worker who fastens two wires to one terminal is an operative.

job specialization
The degree to which a job holder performs only a limited number of tasks.

A generalized job requires the handling of many different tasks. The motivational approach to job design favors generalized jobs. An extreme example of a top-level generalist is the owner of a small business who performs such varied tasks as making the product, selling it, negotiating with banks for loans, and hiring new employees. An extreme example of a generalist at the first (or entry) occupational level is the maintenance worker who packs boxes, sweeps, shovels snow in winter, mows the lawn, and cleans the lavatories.

Exhibit 8-1
The Four Types of Job
Design

Approach	Characteristics	Benefits	Costs
MOTIVATIONAL	i Variety	i Satisfaction	i Training
	i Autonomy	i Motivation	i Staffing difficulty
	i Significance	i Involvement	i Errors
	i Skill usage	i Performance	i Mental fatigue
	i Participation	d Absenteeism	i Stress
	i Recognition		i Mental abilities
	i Growth		i Compensation
	i Achievement		
	i Feedback		
MECHANISTIC	i Specialization	d Training	d Satisfaction
	i Simplification	d Staffing difficulty	d Motivation
	i Repetition	d Errors	i Absenteeism
	i Automation	d Mental fatigue	
	d Spare time	d Mental abilities	
		d Compensation	
BIOLOGICAL	d Strength requirements	d Physical abilities	i Financial costs
	d Endurance requirements	d Physical fatigue	i Inactivity
	i Seating comfort	d Aches & pains	
	i Postural comfort	d Medical incidents	
	d Environmental stressors		
PERCEPTUAL/	i Lighting quality	d Errors	i Boredom
MOTOR	i Display and control quality	d Accidents	d Satisfaction
	d Information processing requirements	d Mental fatigue	
	i User-friendly equipment	d Stress	
		d Training	
		d Staffing difficulty	
		d Compensation	
		d Mental abilities	

i = increased
d = decreased

Source: Adapted with permission from Michael A. Campion and Michael J. Stevens, "Neglected Aspects in Job Design: How People Design Jobs, Task-Job Predictability, and Influence of Training," *Journal of Business and Psychology* (Winter 1991): 175.

ADVANTAGES AND DISADVANTAGES OF JOB SPECIALIZATION. The most important advantage of job specialization is that it allows for the development of expertise at all occupational levels. When employees perform the same task repeatedly, they become highly knowledgeable. Many employees derive status and self-esteem from being experts at some task.

Specialized jobs at lower occupational levels require less training time and less learning ability. This can prove to be a key advantage when the available labor force lacks special skills. For example, McDonald's could never have grown so large if each restaurant needed to be staffed by expert chefs. Instead, newcomers to the work force can quickly learn such specialized skills as preparing hamburgers and french fries. These newcomers can be paid entry-level wages—an advantage from a management perspective only!

Job specialization also has disadvantages. Coordinating the work force can be difficult when several employees do small parts of one job. Somebody has to be responsible for pulling together the small pieces of the total task. Some employees prefer narrowly specialized jobs but the majority prefer broad tasks that give them a feeling of control over what they are doing. Although many technical and professional workers join the work force as specialists, they often become bored by performing a narrow range of tasks.

From an organization's standpoint, job specialization can often result in low productivity because there is not enough work to keep the specialist fully occupied. The volume of work thus places a limit on the specialization of labor. Many organizations attempt to solve this problem by hiring highly trained specialists on a temporary basis when they need certain services.

AUTOMATION AND JOB SPECIALIZATION

Ever since the Industrial Revolution, automation has been used to replace some aspects of human endeavor in the office and the factory. Automation typically involves a machine performing a specialized task previously performed by people. Automation is widely used in factories, offices, and in stores (stores use optical scanners, for example). Managers rely upon automated equipment to perform many clerical chores, such as typing correspondence and mailing out photocopies. In most firms, managers routinely use fax machines to quickly send photocopies of documents to other locations.

A prime example of task specialization through automation is the use of industrial robots. Industrial robots are mechanical arms that are controlled by a computer. (In contrast to science-fiction robots, real robots seldom appear humanoid.) Robots perform many specialized human tasks, such as welding, assembling, spray-painting, loading, and bolting.

Robots have been widely used in the automobile industry. Other applications include food processing, furnace construction, the inspection of computer chips, and the salvaging of nuclear fuel. Robots are highly adaptive and can work under conditions that would be unsafe for humans. Robots can also play a key role in helping people with physical impairments. For example, a robotic arm has been developed that responds to voice commands by dialing a telephone, accessing information on a computer, and even lifting a cup of coffee. The arm enabled a partially paralyzed man to become a customer-service representative at PNC Bank in Pittsburgh.

Robots can work continuously and have high reliability, yet their worldwide use has not met expectations. Japan uses nearly 70 percent of the world's industrial robots. The United States uses 12 percent and Germany uses 7 percent. A major contributor to the growth of robotics in Japan has been an increasing labor shortage. A problem in the United States has been the complexity of some robots and the fact that they do not always fit smoothly into factory operations.

> **job enrichment**
> *An approach to making jobs involve more challenge and responsibility, so they will be more appealing to most employees.*

JOB ENRICHMENT AND THE JOB CHARACTERISTICS MODEL

LEARNING OBJECTIVE

Describe job enrichment, including the job characteristics model.

Job enrichment is an approach to making jobs involve more challenge and responsibility, so they will be more appealing to most employees. At its best, job en-

Exhibit 8-2
Characteristics and
Consequences of an
Enriched Job

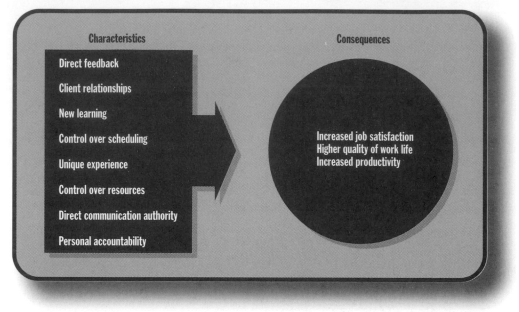

richment gives workers a sense of ownership, responsibility, and accountability for their work. Because job enrichment leads to a more exciting job, it often increases employee job satisfaction and motivation. People are usually willing to work harder at tasks they find enjoyable and rewarding, just as they will put effort into a favority hobby. The general approach to enriching a job is to build into it more planning and decision making, controlling, and responsibility. Most managers have enriched jobs; most data entry specialists do not.

CHARACTERISTICS OF AN ENRICHED JOB

According to Frederick Herzberg, the way to design an enriched job is to include as many of the following characteristics as possible.[4] (Exhibit 8-2 summarizes the characteristics and consequences of enriched jobs.)

1. *Direct feedback.* Employees should receive immediate evaluation of their work. This feedback can be built into the job (such as the feedback that closing a sale gives a sales representative) or provided by the supervisor.
2. *Client relationships.* A job is automatically enriched when an employee has a client or customer to serve, whether that client is inside or outside the firm. Serving a client is more satisfying to most people than performing work solely for a manager.
3. *New learning.* An enriched job allows its holder to acquire new knowledge. The learning can stem from job experiences themselves or from training programs associated with the job.
4. *Control over scheduling.* The ability to schedule one's own work contributes to job enrichment. Scheduling includes the authority to decide when to tackle which assignment and having some say in setting working hours.
5. *Unique experience.* An enriched job has some unique qualities or features. A public-relations assistant, for example, has the opportunity to interact with visiting celebrities.

6. *Control over resources.* Another contributor to enrichment is having some control over resources, such as money, material, or people.
7. *Direct communication authority.* An enriched job provides workers the opportunity to communicate directly with other people who use their output. A software specialist with an enriched job, for example, handles complaints about the software he or she developed. The advantages of this dimension of an enriched job are similar to those derived from maintaining client relationships.
8. *Personal accountability.* In an enriched job, workers are responsible for their results. They accept credit for a job done well and blame for a job done poorly.

A highly enriched job has all eight of the preceding characteristics and gives the job holder an opportunity to satisfy high-level psychological needs, such as self-fulfillment. Sometimes the jobs of managers are too enriched; they have too much responsibility and too many risks. A job with some of these characteristics would be moderately enriched. An impoverished job has none.

GUIDELINES FOR IMPLEMENTING JOB ENRICHMENT

Before implementing a program of job enrichment, a manager must first ask if the workers need or want more responsibility, variety, and growth. Some employees already have jobs that are enriched enough. Many employees do not want an enriched job because they prefer to avoid the challenge and stress of responsibility. Brainstorming is useful in pinpointing changes that will enrich jobs for those who want enrichment.[5] The brainstorming group would be composed of job incumbents, supervisors, and perhaps an industrial engineer. The workers' participation in planning changes can be useful. Workers may suggest, for example, how to increase client contact.

THE JOB CHARACTERISTICS MODEL OF JOB ENRICHMENT

The concept of job enrichment has been expanded to create the **job characteristics model,** a method of job enrichment that focuses on the task and interpersonal dimensions of a job.[6] As Exhibit 8-3 shows, five measurable characteristics of jobs improve employee motivation, satisfaction, and performance. These characteristics are:

job characteristics model
A method of job enrichment that focuses on the task and personal dimensions of a job.

1. *Skill variety,* the degree to which there are many skills to perform.
2. *Task identity,* the degree to which one worker is able to do a complete job, from beginning to end, with a tangible and visible outcome.
3. *Task significance,* the degree to which work has a heavy impact on others in the immediate organization or the external environment.
4. *Autonomy,* the degree to which a job offers freedom, independence, and discretion in scheduling and in determining procedures involved in its implementation.
5. *Feedback,* the degree to which a job provides direct information about performance.

As Exhibit 8-3 reported, these core job characteristics relate to critical psychological states or key mental attitudes. Skill variety, task identity, and task significance lead to a feeling that the work is meaningful. The task dimension of autonomy leads quite logically to a feeling that one is responsible for work outcomes. And the feedback dimension leads to knowledge of results. According to the model, a redesigned job must lead to these three psychological states for workers

Exhibit 8-3
The Job Characteristics
Model of Job Enrichment

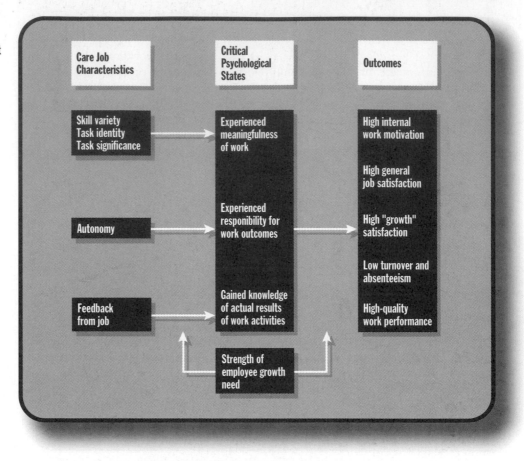

to achieve the outcomes of internal motivation, job satisfaction, low turnover and absenteeism, and high-quality performance.

The notation in Exhibit 8-3, *strength of employee growth need,* provides guidelines for managers. It signifies that the link between the job characteristics and outcomes will be stronger for workers who want to grow and develop. Chapter 12 will say much more about the importance of psychological needs in motivation.

The job characteristics model combines the five characteristics into a single index that reflects the overall potential of a job to trigger high internal work motivation. The index, called the Motivating Potential Score (MPS) is computed as follows:

$$MPS = \frac{\text{Skill variety} + \text{Task identity} + \text{Task significance}}{3} \times \text{Autonomy} \times \text{Feedback}$$

Numeric values for each of the five job characteristics are obtained by tabulating job holders' answers to the Job Diagnostic Survey, a formal questionnaire. After computing the MPS, a researcher can evaluate whether redesigning a job actually changed employees' perceptions of its motivational value.

EFFECTIVENESS OF JOB ENRICHMENT

Programs of job enrichment have become standard practice at thousands of organizations, and the results have often been favorable. Job enrichment has often led to an increase in productivity, quality, and job satisfaction. Quality is likely to increase because job enrichment sometimes includes worker responsibility for quality control.[7]

A current study illustrates the potential of the job characteristics model of job enrichment. A large Southwestern bank–holding company decided to enrich the job of bank teller. The enrichment involved making tellers feel more professional and fulfilled by enhancing responsibility, authority, and accountability. For example, tellers no longer had to refer commercial check customers to special tellers. A total of 526 tellers participated in the study at intervals of 6, 24, and 48 months.

Enriching the job of bank tellers improved the tellers' perceptions. They though the newly defined job was more motivational, as measured by increases in the motivating potential scores. Job satisfaction and commitment increased quickly but then returned to its initial level. Performance did not increase within 6 months. Interestingly, however, performance did increase significantly when measured at 24 and 48 months.[8]

JOB INVOLVEMENT, ENLARGEMENT, AND ROTATION

Job enrichment, including the job characteristics model, is a comprehensive program. Managers can also improve the motivational aspects of job design through less complicated procedures: job involvement, job enlargement, and job rotation. All three processes are built into the more comprehensive job enrichment.

Job involvement is the degree to which individuals are identified psychologically with their work. It also refers to the importance of work to a person's total self-image. If an insurance claims examiner regards his job as a major part of his identity, he experiences high job involvement. For example, at a social gathering the claims examiner would inform people shortly after meeting them, "I'm a claims examiner with Nationwide Insurance." The employee-involvement groups in total quality management are based on job involvement. By making decisions about quality improvement, the team members ideally identify psychologically with their work. Skill-Building Exercise 8-A, at the end of the chapter, gives you an opportunity to examine your own job involvement.

Job enlargement refers to increasing the number and variety of tasks within a job. Because the tasks are approximately at the same level of responsibility, job enlargement is also referred to as *horizontal job loading*. In contrast, job enrichment is referred to as *vertical job loading*, because the job holder takes on higher-level job responsibility. The claims examiner would experience job enlargement if he were given additional responsibilities such as examining claims for boats and motorcycles as well as automobiles.

Job rotation is a temporary switching of job assignments. In this way workers experience skill variety. However, the potential advantages of job rotation are lost if a person is rotated from one dull job to another. An example of an ineffective rotation is having a worker count inventory one day and sort mail the next. A motivational form of job rotation would be for our claims examiner to investigate auto and small-truck claims one month, and large trucks the next. Job rotation helps workers prevent burnout (a feeling a total exhaustion due to long-term stress).

LEARNING OBJECTIVE

Describe job involvement, enlargement, and rotation.

job involvement
The degree to which individuals are identified psychologically with their work.

job enlargement
Increasing the number and variety of tasks within a job.

job rotation
A temporary switching of job assignments.

WORK TEAMS AND JOB DESIGN

Recognize how work teams
are related to job design.

work team
*A group of employ-
ees responsible for
an entire work
process or segment
that delivers a
product or service
to an internal or
external customer.*

An extension of enriching individual jobs has been enriching the job of group members by forming a work team. Teams have already been mentioned at several places in the text. Given their importance in the modern workplace, they will also receive separate mention in Chapter 14. A **work team** is a group of employees responsible for an entire work process or segment that delivers a product or service to an internal or external customer. Terms for the same type of group include *self-managing work team, semi-autonomous group*, and *production work team*.

Working in a team is enriching because it broadens the responsibility of team members. The managerial activities performed by team members have been divided into three levels of responsibility (or complexity):[9]

Level 1 begins with quality responsibilities, followed by continuous improvement in work methods, managing suppliers, external customer contact, and hiring team members.

Level 2 begins with forming teams of people from different functions, followed by vacation scheduling, choosing team leaders, equipment purchase, and facility design.

Level 3 begins with budgeting, followed by product modification and development, team member performance appraisal, handling the disciplinary process, and making compensation decisions.

A survey by a consulting firm indicated that 27 percent of respondents reported that their organization uses self-directed teams. Half of the respondents predicted that the majority of their work force will be organized into work teams within five years.[10] Small as well as large companies are making use of this form of job design. Work teams are found in businesses as diverse as food processing, furniture manufacturing, telecommunications, insurance, and non-profit firms.

ERGONOMICS AND JOB DESIGN

Illustrate how ergonomic
factors can be part of job
design.

**cumulative trauma
disorders**
*Injuries caused by
repetitive motions
over prolonged pe-
riods of time.*

As mentioned in the biological approach to job design, a job should be laid out to decrease the chances that it will physically harm the incumbent. A basic example is that jackhammer operators are required to wear sound dampeners and kidney belts to minimize trauma. A major hazard in the modern workplace is **cumulative trauma disorders**, injuries caused by repetitive motions over prolonged periods of time. These disorders now account for almost half the occupational injuries and illnesses in the United States. According to estimates by Aetna Life & Casualty Co., cumulative trauma disorders cost about $20 billion a year in worker compensation claims, lost productivity, and related expenses.[11]

Any occupation involving excessive repetitive motions, including bricklayer and meat cutter, can lead to cumulative trauma disorder. The surge in the number of cumulative trauma disorders stems from the use of computers and other high-tech equipment such as price scanners. Extensive keyboarding places severe strain on hand and wrist muscles, often leading to *carpal tunnel syndrome*. This syndrome occurs when frequent bending of the wrist causes swelling in a tunnel of

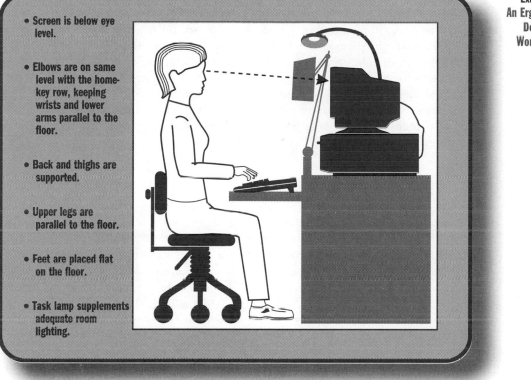

**Exhibit 8-4
An Ergonomically
Designed
Workstation**

- Screen is below eye level.

- Elbows are on same level with the home-key row, keeping wrists and lower arms parallel to the floor.

- Back and thighs are supported.

- Upper legs are parallel to the floor.

- Feet are placed flat on the floor.

- Task lamp supplements adequate room lighting.

bones and ligaments in the wrist. The nerve that gives feeling to the hand is pinched, resulting in tingling and numbness in the fingers.

The symptoms of carpal tunnel syndrome are severe. Many workers suffering from the syndrome are unable to differentiate hot and cold by touch and lose finger strength. They often appear clumsy because they have difficulty with everyday tasks such as tying their shoes or picking up small objects. Treatment of carpal tunnel syndrome may involve surgery to release pressure on the median nerve. Another approach is anti-inflammatory drugs to reduce tendon swelling.

To help prevent and decrease the incidence of cumulative trauma disorders, many companies are selecting equipment designed for this purpose. In addition, many companies are increasing the frequency of rest breaks and offering job rotation. Exhibit 8-4 depicts a workstation based on ergonomic principles developed to engineer a good fit between person and machine.

**modified work
schedule**

Any formal departure from the traditional hours of work, excluding shift work and staggered work hours.

MODIFIED WORK SCHEDULES AND JOB DESIGN

One of the key characteristics of job enrichment is to give workers authority in scheduling their own work. Closely related is the widespread practice of giving workers some choice in deviating from the traditional five-day, 40-hour work week. A **modified work schedule** is any formal departure from the traditional hours of work, excluding shift work and staggered work hours. Yet shift work presents enough unique managerial challenges that it will be described here. Modified work schedules include flexible working hours, a compressed work week, job sharing, working at home, and part-time work.

LEARNING OBJECTIVE

Summarize the various modified work schedules.

Modified work schedules serve several important organizational purposes in addition to being part of job design. They are intended to increase job satisfaction and motivation and to recruit workers who prefer to avoid a traditional schedule. Many single parents need flexible working hours to cope with child care. Flexible working hours are popular with many employees. Working at home is popular with a subset of the work force. Yet, as companies continue to remain thinly staffed, employees have shown less willingness to volunteer for job sharing and part-time work. A prevailing attitude is to cling to a full-time job. Many workers also feel that not being seen around the office regularly might hurt their chances for promotion.

FLEXIBLE WORKING HOURS

flexible working hours

A system of working hours wherein employees must work certain core hours but can choose their arrival and departure times.

For many office employees, the standard eight-hour day with fixed starting and stopping times is a thing of the past. Instead, these employees exert some control over their work schedules through a system of **flexible working hours.**

Employees with flexible working hours are required to work certain core hours, such as 10:00 A.M. to 3:30 P.M. However, they are able to choose which hours they work from 7:00 A.M. to 10:00 A.M. and from 3:30 P.M. to 6:30 P.M. Exhibit 8-5 presents a basic model of flexible working hours. Time-recording devices are frequently used to monitor whether employees have put in the required work for the week.

Employees are often more satisfied but not necessarily more productive under flexible working hours. One study conducted in two government agencies was able to pinpoint the condictions under which flexible working hours do contribute to productivity. Reserachers found that, when busy workers had to share physical resources, flexible working hours did contribute to productivity. Specifically, computer programmers who shared a mainframe computer became more productive under flexible working hours. Data entry operators who did not share resources were as productive in flexible-hours jobs as they were with fixed hours.[12]

Flexible working hours create some supervisory problems. Managers must either be present for the entire band of working hours or arrange tasks so that the employees can function well without supervision. A fully functioning, self-managing team, however, should require less supervison than a traditional work group. Another problem is that some employees subvert the system. They duck away from the office periodically, claiming they are "on flextime." Finally, flexible working hours are only suitable when workers are not dependent upon one another during a specific time period. In a just-in-time inventory environment, for example, employees are dependent on each other.

COMPRESSED WORK WEEK

compressed work week

A full-time work schedule that allows 40 hours in less than five days.

A **compressed work week** is a full-time work schedule that allows 40 hours in less than five days. The usual arrangement is 4-40 (working four 10-hour days). Many employees enjoy the 4-40 schedule because it enables them to have three consecutive days off from work. Employees often invest this time in leisure activities or part-time jobs. A 4-40 schedule usually allows most employees to take off Saturdays and Sundays. Important exceptions include police workers, hospital employees, and computer operators.

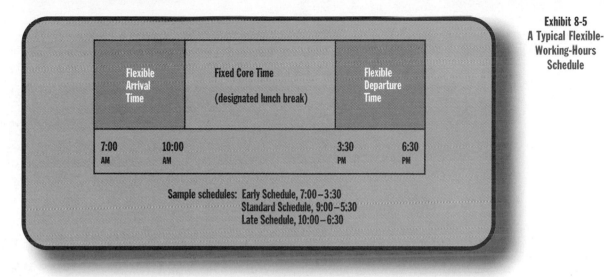

Exhibit 8-5
A Typical Flexible-
Working-Hours
Schedule

A compressed work week currently gaining favor is the 9-80. The numerals signify nine-hour days and 80 hours worked every two weeks. Employees on 9-80 work nine-hour days from Monday through Thursday, and an eight-hour day on Friday. The following Friday is a day off.

Compressed work weeks are well liked by employees whose lifestyle fits such a schedule. However, the 4-40 week has many built-in problems. Many workers are fatigued during the last two hours and suffer from losses in concentration. From a personal standpoint, working for 10 consecutive hours can be inconvenient.

Even in situations where employees are strongly in favor of the compressed work week, employers may discover significant problems. An engineering service group conducted a four-month experiment with a 4-40 schedule. In evaluating the schedule, the white-collar employees cited such advantages as the ability to conduct personal business more efficiently, the ability to avoid difficult morning commutes, and improved productivity due to work continuity. Management stopped the program, however, when it appeared that customer service had not really improved.[13]

TELECOMMUTING

Another deviation from the traditional work schedule is **telecommuting,** an arrangement in which employees use computers to perform their regular work duties at home or in a satellite location. Employees who telecommute usually use computers tied into the company's main office. A worker need not use a computer to work at home, however. An employee might work at home as an insurance claims processor, a telemarketer, or a garment maker. People who work at home are also referred to as *teleworkers.*

In addition to using computers to communicate to their employer's office, telecommuters attend meetings on company premises and stay in telephone contact. Teleworking has become widespread. According to one market research firm, approximately 37 million U.S. households contain at least one person doing income-generating work at home. Many teleworkers are self-employed, but 8.4 million of them are corporate employees working full- or part-time during business

telecommuting
An arrangement in which employees use computers to perform their regular work duties at home or in a satellite location.

BUSINESS OWNER IN ACTION: KELLY'S BALLOONS UNLIMITED

Eleanor Kelly is the founder and owner of Kelly's Balloons Unlimited, of Lexington, Kentucky. She knows balloons, along with teddy bears, chocolate roses, Kentucky gourmet cookies, and a wide range of other gift items. Her small firm began as a one-person operation run from her kitchen table and a telephone. Balloons Unlimited is now a full-time enterprise that employs five part-time workers in the converted basement in Kelly's home.

"About one-forth of our customers are out of state," Kelly says, sitting in front of her computer and scrolling through a database of more than 4,800 customers nationwide. "I don't like to repeat an order. I can call up a customer's records because we want to make sure each order is very different."

Kelly cut costs considerably to get her business launched. Back in 1981 she borrowed $500 from a bank to purchase a used van. Her annual total retail sales are now close to $200,000.

Source: Based on facts reported in Annette Kondo, "Home Office: Flexibility Nice, but Consider Cash Needs," Knight-Ridder story (15 July 1995).

hours.[14] Many small businesses also give selected employees an opportunity to conduct all or some of their work at home. The accompanying Business Owner in Action insert describes a full-time teleworker.

ADVANTAGES OF TELECOMMUTING PROGRAMS. Telecommuting can work well with self-reliant and self-starting employees who have relevant work experience. Work-at-home employees usually volunteer for such an arrangement; therefore, they are likely to experience high job satisfaction from it. Employees derive many benefits from working at home, including easier management of personal life, lowered commuting and clothing costs, and fewer distractions from coworkers. Telecommuting offers these advantages to the employer:[15]

1. *Increased productivity.* Studies have shown consistently that telecommuting programs increase productivity, usually by approximately 25 percent. A survey of 1,002 executives found that 29 percent of companies permit telecommuting, and 86 percent of these firms reported an accompanying productivity increase. Storage Tek in Boulder, Colorado, reported a 144 percent increase in productivity among engineers and other employees. Another productivity gain reported by many companies is that telecommuters rarely have sick days.
2. *Low overhead.* Because the employees are providing some of their own office space, the company can operate with smaller offices. A vice-president of marketing research operations noted that, because of its work-at-home program, the company was able to greatly expand its client load without acquiring additional space. AT&T saved $80 million in 1994 by shutting offices and having sales people work from their homes.
3. *Access to a wider range of employee talent.* Companies with regular work-at-home programs are almost always deluged with résumés from eager job applicants. The talent bank includes parents (mostly mothers) with young children, employees who find commuting unpleasant, and others who live far away from their firms.

DISADVANTAGES OF TELECOMMUTING. Work-at-home programs must be used selectively because they pose disadvantages for both employee and employer. The careers of telecommuters may suffer because they are not visible to management. Many telecommuters complain of the isolation from coworkers.

Also, telecommuters can be exploited if they feel compelled to work on company problems late into the night and on weekends. The many potential distractions at home make it difficult for some telecommuters to concentrate on work. Finally, telecommuters are sometimes part-time employees who receive limited benefits and are paid only for what they produce. As one telecommuter, a data entry specialist, said, "If I let up for an afternoon, I earn hardly anything."

Telecommuting programs can be disadvantageous to the employer because building loyalty and teamwork is difficult when so many workers are away from the office. Telecommuters who are not performing measured work are difficult to supervise—working at home gives an employee much more latitude in attending to personal matters during work time. Another problem is that the organization may miss out on some of the creativity that stems from the exchange of ideas in the traditional office.

SUGGESTIONS FOR MANAGERS OF TELEWORKERS. To maximize the advantages and minimize the disadvantages of telecommuting, managers should follow a few key suggestions:

1. Teleworkers should be chosen with care. Working at home is best suited for self-disciplined, well-motivated, computer-literate, and deadline-conscious workers.
2. Make sure the teleworker has a suitable home environment for telecommuting. The designated work area should be as separate from the household as possible and relatively free from distractions.
3. Clearly define productivity goals and deadlines. The more measurable the output of work, the better suited it is for telecommuting.
4. Agree on the working hours during which the teleworker can be reached. Remember, the manager is not disturbing the worker at home by telephoning that person during regularly scheduled working hours.
5. Discuss how telecommuters will deal with family and personal obligations during working hours. A teleworker should take work as seriously as the company-office employee.
6. Keep in regular contact with teleworkers. Encourage them to use e-mail and the telephone in order to stay in the communications loop.[16]

JOB SHARING

Job sharing is a work arrangement in which two people who work part-time share one job. The sharers divide up the job according to their needs. Each may work selected days of the work week, for example. Or, one person might work mornings and the other work afternoons. The job sharers might be two friends, a husband and wife, or two employees who did not know each other before sharing a job. If the job is complex, the sharers have to spend work time discussing it.

> **job sharing**
> *A work arrangement in which two people who work part-time share one job*

Job sharing has its greatest appeal to workers whose family commitments do not allow full-time work. A typical situation of job sharing involves two friends who want a responsible position but can only work part-time. Job sharing offers the employer an advantage in that two people working half-time usually produce more than one person working full-time. (This is particularly noticeable in creative work.) Also, if one employee is sick, the other is still available to handle the job for the half day.

Job sharing has been proposed as a method of reducing the sting of unemployment. Under this proposal, many workers with full-time jobs would either volunteer for or be forced to work part-time. In this way, they would share their jobs with other workers. Employers would be required to hire more employees to do the same amount of work; total wages and benefits, however, would not increase, because compensation would be shared.

Job sharing has several disadvantages to employee and employer. A part-time worker is unlikely to be recommended for promotion if he or she can only make a half-time commitment to the firm. The firm may have difficulty evaluating, supervising, and rewarding job sharers. For example, should both receive identical raises? How does the company know which should receive credit or blame when something goes right or wrong?

PART-TIME AND TEMPORARY WORK

Part-time work is a work option offered by virtually all large employers today. The category of part-time workers includes employees who work reduced weekly, annual, or seasonal hours and those who have project-based, occasional work. For example, a marketing brand manager might work full days on Mondays, Wednesdays, and Fridays. After returning from maternity leave, a brand manager at Quaker Oats negotiated such an arrangement with the company.

Many people, such as students and semi-retired people, choose part-time work because it fits their lifestyles. Also, many people work part-time because they cannot find full-time employment.

Temporary employment is at an all-time high, with some employers even hiring part-time managers, engineers, lawyers, and other high-level workers. Collectively, part-time and temporary employees constitute one-fourth to one-third of the work force. Because they are hired according to, or contingent upon, an employer's need, they are referred to as **contingent workers.** Some contingent workers receive modest benefits. Another contingent worker is the independent contractor, who is paid for services rendered but does not receive benefits. A familiar example is a plumber hired by a homeowner to make a repair. The plumber sets the wage, and receives no benefits.

> **contingent workers**
> *Part-time or temporary employees who are not members of the employer's permanent work force.*

Many employees enjoy part-time work because they are willing to trade off the low pay for personal convenience. Employers are eager to hire contingent workers to avoid the expense of hiring full-time workers. Paying limited or no benefits to part-time workers can save employers as much as 35 percent of the cost of full-time compensation. Also, contingent workers can be readily laid off if business conditions warrant. Some seasonally oriented businesses, such as gift-catalog sales firms, hire mostly part-time workers. The disadvantage to the employer is that part-time employment works best for entry-level workers. Building a stable, professional staff composed of part-time employees is difficult in most industries. A long-standing exception is colleges and technical schools, which rely heavily on a stable and professional group of part-time faculty.

To optimize the contribution of part-time or temporary workers, they should be assigned projects rather than performing a series of unrelated tasks. Completing an entire project helps define the contribution of the part-time or temporary worker and also contributes to job enrichment. The manager should be clear about what is expected and should set a specific direction. A representative project would be for a contingent worker to update the addresses and telephone numbers on a customer database.

SHIFT WORK

To accommodate the needs of employers rather than employees, many workers are assigned to shift work. The purpose of shift work is to provide coverage during nonstandard hours. The most common shift schedules are days (7 A.M. to 3 P.M.), evenings (3 P.M. to 11 P.M.), and nights (11 P.M. to 7 A.M.). Shift work is used in manufacturing to meet high demand for products without having to expand facilities. It is more economical to run a factory 16 or 24 hours per day than to run two or three factories eight hours per day. Service industries make even more extensive use of shift work to meet the demands of customers around the clock, such as in a hotel. Shift work is also necessary in public-service operations such as police work, fire fighting, and health care.

Shift work is more than a deviation from a traditional work schedule. It is a lifestyle that affects productivity, health, family, and social life. Shift work unfortunately disrupts the natural rhythm of the body and creates job problems. Three times the average incidence of drug and alcohol abuse fosters an increased risk of errors and accidents. Many industrial catastrophes, such as ship wrecks, oil spills, and chemical leaks have taken place during the night ("graveyard") shift. Shift workers also experience difficulty in integrating their schedules with the social needs of friends and families.

With proper training, employees can adjust better to shift work. A shift-work consultant, for example, recommends: "Create healthy sleep environments by keeping rooms cool and eliminating daylight with dark shades and curtains or even styrofoam cutouts or black plastic taped to the window frame."[17]

SUMMARY OF KEY POINTS

1
Identify the major dimensions and different types of job design.
Job design involves establishing job responsibilities and duties and the manner in which they are to be performed. Four approaches to job design are (1) the motivational approach, (2) the mechanistic approach (which emphasizes efficiency), (3) the perceptual/motor approach, and (4) the biological approach (which emphasizes safety). Each of these approaches has benefits and costs.

Job specialization is the degree to which a job holder performs a only a limited number of tasks. Specialists are found at different occupational levels. Job specialization enhances work force expertise at all levels and can reduce training time at the operative level. Specialization, however, can lead to problems. Coordinating the work of specialists can be difficult, and some employees may become bored. Automation, including robotics, contributes to job specialization. Robots perform many specialized tasks, including those that would be unsafe for humans.

2
Describe job enrichment, including the job characteristics model.
Job enrichment is a method of making jobs involve more challenge and responsibility so they will be more appealing to most employees. An enriched job provides direct feedback,

client relationships, new learning, scheduling by the employee, unique experience, control over resources, direct communication authority, and personal accountability.

Job enrichment has been expanded to create the job characteristics model, which focuses on the task and interpersonal dimensions of a job. Five characteristics of jobs improve employee motivation, satisfaction, and performance: skill variety, task identity, task significance, autonomy, and feedback. These characteristics relate to critical psychological states which, in turn, lead to outcomes such as internal motivation, satisfaction, low absenteeism, and high quality.

3

Describe job involvement, enlargement, and rotation.

Job involvement reflects psychological involvement with one's work and how much work is part of the self-image. Job enlargement is about increasing the number and variety of job tasks. Job rotation is switching assignments.

4

Recognize how work teams are related to job design.

Work teams are groups of employees responsible for an entire work process or segment. Work team members are multi-skilled generalists who plan, control, improve their own work processes, and sometimes even make compensation decisions.

5

Illustrate how ergonomic factors can be part of job design.

Cumulative trauma disorders are injuries caused by repetitive motions over prolonged periods of time. Workstations can be designed to minimize these problems by such measures as supporting the back and thighs, and placing the feet flat on the floor.

6

Summarize the various modified work schedules.

Work scheduling is another aspect of job design. A modified work schedule departs from the traditional hours of work. Modified work scheduling options include flexible working hours, a compressed work week, telecommuting, job sharing, and part-time and temporary work. Shift work deviates from a regular day schedule, and can lead to health problems, accidents, and family problems.

KEY TERMS AND PHRASES

Job Design *pg. 170*

Job Description *pg. 171*

Job Specialization *pg. 171*

Job Enrichment *pg. 173*

Job Characteristics model *pg. 175*

Job Involvement *pg. 177*

Job Enlargement *pg. 177*

Job Rotation *pg. 177*

Work Team *pg. 178*

Cumulative Trauma Disorder *pg. 178*

Modified Work Schedule *pg. 179*

Flexible Working Hours *pg. 180*

Compressed Work Week *pg. 180*

Telecommuting *pg. 181*

Job Sharing *pg. 183*

Contingent Workers *pg. 184*

QUESTIONS

1. Is an executive (top-level manager) a specialist or a generalist? Explain your reasoning.
2. A study showed that high mental ability is generally required to perform well in jobs designed by the motivational approach. Why might this be true?

3. Using the characteristics of an enriched job presented in this chapter, analyze the extent to which the job of the instructor for this course is enriched.

4. How would a manager go about *enlarging* but not *enriching* a job?

5. Assume that many of a company's employees telecommute full-time or part-time. Should that company conduct an ergonomics audit of the home offices of the telecommuters?

6. What factors in the external environment have contributed to the popularity of flexible working hours?

7. At what stage in a person's career might telecommuting be particularly inadvisable?

SKILL-BUILDING EXERCISE 8-A: HOW INVOLVED ARE YOU?

Indicate the strength of your agreement with the following statements by circling the number that appears below the appropriate heading: DS = disagree strongly; D = disagree; N = neutral; A = agree; AS = agree strongly. Respond in relation to a present job, the job you hope to have, or school work.

	DS	D	N	A	AS
1. The major satisfaction in my life comes from my work.	1	2	3	4	5
2. Work is just a means to an end.	5	4	3	2	1
3. The most important things that happen to me involve my work.	1	2	3	4	5
4. I often concentrate so hard on my work that I'm unaware of what is going on around me.	1	2	3	4	5
5. If I inherited enough money, I would spend the rest of my life on vacation.	5	4	3	2	1
6. I'm a perfectionist about my work.	1	2	3	4	5
7. I am very much involved personally in my work.	1	2	3	4	5
8. Most things in life are more important than work.	5	4	3	2	1
9. Working full-time is boring.	5	4	3	2	1
10. My work is intensely exciting.	1	2	3	4	5

Score _____

Scoring and interpretation: Total the numbers circled, and then use the following guide to interpretation.

45–50 Your attitudes suggest intense job involvement. Such attitudes should contribute highly to productivity, quality, and satisfaction.

28–44 Your attitudes suggest a moderate degree of job involvement. To sustain a high level of productivity and quality, you would need to work toward becoming more involved in your work.

10–27 Your attitudes suggest a low degree of job involvement. It would be difficult to sustain a successful, professional career with such low involvement.

Source: Six of the above statements are quoted or adapted from Myron Gable and Frank Dangello, "Job Involvement, Machiavellianism, and Job Performance," *Journal of Business and Psychology* (Winter 1994): 163.

SKILL-BUILDING EXERCISE 8-B: THE IDEAL HOME-BASED OFFICE

GROUP ACTIVITY Gather into teams of about five people to design an ideal office at home for a professional worker. Take about 20 minutes to develop suggestions for the following aspects of a home office: (1) hardware and software, (2) equipment other than computers, (3) furniture, (4) ergonomics design, (5) office layout, (6) location within the house or apartment. Consider both productivity and job satisfaction when designing your office. After the designs are complete, the team leaders can present them to the rest of the class.

VIDEO DISCUSSION QUESTIONS

1. What type of job design or organization structure was used by Union Carbide management to manage the aftermath of the Bhopal crisis? **[Bhopal]**
2. What are the enriched elements of the jobs for sales representatives at General Tire? **[General Tire]**
3. To what extent does an entrepreneur have a modified work schedule? **[Entrepreneurial Spirit]**

CASE PROBLEM 8-A: THE AIRPORT SECURITY GUARD BLUES

Patti Freeman, supervisor of airport security at an international airport, met with her boss, Jack Indino, to discuss the job performance of her staff.

"Jack," said Patti, "we're developing a group performance problem with my security staff. I want to lay out the problem with you and then suggest a solution."

"Go ahead," said Indino. "What's one more problem in the life of an airport operations manager?"

"As I see it," said Freeman, "our security guards are bored stiff. Each one of them has told me so either directly or indirectly. The general complaint is that they get bored—after a while, each face is the same, and every attaché case or handbag looks the same."

"I think the job boredom is also creating performance problems. Some of the guards have become so lethargic that they don't pay serious attention to any potential security violation. Thank goodness no terrorist or hijacker has gotten through."

"What are you proposing to do about this problem?" asked Indino.

"My tentative solution is to enrich the jobs of the guards in some way. We could work out some way to give them more responsibility and challenge. Perhaps we can allow them to interview passengers to get their thoughts about airline safety."

"I don't see that as a solution," said Indino. "FAA regulations require that the guards be on duty all the time, checking passengers. The guards may be bored, but if the airport wants to stay in business, we need security guards doing exactly what they are doing. If our present crew of guards find their jobs boring, we may have to replace them with people who can concentrate on their jobs for a full shift."

"I'll get back to you again about this problem," said Freeman. "I understand your viewpoint, but I've got to find some way to get the security guards more wrapped up in their jobs."

CASE QUESTIONS

1. How effective might job enrichment be for purposes of curing the inattention problem that Freeman observes?
2. What is your evaluation of the tactic of replacing the security guards with others who might be more attentive?
3. What is your evaluation of Freeman's contention that boredom might be adversely affecting the security guards' job performance?

CASE PROBLEM 8-B: CAUTION AT COMPAQ

Klaus Marteen is the manufacturing director at Northstar, a maker of IBM-compatible personal computers. One Monday morning he was holding his regularly scheduled staff meeting. In addition to reviewing the status of current projects, the agenda included discussions about product refinements. Northstar president Girard Logenmuth attended this meeting because a key competitive issue was scheduled for discussion.

Ten minutes into the meeting, director of quality Linda Snell presented her part of the agenda. She informed the group that a new era in computer manufacturing had arrived. "From now on," she said, "the consumer must be warned of any possible hazards in the regular use of our machines. Our mission may be to become a key player in the information revolution. Yet we don't want to harm unknowing consumers."

"What harm are you talking about?" asked Marteen. Logenmuth also looked at Snell quizzically.

Snell answered, "I'm talking about the high probability of succumbing to a repetitive motion disorder if a person uses our product excessively. The injury claims for RMDs under worker compensation are skyrocketing. As a quality organization, I don't think we should contribute to the problem."

Marteen commented, "Our job is not to police the world. Nor should we be every computer worker's parent. If our end-users are smart enough to use Northstar computers, they're smart enough not to abuse their bodies."

"Look at what the competition is doing," said Snell. "Compaq is now putting warning labels on computer keyboards. The labels direct people to read a safety guide with tips to avoid hand and wrist injuries. Microsoft is also placing warning labels on a specially designed keyboard. Hand-tool manufacturers post warning labels. Let's get with it."

Logenmuth pondered for a moment, and then said: "Hold on, Linda, you're talking about much bigger players than we are. The giant computer companies can afford a few lost sales because of a warning label. Every sane computer user already knows about carpal tunnel syndrome and related disorders. If they follow normal precautions, they have no problem. We don't have to be as cautious as Compaq or Microsoft."

Somewhat irritated, Snell replied, "Can we at least discuss this labeling issue further at out next staff meeting?"

CASE QUESTIONS

1. What should Northstar do about warning labels on its personal computers?
2. Are Compaq Computer Corp. and Microsoft Corp. being too cautious?
3. What ethical issues are facing Northstar?

Source: Several of the above facts are from "Compaq to Add Warning Label," Associated Press story (17 August 1994).

CASE PROBLEM 8-C: THE INDEPENDENT TEMPORARIES

Modern Designs, a home and office furniture company in South Carolina, has two general categories of employees. The core group of full-time, permanent workers consists of close to 1,100 people. Among these workers are managers, professionals, technicians, sales personnel, clerical support, and production workers. Modern Designs supplements the core group with approximately 350 full- and part-time temporary workers. The temporary workers are found mostly in clerical and production positions, but also include engineers, technicians, software specialists, and a few managers.

Kimberly Blake, the director of human resources, was reviewing the contingent work force program with L.C. Shaheen, the president of Modern Designs. She noted that the program had been in full swing for 38 months—a long enough time to judge its effectiveness. Blake's reports showed that, by hiring contingent workers as needed, the company was saving about $350,000 per year in payroll costs. She expressed some concern that much of this savings was being drained by decreased productivity among the temporary and part-time workers.

Shaheen, who had been studying the figures himself on the company information system, expressed some confusion. "I thought part-time and temporary workers hustle quite hard so their contract can be renewed. That should boost productivity."

"You are right, L.C.," said Blake, "Many contingent workers are crackerjacks. They work hard, and hope to be hired for full-time work. But there are exceptions. Many of our best temporary workers have an independent streak. We need them more than they need us."

"In what way are they independent?" asked Shaheen.

Blake explained, "Based on some of my own observations in the clerical support areas, and my conversations with managers, I have reached a few conclusions. Our most talented temporary workers often leave as soon as their contract allows. They are in demand by other companies also, and they know it. These people enjoy the freedom and independence that comes from moving from one employer to another. It is these temporaries who boost productivity when they are here.

"A good example is Jenny Wilcott, a supervisor we hired for three months to help us ram through an unexpected order for 1,000 desks and chairs. She may have created stress for a few of our workers, but she was dynamite. Her reputation was so good that she moved on to help another company meet an unanticipated surge in demand for product."

"So what's wrong with the contingent workers who want to stay with us on renewed assignments?" asked Shaheen.

"Oh, they have about average productivity. However, as we replace the best temporaries with others, there is usually a learning curve problem. Even the best-trained temporaries take a few weeks to get to the top of their learning curve. So the replacements for departed workers tend to pull down productivity."

L.C. said with a sigh, "You make it all sound so complicated. I would like you to work with our managers to devise a plan for raising the productivity of contingent workers. But whatever you do, don't let the solution become too expensive."

CASE QUESTIONS

1. What should management at Modern Designs do to boost the productivity of contingent workers?
2. What impact might job design have on the productivity problem with temporary workers?

CASE PROBLEM 8-D: THE RIGID FLEXIBLE WORKING HOURS

Austin Paulino, division manager of Imaging Industries, called a meeting with his supervisors to make an important announcement. He said, "Results of this year's opinion survey indicate that 90 percent of the employees in our division would prefer flexible working hours. Upper management is convinced that flexible working hours is an inexpensive way to boost morale. Flextime also helps workers balance work and family demands. The company might even get a productivity boost as a result of the program.

"I'd like to get your opinions on how best to implement flexible working hours. Please turn in your recommendations within two weeks."

After the supervisors presented six drafts of a proposal to management over a period of three months, the flextime program was implemented. The key provisions of the flexible working hours program were as follows:

1. Starting times will fluctuate between 7 A.M. and 8 A.M. The minimum lunch break will be 42 minutes, but it can be extended to 90. Quitting time can fluctuate between 3:42 P.M. and 5:30 P.M. depending on starting time and lunch break.
2. All employees will work during core hours that include start times between 8 A.M. and 11:30 A.M. and ending times between 1:00 P.M. and 3:42 P.M.
3. Employees interested in using flextime for a certain week are required to schedule and post a notice by their desk the preceding Friday. Copies of the schedule must be available to the employee's supervisor and the unit administrative assistant.
4. Meetings will be scheduled when possible during core hours. The employee is responsible for attending meetings called outside of core hours.

After the flexible working hours program was in operation for six months, Austin called a meeting to discuss progress. He began by expressing his concerns: "It appears that something isn't right. The latest figures show that less than 5 percent of our employees are using flextime. I'm disappointed. I'd like for you folks to survey your workers and get some feedback."

Sara, one of the production supervisors, held a feedback session with her group members several days after learning that Austin wanted feedback. Jack, a manufacturing technician, offered these observations: "This flextime program is a joke. Flexibility to me means the ability to make decisions day by day, depending on my personal situation. Having to schedule my work time isn't flexibility in my dictionary. Unfortunately, I cannot schedule either my children's illnesses or my baby-sitting conflicts. My wife and I take turns covering sick days and emergencies."

Ted, a production specialist, said, "I must be one of that 5 percent who consistently use flextime. I live close to work and my kids are still very young. It is therefore a good opportunity for me to have lunch with them. A ninety-minute lunch break is fabulous."

Stan, another production supervisor, learned from his group that workers didn't want to do so much paperwork just to get half an hour of flexibility.

When the supervisor met again with Austin, Stan served as a spokesperson. He informed Austin, "After meeting with all our employees, we've concluded that our current flextime program isn't going to boost productivity or raise morale. It looks like we've set up a system to serve our convenience. We were too conservative in our approach. The program has to be changed. Maybe we should do something radical like the 9-80 program that's becoming popular. Our workers would love to have a couple of Fridays off per month."

Austin thanked the supervisors for their input and proposed that they meet to discuss a plan modification in two weeks. The group accepted the challenge.

CASE QUESTIONS

1. What did the company do wrong in planning its flextime program?
2. What changes should be made to the program?

Source: Case researched by Edna H. Soltero, Rochester Institute of Technology.

REFERENCES

1. Patti Bond, "Home Work to Housework, Easy for Telecommuters," Cox News Service (24 July 1995).
2. Saul Gellerman, *Motivating Superior Performance* (Portland, OR: Productivity Press, 1994).
3. Michael A. Campion and Michael J. Stevens, "Neglected Aspects in Job Design: How People Design Jobs, Task-Job Predictability, and Influence of Training," *Journal of Business and Psychology* (Winter 1991): 169–192.
4. Frederick Herzberg, "The Wise Old Turk," *Harvard Business Review* (September–October 1974): 70–80.
5. J. Barton Cunningham and Ted Eberle, "A Guide to Job Enrichment and Redesign," *Personnel* (February 1990): 59.
6. John Richard Hackman and Greg R. Oldham, *Work Redesign* (Reading, MA: Addison-Wesley, 1980): 77.
7. Robert E. Kopelman, "Job Redesign and Productivity: A Review of the Evidence," *National Productivity Review* 4 (3), 1985: 237–255.
8. Ricky W. Griffin, "Effects of Work Redesign on Employee Perceptions, Attitudes, and Behaviors: A Long-Term Investigation," *Academy of Management Journal* (June 1991): 425–435.
9. Richard S. Wellins, William C. Byham, and Jeanne M. Wilson, *Empowered Teams: Creating Self-Directed Work Groups That Improve Quality, Productivity, and Participation* (San Francisco: Jossey-Bass, 1991): 24–28.
10. Survey cited in Shari Caudron, "Are Self-Directed Teams Right for Your Company?" *Personnel Journal* (December 1993): 78.
11. Michael J. Lotito and Francis P. Alvarez, "Integrate Claims Management with ADA Compliance Strategy," *HRMagazine* (August 1993): 87.
12. David A. Ralston, William P. Anthony, and David J. Gustafson, "Employees May Love Flextime, But What Does It Do to the Organization's Productivity?" *Journal of Applied Psychology* (May 1985): 272–279.
13. Spyros Economides, D. N. Beck, and Allen J. Shus, "Longer Days and Shorter Weeks Improve Productivity," *Personnel Administrator* (May 1989): 112–114.
14. Amy Dunkin, "Taking Care of Business—Without Leaving the House," *Business Week* (17 April 1995): 106.
15. "Telecommuting Raises Productivity," *Human Resources Forum* (July 1995): 4; Julian M. Weiss, "Telecommuting Boosts Employee Output," *HRMagazine* (February 1994): 51–53.
16. "Tips for Managing Telecommuters," *Human Resources Forum* (January 1995): 2.
17. Ellen Hale, "Lack of Sleep is Now Groups for Filing Suit—Or Being Sued," Gannett News Service (15 August 1993).

Organization Structure, Reengineering, and Culture

LEARNING OBJECTIVES

After studying this chapter and doing the exercises, you should be able to:

1 Describe the bureaucratic form of organization and discuss its advantages and disadvantages.

2 Explain the major ways in which organizations are divided into departments.

3 Describe three modifications of the bureaucratic structure: matrix, flat, and network.

4 Present an overview of reengineering and the horizontal structures it creates.

5 Specify how delegation, empowerment, and decentralization spread authority in an organization.

6 Identify major aspects of organizational culture, including its management and control.

© Comstock

Michael Mahar, the director of marketing at Frontier Network Systems Inc., believes that his company is undertaking reengineering from a position of strength. Frontier, a telephone, data, and telecommunications equipment service company, changed to one management information system after it had been operating with two. The new Infocon system reduces the number of steps from receiving a customer lead to closing a sale. Now the company can expand its customer base without adding support staff, because one person, instead of several, handles the entire process. • Mahar explains that the new organization structure did result in the loss of several administrative positions. But the reorganization was intended to eliminate tasks as the company assigned more employees to its growing customer base, not squeeze more work out of a smaller group of people. "I don't think we would have been able to downsize and keep our customer service at an acceptable level," he says. • Top management at Frontier gave the restructuring and reengineering total support, added Michele Palermo, the service center manager.[1]

organization structure
The arrangement of people and tasks to accomplish organizational goals.

organizational design
The process of creating a structure that best fits a purpose, strategy, and environment.

The type of activity just described occurs frequently in private and public organizations. Managers are carefully examining their organization structures, and modifying (or redesigning) them if necessary, to enhance effectiveness. The previous chapter described how the tasks of an organization are divided into jobs for individuals and groups. Work is also subdivided through an **organization structure**—the arrangement of people and tasks to accomplish organizational goals.

The structure specifies who reports to whom and who does what. An organization is similar to the framework of a building or the skeleton of the body. **Organizational design** is the process of creating a structure that best fits a purpose, strategy, and environment. For example, Frontier Network Systems changed to a simpler structure to better serve customers.

The purpose of this chapter is to explain how organizations subdivide work among their units. To this end, we will describe various types of structures, delegation, and decentralization. Organizational culture will be described in this chapter because it can support or undermine the structure, and influence the success of overhauling the organization.

BUREAUCRACY AS A FORM OF ORGANIZATION

LEARNING OBJECTIVE 1

Describe the bureaucratic form of organization and discuss its advantages and disadvantages.

A **bureaucracy** is a rational, systematic, and precise form of organization in which rules, regulations, and techniques of control are precisely defined. It is helpful to think of bureaucracy as the traditional form of organization. Other structures are usually variations of, or supplements to, bureaucracy. Do not confuse the word bureaucracy with bigness. Although most big organizations are bureaucratic, small firms can also follow the bureaucratic model. An example might be a small, carefully organized bank.

bureaucracy
A rational, systematic, and precise form of organization in which rules, regulations, and techniques of control are precisely defined.

PRINCIPLES OF ORGANIZATION IN A BUREAUCRACY

The entire traditional, or classical, school of management contributes to our understanding of bureaucracy. Yet the essence of bureaucracy can be understood by identifying its major characteristics and principles as listed next:

1. *Hierarchy of authority.* The dominant characteristic of a bureaucracy is that each lower organizational unit is controlled and supervised by a higher one. The person granted the most formal authority (the right to act) is placed at the top of the hierarchy. Exhibit 9-1 presents a bureaucracy as pyramid-shaped. The number of employees increases substantially as you move down to each successive level. Most of the formal authority is concentrated at the top. Observe that the amount of formal authority decreases as you move to lower levels.

2. *Unity of command.* A classic management principle, **unity of command,** states that each subordinate receives assigned duties from one superior only and is accountable to that superior. In the modern organization many people serve on projects and teams in addition to reporting to their regular boss, thus violating the unity of command.

unity of command
The classical management principle stating that each subordinate receives assigned duties from one superior only and is accountable to that superior.

3. *Task specialization.* In a bureaucracy, division of labor is based on task specialization (described in Chapter 8). To achieve task specialization, organizations have separate departments, such as manufacturing, customer service, and information systems. Employees assigned to these organizational units have specialized knowledge and skills that contribute to the overall effectiveness of the firm.

Exhibit 9-1
The Bureaucratic
Form of Organization

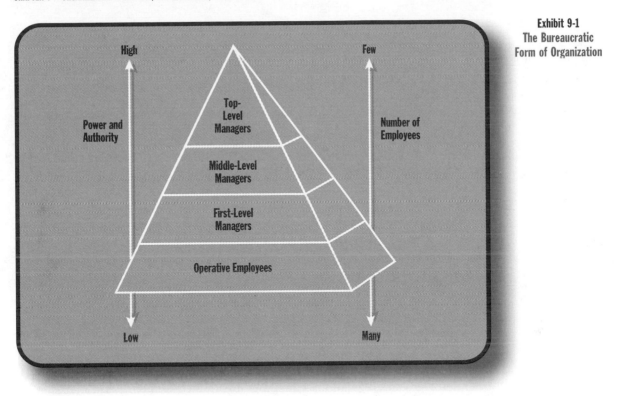

4. *Duties and rights of employees.* Bureaucracies are characterized by rules that define the rights and duties of employees. In a highly bureaucratic organization, each employee has a precise job description, and policy and procedure manuals are current and accessible.

5. *Definition of managerial responsibility.* In a bureaucracy, the responsibility and authority of each manager is defined clearly in writing. When responsibility is defined in writing, managers know what is expected of them and what limits are set to their authority. This approach minimizes overlapping of authority and accompanying confusion.

6. *Line and staff functions.* A bureaucracy identifies the various organizational units as being line or staff. Line functions are those involved with the primary purpose of an organization or its primary outputs. In a bank, people who supervise work related to borrowing and lending money are line managers. Staff functions assist the line functions. Staff managers are responsible for important functions such as human resources (or personnel) and purchasing. Although staff functions do not deal with the primary purposes of the firm, they are essential for achieving the organization's mission.

ADVANTAGES AND DISADVANTAGES OF BUREAUCRACY

Bureaucracy has made modern civilization possible. Without large, complex organizations to coordinate the efforts of thousands of people, we would not have airplanes, automobiles, skyscrapers, universities, vaccines, or space satellites.

Many large bureaucratic organizations are successful and continue to grow at an impressive pace. Among the leading giants are Wal-Mart, Hewlett-Packard, Motorola, Intel, U.S. Healthcare, and Southwest Airlines.[2] The accompanying Organizations in Action feature explains some of the reasons for the continuing success of these agile giants.

ORGANIZATIONS IN ACTION: LESSONS FROM THE THRIVING GIANTS

Large and successful firms that still follow many bureaucratic principles offer certain lessons to other organizations:

1. *Accept change.* Since the marketplace is in flux, firms must continually review their goals and procedures and renew their product lines.
2. *Listen to customers.* Involving customers in the development of new products and services helps guard against isolation and arrogance.

3. *Decentralize authority.* Lower-level managers who are close to customers and markets need the clout to make decisions.
4. *Hire carefully.* Bring on board skilled workers at all levels who are versatile and responsive.
5. *Teach continuously.* Improving employee skill is vital to a company's ability to identify fresh opportunities and respond rapidly to changing markets.
6. *Control costs.* Top management should set the example of frugality to help create a culture of thriftiness.

Source: "Go-Go Goliaths," *Business Week* (13 February 1995): 66–67.

Despite the contributions of bureaucracy, it has several key disadvantages. Above all, a bureaucracy can be rigid in handling people and problems. Its well-intended rules and regulations sometimes create inconvenience and inefficiency. For example, if several layers of approval are required to make a decision, the process takes a long time. Another frequent problem in the bureaucratic form of organization is frustration and low job satisfaction. The sources of these negative feelings include red tape, slow decision making, and an individual's limited influence on how well the organization performs.

DEPARTMENTALIZATION

LEARNING OBJECTIVE 2

Explain the major ways in which organizations are divided into departments.

departmentalization
The process of subdividing work into departments.

In bureaucratic and other forms of organization, the work is subdivided into departments, or other units, to prevent total confusion. Can you imagine an organization of 300,000 people, or even 300, in which all employees worked in one large department? The process of subdividing work into departments is called **departmentalization.**

This chapter will use charts to illustrate four frequently used forms of departmentalization: functional, territorial, product-service, and customer. In practice, most organization charts show a combination of the various types. Exhibit 9-2, which represents the major businesses of Eastman Kodak Company, illustrates functional authority, and organization by customer and territory. This chapter will refer back to Exhibit 9-2 several times to illustrate different types of departmentalization.

The most appropriate form of departmentalization is the one that provides the best chance of achieving the organization's objectives. The organization's environment is an important factor in this decision. Assume that a company needs to use radically different approaches to serve different customers. It would organize the firm according to the customer served. A typical arrangement of this nature is to have one department serve commercial accounts and another department serve the government.

**Exhibit 9-2
Customer and
Territorial
Departmentalization**

Kodak Imaging Group

Consumer Imaging

Office Imaging

Professional Imaging

Entertainment Imaging

Printing and Publishing Imaging

Kodak Imaging U.S and Canada

Kodak Imaging Europe, Africa, and Middle East

Kodak Imaging Asia/Pacific

Kodak Imaging Latin America

FUNCTIONAL DEPARTMENTALIZATION

Functional departmentalization is an arrangement in which departments are defined by the function each one performs, such as accounting or purchasing. Dividing work according to activity is the traditional way of organizing the efforts of people. In a functional organization, each department carries out a specialized activity, such as information processing, purchasing, sales, accounting, or maintenance. Exhibit 9-3 illustrates an organization arranged on purely functional lines.

The advantages and disadvantages of the functional organization, the traditional form of organization, are the same as those of the bureaucracy. Functional departmentalization works particularly well when large batches of work have to be processed on a recurring basis and when the expertise of specialists is required.

The disadvantages of a functional organization derive from its large size and complexity. One result of these characteristics is delay in decision making. A problem might have to pass up the chain of command through many layers of management before a decision is finally reached. Another disadvantage of the functional organization is that it leads to a narrow viewpoint. Department members often develop the false belief that their view is right and the views of those in other units are wrong. For example, the marketing executive might say, "If we don't sell the product, all manufacturing can do is make scrap." The manufacturing point of view is "If we don't make something worthwhile, marketing will have nothing to sell. Besides, a well-manufactured product sells itself."

> **functional departmentalization**
> *An arrangement in which departments are defined by the function each one performs, such as accounting or purchasing.*

TERRITORIAL DEPARTMENTALIZATION

Territorial departmentalization is an arrangement of departments according to the geographic area served. In this organization structure, all the activities for a firm in a given geographic area report to one manager. Marketing divisions often use territorial departmentalization; the sales force may be divided into the northeastern, southeastern, midwestern, northwestern, and southwestern regions. The bottom row of Exhibit 9-2 shows that territorial departmentalization has divided activities into four major geographic categories.

> **territorial departmentalization**
> *An arrangement of departments according to the geographic area served.*

**Exhibit 9-3
Functional
Departmentalization**

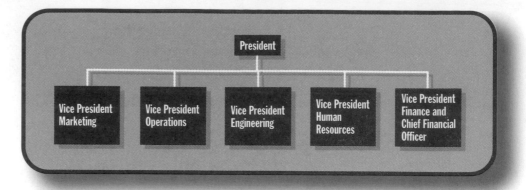

Given that territorial departmentalization divides an organization into geographic regions, it is generally well suited for international business. Yet a new global business trend is to develop a central structure that serves operations in various geographic locations. A case in point is Ford Motor Company. To economize, Ford has merged its manufacturing, sales, and product-development operations in North America and Europe. Latin America and Asia are soon to follow. The company is also establishing five program centers with worldwide responsibility to develop new cars and trucks.[3]

A key advantage of territorial departmentalization is that it allows decision making at a local level, where the personnel are most familiar with the problems. Territorial departmentalization also has some potential disadvantages. The arrangement can be quite expensive because of duplication of costs and effort. For instance, each region may build service departments (such as for purchasing) that duplicate activities carried out at headquarters. A bigger problem is that top-level management may have difficulty controlling the performance of field units.

PRODUCT-SERVICE DEPARTMENTALIZATION

**product-service
departmentalization**
*The arrangement
of departments
according to the
products or services
they provide.*

Product-service departmentalization is the arrangement of departments according to the products or services they provide. When specific products or services are so important that the units that create and support them almost become independent companies, product departmentalization makes sense.

Exhibit 9-4 presents a version of product-service departmentalization. Notice that the organization depicted offers products and services with unique demands of their own. For example, the manufacture and sale of airplane engines is an entirely different business from the development of real estate.

Organizing by product line is beneficial because employees focus on a product or service, which allows each department the maximum opportunity to grow and prosper. Similar to territorial departmentalization, grouping by product or service helps train general managers, fosters high morale, and allows decisions to be made at the local level.

Departmentalization by product has the same potential problems as territorial departmentalization. It can be expensive, because of duplication of effort, and top-level management may find it difficult to control the separate units.

CUSTOMER DEPARTMENTALIZATION

**customer depart-
mentalization**
*An organization
structure based on
customer needs.*

Customer departmentalization creates a structure based on customer needs. When the demands of one group of customers are quite different from the demands of another, customer departmentalization is often the result. Many insurance companies,

Exhibit 9-4
Product-Service
Departmentalization

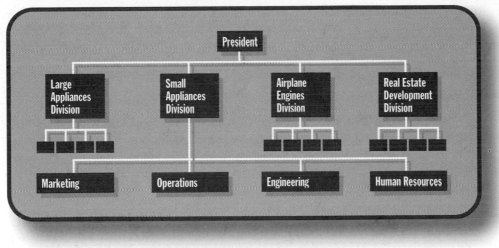

for example, organize their efforts into consumer and commercial departments. Manufacturers of sophisticated equipment typically consist of different groups for processing government and commercial accounts. Customer departmentalization is similar to product departmentalization, and sometimes the distinction between these two forms of organization is blurry. For example, is a bank department that sells home mortgages catering to homeowners, offering a special service, or both?

The second row from the top in Exhibit 9-2 reflects customer departmentalization. Eastman Kodak manufacturers equipment and supplies that differ according to customer group. For example, the company manufactures camera equipment and related film for its Consumer Imaging Group; it manufactures photocopiers for the Office Imaging Group.

MODIFICATIONS OF THE BUREAUCRATIC ORGANIZATION

To overcome some of the problems of the bureaucratic and functional forms of organization, several other organization structures have been developed. Typically, these nonbureaucratic structures are used to supplement or modify the bureaucratic structure. Virtually all large organizations are a combination of bureaucratic and less bureaucratic forms. This section will describe three popular modifications of bureaucracy: the matrix, flat structures, and the virtual corporation. The discussion of reengineering will emphasize horizontal structures that are also a departure from bureaucracy.

THE MATRIX ORGANIZATION

Departmentalization tends to be poorly suited to performing special tasks that differ substantially from the normal activities of a firm. One widely used solution to this problem is **project organization,** in which a temporary group of specialists works under one manager to accomplish a fixed objective. The project organization is used most extensively in the military, aerospace, construction, motion-picture, and computer industries. Project management is so widespread that software has been developed to help managers plot out details and make all tasks visible.

The best-known application of project management is the **matrix organization,** a project structure imposed on top of a functional structure. Matrix organizations evolved to capitalize on the advantages of project and matrix structures while min-

LEARNING OBJECTIVE

Describe three modifications of the bureaucratic structure: matrix, flat, and network.

project organization
A temporary group of specialists working under one manager to accomplish a fixed objective.

matrix organization
A project structure superimposed on top of a functional structure.

imizing their disadvantages. The project groups act as minicompanies within the firm in which they operate. However, the group usually disbands when its mission is completed. In some instances, the project is so successful that it becomes a new and separate division of the company.

Exhibit 9-5 shows a popular version of the matrix structure. Notice that functional managers exert some functional authority over specialists assigned to the projects. For example, the quality manager would occasionally meet with the quality specialists assigned to the projects to discuss their professional activities. The project managers have line authority over the people assigned to their projects.

A distinguishing feature of the matrix is that the project managers borrow resources from the functional departments. Also, each person working on the project has two superiors: the project manager and the functional manager. For example, observe the quality analyst in the lower right corner of Exhibit 9-5. The analyst reports to the manager of quality three boxes above him or her *and* to the project manager for the personal digital assistant located five boxes to the left.

Users of the matrix structure include banks, insurance companies, aerospace companies, and educational institutions. Colleges often use matrix structures for setting up special-interest programs. Among them are African-American studies,

Exhibit 9-5
Matrix Organization Structure in an Electronics Company

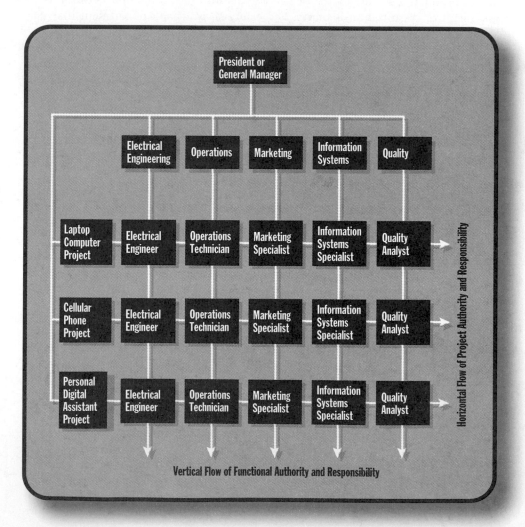

adult education, and industrial training. Each of these programs is headed by a director who uses resources from traditional departments.

RESTRUCTURING AND FLAT STRUCTURES

Organizations with a traditional structure tend to accumulate too many layers of management, and often too many employees in general. Top management may then decide to restructure (or downsize the firm). Restructuring often leads to a **flat organization structure,** a form of organization with relatively few layers. A flat organization is less bureaucratic for two reasons. First, few managers are available to review the decisions of other workers. Second, because the chain of command is shorter, people are less concerned about authority differences.

> **flat organization structure**
> *A form of organization with relatively few layers.*

PURPOSES OF FLAT STRUCTURES. Flat structures are used for several important purposes. The most frequent is to reduce personnel costs by eliminating some managerial positions. Reducing the number of managerial layers also speeds up decision making. With more layers of management, more approvals are required; getting each approval increases the amount of time required to make a decision. With rapid decision making, customer service may improve. A company spokesperson for Xerox Corporation cited improved customer service as a reason for reducing management layers: "The first reason for the cuts, obviously, is the economy. The recession has been longer and deeper than we anticipated. Our second objective is to improve customer service, Xerox's stock-in-trade, by reducing middle management.[4]

SPAN OF CONTROL AND FLAT STRUCTURES. An important consequence of creating flat structures is that the remaining managers now have more workers reporting to them. (**Span of control** is the number of workers reporting directly to a manager.) An exception is when large numbers of individual contributors are laid off along with the managers. The optimum span of control depends on many factors. According to the span-of-control principle, there is a limit to the number of workers a manager can supervise or lead efficiently. Nine factors are of particular significance in determining whether the span of control should be wide (many subordinates) or narrow (few subordinates). Exhibit 9-6 summarizes these factors.

> **span of control**
> *The number of workers reporting directly to a manager.*

EFFECTIVE IMPLEMENTATION OF RESTRUCTURING AND DOWNSIZING. At its best, restructuring achieves it intended purpose of boosting organizational productivity. A prime example is IBM, which reached record profits in 1995 after a decade of restructuring. The accompanying Organization in Action presents details about a successful restructuring. Large-scale elimination of jobs has some serious disadvantages, however. Unemployment leads to human suffering. The human toll includes the physical abuse of family members, family breakups, increased alcoholism, suicides, and decreased self-esteem. The economy suffers because fewer people with good-paying jobs are available to purchase expensive consumer goods.

Unless downsizing is done carefully, it can lead to severe morale problems, confusion, and inefficiency. A nationwide survey of 4,300 working Americans found that only 57 percent of workers in downsizing companies indicated they were generally satisfied with their jobs. In contrast, 72 percent of workers in expanding firms were generally satisfied. A specific complaint about downsizing is that it creates job demands that surviving managers do not have the experience or skill to handle.[5]

A starting point in effective restructuring is to *eliminate low-value and no-value activities.* This is called *activity-based reduction*—a new term for systematically comparing the costs of a firm's activities to their value to the customer. A starting point in searching for low-value activity is workers monitoring the output of others. *Keep-*

1. **Capabilities of the manager.** Experienced, well-trained, and knowledgeable managers can supervise more subordinates than can less capable managers.
2. **Capabilities of the subordinates.** Capable subordinates consume much less managerial time than do their less capable counterparts. Employees of low capability require more instruction, guidance, discipline, and follow-up.
3. **Outside help available to the manager.** If managers can readily obtain help from staff groups, they can direct the activities of a larger number of subordinates.
4. **Amount of flux within the work setting.** Frequent changes in the nature and scope of work assignments make it difficult for managers to sustain a wide span of control. Conversely, if the work is relatively stable, managers can supervise a larger number of employees.
5. **Similarities of work activities supervised.** When all direct subordinates perform similar work, managers can effectively handle a wide span of control. One reason for this is that the managers need be familiar with fewer work activities.
6. **Amount of analytical work and paperwork required in the managerial job.** When managers have to invest considerable time in tasks other than direct supervision, they have less time to deal with human problems. If the managers must do a lot of analytical work and paperwork, the situation requires a narrow span of control.
7. **Amount of coordination among work activities.** A narrow span of control is called for when considerable coordination among members of the work group is required.
8. **External pressures.** If contacts with people outside the unit are extensive, managers will have less time available for supervisory work. The number of subordinates managers can effectively handle is therefore restricted.
9. **Physical dispersion of employees.** When employees are physically dispersed, managers must spend time traveling to meet with them. Therefore, they can handle only a narrow span of control. When employees are in proximity to each other, the span of control can be wider.

**Exhibit 9-6
Factors Influencing
Span of Control**

ing the future work requirements in mind is another factor contributing to effective restructuring. The answer to overstaffing is not to let go of people who will be an important part of the firm's future. *Sensible criteria should be used to decide which workers to let go.* In general, the poorest performers should be released first. Offering early retirement and asking for voluntary resignations also leads to less disruption.

An important strategy for getting layoff survivors refocused on their jobs is for *management to share information with employees.* Information sharing helps quell rumors about further reductions in force. *Listening to employees* helps soften the shock of restructuring. Many survivors will need support groups and other sympathetic ears to express sorrow over the job loss suffered by coworkers. A final suggestion here is for management to *be honest with workers.* Managers should inform people ahead of time if layoffs are imminent or even a possibility. Workers should be told why layoffs are likely, who might be affected, and in what way. Employees will want to know how the restructuring will help strengthen the firm and facilitate growth.[6]

THE NETWORK (VIRTUAL) ORGANIZATION

network structure (or virtual corporation)

A temporary association of otherwise independent firms linked by technology to share expenses, employee talents, and access to each other's markets.

A new form of organization meeting with rapid acceptance involves several firms interacting with each other. A **network structure** (or **virtual corporation**) is a temporary association of otherwise independent firms linked by technology to share expenses, employee talents, and access to each other's markets.[7] Network members can be suppliers, customers, or even rival firms.

A pure virtual corporation would have neither corporate headquarters nor an organization chart. Hierarchy is sacrificed for speed of decision making. Each contributor to the network sticks to its core competency—what it does best, such as manufacturing, new product development, or marketing. Many large organizations today have small units that use the network structure for forming strategic alliances with other companies.

Proponents of the network structure see it as a fluid and flexible entity taking the form of a group of collaborators who link together to capitalize upon a specific opportunity. After the opportunity has been met, the venture will typically disband. A representative network structure is MCI Communications, which forms partnerships with as many as 100 companies in order to win jumbo contracts from major customers. In some strategic alliances the resources of many firms are combined to bring a product to market more quickly than one firm could by itself.

Information technology is facilitating the growth of the virtual corporation built on a network structure. As computer networking becomes more advanced, more and more companies will be able to use information clearinghouses to gain access to potential partners. Such access to each other's capabilities will enable companies to rapidly locate the suppliers, designers, manufacturers, or marketers they need to launch a new venture. An essential requirement is that members of the alliance must trust each other. One incompetent or dishonest member of the network can ruin or severely damage the multiple venture.

REENGINEERING AND HORIZONTAL STRUCTURES

As mentioned in Chapter 1, reengineering involves the radical redesign of business processes to achieve substantial improvements in performance. Reengineering is also called *business-process reengineering* because it has been applied mostly to overhauling certain aspects of business. Here we describe a general approach to reengineering and how it results in a horizontal structure.

LEARNING OBJECTIVE

Present an overview of reengineering and the horizontal structures it creates.

THE FIVE STEPS IN REENGINEERING

Reengineering searches for the most efficient way to perform a large task. The emphasis is on uncovering wasted steps, such as people handing off documents to one another to obtain their approval. After reengineering a work process, there are usually fewer handoffs, as illustrated by the following classic example. IBM Credit Corporation reduced the time it took to process a routine credit application from six days to four hours. At the same time, it increased its workload 100-fold without increasing the number of workers. The feat was accomplished by having routine applications approved by one individual, rather than passing the application through four different specialized departments. A high level of expertise was required on about 5 percent of the applications.

Reengineering takes many forms. A representative approach to reengineering was developed by consultant Robert M. Tomasko. It consists of five steps:[8]

1. *Give control of the process to one person.* Time will be saved if one person in placed in charge of completing an entire process such as order fulfillment or handling a mortgage application.
2. *Map the process.* Reengineering requires the clear identification of key processes, or the actual steps involved in a business transaction. Exhibit 9-7 presents a typical process map. Observe how the customer request loops through various departments before it results in order fulfillment. A major purpose of process mapping is to reduce the number of steps that add little value to the final product or service. An example would be a manager who approves and initials every report passing over his or her desk.
3. *Eliminate potential trouble spots in the system.* Having fewer moving parts in a system means fewer parts are available to create friction. Equally important, fewer

Exhibit 9-7
A Process Map

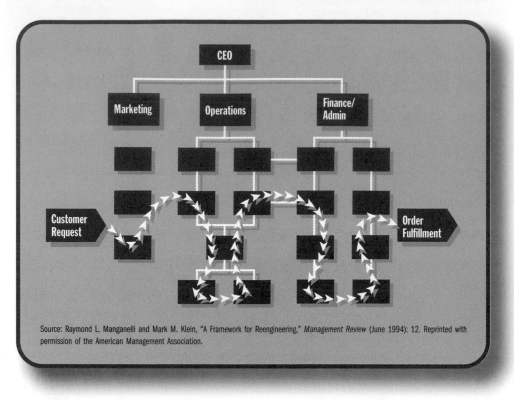

Source: Raymond L. Manganelli and Mark M. Klein, "A Framework for Reengineering," *Management Review* (June 1994): 12. Reprinted with permission of the American Management Association.

people involved in a process means fewer errors and delay. Handoffs from department to department are another source of friction that can be eliminated by reengineering.

4. *Complete the task.* Becoming a fast-cycle company requires a change in mind-set as well as the adoption of a new technique. Under reengineering, important work is done in a hurry. Reengineering specialists attempt to avoid the same mistake committed in so many organizational-improvement efforts—the generation of exhaustive statistics, charts, and reports but little change.

5. *Make reengineering an ongoing process.* After a reengineering program has been implemented, it is usually necessary to reengineer again in the future. One authority on reengineering contends that a complete reengineering effort may take 10 years.[9] New technologies make more improvements possible, and the nature of the reengineered task itself may change.

REENGINEERING AND THE HORIZONTAL ORGANIZATION

horizontal organization
The arrangement of work by teams that are responsible for accomplishing a process.

As a result of reengineering, work is organized horizontally rather than vertically. A **horizontal organization** is the arrangement of work by teams that are responsible for accomplishing a process. The process owners function as team leaders who guide the team toward completion of a core process such as new product development or filling a complicated order. Key performance objectives for the process owner and the team would include "reduce cycle time," "reduce costs," and "reduce throughput time." Another way to understand the horizontal organization that stems from reengineering is to identify the key elements of a horizontal model:[10]

- Making processes rather than functional departments the primary unit of analysis for managerial decision making
- Establishing budgets and allocating resources for process teams instead of functional groups such as sales

- Placing responsibility for establishing and attaining goals with process owners and process teams
- Emphasizing process accomplishments such as "reduce cycle time" as the basis for rewards
- People who are closest to the problem are granted the responsibility for solving it

Reengineering experts speak in glorious terms of its contribution to overhauling businesses. Many good results have been achieved with reengineering. For example, a survey of 100 large firms who underwent reengineering indicated that 70 percent of them achieved productivity gains. The biggest challenge, however, in achieving positive results with reengineering is overcoming employee resistance. Many managers as well as other employees fear reengineering because they think it will result in layoffs.[11]

DELEGATION, EMPOWERMENT, AND DECENTRALIZATION

Collective effort would not be possible, and organizations could not grow and prosper, if a handful of managers did all the work themselves. In recognition of this fact, managers divide up their work. The division can be in one of two directions. Subdividing work in a horizontal direction, through the process of departmentalization, has already been described. The section that follows will discuss subdivision of work in the vertical direction, using the chain of command through delegation and empowerment, and decentralization.

LEARNING OBJECTIVE 5

Specify how delegation, empowerment, and decentralization spread authority in an organization.

DELEGATION OF RESPONSIBILITY

Delegation is an old concept that has been revitalized in the modern organization. It refers to assigning formal authority and responsibility for accomplishing a specific task to another person. If managers do not delegate any of their work, they are acting as individual contributors—not true managers. Delegation is closely tied with **empowerment,** the process by which managers share power with group members, thereby enhancing employees' feelings of personal effectiveness. Delegation is a specific way of empowering employees, thereby increasing motivation.

A major goal of delegation is the transfer of responsibility as a means of increasing one's own productivity. At the same time, delegation allows team members to learn how to handle more responsibility and to become more productive. In downsized organizations, delegation is essential because of the increased work load of managers. As managers are required to assume more responsibility, they must find ways to delegate more work. This feat requires imagination, because in a downsized firm support staff has usually been trimmed as well.

Here we examine two major aspects of delegation: its three components and a variety of suggestions for effective delegation.

delegation
Assigning formal authority and responsibility for accomplishing a specific task to another person.

empowerment
The process by which managers share power with group members, thereby enhancing employees' feelings of personal effectiveness.

THE THREE COMPONENTS OF DELEGATION. Delegation consists of three interdependent components: assigning duties, granting authority, and creating an obligation (responsibility). For delegation to be effective, all three components must be present.

To illustrate the delegation process, consider the example of Murph Ponti, the owner and operator of a new motorcycle dealership. After six months of operation, Ponti realizes he cannot manage the entire business by himself. He asks Peter O'Neill, the more experienced of his two mechanics, to become the manager of the service department. O'Neill accepts the promotion, and Ponti now has the opportunity to delegate some of his managerial tasks.

1. *Assigning duties.* The first step in the delegation process is for the manager to assign duties to somebody else. The delegatee is told what work he or she is to perform. In this case, Ponti provides O'Neill with a careful list of what the manager of the service department at Murph's Cycle Shop is supposed to do.
2. *Granting authority.* To accomplish tasks or duties, the subordinate must have the right or authority to do certain things without constantly checking with the boss. These rights involve using organizational resources—money, material, time, and human effort. If O'Neill is to accomplish his job, Ponti must grant him the authority to do such things as establish the price for each repair job and buy necessary tools and parts.

   The authority of any manager has its limits. Even certain actions of the chief executive officer must be approved by the board of directors. In the case of Murph's Cycle Shop, Murph Ponti limits Peter O'Neill's authority in a general way by saying, "Check with me about any unusual situation." O'Neill must use good judgment in interpreting the meaning of "unusual."
3. *Creating an obligation.* The third key ingredient in delegation is *obligation,* the assumption of responsibility by the subordinate who is to perform the assigned duty. Obligation can also be considered the process of holding the subordinate accountable for the delegated work. If a project fails, it is partially the team member's fault. The delegatee must assume responsibility for getting the work accomplished. For the obligation principle and delegation to work effectively, subordinates must have a strong work ethic. If it does not bother them that assigned duties are neglected, delegation may fail.

A major point about delegation is that, although the manager may hold a group member responsible for a task, the manager has final accountability. (To be accountable is to accept credit or blame for results.) If the group member fails miserably, the manager must accept the final blame. It is the manager who chose the person who failed. As noted in an executive newsletter, "Nothing makes a worse impression than the whining manager who blames a staffer for mishandling a task."[12]

SUGGESTIONS FOR EFFECTIVE DELEGATION AND EMPOWERMENT. Delegation and empowerment lie at the heart of effective management. Following the eight key suggestions that follow improves a manager's chances of increasing productivity by assigning work to others.[13]

1. *Assign duties to the right people.* The chances for effective delegation and empowerment improve when capable, responsible, well-motivated group members receive the delegated tasks. Vital tasks should not be assigned to ineffective performers.
2. *Delegate the whole task.* In the spirit of job enrichment, a manager should delegate an entire task to one subordinate rather than dividing it among several. So doing gives the group member complete responsibility and enhances motivation, and gives the manager more control over results.
3. *Give as much instruction as needed.* Some group members will require highly detailed instructions, while others can operate effectively with general instructions. Many delegation and empowerment failures occur because instruction was insufficient. *Dumping* is the negative term given to the process of dropping a task on a group member without instructions.
4. *Retain some important tasks for yourself.* Managers need to retain some high-output or sensitive tasks for themselves. In general, the manager should handle any task that involves the survival of the unit. However, which tasks the manager should retain always depends on the circumstances.

5. *Obtain feedback on the delegated task.* A responsible manager does not delegate a complex assignment to a subordinate, then wait until the assignment is complete before discussing it again. Managers must establish checkpoints and milestones to obtain feedback on progress.

6. *Delegate both pleasant and unpleasant tasks to group members.* When group members are assigned a mixture of pleasant and unpleasant responsibilities, they are more likely to believe they are being treated fairly. Few group members expect the manager to handle all the undesirable jobs. A related approach is to rotate undesirable tasks among group members.

7. *Step back from the details.* Many managers are poor delegators because they get too involved with technical details. If a manager cannot let go of details, he or she will never be effective at delegation or empowerment.

8. *Evaluate and reward performance.* After the task is completed, the managers should evaluate the outcome. Favorable outcomes should be rewarded, while unfavorable outcomes might either not receive a reward or be punished. It is important, however, not to discourage risk taking and initiative by punishing all mistakes.

DECENTRALIZATION

Decentralization is the extent to which authority is passed down to lower levels in an organization. It comes about as a consequence of managers delegating work to lower levels. **Centralization** is the extent to which authority is retained at the top of the organization. In a completely centralized organization, one chief executive would retain all the formal authority. Complete centralization can exist only in a one-person firm. Decentralization and centralization are, therefore, two ends of a continuum. No firm is completely centralized or decentralized.

The term *decentralization* generally refers to the decentralization of authority. However, the term also refers to decentralization by geography. A multidivision firm departmentalized on the basis of territory has a flat organization structure. A flat organization is often referred to as decentralized, but the reference is to geography, not authority. Unless so noted, this text uses the term *decentralization* in reference to authority.

Certain conditions usually foster decentralization. Organizations favor decentralization when a large number of decisions must be made at lower organizational levels, when important decisions are made low in the management hierarchy, and when several functions are affected by decisions made at lower levels. Some companies permit only operational decisions at the plant or branch level. These are less decentralized than companies that permit operational, financial, and personnel decisions at the plant or branch level. Also, decentralized firms engage in less checking on decisions. Decentralization is greatest when the company requires no check at all. The fewer the people consulted and the lower their positions in the firm, the greater the degree of decentralization.

In general, a centralized firm exercises more control over organizational units than a decentralized firm. New structures, such as horizontal organizations, are willing to surrender much control in order to increase employee motivation and commitment.

Another important point is that many firms are centralized and decentralized simultaneously. Certain aspects of their operations are centralized, whereas others are decentralized. Fast-food franchise restaurants such as McDonald's, Long John Silver's, and Wendy's illustrate this trend. Central headquarters exercises tight control over such matters as menu selection, food quality, and advertising. Individual franchise operators, however, make human resource decisions on their own.

decentralization
The extent to which authority is passed down to lower levels in an organization.

centralization
The extent to which authority is retained at the top of the organization.

ORGANIZATIONAL CULTURE

Identify major aspects of organizational culture, including its management and control.

---

organizational culture (or corporate culture)

The system of shared values and beliefs that actively influence the behavior of organization members.

Organization structure has sometimes been referred to as the "hard side" of understanding how a firm operates. However, each firm has a "soft side" as well; an understanding of this aspect of an organization contributes to an understanding of how the organization operates. **Organizational culture, or corporate culture,** is the system of shared values and beliefs that actively influence the behavior of organization members. The term *shared* is important because it implies that many people are guided by the same values and that they interpret them in the same way. Values develop over time and reflect a firm's history and traditions. Culture consists of the customs of a firm, such as being helpful and supportive toward new employees and customers. This section will describe two important aspects of organizational culture: its dimensions, consequences, organizational learning, and the management and control of culture.

DIMENSIONS OF ORGANIZATIONAL CULTURE

The dimensions of organizational culture help explain the subtle forces that influence employee actions. Recognize that large units within an organization may have a different culture. For example, the culture of a company's lumber mill may be quite different than the culture of its marketing department. Five dimensions are of major significance in influencing organizational culture.[14]

1. *Values.* Values are the foundation of any organizational culture. The organization's philosophy is expressed through values, and values guide behavior on a day-to-day basis. Representative values of a firm might include concern for employee welfare, a belief that the customer is always right, a commitment to quality, or a desire to please stakeholders.
2. *Relative diversity.* The existence of an organizational culture assumes some degree of homogeneity. Nevertheless, organizations differ in terms of how much deviation can be tolerated. Many firms are highly homogeneous; executives talk in a similar manner and even look alike. Furthermore, people from similar educational backgrounds and fields of specialty are promoted into key jobs.
3. *Resource allocation and rewards.* The allocation of money and other resources has a critical influence on culture. The investment of resources sends a message to people about what is valued in the firm. If a customer-service department is fully staffed and nicely furnished, employees and customers can assume that customer service is important to the company.
4. *Degree of change.* A fast-paced, dynamic organization has a culture different from that of a slow-paced, stable one. Top-level managers, by the energy or lethargy of their stance, send messages about how much they welcome innovation.
5. *Strength of the culture.* The strength of a culture, or how much influence it exerts, is partially a byproduct of the other dimensions. A strong culture guides employees in many everyday actions. It determines, for example, whether an employee will inconvenience himself or herself to satisfy a customer. If the culture is not so strong, employees are more likely to follow their own whims—they may decide to please customers only when convenient.

CONSEQUENCES AND IMPLICATIONS OF ORGANIZATIONAL CULTURE

Organizational culture has received much attention because it has a pervasive impact on organizational effectiveness. Exhibit 9-8 outlines several key consequences and implications of organizational culture.

1. *Productivity, quality, and morale.* A culture that emphasizes productivity and quality encourages workers to be productive and quality conscious. Similarly, a culture that values the dignity of human beings tends to foster high morale and job satisfaction. Cultures that deemphasize productivity, quality, or morale achieve the opposite results.

2. *Competitive advantage.* Developing a competitive advantage is a consequence of having a culture that favors high productivity, quality, and morale. A unique culture is important because it prevents other firms from becoming directly competitive.[15] One of the many factors shaping the success of Microsoft, a software firm, is the extraordinary commitment of its professional and technical staffs. A culture like the one at Microsoft is difficult to imitate because it developed over such a long period of time.

3. *Compatibility of mergers and acquisitions.* Approximately 60 percent of corporate mergers and acquisitions lead to poor results. The major reason for these failed mergers is incompatibility between the cultures of the merged firms.[16] Correspondingly, a reliable predictor of the success of a merger is the compatibility of the cultures involved. The problem of incompatible cultures often arises when two companies from different countries merge. Such was the experience of a joint venture between two glass manufacturers, Corning from the U.S. and Vitro from Mexico. Twenty-five months after the start of the joint venture, Corning returned Vitro's $130 million investment and cancelled the joint venture. The joint venture was beset by constant culture clashes, such as differences in how urgently marketing should be carried out.

4. *Direction of leadership activity.* Culture directs the activities of an organization's leaders. Much of an executive's time is spent working with the subtle forces that shape the values of organization members. Of significance, many chief executive officers regard shaping the culture as their most important responsibility. Leaders are also influenced by the existing culture of a firm. It is part of their role to perpetuate a constructive culture.

ORGANIZATIONAL LEARNING AND CULTURE

An important new way of understanding organizations and their cultures is to examine how well they learn. An effective organization engages in continuous learning by proactively adapting to the external environment. In the process, the organization profits from its experiences. Instead of repeating the same old mistakes, the organization *learns.* A **learning organization** is one that is skilled at creating, acquiring, and transferring knowledge. It also modifies its behavior to reflect new knowledge and insights.[17] Although organizational theorists speak of a learning *organization,* it is still the workers who do the learning.

Organizational learning is related to culture, because the culture must support learning for it to take place. Organizational learning gradually becomes part of the

learning organization
An organization that is skilled at creating, acquiring, and transferring knowledge.

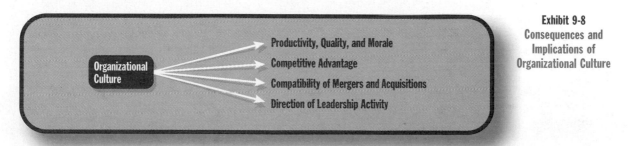

Exhibit 9-8
Consequences and Implications of Organizational Culture

Organizational Culture
- Productivity, Quality, and Morale
- Competitive Advantage
- Compatibility of Mergers and Acquisitions
- Direction of Leadership Activity

organizational culture. The accompanying Organization in Action illustrates how organizations learn from their customers—a major component of the environment.

MANAGING AND CONTROLLING THE CULTURE

A major responsibility of top management is to shape, manage, and control the organizational culture. After a new CEO is appointed, the person typically makes a public statement to the effect: "My number one job is to change the culture." The executive would then have to use his or her best leadership skills to inspire and persuade others toward forming a new culture. Many executives, for example, attempt to move the culture in the direction of higher creativity and risk taking.

Another general way of changing an organization's culture is to undergo organization development, a set of specialized techniques for transforming an organization. Among these techniques would be conducting surveys about the need for change, and then involving many people in making the desirable changes. In addition to working with an organization development consultant to bring about cultural change, a manager might do the following:

- Serve as a role model for the desired attitudes and behaviors. Leaders must behave in ways that are consistent with the values and practices they wish to see imitated throughout the organization. For example, CEO and Chairman George Fisher of Eastman Kodak wanted to move the culture even further into valuing information technology. He personally makes extensive use of the information superhighway, including accessing the Internet.
- Establish a reward system that reinforces the culture, such as giving huge suggestion awards to promote an innovative culture.
- Select candidates for positions at all levels whose values mesh with the values of the desired culture. At SONY Corporation all new-hires must demonstrate that they care about quality (such as having produced something of quality as a hobby) in order to be hired.

ORGANIZATION IN ACTION: BALLY ENGINEERING LEARNS FROM ITS CUSTOMERS

Bally Engineering Structures, Inc., of Bally, Pennsylvania, emphasizes a strategic intent (a desired leadership position) to learn from its customers. Tom Pietrocini, the company president, decided that Bally's survival depended on changing to a firm that could custom-manufacture many products. Bally's regular business had been to make specific products such as refrigerated rooms and walk-in coolers.

After Pietrocini joined the company in 1983, he repositioned it to continue producing high-quality products, but at low cost. Determined that Bally would learn how to be the number one walk-in refrigerator company, Pietrocini had to convince employees they were a key part of the company's success. He encour-

aged employees to learn to listen more closely to customer complaints and suggestions rather than relying so heavily on customer-reported defects or customer-satisfaction surveys.

Employees learned to apply new technologies in unanticipated ways. For example, a customer complained that his floor kept wearing out every 18 months from the hot steam he was using to clean the freezers. In response, a cross-functional team of Bally employees developed a completely new technology to prevent moisture from entering the crevices and destroying the floor. Bally won back the customer. Also, in rising to the challenge of meeting one customer's specific needs, it created and leveraged a technology that gave it substantial competitive advantage in its market.

Source: John W. Slocum, Jr., Michael McGill, and David T. Lei, "The New Learning Strategy: Anytime, Anything, Anywhere," *Organizational Dynamics* (Autumn 1994): 38–39.

- Sponsoring new training and development programs that support the desired cultural values. Among many examples, top management at Levi Strauss wants to support a culture favoring diversity. Training programs in valuing differences therefore receive high levels of encouragement from Levi Strauss executives.

SUMMARY OF KEY POINTS

1

Describe the bureaucratic form of organization and discuss its advantages and disadvantages.

The most widely used form of organization is the bureaucracy, a multilevel organization in which authority flows downward and rules are regulations are carefully specified. Bureaucracies can be highly efficient organizations that are well suited to handling repetitive, recurring tasks. However, they may be rigid in terms of rule interpretation, and they may result in decision-making delays.

2

Explain the major ways in which organizations are divided into departments.

The usual way of subdividing effort in organizations, particularly in bureaucracies, is to create departments. Four common types of departmentalization are functional, territorial, product-service, and customer.

3

Describe three modifications of the bureaucratic structure: matrix, flat, and network.

The matrix organization consists of a project structure superimposed on a functional structure. Personnel assigned to the projects within the matrix report to a project manager, yet they report to a functional manager also.

Flat organizations have fewer layers than traditional hierarchies, and are often a byproduct of downsizing. They are created for such purposes as reducing personnel costs, speeding up decision making, and fitting in with the spirit of the time. After the flat structure has been created, low-value work should be eliminated. The rapidly growing network organization model is a temporary alliance of otherwise independent firms interacting with each other. Network members of the virtual corporation (same as the network organization) can be suppliers, customers, or even rival firms.

4

Present an overview of reengineering and the horizontal structures it creates.

Reengineering involves the radical redesign of a work process, and can be divided into five steps: (1) Give control of the process to one person; (2) map the process; (3) eliminate potential trouble spots in the system; (4) complete the task; and (5) make reengineering an ongoing process. As a result of reengineering, work is organized horizontally (such as in a team) rather than vertically. The team is responsible for a process such as order fulfillment.

5

Specify how delegation, empowerment, and decentralization spread authority in an organization.

Delegation is assigning formal authority and responsibility for accomplishing a task to another person. Delegation fosters empowerment, and consists of three interdependent components: duties, authority, and obligation. The manager remains accountable for the results of subordinates. Effective delegation includes assigning duties to the right people and obtaining feedback on the delegated task. Decentralization stems from delegation. It is the extent to which authority is passed down to low levels in an organization. Decentralization sometimes refers to geographic dispersion.

6

Identify major aspects of organizational culture, including its management and control.

The five key dimensions of organizational culture are values, relative diversity, resource allocation and rewards, degree of change, and the strength of the culture. Culture has important consequences and implications, such as productivity, quality, and morale. How well an organization learns (or profits from its experiences) is also part of its culture. Top management is responsible for shaping, managing, and controlling culture. Although culture is slow to change, the manager can lead the firm through organization development. The manager can also act as a role model and reward behaviors that fit the desired cultural values.

KEY TERMS AND PHRASES

Organization Structure *pg. 194*
Organizational Design *pg. 194*
Bureaucracy *pg. 194*
Unity of Command *pg. 194*
Departmentalization *pg. 196*
Functional Departmentalization *pg. 197*
Territorial Departmentalization *pg. 197*
Product-Service Departmentalization *pg. 198*
Customer Departmentalization *pg. 198*
Project Organization *pg. 199*
Matrix Organization *pg. 199*

Flat Organization Structure *pg. 201*
Span of Control *pg. 201*
Network Structure (or Virtual Corporation) *pg. 202*
Horizontal Organization *pg. 204*
Delegation *pg. 205*
Empowerment *pg. 205*
Decentralization *pg. 207*
Centralization *pg. 207*
Organizational Culture (or Corporate Culture) *pg. 208*
Learning Organization *pg. 209*

QUESTIONS

1. Why do some people particularly enjoy working in a bureaucracy?
2. It has been said that the complete opposite of a bureaucracy is anarchy. Why might this be true?
3. What is the basis for departmentalization in most department stores?
4. Why is the span of control of first-level supervisors typically much wider than that of executives?
5. What similarity do you see between a network organization and a horizontal organization?
6. Visualize your favorite worldwide franchise restaurant such as Pizza Hut or McDonald's. In what ways is this restaurant centralized, and in what ways is it decentralized?
7. What can first- and second-level managers, as well as team leaders, do about shaping the culture of a firm?

SKILL-BUILDING EXERCISE 9-A: UNDERSTANDING YOUR BUREAUCRATIC ORIENTATION

Answer each question "mostly agree" (MA) or "mostly disagree"(MD). Assume the mental set of attempting to learn something about yourself rather than impressing a prospective employer.

	MA	MD
1. I value stability in my job.		
2. I like a predictable organization.		
3. I enjoy working without the benefit of a carefully specified job description.		
4. I would enjoy working for an organization in which promotions were generally determined by seniority.		
5. Rules, policies, and procedures generally frustrate me.		
6. I would enjoy working for a company that employed 95,000 people worldwide.		
7. Being self-employed would involve more risk than I'm willing to take.		
8. Before accepting a position, I would like to see an exact job description.		
9. I would prefer a job as a freelance landscape artist to one as a supervisor for the Department of Motor Vehicles.		
10. Seniority should be as important as performance in determining pay increases and promotion.		
11. It would give me a feeling of pride to work for the largest and most successful company in its field.		
12. Given a choice, I would prefer to make $90,000 per year as a vice president in a small company than $100,000 per year as a middle manager in a large company.		
13. I would feel uncomfortable if I were required to wear an employee badge with a number on it.		
14. Parking spaces in a company lot should be assigned according to job level.		
15. I would generally prefer working as a specialist to performing many different tasks.		
16. Before accepting a job, I would want to make sure that the company had a good program of employee benefits.		

17. A company will not be successful unless it establishes a clear set of rules and regulations.
18. I would prefer to work in a department with a manager than to work on a team where managerial responsibility is shared.
19. You should respect people according to their rank.
20. Rules are meant to be broken.

Score: _____

Scoring and interpretation. Give yourself one point for each question you answered in the bureaucratic direction, then total your score.

1. Mostly agree	9. Mostly disagree
2. Mostly agree	10. Mostly agree
3. Mostly disagree	11. Mostly agree
4. Mostly agree	12. Mostly disagree
5. Mostly disagree	13. Mostly disagree
6. Mostly agree	14. Mostly agree
7. Mostly agree	15. Mostly disagree
8. Mostly agree	16. Mostly agree

17. Mostly agree   19. Mostly agree
18. Mostly agree   20. Mostly disagree

15–20   You would enjoy working in a bureaucracy.
8–14   You would experience a mixture of satisfactions and dissatisfactions if working in a bureaucracy.
0–7   You would most likely be frustrated by working in a bureaucracy, especially a large one.

Source: Adapted and updated from Andrew J. DuBrin, *Human Relations: A Job Oriented Approach*, 5th edition (Englewood Cliffs, NJ: Prentice Hall, 1991): 434–435.

SKILL-BUILDING EXERCISE 9-B: DESIGNING A FLAT ORGANIZATION

GROUP ACTIVITY You and your teammates are assigned the task of creating a flatter structure for the organization depicted in Exhibit 9-9. Draw a new organization chart, with each box carefully labeled. Explain what happens to any managers who might be downsized and why your new structure is an improvement.

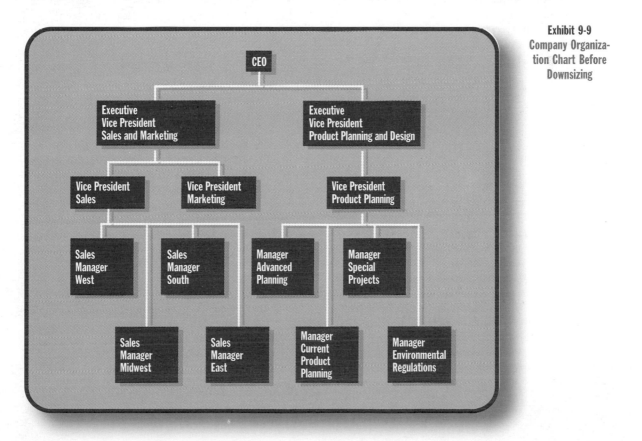

Exhibit 9-9
Company Organization Chart Before Downsizing

VIDEO DISCUSSION QUESTIONS

1. How does downsizing affect the organization structure? **[Morale Crisis]**
2. In what way does McCall, the CEO of Glaxo, intend to reengineer the work of nurses? **[Glaxo]**

3. What message about organization culture is contained in the video about IBM? **[Gerstner]**

CASE PROBLEM 9-A: CONFESSIONS OF A REENGINEERED MANAGER

Bill Arnold (a pseudonym), a former advertising manager at a national magazine, admits to liking hierarchy. As he explains, "I find it highly motivating to know that if I perform well at my job, I will be heartily rewarded with money and career advancement."

The company president told Arnold that the publication he had been working for had lost a third of its advertising during the past six years. He wanted quick action to boost revenues in the ad department. The president thought Arnold could achieve the turnaround. He was therefore transferred from the position of business head of a national magazine to the advertising director in another division of the same organization.

When Arnold arrived in his new position, he found a low-performing sales department that offered staff members no incentives to improve their performance. No formal standards existed by which work was evaluated. Before Arnold could implement a plan to improve the situation, his boss hired a reengineering consulting firm to find a way to bring the sales force closer to customers. Arnold was confused. He said, "I thought I had been hired to turn the business around. Now that challenge was being turned over to consultants."

Arnold's official role was to help educate the consultants about the workings of the 500-person sales department. He regularly attended three- and four-hour meetings to analyze the project's progress. The sales staff was required to put together exhaustive five-year profiles of hundreds of accounts.

During the four-month period of data collection, Arnold's managers sat in a windowless, airless, overcrowded conference room, working alongside the consultants' junior associates for eight hours a day. At the end of the day, the staff would return to their offices to sort through their mail, faxes, phone messages, and other details neglected while working on the reengineering project.

The sales staff became unresponsive to their major accounts because they were too tied up with the reengineering project to visit clients or even answer their telephone calls. The consultants insisted that any short-term problems the sales staff encountered during the transition phase would be overshadowed by the positive impact the new strategy would have.

Five months into the project, the consultants made their recommendations. The hierarchical sales organization with several layers of management would be changed to a team concept. Many employees with different areas of expertise and varying stature would participate in the sales process. Instead of making an individual sales call on a client, the team leader (formerly called the sales manager) would bring along people from promotion, marketing, and finance. Arnold found that most of the busy executives the sales staff were trying to see preferred to be called on by like-minded managers from his publication. The busy executives had little patience for the team approach.

Several weeks later, the top five sales executives and Arnold were given the functional title "co-champions." The change stripped Arnold's position of most of its power. Key decisions were to be made by consensus. The sales organization hierarchy was turned on its side and made into a scaffold, balancing loads of people at the same level. Other people at the same level were formerly on Arnold's support staff. He reflected, "All of my career had been spent climbing the corporate ladder, gaining responsibility and winning financial and ego rewards along the way. The new organizational structure was not only disheartening to me, but downright insulting. After a lot of soul-searching, I quit."

In the year since Arnold left, the staff has been downsized by 20 percent. With little hope for advancement, most of the former sales managers (now called team leaders) are looking for other jobs. Furthermore, the financial gains have fallen far short of the consultants' projections.

CASE QUESTIONS

1. How might the company have implemented reengineering more smoothly?
2. What advice can you offer Arnold about the career rewards in a horizontal (post-reengineered) organization?
3. To what extent do you think Arnold might simply be a disgruntled former employee?

Source: Adapted from Jacky Seyegorf, "Confessions of a Reengineered Manager," *Working Woman* (August 1995): 19–23.

CASE PROBLEM 9-B: PAY AND CHASE AT MEDICARE

Several years ago, Medicare paid a large number of insurance claims that should have been paid by private insurers. (Medicare is the medical care component of Social Security in the United States.) Linda Ruiz was acting director of the Office of Medicare Benefits and Administration at the time. She explained that the government has demanded repayment. Yet because of the agency's record-keeping system, it may be impossible to know how much was recovered. "I know that we had a backlog of $445 million, but what has actually been collected, I don't know," she said. "We put out the demands." (A demand is a request for payment to the private insurance company.)

The collection problem is part of a work process called "Medicare as secondary payer." By law, Medicare has secondary responsibility for medical claims incurred by enrollees who are eligible for Medicare but who also are covered by private medical insurance. Previous to this legislation, Medicare was the primary payer. The purpose of the change was to shift most of the burden to private insurers when senior citizens had dual coverage. Medicare has continued to pay claims as the primary insurer since it cannot accurately determine when an enrollee also has dual coverage.

According to several estimates, Medicare has paid about $1 billion worth of private insurance obligations each year for a decade. The Health Care Financing Administration (HCFA) is the group that runs the Medicare program. After HCFA discovers it has paid a claim that should have been the primary responsibility of a private insurer, it attempts to collect money from the insurance company. The process is labelled "pay and chase" because the government pays the bill and then chases the insurer for its share.

Part of the problem is that claims are processed for Medicare by private contractors. Under the law Medicare is obliged to hire insurance companies to process the claims. Sometimes an insurance company contracted to process Medicare claims is the insurer that should have paid Medicare the primary portion of the same claims.

Under the present system, there is no way of knowing how much money is legitimately owed the government until a demand for payment is issued to the insurance companies. The insurance companies hired to represent Medicare's interests sometimes neglect to send demands for payments to other insurance companies.

CASE QUESTIONS

1. What disadvantages of bureaucracy are illustrated in this case?
2. What can Medicare do to collect more of its money?
3. How might reengineering help Medicare?

Source: Based on facts reported in Jeff Nesmith, "Medicare May Never Heal Its Wallet Wound," Cox News Service (1 August 1993).

CASE PROBLEM 9-C: BIG CHANGES BREWING AT DEUTSCHE TELEKOM

Ron Sommer recently began his new position as CEO of Deutsche Telekom, Europe's largest telecommunication company. Sommer, who speaks German, English, and French, held previous positions as president of Sony Corp. of America and president of Sony Europe. He was in a big hurry in his new position because he had only 26 months to prepare his company to face wide-open competition. On January 1, 1998, the European Union planned to allow open-market competition in telecommunications.

Sommer perceived his role as having to ignite a competitive spirit in a work force long overprotected by Germany's biggest monopoly. He also had to formulate plans for massive cost-cutting and get workers to serve customers it has taken for granted. An equally tough challenge will be to attract investors to Telekom. Sommer has to convince investors that his company will be a worthy competitor to firms such as AT&T and British Communications. New domestic telecommunications companies will also be part of the competition. Telekom has $10 billion in government-owned stock it is attempting to sell to private investors.

Preliminary estimates are that Sommer may have to eliminate 60,000 jobs, a quarter of the company's work force. He plans to offer early retirement and severance packages. So far, the company's union has only agreed to eliminate 30,000 positions. Financial advisors believe that these labor problems will have to be resolved before investors will readily purchase Telekom stock.

After taking the company private, he will have to increase prices enough to cover $86 billion in debt and pay a dividend. Another challenge is that Telekom must begin to offer modern multimedia services that global corporations demand.

In Sommer's evaluation, "The company has an extremely high level of know-how, but it needs to be more customer friendly." One of the company's many pitfalls is that it takes a long time to process orders for equipment, service upgrades, and installation. A major task the new CEO faces is to motivate Telekom employees to be productive in a deregulated environment.

Sommer has informed his managers that he wants Telekom to have the same level of brand awareness as Coca-Cola, IBM, or Kodak. He says, "I want us to be recognized as a great company."

CASE QUESTIONS

1. Identify several cultural changes that will have to take place for Telekom to achieve its goals.
2. What recommendations can you offer Sommer to bring about these cultural changes?

Source: Based on facts in "The Toughest Job In Europe: Can Ron Sommer Transform Bloated Deutsche Telekom In Time?" *Business Week* (9 October 1995).

REFERENCES

1. Kara Fitzsimmons, "Firms Find Potholes On Re-engineering Road," *Rochester Business Journal* (26 May 1995): 17.
2. "Go-Go Goliaths: These Giants Keep on Expanding—Just Like Scrappy Startups," *Business Week* (13 February 1995): 66.
3. "Borderless Management: Companies Strive to Become Truly Stateless," *Business Week* (23 May 1994): 25.
4. William Patalon III, "Xerox to Cut Jobs, Up to 800 Locally," *Rochester Democrat and Chronicle* (12 December 1991): 1A.
5. "Morale Got Downsized, Too: Can Managers Repair the Damage?" *Business Week* (20 February 1995): 26; Kim S. Cameron, Sarah J. Freeman, and Aneil K. Mishra, "Best Practices in White-Collar Downsizing: Managing Contradictions," *The Academy of Management Executive* (August 1991): 63–64.
6. The last suggestion is from Oren Harari, "Layoffs: An Internal Debate," *Management Review* (October 1993): 31.
7. John A. Byrne, "The Virtual Corporation," *Business Week* (8 February 1993): 101.
8. Robert M. Tomasko, "Intelligent Resizing (Part II): View from the Bottom Up," *Management Review* (June 1993): 20–22.
9. "Breathless and the Race Is Hardly Begun," *Management Review* (January 1995): 17.
10. "After Re-engineering, What's Next?" *Supervisory Management* (May 1995): 6.
11. "Employees: The Toughest Challenge for Reengineering," *Human Resources Forum* (April 1995): 4.
12. "The Right Look: How to Get the Most Out of Your Delegating Skills," *Executive Strategies* (January 1993): 7.
13. Several of the ideas on this list are based on David A. Whetton and Kim S. Cameron, *Developing Management Skills,* 2e (Glenview, IL: Scott Foresman, 1991): 116–118; Thomas R. Horton, "Delegation and Team Building: No Solo Acts Please," *Management Review* (September 1992): 58–61.
14. J. Steven Ott, *The Organizational Culture Perspective* (Chicago: Dorsey Press, 1989): 20–48; Terrence Deal and Allan Kennedy, *Corporate Cultures: The Rites and Rituals of Corporate Life* (Reading, MA: Addison-Wesley, 1982): 13–14.
15. Jay B. Barney, "Organizational Culture: Can It Be a Source of Sustained Competitive Advantage?" *Academy of Management Review* (July 1986): 662.
16. Richard J. Petronio, "Why Mergers Fail: The Clash of Cultures," *The Surcon Report* (Special Issue, 1989): 5.
17. David A. Garvin, "Building a Learning Organization," *Harvard Business Review* (July–August 1993): 80.

CHAPTER 10

Staffing and Human Resource Management

Siemens Corporation

Janet Smith strolls by a Pic N' Pay shoe store, sees the "Help Wanted" sign in the window, and walks in. The store manager has her complete a job application form, then directs her to a telephone where he punches in a 1-800 number. "Don't be nervous," the manager says, handing her the receiver. "Welcome to the HR Easy applicant-screening process," a computerized voice tells Smith. She will be interviewed via voice mail, the first step in the centralized employee-selection process developed by Pic N' Pay Stores Inc., a 923-store chain selling popularly priced shoes. • During a 10- to 15-minute period a computerized voice will ask Smith a series of about 100 yes and no job-related questions. A computer analyzes Smith's answers and her response times to "trigger questions." The premise is that it takes longer to tell a lie than tell the truth. The computerized results are reviewed by one of six professional interviewers whose job it is to analyze the report and conduct a follow-up interview. Employee responses to the telephone questions serve as clues to areas requiring further probing. • Since initiating the telephone screening process, there has been a 39 percent reduction in inventory shrinkage and a 50 percent drop in employee turnover. "The system has paid for itself 10 times over," commented Jeff Shepard, the Pic N' Pay CEO and president.[1]

The success of the job-applicant screening process used at the shoe-store chain illustrates but one way in which human resource management contributes to company productivity. This final chapter about organizing and staffing deals with the heart of human resources management—staffing the organization. Staffing an organization requires many subactivities, as indicated shortly. The purpose of this chapter is to explain the basics of human resource management as needed by managers to perform their job.

THE STAFFING MODEL

LEARNING OBJECTIVE 1

Describe the components of organizational staffing.

The model in Exhibit 10-1 indicates that the staffing process flows in a logical sequence. Although not every organization follows the same steps in the same sequence, staffing ordinarily proceeds in the way this section will discuss.

Human resources (or personnel) specialists are heavily engaged in the staffing function. Their staffing activities include providing tools for making human resources forecasts, setting up selection procedures, and conducting training programs. Line managers, however, are the ones with ultimate responsibility for staffing their own departments. Typically, specialists work with managers to help the managers make better staffing decisions. For example, in addition to your prospective boss, an employment specialist may interview you for a job.

Most of the principles and procedures described in this chapter have some applicability for organizations of all sizes. However, because large organizations have

Exhibit 10-1
The Organizational Staffing Model

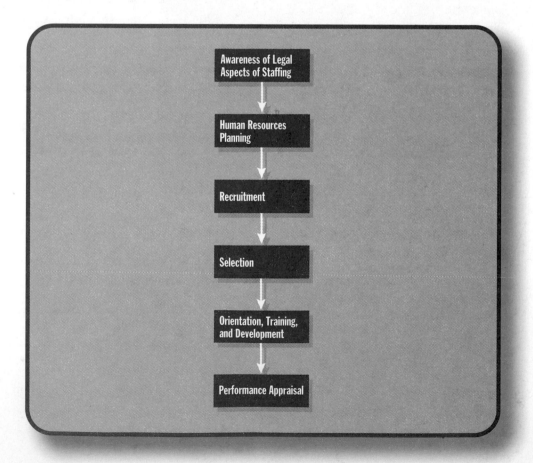

Awareness of Legal Aspects of Staffing

Human Resources Planning

Recruitment

Selection

Orientation, Training, and Development

Performance Appraisal

more resources than small ones, large organizations can engage more fully in most aspects of the staffing model.

LEGAL ASPECTS OF STAFFING

Federal, state, provincial, and local laws influence every aspect of organizational staffing. Managers and human resources specialists must keep the major provisions of these laws in mind whenever they make decisions about any phase of employment.

Exhibit 10-2 summarizes major pieces of U.S. federal legislation that influence various aspects of staffing—not just employee selection. Exhibit 10-3 presents highlights of comparable Canadian legislation. Managers need to be aware that such legislation exists, and also be familiar with the general provisions of each law or executive order. When a possible legal issue arises, the manager should review the relevant legislation in depth and confer with a company specialist in employment law.

A key aspect of implementing the spirit and letter of employment discrimination law in the United States has been affirmative action programs. To comply with the Civil Rights Act of 1964, employers with federal contracts or subcontracts must develop such programs to end discrimination. **Affirmative action** consists of complying with anti-discrimination law *and* correcting past discriminatory practices. Under an affirmative action program, employers actively recruit, employ, train, and promote minorities and women who may have been discriminated against by the employer in the past. As a result, they are under-represented in certain positions. Part of an affirmative action plan might include a career development program for women to help them qualify for management positions.

The major intent of affirmative action programs is to overcome past injustices against minorities and women. To achieve this goal, there have been times when members of a majority group have been denied access to jobs or promotion—a condition referred to as **reverse discrimination.** In 1995, the U.S. Supreme Court reached a decision that made it substantially easier for white males to challenge affirmative action programs. The Supreme Court case involved Adarand Constructors, Inc. The company lost a job bid for guard-rail work on a federal highway in southern Colorado to a Hispanic-owned firm, despite being the low bidder. The Hispanic-owned firm received the contract under a Transportation Department Program benefiting minority contractors. The Supreme Court ruled that the 160 federal laws and regulations must meet the same tough standard that state programs have to follow: They must show that they are dealing with the effects of past discrimination.

The Supreme Court decision arrived at a time of national debate over whether any person in a competitive situation deserves a preference because of race, ethnicity, or sex. The opposing point of view to affirmative action programs is that race, ethnicity, or sex should *not* be a factor in making employment or business decisions.[2] For example, a job candidate should not be given an edge over other applicants because she is an Hispanic female. What is your opinion on this issue?

A misperception of affirmative action is that it always means preferences or goals. Affirmative action can often be accomplished through recruitment in minority areas or publications geared toward affected minorities. Candidates thus flow naturally to the firm without having to establish a quota such as "hiring only a Hispanic woman for our next opening as a credit analyst."

LEARNING OBJECTIVE

Be aware of the legal aspects of staffing.

affirmative action
An employment practice that complies with anti-discrimination law and *correcting past discriminatory practices.*

reverse discrimination
The situation in which members of a majority group are denied access to jobs or promotion.

Civil Rights Act of 1964

Title VII of the Civil Rights Act of 1964 prohibits discrimination in all employment decisions on the basis of race, sex, religion, color, or national origin. Sexual harassment is in violation of Title VII.

Equal Employment Opportunity Commission

The Equal Employment Opportunity Commission (EEOC) administers Title VII and investigates complaints about violations. In addition, it has the power to issue guidelines for interpretation of the act. The EEOC's guidelines are not federal law. Instead, they are administrative rules and regulations.

Civil Rights Act of 1991

According to this act, victims of discrimination have rights to compensatory and punitive damages as well as jury trial. In general, in cases of intentional discrimination, the act shifts the burden of proof from employee to employer. Under earlier civil rights legislation, employees could only receive reinstatement, back pay, and attorneys' fees. The act places limits on how much employees can collect in compensatory and punitive damages. The amount depends on the size of the employer, with limits ranging from $50,000 to $300,000.

Age Discrimination in Employment Act, 1967

This act applies to employers with at least 25 employees. As later amended, it prohibits discrimination against people 40 years or older, in any area of employment, because of age. The act ended mandatory retirement for most employees covered by its provisions. Many employees laid off during downsizings have claimed to be victims of age discrimination.

Pregnancy Discrimination Act of 1978

This act broadens the definition of sex discrimination to cover pregnancy, childbirth, or related medical conditions. It also prohibits employers from discrimination against pregnant women in employment benefits if they are capable of performing their job duties.

Equal Pay Act, 1963

This act prohibits employers from paying unequal wages on the basis of sex. Equal pay must be paid for equal work, regardless of sex. Yet the act still allows employers to pay men and women different wages if the difference is based on ability or seniority.

Americans with Disabilities Act of 1990

The Americans with Disabilities Act (ADA) is designed to protect disabled and chronically ill people from discrimination in employment, public accommodations, transportation, and telecommunications. The act applies to employers with at least 15 employees.

A **disability** is defined as a physical or mental condition that substantially limits an individual's major life activities. Among the physical impairments covered by the ADA are severe vision problems, severe hearing problems, wheelchair confinement, muscular dystrophy, epilepsy, and severe physical disfigurement. Among the mental disabilities included are mental illness, alcoholism, and drug addiction. People who experienced these problems in the past cannot be discriminated against if they can perform the job.

If an employee can perform the essential functions of a job (even with special equipment), he or she should be considered qualified. Employers must accommodate the known disabilities of applicants and employees, unless the accommodations would impose "undue hardship" on the firm.

Family and Medical Leave Act, 1993

The Family and Medical Leave Act applies to employers having 50 or more employees. It requires the employer to provide up to 12 weeks of unpaid, job-protected leave to eligible employees for certain family and medical leave reasons such as caring for a newborn, newly adopted, or seriously ill child. The leave can also be used to take care of an employee's spouse or parent, or to take medical leave for the employee's own illness. The employer must also maintain the employee's health coverage during the leave.

Exhibit 10-2
Major U.S. Federal Anti-Discrimination Legislation and Agreements

disability

A physical or mental condition that substantially limits an individual's major life activities.

STRATEGIC HUMAN RESOURCE PLANNING

Staffing begins with a prediction about how many and what types of people will be needed to conduct the work of the firm. Such activity is referred to as **strategic human resources planning.** It is the process of anticipating and providing for

Canadian Federal Equal Pay for Equal Work Legislation

The Canadian federal government has had pay equity (equal pay for equal work) legislation since the 1950s. The legislation prohibits paying different wages to men and women who perform the same or substantially similar work. Examples include janitors and housekeepers, and orderlies and nurses' aides.

Employment-Equity Legislation, 1995 (Ontario, Canada)

Much employment legislation in Canada is at the provincial rather than the national level. In 1995, the New Democratic Party introduced employment-equity legislation. It requires most employers to meet targets for employment of specified groups, including racial minorities, women, aboriginal people, and the handicapped.

Commission on the Rights of People (Québec, Canada)

The Québec Charter of Human Rights and Freedoms was adopted in 1975. The Commission *des droits de la personne* (rights of people) is responsible for seeing that situations jeopardizing human rights and freedoms are corrected. The Charter provides that every person has a right to full and equal recognition and exercise of his or her human rights and freedoms, without distinction, exclusion, or preference, based on such factors as: race, color, ethnic or national origin, pregnancy, sexual orientation, age, religion, political convictions, language, social condition, or handicap. Citizens who feel their rights have been violated can file complaints through channels provided by the Québec government.

Exhibit 10-3
Major Canadian Federal and Provincial Employment Anti-Discrimination Legislation

the movement of people into, within, and out of an organization to support the firm's business strategy. Management attempts, through planning, to have the right number and right kinds of people at the right time.

Business strategy addresses the financial priorities of the organization with respect to identifying what business the firm should be in, product direction, profit targets, and so forth. Human resources planning addresses the question "What skills are needed for the success of this business?" Planning helps identify the gaps between current employee competencies and behavior and the competencies and behavior needed in the organization's future.[3] Strategic human resources planning consists of four basic steps.[4]

LEARNING OBJECTIVE

Explain the importance of strategic human resource planning.

1. *Planning for future needs.* A human resources planner estimates how many people, and with what abilities, the firm will need to operate in the foreseeable future.
2. *Planning for future turnover.* A planner predicts how many current employees are likely to remain with the organization. The difference between this number and the number of employees needed leads to the next step.
3. *Planning for recruitment, selection, and layoffs.* The organization must engage in recruitment, employee selection, or layoffs to attain the required number of employees.
4. *Planning for training and development.* An organization always needs experienced and competent workers. This step involves planning and providing for training and development programs that ensure the continued supply of people with the right skills.

Strategic business plans usually involve shifting around or training of people. Human resources planning can therefore be an important element in the success of strategies. Human resources planning can also be a strategic objective in itself. For example, one strategic objective of Pepsi Cola International is the development of talented people. Human resources planning contributes to attaining this objective by suggesting on- and off-the-job experiences to develop talent.

> **strategic human resources planning**
>
> *The process of anticipating and providing for the movement of people into, within, and out of an organization to support the firm's business strategy.*

RECRUITMENT

LEARNING OBJECTIVE

Present an overview of recruitment and selection.

Recruitment is the process of attracting job candidates with the right characteristics and skills to fill job openings. This section will describe the major aspects of recruiting.

PURPOSES OF RECRUITMENT

A major purpose of recruiting and selection is to find employees who fit well in the organization. A *person-organization fit* occurs when the characteristics of the individual complement the organizational culture or subculture.[5] For example, a person who values technology and diversity among people—and is qualified— would be a good candidate for work at Digital Equipment Corp.

Another important purpose of recruiting is to sell the organization to high-quality prospective candidates. Recruiters must select candidates who can function in one job today and be retrained and promoted later, as company needs dictate. Flexible candidates of this type are in demand; therefore, a recruiter may need to sell the advantages of his or her company to entice them to work there.[6]

> **recruitment**
> *The process of attracting job candidates with the right characteristics and skills to fill job openings.*

JOB DESCRIPTIONS AND JOB SPECIFICATIONS

An essential starting point in recruiting is to understand the nature of the job to be filled and the qualifications sought. Toward this end, the recruiter should be supplied with job descriptions and specifications. The **job description** explains in detail what the job holder is supposed to do. It is therefore a vital document for human resources planning and performance appraisal.

A **job specification** (or person specification) stems directly from the job description. It is a statement of the personal characteristics needed to perform the job. A job specification usually includes the education, experience, knowledge, and skills required to perform the job successfully. Both the job description and the job specification should be based on a careful job analysis. A job analysis is a gathering of basic facts about the job. Exhibit 10-4 presents a brief job description and the accompanying person specification.

> **job description**
> *A written statement of the key features of a job, along with the activities required to perform it effectively.*

> **job specification**
> *A statement of the personal characteristics needed to perform the job.*

RECRUITMENT OF TRADITIONAL AND CONTINGENT WORKERS

Recruitment applies to searching for full-time employees, part-time employees, and temporary workers. The last two groups are referred to as contingent work-

Exhibit 10-4
Job Description and Accompanying Job Specification

> **Human Resources Assistant:** Prepares personnel change forms, compiles other human resource data, answers routine employment inquiries, maintains appraisal and position description files. Under supervision, performs as required, assignments in the areas of wage and salary administration, job evaluation, employee benefits, and employment activities.
>
> **Job Specification:** Several years of business experience desirable but not mandatory. Person should have business degree from two-year or four-year college, good problem-solving ability, good interpersonal skills, and ability to learn how to run a human resources information system. Person should be well organized and pay careful attention to details.

ers—people who perform work for a firm but are not members of the permanent work force. The number of contingent workers is growing rapidly.

Some contingent workers are hired through agencies. In some cases, companies keep the names of contingent workers on file and, when necessary, hire the workers directly.

To maximize advantages from recruiting contingent workers, they must receive the same serious attention paid to full-time, permanent employees. Contingent workers must receive appropriate training, although temporary workers are sometimes billed as being fully trained. Motivational techniques, such as offering salary increases for good performance, should also be applied to the contingent workforce.[7] Another motivational approach is to offer contingent workers more exciting work.

SOURCES OF RECRUITING

The term *recruitment* connotes newspaper advertisements and campus recruiters. Yet about 85 percent of jobs are filled by word of mouth. The remaining 15 percent are filled through external means, such as classified advertisements. Recruiting sources can be classified into three categories:

1. *Present employees.* A standard recruiting method is to post job openings so that current employees may apply. Another way to recruit current employees is for managers to recommend them for transfer or promotion. A human resources information system is helpful in identifying current employees with the right skills. It minimizes the need to reject unqualified internal applicants.
2. *Referrals by present employees.* If a firm is established, present employees can be the primary recruiters. Satisfied employees may be willing to nominate relatives, friends, acquaintances, and neighbors for job openings.
3. *External sources.* There are a number of ways to reach potential employees outside an organization. The best known of these methods is a recruiting advertisement. Other external sources include: (a) placement offices, (b) private and public employment agencies, (c) labor union hiring halls, (d) walk-ins (people who show up at the firm without invitation), and (e) write-ins (people who write unsolicited job-seeking letters). As illustrated in the accompanying Organization

ORGANIZATION IN ACTION: JOB SEEKERS SEARCH FOR FUN OPPORTUNITIES AT SOUTHWEST AIRLINES

During a recent Southwest Airlines flight, a flight attendant outfitted with bunny ears popped out of an overhead bin and yelled "Su-u-r-prise!" At the end of the trip, another flight attendant requested, "Please pass all the plastic cups to the center aisle so we can wash them out and use them for the next group of passengers." Stunts like these have endeared Southwest to customers and employees. The emphasis on fun, combined with its reputation for excellent human resource management and profitability, have also served as a magnet for job seekers.

In a recent year alone, Southwest received 126,000 applications for a variety of positions: flight attendants, pilots, reservation agents, and mechanics. Many of the applications are from Southwest Airlines customers. Elizabeth Pedrick Sartain, Vice President of People, notes that many times people will drop by a Southwest office and say, "I want to work for Southwest because it's so much fun." Sometimes the company has to downplay the fun image by talking about the hard work involved. Despite the admonition, the company recently interviewed more than 35,000 individuals for 4,500 positions.

Source: Based on facts reported in Brenda Paik Sunoo, "How Fun Flies At Southwest Airlines," *Personnel Journal* (June 1995): 62–64.

in Action, firms with an outstanding reputation receive a steady stream of inquiries about job opportunities.

4. *Recruiting through computer networks.* A rapidly growing external source of job candidates is the Internet and other on-line services. Posting positions on an on-line service can attract thousands of computer-literate candidates. A case in point is Cisco Systems, a self-described "internetworking" firm. Almost all open positions are posted on the firm's World Wide Web home page. Internet browsers can view as many as 400 ads at a time. Cisco receives as many as 700 resumes electronically every month. All resumes are routed into a company database.[8]

GLOBAL RECRUITING

Global recruiting presents unique challenges. Multinational businesses must have the capability to connect with other parts of the globe to locate talent anywhere in the world. Company recruiters must meet job specifications calling for multiculturalism (being able to conduct business in other cultures) on top of more traditional skills. To fill international positions, the recruiter may have to develop overseas recruiting sources.[9] The recruiter may also require the assistance of a bilingual interviewer to help assess the candidate's ability to conduct business in more than one language.

SELECTION

Selecting the right candidate for a job is part of a process that includes recruitment. Exhibit 10-5 shows the steps in the process. A hiring decision is based on information gathered in two or more of these steps. For instance, a person might receive a job offer if he or she was impressive in the interview, scored well on the tests, and had good references. Another important feature of this selection model is that an applicant can be rejected at any point. An applicant who is abusive to the employment specialist might not be asked to fill out an application form.

Careful screening of job applicants has always been important because competent employees are the lifeblood of any firm. Current judicial rulings have added another reason for employers to evaluate candidates carefully. According to the doctrine of *negligent hiring and retention,* an employer can be liable for the job-

Exhibit 10-5
A Model for Selection

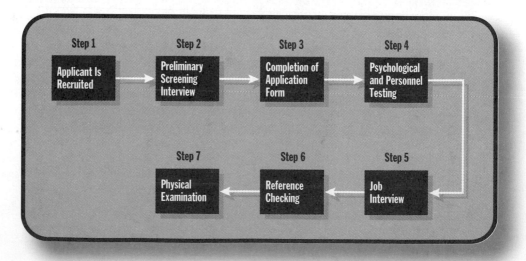

related misdeeds of its employees, whether the wrongs affect customers or cowork-ers.[10] Assume that a supervisor had a pre-employment history of sexual harassment and then sexually harasses another employee during working hours. The employer might be considered negligent for having hired the supervisor. Employers can also be held liable for retaining an employee who commits physically harmful acts.

PRELIMINARY SCREENING INTERVIEWS

Selection begins as soon as candidates come to the attention of the recruiter. If candidates appear to come close to fitting the job specifications, a brief screening interview follows. The purpose of the screening interview is to determine if the candidate should be given further consideration. "Knockout" questions are some-times used for this purpose. Should the candidate give an unacceptable answer to a key question, he or she is knocked out of further consideration. Assume a per-son applying for a supervisory position in a nursing home is asked, "How well do you get along with senior citizens?" A candidate who responds, "Very poorly" is immediately disqualified.

Candidates who pass the screening interview are asked to fill out a job appli-cation form. Sometimes this process is reversed, and a screening interview is con-ducted after the candidate successfully completes the application form.

JOB APPLICATION FORMS

Job application forms are a standard part of any selection procedure. They serve two important purposes. First, they furnish basic biographical data about the candidate, including his or her education, work experience, and citizenship. Second, they pro-vide information that could be related to success on the job. A sloppily completed application form *could* indicate that the candidate had poor work habits, whereas, a carefully completed form *could* indicate that the candidate has careful work habits.

Job application forms and employment interviewers should not ask direct or indirect questions that could be interpreted as discriminatory. Discussing the fol-lowing topics in a job interview could be a violation of antidiscrimination laws.[11]

1. Race
2. Religion
3. Gender (male or female)
4. Pregnancy
5. Number of children
6. Ages of children
7. Marital status
8. Child-care plans
9. Height or weight
10. Handicap
11. Age
12. Criminal record
13. Union affiliation
14. Workers' compensation claims on previous job

Questions about any of these topics would be discriminatory if they were not job-related. A *job-related* question or selection device deals with behavior and skills that are required for job success. Asking an applicant for a child-care specialist position if she or he has ever been convicted of child molestation is job-related.

PSYCHOLOGICAL AND PERSONNEL TESTING

Hundreds of different tests are used in employment testing. All tests are psycho-logical tests in the sense that measuring human ability is an important part of psy-chology. This book uses the term *personnel testing* as well as *psychological testing*, be-cause many people think psychological tests deal with personality and personnel tests deal with job skills.

TYPES OF PSYCHOLOGICAL AND PERSONNEL TESTS. The five principal types of psychological and personnel tests are achievement, aptitude, personality, integrity, and interest.

1. *Achievement tests* sample and measure an applicant's knowledge and skills. They require applicants to demonstrate their competency on job tasks or related subjects. For example, Connecticut General uses a computerized testing system based on job scenarios to screen experienced applicants. The system tests an applicant's ability to process a claim document, typing speed, and typing accuracy. This computerized achievement test saved the company $300,000 in turnover costs in one year.[12]

2. *Aptitude tests* measure the potential for performing satisfactorily on the job, given sufficient training. Mental-ability tests, the best-known variety of aptitude tests, measure the ability to solve problems and learn new material. Mental-ability tests measure such specific aptitudes as verbal reasoning, numerical reasoning, and spatial relations (the ability to visualize in three dimensions).

3. *Personality tests* measure personal traits and characteristics that could be related to job performance. Personality tests have been the subject of considerable controversy for many years. Critics are concerned that these tests invade privacy and are too imprecise to be useful. Nevertheless, personality factors have a profound influence on job performance. Exhibit 10-6 lists the major personality factors related to job performance.

4. *Integrity tests* are designed to measure the extent of a person's integrity as it relates to job behavior. These tests are frequently used in workplaces such as retail stores, banks, and warehouses, where employees have access to cash or merchandise. A major factor measured by integrity tests is social conscientiousness. People who score high on this personality factor are much more likely to follow organizational rules. Despite controversy over their use, integrity tests are widely used. One justification for their use is that several studies have shown that about one-third of employees admit to engaging in some type of company theft. The theft could be as small as taking home a few office supplies or giving generous discounts to friends.[13]

5. *Interest tests* measure preferences for engaging in certain activities, such as mechanical, clerical, literary, or managerial work. They also measure a person's interest in specific occupations, such as accountant, veterinarian, or sales representative. Interest tests are designed to indicate whether a person would en-

Exhibit 10-6
The Big Five Personality Factors

Many psychologists believe that the basic structure of human personality is represented by what they call the Big Five factors. These factors, which follow, influence job performance. Conscientiousness, for example, is related to the tendency to produce quality work. Furthermore, these factors can be measured by psychological tests.

I. **Extraversion.** Extraversion (which is the same as extroversion) relates to whether a person is social, gregarious, assertive, talkative, or active.

II. **Emotional stability.** This factor relates to whether a person is anxious, depressed, angry, embarrassed, emotional, or worried.

III. **Agreeableness.** This factor relates to whether a person is courteous, flexible, trusting, good-natured, cooperative, forgiving, soft-hearted, or tolerant.

IV. **Conscientiousness.** This factor relates to whether a person is careful, thorough, responsible, organized, or prepared. This factor also relates to whether a person is hard-working, achievement-oriented, and persevering.

V. **Openness to experience.** This factor relates to whether a person is imaginative, cultured, curious, original, broad-minded, intelligent, or artistically sensitive.

joy a particular activity or occupation. They do not attempt, however, to measure a person's aptitude for it.

VALIDITY AND EQUAL EMPLOYMENT OPPORTUNITY. The EEOC insists that selection tests be scientifically accurate, job-related, and not discriminatory against any group. These rules also apply to other selection instruments, including application forms and interviews. A specific provision requires a validity study when a selection procedure has adverse impact on any race, sex, or ethnic group. A *validity study* is a statistical and scientific method of seeing if a selection device does predict job performance. Do high scorers perform well on the job? Do low scorers tend to be poor performers?

Thousands of studies have been conducted about the ability of tests to predict job performance. Some studies explore how well groups of tests used in combination predict job performance. These studies are considered the most valuable because, in practice, employment tests are often used in combinations referred to as test batteries. There is considerable disagreement about the contribution of employment tests to the selection process. Nevertheless, it appears that, used as intended, employment testing does improve the accuracy of selection decisions. As a result, productivity improves.

For example, long-term research conducted at the U.S. Job Service concluded that standardized ability tests are fair and valid predictors of performance for all jobs.[14] Another study indicated that ability tests and skills tests have success rates of 80 percent and 75 percent, respectively, in selecting job applicants. The success rate of predicting by experience, interview, or education was only about 58 percent.[15]

THE JOB INTERVIEW

The interview that follows testing is more thorough and comprehensive than the screening interview. The topics covered in a job interview include education, work experience, special skills and abilities, hobbies, and interests. Interviewers frequently use the candidate's résumé as a source of topics. For example, "I notice you have worked for four employers in three years. Why is that?" Testing results may also provide clues for additional questioning. If a candidate scored very low on a scale measuring conscientiousness, the interviewer might ask about the candidate's punctuality and error rate.

Validity increases when interviews are carefully structured (tightly organized) and all applicants are asked the same standard questions. Yet unique questions can still be asked of each candidate. Employment interviews are also more valid when the interviewer is trained and experienced. Validity may also increase when several candidates are interviewed for each position, because comparisons can be made among the applicants. In general, the higher the level the position, the more candidates are interviewed. Southwest Airlines, for example, interviews many more people for a pilot's position than for a baggage handler.

Job interviews have a dual purpose. The interviewer is trying to decide whether the interviewee is appropriate for the organization. At the same time, the interviewee is trying to decide if the job and the organization fit him or her. Exhibit 10-7 presents guidelines for conducting a productive job interview.

REFERENCE CHECKING AND BACKGROUND INVESTIGATION

A **reference check** is an inquiry to a second party about a job candidate's suitability for employment. The two main topics explored in reference checks are past job performance and the ability to get along with coworkers. Concerns about neg-

reference check
An inquiry to a second party about a job candidate's suitability for employment.

ligent hiring are causing the comeback of the reference check as an important part of the screening process. Former and prospective employers have a *qualified privilege* to discuss an employee's past performance. As long as the information is given to a person with a legitimate interest for receiving it, discussion of an employee's past misconduct or poor performance is permissible under law.[16]

Despite such rulings, many past employers are hesitant to provide complete references for two key reasons. First, job applicants have legal access to written references unless they specifically waive this right in writing (Privacy Act of 1974). Second, people who provide negative references worry about being sued for libel.

Reference checks overlap with background investigations. The latter are usually conducted by a firm that authenticates background facts. The investigation might also uncover facts not mentioned during the interview, such as a criminal record or bankruptcy.

THE PHYSICAL EXAMINATION AND DRUG TESTING

The physical examination is important for at least two reasons. First, it gives some indication as to the person's physical ability to handle the requirements of a particular job. Second, the physical exam provides a basis for later comparisons. This lessens the threat of an employee claiming that the job caused a particular injury or disease.

**Exhibit 10-7
Guidelines for
Conducting an Effective
Selection Interview**

1. **Prepare in advance.** Prior to the interview, carefully review the applicant's job application form and résumé. Keep in mind several questions worthy of exploration, such as "I notice you have done no previous selling. Why do you want a sales job now?"
2. **Find a quiet place free from interruptions.** Effective interviewing requires careful concentration. Also, the candidate deserves the courtesy of an uninterrupted interview.
3. **Take notes during the interview.** Take notes on the content of what is said during the interview. Also, record your observations about the person's statements and behavior. For example, "Candidate gets very nervous when we talk about previous work history."
4. **Use a brief warm-up period.** A standard way of relaxing a job candidate is to spend about five minutes talking about neutral topics, such as the weather. This brief period can be extended by asking about basic facts, such as the person's address and education.
5. **Ask open-ended questions.** To encourage the employee to talk, ask questions that call for more than a one- or two-word answer. Sometimes a request for information—a question like "Tell me about your days at business school"—works like an open-ended question.
6. **Follow an interview format.** Effective interviewers carefully follow a predetermined interview format. They ask additional questions that are based on responses to the structured questions.
7. **Give the job candidate encouragement.** The easiest way to keep an interviewee talking is to give that person encouragement. Standard encouragements include "That's very good," "How interesting," "I like your answer," and "Excellent."
8. **Dig for additional details.** When the interviewee brings up a topic worthy of exploration, dig for additional facts. Assume the interviewee says, "I used to work as a private chauffeur, but then I lost my driver's license." Noticing a red flag, the interviewer might respond: "Why did you lose your license?"
9. **Make very limited use of a stress interview.** The purpose of a stress interview is to see how well the interviewee responds to pressure. Among the stress tactics are to insult the interviewee, to ignore him or her, or to stare at the interviewee and say nothing. These tactics create so much ill will that they are hardly worth pursuing. Besides, a job interview is stressful enough.
10. **Spend most of the interview time listening.** An experienced job interviewer spends little time talking. It is the interviewee who should be doing the talking.
11. **Provide the candidate ample information about the organization.** Answer any relevant questions.

For example, after one year on the job, an employee might claim that job stress led to heart disease. If the pre-employment physical showed evidence of heart disease before the employee was hired, the employer would have little to fear from the claim.

The physical examination has increased in importance since the passage of the Americans with Disabilities Act. An employer cannot deny a disabled individual a job because of increased insurance costs or the high cost of health benefits. However, the employer can deny employment to a disabled person if having the individual in the workplace poses a threat to his or her safety or the safety of others.[17] If safety is an issue, the applicant might be offered a less hazardous position.

Sixty-seven percent of large companies test job applicants for use of illegal drugs. Many small companies also use some form of drug testing. Testing for substance abuse includes blood analysis, urinalysis, observation of eyes, and examination of skin (for punctures). Some people are concerned that inaccurate drug testing may unfairly deny employment to worthy candidates. A strong argument in favor of drug testing is that employees who are drug abusers may create such problems as lowered productivity, lost time from work, and misappropriation of funds. Workplace substance abuse costs employers an estimated $120 billion annually.[18]

CROSS-CULTURAL SELECTION

As with cross-cultural recruitment, most of the selection guidelines and techniques already mentioned can be applied cross-culturally. Many selection devices, such as widely used personnel tests, are published in more than one language, especially Spanish. Managers and employment interviewers gathering information about job candidates from other countries should familiarize themselves with key facts about the other culture. For example, in France a *grand école* is a high-prestige college of business that qualifies graduates for positions in the best firms. An interviewer unfamiliar with the French culture might miss the significance of an interviewee talking about his diploma from a *grand école*.

An example of adapting selection techniques to cross-cultural requirements took place at a Japanese-American manufacturer of automobile parts. Management practices at the 80 percent Japanese-owned firm emphasized interpersonal skill, team orientation, and high product quality. The U.S.-based company was hiring Americans for assembly jobs who would fit the Japanese organizational culture. Work simulations (or work samples) proved to be the most effective selection device. It was found that applicant characteristics important in a Japanese culture (such as team and quality orientation) could be measured by the simulation. Trained observers rated the candidates on various factors including the following:[19]

- Attention to maintenance and safety
- Team attitude and participation
- Work motivation and involvement
- Quality orientation

After job candidates have been recruited and passed through all the selection screens, such as the physical exam, they are hired. After the hiring decision is made, human resource specialists make sure all the necessary forms are completed such as those relating to taxes and benefits. Next comes orientation.

ORIENTATION, TRAINING, AND DEVELOPMENT

LEARNING OBJECTIVE 5

Present an overview of employee orientation, training, and development.

Most firms no longer operate under a "sink or swim" philosophy when it comes to employee learning. Instead, employees receive ample opportunity to become oriented to the firm. Later the firm trains and develops them.

EMPLOYEE ORIENTATION

employee orientation program
A formal activity designed to acquaint new employees with the organization.

A new employee usually begins his or her new job by attending an orientation program. An **employee orientation program** acquaints new employees with the company. Part of the orientation may deal with small but important matters, such as telling the employee how to get a parking sticker. Large firms offer elaborate orientation programs conducted by human-resources specialists. The program may include tours of the buildings, talks by department heads, videotape presentations, and generous supplies of printed information.

Employee orientation also includes a manager telling a new employee specifically what his or her job is and what is expected in terms of performance. It is also valuable to hold periodic discussions of this same topic during the employee's time with the firm. In some firms, a *buddy system* is part of the orientation. A buddy, a peer from the new employee's department, shows the new employee around and fills in information gaps.

Another aspect of orientation is informal socialization. In this process, coworkers introduce new employees to aspects of the organizational culture. Coworkers might convey, for example, how well-motivated a new employee should be or the competence level of key people in the organization. The disadvantage of informal orientation is that it may furnish the new employee with misinformation.

TRAINING AND DEVELOPMENT

training
Any procedure intended to foster and enhance learning among employees, particularly directed at acquiring job skills.

Training and development deal with systematic approaches to improving employee skills and performance. **Training** is any procedure intended to foster and enhance learning among employees. It is particularly directed at acquiring job skills.

Rapid changes in technology and the globalization of business have spurred the growth of training programs. Today a wide range of employees receive training on the business applications of the Internet and in international business.

Training programs exist to teach hundreds of different skills, such as equipment repair, performance appraisal, and budget preparation. Literacy training has become widespread because such a large proportion of the work force is functionally illiterate. For example, almost 90 percent of applicants for entry-level jobs at a new Motorola, Inc. plant failed a work-related test.[20] They failed the test because they could not read well enough to perform job-related tasks.

computer-based training
A learning experience based on the interaction between the trainee and a computer.

A substantial amount of skills training in industry is delivered through computers. **Computer-based training** is a learning experience based on the interaction between the trainee and a computer. The computer provides a stimulus or prompt, to which the trainee responds. The computer then analyzes the response and provides feedback to the student.[21] A question in a customer service course might ask if the following is a good response to a customer complaint: "If you don't like my answer, go speak to my boss." A message would then appear suggesting that the trainee take more ownership of the problem. The retail giant Hudson's Bay Co. uses computer-based training for its 65,000 store associates throughout Canada.

development
A form of personal improvement that usually consists of enhancing knowledge and skills of a complex and unstructured nature.

Development is a form of personal improvement that usually consists of enhancing knowledge and skills of a complex and unstructured nature. An example of a development program is one that helps managers become better leaders.

Most of this text and its accompanying course could be considered an experience in management training and development. The next paragraphs will describe two vital aspects of training and development for employees and managers: needs assessment and selection of an appropriate program.

NEEDS ASSESSMENT. Before embarking upon a training program, it is important to determine what type of training is needed. This involves such steps as conducting a job analysis and asking the managers themselves, their bosses, and their subordinates about the managers' needs for training. Also, the trainer observes the managers performing their regular duties to identify needs for improvement.

Despite the importance of matching training and development programs to specific needs, there are universal training needs. These include training in communication, motivation, decision making, counseling and coaching, and time management.

Entertainment in various forms is currently emphasized as a way of both training and developing workers. Among these forms of entertainment are games, quizzes, magic, props, costumes, theater, video, and comedy. One rationale for making training lighter is to capture the attention of trainees. Another is to involve as many perceptual processes as possible with the intent of stimulating creative thinking. One trainer believes that traditional training is too linear, or left-brained.[22] Amusement in training helps stimulate the emotions. What is your opinion of the contribution of amusement to training?

SELECTING AN APPROPRIATE TRAINING PROGRAM. After needs are assessed, they must be carefully matched to training and development programs. A program must often be tailored to fit company requirements. The person assigning employees to training and development programs must be familiar with their needs for training and development, know the content of various programs, and enroll employees in programs that will meet their needs. Exhibit 10-8 presents a sample listing of training and development programs.

A current trend is for nonmanagers to participate in training and development usually reserved for managers and future managers. The rationale is that workers assigned to teams manage themselves to some extent. They also deal directly with many managerial activities, such as selection interviewing and budgeting.[23]

Explain the basics of a fair and reliable method of evaluating employee performance.

PERFORMANCE APPRAISAL

Up to this point in the staffing model, employees have been recruited, selected, oriented, and trained. The next step is to evaluate performance. A **performance appraisal** is a formal system for measuring, evaluating, and reviewing performance. Whichever performance appraisal system or technique is chosen, it should meet the same legal standards of fairness as selection devices. One requirement is that categories of evaluation should be job-related, such as rating a worker on creativity only if his or her job requires creative thinking.

The traditional appraisal involves a manager who evaluates an individual team member. With the current emphasis on various team structures, performance appraisals are now used to evaluate group performance. At times team members contribute to the evaluation of each other and the group. A developing trend in performance appraisals is the **360-degree appraisal,** in which a person is evaluated by a sampling of all the people with whom he or she interacts. An appraisal form for a manager might receive input from the boss, all subordinates, other managers at his or her level, and a sampling of customers. Self-assessment is also included. The sales manager's manager would then synthesize all the information and discuss it with the sales manager. The rationale for the 360-degree appraisal is that it presents a complete picture of performance.

performance appraisal

A formal system for measuring, evaluating, and reviewing performance.

360-degree appraisal

A performance appraisal in which a person is evaluated by a sampling of all the people with whom he or she interacts.

Training Programs	Management Development
Interviewing candidates	Effective leadership
Listening to employees	Mentoring
Motivating subordinates	International management
Coaching and counseling	Strategic thinking
Telemarketing skills	Business ethics
Writing better reports	Policy making
Improving communication skills	Development of quality awareness
Using the Internet	Crisis management
Creativity training	Downsizing the organization
Preventing and controlling sexual harassment	Development of cultural sensitivity
Preventing accidents	Managing for total customer satisfaction
Improving negotiating skills	

Note: Training programs mentioned in the left column are often included in a program of management development. The programs in the right, however, are rarely considered to be specific skill-based training programs.

Performance appraisals help managers determine if the previous steps in the staffing model have been effective. For example, if most employees are performing well, recruitment and selection are probably adequate.

PURPOSES OF PERFORMANCE APPRAISAL

Peformance appraisals serve a number of important administrative purposes and can also help the manager carry out the leadership function. A major administrative purpose of performance appraisals is to decide who should receive merit increases and the relative size of the increases. The appraisal process also helps identify employees with potential for promotion. High-performing teams can be identified as well. Employee reviews are widely used to provide documentation for discharging, demoting, and downsizing employees who are not meeting performance standards.

Performance appraisals help managers carry out the leadership function in several ways. Productivity can be increased by suggesting areas for needed improvement. Also, the manager can help employees identify their needs for self-improvement and self-development. Appraisal results can be used to motivate employees by providing feedback on performance. Finally, a performance appraisal gives employees a chance to express their ambitions, hopes, and concerns. In the process, career development is enhanced.

DESIGN OF THE PERFORMANCE-APPRAISAL SYSTEM

traits
Stable aspects of people, closely related to personality.

behavior
In performance appraisal, what people actually do on the job.

results
In performance appraisal, what people accomplish, or the objectives they attain.

A number of different formats and methods of performance appraisal are in current use. They are designed to measure traits, behavior, or results. **Traits** are stable aspects of people, closely related to personality. Job-related traits include enthusiasm, dependability, and honesty. **Behavior,** or activity, is what people do on the job. Job-related behavior includes working hard, keeping the work area clean, maintaining a good appearance, and showing concern for quality and customer service. **Results** are what people accomplish, or the objectives they attain. Under a system of management by objectives, a performance appraisal consists largely of reviewing whether people achieved their objectives.

At first glance, measuring performance on the basis of results seems ideal and fair. Critics of the results method of appraisal, however, contend that personal qualities are important. A performance-appraisal system that measures only results ignores such important traits and behavior as honesty, loyalty, and creativity. Many managers believe that people with good qualities will achieve good results in the long run.

Many performance-appraisal systems attempt to measure both results and behavior or traits. Exhibit 10-9 shows a portion of a peer-rating system that includes both behavior and results. A group of peers indicates whether a particular aspect of job performance or behavior is a strength or a *developmental opportunity*. The initials under "peer evaluations" refer to coworkers doing the evaluation. The person being evaluated then knows who to thank or blame for the feedback. In addition to indicating whether a job factor is a strength or an opportunity, raters can supply comments and developmental suggestions. The results of the peer ratings might then be supplemented by the manager's ratings to achieve a total appraisal.

COMPENSATION

Compensation, the combination of pay and benefits, is closely related to staffing. A major reason compensation requires so much managerial attention is that it constitutes about two-thirds of the cost of running an enterprise. Here we look at several types of pay and employee benefits. Chapter 12 will describe how compensation is used as a motivational device.

LEARNING OBJECTIVE 7

Summarize the basics of employee compensation.

Exhibit 10-9
Peer Evaluation of Customer Service Technician

PERSON EVALUATED: Chris Marina

Skill Categories and Expected Behaviors	Peer Evaluations for Each Category and Behavior					
Customer Care	TR	JP	CK	JT	CJ	ML
Takes ownership for customer problems	O	S	S	S	S	S
Follows through on customer commitments	S	S	S	S	S	S
Technical Knowledge and Skill						
Engages in continuous learning to update technical skills	O	S	S	S	S	O
Corrects problems on the first visit	O	O	S	S	S	S
Work Group Support						
Actively participates in work group meetings	S	S	S	S	O	S
Backs up other work group members by taking calls in other areas	S	O	O	S	S	S
Minimal absence	S	O	S	S	O	S
Finance Management						
Adheres to work group parts expense process	S	S	S	O	S	S
Passes truck audits	S	S	S	O	S	S

Note: S refers to a strength; O refers to developmental opportunity.

TYPES OF PAY

Wages and salary are the most common forms of pay. Wages are payments to employees for their services, but computed on an hourly basis or on the amount of work produced. A part-time airline reservations agent might be paid $7.25 per hour, or a garment worker might be paid $2.00 per jogging suit fabricated. Salary is an annual amount of money paid to a worker that does not depend directly on output or hours worked.[24] Nevertheless, future salary is dependent to some extent on how well the worker produced in the previous year. Many workers are eligible for bonuses or incentives to supplement their salary.

Skill-based pay is another way of establishing pay levels. Under a pay-for-knowledge-and-skills system, managers calculate starting pay based on the knowledge and skill level required for a given job. Subsequent increases depend on the worker's mastering additional skills and knowledge specified by the firm. Skill-based pay is gaining acceptance for work teams because members must be multi-skilled. The Organization in Action presents more details about skill-based pay.

broadbanding
In salary administration, basing pay more on the person than the position, thus reducing the number of pay grades.

A major new concept in salary administration is **broadbanding,** or basing pay more on the person rather than the position. As a result of broadbanding, the company reduces the number of pay grades and replaces them with several pay ranges (or broad bands). For example, a multiskilled employee exceeding goals might receive 115 percent to 135 percent of a target pay range. A new employee or one not achieving goals might receive 80 percent to 95 percent of the target pay range. Broadbanding fits the new, flexible organization because employees are encouraged to move to jobs where they can develop their careers and add value to the firm. The point is that employees take their salaries with them from job to job instead of being paid according to the range for a given job.[25]

ORGANIZATION IN ACTION: SKILL-BASED PAY SYSTEM AT MCDONNELL DOUGLAS

McDonnell Douglas Helicopter Co., based in Mesa, Arizona, needed a new compensation system to reduce costs, enhance productivity, and promote employee self-development and work-force flexibility. After a two-year trial period, the company chose to implement a pay-for-skill compensation system. The company wanted the new pay system to reflect accurately the capabilities of employees, as well as the skills required for each job.

Multidisciplinary teams, composed of company employees as well as human resource professionals, were formed to design and implement the skill-based pay system. Employee input helped ensure that the skills qualifying for pay were those most necessary to perform the job, and also facilitated gaining support for the new system.

The teams worked with cards for listing each skill, the tasks required to verify proficiency of the skill, and the training requirements to learn the skill. Employees who qualified for a salary increase received a pay increase of 35 cents per hour every 26 weeks after demonstrating proficiency in a skill. Among the many criteria for receiving a pay increase were the following:

- Skills must be demonstrated and be current.
- Skills must meet quality and time standards specified.
- Skills must be witnessed by at least one review-team member.
- Skills must be related to the employee's job (such as running the controls for testing an Apache helicopter's performance).

According to a company spokesperson, the skill-based pay system contributes to greater productivity improvements than the standard learning curve would predict. Also, management now has a better understanding of their worker's abilities, and how they can progress in their careers.

Source: Based on facts reported in Bradford A. Johnson and Harry H. Ray, "Employee-developed Pay System Increases Productivity," *Personnel Journal* (November 1993): 112–118.

EMPLOYEE BENEFITS

An **employee benefit** is any noncash payment given to workers as a condition of their employment. Employee benefits cost employers about 35 percent of salaries. Therefore, an employee earning $30,000 per year in salary probably receives a combined salary and benefit package of $40,500. Health care illustrates the costliness of benefits. In the American auto industry, employee health care adds $1,086 (including $383 for retiree coverage) to the cost of an average vehicle. The comparable figure is $175 for a Japanese auto plant in the U.S.[26]

The fastest-growing trend in benefits is the **flexible benefit package**. A benefit plan of this nature allows employees to select a group of benefits tailored to their preferences. Flexible compensation plans generally provide employees with one category of fixed benefits—minimum standards such as medical and disability insurance. The second category is flexible, with a menu of benefits from which each employee is allowed to select up to a certain total cost. An employee who prefers less vacation time, for instance, might choose more life insurance.

Exhibit 10-10 presents a comprehensive list of employee benefits. Organizations vary considerably in the benefits and services they offer employees. No one firm is likely to offer all the benefits listed.

employee benefit
Any noncash payment given to workers as a condition of their employment.

flexible benefit package
A benefit plan that allows employees to select a group of benefits tailored to their preferences.

Exhibit 10-10
Employee Benefits

Usually Mandatory

Social security	Group life insurance
Workers' compensation	Disability insurance
Unemployment compensation	Retirement pensions
Family leave	Paid vacations

Optional But Frequently Offered

Group life insurance	Tuition assistance
Retirement pensions	Paid rest or refreshment breaks
Disability insurance	Employee assistance program
Accidental health insurance	Company-subsidized cafeteria
Paid lunch breaks	Employee training
Paid sick leave	Personal time off
Health insurance	Paid maternity leaves
Relocation allowance, moving costs	Child adoption grants

Optional and Less Frequently Offered

Paid travel time to work	Retirement counseling
Physical fitness and wellness programs	Outplacement counseling
Stress management programs	Child-care centers
Credit unions	Payment of adoption fees
Cash payments for unused vacation time	Paid paternity leave
Discount-purchasing programs	Parental leave
Funeral pay	Vision-care plans
Assistance with adoption fees	Rape counseling
Car-pooling services	Massage therapy
Prepaid legal fees	

SUMMARY OF KEY POINTS

1

Describe the components of organizational staffing.

The staffing model consists of six phases: awareness of the legal aspects of staffing; strategic human resources planning; recruitment; selection; orientation, training, and development; and performance appraisal. Compensation is also part of staffing.

2

Be aware of the legal aspects of staffing.

Legislation influences all aspects of staffing. Exhibits 10-1 and 10-2 summarize key legislation relating to equal employment opportunity. Managers should be generally familiar with these laws. Affirmative action consists of complying with antidiscrimination law *and* correcting past discriminatory practices.

3

Explain the importance of strategic human resource planning.

Strategic human resource planning provides for the movement of people into, within, and out of the organization. At the same time, it relates these activities to business strategy.

4

Present an overview of recruitment and selection.

Recruitment is the process of attracting job candidates with the right characteristics and skills to fit job openings and the organizational culture. External and internal sources are used in recruiting. A new approach is recruiting through on-line computer services.

Selecting the right employees helps build a firm and minimizes the problem of negligent hiring. Selecting the right candidate from among those recruited may involve a preliminary screening interview, completion of an application form, psychological and personnel testing, a job interview, reference checking, and a physical examination. The five types of psychological and personnel tests used most frequently in employee selection are achievement, aptitude, personality, integrity, and interest tests. Most job interviews are semistructured. They follow a standard format, yet they give the interviewer a chance to ask additional questions. Reference checks play an important role in helping employers prevent the problem of negligent hiring.

5

Present an overview of employee orientation, training, and development.

An employee orientation program helps acquaint the newly hired employee with the firm. Training includes any procedure intended to foster and enhance employee skills. Development is a form of personal improvement that generally enhances knowledge and skills of a complex and unstructured nature. A needs assessment should be conducted prior to selecting training and development programs.

6

Explain the basics of a fair and reliable method of evaluating employee performance.

A performance appraisal is a standard method of measuring, evaluating, and reviewing performance of individuals as well as teams. A recent appraisal technique, the 360-degree appraisal, involves feedback from multiple people. Performance appraisals serve important administrative purposes, such as helping managers make decisions about pay increases and promotions. Appraisals also help managers carry out the leadership function. Appraisal systems measure traits, behavior, and results, with some systems taking into account more than one factor.

7

Summarize the basics of employee compensation.

Workers are typically paid salaries, bonuses, and sometimes payment for job skills. Broadbanding, which results in fewer pay grades, supports the modern, less hierarchical organization. Employee benefits are a major part of compensation. Flexible benefit packages allow employees to select a group of benefits tailored to their preferences.

KEY TERMS AND PHRASES

Affirmative Action *pg. 219*
Reverse Discrimination *pg. 219*
Disability *pg. 220*
Strategic Human Resources Planning *pg. 221*
Recruitment *pg. 222*
Job Description *pg. 222*
Job Specification *pg. 222*

Reference Check *pg. 227*
Employee Orientation Program *pg. 230*
Training *pg. 230*
Computer-Based Training *pg. 230*
Development *pg. 230*
Performance Appraisal *pg. 231*
360-Degree Appraisal *pg. 231*

QUESTIONS

1. In your own words, what is employment (or job) discrimination?
2. How can human resource management be made to support business strategy?
3. What conflict do you see between selecting for a good person-organization fit and valuing diversity?
4. When performance appraisals are used to help make downsizing decisions, should the company use already existing appraisal information? Or should the company conduct new performance appraisals just for the purposes of downsizing?
5. Many training directors contend that the best way to enhance productivity is through training. What is your opinion on this issue?
6. Many researchers and union officials think that pay should be based mostly on seniority (time with the company) because performance appraisals are so biased. What is your opinion?
7. In what way is "compensation" linked to the performance of students?

SKILL-BUILDING EXERCISE 10-A: THE SELECTION INTERVIEW

GROUP ACTIVITY Assume the role of a sales manager or employment interviewer who works for Met Life (Metropolitan Life Insurance Company). After thinking through the job demands of a sales rep for your company, conduct about a 20-minute interview of a classmate who pretends to apply for the sales position. Before conducting the interview, review the guidelines in Exhibit 10-7. Other students on your team might observe the interview and then provide constructive feedback.

SKILL-BUILDING EXERCISE 10-B: ASSESSING TRAINING NEEDS

GROUP ACTIVITY Each student in the class assumes the role of the manager of one store among a chain of stores owned by your company. All the managers have assembled for a national meeting to discuss business strategy and training needs. Each manager will give a two-minute class presentation of his or her needs for development. All class members keep brief notes about these training needs.

After all the store managers have presented their training needs, the class breaks up into groups of about six managers. Each group then identifies the three most important training and development programs the company should offer to meet these developmental needs. A team leader informs the rest of the class of the nature of these programs. The various groups can then compare the various interpretations they made of the training needs of the other managers.

VIDEO DISCUSSION QUESTIONS

1. How much emphasis does Bossidy place on training and development? **[Allied Signal]**
2. How is 360-degree evaluation used to improve productivity in the downsized organization? **[360 Degrees of Evaluation]**
3. How is 360-degree evaluation used for purposes of making compensation decisions? **[360 Degrees of Evaluation]**

CASE PROBLEM 10-A: MANOR CARE REACHES OUT TO EMPLOYEES

Manor Care, based in Silver Spring, Maryland, is the parent of two companies. One of them, Choice Hotels International, manages a franchise systems that includes 2,350 hotels in 22 countries. Manor HealthCare Corp. is the other organization. It operates 167 nursing-care centers nationwide, an acute-care hospital, retirement living units, a wholesale pharmacy business, and medical training schools. Manor also has a hotel-operating division.

Company president Stewart Bainum Jr. is committed to making Manor Care a great service provider. He realizes that attaining this goal depends to a large extent on Manor Care's front-line service employees. The service employees make up most of the employee base. In the health-care side of the business alone, 10,000 of the 20,000 employees are certified nursing assistants. The primary role of a nursing assistant is to help clients dress, eat, and bathe.

To maintain a high level of service, company management decided that turnover must be reduced. One strategy chosen for reducing turnover was to enhance the benefits package. The company discovered that, although its benefits package is good by industry standards, it is not meeting the needs of employees. One example is that only 15 percent of the employees used the medical benefit called Preferred Provider Organization (PPO). The company also discovered that of the employees making $12,000 a year or less, only 20 percent participate in the 401(k) program. (A 401(k) program allows for voluntary employee contributions to a retirement fund. The company provides some matching funds.)

Chairman Bainum met with his top management team, including the human resource director, to develop a benefits package that would suit the needs of the company's thousands of hotel and healthcare workers. The twin goal was to enhance employee satisfaction and reduce turnover.

CASE QUESTIONS

1. To what extent do you think the employee benefits package can increase satisfaction and reduce turnover?
2. Design an affordable benefits package that you think will retain and attract competent employees for Manor Care.

Source: Based on facts reported in Dawn Gunsch, "Benefits Program Helps Retain Frontline Workers," *Personnel Journal* (February 1993): 88–89.

CASE PROBLEM 10-B: SENTRY SEARCHES FOR THE RIGHT EMPLOYEES

The Sentry Group, a 60-year-old company, makes safes, security chests, and insulated two-drawer files for homes and small businesses. Sentry employees 700 people, and its annual sales exceed $70 million. The firm is non-union and family owned. Among its customers are mass-market retailers such as Wal-Mart and Kmart.

As company management recently looked toward an upcoming selling season, it realized that the demand for its products exceeded its capacity to produce. Top management decided to hire 50 production workers to boost output. The beginning pay rate was $7.25 an hour for first-shift jobs, $7.70 for second-shift (3:30 P.M. to midnight), and $7.80 for third-shift (11 P.M. to 7:30 A.M.) jobs. All positions are full-time and permanent, but the company agreed to accept applications for short-term assignments.

The company requires a two-year verifiable work history. Experience in production work, however, is not required. Sentry offers a profit-sharing program for employees with annual bonus checks that could be a double-digit percentage of yearly pay.

Bob Legge, vice president of human resources, says the company is "fairly picky" in its selection process. An important factor in choosing employees is how well the employees fit the corporate culture, which is built on teamwork, quality, and keeping costs low. Legge said the company is interested in people whose attitude is not just "Go to work, do your job, and go home."

CASE QUESTIONS

1. Is Sentry management establishing unrealistic criteria for its new production workers?
2. What is your opinion of the fairness of the pay differential for the three shifts?
3. Which selection methods do you recommend to find employees who fit the Sentry culture and have the right attitude?

Source: Based on facts reported in J. Leslie Sopko, "Sentry Planning for Hire," Rochester *Democrat and Chronicle* (4 August 1995): 8B.

CASE PROBLEM 10-C: CONTINENTAL AIRLINES SETS ITS STANDARDS

To help maintain the company's growth, Continental Airlines recently ran the following classified advertisement in newspapers throughout North America.

THE DIFFERENCE IS THE COMPANY YOU'LL KEEP

When you join the 40,000 people of Continental Airlines, you'll be in great company. Continental people share a unique feeling of loyalty, a particular drive for excellence, and a winning team attitude that won't quit. The reason is simple. It's our philosophy. Every Continental employee is someone special. Just like our customers.

FLIGHT ATTENDANTS

As part of the Continental team, you'll not only enjoy unique travel privileges, you'll earn a starting salary of $14.00 per flight hour, with a guaranteed minimum of 83 hours a month as a reserve Flight Attendant.

To turn your ability to work with people into a respected career, you must be at least 20 years old, be willing to relocate to Newark, NJ, Cleveland, OH, Houston, TX, or Greensboro, NC, and have U.S. work eligibility. A two- or four-year college degree is preferred. Bilingual abilities in Italian are highly desired. Bilingual abilities in French, German, or Spanish are a plus. Phys-

ical qualifications include vision correctable to 20/30 or better (uncorrected 20/200 or better), height between 5′00″ and 6′2″, and weight in proportion to height. Please apply in person with your résumé on. . . .

(Limited seating available. Please be prompt and plan on spending 3 hours.)

DATE AND SITE OF INTERVIEWS

If unable to attend please call 1-800-444-8414 and enter ID# FLT JOBS or send your resume with 2 self-addressed stamped envelopes to: P.O. Box 4748, Hou. TX 77210-4748. If you have been interviewed within the last six months, there is no need to re apply. An Equal Opportunity Employer.

CASE QUESTIONS

1. What recommendations can you offer Continental Airlines to enhance the effectiveness of the above recruiting ad?
2. What is your reaction to the legality of the minimum age requirement mentioned in the ad?
3. What is your reaction to the legality of the size requirements for a flight attendant?

CASE PROBLEM 10-D: ADA BREEDS BAD BACKS AND STRESS DISORDERS

U.S. employers are attempting to cope with claims related to the Americans with Disabilities Act that went into effect in 1992. The law was designed to open the job market to severely disabled Americans. Instead, it has brought a stream of bad-back and psychological-stress cases. More than one-third of the complaints filed with the Equal Employment Opportunity Commission have been from employees with back pain and emotional problems. Ailments caused by alcoholism and other forms of substance abuse are also included in the one-third of complaints.

No more than 6 percent of the people complaining have impaired vision or hearing, and only 12 percent have neurological problems. About 85 percent of the complaints are filed by people who already have jobs.

Russell Redenbaugh, a blind member of the U.S. Commission on Civil Rights, says, "The goal of increasing employment opportunities for those of us who are seriously disabled has not been met at all. I believe there are a vast number of people with disabilities who want to work, can work, and only need the most modest of accommodations."

According to an EEOC analysis of 39,927 complaints filed under ADA employment provisions through the first

three years, the largest proportion, 19.5 percent, concerned back problems. Another 11.4 percent involved emotional/psychiatric impairment. Corporate and private attorneys who specialize in human resources cases say the act threatens to force far more expensive litigation in the future than have cases about racial preferences.

An example of the unintended type of claim being filed because of the ADA took place at GTE Data Services in Tampa. The company discovered that Joseph Hindman, a computer programmer, had been stealing money from other employees and brought a loaded gun to the office. After being fired for having the gun, he sued for reinstatement under ADA. Hindman said he was the victim of mental illness that was aggravated by improper medication. He was therefore disabled under the provisions of the act.

The company disagreed, pointing out that irresponsibility and impulsiveness were personality traits not covered under ADA. Furthermore, even if disabled, Hindman still threatened the safety of other employees. The first tentative court ruling favored Hindman. "When poor judgment is a symptom of a mental or psychological disorder, it is defined as an impairment that would qualify as a disability under the ADA," said the court. The second ruling by the court changed directions. This time the judge ruled that Hindman did not have sufficient evidence to reverse the firing.

Some advocates of the ADA contend that cases should be judged individually. At times bad-back or stress claims are likely to be frivolous, while others will be well founded. "Each person is an individual and has to be judged on that," said Evan Kemp, a disability rights advocate and former chairman of the EEOC.

A human resources manager at an auto plant in Toledo, Ohio, looks at the problem differently: "Using the Americans with Disabilities Act as justification for filing questionable claims and lawsuits is expensive and time consuming. And it's putrid from an ethical standpoint. It also increase the cost of doing business which can hurt the sales of American cars."

CASE QUESTIONS

1. Do you think it is unfair for current employees to use the ADA as a basis for filing complaints for back problems and psychological stress?

2. What can employers do to minimize the use of the ADA to justify so many claims for back pain and mental stress?

Source: Most of the facts in this case are based on "Bad-back Cases Sour Civil-Rights Act: Disabled-Access Law Not Meeting Its Goals," *The Washington Post* (16 April 1995).

REFERENCES

1. Based on facts reported in Pamela McNally, "A Job at Pic 'N Pay Just a Phone Call Away," *Footwear News* (23 May 1994): 1, 6.
2. Charlene Marmer Solomon, "Affirmative Action: What You Need to Know," *Personnel Journal* (August 1995): 56–67.
3. Arthur Sherman, George Bohlander, and Scott Snell, *Managing Human Resources*, 10th ed. (Cincinnati: South-Western College Publishing, 1996): 157; William J. Morin, "HR as Director of People Strategy," *HRMagazine* (December 1994): 52–54.
4. James A. F. Stoner and R. Edward Freeman, *Management*, 4e (Englewood Cliffs, NJ: Prentice Hall, 1989): 331.
5. David E. Bowen, Gerald E. Ledford, Jr., and Barry R. Nathan, "Hiring for the Organization, Not the Job," *The Academy of Management Executive* (November 1991): 35–51.
6. Patricia Martin, "Jobs Must be Marketed," *Personnel Journal* (April 1991): 87–91.
7. Gillian Flynn, "Contingent Staffing Requires Serious Strategy," *Personnel Journal* (April 1995): 50–58.
8. Samuel Greengard, "Catch the Wave as HR Goes Online," *Personnel Journal* (July 1995): 60.
9. Charlene Marmer Solomon, "Navigating Your Search for Global Talent," *Personnel Journal* (May 1995): 95.
10. Ann Marie Ryan and Maria Lasek, "Negligent Hiring and Defamation: Areas of Liability Related to Pre-Employment Inquiries," *Personnel Psychology* (Summer 1991): 293–319.
11. Philip Ash, "Law and Regulation of Preemployment Inquiries," *Journal of Business and Psychology* (Spring 1991): 291–308.
12. Sandy Sillup, "Applicant Screening Cuts Turnover Costs," *Personnel Journal* (May 1992): 115–116.
13. Michael R. Cunningham, Dennis T. Wong, and Anita P. Barbee, "Self-Presentation Dynamics on Overt Integrity Tests: Experimental Studies of the Reid Report," *Journal of Applied Psychology* October 1994): 643.
14. Robert M. Madigan, K. Dow Scott, Diana L. Deadrick, and Jil A. Stoddard, "Employment Testing: The U.S. Job Service Is Spearheading a Revolution," *Personnel Administrator* (September 1986): 102.
15. " 'Is This Test Valid?' A Guide for Determining the Validity of a Pre-Employment Test," *Human Resource Measurements* (a supplement to the April 1992 *Personnel Journal*, Wonderlic Personnel Test, Inc.).
16. Marlene Brown, "Reference Checking: The Law Is on Your Side," *Human Resource Measurements* (a supplement to the December 1991 *Personnel Journal*, Wonderlic Personnel Test, Inc.).
17. Gene Carmean, "The Medical Screening to the Job," *HRMagazine* (July 1992): 85.
18. Rob Brookler, "Industry Standards in Workplace Drug Testing," *Personnel Journal* (April 1992): 128; Sara L. Rynes and Mary L. Connerley, "Participant Reactions to Alternative Selection Procedures," *Journal of Business Psychology* (Spring 1993): 261.
19. Kevin G. Love, Ronald C. Bishop, Deanne A. Heinisch, and Matthew S. Montei, "Selection Across Two Cultures: Adapting the Selection of American Assemblers to Meet Japanese Performance Demands," *Personnel Psychology* (Winter 1994): 837–846.
20. Jane A. Halpert and Lisa K. Gundry, "Issues and Options in Literacy Training," *Journal of Business and Psychology* (Summer 1991): 489.
21. Kelly Allan, "Computer Courses Ensure Uniform Training," *Personnel Journal* (June 1993): 65.
22. Kate Walter, "Bring on the Entertainment," *Personnel Journal* (July 1995): 84–90.
23. "Management Training for Nonmanagers," *Human Resources Forum* (July 1994): 1–2.
24. Gregory M. Bounds, Gregory H. Dobbins, and Oscar S. Fowler, *Management: A Total Quality Perspective* (Cincinnati: South-Western College Publishing, 1995): 335–336.
25. Sandra L. O'Neil, "Aligning Pay with Business Strategy," *HRMagazine* (August 1993): 79–86.
26. Rick Stephan Hayes and C. Richard Baker, "New Health Benefits Rule Has Big Impact on Businesses and Workers," *Business Forum* (Fall 1993): 27.

Leadership

© Ann States/SABA 1995

Forty-two-year old Marilyn Marks is the CEO of Dorsey Trailers, the truck-trailer manufacturer. She bought the company in 1987, using borrowed money and paying back the debt with subsequent earnings (a leveraged buyout). Under Marks' leadership, sales have escalated to over $200 million per year. She has also guided the company toward major productivity gains. • Marks faced her biggest challenge at the time the company was about to go public. As she was packing for a tour with potential investors, Marks received an emergency telephone call from the main plant in Elba, Alabama. Due to a flood, the town was being evacuated. A similar problem occurred in 1990, and the company almost went under. When it looked like history was going to repeat itself, the people who were setting up the financing said, "We *can't* take this company public." But Marks and her staff sat tight. She remembers, "We monitored the situation every hour, and the rebuilt levee held. We felt it withstood the ultimate test."[1]

he CEO of the truck-trailer manufacturer just described illustrated excellent leadership: She stayed calm under pressure and guided her company through a crisis. Today attention focuses on people in the workplace like Marks who can inspire and stimulate others to achieve worthwhile goals. The people who can accomplish these important deeds practice **leadership,** the ability to inspire confidence and support among the people who are needed to achieve organizational goals.[2]

Leadership can be exercised in many settings. This chapter describes the characteristics and behaviors of leaders in organizations, as well as several useful leadership theories. Leadership is important to an organization because effective leaders can make a significant contribution to organizational performance. Similarly, ineffective leadership can impair organizational performance.

THE LINK BETWEEN LEADERSHIP AND MANAGEMENT

Differentiate between leadership and management.

According to John P. Kotter, today's managers must know how to *lead* as well as manage, or their companies will become extinct. (You will recall that leadership—along with planning, organizing, and controlling—is one of the basic functions of management.) Kotter makes these distinctions between management and leadership:[3]

* Management is more formal and scientific than leadership. It relies on universal skills, such as planning, budgeting, and controlling. Management is a set of explicit tools and techniques, based on reasoning and testing, that can be used in a variety of situations.
* Leadership, by contrast, involves having a vision of what the organization can become. Leadership requires eliciting cooperation and teamwork from a large network of people and keeping the key people in that network motivated, using every manner of persuasion.

Exhibit 11-1 presents a stereotype of the difference between leadership and management. Effective leadership and management are both required in the modern workplace. Managers must be leaders, but leaders must also be good managers. Workers need to be inspire and persuaded, but they also need assistance in developing a smoothly functioning workplace.

Exhibit 11-2 presents an overview of the link between leadership and management. It also highlights several of the major topics presented in this chapter. The figure illustrates that, to bring about improved productivity and morale, managers do two things. First, they use power, authority, influence, and personal traits and characteristics. Second, they apply leadership behaviors and practices.

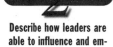

Describe how leaders are able to influence and empower team members.

THE LEADERSHIP USE OF POWER AND AUTHORITY

Leaders influence people to do things through the use of power and authority. **Power** is the ability or potential to influence decisions and control resources. Powerful people have the potential to exercise influence, and they exercise it frequently. For example, a powerful executive might influence an executive from another company to do business with his or her company. **Authority** is the formal right to get people to do things or the formal right to control resources. Factors within a person, such as talent or charm, help them achieve power. Only the organization, however, can grant authority. To understand how leaders use power and authority, we examine the various types of power, influence tactics, and how leaders share power with team mem-

**Exhibit 11-1
Leaders Versus
Managers**

LEADER	MANAGER
Visionary	Rational
Passionate	Consulting
Creative	Persistent
Flexible	Problem-solving
Inspiring	Tough-minded
Innovative	Analytical
Courageous	Structured
Imaginative	Deliberative
Experimental	Authoritative
Independent	Stabilizing

Source: Adapted from Genevieve Capowski, "Anatomy of a Leader: Where Are the Leaders of Tomorrow?" *Management Review* (March 1994): 12.

bers. Understanding these different approaches to exerting influence can help a manager become a more effective leader.

TYPES OF POWER

Leaders use various types of power to influence others. However, the power exercised by team members, or subordinates, acts as a constraint on how much power

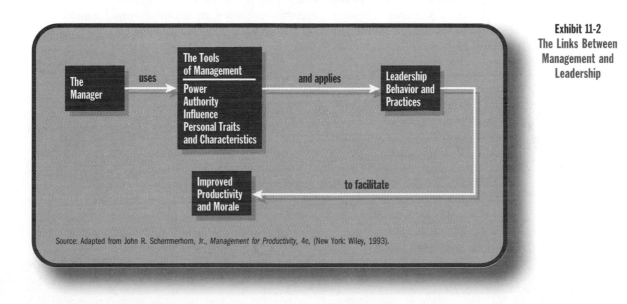

**Exhibit 11-2
The Links Between
Management and
Leadership**

Source: Adapted from John R. Scherrmerhorn, Jr., *Management for Productivity*, 4e, (New York: Wiley, 1993).

leaders can exercise. The list that follows describes the types of power exercised by leaders and sometimes by group members.[4]

1. **Legitimate power** is the authentic right of a leader to make certain types of requests. These requests are based on internalized social and cultural values in an organization. It is the easiest type of influence for most subordinates to accept. For example, virtually all employees accept the manager's authority to conduct a performance appraisal. Legitimate power has its limits, however, as described later under "subordinate power."

2. **Reward power** is a leader's control over rewards of value to the group members. Exercising this power includes giving salary increases and recommending employees for promotion.

3. **Coercive power** is a leader's control over punishments. Organizational punishments include assignment to undesirable working hours, demotion, and firing. Effective leaders generally avoid heavy reliance on coercive power, because it creates resentment and sometimes retaliation.

4. **Expert power** derives from a leader's job-related knowledge as perceived by group members. This type of power stems from having specialized skills, knowledge, or talent. Expert power can be exercised even when a person does not occupy a formal leadership position. An advertising copywriter with a proven record of writing winning ad slogans has expert power. A widely used form of expert power is the control of vital information. If a person controls information other people need, power will flow to that person. Having valuable contacts, such as knowing people prepared to invest in startup companies, is a form of controlling vital information.

5. **Referent power** is based on the desire of followers to identify with their leaders and to be accepted by them. The identification occurs when the leader has characteristics others find desirable. To say a leader has *charisma* means that the leader has unusual charm, or referent power. An inspiring leader scores high on charisma.

6. **Subordinate power** is any type of power that employees can exert upward in an organization, based on justice and legal considerations. For example, certain categories of workers cannot be asked to work overtime without compensation. Group members can always exercise expert power, but subordinate power restricts the extent to which power can be used to control them. As Exhibit 11-3 shows, when subordinates perceive an order as being outside the bounds of legitimate authority, they rebel.

Legitimate orders lie within a range of behaviors that the group members regard as acceptable. A legitimate order from above is acceptable to employees and falls within the **zone of indifference.** That zone encompasses those behaviors toward which the employees feel indifferent (do not mind following). If the manager pushes beyond the zone of indifference, the leader loses power. For example, few group members would accept an order to regularly carry out actions that harm the environment, such as dumping toxins.

Through subordinate power, group members control and constrain the power of leaders. Legal rights contribute to subordinate power. For example, an employee has the legal right to refuse sexual advances from the boss.

zone of indifference
The psychological zone that encompasses acceptable behaviors toward which employees feel indifferent (do not mind following).

INFLUENCE TACTICS

In addition to various types of power, leaders use many other influence tactics to get things done. Seven frequently used influence tactics are as follows.

Exhibit 11-3
Subordinate Power
and the Zone of
Indifference

Power Flows Down	Zone of Indifference	Zone of Noncompliance	Power Flows Up
	Orders are acceptable; employees do not exercise subordinate power, but comply with requests and orders.	Orders are unacceptable; employees exercise subordinate power and refuse to comply.	

Leading by example means that the leader influences group members by serving as a positive model of desirable behavior. A manager who leads by example shows consistency between actions and words. For example, suppose a firm has a strict policy on punctuality. The manager explains the policy and is always punctual. The manager's words and actions provide a consistent model.

Assertiveness refers to being forthright in your demands. It involves a manager expressing what he or she wants done and how the manager feels about it. A leader might say, for example, "Your report is late, and that makes me angry. I want you to get it done by noon tomorrow." Assertiveness, as this example shows, also refers to making orders clear.

Rationality means appealing to reason and logic. Strong leaders frequently use this influence tactic. Pointing out the facts of a situation to group members to get them to do something is an example of rationality. A middle manager might tell a supervisor, for example, "If our department goes over budget this year, the department is likely to be cut further next year." Knowing this, the supervisor will probably become more cost conscious.

Ingratiation refers to getting somebody else to like you, often through the use of political skill. A typical ingratiating tactic would be to act in a friendly manner just before making a demand. Effective managers treat people well consistently to get cooperation when it is needed.

Exchange is a method of influencing others by offering to reciprocate if they meet your demands. Leaders with limited expert, referent, and legitimate power are likely to use exchange and make bargains with subordinates. A manager might say to a group member, "If you can help me out this time, I'll go out of my way to return the favor." Using exchange is like using reward power. The emphasis in exchange, however, is that the manager goes out of his or her way to strike a bargain that pleases the team member.

Coalition formation is a way of gaining both power and influence. A **coalition** is a specific arrangement of parties working together to combine their power, thus exerting influence on another individual or group. Coalitions in business are a numbers game—the more people you can get on your side, the better. For example, a manager might band with several other managers to gain support for a major initiative such as merging with another company.

Joking and kidding, according to one survey, are widely used to influence others on the job.[5] Good-natured ribbing is especially effective when a straightforward statement might be interpreted as harsh criticism. In an effort to get an employee to use the electronic-mail system, one manager said, "We don't want you to suffer from technostress. Yet you're the only supervisor here who can be reached only by telephone, paper memo, or carrier pigeon." The supervisor smiled and proceeded to ask for help in learning how to use electronic mail.

coalition
A specific arrangement of parties working together to combine their power, thus exerting influence on another individual or group.

WHICH INFLUENCE TACTIC TO CHOOSE? Leaders are unlikely to use all the influence tactics in a given situation. Instead, they tend to choose an influence tactic that fits the demands of the circumstances. Researchers found support for this conclusion in a study with 125 leaders employed by a bank. To determine the influence tactics the leaders used, the researchers asked the leaders' superiors and subordinates to complete a questionnaire. The study found that in crisis situations, the leaders used more expert power, legitimate power, referent power, and upward influence than in noncrisis situations. (Upward influence refers to using power to get higher-ranking people to act on one's behalf.) The study also concluded that the leaders were less likely to consult with subordinates in a crisis situation than in a noncrisis situation.[6]

EMPLOYEE EMPOWERMENT

An important trend in the use of power is for managers to systematically share power and control with group members. When they share power, employees experience a greater sense of personal effectiveness and job ownership. Sharing power with group members enables members to feel better about themselves and perform at a higher level. Empowered employees perform better to a large extent because they become better motivated. The extra motivation stems from a feeling of being in charge. An important use of empowerment is to enhance customer service. As employees acquire more authority to take care of customer problems, these problems can be handled promptly—sometimes right on the spot.

A key component of empowerment is the leader's acceptance of the employee as a partner in decision making. Because the team members' experience and information are regarded as equal to those of the leader, he or she shares control. Both the leader and team member must agree on what is to be accomplished. The partnering approach to empowerment builds trust between the employee and the leader.[7]

CHARACTERISTICS, TRAITS, AND BEHAVIORS OF EFFECTIVE LEADERS

LEARNING OBJECTIVE

Identify important leadership characteristics and behaviors.

Understanding leadership takes an understanding of leaders. This section will highlight findings about the personal attributes and behaviors of effective managerial leaders. *Effective*, in this context, means that the leader achieves both high productivity and morale, as Exhibit 11-2 illustrated. Be aware that, in this discussion, quality is an aspect of productivity.

CHARACTERISTICS AND TRAITS

Possessing certain characteristics and traits does not in itself guarantee success. Yet dozens of studies demonstrate that effective leaders differ from others in certain respects.[8] Justification for studying leadership traits is that the traits of leaders are related closely to the degree to which they are perceived to be leaders. For example, managers who are perceived to be good problem solvers are more likely to be accepted as leaders than those who are not.[9]

Hundreds of human qualities can enhance leadership effectiveness in some situations. The list of traits and characteristics that follows is based on several research studies. It presents the factors we believe are the most relevant to the largest number of situations.[10]

1. *Drive and achievement motive.* Leaders are noted for the strong effort they invest in achieving work goals. *Drive* refers to such behaviors as ambition, energy, tenacity, and initiative. Above all, it refers to **achievement motivation,** finding joy in accomplishment for its own sake. High achievers find satisfaction in completing challenging tasks, attaining high standards, and developing better ways of doing things.

2. *Power motive.* Successful leaders have a strong need to control other people and resources. **Power motivation** is a strong desire to control others or get them to do things on your behalf. A leader with a strong power need enjoys exercising power and using influence tactics. Only a manager who uses power constructively could be promoted so rapidly in a modern, well-managed corporation.

3. *Self-confidence.* Self-confidence contributes to effective leadership in several ways. Above all, self-confident leaders project an image that encourages subordinates to have faith in them. Self-confidence also helps leaders make some of the tough business decisions they face regularly.

4. *Honesty, integrity, and openness.* Leadership is undermined without honesty and integrity. Consistency between word and deed creates a reputation of integrity. Honesty simply means being truthful or avoiding deceit. One study found that, compared to low-level managers, managers who reached the top were more likely to endorse this statement: "I will do exactly what I say I will do when I say I will do it. If I change my mind, I will tell you well in advance so you will not be harmed by my actions."[11]

Closely related to honesty and integrity is being open with employees about sensitive company information. A recent trend in leadership is to use *open-book management,* a system by which employees are exposed to financial details of the firm. In addition to conveying openness, the approach helps employees become more knowledgeable about the business. The accompanying Leader in Action provides more details about open-book management.

> **achievement motivation**
> *Finding joy in accomplishment for its own sake.*

> **power motivation**
> *A strong desire to control others or get them to do things on your behalf.*

LEADER IN ACTION: JACK STACK OPENS THE BOOKS

Representatives of more than 1,700 companies have visited Springfield Remanufacturing Corp. (SRC) in Springfield, Missouri, to learn about open-book management. SRC overhauls gas and diesel engines for cars, trucks, and farming and construction equipment. The company has 750 employees in 12 divisions in 16 locations.

Open-book companies teach employees to understand expenses, revenues, assets, liabilities, and related accounting principles. The intent is to create companies with knowledgeable employees who think, act, and are rewarded like owners. The leader of the open-book approach is Jack Stack, the SRC chief operating officer. He believes that a business should be run like an aquarium, where everyone can see what's going on. In this way business can be played like a game in which workers can keep score with financial statements to see whether they are winning or losing.

Stack believes that educating employees about how a company makes money, what its profits are, and other financial information is important. It can reduce suspicion and ignorance about company finances, improve morale, and curb counterproductive behavior.

Source: Based on facts reported in Leon Rubis, "Playing by the Books," *HRMagazine* (May 1995): 39–41.

5. *Good intellectual ability and technical competence.* Intelligence contributes to leadership effectiveness. Intelligence, or problem-solving ability, is becoming increasingly important because managerial jobs are becoming more complex. As the developers of a recent leadership theory explained: "Intelligent and competent leaders make more effective plans, decisions, and action strategies than do leaders with less intelligence and competence."[12] Intellectual ability is closed related to being technically competent, or having knowledge of the business. A case in point is Jerry Reinsdorf, the owner of the Chicago White Sox and the Chicago Bulls. Reinsdorf has been described in these terms: "He is an executive whose only business is sports, not a sport who is an executive in some other business."[13]

6. *Sensitivity to people.* Sensitivity to people means taking people's needs and feelings into account when dealing with them. An effective leader tries not to hurt people's feelings or frustrate their needs. A sensitive leader gives encouragement to subordinates who need it and does not belittle or insult poor performers. Insensitivity, in terms of being abrasive and tactless, can sidetrack a manager's career.

7. *Sense of humor.* The effective use of humor is now regarded as an important part of a leader's job. In the workplace, humor relieves tension and boredom and defuses hostility. Because humor helps a leader dissolve tension and defuse conflict, it can help him or her exert power over the group. Psychologist Barbara Mackoff contends: "Humor is the ultimate power tool on the job."[14]

BEHAVIORS AND SKILLS OF EFFECTIVE LEADERS

Traits alone are not sufficient to lead effectively. A leader must also behave in certain ways and possess key skills. As Chapter 1 described, managers must have sound conceptual, interpersonal, technical, and political skills. The following actions or behaviors are linked to leadership effectiveness. Recognize, however, that behaviors are related to skills. For example, a leader who gives emotional support to team members is using interpersonal skills. An effective leader:

1. *Is adaptable to the situation.* Adaptability reflects the contingency viewpoint: a strategy is chosen based on the unique circumstances at hand. For instance, if a leader were dealing with psychologically immature subordinates, he or she would have to supervise them closely. Mature and self-reliant subordinates would require less supervision. Also, the adaptive leader selects an organization structure best suited to the situation. The circumstances would determine, for example, if the manager chose a brainstorming group or a committee.

    The ability to size up people and situations and adapt tactics accordingly is a vital leadership behavior. It stems from an inner quality called insight or intuition, a direct perception of a situation that seems unrelated to any specific reasoning process.

2. *Provides stable performance.* A manager's steadiness under heavy work loads and uncertain conditions helps subordinates cope with the situation. Most people become anxious when the outcome of what they are doing is uncertain. When the leader remains calm, employees are reassured that things will work out satisfactorily. Stability also helps the leader meet the expectation that a manager should be cool under pressure. Do you recall how Marilyn Marks helped her company get through a weather crisis?

3. *Demands high standards of performance for group members.* Effective leaders consistently hold group members to high standards of performance, which raises

productivity. Setting high expectations for subordinates becomes a self-fulfilling prophecy. People tend to live up to the expectations set for them by their superiors. Setting high expectations might take the form of encouraging team members to establish difficult objectives.

4. *Provides emotional support to group members.* Supportive behavior toward subordinates usually increases leadership effectiveness. A supportive leader is one who gives frequent encouragement and praise. The emotional support generally improves morale and sometimes improves productivity. Being emotionally supportive comes naturally to the leader who has empathy for people and who is a warm person.

5. *Gives frequent feedback.* Giving group members frequent feedback on their performance is another vital leadership behavior. The manager rarely can influence the behavior of subordinates without appropriate performance feedback. Feedback helps in two ways. First, it informs employees of how well they are doing, so they can take corrective action if needed. Second, when the feedback is positive, it encourages subordinates to keep up the good work.

6. *Has a strong customer orientation.* Effective leaders are strongly interested in satisfying the needs of customers, clients, or constituents. Their strong customer orientation helps inspire employees toward satisfying customers. Clark Johnson, the CEO of Pier 1 Imports, Inc., is a prime example. His company is a highly successful retail chain that specializes in imported household goods and gifts. Asked what his job entails, he replied, "I'm the head salesman." Johnson sells his company and his products to customers, and he sells a consistent vision of winning to his employees.[15]

7. *Recovers quickly from setbacks.* Effective managerial leaders are resilient: They bounce back quickly from setbacks such as budget cuts, demotions, and being fired. Leadership resiliency serves as a positive model for employees at all levels when the organization confronts difficult times. During such times effective leaders sprinkle their speech with clichés such as "Tough times don't last, but tough people do," or "When times get tough, the tough get going." Delivered with sincerity, such messages are inspirational to many employees.

LEADERSHIP STYLES

Another important part of the leadership function is **leadership style.** It is the typical pattern of behavior that a leader uses to influence his or her employees to achieve organizational goals. Several different approaches to describing leadership styles have developed over the years. Most of these involve how much authority and control the leader turns over to the group.

First, this section will describe two classical approaches for categorizing leadership styles. We will then discuss the Leadership Grid® styles of leadership, followed by the situational theory of leadership, which emphasizes its contingency nature. We will also describe the entrepreneurial leadership style. Skill Building Exercise 11-A, at the end of the chapter, gives you a chance to measure certain aspects of your leadership style.

THE LEADERSHIP CONTINUUM

The leadership continuum, or classical approach, classifies leaders according to how much authority they retain for themselves versus how much they turn over to a group.

LEARNING OBJECTIVE

Describe the leadership continuum, Theory X and Theory Y, leadership grid, situational, and entrepreneurial styles of leadership.

leadership style
The typical pattern of behavior that a leader uses to influence his or her employees to achieve organizational goals.

Three key points on the continuum represent autocratic, participative, and free-rein styles of leadership. Exhibit 11-4 illustrates the leadership continuum.

autocratic leader
A task-oriented leader who retains most of the authority for himself or herself and is not generally concerned with group members' attitudes toward decisions.

AUTOCRATIC LEADERSHIP STYLE. **Autocratic leaders** retain most of the authority for themselves. They make decisions in a confident manner and assume that group members will comply. An autocratic leader is not usually concerned with the subordinates' attitudes toward the decision. Autocratic leaders are considered task-oriented because they place heavy emphasis on getting tasks accomplished. Typical autocratic leaders tell people what to do, assert themselves, and serve as models for group members.

participative leader
A leader who shares decision making with group members.

PARTICIPATIVE LEADERSHIP STYLE. A **participative leader** is one who shares decision making with group members. There are three closely related subtypes of participative leaders: consultative, consensual, and democratic. *Consultative leaders* confer with subordinates before making a decision. However, they retain the final authority to make decisions. *Consensual leaders* encourage group discussion about an issue and then make a decision that reflects the general opinion (consensus) of group members. All workers who will be involved in the consequences of a decision have an opportunity to provide input. A decision is not considered final until all parties involved agree with the decision. *Democratic leaders* confer final authority on the group. They function as collectors of opinion and take a vote before making a decision.

free-rein leader
A leader who turns over virtually all authority and control to the group.

FREE-REIN LEADERSHIP STYLE. The **free-rein leader** turns over virtually all authority and control to the group. Leadership is provided indirectly rather than directly. Group members are presented with a task to perform and are given free rein to figure out the best way to perform it. The leader does not get involved unless requested. Subordinates are allowed all the freedom they want as long as they do not violate company policy. In short, the free-rein leader delegates completely.

THEORY X AND THEORY Y

Autocratic and participative leaders see people differently. This difference in perception is the basis for the Theory X and Theory Y explanation of leadership style, as summarized in Exhibit 11-5. Douglas McGregor developed these distinctions to help managers critically examine their assumptions about workers. Theory X and Theory Y form part of the foundation of the human relations approach to management.

Exhibit 11-4
The Leadership
Continuum

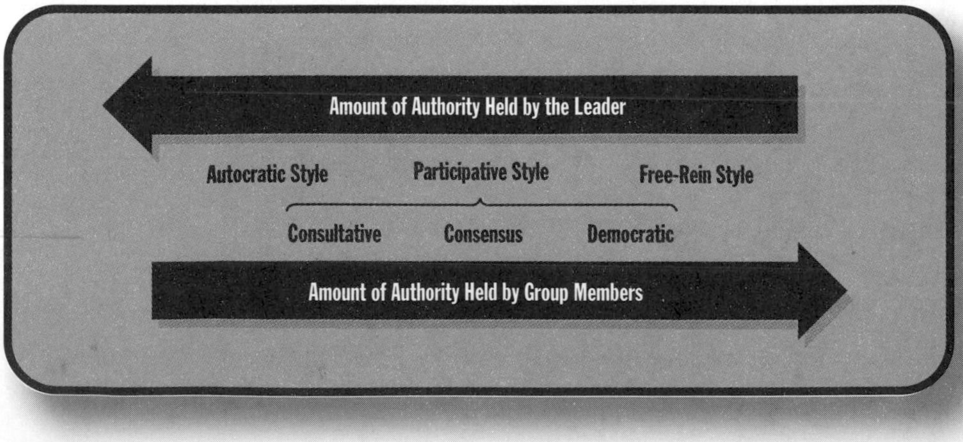

According to Douglas McGregor, leadership approaches are influenced by a leader's assumptions about human nature. Managers make two contrasting assumptions about workers:

Theory X Assumptions. Managers who accept Theory X believe that:

1. The average person dislikes work and will avoid it if possible.
2. Because of this dislike of work, most people must be coerced, controlled, directed, or threatened with punishment to get them to put forth enough effort to achieve organizational objectives.
3. The average employee prefers to be directed, wishes to shirk responsibility, has relatively little ambition, and puts a high value on security.

Theory Y Assumptions. Managers who accept Theory Y believe the statements in the list that follows. Equally important, these managers diagnose a situation to learn what type of people they are supervising.

1. The expenditure of physical and mental effort in work is as natural as play or rest for the average human being.
2. People will exercise self-direction and self-control to achieve objectives to which they are committed.
3. Commitment to objectives is related to the rewards associated with their achievement.
4. The average person learns, under proper conditions, not only to accept but to seek responsibility.
5. Many employees have the capacity to exercise a high degree of imagination, ingenuity, and creativity in the solution of organizational problems.
6. Under the present conditions of industrial life, the intellectual potential of the average person is only partially utilized.

Source: Adapted from Douglas McGregor, *The Human Side of Enterprise* (New York: McGraw-Hill, 1960), 33–48.

Exhibit 11-5
Theory X and Theory Y

LEADERSHIP GRID® LEADERSHIP STYLES

Several approaches to understanding leadership styles focus on two major dimensions of leadership: tasks and relationships. The best known of these approaches is the **Leadership Grid.** It is based on different integrations of the leader's concern for production (tasks) and people (relationships). As Exhibit 11-6 shows, Grid terms are levels of concern on a scale of 1 to 9, with concern for production listed first and concern for people listed second. The Leadership Grid is part of a comprehensive program of leadership training and organizational development.

> **Leadership Grid**
> *A visual representation of different combinations of a leader's degree of concern for task-related issues.*

Concern for production is rated on the Grid's horizontal axis. Concern for production includes results, bottom line, performance, profits, and mission. Concern for people is rated on the vertical axis, and it includes concern for subordinates and coworkers. Both concerns are leadership attitudes or ways of thinking about leadership. The Grid identifies seven styles, yet a leader's approach could fall into any of 81 positions on the Grid.

The developers of the Grid argue strongly for the value of team management (9,9). According to their research, the team management approach pays off. It results in improved performance, low absenteeism and turnover, and high morale. Team management relies on trust and respect, which help bring about good results.[16]

The Grid has an important message. When leading others, think first of striving to use the team management style. By so doing you will keep focused on obtaining high productivity, quality, and morale. As a team manager, you will also apply knowledge of human behavior to obtaining results through people.

THE SITUATIONAL LEADERSHIP MODEL

> **situational leadership model**
> *An explanation of leadership that explains how to match leadership style to the readiness of group members.*

A major perspective on leadership is that effective leaders adapt their style to the requirements of the situation. The characteristics of the group members is one key requirement. The **situational leadership model** of Paul Hersey and Kenneth

task behavior
The extent to which the leader spells out the duties and responsibilities of an individual or group.

H. Blanchard explains how to match leadership style to the readiness of group members.[17]

BASICS OF THE MODEL. Leadership in the situational model is classified according to the relative amount of task and relationship behavior the leader engages in. **Task behavior** is the extent to which the leader spells out the duties and responsibilities

Exhibit 11-6
The Leadership Grid

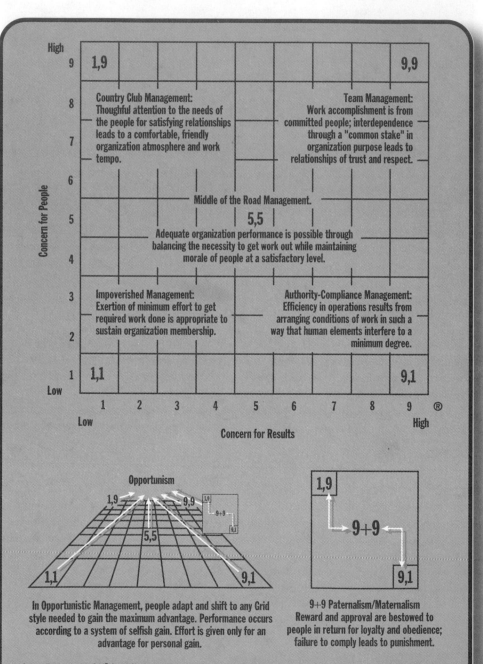

Source: The Leadership Grid® figure, Paternalism Figure and Opportunism from *Leadership Dilemmas—Grid Solutions*, by Robert R. Blake and Anne Adams McCanse (Formerly the Managerial Grid by Robert R. Blake and Jane S. Mouton). Houston: Gulf Publishing Company, (Grid Figure: P. 29, Paternalism Figure: p. 30, Opportunism Figure: p. 31). Copyright 1991 by Scientific Methods, Inc. Reproduced by permission of the owners.

of an individual or group. **Relationship behavior** is the extent to which the leader engages in two-way or multi-way communication. It includes such activities as listening, providing encouragement, and coaching. As Exhibit 11-7 shows, the situational model places combinations of task and relationship behaviors into four quadrants. Each quadrant calls for a different leadership style.

The situational leadership model states there is no one best way to influence group members. The most effective leadership style depends on the readiness level of group members. **Readiness** in situational leadership is defined as the extent to which a group member has the ability and willingness or confidence to accomplish a specific task. The concept of readiness is therefore not a characteristic, trait, or motive—it relates to a specific task.

Readiness has two components, ability and willingness. Ability is the knowledge, experience, and skill an individual or group brings to a particular task or activity. Willingness is the extent to which an individual or group has the confidence, commitment, and motivation to accomplish a specific task.

> **relationship behavior**
> *The extent to which the leader engages in two-way or multi-way communication.*

> **readiness**
> *In situational leadership, the extent to which a group member has the ability and willingness or confidence to accomplish a specific task.*

**Exhibit 11-7
The Situational Model
of Leadership**

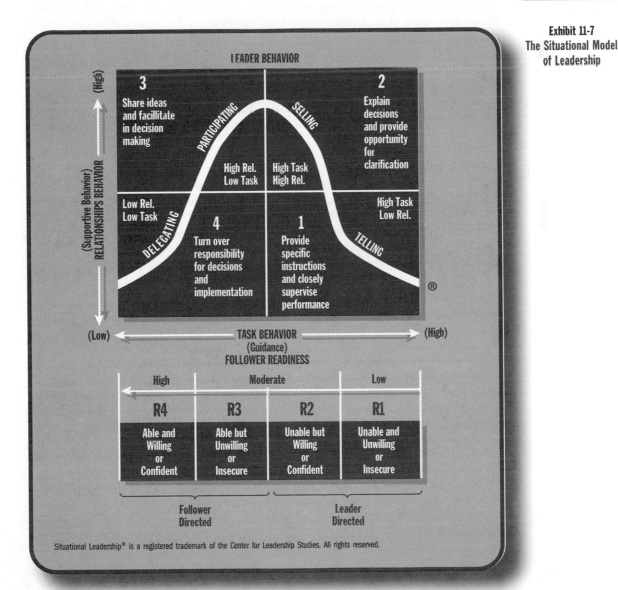

The key point of situational leadership theory is that as a group member's readiness increases, a leader should rely more on relationship behavior and less on task behavior. When a group member becomes very ready, a minimum of task or relationship behavior is required of the leader. Notice that in the readiness condition R4 (as shown in Exhibit 11-7), the group member is able and willing or confident. The manager therefore uses a delegating leadership style (quadrant 4). He or she turns over responsibility for decisions and implementation.

EVALUATION OF THE SITUATIONAL MODEL. The situational model represents a consensus of thinking about leadership behavior in relation to group members: competent people require less specific direction than do less competent people. The situational model also supports common sense and is therefore appealing. You can benefit from the model by attempting to diagnose the readiness of group members before choosing the right leadership style.

Nevertheless, the model presents categories and guidelines so precisely that it give the impression of infallibility. In reality, leadership situations are less clear-cut than the four quadrants suggest. Also, the prescriptions for leadership will work only some of the time. For example, many supervisors use a telling style with unable and unwilling or insecure team members (R1) and still achieve poor results.

THE ENTREPRENEURIAL LEADERSHIP STYLE

Managers who initiate one or more innovative business enterprises show some similarity in leadership style. In overview, they tend to be task-oriented and charismatic. Entrepreneurs often possess the following personal characteristics and behaviors:

1. *A strong achievement need.* Entrepreneurs have stronger achievement needs than most managers. Building a business is an excellent vehicle for accomplishment. The high achiever shows three consistent behaviors and attitudes. He or she (a) takes personal responsibility to solve problems, (b) attempts to achieve moderate goals at moderate risks, and (c) prefers situations that provide frequent feedback on results (readily found in starting a new enterprise).[18]
2. *High enthusiasm and creativity.* Related to the achievement need, entrepreneurs are typically enthusiastic and creative. Their enthusiasm in turn makes them persuasive. As a result, entrepreneurs are often perceived as charismatic by their employees and customers. Some entrepreneurs are frequently so emotional that they are regarded as eccentric.
3. *Always in a hurry.* Entrepreneurs are always in a hurry. When engaged in one meeting, their minds typically begin to focus on the next meeting. Their flurry of activity rubs off on subordinates and others around them. Entrepreneurs often adopt a simple style of dressing to save time. A male entrepreneur may wear slip-on shoes so he doesn't have to bother with laces in the morning. A female entrepreneur may wear an easy-to-maintain short haircut.
4. *Visionary perspective.* Successful entrepreneurs carefully observe the world around them, in constant search for their next big marketable idea. They see opportunities others fail to observe. After the riots in South Central Los Angeles in 1992, for example, many entrepreneurs looked for ways to profit from rebuilding, such as founding a minority-owned bank.
5. *Uncomfortable with hierarchy and bureaucracy.* Entrepreneurs, by temperament, are not ideally suited to working within the mainstream of a bureaucracy. Many successful entrepreneurs are people who were frustrated by the constraints of a bureaucratic system. Once the typical entrepreneur launches a successful business,

he or she would be wise to hire a professional manager to take over the internal workings of the firm. The entrepreneur would then be free to concentrate on making sales, raising capital, and pursuing other external contacts.

6. *A much stronger interest in dealing with customers than employees.* One of the reasons entrepreneurs have difficulty with bureaucracy is that they focus their energies on products, services, and customers. Some entrepreneurs are gracious to customers and moneylenders but brusque with company insiders.

The preceding list implies that it is difficult to find a classic entrepreneur who is also a good organizational manager. Many successful entrepreneurs therefore hire professional managers to help them maintain what they (the entrepreneurs) have built.

THE TRANSFORMATIONAL LEADER

The major new emphasis in the study of leadership is the **transformational leader**— one who helps organizations and people make positive changes in the way they do things. Transformational leadership is a combination of charisma, inspirational leadership, and intellectual stimulation. It is especially critical to the revitalization of existing business organizations. The transformational leader develops new visions for the organization and mobilizes employees to accept and work toward attaining these visions. Recent research indicates that the transformational style of leader, in contrast to a more traditional leader, actually does improve business-unit performance.[19] This section will describe how transformations take place, the role of charisma, how to become charismatic, and the downside of charismatic leadership.

> **transformational leader**
> *A leader who helps organizations and people make positive changes in the way they do things.*

HOW TRANSFORMATIONS TAKE PLACE

The transformational leader attempts to overhaul the organizational culture or subculture. To bring about the overhaul, transformations take place in one or more of three ways.[20] First, the transformational leader raises people's awareness of the importance and value of certain rewards and how to achieve them. The leader might point out the pride workers would experience if the firm became number one in its field. He would also highlight the accompanying financial rewards.

Second, the transformational leader gets people to look beyond their self-interests for the sake of the work group and the firm. Such a leader might say, "I know you would like more support workers. But, if we don't cut expenses, we'll all be out of a job." Third, the transformational leader helps people go beyond a focus on minor satisfactions to a quest for self-fulfillment. He or she might explain, "I know that a long lunch break is nice. But, just think, if we get this project done on time, we'll be the envy of the company."

THE LINK BETWEEN CHARISMA AND TRANSFORMATIONAL LEADERSHIP

Transformational leaders have charisma and, therefore, referent power. To label a leader as charismatic does not mean that everybody perceives him or her in this manner. Even the most popular and inspiring leaders are perceived negatively by some members of their organization.

Transformational and charismatic leaders have the leadership characteristics and behaviors described at the start of this chapter. The list that follows presents transformational leaders' qualities and actions that relate specifically to charisma.[21]

1. *Vision.* A charismatic leader offers an exciting image of where the organization is headed and how to get there. A vision is more than a forecast, because it describes an ideal version of the future of an organization or organizational unit.

2. *Masterful communication style.* To inspire people, charismatic and transformational leaders use colorful language and exciting metaphors and analogies. The president of Coca-Cola tells people, "We give people around the world a moment of pleasure in their daily lives."

3. *Inspire trust.* People believe so strongly in the integrity of charismatic leaders that they will risk their careers to pursue the leader's vision.

4. *Help group members feel capable.* A technique that charismatic leaders often use to boost their followers' self-images is to let them achieve success on relatively easy projects. The group members are then praised and given more-demanding assignments.

5. *Energy and action orientation.* Similar to entrepreneurs, most charismatic leaders are energetic and serve as a model for getting things done on time.

6. *Intellectual stimulation to others.* Transformational leaders actively encourage group members to look at old problems or methods in new ways. They emphasize getting people to rethink problems and reexamine old assumptions.

DEVELOPING CHARISMA

Managers can improve their chances of being perceived as charismatic by engaging in favorable interactions with group members, using a variety of techniques.[22] A starting point is to *use visioning.* Develop a dream about the future of your unit and discuss it with others. *Make frequent use of metaphors.* Develop metaphors to inspire the people around you. A commonly used one after the group has experienced a substantial setback is to say, "Like the phoenix, we will rise from the ashes of defeat." It is important to *inspire trust and confidence.* Get people to believe in your competence by making your accomplishments known in a polite, tactful way.

Remember to *make others feel capable* by giving out assignments on which others can succeed, and lavishly praising their success. *Be highly energetic and goal oriented* so you can impress others with your energy and resourcefulness. To increase your energy supply, exercise frequently, eat well, and get ample rest. It is important to *express your emotions frequently.* Freely express warmth, joy, happiness, and enthusiasm. *Smile frequently, even if you are not in a happy mood.* A warm smile indicates a confident, caring person, which contributes to perceptions of charisma. Finally, *make everybody you meet feel that he or she is quite important.* For example, at a company meeting shake the hand of every person you meet.

THE DOWNSIDE OF CHARISMATIC LEADERSHIP

Charismatic business leaders are seen as corporate heroes when they can turn around a failing business or launch a new enterprise. Nevertheless, this type of leadership has a dark side. Some charismatic leaders manipulate and take advantage of people, such as by getting them to invest retirement savings into risky company stock. Some charismatic leaders are unethical and lead their organizations toward illegal and immoral ends. People are willing to follow the charismatic leader down a quasi-legal path because of his or her referent power. For example, the legendary junk bond king Michael Milken was convicted of illegal securities transactions that contributed to his earning over $500 million in one year. Yet he inspired hundreds of people. One former disciple said of Milken, "If he walked off the cliff, everyone in that group would have followed him."[23]

SUPERLEADERSHIP: LEADING OTHERS TO LEAD THEMSELVES

An important goal for leaders is to become a **SuperLeader,** one who leads others to lead themselves.[24] When people are self-directing, they require a minimum of external control. A SuperLeader leads others to lead themselves by acting as a teacher and a coach, not a director. The key aspect of SuperLeadership deals with learning the right thought patterns. The formulators of the SuperLeadership theory, Charles Manz and Henry Sims, contend that the leader must teach team members how to develop productive thinking. He or she should reward employees when they think constructively. The purpose of productive, or constructive, thinking is to enable workers to gain control over their own behavior. The SuperLeader serves as a model of constructive thought patterns. For example, the leader should minimize expressing pessimistic, self-critical thoughts to team members.

Charles Manz recommends several desirable ways of establishing and altering thought patterns in order to practice self-leadership.[25]

1. *Identify destructive beliefs and assumptions.* After identifying negative thoughts, replace them with more accurate and constructive ones. For example, an employee might regard the manager's criticism as an indicator of personal dislike. A more productive thought is that the manager is just trying to help him or her perform at a higher level.
2. *Make a habit of talking to yourself positively and constructively.* Convert negative thoughts into positive ones. Avoid a statement such as, "My math skills are too poor to prepare a budget." Instead say, "In order to prepare a budget, I will have to improve my math skills. I'll get started tonight."
3. *Visualize methods for effective performance.* Imagine yourself moving effortlessly through a challenging assignment, using methods that have worked in the past. For example, visualize yourself making a hard-hitting presentation to management, a presentation similar to one with lesser stakes that you made in the past.

In summary, the SuperLeader helps create conditions whereby team members require very little leadership. Achieving such a goal is important because organizations have reduced the number of managers. Also, work arrangements such as teams and horizontal structures require self-management.

THE LEADER'S ROLE IN MANAGING CONFLICT

Conflict is the simultaneous arousal of two or more incompatible motives. It is often accompanied by tension and frustration. Whenever two or more people in the workplace compete for the same resource, conflict occurs—for example, when two employees want the office's only fax machine on their own desks. Conflict can also be considered a hostile or antagonistic relationship between people.

Conflict is also built into the relationship between managers and group members. A certain amount of hostility and resentment from subordinates is an inevitable part of work relationships, especially those with an inequality of power.[26]

LEARNING OBJECTIVE 6

Explain how to exercise SuperLeadership.

SuperLeader
A person who leads others to lead themselves.

LEARNING OBJECTIVE 7

Explain the leader's role in managing conflict.

conflict
The simultaneous arousal of two or more incompatible motives.

Because resources in any organization are limited, not everybody's motives and desires can be satisfied. The leader must help people deal with conflict in order to keep the organizational unit running smoothly. A manager must, therefore, act as a mediator and settle disputes among subordinates. Two aspects of conflict of particular interest to the leader are its consequences and the methods for its resolution.

CONSEQUENCES OF CONFLICT

Conflict is a source of stress. The right amount of conflict may enhance job performance, but too much or too little stress lowers performance. If the manager observes that job performance is suffering because of too much conflict, he or she should reduce it. If performance is low because employees are too placid, the manager might profitably increase conflict. For example, the manager might establish a prize for top performance in the group.

POSITIVE CONSEQUENCES OF CONFLICT. Many managers and scholars believe that job conflict can have positive consequences. When the right amount of conflict is present in the workplace, one or more of the following outcomes can be anticipated.

1. *Increased creativity.* Talents and abilities surface in response to conflict. People become inventive when they are placed in intense competition with others.
2. *Increased effort.* Constructive amounts of conflict spur people to new heights of performance. People become so motivated to win the conflict that they may surprise themselves and their superiors with their work output.
3. *Increased diagnostic information.* Conflict can provide valuable information about problem areas in the department or organization. When leaders learn of conflict, they may conduct investigations that will lead to the prevention of similar problems.
4. *Increased group cohesion.* When one group in a firm is in conflict with another, group members may become more cohesive. They perceive themselves to be facing a common enemy.

NEGATIVE CONSEQUENCES OF CONFLICT. When the wrong amount or type of conflict exists, job performance may suffer. Some types of conflict have worse consequences than others. A particularly bad form of conflict is one that forces a person to choose between two undesirable alternatives. Negative consequences of conflict include the following:

1. *Poor physical and mental health.* Intense conflict is a source of stress. A person under prolonged and intense conflict may suffer stress-related disorders.
2. *Wasted resources.* Employees and groups in conflict frequently waste time, money, and other resources while fighting their battles. One executive took a personal dislike to one of his managers and therefore ignored his cost-saving recommendations.
3. *Sidetracked goals.* In extreme forms of conflict, the parties involved may neglect the pursuit of important goals. Instead, they are intent on winning their conflicts. A goal displacement of this type took place within an information systems group. The rival factions spent so much time squabbling over which new hardware and software to purchase that they neglected some of their tasks.
4. *Heightened self-interest.* Conflict often results in extreme demonstrations of self-interest at the expense of the larger organization. Individuals or departments place their personal interests over those of the rest of the firm or customers.

One common result of this type of self-interest is empire building. Managers are using this tactic when they expend considerable effort to increase the size of their organizational units, whether or not this expansion serves the interests of the firm.

METHODS OF CONFLICT RESOLUTION

Managers spend as much as 20 percent of their work time dealing with conflict. A leader who learns to manage conflict effectively can increase his or her productivity. In addition, being able to resolve conflict enhances one's stature as a leader. Employees expect their boss to be able to resolve conflicts. Here we describe the five basic styles or methods of resolving conflict: forcing, accommodation, sharing, collaboration, and avoiding. An effective leader will choose the best approach for the situation.

FORCING. The forcing, or competitive, style is based on the desire to win one's own concerns at the expense of the other party, or to dominate. Autocratic leaders, such as Robert Crandall of American Airlines, choose to resolve conflict in this way. A person with a forcing style is likely to engage in win-lose ("I win, you lose") power struggles.

ACCOMMODATION. The accommodative style favors appeasement, or satisfying the other's concerns without taking care of one's own. People with this orientation may be generous or self-sacrificing just to maintain a relationship. An irate customer might be accommodated with a full refund "just to shut him (or her) up." The intent of such accommodation might also be to retain the customer's loyalty.

SHARING. The sharing style is midway between domination and appeasement. Sharers prefer moderate but incomplete satisfaction for both parties. The result is compromise. The term *splitting the difference* reflects this orientation. The sharing style of conflict resolution is commonly used in such activities as purchasing a house or car.

COLLABORATION. In contrast to the sharing style, collaboration reflects an interest in fully satisfying the desire of both parties. It is based on an underlying win-win philosophy, the belief that after conflict has been resolved both sides should gain something of value. For example, a company president might offer employees stock options if they are willing to take a pay cut to help the firm through rough times. If the firm succeeds, both parties have scored a victory.

All parties benefit from collaboration, or a win-win approach to resolving conflict. In addition, compliance with the solution occurs readily, and the relationship between those in conflict improves.

A conflict-resolution technique built into the collaboration style is *confrontation and problem solving*. Its purpose is to identify the real problem and then arrive at a solution that genuinely solves it. First the parties are brought together and the real problem is confronted. The accompanying Manager in Action illustrates the application of confrontation and problem solving in relation to political conflict.

Another collaborative approach involves asking what action can break an impasse. When a conflict reaches a point where progress has reached a standstill, one of the parties asks, "What would you like me to do?" The other side often reacts with astonishment and then the first party asks, "If I could do anything to

MANAGER IN ACTION: TOM MELOHN TACKLES OFFICE POLITICS

Tom Melohn, owner of North American Tool and Die, believes that politicking can be halted by simply not putting up with it. He recalls that soon after he bought the company, the plant manager came into his office and began criticizing the chief engineer.

Melohn told the manager to hold his comments for a minute, and then telephoned the chief engineer and invited him to join them. When the chief engineer arrived, Melohn asked the plant manager to repeat what he had said. A long pause followed, accompanied by a red face, a couple of grunts, then silence.

Melohn closed the meeting with this request: "You're entitled to your opinion. But if you have a problem with someone, sit down with him and talk it through. If you still can't reach an understanding, them come on in here together. I'll try to adjudicate. But don't ever come back in here alone and talk behind someone's back."

The plant manager never again made negative comments about someone else in front of Melohn. A major reason was that Melohn deliberately leaked the episode to others without using names. The message was clear. Back stabbing would not be permitted.

Source: Tom Melohn, *The New Partnership: Profit by Bringing Out the Best In Your People, Customers, and Yourself* (Essex Junction, VT: Oliver Wright Publications, 1994).

make this situation okay in your eyes, what would that be?"[27] Frequently the desired action—such as "Treat me with more respect"—can be implemented.

AVOIDING. The avoider combines uncooperativeness and unassertiveness. He or she is indifferent to the concerns of either party. The person may actually be withdrawing from conflict or relying upon fate. The avoiding style is sometimes used by a manager who stays out of a conflict between team members. The members are left to resolve their own differences.

SUMMARY OF KEY POINTS

1
Differentiate between leadership and management.
Management is a set of explicit tools and techniques, based on reasoning and testing, that can be used in a variety of situations. Leadership is more concerned with vision, change, motivation, persuasion, creativity, and influence.

2
Describe how leaders are able to influence and empower team members.
Power is the ability to get other people to do things or the ability to control resources. Authority is the formal right to wield power. This chapter described six types of power: legitimate, reward, coercive, expert, referent (stemming from charisma), and subordinate. Through subordinate power, team members limit the authority of leaders. To get others to act, leaders also use tactics such as leading by example, assertiveness, rationality, in-

gratiation, exchange, coalition formation, and joking and kidding.

Empowerment is the process of sharing power with team members to enhance their feelings of personal effectiveness. Empowerment increases employee motivation, because the employee is accepted as a partner in decision making.

3
Identify important leadership characteristics and behaviors.
Certain personal characteristics are associated with successful managerial leadership in many situations. These characteristics include a strong drive and achievement motive, the power motive, self-confidence, honesty, integrity, and openness, good intellectual ability and technical competence, sensitivity to people, and a sense of humor.

Effective leaders need to demonstrate adaptability, stable performance, high standards of performance, and the ability to give emotional support to subordinates. They should provide frequent feedback to subordinates, have a strong customer orientation, and recover quickly from setbacks.

4

Describe the leadership continuum, Theory X and Theory Y, leadership grid, situational, and entrepreneurial styles of leadership.

Leadership style is the typical pattern of behavior that a leader uses to influence employees to achieve organizational goals. Autocratic leaders attempt to retain most of the authority. Participative leaders share decision making with the group. One subtype of participative leader is the consultative leader, who involves subordinates in decision making but retains final authority. A consensus leader also involves subordinates in decision making and bases the final decision on group consensus. A democratic leader confers final authority on the group.

Autocratic managers make Theory X assumptions about people. They believe people basically dislike work and need to be controlled. Participative managers make Theory Y assumptions about people. They believe that people enjoy their work and want to be self-directing.

Participative leadership works well with competent and self-motivated employees. Free-rein leaders turn over virtually all authority and control to the group.

The Leadership Grid classifies leaders according to how much concern they have for both production and people. Team management, with its high emphasis on production and people, is considered the ideal.

The situational leadership model explains how to match leadership style to the readiness of group members. The model classifies leadership style according to the relative amount of task and relationship behavior the leader engages in. *Readiness* refers both to ability and willingness to accomplish a specific task. As group member readiness increases, a leader should rely more on relationship behavior and less on task behavior. When a group member becomes very ready, however, minimum task or relationship behavior is required.

Entrepreneurial leaders are generally task-oriented and charismatic. They have a strong achievement need, high enthusiasm and creativity, and a visionary per-

spective. They are uncomfortable with hierarchy and bureaucracy and are always in a hurry.

5

Describe transformational and charismatic leadership.

The transformational leader helps organizations and people make positive changes. He or she combines charisma, inspirational leadership, and intellectual stimulation. Transformations take place through such means as pointing to relevant rewards, getting people to look beyond self-interest, and encouraging people to work toward self-fulfillment. Charismatic leaders provide vision and masterful communication. They can inspire trust and help people feel capable, and they are action-oriented. Some charismatic leaders are unethical and use their power to accomplish illegal and immoral ends.

6

Explain how to exercise SuperLeadership.

An important goal for leaders is to become a Super-Leader, one who leads others to lead themselves. Teaching team members to develop productive thought patterns, such as encouraging them to talk to themselves positively and constructively, helps develop self-leadership.

7

Explain the leader's role in managing conflict.

The leader must help people deal with conflict in order to keep the organization running smoothly. Conflict is a source of stress. The right amount of conflict may enhance job performance, but too much or too little stress lowers job performance. Conflict has positive consequences such as increasing creativity, and negative consequences such as wasting resources.

Five major modes of conflict management have been identified: competitive, accommodative, sharing, collaborative, and avoidant. Each style is based on a combination of satisfying one's own concerns (assertiveness) and satisfying the concerns of others (cooperativeness). Confrontation and problem solving is a widely applicable collaborative technique of resolving conflict.

KEY TERMS AND PHRASES

Leadership *pg. 242*
Power *pg. 242*
Authority *pg. 242*
Legitimate Power *pg. 244*
Reward Power *pg. 244*
Coercive Power *pg. 244*
Expert Power *pg. 244*
Referent Power *pg. 244*

Subordinate Power *pg. 244*
Zone of Indifference *pg. 244*
Coalition *pg. 245*
Achievement Motivation *pg. 247*
Power Motivation *pg. 247*
Leadership Style *pg. 249*
Autocratic Leader *pg. 250*
Participative Leader *pg. 250*

QUESTIONS

1. Give an example of a business situation that might require a leader rather than a manager.
2. What kinds of power does your instructor exercise for this course?
3. Visualize yourself as a special assistant to a senior executive. What job-related request might the executive make that would lie around the outer edge of your zone of indifference?
4. What concerns might many experienced businesspeople have about open-book management?
5. For what type of work situation might the "delegating" style of leadership be the most effective?
6. For what type of leadership situation might a transformational leader be inappropriate?
7. Why might the practice of SuperLeadership make charisma less important?

SKILL-BUILDING EXERCISE 11-A: HOW PARTICIPATIVE IS YOUR LEADERSHIP STYLE?

The purposes of this quiz are to: (1) specify what kind of behaviors are represented by an ideal participative leader, and (2) give you an opportunity to compare your behavior (or potential behavior) to that ideal. Be more concerned about giving yourself the gift of candid self-appraisal than attempting to give the "right" answer. Grade your leadership style by rating the frequency with which you use (or would use if placed in the situation) the behaviors listed: 3 = almost always; 2 = sometimes; 1 = never.

	AA	S	N
1. I believe that employee involvement is critical to my work group's success.	3	2	1
2. I hardly ever review our corporate mission statement with our group.	3	2	1
3. My work group develops their own measurable goals.	3	2	1
4. I communicate how my work group contributes to the success of the entire organization.	3	2	1
5. I allow my group to establish its own performance measures.	3	2	1
6. I provide informal performance feedback to my group.	3	2	1
7. My group plays an active role in determining their own recognition and rewards.	3	2	1
8. I appropriately delegate my responsibilities to my work group.	3	2	1
9. I support my work group by providing the resources they need.	3	2	1
10. I emphasize the importance of work.	3	2	1

Scoring and interpretation: Subtract your answers to questions 2, 3, 5, and 7 from the sum of your remaining answers.

11–14 You are already a participative leader (or already think and act like one).
7–10 You are well on your way to becoming a participative leader.
4–6 You have begun the shift to participative leadership (or are beginning to think in that direction).
0–3 You are still leading in a traditional manner (or are thinking like one who does).

Source: Adapted from a quiz from Suzanne W. Zoglio, *The Participative Leader* (Doylestown, PA: Tower Hill Press, 1994).

SKILL-BUILDING EXERCISE 11-B: IDENTIFYING CHARISMATIC LEADERS

Take a poll of the next 10 persons convenient to you. Define charisma, and then ask the person to identify the most charismatic person who comes to his or her mind.

Search for an explanation as to why the leader is perceived as charismatic.

VIDEO DISCUSSION QUESTIONS

1. What type of leadership was expected from Gerstner when he joined IBM? **[Gerstner]**
2. What characteristics of an entrepreneurial leader does the founder of How Sweet It Is exhibit? **[Entrepreneurial Spirit]**
3. To what extent was the Bhopal incident caused by job conflict? **[Bhopal]**

CASE PROBLEM 11-A: HOW DO WE INSPIRE STORE MANAGERS?

Pearle Vison has 1,057 retail stores in 46 states and 10 countries selling eye-wear products and services. Including the headquarters staff in Dallas, Texas, the company has 5,000 corporate employees. The other employees work for the franchisees who operate Pearle Vision stores.

A few years ago, senior management at Pearle was examining reports that compared 557 franchise stores with 500 corporate-owned stores. The results showed that franchisees consistently outperformed corporate store managers in total profits. One executive observed that corporate store managers were required to adhere closely to corporate rules and regulations. All the stores were operated exactly the same way, regardless of their location, size, projected growth, or profit history.

Other members of senior management turned to the vice president of human resources, Roy J. Wilson. He was given 30 days to develop a plan to inspire corporate managers to perform as well as the franchisees. Wilson was told that somehow the corporate managers had to start acting like entrepreneurs for company profits to improve. Senior management also agreed that the store managers must start thinking and acting like business owners.

Wilson recognized that 30 days was not enough time to make much progress on this assignment. But he also felt pressure to get Pearle Vision moving in the right direction.

CASE QUESTIONS

1. In what way is the problem facing Pearle Vision a leadership problem?
2. What steps should top management take to instill a spirit of ownership among the corporate store managers?

Source: Based on facts reported in Jennifer J. Laabs, "Pearle Vision's Managers Think Like Entrepreneurs," *Personnel Journal* (January 1993): 38–46.

CASE PROBLEM 11-B: RICK PITINO, THE LEADER

Back in 1990 the men's basketball team of the University of Kentucky, the Wildcats, was experiencing rough times. The team had received a two-year suspension from tournament competition and was banned from television while the NCAA investigated alleged recruiting violations. Several key players transferred, team morale was low, and player confidence sank. To improve this situation, university officials hired Rick Pitino as the new head coach. Pitino had received credit for impressive turnarounds at Boston University, at Providence College, and with the New York Knicks. Now he turned his attention to Kentucky. After studying the situation briefly, Pitino said he would teach team members to win.

Reggie Hanson, one of the Kentucky players, recalls that the team began its comeback the moment the new coach spoke. "People tell me you can't play," prodded Pitino. "They say you don't have enough talent, that it will take me five or six years to get a winning program here. But I don't believe that. If you stick with me, I guarantee that you'll be better than what you expect and what people expect."

To get players to share his enthusiasm, Pitino relies on hard work. He explains, however, that "hard work itself is not the key to success. The key is to get people to like working hard. Some coaches get their players to work by browbeating and intimidating them. The only way to get people to *like* working hard is to motivate them. Today, they must understand *why* they're working so hard." Pitino himself works hard, getting up before sunrise, shooting baskets, working on his game plans, and meeting with his staff.

Pitino emphasizes teamwork both on and off the court. He told his players that they would have to begin communicating with one another. In Pitino's view, the teamwork that takes place on the court results from players being deeply committed to working together in their lives. As he helped the Wildcats make a comeback, Pitino checked over downtown Lexington, Kentucky. Seeing quiet streets and no bustling restaurants, his verdict was that what the town needed was a good, East Coast-style Italian bistro. Shortly thereafter, a new restaurant emerged. It became an immediate success with sell-out crowds and long lists for reservations. Pitino ran the restaurant for several years before he sold it to concentrate on other interests. He managed the restaurant in the same style he manages basketball teams. He recruited top talent because he persuaded people that he would help them reach their potential. He attended staff meetings regularly, and praised everyone from dishwashers to the maitre d'.

Colleagues think Pitino is a nice guy to be around when the game clock is not running. "When he steps off the court, he's a completely different person," said Bernadette Locke-Mattox, one of his assistant coaches. "He's a caring, giving individual. He loves his family and team. His players are like his children."

Pitino is hired frequently as a motivational speaker by business firms. He believes that his style of coaching and motivating applies equally well to business. The way to motivate a sales representative, for example, is to tell

him or her, "I know you've got the potential to get the job done." This is much better than threatening the sales rep with being fired if the quota is not reached.

By the start of the 1995–96 season, the Wildcats were back to regularly ranking in the top ten. In the 1993–94 season, for example, the team record was 30–4. Pitino had accomplished his goal of returning the team to consistent prominence. And in 1996 Pitino reached a milestone in his career when the Kentucky Wildcats beat the Syracuse Orangemen for the NCAA men's basketball championship.

CASE QUESTIONS

1. How would you characterize Pitino's leadership style?
2. What elements of SuperLeadership does Pitino practice?
3. In what way is Pitino a transformational leader?
4. What leadership traits and practices does Pitino demonstrate?

Source: Based on facts in Michael Maren, "Win!" *Success* (April 1992): 36–41; Gary Falleson, "Pitino Always Up to the Challenge," Rochester *Democrat & Chronicle* (12 February 1994): 6D.

REFERENCES

1. Janet Bamford, "The Working Woman 50: America's Top Women Business Owners," *Working Woman* (May 1995): 42.
2. W. Chan Kim and Renee A. Mauborgne, "Parables of Leadership," *Harvard Business Review* (July–August 1992): 123.
3. John P. Kotter, *A Force for Change: How Leadership Differs from Management* (New York: Free Press, 1990).
4. John R. P. French, Jr., and Bertram Raven, "The Bases of Social Power," in Dorwin Cartwright and Alvin Zander (eds.), *Group Dynamics: Research and Theory* (New York: Harper & Row, 1960): 607–623.
5. Andrew J. DuBrin, "Sex and Gender Differences in Tactics of Influence," *Psychological Reports*, 1991, (68): 645–646.
6. Mauk Mulder et al., "Power, Situation, and Leaders' Effectiveness: An Organizational Field Study," *Journal of Applied Psychology* (November 1986): 556–570.
7. Frank J. Navran, "Empowering Employees to Excel," *Supervisory Management* (August 1992): 5.
8. Shelley A. Kirkpatrick and Edwin A. Locke, "Leadership: Do Traits Matter?" *The Executive* (May 1991): 48–60.
9. Robert G. Lord et al., "A Meta-Analysis of the Relationship Between Personality Traits and Leadership Perceptions: An Application of Validity Generalization Procedures," *Journal of Applied Psychology* (August 1986): 402–410.
10. Kirkpatrick and Locke, "Leadership: Do Traits Matter?"; Bernard M. Bass, *Bass & Stogdill's Handbook of Leadership: Theory, Research, and Managerial Applications*, 3e (New York: Free Press, 1990): 78–96.
11. Kirkpatrick and Locke, "Leadership: Do Traits Matter?": 53.
12. Fred E. Fiedler and Joseph E. Garcia, *New Approaches to Effective Leadership: Cognitive Resources and Organizational Performance* (New York: Wiley, 1987).
13. David Greising, "The Toughest #&?!% in Sports," *Business Week* (15 June 1992): 100.
14. Glenn Collins, "Humor is Newest Tool To Lessen Stress, Motivate Workers," *The New York Times* (2 May 1988).
15. "The Chief Salesman," *Success* (May 1991): 14.
16. Robert R. Blake and Anne Adams McCanse, *Leadership Dilemmas—Grid Solutions* (Houston: Gulf Publishing, 1991).
17. Paul Hersey and Kenneth H. Blanchard, *Management of Organizational Behavior: Utilizing Human Resources*, 5th ed. (Englewood Cliffs, NJ: Prentice Hall, 1988): 170–177.
18. David C. McClelland, *The Achieving Society* (New York: Van Nostrand Reinhold, 1961).
19. Jane M. Howell and Bruce J. Avolio, "Transformational Leadership, Transactional Leadership, Locus of Control, and Support for Innovation: Key Predictors of Consolidated-Business-Unit Performance," *Journal of Applied Psychology* (December 1993): 891–902.
20. John J. Hater and Bernard M. Bass, "Superiors' Evaluations and Subordinates' Perceptions of Transformational and Transactional Leadership," *Journal of Applied Psychology* (November 1988): 695.
21. Alan J. Dubinsky et al., "An Examination of Linkages Between Personal Characteristics and Dimensions of Transformational Leadership," *Journal of Business and Psychology* (Spring 1995): 315; Jay A. Conger, *The Charismatic Leader: Beyond the Mystique of Exceptional Leadership* (San Francisco: Jossey-Bass, 1989).
22. The last two suggestions are from Roger Dawson, *Secrets of Power Persuasion* (Englewood Cliffs, NJ: Prentice Hall, 1992).
23. Jane M. Howell and Bruce Avolio, "The Ethics of Charismatic Leadership: Submission or Liberation?" *The Executive* (May 1992): 52–53.
24. Charles C. Manz and Henry P. Sims, Jr., "SuperLeadership: Beyond the Myth of Heroic Leadership," *Organizational Dynamics* (Spring 1991): 18.
25. Charles C. Manz, "Helping Yourself and Others to Master Self-Leadership," *Supervisory Management* (November 1991): 9.
26. "How Managers Get The Job Done," *Harvard Business Review* (January–February 1995): 10.
27. James A. Autry, *Love & Profit* (New York: Morrow, 1991).

CHAPTER 12

Motivation

LEARNING OBJECTIVES
After studying this chapter and doing the exercises, you should be able to:

1
Explain the relationship between motivation and performance.

2
Present an overview of major theories of need satisfaction in explaining motivation.

3
Explain how goal setting is used to motivate people.

4
Describe the application of behavior modification to worker motivation.

5
Describe the role of financial incentives, including gainsharing, in worker motivation.

6
Explain the conditions under which a person will be motivated according to expectancy theory.

© Jose L. Pelaez/
The Stock Market

Several years ago, top management at IBM decided they wanted the sales force to bring home greater profits, not just sales. In a step never taken previously, IBM tied sales-force commissions to the profits on the deals they signed. Previously there was a smaller tie between commissions and profits. The senior vice-president in charge of sales and marketing in the United States and Canada said, "We have gone from different sales objectives to financial objectives." • To reinforce these behaviors, IBM management established the following standards for how the sales force earns commissions: Sixty percent of commission is based on profitability, not overall revenues, on an order. Forty percent of the commission is based on customer satisfaction. Buyers are surveyed to assess if they are happy with the local sales team and if the sales reps helped them achieve their business objectives. Now sales representatives only have to worry about two outcomes: satisfying the customers and profits. • The reinforcement strategy appears to be working: 1994 was a banner year for IBM in terms of profits—$2.8 billion profit on revenues of $63.9 billion—followed by comparable success in 1995 and the first quarter of 1996.[1]

The incident about changing the incentive plan for IBM sales representa- tives illustrates a fundamental point about the practice of management. A working knowledge of motivation theory and techniques (in this case reinforcement theory) can help managers achieve good business results. Un- derstanding motivation is also important because how to motivate employees is a perennial challenge faced by managers. Low motivation contributes to low- quality work, superficial effort, indifference toward customers, and high absen- teeism and tardiness.

The term *motivation* refers to two different but related ideas. From the stand- point of the individual, motivation is an internal state that leads to the pursuit of objectives. Personal motivation affects the initiation, direction, intensity, and per- sistence of effort. (A motivated worker gets going, focuses effort in the right di- rection, works with intensity, and sustains the effort.) From the standpoint of the manager, motivation is the process of getting people to pursue objectives. Both concepts have an important meaning in common. **Motivation** is the expenditure of effort to accomplish results. The effort results from a force to perform that stems from one or more of three sources: the individual, the manager, or the group. The purpose of motivating team members is to get them to achieve results that help the organization.

motivation
The expenditure of effort to accomplish results.

This chapter will present several theories or explanations of motivation in the workplace. In addition, it will provide descriptions of specific approaches to motivating employees. Exhibit 12-1 presents an overview of the various mo- tivation theories and techniques this chapter will discuss. Referring back to this figure will help you integrate the information in this chapter. All the ideas presented in this chapter can be applied to motivating oneself as well as oth- ers. For instance, when you read about the expectancy theory of motivation, ask yourself: "What rewards do I value strongly enough for me to work extra hard?"

Exhibit 12-1
Overview of Motivation
Theories and Techniques

I. Theories and explanations of motivation
    1. Motivation through need satisfaction
        a. Maslow's need hierarchy
        b. Satisfaction of needs such as achievement, power, affiliation, and recognition
        c. Herzberg's two-factor theory
    2. Goal theory
    3. Behavior modification
    4. Expectancy theory
II. Specific motivational techniques stemming from theories
    1. Recognition programs
    2. Positive reinforcement programs
    3. Motivation through financial incentives
        a. Linking pay to performance
        b. Gainsharing
        c. Employee stock-ownership programs (ESOP)
        d. Team incentives

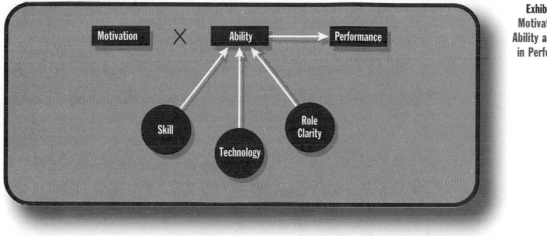

Exhibit 12-2
Motivation and
Ability as Factors
in Performance

THE RELATIONSHIP BETWEEN MOTIVATION AND PERFORMANCE

Many people believe the statements "You can accomplish anything you want" and "Think positively and you will achieve all your goals." In truth, motivation is but one important contributor to productivity and performance. Abilities, skills, and the right equipment are also indispensable. An office supervisor at a bank desperately wanted to become chairperson of the board within three years. Despite the intensity of his motivation, he did not reach his goal. The factors against him included his lack of formal business education, limited conceptual skills, underdeveloped political skills, and inadequate knowledge of high finance. Furthermore, the current chairperson had no intention of leaving the post.

Exhibit 12-2 shows the relationship between motivation and performance. It can also be expressed by the equation $P = M \times A,$ where P refers to performance, M to motivation, and A to ability. Note that skill, technology, and role clarity contribute to ability.[2] For instance, if you are skilled at using a computer, if you have the right hardware and software, and if your assignment is clear, you can accomplish desktop publishing.

Group norms are another contributor to both motivation and performance. If group norms and organizational culture encourage high motivation and performance, the individual worker will feel compelled to work hard. To do otherwise is to feel isolated from the group. Group norms favoring low motivation and performance will often lower individual output.

A manager contributes to performance by motivating group members, improving their ability, increasing role clarity, and helping to create a positive work culture. Has a manager ever contributed to your performance?

MOTIVATION THROUGH NEED SATISFACTION

The simplest explanation of motivation is one of the most powerful: people are willing to expend effort toward achieving a goal because it satisfies one of their important needs. A **need** is a deficit within an individual, such as a craving for water or affection. Self-interest is thus a driving force. The principle is referred to as "What's in it for me?" or WIIFM (pronounced wiff′ em). Reflect on your own experiences. Before working hard to accomplish a task, you probably want to know how you will

LEARNING OBJECTIVE

Explain the relationship between motivation and performance.

$P = M \times A$
An expression of the relationship be tween motivation and performance, where P *refers to performance,* M *to motivation, and* A *to ability.*

need
A deficit within an individual, such as a craving for water or affection.

LEARNING OBJECTIVE

Present an overview of major theories of need satisfaction in explaining motivation.

benefit. If your manager asks you to work extra hours to take care of an emergency, you will most likely oblige. Yet underneath you might be thinking, "If I work these extra hours, my boss will think highly of me. As a result, I will probably receive a good performance evaluation and maybe a better-than-average salary increase.

People are motivated to fulfill needs that are not currently satisfied. An important implication of the need-satisfaction approach is that there are two key steps in motivating workers. First, you must know what people want—what needs they are trying to satisfy. To learn what the needs are, you can ask directly or observe the person. You can obtain knowledge indirectly by getting to know employees better. To gain insight into employee needs, find out something about the employee's personal life, education, work history, outside interests, and career goals.

Second, you must give each person a chance to satisfy needs on the job. To illustrate, one way to motivate a person with a strong need for autonomy is to allow that person to work independently.

This section examines needs and motivation from three related perspectives. First, we describe the best-known theory of motivation, Maslow's need hierarchy. Then we discuss several specific needs related to job motivation and move on to another cornerstone idea, Herzberg's two-factor theory.

MASLOW'S NEED HIERARCHY

Maslow's need hierarchy

The motivation theory that arranges human needs into a pyramid-shaped model with basic physiological needs at the bottom and self-actualizing needs at the top.

deficiency needs

Lower-order needs that must be satisfied to ensure a person's existence, security, and requirements for human contact.

growth needs

Higher-order needs that are concerned with personal development and reaching one's potential.

Based on his work as a clinical psychologist, Abraham M. Maslow developed a comprehensive view of individual motivation.[3] **Maslow's need hierarchy** arranges human needs into a pyramid-shaped model with basic physiological needs at the bottom and self-actualization needs at the top. (See Exhibit 12-3.) Lower-order needs, call **deficiency needs,** must be satisfied to ensure a person's existence, security, and requirements for human contact. Higher-order needs, or **growth needs,** are concerned with personal development and reaching one's potential. Before higher-level needs are activated, the lower-order needs must be satisfied. The five levels of needs are described next.

1. *Physiological needs* refers to basic bodily requirements such as nutrition, water, shelter, moderate temperatures, rest, and sleep. Most office jobs allow us to satisfy physiological needs. Fire fighting is an occupation with potential to frustrate some physiological needs. Smoke inhalation can block need satisfaction.
2. *Safety needs* include the desire to be safe from both physical and emotional injury. Many operatives who work at dangerous jobs would be motivated by the prospects of obtaining safety. For example, computer operators who are suffering from cumulative trauma disorder would prefer a job that requires less intense pressure on their wrists. Any highly stressful job can frustrate the need for emotional safety.
3. *Social needs* are the needs for love, belonging, and affiliation with people. Managers can contribute to the satisfaction of these needs by promoting teamwork and allowing people to discuss work problems with each other. Many employees see their jobs as a major source for satisfying social needs.
4. *Esteem* needs reflect people's desire to be seen by themselves and others as a person of worth. Occupations with high status are a primary source for the satisfaction of esteem needs. Managers can help employees satisfy their esteem needs by praising the quality of their work.
5. *Self-actualization* needs relate to the desire to reach one's potential. They include needs for self-fulfillment and personal development. True self-actualization is an ideal to strive for, rather than something that automatically stems

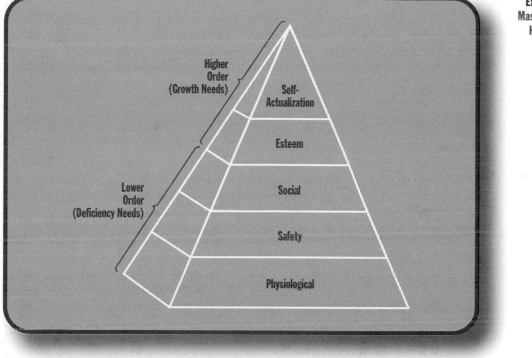

Exhibit 12-3
Maslow's Need
Hierarchy

from occupying a challenging position. Self-actualized people are those who are becoming all they are capable of becoming. Managers can help subordinates move toward self-actualization by giving them challenging assignments and the chance for advancement and new learning.

THE NEED HIERARCHY IN PERSPECTIVE. Maslow's need hierarchy is a convenient way of classifying needs and has spurred thousands of managers to take the subject of human motivation more seriously. Its primary value has been that it dramatizes the importance of satisfying needs in order to motivate employees. Furthermore, Maslow has shown why people are difficult to satisfy. As one need is satisfied, people want to satisfy other needs or different forms of the same need. The need hierarchy has helped three generations of students understand that it is normal to be constantly searching for new satisfactions.

Despite its contribution, Maslow's need hierarchy does not apply universally. Not everybody wants to satisfy needs in a stepwise fashion. Some people try to achieve esteem before satisfying their social needs. Others try to satisfy more than one group of needs simultaneously.

SPECIFIC NEEDS PEOPLE ATTEMPT TO SATISFY

Maslow's need hierarchy refers to classes of needs. The work setting offers the opportunity to satisfy dozens of psychological needs included somewhere in the need hierarchy. This section will describe four of the most important of these needs.

ACHIEVEMENT, POWER, AND AFFILIATION. According to David McClelland and his associates, much job behavior can be explained by the strength of people's needs for achievement, power, and affiliation.[4] The achievement and power needs (or motives) have already been described in relation to leadership. The **affiliation need** is a de-

> **affiliation need**
> *A desire to have close relationships with others and be a loyal employee or friend.*

sire to have close relationships with others and to be a loyal employee or friend. Affiliation is a social need, while achievement and power are self-actualizing needs.

A person with a strong need for affiliation finds compatible working relationships more important than high-level accomplishment and the exercise of power. Successful executives, therefore, usually have stronger needs for achievement and power than for affiliation. Workers with strong affiliation needs, however, typically enjoy contributing to a team effort. Befriending others and working cooperatively with them satisfies the need for affiliation.

recognition need
The desire to be acknowledged for one's contributions and efforts and to feel important.

RECOGNITION. The workplace provides a natural opportunity to satisfy the **recognition need,** the desire to be acknowledged for one's contributions and efforts and to feel important. A manager can thus motivate many employees by making them feel important. Employee needs for recognition can be satisfied both through informal recognition and by giving formal recognition programs. In regard to informal interactions, a study asked older workers what would make them stay beyond their company's usual retirement age. A representative answer was that an older worker would stay if the manager came to him or her and said, "You're a key player. We need you."[5]

Company recognition programs, such as awarding watches and jewelry for good service, are direct appeals to the need for recognition. Less expensive awards, such as T-shirts and beverage mugs, are also useful for providing recognition. Virtually every large and small organization has some type of recognition program. The program might be as simple as posting an "employee of the month" plaque on the wall. The accompanying Organization in Action feature presents a well-publicized recognition program.

Praising workers for good performance is closely related to recognition. An effective form of praise describes the worker's performance rather than merely making an evaluation. Describing good performance might take this form: "You turned an angry customer into an ally who has referred new business to us." A straightforward evaluation would be "You did a great job with that angry customer." Even more effective would be to combine the two statements.

HERZBERG'S TWO-FACTOR THEORY

two-factor theory of work motivation
The theory contending that there are two different sets of job factors. One set can satisfy and motivate people, and the other set can only prevent dissatisfaction.

The study of the need hierarchy led to the **two-factor theory of work motivation.** The key point to the theory is that there are two different sets of job factors. One set of factors can satisfy and motivate people. The other can only prevent dissatisfaction.

Psychologist Frederick Herzberg and his associates interviewed hundreds of professionals about their work.[6] They discovered that some factors of a job give people a chance to satisfy higher-level needs. Such elements are satisfiers or motivators. A *satisfier* is a job factor that, if present, leads to job satisfaction. Similarly, a *motivator* is a job factor that, if present, leads to motivation. When a motivator is not present, the effect on motivation is neutral rather than negative. Herzberg's theory originally dealt with job satisfaction, but now it is also considered a theory of job motivation.

Individuals vary somewhat in the particular job factors they find satisfying or motivating. However, satisfiers and motivators generally refer to the content (the heart or guts) of a job. These factors are achievement, recognition, challenging work, responsibility, and the opportunity for advancement. All the factors are self-rewarding. The important implication for managers is that, as managers, they can motivate most people by giving them the opportunity to do interesting work or to be promoted. The two-factor theory is thus the psychology that underlies the philosophy of job design through job enrichment and the job characteristics model, as described in Chapter 8.

ORGANIZATION IN ACTION: BRAVO-ZULU AT FEDERAL EXPRESS

The formal method for recognizing employees at Federal Express Corp. is the Bravo-Zulu Award Program. "Bravo-Zulu" is a U.S. Navy expression for a job well done, and recognition of excellence is shown by the B and Z signal flags flying from a ship's mast. Federal Express managers are authorized to make Bravo-Zulu awards on the spot by giving an employee a small set of flags and a check for from $50 to $100. For example, a driver who made it through a snowstorm to de-

liver urgently needed supplies might receive a Bravo-Zulu award from the supervisor.

Fred A. Manske, Jr., the senior vice-president who started the program, never conducts a staff meeting without some form of planned recognition. He praises outstanding performance and, when appropriate, presents employees with a tangible award. The award could be a Bravo-Zulu award or a cash-equivalent award, such as a voucher for dinner for two.

Source: Fred Manske, Jr., *Secrets of Effective Leadership* (Germantown, TN: Leadership Education and Development, 1988); updated with 1995 interview with Federal Express employee.

Herzberg also discovered that some job elements are more relevant to lower-level needs than upper-level needs. Referred to as dissatisfiers, or hygiene factors, these elements are noticed primarily by their absence. A *dissatisfier* is a job element that, when present, prevents dissatisfaction; it does not, however, create satisfaction. People will not be satisfied with their jobs just because hygiene factors are present. For example, not having a handy place to park your car would create dissatisfaction. But having a place to park would not make you happier about your job.

Dissatisfiers relate mostly to the context (the job setting or external elements). These include relationships with coworkers, company policy and administration, job security, and money. All these factors deal with external rewards. Money, however, does work as a satisfier for many people. Some people want or need money so much that high pay contributes to their job satisfaction. (See the discussion of financial incentives later in this chapter.) One reason that money can be a motivator is that high pay is often associated with high status and high esteem.

Exhibit 12-4 summarizes the major aspects of the two-factor theory of job motivation. The exhibit illustrates an important point: The opposite of satisfaction is no satisfaction—not dissatisfaction. Similarly, the opposite of dissatisfaction is no dissatisfaction—not satisfaction.

EVALUATION OF THE TWO-FACTOR THEORY. Herzberg's theory has had considerable influence on the practice of management and job design. The two-factor theory has prompted managers to ask, "What really motivates our employees?" Nevertheless, Herzberg's assumption—that all workers seek more responsibility and challenge on the job—may have been incorrect. It is more likely that people in higher-level occupations strive for more responsibility and challenge. But even in a given occupational group, such as managers or production workers, not everybody has the same motivational pattern. One executive admitted to this author that she finds the status she receives as a company president to be highly motivational. Also, many workers are motivated by a secure job when they have heavy financial obligations.

Another problem with the two-factor theory is that it goes too far in concluding that hygiene factors cannot contribute to satisfaction and motivation. Many people do experience high job satisfaction and motivation because of more job elements such as job security and pleasant working conditions.

Exhibit 12-4
The Two-Factor Theory
of Work Motivation

| **Satisfiers or Motivators** | Presence | Positive effect on motivation and satisfaction |
| | Absence | No negative effect on motivation or satisfaction |

1. Achievement	4. Responsibility
2. Recognition	5. Advancement
3. Work itself	6. Growth

| **Dissatisfiers** | Presence | No positive effect on motivation or satisfaction |
| | Absence | Negative effect on motivation and satisfaction |

1. Company policy	6. Relationships with peers
2. Supervision	7. Personal life
3. Relationship with supervisor	8. Relationships with subordinates
4. Work conditions	9. Status
5. Salary	10. Job security

MOTIVATION THROUGH GOAL SETTING

LEARNING OBJECTIVE

Explain how goal setting is
used to motivate people.

Goal setting, including management by objectives (see Chapter 5), is a pervasive managerial activity. This section is concerned with the psychology behind goal setting: why and how it leads to improved performance.

THE BASICS OF GOAL THEORY

Goal setting is an important part of most formal motivational programs and managerial methods of motivating employees. The premise underlying goal theory is that behavior is regulated by values and goals. A *value* is a strongly held personal standard or conviction. It is a belief about something very important to the individual, such as dignity of work or honesty. Our values create within us a desire to behave consistently with them. If an executive values honesty, the executive will establish a goal of trying to hire only honest employees. He or she would therefore make extensive use of reference checks and honesty testing.

With respect to planning, a goal has been defined as an overall condition one is trying to achieve. Its psychological meaning is about the same. A *goal* is what the person is trying to accomplish, or a conscious intention to act.

Edwin A. Locke and Gary P. Latham have incorporated hundreds of studies about goals into a theory of goal setting and task performance.[7] Exhibit 12-5 summarizes some of the more consistent findings and the list that follows describes them.

1. *Specific goals lead to higher performance than do generalized goals.* Telling someone to "do your best" is a generalized goal. A specific goal would be "Decrease the turnaround time on customer inquiries to an average of two working days."
2. *Performance generally increases in direct proportion to goal difficulty.* The harder one's goal, the more one accomplishes. There is an important exception, however. When goals are too difficult, they may lower performance. Difficulty in reaching the goal leads to frustration, which in turn leads to lowered performance.
3. *For goals to improve performance, the employee must accept them.* If you reject a goal, you will not incorporate it into your planning. This is why it is often helpful

Exhibit 12-5
Goal-Setting Theory

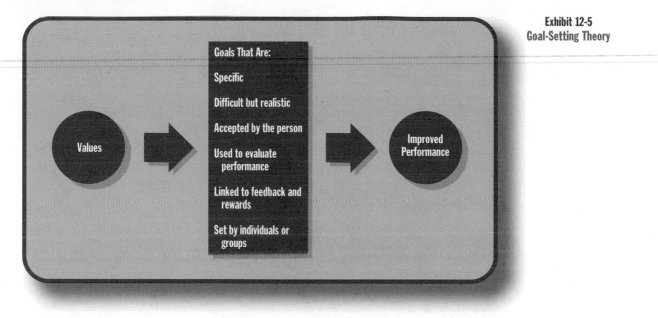

to discuss goals with employees, rather than just imposing the goals on them. Participating in setting goals has no major effect on the level of job performance, except when it improves goal acceptance. Goal acceptance is important for another reason. When a worker is committed to a goal, it is more likely that setting harder goals will lead to improved performance.[8] Without commitment (a strong form of acceptance), the person is more likely to be frustrated in pursuing a difficult goal.

4. *Goals are more effective when they are used to evaluate performance.* When workers know that their performance will be evaluated in terms of how well they attained their goals, the impact of goals increases. Management by objectives is built around this important idea.

5. *Goals should be linked to feedback and rewards.* Workers should receive feedback on their progress toward goals and be rewarded for reaching them.[9] *Feedback* is information about how well someone is doing in achieving his or her goals. Rewarding people for reaching goals is perhaps the best-accepted principle of management.

6. *Group goal setting is as important as individual goal setting.* Having employees work as teams with a specific team goal, rather than as individuals with only individual goals, increases productivity. Furthermore, the combination of the compatible group and individual goals is more effective than either individual or group goals.

Despite the contribution of goals to performance, technically speaking, they are not motivational by themselves. Rather, the discrepancies created by what individuals do and what they aspire to do creates self-dissatisfaction. The dissatisfaction in turn creates a desire to reduce the discrepancy between the real and the ideal.[10] When a person desires to attain something, the person is in a state of mental arousal. The tension created by not having already achieved a goal spurs the person to reach the goal. Assume your goal is to prepare a 25-page report for your manager by 10 days from now. Your dissatisfaction with not having started would propel you into action.

BEHAVIOR MODIFICATION

**behavior
modification**

*A way of chang-
ing behavior by
rewarding the
right responses
and punishing or
ignoring the wrong
responses.*

law of effect

*The underlying
principle of behav-
ior modification
stating that behav-
ior leading to posi-
tive consequences
tends to be repeated
and that behavior
leading to negative
consequences tends
not to be repeated.*

The most systematic method of motivating people is **behavior modification.** It is a way of changing behavior by rewarding the right responses and punishing or ignoring the wrong responses. A reward is something of value received as a consequence of having attained a goal. This section will describe several key concepts and strategies of behavior modification (also referred to as OB Mod). Much of behavior modification is based on the work of B.F. Skinner, the noted psychologist who promoted behaviorism.

KEY CONCEPTS OF BEHAVIOR MODIFICATION

The **law of effect** is the foundation principle of behavior modification. According to this principle, behavior that leads to positive consequences tends to be repeated. Similarly, behavior that leads to negative consequences tends not to be repeated. Perceptive managers rely on the law of effect virtually every day. Assume that a supervisor of a paint shop wants her employees to put on a face mask every time they use a spray gun. When she sees an employee using a mask properly, she might comment, "Good to see that you're wearing the safety mask today." If the supervisor noticed that an employee was not wearing a mask, she might say, "Please put down the spray gun, and go get your mask. If this happens again, I will be forced to suspend you for one day."

Behavior modification offers a different explanation of human motivation than do need theories. According to need theories, people are driven to engage in certain behaviors by internal forces, such as the need for self-fulfillment. According to behavior modification theorists, people engage in certain behaviors because they have been conditioned by past rewards and punishments. Note the fine line between learning and motivation. Learning is a relatively permanent change in behavior and is based on experience. We learn to do something the first time on the basis of rewards and punishments. It is motivation that leads us to repeat that behavior in the future.

Rewards can be extrinsic or intrinsic. An *extrinsic (or external) reward* is received from outside the self. Money and praise are extrinsic rewards. An *intrinsic (or internal)* reward stems from inside the self. The sense of satisfaction for having done something right is an intrinsic reward. Motivational programs such as job enrichment and empowerment incorporate intrinsic rewards. For example, an empowered employee has more opportunity to perform challenging tasks, such as making important decisions, than an unempowered employee.

Behavior modification is generally associated with extrinsic rewards such as financial bonuses and prizes. However, intrinsic rewards are also used. A worker might receive a more challenging assignment as a reward for performing well on the previous assignment.

BEHAVIOR MODIFICATION STRATEGIES

There are four behavior modification strategies used either individually or in combination: positive reinforcement, negative reinforcement, extinction, and punishment.

POSITIVE REINFORCEMENT. *Positive reinforcement* increases the probability that behavior will be repeated by rewarding people for making the right response. The phrase "increases the probability" is noteworthy. No behavior modification strategy guarantees that people will always make the right response in the future. However, it increases the chance that they will repeat the desired behavior. The term *reinforcement* means that the behavior (or response) is strengthened or entrenched. For example, your response of placing your left pinky on the *a* of your keyboard is probably reinforced through thousands of successful attempts.

Positive reinforcement is the most effective behavior modification strategy. Most people respond better to being rewarded for the right response than to being punished for the wrong response. The IBM decision to base sales representative compensation in part on customer satisfaction illustrates rewarding the desired behavior to improve performance.

NEGATIVE REINFORCEMENT (AVOIDANCE MOTIVATION). *Negative reinforcement* is rewarding people by taking away an uncomfortable consequence. It is a method of strengthening a desired response by making the removal of discomfort contingent on the right response. Assume that an employee is placed on probation because of excessive absenteeism. After 20 consecutive days of coming to work, the employer rewards the employee by removing the probation. Because the opportunity for removing punishments is limited, negative reinforcement is not a widely used behavior modification strategy.

Negative reinforcement or avoidance motivation is often confused with punishment. In reality, negative reinforcement is the opposite of punishment. It is rewarding someone by enabling him or her to avoid punishment.

EXTINCTION. *Extinction* is the weakening or decreasing of the frequency of undesirable behavior by removing the reward for such behavior. It is the absence of reinforcement. Extinction often takes the form of ignoring undesirable behavior. It works this way: Suppose an employee engages in undesirable behavior, such as creating a disturbance just to get a reaction from coworkers. If the coworkers ignore the disturbance, the perpetrator no longer receives the reward of getting attention and stops the disturbing behavior. The behavior is said to be extinguished.

Extinction must be used with great care because there are many times when it does not work. An employee may habitually come to work late. If the boss does not reprimand the employee, the employee's tardiness may strengthen. The employee may interpret the boss's attempt at extinction as condoning the behavior.

PUNISHMENT. *Punishment* is the presentation of an undesirable consequence for a specific behavior. Yelling at an employee for making a mistake is a direct form of punishment. Another form of punishment is taking away a privilege, such as working on an interesting project, because of some undesirable behavior. In order to be effective, punishment not only tells people what not to do, it teaches them the right behavior. When used appropriately, punishment can be a motivator for those punished and those observing the punishment. This means delivering it in a manner that is clearly impersonal, corrective, focused on a specific act, and relatively intense and quick.

Punishment has a potential contribution that goes beyond controlling the behavior of the counterproductive worker. Coworkers may welcome punishment for an individual's misconduct because it represents justice. Punishing misconduct is also important because it communicates to the work group which type of behavior is unacceptable.[11]

A serious disadvantage of punishment is that it may cause adverse consequences for managers and the organization. Employees who are punished often become defensive, angry, and eager to seek revenge. A common form of revenge is destroying computer files.

SUCCESSFUL APPLICATION OF POSITIVE REINFORCEMENT

Although behavior modification through positive reinforcement may take the form of an overall company program, managers and professionals use it more frequently on an informal, daily basis. The list that follows presents several suggestions for making effective use of positive reinforcement.[12]

1. *Focus on the positive aspects of job performance.* Most negative job behaviors have a positive counterpart. To improve performance, reward the employee for engaging in positive behavior. Assume, for example, an inventory control technician typically turns in inventory reports with missing data. When the technician turns in a complete report, the manager should offer a compliment.

2. *State clearly what behavior will lead to a reward.* The nature of good performance, or the goals, must be agreed to by both superior and subordinate. Clarification could take this form: "What I need are inventory reports without missing data. When you achieve this, you'll be credited with good performance."

3. *Use appropriate rewards.* An appropriate reward is an effective one because it is valued by the person being motivated. Examine the list of rewards in Exhibit 12-6. Note that some have more appeal to you than do others. The best way to motivate people is to offer them their preferred rewards for good performance. Managers should ask employees what they are interested in attaining.

4. *Make rewards contingent on good performance.* Contingent reinforcement means that getting the reward depends on giving a certain performance. Unless a reward is linked to the desired behavior or performance it will have little effect on whether the behavior or performance is repeated. For example, saying "You're doing great" in response to anything an employee does will not lead to good performance. Yet if the manager reserves the "doing great" response for truly outstanding performance, he or she may reinforce the good performance.

5. *Administer rewards intermittently.* Positive reinforcement can be administered under different types of schedules. The most effective and sensible type is an intermittent schedule, in which rewards are administered often, but not always, when the appropriate behavior occurs. A reward loses its effect if given every time the employee makes the right response. (Would you become tired of receiving praise every time you did something right?) Thus intermittent rewards sustain desired behavior for a long time by helping to prevent the behavior from fading away when it is not rewarded.

   In addition to being more effective, intermittent rewards are generally more practical than continuous rewards. Few managers have enough time to dispense rewards every time team members attain performance goals.

6. *Vary the size of the reward with the size of accomplishment.* Big accomplishments deserve big rewards, and small accomplishments deserve small rewards. Rewards of the wrong magnitude erode their motivational power. An important corollary of this principle is that people become embarrassed when praise is overly lavish.

7. *Administer rewards promptly.* The proper timing of rewards may be difficult because the manager is not present at the time of good performance. In this case, a telephone call or a note of appreciation within several days of the good performance is appropriate.

8. *Change rewards periodically.* Rewards grow stale quickly; they must be changed periodically. A repetitive reward can even become an annoyance. How many times can one be motivated by the phrase "nice job"? Suppose the reward for making a sales quota is a clock radio. How many clock radios can one person use?

Monetary

Salary increases or bonuses
Company-paid vacation trip
Discount coupons
Company stock
Extra paid vacation days
Profit sharing
Paid personal holiday (such as birthday)
Movie or athletic event passes
Free or discount airline tickets
Discounts on company products and services
Gift selection from catalog

Job and Career Related

Challenging work assignments
Job security (relatively permanent job)
Favorable performance appraisal
Freedom to choose own work activity
Promotion
Improved working conditions
More of preferred tasks
Role as boss's stand-in when he or she
   is away
Role in presentations to top-level management
Job rotation
Paid membership in professional group

Food and Dining

Business luncheon paid by company
Company picnics
Department parties
Holiday turkeys and fruit baskets

Social and Pride Related

Compliments
Encouragement
Comradeship with boss
Access to confidential information
Pat on the back
Expression of appreciation in front of others
Note of thanks
Employee-of-the-month award
Wall plaque indicating accomplishment
Special commendation
Company recognition plan

Status Symbols

Bigger desk
Bigger office
Exclusive use of fax machine
Freedom to personalize work area
Private office
Cellular phone privileges
On-line services privileges

Exhibit 12-6
Rewards Suitable for Use in Positive Reinforcement

ARGUMENTS FOR AND AGAINST BEHAVIOR MODIFICATION

Concrete evidence indicates that behavior modification improves productivity more than any other motivational program.[13] Nevertheless, behavior modification is controversial. The most vehement concern is that behavior modification manipulates employees against their will. A counterargument is that behavior modification cannot work if people are offered rewards they do not value. Thus, workers do exert some control over the motivational process.

Behavior modification is also valuable because it can be applied cross-culturally. People from all cultures seek rewards for work, whether they be geared to individuals or groups. The challenge is to find which rewards are effective in the particular culture. A study was conducted in a cotton mill in the Russian Republic of the former Soviet Union. One aspect of the study offered extrinsic rewards in the form of American goods to 99 weavers from different shifts. Praise and recognition were also used as rewards. Receiving the goods as well as recognition and praise were contingent upon increases in the amount of top-grade fabric they produced. The rewards resulted in increased production. Another motivational technique, employee participation, contributed to a performance decline.[14]

Another anti-behavior modification argument is that the system is too mechanistic. It works well with only simple aspects of job performance, such as spotting quality defects. This argument is based on an incomplete understanding of the use of positive reinforcement on the job. Workers at all levels respond well to appropriate rewards. For example, senior vice-presidents were included in a behavior modification program at the Union National Bank in Little Rock, Arkansas.[15]

The most consistent argument against behavior modification is that it focuses the attention of workers on extrinsic rewards such as money and praise. In the process they lose out on intrinsic rewards such as joy in accomplishment. One argument is that external rewards do not create a lasting commitment. Instead, they create temporary compliance, such as working hard in the short run to earn a bonus. Another anti-OB Mod position is that rewards manipulate people, as do bribes.[16] In reality, workers at all levels need a combination of internal and external rewards to sustain motivation. A telling example is that authorities on the evils of external rewards expect to be paid handsomely for their talks on the subject. Furthermore, they will not talk for free, however exciting they find the subject.

MOTIVATION THROUGH FINANCIAL INCENTIVES

LEARNING OBJECTIVE 5

Describe the role of financial incentives, including gainsharing, in worker motivation.

A natural way to motivate workers at any level is to offer them financial incentives for good performance. Linking pay to performance improves the motivation value of money. Using financial incentives as a motivator is an application of behavior modification. Financial incentives, however, pre-date behavior modification in the workplace. Although financial incentives are widely used as motivators, they can create problems. For example, workers may not agree with managers about the value of their contribution. Financial incentives can also pit individuals and groups against each other. The result may be unhealthy competition rather than cooperation. The paragraphs that follow will discuss the concept of linking pay to performance and describe specific applications of the concept (gainsharing and employee stock-ownership programs).

LINKING PAY TO PERFORMANCE

Financial incentives are more effective when they are linked to (or contingent) upon good performance. Linking pay to performance motivates people to work harder. Production workers and sales workers have long received contingent financial incentives. Many production workers receive, after meeting a quota, bonuses per unit of production. Most sales representatives receive salary plus commissions. Exhibit 12-7 presents a typical approach to linking employee pay to performance, a plan that is often referred to as *merit pay*. A cost-of-living adjustment is not considered merit pay because it is not related to performance.

Managers and others continue to fine-tune methods of linking pay to individual performance. A method now in use by many companies calculates base pay according to a variety of factors. Among them are ability to communicate, customer focus, dealing with change, interpersonal skills, and job knowledge. Managers are rated on employee development, team productivity, and leadership. Merit pay for both individual contributors and managers is based on actual results. Merit pay runs from 5 to over 15 percent of total compensation.

TEAM INCENTIVES. The emphasis on teamwork in organizations has led many firms to link pay to team performance as well as individual performance. Team incentives fit in between company-wide profit sharing and individual incentives. Merit

Exhibit 12-7
Guidelines for
Performance-Based
Merit Increases at
a Hospital

Performance Level of Staff Members	Merit Increase (Percentage of Pay)
Demonstrate exceptional performance and make outstanding contributions during the year	4.75–5.50
Give consistently productive performance that meets all standards and exceeds some	3.75–4.74
Give consistently productive performance that meets expectations	2.00–3.74
Demonstrate performance that is not wholly satisfactory, even though some expectations may be met or even exceeded	1.00–1.99
Generally fail to meet key expectations and standards; substantial improvement is necessary and essential	0.00

pay for team members is linked to a team goal, such as processing orders promptly. Individual contribution is evaluated with respect to how well it contributes to the team effort. For example, a team member might earn merit points for doing an exceptional job of sharing useful information.

GAINSHARING

Many organizations attempt to increase motivation and productivity through a company-wide plan of linking incentive pay to increases in performance. **Gainsharing** is a formal program of allowing employees to participate financially in the productivity gains they have achieved. Gainsharing is based on principles of positive reinforcement, and it also recognizes the motivational impact of money.

FORMAT AND PURPOSES OF GAINSHARING PLANS. Gainsharing offers a financial incentive to the work force to improve productivity. Rewards are distributed after performance improves. The work force can consist of the entire organization or a unit within the firm. Gainsharing is accomplished through establishing a payout formula and getting employees involved.

The formulas used in gainsharing vary widely, but there are common elements. Managers begin by comparing what employees are paid to what they sell or produce. Assume that labor costs make up 50 percent of production costs. Any reductions below 50 percent are placed in a bonus pool. Part of the money in the bonus pool is shared among workers. The company's share of the productivity savings in the pool can be distributed to shareholders as increased profits. The savings may allow managers to lower prices, a move that could make the company more competitive.

The second element of gainsharing is employee involvement. Managers establish a mechanism that actively solicits, reviews, and implements employee suggestions about productivity improvement. A committee of managers and employees reviews the ideas and then implements the most promising suggestions. The third key element is employee cooperation. To achieve the bonuses for productivity improvement, group members must work harmoniously with each other. Departments must also cooperate with each other, because some suggestions involve the work of more than one organizational unit.[17]

gainsharing
A formal program allowing employees to participate financially in the productivity gains they have achieved.

RESULTS OF GAINSHARING. Gainsharing plans have over a 60-year history of turning unproductive companies around and making successful companies even more productive. Lincoln Electric Co. of Cleveland, Ohio, is regularly cited as the ideal example of gainsharing. Lincoln manufactures and sells welding machines and motors. Its productivity rate is double to triple that of any other manufacturing operation that uses steel as its raw material and that has 1,000 or more employees. The company offers no paid holidays or sick days, but has a no-layoff policy.

The Lincoln gainsharing plan rewards workers for producing high-quality products efficiently while controlling costs. All employees receive a base salary, and production workers also receive piecework pay (money in relation to units produced). A year-end bonus supplements the piecework pay based on increases in profits. Bonus payments are determined by merit ratings based on output, quality, dependability, and personal characteristics (such as cooperativeness).

Production workers typically receive bonuses averaging around $20,000. Total yearly compensation for these workers, including wages, profit sharing, and bonuses averages $45,000. Lincoln Electric is consistently profitable and has paid out $500 million dollars in year-end bonuses to employees since it began its bonus program in 1934.[18]

Productivity improvements do not inevitably stem from gainsharing. Two critical factors for a successful gainsharing program are support from top management and an atmosphere of trust. In some companies, gainsharing programs have created conflict because the workers did not believe the company calculated bonuses accurately.

EMPLOYEE STOCK-OPTION PLANS

Many companies offer lower-ranking workers, as well as executives, the opportunity to purchase company stock at a reduced rate. Sometimes employees purchase stock by installments through a payroll deduction program. Employee stock-ownership programs can be motivational because employees become part-owners of the firm. If they work hard, the company may become more successful and the value of their stock increases.

Sometimes an employee stock-option plan (ESOP) is used as part of a retirement program. The assets of the plan are invested primarily in company stock. Such plans provide motivation to employees with a long-range point of view. Upon retirement, employees can choose to receive company stock instead of cash. ESOPs are also significant because they offer tax incentives to the employer. For example, a portion of company earnings paid to the retirement fund are tax deductible.

> **expectancy theory of motivation**
> *An explanation of motivation that states that people will expend effort if they expect the effort to lead to performance and the performance to lead to a reward.*

LEARNING OBJECTIVE

Explain the conditions under which a person will be motivated according to expectancy theory.

EXPECTANCY THEORY OF MOTIVATION

According to the **expectancy theory of motivation,** people will put forth the greatest effort if they expect the effort to lead to performance and the performance to lead to a reward. Expectancy theory has an advantage over need theories: It takes into account individual differences and perceptions. Expectancy theory is often preferred to behavior modification because it emphasizes the rational, or thinking, side of people.

Exhibit 12-8
Basic Version of
Expectancy Theory
of Motivation

An individual will be motivated when:

A. The individual believes effort (E) will lead to favorable performance (P)–that is, when $E \rightarrow P$ (also referred to as expectancy).

B. The individual believes performance will lead to favorable outcome (O)–that is, when $P \rightarrow O$ (also referred to as instrumentality).

C. Outcome or reward satisfies an important need (in other words, valence is strong).

D. Need satisfaction is intense enough to make effort seem worthwhile.

A BASIC MODEL OF EXPECTANCY THEORY

Expectancy theory integrates important ideas found in the other generally accepted motivation theories. Exhibit 12-8 presents a basic version of expectancy theory. According to expectancy theory, four conditions must exist for motivated behavior to occur.[19]

Condition A refers to *expectancy*, which means that people will expend effort because they believe it will lead to performance. This is called the $E \rightarrow P$ expectancy, in which subjective probabilities range between 0.0 and 1.0. Rational people ask themselves, "If I work hard, will I really get the job done?" If they evaluate the probability as being high, they probably will invest the effort to achieve the goal. People have higher $E \rightarrow P$ expectancies when they have the appropriate skills, training, and self-confidence.

Condition B is based on the fact that people are more willing to expend effort if they think that good performance will lead to a reward. This is referred to as $P \rightarrow O$ instrumentality, and it too ranges between 0.0 and 1.0. (*Instrumentality* refers to the idea that the behavior is instrumental in achieving an important end.) The rational person says, "I'm much more willing to perform well if I'm assured that I'll receive the reward I deserve." A cautious employee might even ask other employees if they received their promised rewards for exceptional performance. To strengthen a subordinate's $P \rightarrow O$ instrumentality, the manager should give reassurance that the reward will be forthcoming.

Condition C refers to *valence*, the value a person attaches to certain outcomes. The greater the valence, the greater the effort. Valences can be either positive or negative. If a student believes that receiving an A is very important, he or she will work very hard. Also, if a student believes that avoiding a C or a lower grade is very important, he or she will work hard. Valences range from −1 to +1 in most versions of expectancy theory. A positive valence indicates a preference for a particular reward. A clearer picture of individual differences in human motivation spreads valences out over a range of −1,000 to +1,000.

Most work situations present the possibility of several outcomes, with a different valence attached to each. Assume that a purchasing manager is pondering whether becoming a certified purchasing manager (CPM) would be worth the effort. The list that follows cites possible outcomes or rewards from achieving certification, along with their valences (on a scale of −1,000 to +1,000).

- Status from being a CPM, 750
- Promotion to purchasing manager, 950

- Plaque to hang on office wall, 250
- Bigger salary increase next year, 900
- Letters of congratulations from friends and relatives, 500
- Expressions of envy from one or two coworkers, −250

Valences are useful in explaining why some people will put forth the effort to do things with very low expectancies. For example, most people know there is only one chance in a million of winning a lottery, becoming a rock star, or writing a best-selling novel. Nevertheless, a number of people vigorously pursue these goals. They do so because they attach an extraordinary positive valence to these outcomes (perhaps 1,000!).

Condition D indicates that the need satisfaction stemming from each outcome must be intense enough to make the effort worthwhile. Would you walk 2 miles on a very hot day for one glass of ice water? The water would undoubtedly satisfy your thirst need, but the magnitude of the satisfaction would probably not be worth the effort. Similarly, an operative employee turned down a promotion to the position of inspector because the raise offered was only 50 cents per hour. The worker told his supervisor, "I need more money. But I'm not willing to take on that much added responsibility for twenty dollars a week."

IMPLICATIONS FOR MANAGEMENT AND EVALUATION

Expectancy theory has several important implications for the effective management of people. The theory helps pinpoint what a manager must do to motivate subordinates:[20]

1. *Individual differences among employees must be taken into account.* Different people attach different valences to different rewards, so a manager should try to match rewards with individual preferences. Behavior modification also makes use of this principle.
2. *Rewards should be closely tied to those actions the organization sees as worthwhile.* For example, if the organization values quality, people should be rewarded for producing high-quality work.
3. *Employees should be given the appropriate training and encouragement.* This will strengthen their subjective hunches that effort will lead to good performance.
4. *Employees should be presented with credible evidence that good performance does lead to anticipated rewards.* Similarly, a manager should reassure employees that good work will be both noticed and rewarded. As part of this implication, managers must listen carefully to understand the perceived link employees have between hard work and rewards. If instrumentality is unjustifiably low, the manager must reassure the employee that hard work will be rewarded.
5. *The meaning and implications of outcomes should be explained.* It can be motivational for employees to know the values of certain outcomes. If an employee who is interested in working on a special task force knows that assignment to the task force is linked to successful completion of a project, the employee will give special attention to the project.

Expectancy theory has not been widely applied in complete form. However, many managers and others who apply the theory find it useful. Walter B. Newsom has found that managers exposed to expectancy theory find it to be a powerful diagnostic tool in determining why team members have or have not been motivated.[21]

SUMMARY OF KEY POINTS

1

Explain the relationship between motivation and performance.

From the standpoint of the individual, motivation is an internal state that leads to the pursuit of objectives. From the standpoint of the manager, motivation is an activity that gets subordinates to pursue objectives. The purpose of motivating employees is to get them to achieve results. Motivation is but one important contributor to productivity and performance. Other important contributors are abilities, skills, technology, and group norms.

2

Present an overview of major theories of need satisfaction in explaining motivation.

Workers can be motivated through need satisfaction, particularly because most people want to know "What's in it for me?" First, needs must be identified. Second, the person must be given an opportunity to satisfy those needs.

Maslow's need hierarchy states that people strive to become self-actualized. However, before higher-level needs are activated, certain lower-level needs must be satisfied. When a person's needs are satisfied at one level, he or she looks toward satisfaction at a higher level. Specific needs playing an important role in work motivation include achievement, power, affiliation, and recognition.

The two-factor theory of work motivation contends that there are two different sets of job-motivation factors. One set gives people a chance to satisfy higher-level needs. These are satisfiers and motivators. When present, they increase satisfaction and motivation. When satisfiers and motivators are absent, the impact is neutral. Satisfiers and motivators generally relate to the content of a job. They include achievement, recognition, and opportunity for advancement. Dissatisfiers are job elements that appeal more to lower-level needs. When they are present, they prevent dissatisfaction, but they do not create satisfaction or motivation. Dissatisfiers relate mostly to the context of a job. They include company policy and administration, job security, and money.

3

Explain how goal setting is used to motivate people.

Goal setting is an important part of most motivational programs, and it is a managerial method of motivating subordinates. It is based on these ideas: (a) specific goals are better than generalized goals; (b) the more difficult the goal, the better the performance; (c) only goals that are accepted improve performance; (d) goals are more effective when used to evaluate performance; (e) goals should be linked to feedback and rewards; and (f) group goal setting is important.

4

Describe the application of behavior modification to worker motivation.

Behavior modification is the most systematic method of motivating people. It changes behavior by rewarding the right responses and punishing or ignoring the wrong ones. Behavior modification is based on the law of effect: Behavior that leads to positive consequences tends to be repeated, and behavior that leads to negative consequences tends not to be repeated.

There are four behavior modification strategies. Positive reinforcement rewards people for making the right response. Negative reinforcement, or avoidance motivation, rewards people by taking away an uncomfortable consequence. Extinction is the process of weakening undesirable behavior by removing the reward for it. Punishment is the presentation of an undesirable consequence for a specific behavior. Punishment is often counterproductive. If used appropriately, however, it can be motivational.

Suggestions for the informal use of positive reinforcement in a work setting include: (a) focus on the positive, (b) state clearly what behavior leads to a reward, (c) use appropriate rewards, (d) make rewards contingent on good performance, and (e) change rewards periodically.

5

Describe the role of financial incentives, including gainsharing, in worker motivation.

A natural way to motivate workers at any level is to offer financial incentives for good performance. Linking pay to performance improves the motivational value of financial incentives. Pay linked to performance is referred to as merit pay. To encourage teamwork, many firms are offering team incentives as supplements to individual incentives.

Gainsharing is a formal program that allows employees to participate financially in the productivity gains they have achieved. It can be a motivational program. Bonuses are distributed to employees based on how much they decrease the labor cost involved in producing or selling goods. Employee involvement in increasing productivity is an important part of gainsharing.

Employee stock-ownership plans set aside a block of company stock for employees to purchase at a reduced price. The expectation is that the plan will motivate the employees to work harder because improved company performance may elevate the stock price.

6

Explain the conditions under which a person will be motivated according to expectancy theory.

Expectancy theory contends that people will expend effort if they expect the effort to lead to performance and

the performance to lead to a reward. According to the expectancy model presented here, a person will be motivated if the person believes effort will lead to performance, the performance will lead to a reward, the reward satisfies an important need, and the need satisfaction is intense enough to make the effort seem worthwhile.

KEY TERMS AND PHRASES

Motivation *pg. 266*
$P = M \times A$ *pg. 267*
Need *pg. 267*
Maslow's Need Hierarchy *pg. 268*
Deficiency Needs *pg. 268*
Growth Needs *pg. 268*
Affiliation Need *pg. 269*

Recognition Need *pg. 270*
Two-Factor Theory of Work Motivation *pg. 270*
Behavior Modification *pg. 274*
Law of Effect *pg. 274*
Gainsharing *pg. 279*
Expectancy Theory of Motivation *pg. 280*

QUESTIONS

1. What information does this chapter have to offer the manager who is already working with a well-motivated team?
2. It is usually difficult to get workers to concentrate on a management presentation when the talk runs past mealtime. How would you explain this problem, using the need hierarchy?
3. What needs are likely to be satisfied by operating a small business?
4. How might students apply goal theory to themselves to achieve greater success in school?
5. What techniques does the instructor in this class use to motivate students?
6. Identify two occupations in which you think intrinsic (internal) motivation would be particularly high.
7. How might SuperLeadership (discussed in Chapter 11) relate to effort to performance expectancies ($E \to P$)?

SKILL-BUILDING EXERCISE 12-A: MY APPROACH TO MOTIVATING OTHERS[22]

Describe how often you act or think in the way indicated by the statements below when you are attempting to motivate another person. Use the following scale: very infre-

quently (VI); infrequently (I); sometimes (S); frequently (F); very frequently (VF).

	VI	I	S	F	VF
1. I ask the other person what he or she is hoping to achieve in the situation.	1	2	3	4	5
2. I attempt to figure out if the person has the ability to do what I need done.	1	2	3	4	5
3. When another person is heel-dragging, it usually means he or she is lazy.	5	4	3	2	1
4. I tell the person I'm trying to motivate exactly what I want.	1	2	3	4	5
5. I like to give the other person a reward up front so he or she will be motivated.	5	4	3	2	1
6. I give lots of feedback when another person is performing a task for me.	1	2	3	4	5
7. I like to belittle another person enough so that he or she will be intimidated into doing what I need done.	5	4	3	2	1
8. I make sure that the other person feels treated fairly.	1	2	3	4	5
9. I figure that if I smile nicely enough I can get the other person to work as hard as I need.	5	4	3	2	1
10. I attempt to get what I need done by instilling fear in the other person.	5	4	3	2	1

	VI	I	S	F	VF
11. I specify exactly what needs to be accomplished.	1	2	3	4	5
12. I generously praise people who help me get my work accomplished.	1	2	3	4	5
13. A job well done is its own reward. I therefore keep praise to a minimum.	5	4	3	2	1
14. I make sure to let people know how well they have done in meeting my expectations on a task.	1	2	3	4	5
15. To be fair, I attempt to reward people about the same no matter how well they have performed.	5	4	3	2	1
16. When somebody doing work for me performs well, I recognize his or her accomplishments promptly.	1	2	3	4	5
17. Before giving somebody a reward, I attempt to find out what would appeal to that person.	1	2	3	4	5
18. I make it a policy not to thank somebody for doing a job he or she is paid to do.	5	4	3	2	1
19. If people do not know how to perform a task, their motivation will suffer.	1	2	3	4	5
20. If properly designed, many jobs can be self-rewarding.	1	2	3	4	5

Total Score _____

Scoring and interpretation: Add the numbers circled to obtain your total score.

90–100   You have advanced knowledge and skill with respect to motivating others in a work environment. Continue to build on the solid base you have established.

50–89   You have average knowledge and skill with respect to motivating others. With additional study and experience, you will probably develop advanced motivational skills.

20–49   To effectively motivate others in a work environment, you will need to greatly expand your knowledge of motivation theory and techniques.

SKILL-BUILDING EXERCISE 12-B: BEHAVIOR MODIFICATION

GROUP ACTIVITY In both the following scenarios, one student plays the role of the manager attempting to modify the behavior of (motivate) the other individual. Another student plays the role of the recipient of these attempts at motivation.

SCENARIO 1: REWARDING A CUSTOMER-SERVICE REPRESENTATIVE.

The customer-service manager reviews customer-service reports to discover that one service rep has resolved the most complaints for four consecutive weeks. Since this rep has only been on the job for six months, the manager wants to ensure that the rep feels amply rewarded and appreciated. The manager also wants to sustain this high level of performance. The manager calls the rep into the office to discuss this outstanding performance and to administer an appropriate reward.

SCENARIO 2: PUNISHING A CUSTOMER-SERVICE REPRESENTATIVE.

The customer-service manager reviews customer-service reports and discovers that one service rep has resolved the fewest complaints for four consecutive weeks. Furthermore, three customers have written the company complaining of rude treatment by this representative. Since this rep has only been on the job six months, the manager wants to make sure that the rep makes substantial improvements. The manager calls the rep into the office to discuss this poor performance and to administer the appropriate punishment.

Other class members observe the two scenarios so they can provide feedback on how well behavior modification principles were applied.

VIDEO DISCUSSION QUESTIONS

1. How might 360-degree evaluation be used to motivate workers? **[360 Degrees of Evaluation]**
2. How does downsizing affect motivation? **[Morale Crisis]**
3. What were the key motivators for the team investigating the gas tank leak at Union Carbide, Bhopal? **[Bhopal]**

CASE PROBLEM 12-A: THE FORMULA 409 CASES

Wilson Harrell is the former president of the company that manufactured Formula 409, the spray cleaner. He is now a consultant and speaker to entrepreneurial businesspeople. Harrell recalls how Formula 409 was competing profitably against spray cleaners made by industry giants such as Proctor & Gamble and Colgate.

From the beginning, Harrell had employed a simple incentive plan based on case sales. Each month, every sales representative and manager received a bonus check based on the number of cases of 409 he or she sold. Bonuses for the the support staff were also based on monthly case sales. Harrell recalls, "It was a happy time, with everyone making a lot of money, including me."

Yet as the company grew toward becoming a large company, Harrell looked critically at his compensation plan. He attended seminars and read business books with the intent of learning how to run his company more effectively. Harrell also hired a business consultant.

The consultant was horrified at Harrell's incentive plan, especially at how much money so many employees were making. He explained how dangerous it was to pay bonuses before year-end profits could be accurately predicted. The consultant recommended that Harrell abandon the monthly case-sales bonus plan, and institute an annual profit-sharing plan based on performance appraisals.

Harrell studied the recommendations about revamping the sales-incentive plan. He decided to make the switch despite some reluctance about abandoning an incentive system that was working well.

CASE QUESTIONS

1. What effect do you think the new sales-incentive plan had on productivity, morale, and turnover?
2. What principles of behavior modification might be violated by the new incentive plan?
3. Why might money be a key motivator for people selling cases of spray cleaner?

Source: Based on information reported in Wilson Harrell, "Inspire Action: What Really Motivates Your People to Excel?" *Success* (September 1995): 100.

CASE PROBLEM 12-B: MOTIVATING THE WILD DUCKS

Carol Dudick is the manager of technology commercialization at Battelle Pacific Northwest Laboratory in Richland, Washington. Her attitudes about work motivation are somewhat influenced by the ideas of Thomas Watson, the founder of IBM. He uses the term "wild ducks" to refer to creative professionals such as engineers, software developers, and researchers. As Watson saw it, wild ducks are not motivated by traditional incentives such as the promise of a promotion. Instead, they want the freedom to innovate, and recognition for their scientific breakthroughs.

Several years ago, Battelle Pacific Northwest was looking to install a motivation program for professional employees involved in both government-sponsored research and private research projects. The need for the program arose partly because of a government mandate. An even more decisive factor was that Battelle managers wanted staff professionals to work harder at transferring technology to private clients.

When Battelle researchers develop technologies that are licensed for use by private industry, the laboratory benefits enormously. Battelle receives licensing fees for that technology, as well as royalties on products manufactured using the technology.

Dudick worked with the human resource professionals at her laboratory and other managers to design a motivation program for the scientists at Battelle. As she began to design the program, the wild duck metaphor figured heavily into her thinking. She also recognized that scientists, like everybody else, have bills to pay. Furthermore, she thought to herself, "Even wild ducks have bills!"

CASE QUESTIONS

1. What type of motivation program do you think Battelle designed to increase the technology transfer?
2. Which two explanations of motivation presented in this chapter best apply to this motivational situation?
3. To what extent do you think a special program was necessary to motivate the Battelle staff professionals?

Source: Based on information in Shari Caudron, "Motivating Creative Employees Calls for New Strategies," *Personnel Journal* (May 1994): 103–104.

CASE PROBLEM 12-C: THE INCENTIVE HASSLE

Pat Lancaster founded Lantech in 1972. The company manufactures machines for wrapping large bundles of products, such as breakfast cereal, in plastic film for shipment to retailers. Today the company has 325 employees and annual sales of about $65 million.

Lancaster was among the pioneers in company-wide incentive pay. During the mid-1970s, Lantech employees were requested to evaluate one another's job performance. Bonuses were distributed according to workers' scores on these evaluations. The program created so much tension that it was disbanded. Faced with tough competition in the 1980s, Lancaster was determined to make incentive pay work. He also implemented other modern management practices such as just-in-time inventory.

At one time, each of Lantech's five manufacturing divisions was given a bonus based on how much profit it made. A worker could receive a bonus up to as much as 10 percent of base pay. The interdependence of the divisions, however, made it difficult to assess an equitable share for each division. "That led to so much secrecy, politicking, and sucking noise you wouldn't believe it," says CEO Jim Lancaster, the 29-year old son of chairman Pat Lancaster.

An example of interdependency is between the division that manufactures standard machines and the one that adds custom design features to them. The two divisions depend on each other for parts, engineering expertise, and scheduling. The two groups entered into conflict, each one attempting to assign costs to the other and claim credit for revenues.

Pat Lancaster recalls, "By the early 1990s I was spending 95 percent of my time on conflict resolution instead of on how to serve our customers." The divisions argued so long over who would be charged for overhead cranes to haul heavy equipment that their installation was delayed two years. At the end of each month, the divisions would scurry to fill orders from other divisions in the company. As a result, the division that filled the order would earn a profit, but the recipient of the orders was left with piles of unnecessary and costly inventory.

Some employees even argued over who should have to pay for paper toweling in the common restrooms. One employee suggested that employees from another division had dirtier jobs so they should absorb more of the costs for hand soap.

Pat Lancaster concluded, "Incentive pay is toxic because it is open to favoritism and manipulation." As a consequence, Lantech has abandoned individual and division performance pay. Instead it relies on a profit-sharing system in which all employees receive bonuses based on salary. Much of the anger has subsided, and the company is prospering. However, bonuses are still paid to executives and sales representatives.

CASE QUESTIONS

1. What mistakes did Lantech make in designing and implementing the company incentive system?
2. Has Lantech really abandoned incentive pay for all workers?
3. Should the company continue its incentive program for executives and sales personnel?

Source: Based on facts reported in Peter Nulty, "Incentive Pay Can Be Crippling," *Fortune* (13 November 1995): 235.

CASE PROBLEM 12-D: FINDING A SUCCESS FORMULA AT MONSANTO, LULING

Luling, Louisiana, may not appear to be a likely spot for a workplace revolution. The town is located on a back road between New Orleans and Baton Rouge. Yet a Monsanto Co. chemical plant in Luling is a testing ground for a strategic change in the way workers are compensated.

At the modest-sized Luling plant, managers have been struggling to find ways to link employee pay to a meaningful measure of company success. The first attempt was to tie employee bonuses to plant safety.

Yet management backed off when they thought about the negative side effects of this tactic. Workers might cover up accidents just to receive their bonus. The next version of a revised compensation plan was to link pay to the plant's overall success. Workers intensely disliked that pay scheme. Many of the workers expressed this sentiment: "This bonus system has a built-in problem. We have no control over what's happening in someone else's product line. If they mess up, we get penalized."

After eight years of false starts and potentially hazardous turns, plant management thinks they have found the right pay system to boost productivity. A small part of the compensation system is to reward workers for helping to prevent accidents. One such method would be to reward workers who have attended accident-prevention training programs.

The final plan retains up to 95 percent of worker's base pay. The other 5 to 10 percent is variable pay. After about one year with the program, Luling plant manager Tony L. Corley says, "We've gotten back everything we've paid for."

CASE QUESTIONS

1. Based on your knowledge of motivational programs, what do you think was the basis for the 5 to 10 percent bonus?

2. What technique other than bonuses might the managers at Luling have used to motivate workers?

3. What is your evaluation of the concern that workers would cover up accidents just to receive a higher bonus?

Source: Based on information in "Bonus Pay: Buzzword or Bonanza?" *Business Week* (14 November 1994): 62.

REFERENCES

1. Based on facts reported in "IBM Leans On Its Sales Force," *Business Week* (7 February 1994); "Bare Knuckles at Big Blue," *Business Week* (26 December 1994): 60.

2. Ruth Kanfer and Philip L. Ackerman, "Motivation and Cognitive Abilities: An Integrative/Aptitude-Treatment Interaction Approach to Skill Acquisition," *Journal of Applied Psychology* (August 1989): 657.

3. Abraham Maslow, "A Theory of Human Motivation," *Psychological Review* (July 1943): 370–396; Maslow, *Motivation and Personality* (New York: Harper & Row, 1954): Chapter 5.

4. Michael J. Stahl, "Achievement, Power, and Managerial Motivation: Selecting Managerial Talent with the Job Choice Exercise," *Personnel Psychology* (Winter 1983): 775–789; David C. McClelland, *Power: The Inner Experience* (New York: Irvington, 1975).

5. Minda Zetlin, "Older & Wiser: Tips to Motivate the 50s Crowd," *Management Review* (August 1992): 31.

6. Frederick Herzberg, *Work and the Nature of Man* (Cleveland: World, 1966).

7. Edwin A. Locke and Gary P. Latham, *A Theory of Goal Setting & Task Performance* (Englewood Cliffs, NJ: Prentice Hall, 1990).

8. Patrick M. Wright et al., "On the Meaning and Measurement of Goal Commitment," *Journal of Applied Psychology* (December 1994): 795.

9. F. Christopher Earley et al., "Impact of Process and Outcome Feedback on the Relation of Goal Setting to Task Performance," *Academy of Management Journal* (March 1990): 87–105.

10. P. Christopher Earley and Terri R. Lituchy, "Delineating Goal and Efficacy Effects: A Test of Three Models," *Journal of Applied Psychology* (February 1991): 83.

11. Linda Klebe Trevino, "The Social Effects of Punishment in Organizations: A Justice Perspective," *Academy of Management Review* (October 1992): 667.

12. For more information on this topic, *see* Richard L. Bunning, "Rewarding a Job Well Done," *Personnel Administrator* (January 1989): 60–64.

13. W. E. Scott, Jr., and P. M. Podaskoff, *Behavioral Principles in the Practice of Management* (New York: Wiley, 1985).

14. Dianne H. B. Welsh, Fred Luthans, and Steven M. Sommer, "Managing Russian Factory Workers: The Impact of U.S.-Based Behavioral and Participative Techniques," *Academy of Management Journal* (February 1993): 58–79.

15. Wayne Dierks and Kathleen A. McNally, "Incentives You Can Bank On," *Personnel Administrator* (March 1987): 61–65.

16. Alfie Kohn, "Why Incentive Plans Cannot Work," *Harvard Business Review* (September–October 1993): 54–63.

17. Susan C. Hanlon, David C. Meyer, and Robert R. Taylor, "Consequences of Gainsharing: A Field Experiment Revisited," *Group and Organizational Management*, 19 (1), 1994: 87–111.

18. Carolyn Wiley, "Incentive Plan Pushes Production," *Personnel Journal* (August 1993): 86–91.

19. The original explanation of expectancy theory as applied to work motivation is from Victor H. Vroom, *Work and Motivation* (New York: Wiley, 1964). A more recent synthesis is Henry L. Tosi, John R. Rizzo, and Stephen J. Carroll, *Managing Organizational Behavior* (Marshfield, MA: Pitman, 1986): 240–246.

20. Several ideas are from Robert Kreitner, *Management*, 5e (Boston: Houghton Mifflin, 1992): 390–391.

21. Walter B. Newsom, "Motivate, Now!" *Personnel Journal* (February 1990): 51–52.

22. The idea for this quiz, along with a few items, are from David A. Whetton and Kim S. Cameron, *Developing Management Skills*, 2e (New York: HarperCollins, 1991): 336–337.

CHAPTER 13

Communication

LEARNING OBJECTIVES
After studying this chapter and doing the exercises, you should be able to:

1
Describe the steps in the communication process.

2
Recognize the major types of nonverbal communication in the workplace.

3
Explain and illustrate the difference between formal and informal communication channels.

4
Identify major communication barriers in organizations.

5
Develop tactics for overcoming communication barriers.

6
Describe how to conduct more effective meetings.

© Steven Peters/Tony Stone Images

BP Exploration (BPX), a division of British Petroleum, has developed a formal system for letting managers know what group members think of them. The upward feedback process begins with managers distributing a questionnaire describing 23 management practices to group members. Certain other people with whom the managers interact also receive the questionnaires. A typical management practice described would be "meets frequently with employees to review their individual performance." • All respondents rate the manager on each item. The subordinates anonymously enter the completed questionnaire onto an on-line computer system. The system collates, summarizes, and sends the report to managers via E-mail. The manager has the option of discussing the feedback with a trained observer. The discussion helps prepare the manager for the next step in the process—a feedback meeting between the manager and his or her staff. At the meeting, the manager and staff discuss areas of their relationship that might need improvement.[1]

The upward feedback system at BPX illustrates the serious attention successful companies pay to communication in the workplace. So vital is communication that it has been described as the glue that holds the organization together. Poor communication is the number one problem in virtually all organizations and the cause of most problems. Communication problems can be immensely expensive. John O. Whitney says, "I have, as a manager or consultant in business turnarounds, observed losses totalling more than $1 billion in organizations where people, early in the game, either knew absolutely or had strong premonitions about the problem, but were intimidated, squelched, or ignored."[2]

Communication is an integral part of all managerial functions. Unless managers communicate with others, they cannot plan, organize, control, or lead. For example, a manager cannot communicate a vision without superior communication skills. Person-to-person communication is as much a part of managerial, professional, technical, and sales work as running is a part of basketball and tennis. Furthermore, the ability to communicate effectively is closely related to career advancement. Employees who are poor communicators are often bypassed for promotion, particularly if the job includes people contact.

The information in this chapter is designed to improve communication among people in the workplace. Two approaches are used to achieve this end. First the chapter will describe key aspects of organizational communication, including communication channels and barriers. Second, the chapter presents many suggestions about how managers and others can overcome communication barriers and conduct effective meetings.

THE COMMUNICATION PROCESS

LEARNING OBJECTIVE 1

Describe the steps in the communication process.

communication
The process of exchanging information by the use of words, letters, symbols, or nonverbal behavior.

Anytime people send information back and forth to each other they are communicating. **Communication** is the process of exchanging information by the use of words, letters, symbols, or nonverbal behavior. Sending messages to other people, and having the messages interpreted as intended, is both complex and difficult. A major part of the problem is that communication is dependent on perception. People may perceive words, symbols, actions, and even colors differently, depending on their background and interests.

A typical communication snafu took place at quality-improvement meeting. The supervisor said to a technician, "Quality is in the eye of the beholder." The technician responded, "Oh, how interesting." Later the technician told the rest of the team, "It's no use striving for high quality. The boss thinks quality is too subjective to achieve." The message the supervisor was trying to communicate is that the consumer is the final judge of quality.

STEPS IN THE COMMUNICATION PROCESS

Exhibit 13-1 illustrates the complexity of the communication process. This diagram is a simplification of the baffling process of sending and receiving messages. The theme of the model is that two-way communication involves major steps and that each step is subject to interference, or noise. The four steps are: encoding, transmission, decoding, and feedback.

encoding
The process of organizing ideas into a series of symbols designed to communicate with the receiver.

ENCODING THE MESSAGE. Encoding is the process of organizing ideas into a series of symbols, such as words and gestures, designed to communicate with the receiver. Word choice has a strong influence on communication effectiveness. The

Exhibit 13-1
The Communication
Process

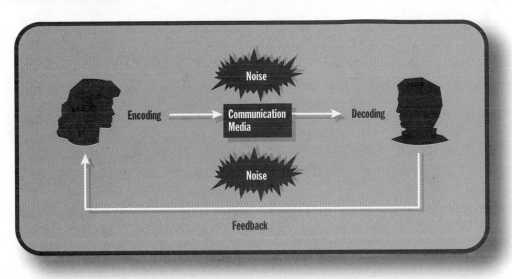

better a person's grasp of language, the easier it is for him or her to encode. If the choice of words or any other symbol is appropriate, the better the chance that communication will proceed smoothly. The supervisor mentioned at the beginning of this section chose to use the somewhat vague phrase, "Quality is in the eye of the beholder." A more effective message would have been: "Quality is measured by customer acceptance."

COMMUNICATION MEDIA. The message is sent via a communication medium, such as voice, telephone, paper, or electronic mail. It is important to select a medium that fits the message. It would be appropriate to use the spoken word to inform a coworker that his shirt was torn. It would be inappropriate to send the same message over an electronic bulletin board. Many messages in organizations are sent nonverbally, through the use of gestures and facial expressions. For example, a smile from a superior in a meeting is an effective way of communicating the message "I agree with your comment." Exhibit 13-2 presents additional ideas about choosing the best medium for your message.

DECODING THE MESSAGE. In **decoding,** the receiver interprets the message and translates it into meaningful information. Barriers to communication are most likely to surface at the decoding step. People often interpret messages according to their psychological needs and motives. The technician mentioned earlier may have been looking for an out—a reason not to be so concerned about achieving high standards. So he interpreted the message in a way that minimized the need to strive for quality.

> **decoding**
> *The communication stage in which the receiver interprets the message and translates it into meaningful information.*

After understanding comes action—the receiver does something about the message. If the receiver acts in the manner the sender wants, the communication has been totally successful. From the manager's perspective, the success of a message is measured in terms of the action taken by a subordinate. Understanding alone is not sufficient. Many people understand messages but take no constructive action.

FEEDBACK. Messages sent back from the receiver to the sender are referred to as *feedback*. Without feedback it is difficult to know whether a message has been received and understood. The feedback step also includes the reactions of the receiver. If the receiver takes actions as intended by the sender, the message has been received satisfactorily.

Several options exist for communicating an important message on the job. Before choosing an option, think of its major pros and cons.

Quick Telephone Call: On the positive side, a quick call is efficient. It is personal, informal, and allows for an exchange of ideas. A disadvantage is that phone calls are intrusive. You are asking the recipient to stop what he or she is doing, and the person may feel pressured into giving you an immediate response.

Face-to-Face Meeting: On the positive side, visiting a person at his or her work area can get a problem resolved quickly. On the negative side, you can annoy people by dropping by without an appointment. Making an appointment can also be disturbing because the person has to place you on his or her schedule. Dropping in on a high-ranking person may be unwelcome in a hierarchical organization.

E-mail: Sending a message by E-mail is excellent for wide distribution, and you will have a permanent record of your message. Your receiver also has control over when to receive the message. A negative is that the tone of an E-mail message can be misinterpreted. Remember too, that once you hit the send button it is too late to change your mind. Also, with so many people sending E-mail, your message might get overlooked.

Hard-Copy Memo: Paper memos appear quite official, and are a standard part of organizational communications. You are also more likely to carefully compose and edit a hard-copy memo than an electronic one. Written memos, however, may appear stiff, and some people will misplace a written memo before or after reading it. If your firm makes extensive use of E-mail, a paper memo will appear out of date.

Scheduled Meeting: If you schedule a meeting, you are in charge and you will be able to interact with several people about your issue. Holding a meeting dramatizes the importance of the topic. A disadvantage of a meeting is that some participants will be annoyed if the topic does not appear substantial enough to justify calling a meeting.

Source: Based on ideas from "The Right Medium for Your Message," *Working Smart* (January 1995): 5.

**Exhibit 13-2
Choosing the Right
Medium for Your
Message**

Action is a form of feedback, because it results in a message being sent back to the original sender from the receiver. Suppose a small-business owner receives this message from a supplier: "Please send us $450 within 10 days to cover your overdue account. If we do not receive payment within 10 days, your account will be turned over to a collection agent." The owner understands the message but decides not to comply, because the parts for which the $450 is owed were defective. The owner's noncompliance is not due to a lack of understanding.

noise
In communication, unwanted interference that can distort or block a message.

Many missteps can occur between encoding and decoding a message. **Noise**, or unwanted interference, can distort or block the message. Later in the chapter the discussion of communication barriers will examine the problem of noise and how it prevents the smooth flow of ideas between sender and receiver.

LEARNING OBJECTIVE

Recognize the major types of nonverbal communication in the workplace.

NONVERBAL COMMUNICATION IN ORGANIZATIONS

The most obvious modes of communication are speaking, writing, and sign language. (Many large business meetings today include an interpreter who *signs* for deaf members of the audience.) A substantial amount of interpersonal communication also occurs through **nonverbal communication**, the transmission of messages by means other than words. Body language refers to those aspects of nonverbal communication directly related to movements of the body such as gestures and posture.

nonverbal communication
The transmission of messages by means other than words.

Nonverbal communication usually supplements rather than substitutes for writing, speaking, and sign language. The general purpose of nonverbal communication is to express the feeling behind a message, such as shaking one's head vigorously to indicate an emphatic "yes." Nonverbal communication incorporates a wide range of behavior. Nevertheless, it can be divided into the following eight categories.[3]

A good voice alone will not make a businessperson successful. Yet, like clothing, voice quality should always add to a person's image, not subtract from it. Here are several practical suggestions, developed by voice coaches, for improving voice quality:

- **Avoid having a nasal-sounding voice.** The only sounds that should come through the nose are the sounds of *m*, *n*, and *ng*. The rest of speech should be sounded in the mouth. There's an easy test to see if you talk through your nose: Say "that." Now, pinch your nose and say "that" again. There should be no difference. If you sound like a duck when you pinch your nose and say "that," then you have a nasal voice. To solve this problem, throw open your mouth and repeat "that" as you yawn. This will bring the vowel down into your mouth. With practice, you will sound the vowels in your mouth and lose the nasal tone.
- **Vary your tone.** If you speak in a monotone, your voice will sound mechanical. One way to overcome a monotone is to practice singing several of your typical presentations. This will help you develop skill in using vocal variety.
- **Decrease voice hesitations.** Vocal hesitations are a nonverbal clue to weakness and insecurity. When you hesitate between words, people may think you have not thought through your comments. This problem can be solved by slowing down your speech.
- **Avoid breathiness.** People who take a breath after almost every word appear anxious. To remedy breathiness, take the time to fill your lungs with air before speaking. Practice until you can speak two sentences without taking a breath.
- **Practice conveying commitment in the sound of your voice.** Tape yourself as you talk extemporaneously about a topic you care about, such as describing your fantasy goals in life. Replaying the tape, you will hear your voice move up and down the musical scale. The emotion shown reflects commitment.

Source: Based on information in Charles Livingston McCain, "Say it in the Voice of Authority," *Success* (May 1984): 48, 51; and Roger Ailes and Jon Kraushar, "Are You a Communications Wimp?" *Business Week Careers* (June 1988): 76.

**Exhibit 13-3
How to Speak with an
Authoritative Voice**

1. *Environment.* The physical setting in which the message takes place communicates meaning. Included here would be office decor, type of automobile, and the restaurant or hotel chosen for a business meeting. What kind of message would you send to people if you drove to work in a Chevy Tahoe or a Land Rover?
2. *Body placement.* The placement of one's body in relation to someone else is widely used to transmit messages. Facing a person in a casual, relaxed style indicates acceptance. Moving close to another person is also a general indicator of acceptance. Yet moving too close may be perceived as a violation of personal space, and the message sender will be rejected.
3. *Posture.* Another widely used clue to a person's attitude is his or her posture. Leaning toward another person suggests a favorable attitude toward the message that person is trying to communicate. Leaning backward communicates the opposite. Standing up straight is generally interpreted as an indicator of self-confidence, while slouching is usually a sign of low self-confidence.
4. *Hand gestures.* Included here are gestures of the hand such as frequent movements to express approval and palms spread outward to indicate perplexity.
5. *Facial expressions and movement.* The particular look on a person's face and movements of the person's head provide reliable cues as to approval, disapproval, or disbelief.
6. *Voice quality.* Aspects of the voice such as pitch, volume, tone, and speech rate may communicate confidence, nervousness, and enthusiasm. Intelligence is often judged by how people sound. Research suggests that the most annoying voice quality is a whining, complaining, or nagging tone.[4] Exhibit 13-3 provides some suggestions for developing impressive voice quality.
7. *Clothing, dress, and appearance.* The image a person conveys communicates such messages as "I feel powerful" and "I think this meeting is important." For example, wearing one's best business attire to a performance appraisal interview

MANAGER IN ACTION: INTERPRETING BODY LANGUAGE

Sandra Johnson, an operations manager, was asked by the recruiting manager why she was leaving her current position. Without hesitation Johnson replied, "Growth opportunities are limited." Not satisfied with that response, the interviewer continued to probe until Johnson finally acknowledged that a disagreement with the operations vice-president over departmental procedures triggered her resignation.

After the interview, Johnson wondered what she had said that prompted the interviewer to pursue the issue. What Johnson didn't realize is that her body language was a tipoff that she was being less than forthright. Up until that moment in the interview, Johnson was sitting with her right leg crossed over her left leg, hands resting in her lap, eyes focused directly at the interviewer's face. When the question about leaving her present position surfaced, without conscious awareness, Johnson shifted slightly in her seat, crossed her left leg over her right, leaned forward slightly, and placed her hands on the desk in front of her. Changes in her body language were enough to suggest to the savvy interviewer that she was not being completely honest.

Source: "The Importance of Body Language," *HRfocus* (June 1995): 22.

would communicate that the person thinks the meeting is important. Another important meaning of dress is that it communicates how willing the employee is to comply with organizational standards. By deviating too radically from standard, such as wearing a suit on "Dress Down" day, the person communicates indifference. As two researchers note, "Employees failing to maintain dress standards suffer consequences that range from insults and ridicule to termination."[5]

8. *Mirroring.* To mirror is to build rapport with another person by imitating his or her voice tone, breathing rate, body movement, and language. Mirroring relies 10 percent on verbal means, 60 percent on voice tone, and 10 percent on body physiology. A specific application of mirroring is to conform to the other person's posture, eye movements, and hand movements. The person feels more relaxed as a result of your imitation.

Keep in mind that many nonverbal signals are ambiguous. For example, a smile usually indicates agreement and warmth, but at times it can indicate nervousness. Even if nonverbal signals are not highly reliable, they are used to judge your behavior as illustrated in the accompanying Manager in Action.

LEARNING OBJECTIVE

Explain and illustrate the difference between formal and informal communication channels.

formal communication channels
The official pathways for sending information inside and outside an organization.

ORGANIZATIONAL CHANNELS AND DIRECTIONS OF COMMUNICATION

Messages in organizations travel over many different channels, or paths. Communication channels can be formal or informal and be categorized as downward, upward, horizontal, or diagonal.

FORMAL COMMUNICATION CHANNELS

Formal communication channels are the official pathways for sending information inside and outside an organization. The primary source of information about formal channels is the organization chart. It indicates the channels messages are supposed to follow. By carefully following the organization chart, a maintenance technician would know how to transmit a message to the chairman of the board. In many large organizations, the worker may have to go through eight management or organizational levels. Modern organizations, however, make it easier for lower-ranking workers to communicate with high-level managers.

In addition to being pathways for communication, formal channels are also means of sending messages. These means include publications such as newsletters and newspapers, meetings, written memos, electronic mail, traditional bulletin boards, and electronic bulletin boards.

One important communication channel can be classified as formal or informal. *Management by walking around* involves managers intermingling freely with workers on the shop floor, in the office, with customers, and at company social events. By spending time in personal contact with employees, the manager enhances open communication. Because management by walking around is systematic, it could be considered formal. However, a manager who circulates throughout the company violates the chain of command. He or she, therefore, is not following a formal communication path.

COMMUNICATION DIRECTIONS

Messages in organizations travel in four directions: downward, upward, horizontally, and diagonally. Over time, an organization develops communication networks corresponding to these directions. A **communication network** is a pattern or flow of messages that traces the communication from start to finish.

> **communication network**
> *A pattern or flow of messages that traces the communication from start to finish.*

Downward communication is the flow of messages from one level to a lower level. It is typified by a supervisor giving orders to a team member or by top-level managers sending an announcement to employees. Downward communication is often overemphasized at the expense of receiving upward communication. A survey of employees from different companies indicated that an area of concern is the quantity and quality of communications that they received from management. A representative employee complaint is as follows:

I still feel like I don't know what's going on around this company. I feel like decisions are being made and I never hear about it and when I do it's often too late.[6]

Upward communication is the transmission of messages from lower to higher levels in an organization. Although it may not be as frequent as downward communication, it is equally important. Remember the $1 billion mistake mentioned at the outset of the chapter? Upward communication tells management how well messages have been received. The same communication path is also the most important network for keeping management informed about problems. Management by walking around and simply speaking to employees facilitates upward communication. In addition, companies have developed many programs and policies to facilitate bottom-up communication. Three such approaches follow:

1. *Open-door policy.* An open-door policy allows any employee to bring a gripe to top management's attention—without first checking with his or her immediate manager. The open-door policy can be considered a grievance procedure that helps employees resolve problems. However, the policy also enhances upward communication because it informs top management about problem employees are experiencing.
2. *Workout program at GE.* General Electric conducts three-day town meetings across the company, attended by a cross-section of about 50 company personnel—senior and junior managers, and salaried and hourly workers. Facilitators are present to encourage the audience to express their concerns freely. Partici-

pants evaluate various aspects of their business, such as reports and meetings. They discuss whether each one makes sense and attempt to "work out" problems. By using upward communication, GE attempts to achieve more speed and simplicity in its operations.

3. *Complaint program.* Many organizations have formal complaint programs. Complaints sent up through channels include those about supervisors, working conditions, personality conflicts, sexual harassment, and inefficient work methods.

Horizontal communication is sending messages among people at the same organizational level. Horizontal communication frequently takes the form of coworkers from the same department talking to each other. When coworkers are not sharing information with and responding to each other, they are likely to fall behind schedules and miss deadlines. Also, efforts are duplicated and quality suffers. Another type of horizontal communication takes place when managers communicate with other managers at the same level.

Horizontal communication is the basis for cooperation. People need to communicate with each other to work effectively in joint efforts. For example, they have to advise each other of work problems and ask each other for help when needed. Horizontal communication is especially important because it is the basis for the horizontal organization described in Chapter 9. Moreover, recent evidence confirms the belief that extensive lateral communication enhances creativity. Exchanging and "batting around" ideas with peers sharpens imagination.[7]

Diagonal communication is the transmission of messages to higher or lower organizational levels in different departments. A typical diagonal communication event occurs when the head of the marketing department needs some pricing information. She telephones a supervisor in the finance department to get his input. The supervisor, in turn, telephones a specialist in the data processing department to get the necessary piece of information. The marketing person has thus started a chain of communication that goes down and across the organization.

INFORMAL COMMUNICATION CHANNELS

informal communication channel
An unofficial network that supplements the formal channels in an organization.

Organizations could not function by formal communication channels alone. Another system of communication, called an **informal communication channel**, is also needed. Informal communication channels are the unofficial network that supplements the formal channels. Most of these informal channels arise out of necessity. For example, people will sometimes depart from the official communication channels to consult with a person with specialized knowledge. Suppose the manager of pension services in a bank was familiar with the methods of calculating exchange rates between the U.S. dollar and other currencies. Bank employees from other departments would regularly consult this manager when they faced an exchange-rate problem. Any time two or more employees consult each other outside formal communication channels, an informal communication channel has been used. Two other major aspects of informal communication channels are the grapevine and the rumors it carries.

grapevine
The informal means by which information is transmitted in organizations.

THE GRAPEVINE AND RUMOR CONTROL. The **grapevine** is the informal means by which information is transmitted in organizations. As such, it is the major informal communication channel. The term *grapevine* refers to tangled pathways that can distort information. This perception is an oversimplification. The grapevine is sometimes used purposely to disseminate information along informal lines. For example, management might want to hint to employees that the plant will be closed unless the employees become more productive. Although the plans are still tentative, feeding them into the grapevine may result in improved motivation and productivity. Some important characteristics of the grapevine are:[8]

- A substantial number of employees consider the grapevine to be their primary source of information about company events. The grapevine often has a bigger effect on employees than do messages sent over formal channels. Messages sent over formal communication channels are often perceived to be stale news.

- Information is usually transmitted along the grapevine with considerable speed. The more important the information, the greater the speed. For example, information about the firing or sudden resignation of an executive can pass through the company in 30 minutes.

- Approximately three-fourths of messages transmitted along the grapevine are true. Because so many grapevine messages are essentially correct, employees believe most of them. They have received intermittent reinforcement for having believed them in the past. Nevertheless, messages frequently become distorted and misunderstood. By the time a rumor reaches the majority of employees, it is likely to contain false elements.

    An example of this is the case of a company president who gave a personal donation to a gay rights group. The funds were to be used to promote local legislation in favor of equal employment opportunities for gay people. The last version of the story that traveled over the grapevine took this form: "The president has finally come out of the closet. He's hiring three gay managers and is giving some year-end bonus money to the Gay Alliance."

- Only about 10 percent of employees who receive rumors pass along the information to others. Those who do, however, usually communicate the information to several other employees, rather than to only one.

The grapevine is the primary medium for transmitting rumors and therefore can create some problems. False rumors can be disruptive to morale and productivity. Some employees will take action that hurts the company and themselves in response to a rumor. It is not unknown for valuable employees to leave a firm in response to rumors about an impending layoff. The reason valuable employees are often first to leave is that they have skills in demand at other firms.

Severe negative rumors, especially about product defects or poisonings, must be neutralized to prevent permanent damage to an organization. In 1991, a soft drink company in Brooklyn, New York, was nearly put out of business by a rumor that its leading brand of soda caused sterility in black males. A public relations firm was hired to help successfully neutralize the rumor. Based on developments in *rumor theory*, following are several suggestions for neutralizing rumors.[9] To begin, if a rumor seems entirely ridiculous, *ignore it* because it will probably die on its own. (A case in point was the recent rumor that IBM was getting out of the hardware business to concentrate on software and computer consulting.) Second, if the rumor contains any truth, *confirm the part that is true.* Third, make a comment rather than saying "no comment," because refusing comment is generally taken as "yes." The manager might explain that the rumor is so absurd that it does not require a lengthy response. Fourth, if the rumor is to be denied, *base the denial on truth.* If the truth is denied, public reaction can be severe. Fifth, make sure every official commenting on the rumor *tells a consistent story.* Sixth, *hold town meetings* with employees and perhaps the public to discuss the rumor. An open discussion can help decrease suspicion about a catastrophic rumor such as that the company has squandered a pension fund.

CHANCE ENCOUNTERS. Unscheduled informal contact between managers and employees can be an efficient and effective informal communication channel. John P. Kotter found in his study of general managers that effective managers do not confine their communications to formal meetings. Instead, they collect valuable information during chance encounters.[10] Spontaneous communication events may occur in the cafeteria, near the water fountain, in the halls, and on the elevator. For example, during an elevator ride, a manager might spot a purchasing agent and ask, "Whatever happened to the just-in-time inventory purchasing proposal?" In 2 minutes the manager might obtain the information that would typically be solicited in a 30-minute meeting. A chance encounter differs from management by walking around in that the latter is a planned event; the former occurs unintentionally.

BARRIERS TO COMMUNICATION

LEARNING OBJECTIVE

Identify major
communication barriers
in organizations.

Messages sent from one person to another are rarely received exactly as intended. Barriers exist at every step in the communication process. Exhibit 13-4 shows how barriers to communication influence the receiving of messages. The input is the message sent by the sender. Ordinarily, the message is spoken or written, but it could be nonverbal. Barriers to communication, or noise, are shown as *throughput*, the processing of input. Noise is always a potential threat to effective communication because it can interfere with the accuracy of a message. Noise creates barriers to effective transmission and receiving of messages. The barriers may be related to the receiver, the sender, or the environment. The output in this model is the message as received.

Which messages are the most likely to encounter the most barriers? Interference is the most likely to occur when a message is complex, arouses emotion, or clashes with a receiver's mental set. An emotionally arousing message deals with such topics as money or personal inconvenience (e.g., being assigned a less convenient work schedule). A message that clashes with a receiver's usual way of viewing things requires the person to change his or her typical pattern of receiving messages. To illustrate this problem, try this experiment. The next time you order food at a restaurant, order the dessert first and the entrée second. The server will probably not hear your dessert order.

LOW MOTIVATION AND INTEREST

Many messages never get through because the intended receiver is not motivated to hear the message or is not interested. The challenge to the sender is to frame the message in such a way that it appeals to the needs and interests of the receiver. This principle can be applied to conducting a job campaign. When sending a message, the job seeker should emphasize the needs of the prospective employer. An example would be: "If I were hired, what problem would you like me to tackle first?" Many job seekers send low-interest messages of this type: "Would this job give me good experience?"

Sending a message at the right time is part of appealing to motives and interest. Messages should be sent at a time when they are the most likely to meet with a good reception. Following this principle, a good time to ask for new equipment is early in the fiscal year, when most of the money has not yet been spent. Sending the message late in the fiscal year can also be effective. The manager might have some unspent money he or she does not want to return to the general fund.

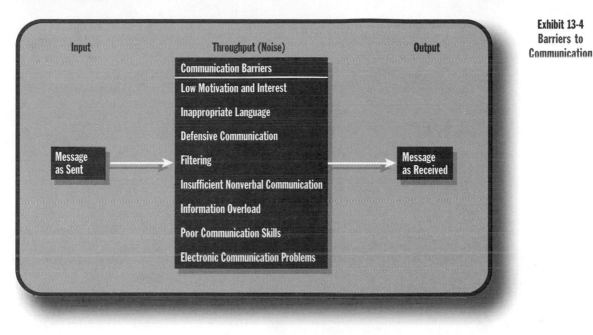

Exhibit 13-4
Barriers to
Communication

INAPPROPRIATE LANGUAGE

The language used to frame a message must be suited to the intended receivers. Language can be inappropriate for a host of reasons. Two factors of particular significance in a work setting are semantics and difficulty level.

Semantics is the study of meaning in language forms. The message sender should give careful thought to what certain terms will mean to receivers. A good example is the term *productive*. To prevent erecting communication barriers, you may have to clarify this term. Assume a manager says to the group members, "Our department must become more productive." Most employees will correctly interpret the term as meaning something like "more efficient," but some employees will interpret it as "work harder and longer at the same rate of pay." Consequently, these latter employees may resist the message.

The *difficulty level of language* is its ease of comprehension. Communicators are typically urged to speak and write at a low difficulty level. There are times, however, when a low difficulty level is inappropriate. For instance, when a manager is communicating with technically sophisticated employees, using a low difficulty level can create barriers. The employees may perceive the manager as patronizing and may tune him or her out. The use of jargon, or insider language, is closely related to difficulty level. When dealing with outsiders, jargon may be inappropriate; with insiders (people who share a common technical language), it may be appropriate. Jargon can help the sender establish a good relationship with the receivers.

DEFENSIVE COMMUNICATION

An important general communication barrier is **defensive communication**—the tendency to receive messages in a way that protects self-esteem. Defensive communication is also responsible for people sending messages to make themselves look good. People communicate defensively through the process of *denial*, the suppression of information one finds to be uncomfortable. It serves as a major barrier to communication because many messages sent in organizations are poten-

> **defensive communication**
> *The tendency to receive messages in a way that protects self-esteem.*

tially uncomfortable. When an anxiety-provoking message is sent, sometimes just part of it is denied. A long-term employee was told that he would be asked to move from his window office to one without windows (a loss of perceived status). He nodded in agreement. When moving day came, the employee discovered that he was being moved to an inside office. He protested to the president, saying that he was never told that the move would mean giving up his window office. The employee denied to himself the reality of losing a window with an office.

FILTERING

filtering
Coloring and altering information to make it more acceptable to the receiver.

Filtering is coloring and altering information to make it more acceptable to the receiver. Telling the manager what he or she wants to hear is part of filtering. It is another variation of defensive communication. For example, suppose an employee becomes aware of information that should be communicated to management. The employee realizes, however, that managers would be upset if they knew the full story. The employee filters the truth, to avoid dealing with the wrath of management.

INSUFFICIENT NONVERBAL COMMUNICATION

Effective communicators rely on both verbal and nonverbal communication. If verbal communication is not supplemented by nonverbal communication, messages may not be convincing, as the following situation illustrates.

A customer service representative at a cable television station approached her manager with a preliminary proposal for increasing the number of subscribers. Her idea was to interview former customers who had dropped the service. With a blank expression on his face, the manager replied, "I see some merit in your idea. Work with it further." Two months later the manager asked the representative if she had completed the proposal. She replied that she had dropped the idea because "you seemed so unresponsive to my proposal."

INFORMATION OVERLOAD

information overload (or communication overload)
A condition in which an individual receives so much information that he or she becomes overwhelmed.

Information overload, or **communication overload**, occurs when an individual receives so much information that he or she becomes overwhelmed. As a result, the person does a poor job of processing information and receiving new messages. Many managers suffer from information overload because of the blitz of memos, reports, advertisements, and telephone calls they receive. Many managers are trying to prevent information overload. They may require that each report be accompanied by a brief summary.

An important strategy for dealing with information overload in the workplace is to learn to differentiate between relevant and less relevant information. When information appears on your desk or in your computer, ask, "Can this information help me function better in my job?" Recognize, however, that intellectual broadening can always help you in the long range. You therefore may not want to quickly exclude all information that cannot help you this week.

POOR COMMUNICATION SKILLS

A message may fail to register because the sender lacks effective communication skills. The sender might garble a written or spoken message so severely that the receiver cannot understand it, or the sender may deliver the message so poorly that the receiver does not take it seriously. Communication barriers can result from deficiencies within the receiver. A common barrier is a receiver who is a poor listener.

ELECTRONIC COMMUNICATION PROBLEMS

Advanced technology in the office has created several new communication barriers. The problems associated with electronic mail are representative of these barriers. One communication barrier associated with electronic mail is its impersonality. Much like any printed document, an electronic message can seem much harsher than a spoken message. A manager can smile and express sympathy through a nod of the head. These messages are difficult to communicate via a computer screen. Electronic mail is, therefore, better suited to communicating routine rather than complex or sensitive messages.[11]

The Internet and on-line computer services such as MCI Mail, CompuServe, Prodigy, and American Online are creating communication barriers of their own. Because of their comprehensiveness and 24-hour-per-day accessibility, they contribute to information overload. Another problem relates to the intrinsic satisfaction associated with "surfing" the information superhighway. Many workers become so preoccupied with searching for information and sending messages to other subscribers that interaction with officemates is perceived as an interference. Customer inquires can also get sidetracked while the on-line service user is perusing computerized information.

Telephone answering machines and voice mail create their own frustrations and communication barriers to both senders and receivers. Senders may dislike the impersonality of not being able to communicate with a live person. If so, they may be less receptive to conducting business with the other party. Receivers who get negative messages by machine may react more strongly than if a person delivered the messages.

Another advanced electronic communication device, videoconferencing, is gaining in acceptance. In a videoconference, people in different locations talk to each other while viewing each other's images on a television screen. With videoconferencing, a meeting can be held with workers in several different locations. One result is decreased travel expenses. The technique also increases productivity, because employees only have to travel to the videoconferencing center near their office. Videoconferencing creates some communication problems because it lacks the give-and-take of in-person interaction. Some nonverbal communication is lost because conference members tend to act more stiffly in front of cameras than in person.

OVERCOMING BARRIERS TO COMMUNICATION

Most barriers to communication are surmountable. The general strategy for overcoming them has two parts. First, you must be aware that these potential barriers exist. Second, you should develop a tactic to deal with each one. For example, when you have an important message to deliver, make sure you answer the following question from the standpoint of the receiver: "What's in it for me?" This section will describe eight strategies and tactics for overcoming communication barriers. Exhibit 13-5 lists the strategies.

LEARNING OBJECTIVE 5

Develop tactics for overcoming communication barriers.

UNDERSTAND THE RECEIVER

To be an effective communicator, you must understand the receiver. Understanding the receiver is a strategy that can assist in overcoming every communication barrier. For example, part of understanding the receiver is to be aware that he or she may be overloaded with information or be poorly motivated. Achieving understanding takes *empathy*, the ability to see things as another person does or to "put yourself in the other person's shoes."

Empathy leads to improved communication, because people are more willing to engage in a dialogue when they feel understood. Managers especially need empathy to communicate with employees who do not share their values. A typical situation involves an employee who does not identify with company goals and is therefore poorly motivated. To motivate this employee, the manager might talk about productivity leading to higher pay rather than to higher returns to stockholders.

Empathy is not sympathy. A manager might understand why an employee does not identify with company goals. The manager does not have to agree, however, that the company goals are not in the employee's best interests.

COMMUNICATE ASSERTIVELY

Many people create their own communication barriers by expressing their ideas in a passive, or indirect, mode. If instead they explained their ideas explicitly and directly—and with feeling—the message would be more likely to be received. Notice the difference between a passive (indirect) phrasing of a request versus an assertive (direct) approach:

Passive

Team member: *By any chance would there be some money left over in the budget? If there would happen to be, I would like to know.*

Manager: *I'll have to investigate. Try me again soon.*

Assertive

Team member: *We have an urgent need for a fax machine in our department. Running to the document center to use their fax is draining our productivity. I am therefore submitting a requisition for a fax machine.*

Manager: *Your request makes sense. I'll see what's left in the budget right now.*

informative confrontation
A technique of inquiring about discrepancies, conflicts, and mixed messages.

Another use of assertiveness in overcoming communication barriers in the workplace is **informative confrontation**, a technique of inquiring about discrepancies, conflicts, and mixed messages.[12] Confronting people about the discrepancies in their message provides more accurate information. As a manager, here is how you might handle a discrepancy between verbal and nonverbal messages:

Exhibit 13-5
Overcoming
Communication
Barriers

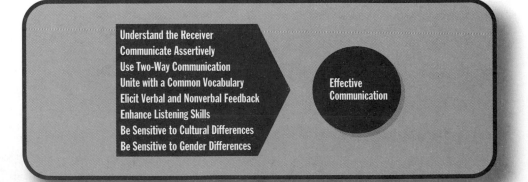

Understand the Receiver
Communicate Assertively
Use Two-Way Communication
Unite with a Common Vocabulary
Elicit Verbal and Nonverbal Feedback
Enhance Listening Skills
Be Sensitive to Cultural Differences
Be Sensitive to Gender Differences

Effective
Communication

You're talking with a team member you suspect is experiencing problems. The person says, "Everything is going great" (verbal message). At the same time the team member is fidgeting and clenching his fist (nonverbal message). Your informative confrontation might be: "You say things are great, yet you're fidgeting and clenching your fist."

Another way of being assertive is to repeat your message and use multiple channels. Communication barriers may prevent messages from getting through the first time they are sent. These barriers include information overload and the receiver's desire not to hear or see the information. By being persistent, your message is more likely to be received. An important message should be repeated when it is first delivered and repeated again one or two days later. Experienced communicators often repeat a message during their next contact with the receiver.

Repetition of the message becomes even more effective when more than one communication channel is used. Effective communicators follow up spoken agreements with written documentation. The use of multiple channels helps accommodate the fact that some people respond better to one communication mode than another. For example, a supervisor asked an employee why she did not follow through with the supervisor's request that she wear safety shoes. The employee replied, "I didn't think you were serious. You didn't put it in writing."

USE TWO-WAY COMMUNICATION

Many communication barriers can be overcome if senders engage receivers in conversation. A dialogue helps reduce misunderstanding by communicating feelings as well as facts. Both receiver and sender can ask questions of each other. Here is an example:

Manager: *I want you here early tomorrow. We have a big meeting planned with our regional manager.*

Employee: *I'll certainly be here early. But are you implying that I'm usually late?*

Manager: *Not at all. I know you come to work on time. It's just that we need you here tomorrow about thirty minutes earlier than usual.*

Employee: *I'm glad I asked. I'm proud of my punctuality.*

UNITE WITH A COMMON VOCABULARY

People from the various units within an organization may speak in terms so different that communication barriers are erected. For example, the information system group and the marketing group may use some words and phrases not used by the other. Steve Patterson recommends that managers should first identify the core work of a business, and then describe it in a shared business vocabulary.[13] All key terms should be clearly defined, and people should agree on the meaning. Assume that a company aims to provided "high-quality long-distance telephone service." Workers should agree on the meaning of high quality in reference to long distance. The various departments might retain some jargon, and their unique perspectives, but they would also be united by a common language.

ELICIT VERBAL AND NONVERBAL FEEDBACK

To be sure that the message has been understood, ask for verbal feedback. A recommended managerial practice is to conclude a meeting with a question such as: "To what have we agreed this morning?" The receiver of a message should also take the responsibility to offer feedback to the sender. The expression "This is what I heard you say" is an effective feedback device. Feedback can also be used to facilitate communication in a group meeting. After the meeting, provide everyone in attendance with written follow-up to make sure they all left with the same understanding.

It is also important to observe and send nonverbal feedback. Nonverbal indicators of comprehension or acceptance can be more important than verbal indicators. For example, the manner in which somebody says "Sure, sure" can indicate if that person is truly in agreement. If the "Sure, sure" is a brush-off, the message may need more selling. The expression on the receiver's face can also be due to acceptance or rejection.

ENHANCE LISTENING SKILLS

active listening
Listening for full meaning, without making premature judgments or interpretations.

Many communication problems stem from the intended receiver not listening carefully. Unless a person receives messages as intended, he or she cannot get work done properly. Managers need to be good listeners because so much of their work involves eliciting information from others in order to solve problems. Reducing communication barriers takes active listening. **Active listening** means listening for full meaning, without making premature judgments or interpretations. The suggestions for effective listening presented in Exhibit 13-6 support active listening. In addition, an active listener should follow these four steps:[14]

1. *The receiver listens for total meaning of the sender's message.* By carefully analyzing what is said, what is not said, and nonverbal signals, you will uncover a fuller meaning in the message.
2. *The listener forms an initial opinion about the information.* Assume that the information is not what the receiver wants to hear. An active listener will nevertheless continue listening.

Exhibit 13-6
Keys to Effective Listening

If you practice these suggestions regularly and are patient, you can become an effective listener. Coaching and feedback by an observer could also be helpful. Learning to be an effective listener may also require breaking habits that conflict with these suggestions.

- **Limit distractions.** Hold telephone calls, close the door, and find a quiet place away from ordinary responsibilities.
- **Discipline yourself to concentrate.** Take notes, maintain eye contact with the speaker, and ask questions to make sure that you understand the message. Such signals assure the speaker that you are actively listening.
- **Don't interrupt.** A poor listener cannot wait for the chance to jump in with his or her opinion or argument. To be a good listener, one has to adopt a passive mode sometimes.

- **Capitalize on the fact that thought is faster than speech.** A poor listener tends to daydream with slow or average speakers. A good listener uses the time to evaluate carefully what the speaker is saying. He or she also listens to voice tone and observes nonverbal signs, thus reading between the lines.
- **Be sincere.** When voice tone, facial expressions, and eye contact convey sincerity, the sender will feel more trusting and at ease.
- **Set aside preconceptions.** View each encounter as something new, and avoid perceiving the message sender in predetermined ways. Avoid such thinking as "Here comes Miguel with another complaint." Instead, start with a fresh slate.

Source: C. Glenn Pearse, "Learning How to Listen Emphatically," *Supervisory Management* (September 1991): 11; "Words to Live By: I'm All Ears," *Working Smart* (January 1993):1.

3. *The receiver reflects the message back to the sender.* Show the sender that you understand by providing summary reflections such as "You tell me you are behind schedule because our customers keep modifying their orders."
4. *The sender and receiver both understand the message and engage in a concluding discussion.* In the preceding situation, the manager and the employee would converse about the challenges of making on-time deliveries despite changes in customer requirements.

BE SENSITIVE TO CULTURAL DIFFERENCES

As organizations have become more culturally diverse, the possibility of culturally based communication barriers has increased. The list that follows presents several strategies and specific tactics to help overcome cross-cultural communication barriers.

- *Be sensitive to the fact that cross-cultural communication barriers exist.* Awareness of these potential barriers will alert you to the importance of modifying your communication approach.
- *Use straightforward language and speak clearly.* When working with people who do not speak your language fluently, speak in an easy-to-understand manner. Minimize the use of idioms and analogies specific to your language. A sales representative from Juarez, Mexico, was attending a company sales meeting in San Antonio, Texas. The sales manager said that the chief competitor was "over the hill." The sales representative was confused because he thought perhaps the competitor had relocated to a new town just "over the hill."
- *Observe cultural differences in etiquette.* Violating rules of etiquette without explanation can erect immediate communication barriers. A major rule of etiquette in many countries is that people address each other by the last name unless they have worked together for a long time. Etiquette expert Letitia Baldridge recommends that you explain the difference in custom to prevent misunderstanding. Particularly if on an overseas assignment, ask your work associate when using his or her first name would be appropriate.[15]
- *Be sensitive to differences in nonverbal communication.* Be alert to the possibility that your nonverbal signal may be misinterpreted by a person from another culture. Hand gestures are especially troublesome. An engineer for a New Jersey company was asked a question by a German coworker. He responded OK by making a circle with his thumb and forefinger. The German worker stormed away because, in Germany, the same gesture is a personal insult.[16]
- *Do not be diverted by style, accent, grammar, or personal appearance.* Although these superficial factors are all related to business success, they are difficult to interpret when judging a person from another culture. It is therefore better to judge the merits of the statement or behavior.[17] A brilliant individual from another culture may still be learning your language and may make basic mistakes in speaking your language.

BE SENSITIVE TO GENDER DIFFERENCES

Despite the trend toward equality in organizations, much has been made recently of identifying differences in communication styles between men and women. Awareness of these differences helps lower potential communication barriers between men and women. Nevertheless, the differences described next are stereotypes that overlook the fact that men and women vary among themselves in communication style. Differences in gender-related communication style include the following:[18]

- Women prefer to use communication for rapport building. In contrast, men prefer to use talk primarily as a means to preserve independence and status by displaying knowledge and skill.
- Men prefer to work their problems out by themselves, whereas women prefer to talk out solutions with another person.
- Women are more likely to compliment the work of a coworkers, while men are more likely to be critical.
- Men tend to be more directive in their conversation, while women emphasize politeness.
- Women tend to be more conciliatory when facing differences, while men become more intimidating.
- Men are more interested than women in calling attention to their accomplishments or hogging recognition. As a result, men are more likely to dominate discussion during meetings.

Understanding the above differences can help you interpret the behavior of people, thus avoiding a communications block. For example, if a team member who is male is stingy with praise, remember that he is simply engaging in gender-typical behavior. Do not take it personally. If a team member who is female talks about a problem without looking for a quick solution, do not get frustrated. She is simply engaging in gender-typical behavior by looking for support.

HOW TO CONDUCT AN EFFECTIVE MEETING

LEARNING OBJECTIVE

Describe how to conduct
more effective meetings.

Much of workplace communication takes place in meetings, including group decision making. When conducted poorly, meetings can represent a substantial productivity drain. Most of the information presented in this chapter and in Chapter 6, which discussed decision making, applies to meetings. The suggestions that follow are for those who conduct meetings. However, many also apply to participants. By following these suggestions, you increase the chance that the meetings you attend are effective communication vehicles.

1. *Meet only for valid reason.* Many meetings lead to no decisions because there was no valid reason for calling them. Meetings are necessary only when there is a need for coordinated effort and group decision making. Memos can be substituted for meetings when factual information needs to be disseminated and discussion is unimportant.
2. *Have a specific agenda and adhere to it.* Meetings are more productive when an agenda is planned and followed carefully. People should see the agenda in advance so they can give some careful thought to the issues—preliminary thinking helps people arrive at more realistic decisions. In addition, assign maximum discussion times to the agenda items.
3. *Rely on qualified members.* Groups often reach poor decisions because those who contribute to those decisions are not qualified from the standpoint of knowledge or interest. An uninformed person is typically a poor decision maker. Also, a person who attends a meeting reluctantly sometimes agrees to any decision just to help bring the meeting to a close.

4. *Share decision-making authority.* A key attribute of an effective problem-solving meeting is authority sharing by the leader. Unless authority is shared, the members are likely to believe that the hidden agenda of the meeting is to seek approval for the meeting leader's tentative decision.

5. *Keep comments brief and to the point.* A major challenge facing the meeting leader is to keep conversation on track. Verbal rambling by participants creates communication barriers because other people lose interest. An effective way for the leader to keep comments on target is to ask the contributor of a non sequitur, "In what way does your comment relate to the agenda?"

6. *Encourage critical feedback and commentary.* Meetings are more likely to be fully productive when participants are encouraged to be candid with criticism and negative feedback. Openness helps prevent groupthink and also brings important problems to the attention of management. It is also within the spirit of total quality management for workers to confront rather than hide problems. Participants at the meeting should also be encouraged to discuss problems they are having with each other and with the manager.

7. *Strive for wide participation.* One justification for conducting a meeting is to obtain multiple input. Although not everybody is equally qualified to voice a sound opinion, everyone should be heard. A skillful leader may have to limit the contribution of domineering members and coax reticent members to voice their ideas.

8. *Provide summaries for each major point.* Many ideas are expressed in the typical meeting, so some members may have trouble following what has been accomplished. Also, decision-making quality improves when members clearly understand the arguments that have been advanced for and against each alternative. Summarizing key points can help members follow what is happening and make better-informed decisions. Without summaries, participants sometimes do not know what, specifically, they are voting for or against.

9. *Strive for consensus, not total acceptance.* Few groups of assertive individuals will reach total agreement on most agenda items. Furthermore, disagreement is healthy because it can sharpen and refine decision making. It is more realistic to strive for *consensus*—a state of harmony, general agreement, or majority opinion. When consensus is achieved, each member should be willing to accept the plan because it is logical and feasible. One way of achieving consensus is to strive for win-win solutions or plans instead of using such methods as majority rule, averaging, and coin flipping.[19]

10. *Congratulate members when they reach a decision.* Complimenting group members when they reach a decision reinforces decision-making behavior and increases the probability that consensus will be reached the next time the group faces a problem.

11. *Ensure that all follow-up action is assigned and recorded.* All too often, even after a decision has been reached, a meeting lacks tangible output. Distribute a memo summarizing who is responsible for taking what action and by what date.

SUMMARY OF KEY POINTS

1

Describe the steps in the communication process.

The communication process involves four basic elements, all of which are subject to interference, or noise. The process begins with a sender encoding a message and then transmitting it over a channel to a receiver. Feedback from receiver to sender is also essential. In successful communication, the receiver decodes the message, understands it, and then acts on it.

2

Recognize the major types of nonverbal communication in the workplace.

The major modes of transmitting nonverbal messages are through the environment (physical setting); body placement; posture; hand gestures; facial expression and movement; voice quality; and clothing, dress, and appearance. Mirroring, the use of nonverbal communication to establish rapport, is also of significance.

3

Explain and illustrate the difference between formal and informal communication channels.

Formal channels are revealed by the organization chart. Management by walking around can also be considered a formal communication channel. Messages are transmitted in four directions: upward, downward, sideways, and diagonally. Informal channels are the unofficial network of communications that supplement the formal pathways. The grapevine is the major informal communication pathway, and it transmits rumors. Management can take steps to neutralize negative rumors, such as publicly discussing them.

4

Identify major communication barriers in organizations.

Barriers exist at every step in the communication process.

Among them are (1) low motivation and interest, (2) inappropriate language, (3) defensive communication, (4) filtering, (5) insufficient nonverbal behavior, (6) information overload, (7) poor communication skills, and (8) electronic communication problems.

5

Develop tactics for overcoming communication barriers.

To overcome communication barriers you must (1) understand the receiver, (2) communicate assertively, (3) use two-way communication, (4) unite with a common vocabulary, (5) elicit verbal and nonverbal feedback, (6) enhance listening skills, (7) be sensitive to cultural differences, and (8) be sensitive to gender differences.

6

Describe how to conduct more effective meetings.

To improve the communication effectiveness (and decision-making quality) of meetings, follow these suggestions: (1) meet only for valid reasons, (2) adhere to an agenda, (3) rely on qualified members, (4) share decision-making authority, (5) keep comments brief and to the point, (6) encourage critical feedback and commentary, (7) strive for wide participation, (8) provide summaries for major points, (9) strive for consensus, (10) congratulate members when they reach a decision, and (11) assign follow-up action.

KEY TERMS AND PHRASES

Communication *pg. 290*
Encoding *pg. 290*
Decoding *pg. 291*
Noise *pg. 292*
Nonverbal Communication *pg. 292*
Formal Communication Channels *pg. 294*
Communication Network *pg. 295*
Informal Communication Channel *pg. 296*

Grapevine *pg. 296*
Defensive Communication *pg. 299*
Filtering *pg. 300*
Information Overload (or Communication Overload) *pg. 300*
Informative Confrontation *pg. 302*
Active Listening *pg. 304*

QUESTIONS

1. Employers continue to emphasize good communication skills as one of the most important qualifications for screening career-school and business graduates. What are some of the reasons for this requirement?
2. How might understanding the steps in the communication process help managers and professionals do a better job?
3. Why is it more important to select the right channel for bad news rather than for good news?
4. Assume you have an urgent message for top-level management. What would be the best way to get the message up through the organization?
5. Why has horizontal communication become so important in the modern organization?
6. How do direct marketers (those who sell by mail) make use of the tactic "Understand the receiver"?
7. How can knowing about gender differences in communication style help you be more effective in your career?

SKILL-BUILDING EXERCISE 13-A: A TEST OF COMMUNICATION EFFECTIVENESS

The following scale consists of opposite descriptions of communication style. Between each pair is a 7-to-1 scale. Assess your communication style in terms of each pair of descriptions and circle the appropriate number. If you are not currently working as a manager, imagine how the situation would be based on your other work or social experiences with people.

I think my communication with people who report to me:

Increases my credibility	7	6	5	4	3	2	1	Decreases my credibility
Is precise	7	6	5	4	3	2	1	Is imprecise
Is clear	7	6	5	4	3	2	1	Is unclear
Answers more questions than it raises	7	6	5	4	3	2	1	Raises more questions than it answers
Is effective	7	6	5	4	3	2	1	Is ineffective
Is competent	7	6	5	4	3	2	1	Is incompetent
Is productive	7	6	5	4	3	2	1	Is unproductive
Gets the results I want	7	6	5	4	3	2	1	Does not get the results I want
Is impressive	7	6	5	4	3	2	1	Is unimpressive
Creates a positive image of me	7	6	5	4	3	2	1	Creates a negative image of me
Is good	7	6	5	4	3	2	1	Is bad
Is skillful	7	6	5	4	3	2	1	Is unskillful
Is relaxed	7	6	5	4	3	2	1	Is strained
Is self-rewarding	7	6	5	4	3	2	1	Is not self-rewarding
Does not embarrass me	7	6	5	4	3	2	1	Does embarrass me

Total score _____ To find your total score, add the numbers you circled.

Interpretation: If your total score is 81 or above, you have analyzed yourself as a very effective communicator. If your total score is 59–80, you have analyzed yourself as an effective communicator. If your total score is 37–58, you have analyzed yourself as an ineffective communicator. If your total score is 15–36, you have analyzed yourself as a very ineffective communicator.

To increase the accuracy of your self-evaluation, ask another person to evaluate your on-the-job communication by taking this test. Many of the ideas contained in this chapter, and in books and articles about communication skills, will help you improve your communication effectiveness.

Source: Adapted from Lyle Sussman and Paul D. Krivnos, *Communication for Supervisors and Managers* (Sherman Oaks, CA: Alfred Publishing, 1979), 10–12.

SKILL-BUILDING EXERCISE 13-B: ACTIVE LISTENING

GROUP ACTIVITY Before conducting the following role plays, review the suggestions for active listening in this chapter. The suggestion about reflecting the message is particularly relevant because the role plays involve an emotional topic.

THE ELATED COWORKER

One student plays the role of a coworker who has just been offered a promotion to supervisor of another department. She will be receiving 10 percent higher pay and be able to travel overseas twice a year for the company. She is eager to describe full details of her good fortune to a coworker. Another student plays the role of the coworker to whom the first worker wants to describe her good fortune. The second worker decides to listen intently to the first worker. Other class members will rate the second student on his or her listening ability.

THE DISCOURAGED COWORKER

One student plays the role of a coworker who has just been placed on probation for poor performance. His boss thinks that his performance is below standard and that his attendance and punctuality are poor. He is afraid that if he tells his girlfriend, she will leave him. He is eager to tell his tale of woe to a coworker. Another student plays the role of a coworker he corners to discuss his problems. The second worker decides to listen intently to his problems but is pressed for time. Other class members will rate the second student on his or her listening ability.

VIDEO DISCUSSION QUESTIONS

1. What is your evaluation of McCall's communication effectiveness? [Glaxo]
2. What is your evaluation of Bossidy's communication skills? [Allied Signal]
3. To what extent does the sales representative for commercial accounts at General Tire engage in active listening? [General Tire]

CASE PROBLEM 13-A: THE E-MAIL QUANDARY

Dan Wells is the chief engineer of electrical engineering at Volvo GM Heavy Truck Corp. in Greensboro, North Carolina. He strongly believes in extensive communication in all directions throughout the organization. Every truck produced by Volvo GM is an enormous capital expenditure, making any communication mistake potentially very expensive.

Wells compares the communication pipeline before and after E-mail was introduced to his company more than 10 years ago. He explains, "The old-fashioned way was for a secretary to type an interoffice memo, take it to the interoffice reproduction department, and print 1,500 copies for distribution to employees at this location."

Wells explains further that on the surface this would seem like a considerable savings of productive time and paper. Yet he is concerned that employees have not made the shift in mental set that they don't have to print out everything they receive. Many employees still print out everything, even only a couple of lines about a meeting. Wells is concerned that E-mail is not yielding the productivity gains his company had anticipated.

CASE QUESTIONS

1. From a productivity standpoint, what's wrong with employees making hard copies of practically all E-mail messages?
2. What can Volvo GM do to prevent employees from making so many E-mail copies?

Source: Adapted from Jayne A. Pearl, "The E-mail Quandary," *Management Review* (July 1993): 48–49.

CASE PROBLEM 13-B: MEMO WARFARE

OFFICE MEMO

TO: Office Staff of Balta Construction
FROM: Sherm Balta, president
SUBJECT: Budget overrun on fax charges

It has been brought to my attention that we are now 34 percent over budget on fax expenses, with a full one-third of the year remaining. Somehow this abuse of fax privileges must stop. This is certainly no way to run a construction company. I see three alternatives facing us. Number one, we can close down the construction company for the year, thus avoiding any more fax expenses (an alternative *most* of you would not enjoy). Number two, we can stop using faxes for the rest of the year. Number three, we can all develop a responsible and mature approach to budget management by making more prudent use of the fax machine.

OFFICE MEMO

TO: Sherm Balta
FROM: Yukiko Inose
SUBJECT: Your memo about fax machine use *with regard to fax expense.*

I read your recent memo with dismay, since it is my department that makes extensive use of the fax machine. We use faxes for very important purposes such as getting cost updates to clients in a hurry. Are we in the business of keeping our clients informed about their construction costs or in the business of pinching quarters on fax machine costs?

OFFICE MEMO

TO: Yukiko Inose
FROM: Sherm Balta, president
SUBJECT: Your response to my memo about fax costs

It is obvious to me, Yukiko, that you are resisting the philosophy of budgeting. In today's business world, both the Bechtels and the Balta Construction companies must learn to respect the limits imposed by budgets. Perhaps it is time that you and I had a serious discussion about this matter. Please make an appointment to see me at your earliest convenience.

CASE QUESTIONS

1. What communication problems are revealed by this incident?
2. Rewrite Balta's first memo in such a way that it will be less likely to make Inose defensive.
3. Rewrite Inose's memo in such a way that it will be less likely to make Balta counterdefensive.

CASE PROBLEM 13-C: WHY DON'T THEY COMPLAIN TO ME?

Business Equipment Corporation is a distributor of photocopying machines, small computers, fax machines, and telecommunication devices. Branch units are responsible for sales and customer service. Kathy Diaz, a branch manager, was conferring with Ned Carter, her regional manager who was visiting her office. Prior to this luncheon conference, Ned had chatted briefly with several of the sales and service employees in Kathy's branch office. Part of the conversation between Kathy and Ned took this form:

Ned: *There's something happening in your branch I want to discuss.*

Kathy: *Nothing too gruesome, I hope. Our results have been pretty good this last quarter, haven't they?*

Ned: *Nothing gruesome, just a question of your management style. Some of your team members think they don't have a big enough say about who is hired into the branch.*

Kathy: *I thought they did have a big say. Before I hire anybody, a support person, a customer service rep, or a sales rep, that person is interviewed by the people he or she would be working most directly with.*

Ned: *Yes, but they think you choose which candidates will even be interviewed. And then you make the final hiring decision.*

Kathy: *If they want to be involved in those aspects of the hiring process, I guess it could be arranged. I'm concerned though that total participation along those lines would be cumbersome and inefficient. We would spend a lot of time on recruiting and selection. Besides, I thought a branch manager was responsible for hiring employees even in today's empowered organization.*

Ned: *Yes, but I think the time invested would pay off. Your people would feel much more like they are part of a team effort.*

Kathy: *By the way, nobody ever told me about these problems. I would have been receptive to their input. I believe in team management. Why don't they complain to me instead of going to you?*

CASE QUESTIONS

1. Why is this problem included in a chapter about interpersonal communication?
2. What might Kathy do in the future to encourage branch members to bring their problems directly to her instead of complaining to the regional manager?
3. Do you think the branch employees were justified in using the communication channel they did to criticize the recruiting procedures?

CASE PROBLEM 13-D: FRENZY AT THE DATE BOOK COMPANY

John Cotter, a book bindery operator for the Date Book Company in Brooklyn, New York, was talking to a sales representative from McCain Book Binding Equipment. The McCain sales rep informed him that the brother of the owner of Date Book was buying some of his competitor's equipment to set up a book binding plant in

nearby New Jersey. After the sales rep left, John spoke to one of the other senior operators, Lorraine Parsons.

"Lorraine, the salesman from McCain Book Binding just told me the owner's brother is setting up a book binding plant in New Jersey. You know how the owner is always complaining about the union. I bet that as soon as the New Jersey plant is up and running, they will shift work over there. I heard they are not going to have a labor union. We will all be out looking for jobs. Let's call a meeting of all of the operators tomorrow after work at the union meeting hall."

Twenty-two people were at the meeting the following day. John was the first to speak. With anger in his voice, he said: "We have all worked hard for the Date Book Company. Now the owner is setting up a non-union bindery to save a few dollars on wages. We will all be out of a job in six months, and there is little we can do about it. I suggest we all start looking for new jobs. We should also teach our employer a good lesson by ruining as much product as possible before they shut us down."

Three weeks later, Peter Reynolds, the plant superintendent, walked into the owner's office. He said, "I don't know what's going on. I had to reject another large batch of date books due to another bindery error. We have had more spoiled product in the last two weeks that we had all last year. Another problem is that two of our most experienced operators quit with no explanation.

"We now not only have to worry about your brother opening up a competitive business, we also have to solve our manufacturing problems."

Larry Stagliano, the owner, responded to Peter: "Why didn't you tell me about the spoilage problem before today? I think I know what's going on. Two weeks ago Arnie, the maintenance man who has worked here for 25 years, told me about a rumor running through the shop. According to the story, I was building the plant with my brother and I was going to close down our bindery operation.

"I figured the rumor would run its course, and that maybe those highly paid bindery operators needed a good scare. I had no idea they would start ruining product and quitting."

CASE QUESTIONS

1. What mistakes did Stagliano make in dealing with the rumor he heard from the maintenance man?
2. What should Stagliano and Reynolds do now to prevent any further damage from the rumor?
3. What should management do to minimize the chances of employees acting on the basis of false rumors in the future?

Source: Case researched by Cliff Grinell, Rochester Institute of Technology.

REFERENCES

1. Based on facts reported in Milan Moravec, Herman Gyr, and Lisa Friedman, "A 21st Century Communication Tool," *HRMagazine* (July 1993) p. 78.
2. John O. Whitney, *The Trust Factor: Liberating Profits and Restoring Corporate Vitality* (New York: McGraw-Hill, 1994).
3. Michael Argyle, *Bodily Communication*, 2e (Madison, CT: International Universities Press, 1990).
4. Research cited in Kathleen Driscoll, "Your Voice Can Make or Break You," Rochester, New York, *Democrat and Chronicle* (26 August 1993): 10B.
5. Anat Rafaeli and Michael G. Pratt, "Tailored Meanings: On the Meaning and Impact of Organizational Dress," *Academy of Management Review* (January 1993): 32.
6. "Mapping Employee Opinions," *The Surcon Report* (July 1995): 2.
7. John B. Bush, Jr., and Alan L. Frohman, "Communication in a 'Network' Organization," *Organizational Dynamics* (Autumn 1991): 23–26.
8. Alan Zarcmba, "Working with the Organizational Grapevine," *Personnel Journal* (March 1989): 34.
9. Nicholas DiFonzo, Prashant Bordia, and Ralph L. Rosnow, "Reining in Rumors," *Organizational Dynamics* (Summer 1994): 57–60.
10. John P. Kotter, *The General Managers* (New York: Free Press, 1991).
11. Lucy A. Newton and Lynn McFarlane Shore, "Genres of Organizational Communication: An Approach to Studying Communication and Media," *The Academy of Management Review* (April 1992): 317.
12. William Cormier and Sherilyn Cormier, *Interviewing Strategies for Helpers* (Monterey, CA: Brooks/Cole, 1990).
13. Steve Patterson, "Returning to Babel," *Management Review* (June 1994): 44–48.
14. Andrew E. Schwartz, "The Importance of Listening: It Can't Be Stressed Enough . . . " *Supervisory Management* (July 1991): 7.
15. "Letitia Baldrige: Arbiter of Business Manners and Mores," *Management Review* (April 1992): 50.
16. Roger E. Axtell, *Gestures: The Do's and Taboos of Body Language Around the World* (New York: Wiley, 1991).
17. David P. Tulin, "Enhance Your Multi-Cultural Communication Skills," *Managing Diversity*, Vol. 1, 1992: 5.
18. Deborah Tannen, *Talking from 9 to 5* (New York: William Morrow, 1994); Tannen, *You Just Don't Understand* (New York: Ballantine, 1990); John Gray, *Men are from Mars, Women are from Venus* (New York: HarperCollins, 1992).
19. Richard A. Cosier and Charles R. Schwenk, "Agreement and Thinking Alike: Ingredients for Poor Decisions," *The Academy of Management Executive* (February 1990): 69–74.

CHAPTER 14

Teams, Groups, and Teamwork

LEARNING OBJECTIVES
After studying this chapter and doing the exercises, you should be able to:

1

Identify various types of teams and groups.

2

Describe the characteristics of effective groups and teams.

3

Specify key roles assumed by team and group members.

4

Summarize managerial actions for building teamwork.

5

Explain the actions and attitudes of an effective team player.

6

Point to the potential problems of teams and groups.

© Charles Thatcher/
Tony Stone Images

Barry Jentz, an organizational consultant, was hired to promote teamwork on the construction of the new world headquarters of Bausch & Lomb, Inc. The construction project was organized to eliminate the usual adversarial relations among architects, contractors, subcontractors, and corporate construction managers. Teamwork was therefore considered especially important on this project. To promote teamwork, Jentz took workers at all levels through a series of exercises, such as breaking up into work teams to solve practical problems. • Anecdotal evidence suggested the team development sessions were effective. One technical challenge was lighting the roof at the top of the tower on the new building. It is a pitched roof with a spire, divided into panels with light coming from squares in each panel. Builders couldn't figure out a practical way to attach light bulbs. An introverted engineer wrote down a suggestion for using optical fiber, with just one light source pumping up through the fiber conduits. Under the old, combative way of hammering out decisions, he might not have been listened to, said the project manager.[1]

Building a world-class office tower is but one example where a knowledge of teams and teamwork skills can make an important contribution. The heavy emphasis on teams and group decision making in the workplace increases the importance of understanding teams and groups. (You will recall the discussion of group decision making in Chapter 6, and teams as part of job design in Chapter 8.)

We approach an understanding of teams, groups, and teamwork here by presenting several key topics on the subject. They include types of groups, characteristics of effective teams and groups, group-member roles, building teamwork, and being a team player. We also look at problems associated with teams and groups.

TYPES OF TEAMS AND GROUPS

group
A collection of people who interact with each other, are working toward some common purpose, and perceive themselves to be a group.

team
A special type of group in which members have complementary skills and are committed to a common purpose, a set of performance goals, and an approach to the task.

teamwork
The situation in which there is understanding and commitment to group goals on the part of all team members.

A **group** is a collection of people who interact with each other, are working toward some common purpose, and perceive themselves to be a group. The head of a customer-service team and her staff would be a group. In contrast, 12 people in an office elevator would not be a group because they are not engaged in collective effort. A **team** is a special type of group. Team members have complementary skills and are committed to a common purpose, a set of performance goals, and an approach to the task. **Teamwork** means that there is understanding and commitment to group goals on the part of all team members.[2]

Groups and teams have been classified in many different ways. Here we describe the distinction between formal versus informal groups, and among four different types of work teams.

The increasingly heavy emphasis on teams in the workplace compels today's managers to understand thoroughly the characteristics of effective teams and groups.

Exhibit 14-1
Types of Work Teams

Type and Examples	Work Cycles	Typical Outputs
Advice and involvement Committees Quality circles Employee involvement groups	Can be brief or long; one cycle can be team life span.	Decisions Selections Proposals Recommendations
Production and service Assembly teams Mining teams Flight attendant crews Data processing groups	Typically repeated or continuous process; cycles often briefer than team life span.	Food Components Retail sales Customer service Equipment repairs
Project and development Research groups Planning teams Engineering teams Development teams Task forces	Differ for each new project; one cycle can be team life span.	Plans, designs Investigations Presentations Prototypes Reports, findings
Action and negotiation Sports teams Cockpit crews Negotiating teams Surgical teams	Brief performance events, often repeated under new conditions.	Combat missions Contracts, lawsuits Surgical work Competitions

Source: Adapted from Eric Sundstrom, Kenneth P. De Meuse, and David Futrell, "Work Teams: Application and Effectiveness," *American Psychologist* (February 1990): 125.

FORMAL VERSUS INFORMAL GROUPS

Some groups are formally sanctioned by management and the organization itself, while others are not. A **formal group** is one deliberately formed by the organization to accomplish specific tasks and achieve goals. Examples of work groups include departments, project groups, task forces, committees, and quality circles. In contrast, **informal groups** emerge over time through the interaction of workers. Although the goals of these groups are not explicitly stated, informal groups typically satisfy a social or recreational purpose. Members of a department who dine together occasionally would constitute an informal group. Yet the same group might also meet an important work purpose of discussing technical problems of mutual interest.

formal group
A group deliberately formed by the organization to accomplish specific tasks and achieve goals.

informal group
A group that emerges over time through the interaction of workers.

TYPES OF WORK TEAMS

All workplace teams have the common element of people working together cooperatively and members possessing a mix of skills. Exhibit 14-1 classifies teams into four types: advice and involvement; production and service; project and development; and action and negotiation. The exhibit also presents information about how quickly the team performs its work (work cycles) and typical outputs of each type of team.

A classification of work teams is not fixed, because new types of work teams evolve to meet organizational needs. A recent addition to the advice and involvement category is the **affinity group**, an employee-involvement group composed of professional level (or knowledge) workers. The members are colleagues who meet regularly to share information, capture opportunities, and solve problems affecting the work group and the larger organization. The group is self-managing and has a formal charter.[3]

Most people today belong to more than one formal and informal group, and more than one work team. For example, a customer-service representative might work in the customer-service department and also be assigned to a task force for redesigning the company benefits program.

affinity group
An employee-involvement group composed of professional-level workers who meet regularly to share information, capture opportunities, and solve problems affecting the work group and the larger organization.

CHARACTERISTICS OF EFFECTIVE WORK GROUPS

LEARNING OBJECTIVE 2

Describe the characteristics of effective groups and teams.

Groups, as do individuals, have characteristics that contribute to their uniqueness and effectiveness. As shown in Exhibit 14-2, these characteristics can be grouped into six categories. Our description of work group effectiveness follows this framework.[4]

JOB DESIGN

Effective work groups follow the principles of job design embodied in job enrichment and the job characteristics model described in Chapter 8. For example, task significance and task identity are both strong. A major theme is self-management, as practiced by self-managing work teams. A closely related attribute is participation in key decisions, such as how to improve quality, by work group members.

INTERDEPENDENCE

Effective work groups are characterized by several types of *interdependence*. Such groups show *task interdependence* in the sense that members interact and depend on one another to accomplish the work. Task interdependence is valuable because it increases motivation and enhances the sense of responsibility for the work of other group members.

Goal interdependence refers to the linking of individual goals to the group's goals. A member of a sales team might establish a compensation goal for herself, but she can realize this goal only if other team members achieve similar success. Aside from the fact of interdependence, clearly defined goals are a major requirement for group effectiveness.[5] *Interdependent feedback and rewards* also contribute to group effectiveness. Individual feedback and rewards should be linked to group performance to encourage good team play.

Exhibit 14-2
Work Group
Characteristics
Related to
Effectiveness

Characteristics	Effectiveness Criteria
Job Design	
Self-Management	
Job Characteristics Model	
Interdependence	
Task Interdependence	
Goal Interdependence	
Interdependent Feedback and Rewards	
Composition	
Heterogeneity	Productivity
Flexibility	
Preference for Group Work	Satisfaction
Context and Resources	
Training	
Managerial Support	Judgments by Manager
Communication/Cooperation Between Groups	
Process	
Potency	
Social Support	
Workload Sharing	
Communication/Cooperation Within Groups	
Familiarity	
Jobs	
Coworkers	
Work Environment	

Source: Adapted from Michael A. Campion, Gina J. Medsker, and A. Catherine Higgs, "Relations Between Work Group Characteristics and Effectiveness: Implications for Designing Effective Work Groups," *Personnel Psychology* (Winter 1993): 825; Paul S. Goodman and Dennis Patrick Leyden, "Familiarity and Group Productivity," *Journal of Applied Psychology* (August 1991): 578.

GROUP COMPOSITION

Member *heterogeneity* generally has a positive effect on group performance, especially when the group has a variety of problems to solve. A diverse group also facilitates members learning from each other. Relevant heterogeneous factors include educational background, field of experience, socioeconomic level, and risk-taking attitudes. Cultural diversity is another aspect of heterogeneity that improves groups' effectiveness, because it enhances creativity.[6] The group should also be composed of members who have *flexible* work assignments, thereby being able to fill in for each other.

Relative size is a key aspect of composition. Groups should be large enough to accomplish their work, but when groups become too large, confusion and poor coordination may result. Also, larger groups tend to be less cohesive. Committees, work teams, and task forces tend to be the most productive with seven to 10 members. *Preference for group work* is also related to effectiveness. A group

ORGANIZATION IN ACTION: CROSS-FUNCTIONAL TEAMS AT GOSSEN CORP.

Gossen Corp., of Milwaukee, supplies components to other companies. The company organized its 120 employees into cross-functional teams eight years ago. When the teams were formed, the employees did not understand how working together in teams would benefit them personally more than performing well on their own. "The goal of teamwork was too abstract," explains Gossen president Jef Butterfield. "We operate in a culture where people don't see the value of their expertise to other departments."

To overcome this misperception, Gossen initiated an employee communication and training effort that continues today. The goal of the initiative is to continually remind employees of the company's mission to satisfy the customer. Team members are empowered to identify customer needs and create work methods to satisfy those needs. Instead of trying to please a boss, employees focus their efforts on pleasing customers.

Butterfield emphasizes that when employees understand the mission of focusing on meeting customer demands, they work in unison. Implementing the mission gives a reason for working together.

Source: Shari Caudron, "Teamwork Takes Work," *Personnel Journal* (February 1994): 42.

composed of members who enjoy working in groups will outperform one whose members prefer working alone. Many individualistic and creative people prefer to avoid the investment of time in interpersonal relations required by group work.

CONTEXT AND RESOURCES

The context (or environment) in which the group works and resources available to the group influence effectiveness. *Training* quite often facilitates work group effectiveness. The training content typically includes group decision making, interpersonal skills, technical knowledge, and the team philosophy or mission. The accompanying Organization in Action illustrates the importance of training the work team to understand its mission.

Managerial support in the form of investing resources and believing in group effort fosters effectiveness. *Communication and cooperation* between groups improve group effectiveness, and management must help create the right environment for it to occur.

PROCESS

Many processes (activities) take place within the group that influence effectiveness. A key process characteristic is *potency*, or the belief by the group that it can be effective. Potency is technical jargon for team spirit. Effectiveness is also enhanced when workers provide *social support* to each other through such means as helping each other have positive interactions. *Workload sharing* is another process characteristic related to effectiveness. By sharing the workload equitably, free riding (not doing one's share) can be minimized. *Communication and cooperation* within the work group also contribute to effectiveness.

Collectively, the right amount of these process characteristics contributes to *cohesiveness*, or a group that pulls together. Without cohesiveness, a group will fail to achieve synergy.

The characteristics of an effective work group or team should also be supplemented by effective leadership. Team leaders must emphasize coaching more than controlling, or make the shift from "cop" to "coach." Instead of being a supervisor, the leader becomes a team developer.[7]

FAMILIARITY

Another important set of factors related to work group effectiveness is familiarity. It refers to the specific knowledge group members have of their jobs, coworkers, and the work environment. The effects of familiarity were studied among 26 crews in two underground coal mines. When absenteeism led to replacements of miners, the lack of familiarity with coworkers was associated with lower productivity.[8] The same phenomenon may occur when new members join an athletic team. Quite often the team loses momentum during the adjustment period.

ROLES FOR TEAM AND GROUP MEMBERS

Another perspective on the group process is to identify team member roles.[9] Positive roles are described here to help you identify areas of possible contribution in group or team effort.

LEARNING OBJECTIVE

Specify key roles assumed by team and group members.

- *Knowledge Contributor.* Being technically proficient, the knowledge contributor provides the group with useful and valid information. He or she is intent upon helping with task accomplishment, and values sharing technical expertise with team members.
- *Process Observer.* A person occupying this role forces the group to look at how it is functioning, with statements such as: "We've been at it for two and one-half hours, and we have only taken care of one agenda item. Shouldn't we be doing better?" The process observer might also point to excellent team progress.
- *People Supporter.* A person occupying this role assumes some of the leader's responsibility for providing emotional support to teammates and resolving conflict. He or she serves as a model of active listening while others are presenting. The people supporter helps others relax by smiling, making humorous comments, and appearing relaxed. He or she supports and encourages team members even when disagreeing with them.

- *Challenger.* To prevent complacency and noncritical thinking, a team needs one or more members who confront and challenge bad ideas. A challenger will criticize any decision or preliminary thinking that is deficient in any way, including being ethically unsound. Effective interpersonal skills are required to be a challenger. Antagonistic, attack-style people who attempt the challenger role lose their credibility quickly.

- *Listener.* Listening contributes so substantially to team success that it comprises a separate role, even though other roles involve listening. If other people are not heard, the full contribution of team effort cannot be realized. As a result of being a listener, a team member or team leader is able to summarize discussion and progress for the team.

- *Mediator.* Disputes within the group may become so intense and prolonged that two people no longer listen or respond to each other. The two antagonists develop such polarized viewpoints that they are unwilling to move toward each other's point of view. Furthermore, they have moved beyond the point that conciliation is possible. At this point the team leader or a team member must mediate the dispute.

- *Gatekeeper.* A recurring problem in group effort is that some members may fail to contribute because other team members dominate the discussion. Even when the viewpoints of the timid team members have been expressed, they may not be remembered because one or two other members contribute so frequently to discussion. When the opportunity gate is closed to several members, the gatekeeper pries it open. He or she requests that a specific team member be allowed to contribute, or that the member's past contribution be recognized.

Skill-Building Exercise 14-B gives you an opportunity to identify and observe the roles just described. Recognize, however, that these roles may overlap; they are not entirely independent of each other.

MANAGERIAL ACTIONS FOR BUILDING TEAMWORK

LEARNING OBJECTIVE

Summarize managerial
actions for building
teamwork.

The team player roles described previously point to actions the individual can take to become a team player. Here we highlight managerial actions and organizational practices that facilitate teamwork.[10] Good teamwork enhances, but does not guarantee, a successful team. For example, a group with excellent teamwork might be working on improving a service no longer offered by the company. No matter what the output of the team, it will probably be ignored.

The manager can begin by helping team members believe they have an urgent, constructive purpose. A demanding performance challenge helps create and sustain the team. A major strategy for teamwork is to promote the attitude that working together effectively is an expected norm. Developing such a culture of teamwork will be difficult when a strong culture of individualism exists within the firm. The team leader can communicate the norm of teamwork by making fre-

Exhibit 14-3
Developing a Culture
of Teamwork

Individual Culture	Team Culture
Workers compete against each other for recognition, raises, and resources.	Workers learn to collaborate with each other.
Workers are paid for their individual efforts.	Workers now rewarded based on own efforts plus efforts of teammates.
Supervisors use authoritarian leadership or management style.	Supervisors become facilitative; they coach workers rather than only giving orders.

Source: Compiled from information in "The 'Facts of Life' for Teambuilding," *Human Resources Forum* (February 1995): 3.

quent use of words and phrases that support teamwork. Emphasizing the words *team members* or *teammates*, and deemphasizing the words *subordinates* and *employees* helps communicate the teamwork norm. Exhibit 14-3 summarizes key culture changes necessary to achieve teamwork.

Using the consensus decision-making style is another way to reinforce teamwork. A sophisticated approach to enhancing teamwork is to feed team members valid facts and information that motivate them to work together. New information prompts the team to redefine and enrich its understanding of the challenge it is facing, thereby focusing on a common purpose. A subtle yet potent method of building teamwork is for the team to use language that fosters cohesion and commitment. In-group jargon bonds a team and sets the group apart from others. An example is a team of computer experts saying "Give me a core dump" to mean "Tell me your thoughts."

To foster teamwork, the manager should minimize **micromanagement**, or supervising group members too closely and second-guessing their decisions. Micromanagement can hamper a spirit of teamwork (potency) because team members do not feel in control of their own work.

Creating physical structures suited for teams is an effective organizational intervention to support teamwork. Group cohesiveness, and therefore teamwork, is enhanced when teammates are located close together and can interact frequently and easily. Frequent interaction often leads to camaraderie and a feeling of belonging. A useful method for getting people to exchange ideas is to establish a shared physical facility, such as a conference room, research library, or beverage lounge. A key strategy for encouraging teamwork is to reward the team as well as individuals. The most convincing team incentive is to calculate compensation partially on the basis of team results.

A more general reward strategy is for managers to apply positive reinforcement whenever the group or individuals engage in behavior that supports teamwork. For example, if team members took the initiative to have an information-sharing session, this activity should be singled out and praised.

micromanagement
Supervising group members too closely and second-guessing their decisions.

ORGANIZATION IN ACTION: TEAM SYMBOLS AT EASTMAN KODAK COMPANY

The black and white film manufacturing group at Eastman Kodak Company had lost its once revered status because color film now dominates the amateur film market. Despite the increase in use of color film by amateurs, the black and white film business has annual sales of about $2 billion. Professional photographers use black and white film regularly, as evidenced by photographs in newspapers. Serious amateurs still shoot in balck and white as well as color. Added to these applications of black and white film are 7,000 products used in printing, X-rays, and spy satellites.

One thousand five hundred Kodak employees work in a horizontal organization structure. To help pick up their spirits, these employees have adopted the symbol Zebra. The group is also referred to as "Team Zebra." A 25-member leadership team watches the flow of work and regularly measures productivity. Zebras are divided into "streams" (manufacturing groups) that supply products to various Kodak business units. The business units are regarded as internal customers. These customers evaluate the streams against customer-satisfaction measures such as on-time delivery.

Within the streams, most employees work in self-directed teams called *flow teams*. When the flow teams began in 1989, the black and white film group exceeded budgeted cost by 15 percent. The group took up to 42 days to fill an order, and it was frequently late. As measured by company surveys, the morale of the group was rock bottom. As the group shifted to a horizontal organization and took on the Zebra team symbol, productivity and morale began to climb. By 1992 the group was under budgeted cost by 15 percent, had reduced its cycle time by half, and was late only 5 percent of the time.

The team spirit that evolved as the concept of Team Zebra took hold is best understood in terms of one particular flow team, or stream, within the larger group. One day Kodak managers were faced with a problem, so they asked Gordon Ackley and four other production workers how to solve it. The first thing Ackley said was, "Will everybody leave the room? We'll let you know how we'll do it." In previous years, few workers would have been brazen enough to assume they could solve problems without extensive involvement by management.

Ackley is part of a flow team at Kodak Park, the company's largest manufacturing facility. Workers are grouped by what product they help make, not by what job they do. Despite the various products they help make, all are united by their status as Zebras.

The problem facing the flow team was how to gear up quickly to make Ektamate paper, an ultra-thick photographic paper used to print copies of microfilm slides. Kodak had stopped making Ektamate. Instead, the Kodak Business Imaging Systems unit had gone outside the company, to 3M Co., for paper to be used with its microfilm machines. The Imaging Systems sales representatives, however, had found that some customers preferred the old Ektamate paper. The sensitized products manufacturing division now had a challenge to get Ektamate manufacturing back. The condition laid down, however, was that the group had to produce Ektamate quickly and at low cost.

The division had recently reorganized into flow teams. In the past, manufacturing was organized around different jobs. These included mixing chemicals, coating film and paper, or cutting and packaging. Now the division is organized around products such as black and white paper (Ektamate included), black and white film, color paper, and color film for professional photographers. A division organized around products translates into a horizontal structure organized around the requirements of internal customers. For example, the Zebra groups provide film to a medical products sales group.

The flow team of five Zebras swung into action and quickly grew to 15 members. The group established 12-hour shifts but did not cancel vacations. To accomplish their mission, the team retrieved old machines from storage. Many of these machines were found to have parts missing. The team figured

ORGANIZATION IN ACTION: TEAM SYMBOLS AT EASTMAN KODAK COMPANY *cont.*

out what help and supplies were needed. Other departments had to increase their output of paper and chemicals. Machinery was modified by maintenance workers who had volunteered for the project.

Sometimes the project needed the help of key workers for as little as two hours at a time. This demand was met, although company procedures allowed only week-long transfers outside departments.

Michael Graves, manager of development and manufacturing materials for Kodak Business Imaging Systems, expressed his positive opinion of the workers: "I'm really impressed by how much these workers really want to bring this business back within Kodak. The team spirit is enormous. They were absolutely determined, and they were up and running in 10 weeks. In an earlier day, workers might have taken many months to achieve this much."

Another Kodak executive compared flow teams to the past. His perception was that the old approach was a "Doberman system." As he put it, accounting "watchdogs" would go after manufacturing units that missed cost productivity and targets. Under the new system, each unit produces not only film and paper, but a profit.

Another option available to organizations for enhancing teamwork is to send members to outdoor training, a form of experiential learning. Participants acquire leadership and teamwork skills by confronting physical challenges and exceeding their self-imposed limitations. Rope activities are typical of outdoor training. Participants attached to a secure pulley with ropes will climb up a ladder and jump off to another spot. All of these challenges are faced in teams rather than individually, hence the development of teamwork. Outdoor training is likely to have the most favorable outcomes when the trainer helps the team members comprehend the link between such training and on-the-job behavior.

The preceding Organization in Action presents a widely publicized successful attempt at building teamwork. Management emphasized the use of a team symbol as part of team building.

BEING AN EFFECTIVE TEAM PLAYER

Being an effective team player is important because without such capability, collaborative effort is not possible. Being an effective team player is also important because of managerial perceptions. A survey of 15 business organizations in 34 industries indicates that employers rate "team player" as the most highly ranked workplace behavior. Approximately 40 percent of the managers surveyed ranked team player as number one among seven desirable traits.[11] Here we describe a number of skills, actions, and attitudes contributing to effective team play. For convenience, five are classified as task-related, and five as people-related.[12] In reviewing these attributes, remember that all team situations do not have identical requirements.

LEARNING OBJECTIVE 5

Explain the actions and attitudes of an effective team player.

TASK-RELATED ACTIONS AND ATTITUDES

Task-related actions and attitudes focus on the work the group or team is attempting to accomplish rather than on interpersonal relationships. An effective team player is likely to behave and think in the following ways:

1. *Possess and share technical expertise.* Most people are chosen to join a particular work team on the basis of their technical or functional expertise. Glenn Parker believes that to use your technical expertise to outstanding advantage, you must be willing and able to share that expertise. It is also necessary for the technical expert to be able to communicate with team members in other disciplines who lack the same technical background.[13]

2. *Assume responsibility for problems.* The outstanding team player assumes responsibility for problems. If a problem is free-floating (not yet assigned to a specific person), he or she says, "I'll do it." The task should be one suited for independent rather than coordinated activity, such as conducting research.

3. *Willingness to commit to team goals.* The exceptional team player will commit to team goals even if his or her personal goals cannot be achieved for now. For instance, the team member seeking visibility will be enthusiastic about pursuing team goals even if not much visibility will be gained.

4. *Ability to see the big picture.* As described in Chapter 1, a basic management skill is to think conceptually. Exceptionally good team players should have the same skill. In team efforts, discussion can get bogged down in small details. As a result, the team might temporarily lose sight of what it is trying to accomplish. The team player (or team leader) who can help the group focus on its broader purpose plays a vital role.

5. *Willingness to ask tough questions.* A **tough question** helps the group achieve insight into the nature of the problem it is facing, what it might be doing wrong, and whether progress is sufficient. Tough questions can also be asked to help the group see the big picture. A major contribution of asking tough questions is that it helps the group avoid groupthink. Here is a representative tough question asked by a team member: "I've been to all our meetings so far. What in the world have we accomplished?"

> **tough question**
> *A question that helps the group achieve insight into the nature of a problem, what it might be doing better, and whether progress is sufficient.*

PEOPLE-RELATED ACTIONS AND ATTITUDES

Outstanding team players are consciously aware of their interpersonal relations within the group. They recognize that effective interpersonal relationships are important for getting tasks accomplished. Outstanding team players are also aware that interpersonal relationships should contribute to task accomplishment. An outstanding team player is likely to do or think the following:

1. *Trusting team members.* The cornerstone attitude of the outstanding team player is to trust team members. If you do not believe that the other team members have your best interests at heart, it will be difficult to share opinions and ideas. Trusting team members includes believing that their ideas are technically

sound and rational until proven otherwise. Another manifestation of trust is taking a risk by trying out a team member's unproven ideas.

2. *Sharing credit.* A not-to-be-overlooked tactic for emphasizing teamwork is to share credit for your accomplishments with the team. Sharing credit is authentic because other members of the team usually have contributed to the success of a project.

3. *Recognizing the interests and achievements of others.* A fundamental tactic for establishing yourself as a solid team player is to recognize the interests and achievements of others. Let others know that you care about their interests by such means as asking, "How do my ideas fit into what you have planned?" Recognizing the achievements of others can be done by complimenting their tangible accomplishments.

4. *Active listening and information sharing.* The skilled team player listens actively both inside and outside of meetings. As described previously, an active listener strives to grasp both the facts and feelings behind what is being said. Information sharing helps other team members do their job well and also communicates concern for their welfare. Information sharing can take many forms. These include bringing in news clips, magazine articles, and printouts from on-line services, and recommending relevant books.

5. *Giving and receiving criticism.* The strong team player offers constructive criticism when needed, but does so diplomatically. A high-performance team demands sincere and tactful criticism among members. In addition to criticizing others in a helpful manner, the strong team player benefits from criticism directed toward him or her. A high-performing team involves much give and take including criticism of each other's ideas. The willingness to accept constructive criticism is often referred to as *self-awareness*. The self-aware team player insightfully processes personal feedback to improve effectiveness.

POTENTIAL PROBLEMS OF TEAMS AND GROUPS

LEARNING OBJECTIVE

Point to the potential problems of teams and groups.

Group activity, including group decision making, does not always lead to superior results. Here we look at two major processes within groups that can hamper their effectiveness: group polarization and social loafing. Certain legal risks with employee-involvement groups will also be mentioned. In Chapter 6, about problem solving and decision making, we described two other problems with teams and groups: time wasting and groupthink.

GROUP POLARIZATION

During group problem solving, or group discussion in general, members often shift their attitudes. Sometimes the group moves toward taking greater risks, called the risky shift. At other times the group moves toward a more conservative

group polarization
A situation in which post-discussion attitudes tend to be more extreme than pre-discussion attitudes.

position. The general term for moving in either direction is **group polarization**, a situation in which post-discussion attitudes tend to be more extreme than pre-discussion attitudes.[14] For example, as a result of group discussion members of an executive team become more cautious about entering a new market.

Group discussion facilitates polarization for several reasons. Discovering that others share our opinions may reinforce and strengthen our position. Listening to persuasive arguments may also strengthen our convictions. The "devil-made-me-do-it" attitude is another contributor to polarization. If responsibility is diffused, a person will feel less responsible—and guilty—about taking an extreme position.

Group polarization has a practical implication for managers who rely on group decision making. Workers who enter into group decision making with a stand on an issue may develop more extreme post-decision positions. For example, a team of employees who were seeking more generous benefits may decide as a group that the company should become an industry leader in employee benefits.

SOCIAL LOAFING

social loafing
Freeloading or shirking individual responsibility, when a person is placed in a group setting and removed from individual accountability.

An unfortunate by-product of group and team effort is that an undermotivated person can often squeeze by without contributing a fair share. **Social loafing** is freeloading, or shirking individual responsibility, when a person is placed in a group setting and removed from individual accountability. Readers who have worked on group projects for courses may have encountered this widely observed dysfunction of collective effort.

Two motivational explanations of social loafing have been offered. First, some people believe that because they are part of a team, they can "hide in the crowd." Second, group members typically believe that others are likely to withhold effort when working in a group. As a consequence they withhold effort themselves to avoid being played for a sucker.

An experiment by Tina L. Robbins demonstrated that social loafing can occur even when a task is thought-provoking, personally involving, and allows for unique contribution. She concludes, "The performance of self-directed work teams or groups which are formed for the purpose of brainstorming, product idea generation, or for making proposal implementation decisions, may suffer the consequences of social loafing."[15]

LEGAL RISKS

Under certain circumstances managers may be in violation of labor law by forming work teams. According to the National Labor Relations Act (the NLRA or Wagner Act) a group is illegal if it can be proved to be employer-dominated and a labor organization under the law. An employee-involvement group, such as a work team or quality-improvement team, is usually employer-dominated. This is true because the employer establishes the group, provides a role for management, and funds the group. The key issue in many cases is whether the groups are classified as labor organizations within the meaning of the NLRA.

Corporate lawyers have developed guidelines to help managers assess whether its work teams violate the Wagner Act. The major recommendation is to determine whether the issues addressed by an employee involvement group constitute *conditions of employment*. Issues in possible violation include attendance policies, bonuses, grievances, labor disputes, wages, and hours of employment. To be legally safe, for now work teams of nonmanagerial personnel should be limited to addressing production, quality, and safety matters.[16] Although the above legal precautions should be heeded, at present very few lawsuits have been filed over the use of various types of teams.

SUMMARY OF KEY POINTS

1
Identify various types of teams and groups.
Formal groups are deliberately formed by the organization, whereas informal groups emerge over time through worker interaction. Work teams can be classified as advice and involvement, production and service, project and development, and action and negotiation.

2
Describe the characteristics of effective groups and teams.
Effective work group characteristics are well documented. Jobs of members should be enriched and include a degree of self-management. Group members should be interdependent in terms of task, goals, and feedback and reward. Group composition should include heterogeneity, flexible members, and preference for group work. The context (or environment) should favor group work, such as training and managerial support. The group process should include potency, social support, and workload sharing. Members should be familiar with the jobs, coworkers, and work environment.

3
Specify key roles assumed by team and group members.
Group member roles include knowledge contributor (technical expert), process observer, people supporter, challenger, listener, mediator, and gatekeeper.

4
Summarize managerial actions for building teamwork.
Managers and leaders can enhance teamwork through many behaviors, attitudes, and organizational actions, including the following: give the team an urgent, constructive purpose; develop a norm of teamwork; minimize micromanagement; and support outdoor training.

5
Explain the actions and attitudes of an effective team player.
Task-related actions and attitudes of effective team players include the following: sharing technical expertise; assuming responsibility for problems; committing to team goals; seeing the big picture; and asking tough questions. People-related actions and attitudes include the following: trusting team members; sharing credit; recognizing others; listening and information sharing; and giving and receiving criticism.

6

Point to the potential problems of teams and groups.

One potential problem of group effort is polarization, or taking extreme positions. Members may engage in social loafing or freeloading. Employee-involvement groups may be in violation of the NLRA if they are employee-dominated and are classified as a labor union under the law.

KEY TERMS AND PHRASES

Group *pg. 314*   Affinity Group *pg. 316*
Team *pg. 314*   Micromanagement *pg. 321*
Teamwork *pg. 314*   Tough Question *pg. 324*
Formal Group *pg. 315*   Group Polarization *pg. 326*
Informal Group *pg. 315*   Social Loafing *pg. 326*

QUESTIONS

1. Does the management use of the word *team* refer to about the same idea as the use of the term in athletics?
2. What type of professional job would you recommend for a person who prefers to work alone rather than in teams?
3. Take any high-performing team familiar to you, and indicate which characteristics of an effective work group it appears to possess.
4. How can you use the information and roles within groups to help you in your career?
5. Outdoor training as a method for developing teamwork has achieved enormous popularity. What factors do you think account for its popularity?
6. Give an example of a *tough question* a manager might ask a team.
7. Which problems associated with groups and teams have you been assigned to at school?

SKILL-BUILDING EXERCISE 14-A: ASSESSING TEAM PLAYER ATTITUDES

Directions: Describe how well you agree with each of the following statements, using the following scale: disagree strongly (DS); disagree (D); neutral (N); agree (A); agree strongly (AS).

	DS	D	N	A	AS
1. I am at my best working alone.	5	4	3	2	1
2. I have belonged to clubs and teams ever since I was a child.	1	2	3	4	5
3. It takes far too long to get work accomplished with a group.	5	4	3	2	1
4. I like the friendship of working in a group.	1	2	3	4	5
5. I would prefer to run a one-person business than to be a member of a large firm.	5	4	3	2	1
6. It's difficult to trust others in the group on key assignments.	5	4	3	2	1
7. Encouraging others comes to me naturally.	1	2	3	4	5
8. I like the give and take of ideas that is possible in a group.	1	2	3	4	5
9. It is fun for me to share responsibility with other group members.	1	2	3	4	5
10. Much more can be accomplished by a team than by the same number of people working alone.	1	2	3	4	5

Total Score _____

Scoring and interpretation: Add the numbers you have circled to obtain your total score.

41–50   You have strong positive attitudes toward being a team member and working cooperatively with other members.

30–31   You have moderately favorable attitudes toward being a team member and working cooperatively with other members.

10–29   You much prefer working by yourself than being a team member. To work effectively in a company that emphasizes teamwork, you may need to develop more positive attitudes toward working jointly with others.

SKILL-BUILDING EXERCISE 14-B: TEAM MEMBER ROLES

GROUP ACTIVITY Small teams are formed to conduct a 45-minute meeting on a significant topic. Possibilities include (a) a management team deciding whether to lay off one-third the work force in order to increase profits, or (b) a group of fans who have volunteered to find a new team mascot name to replace "Redskins."

While the team members are conducting their heated discussion, other class members make notes of which team members carry out which roles. Watching for the seven different roles can perhaps be divided among class members, such as people in the first row looking for examples of Knowledge Contributor. Use the role worksheet provided to help you make your observations. Summarize the comment indicative of the role.

Knowledge Contributor: _____

_____

_____

Process Observer: _____

_____

_____

People Supporter: _____

_____

_____

Challenger: _____

_____

_____

Listener: _____

_____

_____

Mediator: _____

_____

_____

Gatekeeper: _____

_____

_____

VIDEO DISCUSSION QUESTIONS

1. How does 360-degree evaluation contribute to teamwork? **[360 Degrees of Evaluation]**
2. How did Union Carbide capitalize on teams to investigate the Bhopal incident? **[Bhopal]**
3. How effective do you think Bossidy might be in encouraging teamwork? **[Allied Signal]**

CASE PROBLEM 14-A: THE UNBALANCED TEAM

Bluestone Security Systems is one of the largest security systems distributors in its city, with annual sales of $15 million. Two years ago, Bill Scovia, the vice-president of marketing and sales, reorganized the sales force. Previously the sales force consisted of inside sales representatives (who took care of phone-in orders) and outside sales representatives (who called on accounts). The reorganization divided the outside sales force into two groups: direct sales and major accounts. The direct sales representatives were made responsible for small commercial customers and individual homeowners. As before, they would service existing customers and prospect for new accounts. Servicing existing customers usually involves adding fire protection to burglary protection, and upgrading the burglary systems.

Three of the people who were direct sales representatives were promoted to major account executives. The account executives would service Bluestone's largest accounts, including prospecting for new business within those accounts. An example would be expanding the security system to other stores of a retailer. To promote teamwork and cooperation, Scovia assigned group sales quotas to the account representatives. Collectively, their goal was to bring in 21 new large accounts per month.

Given that the sales quota was a group quota, the account representatives were supposed to work together on strategy for acquiring new accounts. If a particular account exec did not have the expertise to handle his or her customer's problems, another account executive was supposed to offer help. Brian Marcos, for example, was the resident expert on the unique security problems of warehouses. If invited, Brian would join one of the two other account executives to call on a customer who owned a warehouse.

After the new sales organization had been in place 19 months, Elizabeth Kato, an account executive, was having lunch with Larry Starks, the manufacturing director at Bluestone. "I've about had it," said Elizabeth, "I'm tired of single-handedly carrying the team."

"What do you mean you are single-handedly carrying the team?" asked Larry.

"You're a trusted friend, Larry. So let me lay out the facts. Each month the group is supposed to bring in 21 new sales. If we don't average those 21 sales per month, we don't get our semiannual bonus. That represents about 25 percent of my income. So a big chunk of my money comes from group effort.

"My average number of new accounts brought in for the last 12 months has been 11. And we are averaging about 18 new sales per month. This translates into the other account execs averaging about seven sales among them. I'm carrying the group, but overall sales are still below quota. This means I didn't get my bonus last month.

"The other account execs are friendly and helpful in writing up proposals. But they just don't bring in their share of accounts."

Larry asked, "What does your boss say about this?"

"I've had several conversations with him about the problem. He tells me to be patient and to remember that the development of a fully balanced team requires time. He also tells me that I should develop a stronger team spirit. My problem is that I can't pay my bills with team spirit."

CASE QUESTIONS

1. What does this case illustrate about teamwork?
2. What role or roles is Elizabeth occupying in the group?
3. To what extent are Elizabeth's complaints justifiable?

CASE PROBLEM 14-B: ROLLS ROYCE LOOKS TO CHANGE

Rolls Royce Motor Cars Ltd. automobiles are still considered the epitome of luxury for the world's super-rich. A bottom-of-the-line Rolls Royce Silver Dawn retails for $149,900, and a top-of-the-line limousine sells for $347,200. Despite the fame of its vehicles, in recent years Rolls Royce has had to reduce costs. The company reduced its payroll by half, and has subcontracted some parts that it used to make.

The Rolls Royce tradition, however, remains in every car the company produces. Leather seats for the cars are made from 10 to 12 hides per vehicle. Workers carefully match the leather before it is dyed. After carefully studying each hide, the workers decide where to cut each piece. Trim for the carpeting is made from less fine leather than the seats. Yet to make an ideal match, the carpeting leather comes from the same hide as the seats.

When sales of their vehicles decreased in the early 1990s, Rolls Royce lost an estimated hundreds of millions of dollars. (These results do not include the sale of Rolls Royce airplane engines.) Top management then decided that employees should be encouraged to use much more initiative in order to increase productivity. As the managing director of operations said, "The managers managed, and the workers worked." He also said that he wanted production workers to act like they were serving customers directly.

CASE QUESTIONS

1. What changes from the traditional assembly line would you recommend for the manufacture of Rolls Royce automobiles?
2. What changes in work arrangements (or organizational design) can be made so that production workers feel they are serving customers?

Source: Based on facts as reported in "Rolls Quickens the Pace of Perfection," Associated Press story (4 December 1994).

CASE PROBLEM 14-C: THE REWARD-CONSCIOUS TEAM

Alliant Health Care System is a hospital and health-care corporation with headquarters in Louisville, Kentucky. Many of the company's 4,800 employees are organized into teams. After three years of team operation, several notable accomplishments have occurred, including the following:

- The Rehabilitation Services Team improved charting of discharges from 60 percent within standard to 90 percent within standard in less than three months.
- The Post Anesthesia Care Unit (recovery) Team eliminated $8,300 annually of on-call pay by revamping the process for weekend call-ins.
- After laboratory employees learned to function as a team, the lab was able to function without a supervisor on the 10:30 P.M. to 7:00 A.M. shift. The company was able to save the salary that would have been paid to the night supervisor.

Over time, each of the teams at Alliant have taken over 11 managerial and supervisory tasks and functions, as follows:

1. Team Liaison—serves as the interface between management and the team.
2. Daily Operations—handles such matters as team scheduling, vacation, sick-time backup, and daily work assignments.
3. Finance and Budget—monitors all team financial activities, including budgets, and time and attendance.
4. Human Resources—coordinates coaching, termination, performance appraisals, and benefits.
5. Quality Management—is responsible for continuous quality improvements.
6. Housekeeping—maintains a clean work environment that meets health regulations.
7. Education and Development—oversees orientation, training, and continuing education.
8. Communications—arranges meetings and resolves conflicts within the team.
9. Purchasing—keeps inventory of supplies and equipment and places orders.
10. Customer Service—handles customer complaints, and surveys external and internal customers.
11. Safety—ensures compliance with regulatory requirements.

Many Alliant employees enjoyed assuming managerial responsibility. However, the initial enthusiasm often dwindled rapidly. Thirty-two teams were formed, but within four years the number of self-directed work teams had fallen below 20. The Geriatric Psychiatry team is one of the groups that had some reservations about the team structure. Team members looked at all their additional responsibility (the 11 tasks listed above) and concluded that compensation should be adjusted. The basis of their demands was that the team had assumed added responsibilities of being self-directed.

The Geriatric Psychiatry team made a strong argument for supplemental team compensation in a memo to the hospital administrator and the vice-president of human resources. Alliant management took the demands seriously, but also realized that a health-care organization must carefully control expenses. Management also worried about the staying power of a team-based organization if no concessions were granted.

CASE QUESTIONS

1. How legitimate is it for teams to want more compensation for the additional responsibilities assumed by team members?
2. Develop a plan management of Alliant can use to deal with the issue of the team wanting to be compensated for being a self-directed team.

Source: Adapted in part from John L. Morris, "Bonus Dollars for Team Players," HRMagazine (February 1995): 76–83.

CASE PROBLEM 14-D: THERE MUST BE A BETTER WAY TO DEVELOP A CORDLESS TELEPHONE

In 1988, AT&T began developing a cordless telephone. A major obstacle the company faced was a tightly formed hierarchical structure. It was clearly spelled out who reported to whom, and employees had carefully defined responsibilities. The clarity was an impediment at times, because employees lost some flexibility and decision making took a lot of time.

John Haney, the vice-president of product development, hoped to cut product development time in half. He knew that the company would have to make major changes to accomplish this goal. In the past, the AT&T approach to product development resembled a relay system: The product development group would hand a design over to manufacturing. Next, manufacturing would hand the product over to marketing, who would sell it to consumers.

Haney knew the old system had helped AT&T achieve greatness, but it was too slow to fit the competitiveness of today's telecommunications industry. So he had to think of a radically different approach to product development.

CASE QUESTIONS

1. How does the AT&T product development experience relate to teams and teamwork?
2. Design a new product development structure and process to help design a cordless telephone more quckly.

Source: Based on information in D. Keith Denton, "Multi-Skilled Teams Replace Old Work Systems," HRMagazine (September 1992): p. 49.

CASE: VALASSIS COMMUNICATIONS: A STUDY IN TEAMWORK

Valassis Communications, which prints coupon inserts for various publications, developed a corporate culture of teamwork to help it achieve its goals of satisfying customer demands. Top management believed strongly that teamwork would provide opportunities for workers to benefit from each other's knowledge in meeting tough challenges. For example, teams figured out how to reduce waste in paper consumption.

The teamwork culture is supported by crosstraining, visiting other departments, and working in open cubicles. Closely related to teamwork is companywide goal setting, in which teams of workers gear their activities to reaching corporate goals.

REFERENCES

1. Phil Ebersole, "Inside Connections," Rochester, New York, *Democrat and Chronicle* (5 February 1995): 1E–2E.
2. Jon R. Katzenbach and Douglas K. Smith, "The Discipline of Teams," *Harvard Business Review* (March-April 1993): 113.
3. Eileen M. Van Aken, Dominic J. Monetta, and D. Scott Sink, "Affinity Groups: The Missing Link in Employee Involvement," *Organizational Dynamics* (Spring 1994): 38.
4. Based in part on literature reviews in Michael A. Campion, Gina J. Medsker, and A. Catherine Higgs, "Relations Between Work Group Characteristics and Effectiveness: Implications for Designing Effective Work Groups," *Personnel Psychology* (Winter 1993): 823–850; Paul S. Goodman and Dennis Patrick Leyden, "Familiarity and Group Productivity," *Journal of Applied Psychology* (August 1991): 578–586.
5. Anne M. O'Leary-Kelly, Joseph J. Martocchio, and Dwight D. Frink, "A Review of the Influence of Group Goals on Group Performance," *The Academy of Management Journal* (October 1994): 1285–1301.
6. Taylor H. Cox and Stacy Blake, "Managing Cultural Diversity: Implications for Organizational Competitiveness," *The Academy of Management Executive* (August 1991): 45–56.
7. Daniel Ray and Howard Bronstein, *Teaming Up: Making the Transition to a Self-Directed, Team-Based Organization* (New York: McGraw-Hill, 1995).
8. Goodman and Leyden, "Familiarity and Group Productivity," 578–586.
9. Glenn M. Parker, *Team Players and Teamwork: The New Competitive Business Strategy* (San Francisco: Jossey-Bass, 1990): 61–98; Thomas L. Quick, *Successful Team Building* (New York: AMACOM, 1992): 40–52.
10. Several of the points are from Katzenbach and Smith, "The Discipline of Teams," 112.
11. "Team Player Gets Top Spot in Survey" (undated sample copy distributed by Dartnell Corporation, 1994): 3.
12. Andrew J. DuBrin, *The Breakthrough Team Player: Becoming the M.V.P. on Your Workplace Team* (New York: AMACOM, 1995): 19–38.
13. Glenn M. Parker, *Cross-Functional Teams: Working with Allies, Enemies & Other Strangers* (San Francisco: Jossey-Bass Publishers, 1994): 170.
14. Gregory Moorhead and Ricky W. Griffin, *Organizational Behavior: Managing People and Organizations*, 4th ed. (Boston: Houghton Mifflin, 1995): 278–270.
15. Tina L. Robbins, "Social Loafing on Cognitive Tasks: An Examination of the 'Sucker Effect', " *Journal of Business and Psychology* (Spring 1995): 337.
16. "When Is a Team Not a Team? When the NLRB Says No," *Human Resources Forum* (February 1994): 1–2.

CHAPTER 15

Control and Information Technology

LEARNING OBJECTIVES

After studying this chapter and doing the exercises, you should be able to:

1 Explain how controlling relates to the other management functions.

2 Understand the different types and strategies of control.

3 Describe the steps in the control process.

4 Explain the use of nonbudgetary control techniques.

5 Summarize the various types of budgets, and the use of budgets and financial ratios for control.

6 Outline the basics of an information system.

7 Present an overview of how information technology influences a manager's job.

8 Specify several characteristics of effective controls.

© David Joel/Tony
Stone Images

Not too long ago, Case-Hoyt Corp., a high-quality printing company, was on the verge of bankruptcy. Jose Arriola Jr. is the owner, president, and chief executive officer of both Case-Hoyt and its parent company, Avanti/Case-Hoyt of Miami. He says that the graphic arts company is back being profitable, and reclaiming its former position as a premier name in the printing industry. Last year, Case-Hoyt's sales were $54 million, or 45 percent of Avanti/Case-Hoyt's total sales of $120 million. • Harris M. DeWeese, an investment banker who specializes in the printing industry, has financially analyzed Case-Hoyt. He estimated Case-Hoyt's gross margin—the difference between sales and the cost of raw materials, equipment, and production workers—to be between 24 percent and 25 percent. He finds that acceptable because the industry average is between 25 and 30 percent. Arriola agrees with the analysis, and regards it as a sign of the company's turnaround.[1]

This description of the financial performance of a printing company illustrates how managers use control measures to evaluate performance. In this case the measure was *gross margin*. The controlling function of management involves measuring performance and then taking corrective action if goals are not being achieved. When goals are being readily achieved, management will sometimes establish new, even more challenging goals.

As you will see in studying this chapter, controls make many positive contributions to the organization. An important purpose of controlling is to align the actions of workers with the interests of the firm. Without the controlling functions, managers have difficulty knowing if people are carrying out their jobs properly. Controls also enable managers to gauge whether the firm is attaining its goals.

Controls often make an important contribution to employee motivation. Achieving the performance standards set in a control system leads to recognition and other deserved rewards. Accurate control measurements give the well-motivated, competent worker an opportunity to be noticed for good work.

In this chapter we emphasize the types and strategies of controls, the control process, budgets and controls, and the use of information systems in control. We also examine how information technology influences a manager's job, because of the close link between information technology and controls. Finally, we describe characteristics of effective controls.

CONTROLLING AND THE OTHER MANAGEMENT FUNCTIONS

LEARNING OBJECTIVE

Explain how controlling relates to the other management functions.

Controlling has been referred to as the terminal management function because it takes place after the other functions have been completed. Controlling is most closely associated with planning, because planning establishes goals and the methods for achieving them. Controlling investigates the extent to which planning has been successful.

The links between controlling and other major management functions are illustrated in Exhibit 15-1. Controlling helps measure how well planning, organizing, and leading have been performed. The controlling function also measures the effectiveness of the control system. On occasion, the control measures are inappropriate. For example, suppose one measure of sales performance is the number of sales calls made. Such a measure might encourage a sales representative to call on a large number of poor prospects, just to meet the performance standard. Spending more time with better prospects would probably boost the sales representative's effectiveness. More will be said about effective control measures later.

The planning and decision-making tools and techniques Chapter 7 described are also tools and techniques of control. For example, a Gantt chart is a tool that keeps track of how well target dates for a project are being met. Keeping track is a control activity. If an event is behind schedule, a project manager usually takes corrective action.

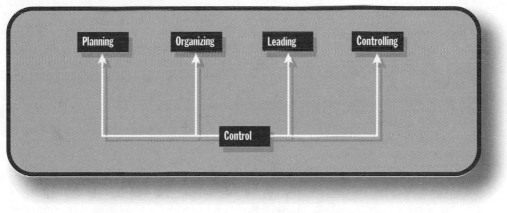

TYPES AND STRATEGIES OF CONTROL

Controls can be described according to their overall perspective: short range, intermediate range, long range. Controls can also be classified according to the time at which the control is applied to the activity—before, during, or after. Another important way of describing controls relates to the source of the control—external versus internal.

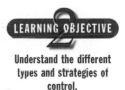

LEARNING OBJECTIVE 2

Understand the different types and strategies of control.

THE TIME ELEMENT OF CONTROLS

A **feedforward control** (or precontrol) takes place prior to the performance of an activity. A feedforward control prevents problems that result from deviation from performance standards. Feedforward controls are generally the most cost-effective controls. A manufacturing company that specifies quality standards for purchased parts has established a feedforward control. By purchasing high-quality parts, the manufacturer prevents many instances of machine failure. Feedforward controls are also used in human resources management. Standards for hiring employees are feedforward controls. For example, a company may require that all job candidates hired are nonsmokers. This precontrol helps decrease lost productivity due to smoking breaks and smoking-related illnesses.

feedforward control
A control that takes place prior to the performance of an activity.

   Concurrent controls monitor activities while they are being carried out. A typical concurrent control takes place when a supervisor observes performance, spots a deviation from standard, and immediately makes a constructive suggestion. For example, suppose a sales manager overhears a telemarketing specialist fail to ask a customer for an order. On the spot, the manager would coach the telemarketer about how to close an order.

concurrent control
A type of control that monitors activities while they are being carried out.

   Feedback controls (or postcontrols) evaluate an activity after it has been performed. Feedback controls measure history by pointing out what went wrong in the past. The process of applying the control may provide guidelines for future corrective action. Financial statements are a form of feedback control. If a financial report indicates that one division of a company has lost money, top level managers can then confer with division managers to see how to improve the situation.

feedback control
A control that evaluates an activity after it has been performed.

**Exhibit 15-2
Three Types of Time-
Based Controls**

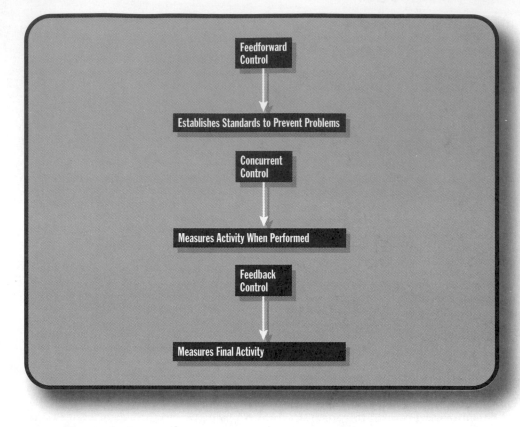

The gross margin index used by an analyst in evaluating the progress of Case-Hoyt illustrates a feedback control.

Exhibit 15-2 summarizes the three types of time-based controls. Most firms use a combination of feedforward, concurrent, and feedback controls. An important part of a manager's job is choosing controls appropriate to the situation.

EXTERNAL VERSUS INTERNAL CONTROLS

external control strategy
An approach to control based on the belief that employees are motivated primarily by external rewards and need to be controlled by their managers.

Controls can be classified according to their underlying strategy. **External control strategy** is based on the belief that employees are motivated primarily by external rewards and need to be controlled by their managers. Autocratic and Theory X management use an external control strategy. An effective external control system involves three steps. First, the objectives and performance standards need to be relatively difficult in order to gain optimum effort of team members and leave little leeway in performance. Second, the objectives and measures must be set in such a way that people cannot manipulate or distort them. For instance, top-level management should make its own investigation of customer satisfaction rather than take the word of field personnel. Third, rewards must be directly and openly tied to performance.

An external control strategy has several different effects. On the positive side, employees may channel considerable energy into achieving objectives. Employees do so because they know that good performance leads to a reward. If the control system is tightly structured, the result will be a high degree of control over employee behavior.

External control can create problems, however. Employees may work toward achieving performance standards, but they may not develop a commitment to the firm. They may reach standards but not be truly productive. Reaching standards without being productive is sometimes referred to as "looking good on paper." Suppose the top-level managers of an outpatient clinic establish as a performance standard a very high number of patients processed. To achieve this standard, the business manager in the clinic instructs the telephone receptionist, "When anybody calls with even a minor complaint, tell that person to come in for a visit." As a result, the medical staff spends brief amounts of time with many people who do not require medical attention. A more effective strategy would be to try to use the receptionist to screen callers so the doctors spend more time with fewer patients who truly need medical care.

Misdirected effort is another problem that can arise from an external control strategy. People may put too much effort into achieving performance standards and, as a result, neglect other important aspects of the job. High sales quotas may result in neglect of customer service. Externally imposed standards may also result in the filtering, or hiding, of poor performance.

Internal control strategy is based on the belief that employees can be motivated by building their commitment to organizational goals. Participative and Theory Y management use internal control strategy, as do self-managing work teams. Part of the success of the development of Windows NT was attributed to an internal control strategy. Two hundred and fifty programmers, testers, and program managers were involved in developing the software for personal computers. Control was directed from the bottom up, meaning that professionals established controls for their own work.[2]

Building an effective internal control system requires three steps. First, group members must participate in setting goals. These goals are later used as performance standards for control purposes. Second, the performance standards (control measures) must be used for problem solving rather than for punishment or blame. When deviations from performance are noted, superiors and subordinates should get together to solve the underlying problem. Third, although rewards should be tied to performance, they should not be tied to only one or two measures. An internal control strategy calls for evaluation of an employee's total contribution, not one or two quantitative aspects of performance.

A positive result of internal controls is that they usually lead to a higher commitment to attain goals. Thus, they may direct greater energy toward task performance. Another good result is that the system encourages the upward and horizontal flow of valid information about problems.

On the negative side, an internal control system may motivate employees to establish easy performance standards for themselves. Another problem is that the supervisor loses control over subordinates and may feel powerless as a result. Fi-

> **internal control strategy**
> *An approach to control based on the belief that employees can be motivated by building their commitment to organizational goals.*

nally, an internal control system creates some problems in giving out equitable rewards. Because performance standards may be loose, it is difficult to measure good performance.

An internal control system is not necessarily good, and an external control system is not necessarily bad. Internal controls work satisfactorily when a high-caliber, well-motivated work force is available. External controls compensate for the fact that not everybody is capable of controlling their own performance. If applied with good judgment and sensitivity, external control systems work quite well. The effective use of controls thus follows a contingency, or "if . . . then," approach to management.

STEPS IN THE CONTROL PROCESS

LEARNING OBJECTIVE

Describe the steps in the control process.

The steps in the control process follow the logic of planning: (1) performance standards are set, (2) performance is measured, (3) performance is compared to standards, and (4) corrective action is taken if needed. The following discussion describes these steps and highlights the potential problems associated with each one. Exhibit 15-3 presents an overview of controlling.

SETTING APPROPRIATE PERFORMANCE STANDARDS

standard

A unit of measurement used to evaluate results.

A control system begins with a set of performance standards that are realistic and acceptable to the people involved. A **standard** is a unit of measurement used to evaluate results. Standards can be quantitative, such as cost of sales, profits, or time to complete an activity. Standards can also be qualitative, such as a viewer's perception of the visual appeal of an advertisement. An effective standard has the same characteristics as an effective objective (see Chapter 5). Effective controls will be discussed later in this chapter.

Historical information about comparable situations is often used when standards are set for the first time. Assume a manufacturer wants to establish a standard for the percentage of machines returned to the dealer for repair. If the return rate for other machines with similar components is 3 percent, the new standard might be a return rate of no more than 3 percent.

At times performance standards are dictated by profit-and-loss considerations. A case in point is the occupancy-rate standard for a hotel. Assume break-even analysis reveals that the average occupancy rate must be 75 percent for the hotel to cover costs. Hotel management must then set an occupancy rate of at least 75 percent as a standard.

MEASURING ACTUAL PERFORMANCE

To implement the control system, performance must be measured. Performance appraisals are one of the major ways of measuring performance. Supervisors often make direct observations of performance to implement a control system. A simple example would be observing to make sure a sales associate always asks a

Exhibit 15-3
Steps in the Control-
ling Process

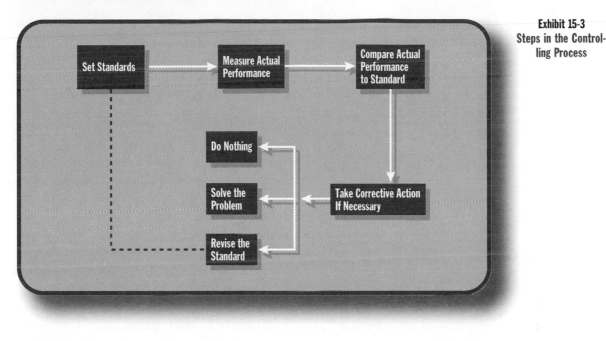

customer, "Is there anything else I could show you now?" A more elaborate performance measure would be a 10-page report on the status of a major project submitted to top-level management. The aspects of performance that accountants
measure are manufacturing costs, profits, and cash flow (a statement of cash receipts and payments).

Measurement of performance is much more complex than it would seem on
the surface. The list that follows presents three important conditions for effective
performance measurement:[3]

1. *Agree on the specific aspects of performance to be measured.* Top-level managers in a
   hotel chain might think that occupancy rate is the best measure of performance. Middle-level managers might disagree by saying, "Don't place so much
   emphasis on occupancy rate. If we try to give good customer service, the occupancy rate will take care of itself. Therefore, let's try to measure customer
   service."

2. *Agree on the accuracy of measurement needed.* In some instances, precise measurement of performance is possible. Sales volume, for example, can be measured
   in terms of customer billing and accounts paid. The absolute number or percentage of customer returns is another precise measurement. In other instances, precise measurement of performance may not be possible. Assume
   top-level managers of the hotel chain buy the idea of measuring customer service. Quantitative measures of customer satisfaction—including the ratings that
   guests submit on questionnaires and the number of formal complaints—are
   available. However, many measurements would have to be subjective, such as
   the observation of the behavior of guests, including their spontaneous comments about service. These qualitative measures of performance might be more
   relevant than the quantitative measures.

3. *Agree on who will use the measurements.* In most firms, managers at higher levels have the authority to review performance measures of people below them in the chain of command. Few people at lower levels object to this practice. Another issue is how much access the staff has to control reports. Line managers sometimes believe that too many staff members make judgments about their performance.

COMPARING ACTUAL PERFORMANCE TO STANDARDS

Once standards have been established and performance measurements taken, the next step is to compare actual performance to standards. Key aspects of comparing performance to standards include measuring the deviation and communicating information about it.

deviation
In a control system, the size of the discrepancy between performance standards and actual results.

Deviation in a control system is the size of the discrepancy between performance standards and actual results. It is important to agree beforehand how much deviation from the standard is a basis for corrective action. When using quantitative measures, statistical analysis can determine how much of a deviation is significant. Recall the 75 percent occupancy-rate standard in the hotel example. A deviation of plus or minus 3 percent may not be considered meaningful but rather caused by random events. Deviations of 4 percent or more, however, would be considered significant. Taking corrective action on significant deviations only is applying the *exception principle.*

There are times when a deviation as small as 1 percent from standard can have a big influence on company welfare. If a division fails by 1 percent to reach $100 million in sales, the firm has $1 million less money than anticipated. At other times, deviations as high as 10 percent might not be significant. A claims department might be 10 percent behind schedule in processing insurance claims. However, the claims manager might not be upset, knowing that all the claims will eventually be processed.

When statistical limits are not available, it takes wisdom and experience to diagnose a random deviation. Sometimes factors beyond a person's influence lead to a one-time deviation from performance. If the manager believes this to be the case, the deviation can be ignored. For example, a person might turn in poor performance one month because he or she faced a family crisis.

For the control system to work, the results of the comparison between actual performance and standards must be communicated to the right people. These people include the employees themselves and their immediate managers. At times, the results should also be communicated to top-level managers and selected staff specialists. They need to know about events such as exceptional deviations from safety and health standards. For example, nuclear power plants are equipped with elaborate devices to measure radiation levels. When a specified radiation level is reached or exceeded, several key people are notified automatically.

TAKING CORRECTIVE ACTION

After making an evaluation of the discrepancy between actual performance and a standard, a manager has three courses of action: do nothing, solve the problem, or revise the standard. Each of these alternatives may be appropriate, depending on the results of the evaluation.

DO NOTHING. The purpose of the control system is to determine if the plans are working. If the evaluation reveals that events are proceeding according to plan, no corrective action is required. Doing nothing, however, does not mean abdicating, or giving up, responsibility. A manager might take the opportunity to compliment employees for having achieved their objectives (thus increasing employee motivation), but do nothing about their approach to reaching objectives, because performance measurements show it to be effective.

SOLVE THE PROBLEM. The big payoff from the controlling process concerns the correction of deviations from substandard performance. If a manager decides that a deviation is signficant (nonrandom), he or she starts problem solving. Typically the manager meets with the team member to discuss the nature of the problem. Other knowledgeable parties might participate in the problem-solving process. At times, the deviation from a performance standard is so large that a drastic solution is required. A severe shortfall in cash, for example, might force a retailer to sell existing inventory at a loss.

Sometimes a manager can correct the deviation from a performance standard without overhauling current operations. An office manager in a group dental practice used a control model to measure the percentage of professional time allotted to patient care. The analysis revealed that nonbilled time had exceeded 10 percent—an unacceptable deviation. The corrective action involved two steps. First, workers scanned dental records to find patients who were overdue for cleaning and checkups. Second, the office manager telephoned these people and asked them if they would like to schedule an appointment for cleaning and checkup. The telemarketing campaign was so successful that virtually all the slack time was filled within 10 days.

REVISE THE STANDARD. Deviations from standard are sometimes attributable to errors in planning rather than to performance problems. Corrective action is thus not warranted because the true problem is an unrealistic performance standard. Consider an analogy to the classroom: If 90 percent of the students fail a test, the real problem could be an unrealistically difficult test.

Standards often must be revised because of changes in the task environment. A sudden shift in consumers' preference—from large to small computer disks, for example—could necessitate the revision of standards. Planning for a new task can also create a need for revised standards. Performance quotas may be based on "guesstimates" that prove to be unrealistically difficult or overly easy to reach. A performance standard is too difficult if no employee can meet it. A performance standard may be too easy if all employees can exceed it. As Exhibit 15-3 shows, revising standards means repeating the control cycle.

> **qualitative control technique**
> *A method of controlling based on human judgments about performance that result in a verbal rather than numerical evaluation.*

NONBUDGETARY CONTROL TECHNIQUES

One way of classifying control techniques is to divide them into those based on budgets versus those not based on budgets. In this section we describe nonbudgetary techniques, and classify them into two types. **Qualitative control techniques**

LEARNING OBJECTIVE

Explain the use of nonbudgetary control techniques.

are methods based on human judgments about performance that result in a verbal rather than a numerical evaluation. For example, customer service might be rated as "outstanding" rather than as 4.75 on a 1-to-5 scale. **Quantitative control techniques** are methods based on numerical measures of performance. Rating customer services as 4.75 on a 1-to-5 scale rather than as "outstanding" would indicate a quantitative control measure.

Exhibits 15-4 and 15-5 summarize qualitative and quantitative control techniques, respectively. The purpose in listing them is primarily to alert you to their existence. Chapter 7 provided details about four of the quantitative control techniques that Exhibit 15-5 describes.

Controls are widely used in firms to keep costs at acceptable levels. Feedback is often used when costs have risen too high. In response, managers begin to reduce as many variable costs as possible. Major cost-reduction activities include trimming payroll, selling off an unprofitable portion of the business, and reducing travel by company personnel. Minor areas of cost-cutting include restricting the use of photocopiers, cancelling magazine subscriptions, and eliminating the purchase of fresh flowers for reception areas.

Some firms use feedforward controls to guard against the need to trim costs. The use of temporary employees can be a feedforward control. By hiring temporaries, a firm prevents a portion of payroll costs from reaching an unacceptable level. A firm pays a temporary worker only for the duration of the assignment. In contrast, permanent workers are often kept on the payroll when they are between assignments, because managers anticipate finding constructive work for them soon.

BUDGETS AND BUDGETARY CONTROL TECHNIQUES

When people hear the word *budget,* they typically think of tight restrictions placed on the use of money. The car-rental agency name Budget Rent-A-Car was chosen because of popular thinking that the adjective *budget* means conservative spending. In management, a budget does place restrictions on the use of money, but the allotted amounts can be quite generous. A **budget** is a plan expressed in numerical terms, for allocating resources. The numerical terms typically refer to money, but they could also refer to such things as the amount of energy or the number of printer ribbons used. A budget typically involves cash outflow and inflow.

Virtually every manager has some budget responsibility, because a budget is a plan for allocating resources. Without budgets, there would be no way of keeping track of how much money is spent in comparison to how much money is available. Two aspects of budgets are of particualr interest to managers: the different types of budgets and how budgets are used for control. Readers who have studied accounting and finance will be familiar with this information.

TYPES OF BUDGETS

Budgets can be classified in many ways. For example, budgets are sometimes described as either fixed or flexible. A *fixed budget* allocates expenditures based on

Exhibit 15-4
Qualitative Control
Techniques

Technique	Definition	Key Features
Audit	Examination of activities or records to verify their accuracy or effectiveness	Usually conducted by someone from outside the area audited
External audit	Verification of financial records by external agency or individual	Conducted by an outside agency, such as a CPA firm
Internal audit	Verification of financial records by an internal group of personnel	Wide in scope, including evaluation of control system
Management audit	Use of auditing techniques to evaluate the overall effectiveness of management	Examines wide range of management practices, policies, and procedures
Personal observation	Manager's first-hand observations of how well plans are carried out	Natural part of manager's job
Performance appraisal	Formal method or system of measuring, evaluating, and reviewing employee performance	Points out areas of deficiency and areas for corrective action; manager and group member jointly solve the problem
Policy	General guideline to follow in making decisions and taking action	Indicates if manager is following organizational intentions

Technique	Definition	Purpose
Gantt chart	Chart depicting planned and actual progress of work on a project	Describes progress on a project
CPM/PERT	Method of scheduling activities and events using time estimates	Measures how well project is meeting schedule
Break-even analysis	Ratio of fixed costs to price minus variable costs	Measures organization's performance and gives basis for corrective action
Economic-order quantity (EOQ)	Inventory level that minimizes ordering and carrying costs	Avoids having too much or too little inventory
ABC analysis	Method of assigning value to inventory; A items are worth more than B or C items	Indicates where emphasis should be placed to control money
Variance analysis	Major control device in manufacturing	Establishes standard costs for materials, labor, and overhead, and then measures deviations from these costs

a one-time allocation of resources. The organizational unit receives a fixed sum of money that must last for the budget period. A *flexible budget* allows for variation in the use of resources on the basis of activity. Under a flexible budget, a sales department would receive an increased telephone budget if the department increased its telemarketing program. Any type of budget can be classified as fixed or flexible.

Many different types of budgets help control costs in profit and nonprofit firms. Below are brief descriptions of seven commonly used budgets. Most other budgets are variations of these basic types.[4]

master budget
A budget consolidated from the budgets of various units.

MASTER BUDGET. A **master budget** is a budget consolidated from the budgets of various units. Its purpose is to forecast financial statements for the entire company. Each of the separate budgets gives the projected costs and revenues for its own operations.

cash budget
A forecast of cash receipts and payments.

CASH BUDGET. A **cash budget** is a forecast of cash receipts and payments. The budget is compared against actual expenditures. The cash budget is an important control measure because it reflects a firm's ability to meet cash obligations. A firm that is working to capacity—such as a restaurant overflowing with customers—can still go bankrupt if its expenses are so high that even full production cannot generate enough revenue to meet expenses. (A typical problem is that the firm in this position has borrowed so much money that having a cash surplus becomes almost impossible. Principal and interest payments on the loans consume most of the cash receipts.)

Cash budgeting also serves the important function of showing the amount of cash available to invest in revenue-producing ventures. In the short range, businesses typically invest cash surpluses in stocks, bonds, and money market funds. In the long range, the cash is likely to be invested in real estate or in the acquisition of another company. Another long-range alternative is to use surplus cash to expand the business. Managers can also use cash surpluses to retire debt and consolidate ownership by buying up shares of the company owned by others.

revenue-and-expense budget
A document that describes plans for revenues and operating expenses in dollar amounts.

REVENUE-AND-EXPENSE BUDGET. A **revenue-and-expense budget** describes in dollar amounts plans for revenues and operating expenses. It is the most widely used, and most readily understood, type of budget. The sales budget used by business firms is a revenue-and-expense budget. It forecasts sales and estimates expenses for a given period of time. Many firms use a monthly revenue-and-expense budget. The monthly budgets are later converted into quarterly, semiannual, and annual budgets. Most revenue-and-expense budgets divide operating expenses into categories. Major operating expenses include salaries, benefits, rent, utilities, business travel, bulding maintenance, and equipment.

production budget
A detailed plan that identifies the products or services that must be produced to match the sales forecast and inventory requirements.

PRODUCTION BUDGETS. After sales forecasts have been established, the units needed from the production area can be estimated. A **production budget** is a detailed plan that identifies the products or services that must be produced or provided to match the sales forecast and inventory requirements. A production budget can be considered a production schedule.

MATERIALS PURCHASE/USAGE BUDGET. After production demands have been forecast, it is necessary to estimate the cost of meeting this demand. A **materials purchase/usage budget** is a plan that identifies the raw materials and parts that must be purchased to meet production demands. In a retail business a comparable budget specifies the merchandise that must be purchased to meet the anticipated sales demand.

HUMAN RESOURCES BUDGET. To satisfy sales and production demands, money must be allocated for the labor to accomplish the work. A **human resources budget** is a schedule that identifies the human resources needs for a future period and the labor (or personnel) costs to meet those needs. Of particular interest to management is whether the number of employees will have to be substantially increased or decreased to meet sales and production forecasts.

CAPITAL-EXPENDITURE BUDGETS. Organizations must invest in new equipment and buildings to stay in operation. A **capital-expenditure budget** is a plan for spending money on assets used to produce goods or services. Capital expenditures are usually regarded as major expenditures and are tied to long-range plans. Capital expenditures include money spent for buildings, machinery, equipment, and major inventories. In a typical budgeting system, the planned purchase of a computer network would be included in the capital budget. The monthly payment for postage and private delivery companies would be an operating expense.

> **materials purchase/ usage budget**
> *A plan that identifies the raw materials and parts that must be purchased to meet production demands.*

> **human resources budget**
> *A schedule that identifies the human resource needs for a future period and the labor costs to meet those needs.*

> **capital-expenditure budget**
> *A plan for spending money on assets used to produce goods or services.*

BUDGETS AND FINANCIAL RATIOS AS CONTROL DEVICES

An important part of the control process is to use budgets and financial ratios as measures of performance. To the extent that managers stay within budget or meet their financial ratios they are performing according to standard.

BUDGETS AND THE CONTROL PROCESS. Budgets are a natural part of controlling. Planned expenditures are compared to actual expenditures, and corrective action is taken if the deviation is significant. Exhibit 15-6 shows a budget used as a control device. The nightclub and restaurant owner described in Chapter 7 operates with a monthly budget. The owner planned for revenues of $40,000 in March. Actual revenues were $42,500, a positive deviation. The discrepancy is not large enough, however, for the owner to change the anticipated revenues for April. Expenses were $150 over budget, a negative deviation the owner regards as insignificant. In short, the performance against budget looks good. The owner will take no corrective action on the basis of March performance.

FINANCIAL RATIOS AND THE CONTROL PROCESS. A more advanced method of using budgets for control is to use financial ratios guidelines for performance. Three

Exhibit 15-6
March Revenue-and-Expense Budget for Nightclub and Restaurant

Item	Budget	Actual	Over	Under
Revenues	$40,000	$42,500	$2,500	
Beginning inventory	3,500	3,500		
Purchases	19,250	19,000		$250
End inventory	3,000	3,000		
Cost of goods sold	19,750	19,500		
Gross profit	20,250	23,000		
Salaries expense	10,500	10,500		
Rent and utilities expense	1,500	1,500		
Miscellaneous expense	100	250	150	
Maintenance expense	650	650		
Total operating expenses	12,750	12,900		
Net income before tax	7,500	10,100		
Taxes (40%)	3,000	4,040		
Net income	$ 4,500	$ 6,060		

Budget summary: Revenues and Net Income exceed budget by $2,500 and $1,560, respectively.

Note: Data analyzed according to *Generally Accepted Accounting Principles* by Jose L. Cruzet of Florida National College.

gross profit margin
A financial ratio expressed as the difference between sales and the costs of goods sold, divided by sales.

such ratios are presented here. One such commonly used ratio is **gross profit margin**, expressed as the difference between sales and the cost of goods sold, divided by sales, or

$$\text{Gross profit margin} = \frac{\text{Sales} - \text{Cost of goods sold}}{\text{Sales}}$$

The purpose of this ratio is to measure the total money available to cover operating expenses and to make a profit. If performance deviates significantly from a predetermined performance standard, corrective action must be taken.

Assume the nightclub owner needs to earn a 10 percent gross profit margin. For March, the figures are as follows:

$$\text{Gross profit margin} = \frac{\$42,500 - \$19,500}{\$42,500} = \frac{\$23,000}{\$42,500} = .54$$

Based on the gross-profit-margin financial ratio, the business is performing better than planned. One could argue that the gross profit margin presents an overly optimistic picture of how well the business is performing. Another widely used financial ratio is the **profit margin,** or return on sales. Profit margin measures profits earned per dollar of sales as well as the efficiency of the operation.

profit margin
A financial ratio measuring return on sales, or net income divided by sales.

$$= \frac{\text{Net income}}{\text{Sales}} = \frac{\$6,060}{\$42,500} = .14 \text{ or } 14\%$$

A profit margin of 14 percent would be healthy for most businesses. It also appears to present a more realistic assessment of how well the nightclub in question is performing as a business.

The last ratio described here is **return on equity**, an indicator of how much a firm is earning on its investment. It is the ratio between net income and the owner's equity, or

$$\text{Return on equity} = \frac{\text{Net Income}}{\text{Owner's Equity}}$$

> **return on equity**
> *A financial ratio of how much a firm is earning on its investment expressed as net income divided by owner's equity.*

Assume that the owner of the nightclub and restaurant invested $400,000 in the restaurant, and that the net income for the year is $72,500. The return on equity is $72,500/$400,000 = .181 or 18.1 percent. The owner should be satisfied, because few investments offer such a high return on equity.

OVERCOMING POTENTIAL PROBLEMS WITH BUDGETS

Budgets are a sensible method of controlling the expenditures of a firm. Without budgets a firm (as well as a family) can get out of financial control quickly. Some people will squander funds, leaving little money for important purposes. Even worse, there will be no systematic way of knowing if funds are available to cover legitimate expenses.

Despite their advantages, major concerns have been expressed about budgets. One concern, particularly in manufacturing, is that they may be based on outmoded accounting concepts. The traditional way of evaluating capital expenditures is to determine how much money they save in labor. If the cost of equipment cannot be justified in labor savings, managers may decide not to purchase the equipment.[5] A broader viewpoint is needed to achieve true productivity increases. Other cost-justification measures include how useful the new equipment is in cutting lead times, boosting quality, increasing customer satisfaction, and helping the company survive in the marketplace. As one small-business owner put it, "I don't care if my accountant says the new labeling machine will not provide a satisfactory return on investment. If we don't supply our customers with a computerized mailing list, we won't have any more customers."

Progress is being made in overcoming the limited view of performance sometimes created by budgets. An accounting professor and a technology consultant worked with 12 companies to devise a *balanced scorecard*—a set of measures that provide a quick but comprehensive view of a business. The scorecard provides managers answers to four key questions:[6]

1. How do customers see us? (the customer's perspective)
2. In what must we excel? (the internal business perspective)
3. Can we continue to improve and create value? (the innovation and improvement perspective)
4. What do shareholders think of us? (the financial perspective)

The four perspectives are related, as Exhibit 15-7 shows. For example, if a company excels at something, good financial results will be forthcoming. When applying the balanced scorecard, a firm will typically use several measures to answer

Exhibit 15-7
How a Balanced Score-card Links Performance Measures

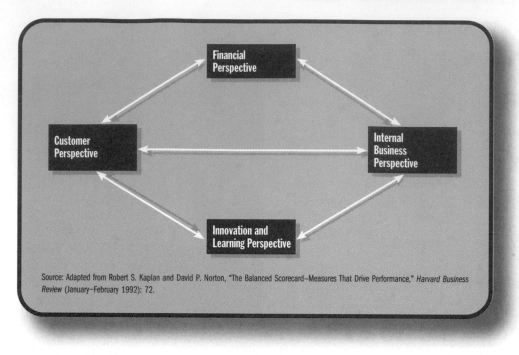

Source: Adapted from Robert S. Kaplan and David P. Norton, "The Balanced Scorecard–Measures That Drive Performance," *Harvard Business Review* (January–February 1992): 72.

each of the four questions. For example, Apple Computer uses five categories in the innovation and improvement category:[7]

- Customer Satisfaction—measures are made of the extent to which Apple is customer-driven.
- Core Competencies—Apple executives want employees to be highly focused on a few key competencies, such as friendly interfaces and effective distribution systems.
- Employee Commitment and Alignment—surveys are conducted to determine how well employees understand the company strategy and whether they achieve results consistent with the strategy.
- Market Share—the company regularly monitors its percentage of computers sold domestically and globally.
- Shareholder Value—the intention is to emphasize investments required today to generate growth for tomorrow.

LEARNING OBJECTIVE

Outline the basics of an information system.

> **information system (or management information system)**
> *A formal system for providing management with information useful or necessary for making decisions.*

INFORMATION SYSTEMS AND CONTROL

An **information system (IS)**, or **management information system (MIS),** is a formal system for providing management with information useful or necessary for making decisions. The IS is usually based on a mainframe computer, but recent advances allow some of these systems to be based on personal computers. Many firms that decentralized their information systems have gone back to using a large centralized corporate mainframe. A centralized system reduces duplication and helps integrate the different functions.

The use of information systems has become widespread throughout all kinds of organizations. Advances in digital technology have helped make this possible—

accessing computers from remote locations is easier than ever. With handheld information tools (or personal digital assistants) field personnel, including technicians, can get information from a central source. Sales representatives equipped with laptop computers or personal digital assistants can get needed information from the home office in seconds. Simultaneously, they can feed back to marketing vital information about customer orders and preferences.

Managerial control is based on valid information, so an IS is an indispensable part of any control system. The next sections describe the basic elements of an information system, how it can function as a control, and the electronic monitoring of work.

ELEMENTS OF AN INFORMATION SYSTEM

Establishing an information system usually involves four basic steps. As Exhibit 15-8 shows, these steps are: analyze the information requirements, develop an information base, design an information processing system, and build controls into the system.

ANALYZE INFORMATION REQUIREMENTS. The first step in designing an information system is to research the kinds of decisions managers and specialists need help in making. A related step is to decide what type of information is needed to provide that help. For example, research might show that managers need help in making decisions about which employees are qualified for overseas assignments. The IS designed to help them would include data about each employee's travel preferences, foreign-language skills, and ability to work without close supervision.

The people who are going to use the data from the information system should decide on the information requirements. This means managers must give the IS specialists a clear picture of their information requirements. This keeps users from getting stuck with an inadequate system; additionally, users are more committed to a system that they help select. Too often, when other people, such as systems analysts, decide on requirements, they make a wrong guess about what the users need. For example, the systems analyst may purchase software that is able to produce only limited information.

DEVELOP AN INFORMATION BASE. A base of valid information is the heart of any information system. Developing relevant information takes ingenuity. Sometimes, much of the information already exists in company records; it simply must be coded and stored in the IS. In other cases, information must be collected. In the overseas assignment example, managers and IS specialists might have to develop a questionnaire for job candidates. The questionnaire could be completed both by the candidate and by the manager during interviews. The results could be combined with the company information about work performance.

DESIGN AN INFORMATION PROCESSING SYSTEM. In this step, a system is designed for collecting, storing, transmitting, and retrieving information. Specialized knowledge about computer systems is required to complete this step successfully, so

Exhibit 15-8
Basic Elements of an
Information System

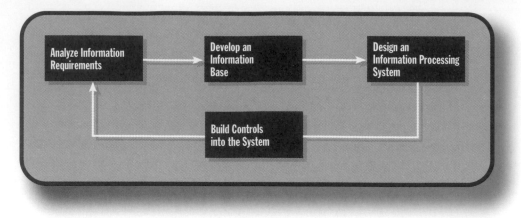

many firms use outside assistance. The total IS is a composite of a number of specific information systems. The same system that helps select candidates for overseas assignments cannot keep track of spare parts.

BUILD CONTROLS INTO THE SYSTEM. At the beginning of this chapter, we mentioned that one part of the controlling function is to evaluate the control system. Building controls into the IS is a special case of this general principle. Most information systems are impressive on the surface because they involve modern electronic equipment. However, despite outward sophistication, an IS can generate invalid or outdated information. The information system for foreign assignments might generate a list of employees at the press of a few buttons. If inaccurate performance-appraisal data had been entered, however, many of these people could be unqualified for overseas work. To use a tired cliché, "garbage in, garbage out."

Another type of control built into an information system is a control against misappropriation, or unauthorized use, of information. Controls against such computer theft include an elaborate system of passwords and other security devices. Programs to counter computer viruses are another aspect of computer security. A *computer virus* is an unauthorized program, placed secretly into a computer, that destroys stored data and other programs. A virus can also be introduced into a system accidentally by a contaminated disk from an outside source.

Effective controls enable managers to pinpoint the deficiencies in an IS. Effective controls are also useful in updating the system as information requirements change.

CONTROL INFORMATION SUPPLIED BY AN INFORMATION SYSTEM

The field of information systems keeps expanding. This growth is partly attributable to the increasing need for useful control information. The control information that can be generated by an information system is virtually unlimited. Exhibit 15-9 shows a sampling of what an IS keeps track of. The accompanying Organization in Action feature illustrates a standard application of an information system to better control inventory purchases.

Information systems can:

- Report on sales of products by territory, sales representative, and customer category
- Supply inventory level information by region, plant, and department
- Describe magazine subscribers by age, income, occupational level, and ZIP code
- Report turnover rates by age, sex, job title, and salary level
- Supply information about budget deviations by location, department, and manager
- Automatically compile financial ratios and compare them to industry standards
- Automatically compile production and operation control indexes and compare them from plant to plant
- Print out a summary of overdue accounts according to customer, and goods or services purchased
- Report hospital-bed occupancy rates according to diagnosis, sex, and age of patient
- Calculate, by subsidiary, the return on investment of cash surpluses

COMPUTER-AIDED MONITORING OF WORK

Increasingly, information systems are being used for *computer-aided monitoring of work*. In this type of monitoring, a computer-based system gathers data about the work habits and productivity of employees. These systems capitalize upon the networking of computer terminals to monitor the work of employees who use com-

ORGANIZATION IN ACTION: RETAILERS RELY ON INFORMATION SYSTEMS

A study commissioned by MasterCard International revealed that retail shopping has lost some of its allure. Dining out has bumped shopping from first place in the ways people treat themselves. Mindful of such findings, retailers are scrambling to find ways to take market share from their competitors. Retailers recognize they must have what customers want, when they want it, or they will fail to make a sale.

Retail analyst Edward Johnson says that retailers must use state-of-the-art technology to remain competitive. Computerized inventory control is a good example. It enables retailers to keep close watch on what's hot and what's not, and to react quickly to buying patterns. It quickens the process of reordering fast-selling hits and canceling orders for slow-moving items.

Johnson says that information technology holds labor costs down in one of the most labor-intensive industries. Reducing overhead costs is vital for retailers who must increasingly battle for business by slashing prices. Competing on price is especially important now that "reverse snob appeal" is motivating shoppers. According to Johnson, the "in thing" is finding quality merchandise at the lowest possible price.

Source: Based on facts reported in Marybeth Nibley, "Shoppers Get Pickier About Their Buying: Stores Need Technology Edge," Associated Press story (17 January 1993).

puter terminals in their jobs or who operate complex machine tools. Once the monitoring software is installed, the central computer processes information from each terminal and records the employee's efficiency and effectiveness.

Office workers, including those who are in frequent telephone contact with the public, are the most likely to be monitored. Word processing specialists are measured by such factors as words keyed per minute, the number of breaks taken, and the duration of each break. The Internal Revenue Service uses an electronic monitoring system to evaluate workers who provide taxpayer assistance by telephone. AT&T uses electronic monitoring to evaluate operators, who must complete calls within a set time. Safeway Stores, Inc. equips its trucks with small, computerized boxes that record truck speed, gas mileage, gear shifting patterns, and whether the truck strays from its route.

The major advantage of an electronic monitoring system is the close supervision it allows managers. Some employees welcome computerized monitoring because it supplements arbitrary judgments by supervisors about their productivity. Computerized work-monitoring systems have substantial disadvantages, however. Many argue that these systems invade employee privacy and violate their dignity. Moreover, electronic monitoring often contributes to low levels of job satisfaction, absenteeism, high turnover, and job stress.

INFORMATION TECHNOLOGY AND THE MANAGER'S JOB

LEARNING OBJECTIVE 7

Present an overview of how information technology influences a manager's job.

The preceding discussion of information systems emphasized how managers use information, gathered primarily through information technology, to improve the control function. Information technology also exerts a profound effect on other aspects of a manager's job and on organizational performance. As but one example, information technology makes it easier for managers to reengineer a business process such as handling a mortgage application. Information technology (IT) has become so important in business that many chief executive officers make decisions about upgrading such technology in their firms. In the past, major decisions about information technology were delegated to the information systems manager. A senior vice-president of a gas company gives this perspective:

The IT function should be run by a great general manager, not by the traditional technology manager. No company can afford to overlook the role information technology can play in spurring organizational change and shaping core business processes. You can no longer delegate the IT function to the back office. Rather, you need to see it as a vital business within your business, run by people with commercial backgrounds who know how to make decisions that are based on ever changing competitive imperatives.[8]

Much of the revolutionary impact of information technology on the jobs of managers, and on organizations, stems from the use of networks. As used in information technology, a **network** is the linking by computer of workers through-

network
The linking by computer of workers throughout the organization with each other.

out the organization with each other. Workers can also connect with internal and external databases, and with customers and suppliers. Networks give all employees who have learned to use the computer system direct access to each other and to information they need to carry out their jobs. In addition to using networks designed for the company only, many workers also join on-line services such as the Internet.[9]

To understand the impact of information technology on the manager's job, we describe the positive consequences of information technology. In addition, we will comment on its possible negative side effects.

THE POSITIVE CONSEQUENCES OF INFORMATION TECHNOLOGY

The information technology revolution would not have lasted so long if it were not helping managers, other workers, and organizations perform better. A brief description of the positive impact of IT follows, with an emphasis on managerial work.

IMPROVED PRODUCTIVITY AND TEAMWORK. A major justification for installing information technology is that it improves productivity. By using computerized information systems, workers can handle a large number of transactions with high accuracy. A specific example is that an investment consultant (stockbroker) can handle many more accounts with computerized than manual record keeping. The productivity of human resource managers and professionals has increased through using ATM-like machines to automate the administrative side of human resources. For example, voice-response systems enable employees to receive updated information on their benefits. Using such systems, human resource departments have downsized by 30 to 40 percent in recent years, thus enhancing productivity.[10]

Small business owners have increased their productivity in many ways by exploiting information technology. An advanced application of IT is using on-line services to find sources of investment capital. The business owner posts a message, and then potential investors can respond. Finding investors on-line can be quicker than an extensive letter-writing and telephone-calling campaign.

Information technology can enhance teamwork because team members can maintain frequent contact with each other through E-mail and pagers. Even if the group does not have the time to hold an in-person meeting, team members can give electronic feedback to each other's ideas. Furthermore, with extensive use of IT, teammates do not even have to work in the same physical location.

GAINING COMPETITIVE ADVANTAGE. Effective use of information technology can give a firm a competitive advantage. A classic example is American Airlines' computerized reservation system (the SABRE system). American Airlines leases the system to other airlines, yet SABRE displays American Airlines flights whenever possible. In addition to the user fees SABRE collects, the system provides American Airlines with useful competitive information such as pricing tactics. Another

illustration of using IT to gain competitive advantage is that many banks now offer on-line banking services. Security First, of Lexington, Kentucky, opened its
doors on the Internet in 1995, with a relatively small $41 million in assets. Yet
by being on the Internet it can compete directly with a banking giant such as
Wells Fargo.[11]

IMPROVED CUSTOMER-SERVICE AND SUPPLIER RELATIONSHIPS. Advances in information technology, including networking, can lead to improved customer service and
smoother working relationships with suppliers. Customer service is improved when
service representatives have immediate access to information that can resolve a
customer problem. USAA, a large financial services firm, is a model for the industry in terms of prompt service. The company sells insurance directly to the public, without the use of external sales representatives or insurance agents. Policy
holders can call an 800 number to receive immediate answers to complex questions such as how much rates will increase if a 16-year-old family member becomes
a licensed driver.

Supplier relationships can be more productive when suppliers and purchasers
are part of the same network. Large retailers such as Wal Mart authorize some of
their suppliers to ship and stock goods based on electronic messages sent from
point of purchase to the suppliers' computers. When inventory gets low on a fast-
moving item, supplies are replenished automatically without a retail store official
having to make a phone call or send a letter.

ENHANCED COMMUNICATION AND COORDINATION. Nowhere is the impact of information technology on the manager's job more visible than in communication and
coordination. By relying on information technology they can be in frequent contact with office members without being physically present. They can also be part
of the **virtual office,** in which employees work together as if they were part of a
single office despite being physically separated. The most familiar tools of the virtual office are fax machines, modems, pagers, and cellular telephones. A more recent advance is the *electronic assistant,* such as Wildfire. The device is a three-way
combination of a computer, telephone, and voice recognition system. In response
to the owner's voice command, Wildfire can telephone any number in its file system and can also relay messages.

Frequent contact with company employees, customers, and suppliers enhances
coordination. The alternative is for the manager to communicate primarily when
back at the office. A high-tech manager is never away from the office—even if he
or she would like to be!

QUICK ACCESS TO VAST INFORMATION. Information technology gives managers quick
access to vast amounts of information. A careful library researcher could always
access vast amounts of business-related information. Advances in information technology, however, allow for fingertip access if the manager has the right computer
skills. For example, a sales manager might want a targeted list of prospects for her
company's new pool tables. She uses an electronic directory to locate sporting-

virtual office
*An arrangement
whereby employees
work together as if
they were part of a
single office despite
being physically
separated.*

goods stores in her region, ranking them by revenue and zip code to streamline her sales strategy.

In general, the manager obtains quick access to vast—and relevant—information by learning how to navigate the information superhighway. The **information superhighway** is the combination of computer, telecommunication, and video technologies for the purpose of disseminating and acquiring information. Managers also use the info superhighway to let others know of their products, services, and job openings. Furthermore, a manager might use an on-line service to list an unusual requirement such as requiring a part for an obsolete machine.

ENHANCED ANALYSIS OF DATA AND DECISION MAKING. Closely related to gathering a wider array of information, IT allows for better analysis of data and decision making. A good example is that Stanley Home Products was able to reduce inventories worldwide by $5 million in one year by using global telecommunication networks. The information obtained on the network gave Stanley managers a more accurate analysis of how much inventory to stock. The manager of corporate systems said, "The main problem was delays and the excess inventories that delays can cause. When that kind of activity is going on worldwide, there can be delays of 10 weeks or more between order and delivery."[12]

Another way in which information technology helps managers make better decisions is through computer-assisted decision making. A variety of software has been designed for such purposes. The most directly relevant for most managers is **decision-making software.** It is any computer program that helps a decision maker work through problem-solving and decision-making steps. Such software usually asks the user questions about values, priorities, and the importance attached to factors such as price and quality.

The decision-making process used in these programs is referred to as "intuitive" because the programs rely more on human judgment than on quantitative analysis. The intent of the programs is to improve the quality of decisions rather than to just make computations or generate data. A decision-making program might help a traffic manager decide whether to make a large shipment by truck, railroad, or airplane.

FACILITATION OF EMPOWERMENT AND FLATTER ORGANIZATIONS. The widespread use of information technology gives more workers access to information they need for decision making. As a result, more workers can be empowered to make decisions. Fewer layers of management are required because so many middle managers are no longer needed to act as information conduits. Instead, workers at lower levels access information directly through computer networks. Information technology therefore provides line employees with the documents they need to perform their jobs more effectively and make decisions on their own.[13]

THE NEGATIVE CONSEQUENCES OF INFORMATION TECHNOLOGY

Information technology's contribution to organizational health has been extraordinary. Nevertheless, the same exciting technology produces some unintended

---

information superhighway
The combination of computer, telecommunications, and video technologies for the purpose of disseminating and acquiring information.

decision-making software
Any computer program that helps a decision maker work through problem-solving and decision-making steps.

negative consequences. Awareness of these potential problems can help managers prevent them from occurring. One subtle problem is that managers and other employees become **computer goof-offs.** They spend so much time attempting new computer routines and accessing information of questionable value that they neglect key aspects of their job. Many managers, for example, would prefer to surf the Internet for low-value information than to confront an employee about a discipline problem.

computer goof-off
A person who spends so much time attempting new computer routines and accessing information of questionable value that he or she neglects key aspects of the job.

A problem of considerable magnitude is that customer service sometimes deteriorates because of information technology. Many banks, for example, force customers with a service problem to call an 800 number rather than allowing them to deal with a branch representative. A voice-response system instructs the customer to punch in lengthy account numbers, along with making choices from a complicated menu. The process is time-consuming and impersonal, and difficult for customers unfamiliar with information technology. A related problem is that highly automated customer-service operations may appear unfriendly and detached.

Information technology has resulted in *wired managerial workers.* As a result of being electronically connected to the office at all times, many managers and professionals complain that their employers expect them to be always available for consultation. Many managers, for example, are expected to bring pagers and cellular telephones on vacation so they can respond to inquiries from the office.

Another potential dysfunction of information technology is that companies sometimes collect a hodgepodge of poorly integrated equipment. Even many of the resident technology experts are baffled by its proper use. As a result, the company achieves a poor return on its investment. To overcome this problem many companies, including financial services giant Aetna, are consolidating software and putting employees on one standardized office system.[14]

CHARACTERISTICS OF EFFECTIVE CONTROLS

LEARNING OBJECTIVE 8

Specify several characteristics of effective controls.

An effective control system improves job performance and productivity by helping workers correct problems. A system that achieves these outcomes has distinct characteristics. The greater the number of the following characteristics a given control system contains, the better the system will be at providing management with useful information and improved performance.

1. *The controls must be accepted.* For control systems to increase productivity, employees must cooperate with the system. If they are more intent on beating the system than on improving performance, controls will not achieve their ultimate purpose. For example, the true purpose of a time-recording system is to ensure that employees work a full day. If workers are intent on circumventing the system through such means as having friends punch in and out for them, the time-recording system will not increase productivity.

2. *The control measures must be appropriate and meaningful.* People tend to resist control measures that they believe do not relate to performance in a meaningful

way. Customer-service telephone representatives, for example, may object to a control measure based primarily on the amount of inquiries processed. Experienced operators contend that giving the right assitance to fewer callers would be a better measure of performance.

3. *An effective control measure provides diagnostic information.* If controls are to improve performance, they must help people correct deviations from performance. A sales manager might be told that he or she was performing well in all categories except selling to small-business owners. This information might prompt the manager to determine what services the company sells that would have more appeal to small businesses.

4. *Effective controls allow for self-feedback and self-control.* A control system that is self-administering saves considerable time. Employees can do much of their own controlling if the system permits them access to their own feedback. An example is a system whereby clients complain directly to the employee instead of going to management.

5. *Effective control systems provide timely information.* Controls are more likely to lead to positive changes in behavior when the control information is available quickly. It is more helpful to give workers daily rather than monthly estimates of their performance against quota. Given day-by-day feedback, an employee can make quick adjustments. If feedback is withheld until the end of a month or a quarter, the employee may be too discouraged to make improvements.

6. *Control measures are more effective when employees have control over the results measured.* People rebel when they are held responsible for performance deviations beyond their control. For example, a resort hotel manager's profits might fall below expectations because of a factor beyond his or her control such as a sudden shift in weather that results in cancellations.

7. *Effective control measures do not contradict each other.* Employees are sometimes asked to achieve two contradictory sets of standards. As a result, they resist the control system. If employees are told to increase both quantity and quality, for example, the result can be confusion and chaos. A compromise approach would be to improve quality with the aim of increasing net quantity in the long run. If care is taken in doing something right the first time, less rework is required. With less time spent on error correction, eventually the quantity of goods produced increases.

8. *Effective controls allow for random variations from standard.* If a control allows for random variations that do not differ significantly from the standard, then it is more effective. An ineffective way of using a control system is to quickly take action at the first deviation from acceptable performance. A one-time deviation may not indicate a genuine problem. It could simply be a random or insignificant variation that may not be repeated for years. For example, would you take action if a team member exceeded a $3,000 travel-expense allowance by $2.78?

9. *Effective controls are cost-effective.* Control systems should result in satisfactory returns on investment. In many instances they don't because the costs of con-

trol are too high. Having recognized this fact, some fast-food restaurants allow employees to eat all the food they want during working hours. The cost of trying to control illicit eating is simply too high. (This policy has the added benefit of building worker morale.)

10. *A cross-functional team's measurement system must empower the team instead of top management retaining the power.* The ascendance of teams in organizations often requires that control measures for teams be given special consideration. Traditional performance measures may inhibit empowerment because team members do not have full control. One suggestion is for teams to create measures that track the process of delivering value. An example is that a product-development team might decide to measure the number or percentage of new parts to be used in a product. The rationale is that the more parts a product contains, the greater the possibility for malfunction.[15]

SUMMARY OF KEY POINTS

1
Explain how controlling relates to the other management functions.
Controlling is used to evaluate whether the manager has done a good job planning, organizing, and leading. Controls can also be used to evaluate control systems.

2
Understand the different types and strategies of control.
Controls can be classified according to the time when they are applied. Feedforward controls are applied prior to the performance and are thus preventive. Concurrent controls monitor activities while they are being carried out. Feedback controls evaluate and take corrective action after an activity has been performed.

Controls can also be classified according to their underlying strategy. An external control strategy is based on the assumption that employees are motivated primarily by external rewards and need to be controlled by their managers. An internal control strategy assumes that managers can motivate employees by building commitment to organizational goals.

3
Describe the steps in the control process.
The steps in the controlling process are to set standards, measure actual performance, compare actual performance to standards, and take corrective action if necessary. To measure performance, agreement must be reached on the aspects of performance to be measured, the degree of accuracy needed, and who will use the measurements.

The three courses of action open to a manager are to do nothing, to solve the problem, or to revise the standard. Taking corrective action on significant deviations only is called the exception principle.

4
Explain the use of nonbudgetary control techniques.
Nonbudgetary control techniques can be qualitative or quantitative. Qualitative techniques include audits, personal observation, and performance appraisal. Quantitative techniques include Gantt charts, PERT, and economic-order quantity. Cost cutting is closely tied to the control function.

5

Summarize the various types of budgets, and the use of budgets and financial ratios for control.

A budget is a spending plan for a future period of time, and it is expressed in numerical terms. A fixed budget allocates expenditures based on a one-time allocation of resources. A flexible budget allows variation in the use of resources on the basis of activity. Seven widely used types of budgets are the (1) master budget, (2) cash budget, (3) revenue-and-expense budget, (4) production budget, (5) materials purchase/usage budget, (6) human resources budget, and (7) capital-expenditure budget.

Budgets are a natural part of controlling. Managers use budgets to compare planned expenditures to actual expenditures, and they take corrective action if the deviation is significant. Three key financial ratios are gross profit margin, profit margin, and return on equity.

Budgets are a sensible method of controlling the expenditures of a firm. However, budgets can lead to rigidity in behavior, and they can be time-consuming to prepare. To help overcome the limited view of performance created by budgeting, the balanced scorecard has been developed. Using this tool, managers view an organization from four perspectives: financial, internal business, innovation and improvement, and the customer.

6

Outline the basics of an information system.

An information system (IS), or management information system (MIS), is a formal system for providing management with information useful or necessary for making decisions. To develop an IS, you must analyze the information requirements, develop an information base, design an information processing system, and build controls into the system. An IS can keep track of a wide range of facts that are used for control purposes. Increasingly, information systems are being used for the electronic monitoring of the work habits and productivity of employees. Although the method helps managers monitor employee performance, it has met with considerable criticism. Electronic monitoring works best when its results are used for constructive feedback.

7

Present an overview of how information technology influences a manager's job.

Information technology has its greatest impact on managerial work through the use of computer networks. Positive consequences of IT on the manager's job include: improved productivity and teamwork; gaining competitive advantage; improved customer-service and supplier relationships; enhanced communication and coordination; quick access to information; enhanced analysis of data and decision making; and facilitation of empowerment and flatter organizations. Negative consequences of information technology include computer goofing off, rude customer service, wired managerial workers, and poorly integrated equipment leading to no productivity gain.

8

Specify several characteristics of effective controls.

An effective control system results in improved job performance and productivity, because it helps people correct problems. An effective control measure is accepted by workers, appropriate, provides diagnostic information, allows for self-feedback and self-control, and provides timely information. It also allows employees some control over the behavior measured, does not embody contradictory measures, allows for random variation, is cost-effective. Teams can sometimes select their own relevant control measures.

KEY TERMS AND PHRASES

Feedforward Control *pg. 339*
Concurrent Control *pg. 339*
Feedback Control *pg. 339*
External Control Strategy *pg. 340*
Internal Control Strategy *pg. 341*
Standard *pg. 342*
Deviation *pg. 344*
Qualitative Control Technique *pg. 345*
Quantitative Control Technique *pg. 346*
Budget *pg. 346*
Master Budget *pg. 348*
Cash Budget *pg. 348*
Revenue-and-Expense Budget *pg. 348*
Production Budget *pg. 348*

Materials Purchase/Usage Budget *pg. 349*
Human Resources Budget *pg. 349*
Capital-Expenditure Budget *pg. 349*
Gross Profit Margin *pg. 350*
Profit Margin *pg. 350*
Return on Equity *pg. 351*
Information System (or Management
    Information System) *pg. 352*
Network *pg. 356*
Virtual Office *pg. 358*
Information Superhighway *pg. 359*
Decision-Making Software *pg. 359*
Computer Goof-Off *pg. 360*

QUESTIONS

1. To what extent do controls fit in the modern organization?
2. Which style of leader would most likely establish and implement controls?
3. What corrective action should a manager take when the department has spent all its budget for office supplies three months before the end of the fiscal year?
4. A sales manager was criticized for going over budget on expenses for entertainment and travel. His response was, "You can't make money if you don't spend money. Our customers want to be entertained." What is your reaction to his statement?
5. Identify two control techniques used in the classroom.
6. What do you regard as the most important use a manager can make of information technology?
7. In what way does information technology contribute to unemployment?

SKILL-BUILDING EXERCISE 15-A: FINANCIAL RATIOS

GROUP ACTIVITY Jessica Albanese invested a $50,000 inheritance as equity in a franchise print and copy shop. Similar to well-established national franchises, the shop also offers desktop publishing, fax, and computer graphics services. Listed below is Jessica's revenue-and-expense statement for her first year of operation.

Item	Financial Result
Revenues	$255,675
Beginning inventory	15,500
Purchases	88,000
End inventory	14,200
Cost of goods sold	89,300
Gross profit	166,375
Salaries expense	47,000
Rents and utilities expense	6,500
Miscellaneous expense	1,100
Maintenance expense	750
Total operating expenses	55,350
Net income before taxes	111,025
Taxes (40%)	44,410
Net income	66,615

Working individually or in small groups, compute the following ratios: gross profit margin, profit margin (return on sales), and return on equity. Groups might compare answers. Discuss whether you think that Jessica is operating a worthwhile business.

SKILL-BUILDING EXERCISE 15-B: INVENTORY SHRINKAGE

Assume you are the production manager for a firm that manufactures personal digital assistants. An audit shows that many of these devices are disappearing from finished inventory. Design a control system to reduce this inventory shrinkage.

VIDEO DISCUSSION QUESTIONS

1. Which financial control measures does Bossidy mention? **[Allied Signal]**
2. How might 360-degree evaluation be used as a control device? **[360 Degrees of Evaluation]**
3. How can learning about interactive television help managers perform better on the job? **[Technology]**

CASE PROBLEM 15-A: THE ATM FRAUD

Karen Smith was not aware that her bank card was missing until her credit union informed her that her account was more than $346,000 overdrawn. Two men and a woman now face charges that they used Smith's card to make 724 withdrawals during a 54-hour period. Authorities say this rampage was one of the five largest automated-teller fraud cases in U.S. history.

The thieves' assault on automatic-teller machines (ATMs) was like winning repeatedly at playing a slot machine. The trio cruised from one automated-teller machine to another in a maroon, gold-trimmed Cadillac. Police said they spent hours at a time withdrawing money. Police detective Jim Muzyn said, "They did it just as fast as you could punch in the

CASECASECASECAS

card, punch in the number and pull out the card, time and time again, many, many, many consecutive withdrawals."

By the time the three thieves finished, they withdrew $346,770 from 48 bank machines. A secret service agent noted that they drained a few of the machines dry. The three people found a way around the problem of the account becoming empty. They used empty envelopes to make phony deposits totaling $820,000.

"Many banks will believe the card user and trust their customers," Muzyn said. "If you're putting in some money, it will post it immediately."

The episode began when Smith left her van locked in a parking lot while she attended a football game in Gresham, a suburb of Portland, Oregon. Somebody broke into the van, and stole the bank card from Smith's purse. She had written the card's personal identification number (PIN) on her Social Security card.

Investigators used bank-machine records to trace the thieves' route more than 100 miles through five counties. Four of the machines were equipped with cameras that photographed the three people. The suspects are a man who has been imprisoned five times, his wife, and the Cadillac owner.

CASE QUESTIONS

1. Why is this case included in a chapter about control systems?
2. What controls should bank management implement that will prevent such thievery in the future?
3. What precontrols should Karen Smith have implemented to prevent this incident?

Source: Adapted from "Automated Tellers Become Slot Machines, Net Crooks $346,000," Associated Press story (11 February 1995).

CASE PROBLEM 15-B: BUSINESS MAIL EXPRESS TACKLES A BIG ONE

Some companies, such as Fingerhut, Citibank, Mastercard International, and BankOne rely on mass mailings to collect their money. To such large mailers, time is definitely money. The initial problem these companies face is that after a first-class letter is dropped off in the company mail room, it takes an average of five days to reach the destination. In 1996, the postage was 32 cents plus printing and handling.

According to these high-volume mailers, the cost may actually be 10 times higher. For every day the bill is in the mail, that's one day less the customer's check is not yet on the way. As a consequence, a company such as BankOne does not have the customer's money credited to its account. The money therefore does not collect interest in the bank nor can it be invested.

Paul Carlin, the former Postmaster General, and Eugene C. Johnson, the creator of the Mailgram, saw the delays in getting a check in hand as an entrepreneurial opportunity. For the foreseeable future, the mass mailers of bills would still have to put bills in the hands of their customers. And they would also need to receive checks or money orders back from their customers. Not many customers were prepared or willing to use electronic transfers of funds.

Carlin and Johnson decided to form a new company to deal with the challenge, Business Mail Express. What they needed was a unique synergy of what the post office did best—delivery of mail to its final destination in homes—and electronic transfer. The transfer would have to bypass the least efficient steps in the postal process: collection, long-haul transportation, and mail processing.

Cash flow is a big problem with many potential clients of Business Mail Express. A marketing manager explained that 17 percent of credit-card users paid their bills on receipt of the invoice. Another 7 percent paid within one week, and 39 percent paid within two weeks. If the bill could get into the credit-card issuer's hands within one or two days, cash flow would be much improved.

"The challenge was to cut the five-day, coast-to-coast delivery of the Postal Service to two days or less," said Johnson. Carlin and Johnson agreed that the heart of their business would be to use information technology to reduce coast-to-coast delivery time.

CASE QUESTIONS

1. What type of system would help Business Mail Express carry out its mission? Whether or not you are an expert in information technology, how would IT contribute to the system you describe?
2. How might this case be considered a problem of reengineering?

Source: Based on facts reported in David A. Andelman, "Mail-by-Wire," *Management Review* (November 1994): 16–17.

CASE PROBLEM 15-C: HOW WELL IS EFTEK DOING?

EFTEK is a package engineering and design company, whose primary product is called the Water Ballast/Rinser System. The system helps soft-drink bottling companies cope with the problem of top-heavy plastic bottles that tend to tip over before being filled at the plant. The result is that these bottles cannot be run through filling lines at anywhere near the speeds and efficiencies normally associated with glass or base-cup-equipped plastic bottles.

The heart of the patented systems is injection of rinse water into the bottles in quantities sufficient to act as ballast. The bottles can then be moved on standard glass conveyor lines at speeds in excess of 1,000 per minute. The bottles are then emptied of rinse water, rinsed again, and then filled and capped.

The enhancement pays for itself financially in less than six months, making it appealing to cost-conscious managers at major bottlers like Coca-Cola, Pepsico, and Perrier. According to the research of a group of financial analysts, the potential market for the ballaster in the U.S. and Canada is an estimated 4,000 packagers of beverage products. Added to this figure is another 6,000 units internationally. Following is a portion of projected financial information for EFTEK for 1998:

Units Sold	150
NET SALES	$21,235,500
Cost of Goods	8,167,500
GROSS PROFIT	13,068,000
Gross Margin	61.5%

CASE QUESTIONS

1. Do you think the EFTEK Corp. has a product that meets customer requirements?
2. Apply financial ratio analysis to decide whether EFTEK is projected to have outstanding financial results.

Source: *Letter from the Publisher*, Berkshire Information Services, Inc., One Evertrust Plaza, Jersey City, N.J. 07032. E-Mail: berkshire@growth.com

CASE PROBLEM 15-D: INFORMATION TECHNOLOGY AT TAKEOUT TAXI

Takeout Taxi is the world's largest multi-restaurant marketing-and-delivery business, with annual sales of over $50 million. The company delivers restaurant meals directly to a customer's home or office from its 150-plus franchise stores. When a customer telephones, a Takeout Taxi employee seated at a terminal is prepared to enter the order into the company's computer system. While the order is sent by fax to the restaurant, a dispatcher locates a driver to pick up and deliver the food as soon as it's ready. In any given area, Takeout Taxi works with from 12 to 50 restaurants.

Takeout Taxi CEO Kevin Abt, age 37, is in total control of his business. From his office in Herndon, Virginia, he can obtain information from each of the 150 stores in his system. His software system gives him access to even small details of his operation. Abt says, "I can track sales down to the last egg roll we have delivered anywhere in the world."

Computers are the foundation of the business at Takeout Taxi. Abt thought of establishing a restaurant-food delivery service because he was too busy working to spend the time going out for dinner. He believed that information technology would be the key to success in a restaurant delivery service.

The company information system enables Abt to have a direct hand in the business even as Takeout Taxi becomes more geographically dispersed. Every Saturday night, data from the previous week is sent by modem to headquarters from each location. "It's like we're sitting there in the store," says Abt. "If I have a quick analytical question on a certain franchisee, I can log in from my office or from home. I can then take a quick look into the specific market, run a five-second sales report, and cut the data in a number of different ways. It's a fingertip away."

CASE QUESTIONS

1. Describe what the information system at Takeout Taxi has to accomplish to enable the company to perform its delivery service. (In other words, what tasks must the system perform for the business to fulfill its purpose?)
2. Identify the control system Takeout Taxi currently uses.
3. Can you suggest any other controls Takeout Taxi should be using to run its food-delivery service?

Source: Based on facts reported in Niklas von Daehne, "The New CEO," *Success* (November 1994): 46–48.

REFERENCES

1. Jill A. Zelickson, "Black Ink Flows Again at Case-Hoyt," *Rochester Inc.* (27 March 1995): 1.
2. C. Pascal Zachary, *Showstopper! The Breakneck Race to Create Windows NT and the Next Generation at Microsoft* (New York: The Free Press, 1994).
3. Richard O. Mason and E. Burton Swanson, "Measurement for Management Decision: A Perspective," *California Management Review* (Spring 1979): 70–81.
4. Belverd E. Needles, Jr., Henry R. Anderson, and James C. Caldwell, *Principles of Accounting,* 4e (Boston: Houghton Mifflin, 1990): 1099–1113.
5. Karren Pennar, "The Productivity Paradox," *Business Week* (6 June 1988): 101.
6. Robert S. Kaplan and David P. Norton, "The Balanced Scorecard–Measures That Drive Performance," *Harvard Business Review* (January–February 1992): 71–72.
7. Robert S. Kaplan and David P. Norton, "Putting the Balanced Scorecard to Work," *Harvard Business Review* (September–October 1993): 134.
8. "The End of Delegation? Information Technology and the CEO," *Harvard Business Review* (September–October 1995): 162.
9. Gregory M. Bounds, Gregory H. Dobbins, and Oscar S. Fowler, *Management: A Total Quality Perspective* (Cincinnati: South-Western College Publishing, 1995): 693.
10. "Technology Update: Welcome to Virtual HR," *Human Resources Forum* (September 1995): 1.
11. "The Competition Heats Up in Online Banking," *Fortune* (26 June 1995): 18–19.
12. Patrick Flanagan, "Managing Network Technology," *Management Review* (October 1993): 13.
13. Liz Thach and Richard E. Woodman, "Organizational Change and Information Technology," *Organizational Dynamics* (Summer 1994): 30.
14. Jenny C. McCune, "Information Systems Get Back to Basics," *Management Review* (January 1994): 55.
15. Christopher Meyer, "How the Right Measures Helps Teams Excel," *Harvard Business Review* (May–June 1994): 96.

CHAPTER 16

Managing Ineffective Performers

LEARNING OBJECTIVES

After studying this chapter and doing the exercises, you should be able to:

1
Identify factors contributing to poor performance.

2
Describe in detail the control process for managing ineffective performers.

3
Know what is required to coach and constructively criticize employees.

4
Understand how to discipline employees.

5
Explain the purpose and operation of an employee assistance program.

6
Develop an approach to dealing with difficult people.

7
Explain the recommended approach to terminating employees.

© UPI/Bettman

During August, a few years back, a Manhattan subway accident killed five people and injured 170 others. Investigators discovered a vial of crack cocaine in the conductor's cab, but no conductor. He was caught later, drunk. The incident brought support for random drug and alcohol testing from transit authorities as well as unions. The next year, the U.S. Department of Transportation (DOT) added alcohol testing to its requirements.[1]

The tragic subway accident dramatizes management's responsibility for dealing with individual behavior that can lead to ineffective performance, and sometimes catastrophic consequences. An important aspect of managerial control is dealing constructively with **ineffective job performance.** Job performance is considered ineffective when it lowers productivity below an acceptable standard. Ineffective performers are also referred to as problem employees because they create problems for management.

> **ineffective job performance**
>
> *Job performance that lowers productivity below an acceptable standard.*

Ineffective performers lower organizational performance directly by not accomplishing their fair share of work. They also lower organizational productivity indirectly. Poor performers decrease the productivity of their superiors by consuming managerial time. Additionally, the productivity of coworkers is often decreased because coworkers must take over some of the ineffective performer's tasks. The relatively high turnover rate of poor performers also lowers productivity, because of the time and expense involved in recruiting and training replacements.

The consequences of ineffective performance are enormous. For example, one set of factors contributing to poor performance is employee deviancy. It includes behaviors such as stealing, cheating, and substance abuse. Alone these factors produce organizational losses estimated to range from $6 billion to $200 billion annually.[2] In this chapter, ineffective performance is regarded as a control problem for which the manager can take corrective actions. Poor performance, however, can also be viewed as a problem of motivation or staffing. Poor performers sometimes require effective motivation, and poor performance sometimes occurs because people are placed in the wrong job.

FACTORS CONTRIBUTING TO INEFFECTIVE PERFORMANCE

LEARNING OBJECTIVE 1

Identify factors contributing to poor performance.

Employees are or become ineffective performers for many different reasons. The cause of poor job performance can be rooted in the person, the job, the manager, or the company. At times, the employee's personal traits and behaviors create so much disturbance that he or she is perceived as ineffective.

Exhibit 16-1 summarizes factors that can contribute to ineffective performance. Factors not listed here can also be contributors. These factors fall into one of four categories: personal, or related to the job, manager, or company. Usually, the true cause of ineffective performance is a combination of several factors. Assume that an employee is late for work so frequently that his or her performance becomes substandard. The contributing factors in this situation could be the worker's disrespect for work rules, an unchallenging job, and an unduly harsh supervisor. One factor may be more important than others, but they are all contributors.

A manager and a company can contribute significantly to ineffective performance through improper implementation of the various functions of management. For example, with poor planning and leadership, workers receive little guidance and may drift into poor work habits. Too much supervision can also cause problems. A system of tight controls can create enough stress to lower performance.

The following list expands on how the factors listed in Exhibit 16-1 are related to ineffective performance:

THE EMPLOYEE

- *Insufficient mental ability and education.* The employee lacks the problem-solving ability necessary to do the job. Poor communication skills are included here.

Factors Related to the Employee	Factors Related to the Job
Insufficient mental ability and education	Ergonomics problems
Insufficent job knowledge	Cumulative trauma disorder
Emotional problem or personality disorder	Repetitive, physically demanding job
Alcoholism and drug addiction	Built-in conflict
Tobacco addiction or withdrawal symptoms	Night-shift work assignments
Job stress and burnout	Substandard industrial hygiene
Technological obsolescence	A "sick" building
Excessive absenteeism and tardiness	**Factors Related to the Company**
Conducting outside business on the job	
Chronic complaining	Organizational culture that tolerates poor performance
Family and personal problems	Counterproductive work environment
Physical limitations	Negative work-group influences
Brain injury	Intentional threats to job security
Factors Related to the Manager	Violence or threats of violence
Inadequate communication about job responsibilities	
Inadequate feedback about job performance	
Inappropriate leadership style	

Exhibit 16-1
Factors Contributing to Ineffective Performance

A report by the Commission on the Skills of the American Workforce concluded that the knowledge and skill deficiency of the majority of American workers reduces productivity.[3]

- *Insufficient job knowledge.* The employee is a substandard performer because he or she comes to the job with insufficient training or experience.

- *Emotional problem or personality disorder.* The employee may have emotional outbursts, periods of depression, or other abnormal behaviors that interfere with human relationships and work concentration. Cynical behavior may lower the performance of an entire work group if the negative attitude spreads to others.

- *Alcoholism and drug addiction.* The employee cannot think clearly because his or her mental or physical condition has been temporarily or permanently impaired by alcohol or other drugs. Attendance is also likely to suffer.

- *Tobacco addiction or withdrawal symptoms.* The employee who smokes is often fatigued and takes so many cigarette breaks that his or her work is disrupted. Sick leave may also increase. Even workers who stop smoking may suffer performance problems for a while. Recent quitters report higher depression, anxiety, lower job satisfaction, more job tension, and increased short-term absence.[4]

- *Job stress and burnout.* Severe short-term stress leads to errors in concentration and judgment. As a result of prolonged job stress, an employee may become apathetic, negative, and impatient. He or she can no longer generate the energy to perform effectively.

- *Technological obsolescence.* Employee does not keep up with the state of the art in his or her field. He or she avoids using new ideas and techniques and becomes ineffective.

- *Excessive absenteeism and tardiness.* The employee is often not at work for a variety of personal or health reasons. Lost time leads to low productivity.

- *Conducting outside business on the job.* The employee may be an "office entrepreneur" who sells merchandise to coworkers or spends time on the phone working on investments or other outside interests. Time spent on these activities lowers productivity.
- *Chronic complaining.* The employee spends so much time complaining about working assignments, working conditions, and coworkers that the employee wastes his or her time and that of supervisors.
- *Family and personal problems.* The employee is unable to work at full capacity because of preoccupation with an off-the-job problem such as a marital dispute, conflict with children, a broken romance, or indebtedness.
- *Physical limitations.* Job performance decreases as a result of injury or illness. For example, in the United States, lower-back problems account for approximately one-fourth of all workdays lost and cost between $15 and $20 billion per year.[5]
- *Brain injury.* The employee receives brain injury through physical trauma or substance abuse. Concentration, judgment, and physical mobility may be impaired. The employee may also suffer from temper trantrums and depression.

THE JOB

- *Ergonomic problems.* If equipment or furniture used on the job contributes to fatigue, discomfort, or injury, performance problems result. For example, if an employee develops neck pain and eyestrain from working at a poorly designed computer configuration, performance will suffer.
- *Cumulative trauma disorder.* The worker experiences physical injuries caused by repetitive motions over prolonged periods of time. Carpal tunnel syndrome is a leading cumulative trauma disorder. The syndrome occurs when frequent bending of the wrist causes swelling that pinches a key nerve. Among those affected are data entry specialists, cashiers who work with optical scanners, and interpreters who use sign language.
- *Repetitive, physically demanding job.* A repetitive, physically demanding job can cause the employee to become bored and fatigued, leading to lowered performance.
- *Built-in conflict.* The nature of the job involves so much conflict that job stress lowers performance. The position of collection agent for a consumer-loan company might fit this category.
- *Night-shift work assignments.* Employees assigned to all-night shifts suffer many more mental lapses and productivity losses than those assigned to daytime or evening shifts.
- *Substandard industrial hygiene.* Excessive noise, fumes, uncomfortable temperatures, inadequate lighting, high humidity, and fear of injury or contamination engender poor performance.
- *A "sick" building.* In some office buildings a diverse range of airborne particles, vapors, and gases pollute the indoor environment. The results can be headaches, nausea, and respiratory infections. Performance suffers and absenteeism increases.

THE MANAGER

- *Inadequate communication about job responsibilities.* The employee performs poorly because he or she lacks a clear picture of what the manager expects.
- *Inadequate feedback about job performance.* The employee makes a large number of errors because he or she does not receive the feedback—early enough or at all—to prevent them.

CONSULTANT IN ACTION: EARLY-WARNING SIGNALS OF VIOLENCE

Psychologists and crisis specialists contend that more than 99 percent of the workplace homicides involving coworkers had telltale signs. Furthermore, alert observers could have noticed these signs. "The perpetrator always give you an indicator," says John Nicoletti, a police psychologist and crisis consultant in Lakewood, Colorado. "The typical public belief is that these people just snap; that just isn't true."

Coworkers tend to ignore evidence such as threats or a smashed windshield. According to Nicoletti, virtually every would-be murderer begins with threats of three forms. One form is direct threats, such as "I'm gonna get you for this." Another form is conditional threats such as "If I don't get my job back,

I'm going to hold you responsible." The third form is veiled threats, such as "I can see how someone might want to blow up the place." The veiled threats are often the most dangerous. An effective antidote to such a threat is to confront the person and say, "Time out; why did you say that?"

A recent study revealed that 58 percent of workers who had been harassed, 24 percent of those who had been attacked, and 43 percent of those who had been threatened did not report the incident. The result may range from damaged property to murders. Nicoletti said that a lot of people are left shaking their heads and saying they should have known.

Source: "Violent Workers Usually Give Warning Signs, Experts Say," Knight Ridder News Service (15 September 1995).

- *Inappropriate leadership style.* The employee performs poorly because the manager's leadership style is inappropriate to the employee's needs. For example, an immature employee's manager gives him or her too much freedom and the result is poor performance. This employee needs closer supervision.

THE COMPANY

- *Organizational culture that tolerates poor performance.* Suppose an organization has a history of not imposing sanctions on employees who perform poorly. When managers demand better performance, many employees may not respond to the new challenge.
- *Counterproductive work environment.* The employee lacks proper tools, support, budget, or authority to accomplish the job. An example would be a sales representative who does not have an entertainment budget sufficient to meet customers' expectations.
- *Negative work-group influences.* Group pressures restrain good performance or the work group penalizes a high-performance worker. Similarly, peer group social pressure may cause an employee to take overly long lunch breaks, neglecting job responsibilities.
- *Intentional threats to job security.* A company, for example, makes excessive work demands on an employee in the context of a veiled threat that the job will be eliminated unless the extra work is done. Performance suffers as the worker becomes fearful and anxious.
- *Violence or the threat of violence.* Employees witness violent behavior in the workplace such as physical assaults, knifings, shootings, or threats of violence. Many employees not directly affected are nevertheless distracted and fearful, leading to lowered productivity. The accompanying Consultant in Action presents more details about workplace violence.

Many performance problems described above can be viewed from the perspective of a **behavior mismatch.** Such a mismatch happens when one person's ac-

behavior mismatch
A condition that occurs when one person's actions do not meet another's expectations.

tions do not meet another's expectations.[6] In the present context, it is the worker's actions and the manager's expectations. A lack of understanding between the manager and the group member that stems from their different perspectives leads to different expectations. The perception of poor performance results from differing views and expectations.

Assume that a worker is experiencing the problem of a personal bankruptcy. His perception is that because he has personal problems, less should be expected of him. Perhaps he believes that 75 percent of his usual productivity is adequate performance. Yet his supervisor perceives him as not meeting job expectations.

THE CONTROL PROCESS FOR MANAGING INEFFECTIVE PERFORMERS

LEARNING OBJECTIVE

Describe in detail the control process for managing ineffective performers.

The approach to improving ineffective performance presented here follows the logic of the control process shown in Exhibit 16-2. Problem identification and problem solving lie at the core of this approach. The control process for managing ineffective performers is divided into the eight steps illustrated in Exhibit 16-2, and should usually be followed in sequence. This section will describe each of these steps in detail. Two key methods of improving ineffective performance— discipline and employee assistance programs—receive separate attention later in the chapter.

DEFINE PERFORMANCE STANDARDS

Penalizing employees for not achieving performance standards that have not been carefully communicated is unfair. Therefore, the first step in the controlling process for managing ineffective performers is to clearly define what is expected of employees. (This step is identical to the step labeled "Set Standards" in the controlling process shown in Exhibit 15-3.) Performance standards are commonly established by such means as job descriptions, work goals, production quotas, and formal discussions of what is to be accomplished in a position.

DETECT DEVIATION FROM ACCEPTABLE PERFORMANCE

Detection is the process of noting when an employee's performance deviates from an acceptable standard. Managers use the various control measures Chapter 15 described to detect deviations from acceptable performance. For performance to be considered ineffective or poor, it must deviate significantly from the norm.

At times, quantitative measures can be used to define ineffective performance. For some jobs, ineffective performance might begin at 30 percent below standard. For other jobs, the cutoff point could be 20 or 50 percent, or any other percentage of deviation that fits the situation. What percentage of deviation from standard do you think would be acceptable for a quality inspector? For a loan specialist in a bank?

Personal observation plays a key role in detecting ineffective performance. One reason that observation is so important is that it is a concurrent control. By the time quantitative indicators of poor performance have been collected, substantial damage may have been done. Assume a bank manager observes that one of the loan officers is taking unduly long lunch hours on Fridays. Upon return, the officer appears to be under the influence of alcohol. Eventually, this unacceptable behavior will show up in quantitative indicators of performance. However, it might take a year to collect these data.

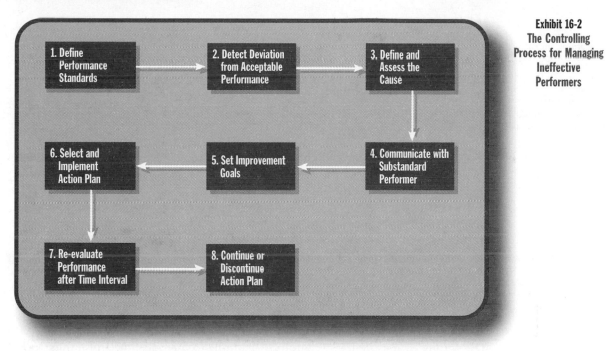

DEFINE AND ASSESS THE CAUSE

At this stage the manager attempts to diagnose the real cause of the problem. Following the logic of Exhibit 16-1, the primary contributor to the problem could be a personal factor or a factor related to the job, the company, or the manager. A discussion with the employee (the next step in the controlling process) may be necessary to reveal the major cause of the problem. For example, an office assistant was absent so frequently that her performance suffered. She claimed that extensive photocopying made her sick. The supervisor investigated further and called in the company health and safety expert. A medical examination confirmed that the office assistant was allergic to the trace fumes from the toner in the large-volume photocopier. After the office assistant was reassigned, her attendance became satisfactory.

COMMUNICATE WITH THE SUBSTANDARD PERFORMER

After the unacceptable performance or behavior is detected, the manager must communicate concern to the worker. At times, a simple discussion will suffice. At other times, confrontation may be necessary. **Confrontation** means dealing with a controversial or emotional topic directly. Confrontation is necessary whenever the employee does not readily admit to experiencing a problem.

Managers often avoid confrontation for several reasons. They may have limited skill in criticizing employees. Or, they may prefer not to deal with the anger and resentment that confrontation is likely to trigger. A third reason is not wanting to make the employee feel uncomfortable.

A recommended confrontation technique is to communicate an attitude of concern about the confronted person's welfare. To do this, confront the person is a sincere and thoughtful manner. Using the words *care* and *concern* can be helpful. For instance, a manager might begin by saying: "The reason I'm bringing up this problem is that I care about your work. You have a good record with the company, and I'm concerned that your performance has slipped way below its former level."

confrontation
Dealing with a controversial or emotional topic directly.

SET IMPROVEMENT GOALS

The fifth step in the control process is to set improvement goals. An **improvement goal** is one that, if attained, will correct unacceptable deviation from a performance standard. The goals should be documented on paper or electronically. Improvement goals should have the same characteristics as other objectives (see Chapter 5). Above all, improvement goals should specify the behavior or result that is required. Vague improvement goals are not likely to cause changes in performance.

An example of a specific improvement goal is: "During this month, nine of your ten customer-service reports must be in on time." This specific goal is likely to be more effective than a general improvement goal, such as "Become more prompt in submitting customer-service reports."

If the ineffective performer expresses an interest in improvement, joint goal setting is advisable. By providing input into goal setting, the substandard performer stands a good chance of becoming committed to improvement. At times improvement goals have to be imposed on substandard performers, especially in cases involving a motivation problem. If substandard employees were interested in setting improvement goals, they would not have a motivation problem.

SELECT AND IMPLEMENT AN ACTION PLAN

The setting of improvement goals leads logically to the selection and implementation of action plans to attain those goals. Much of the art of remedying ineffective performance is contained in this step. Unless appropriate action plans are developed, no real improvement is likely to take place. Many attempts at improving substandard performance fail because the problem is discussed and then dropped. Thus the employee has no concrete method of making the necessary improvements.

TYPES OF ACTION PLANS. An action plan for improvement can include almost any sensible approach tailored to the specific problem. An action plan could be formulated to deal with every cause of ineffective performance listed in Exhibit 16-1.

Action plans for improving ineffective performance can be divided into two types. One type is within the power of the manager to develop and implement. Plans of this type include coaching, encouraging, and offering small incentives for improvement. The other type of action plan is offered by the organization or purchased on the outside. These include training programs, stress-management programs, and stays at alcoholism-treatment centers. Exhibit 16-3 lists a selection of feasible corrective actions.

IMPLEMENTATION OF THE ACTION PLAN. After the action plan is chosen, it must be implemented. As shown in Exhibit 16-2, implementation begins in step 6 and continues through step 8. The manager has to utilize the approaches listed under "Managerial Actions and Techniques" in Exhibit 16-3. Human resources specialists outside the manager's department usually implement organizational programs.

An important part of effective implementation is continuation of the remedial program. Given the many pressures facing a manager, it is easy to forget the substandard performer who needs close supervision or a motivational boost. Often, a brief conversation is all that is needed.

RE-EVALUATE PERFORMANCE AFTER A TIME INTERVAL

Step 7 in the controlling process helps ensure that the process is working. In this step the manager measures the employee's current performance. If the remedial process is working, the team member's performance will move up toward stan-

Managerial Actions and Techniques

- **Coaching.** The manager points out specifically what the performer could be doing better or should stop doing. In daily interaction with the team members, the manager makes suggestions for improvement. One estimate is that coaching takes approximately 85 percent of the time a manager spends on performance improvement.[7]
- **Closer supervision.** The manager works more closely with the subordinate, offering frequent guidance and feedback.
- **Reassignment or transfer.** The manager reassigns the ineffective performer to a position that he or she can handle better.
- **Referral for personal counseling.** The manager refers the problem employee to an employee assistance program or other resource for personal counseling.
- **Use of motivational techniques.** The manager attempts to improve employee motivation by using positive reinforcement or some other motivational technique.
- **Corrective discipline.** The manager informs the employee that his or her behavior is unacceptable and that corrections must be made if the worker is to remain employed by the firm. The employee is counseled as part of corrective discipline.
- **Temporary leave.** The manager offers the employee an opportunity to take a leave of absence for a specified time in order to resolve the problems causing the poor performance.
- **Lower performance standards.** If performance standards have been too high, the manager lowers expectations of the team member. Consultation with higher management would probably be necessary before implementing this step.
- **Job rotation.** If ineffective performance results from staleness or burnout, changing to a different job of comparable responsibility may prove helpful.

Organizational Programs

- **Employee assistance programs (EAPS).** The employee is referred to a counseling service specializing in rehabilitating employees whose personal problems interfere with work.
- **Wellness programs.** The organization encourages employees to participate in specialized programs that help them stay physically and mentally healthy. By doing so, employees may prevent or cope with health problems—such as heart disease or an eating disorder—that interfere with job performance or lead to absenteeism. The wellness program usually includes stress management.
- **Career counseling and outplacement.** The employee receives professional assistance in solving a career problem, including being counseled on finding a job outside the firm.
- **Job redesign.** Specialists in human resources management and industrial engineering redesign job elements that could be causing poor performance. For example, the job is changed so that the employee has less direct contact with others, leading to reduced conflict.
- **Training and development programs.** The employee is assigned to a training or development program directly linked to his or her performance deficiency. For example, a very reserved sales representative receives assertiveness training.

**Exhibit 16-3
Corrective Actions for
Ineffective Performers**

dard. The greater the performance problem, the more frequent the re-evaluations of performance should be. In instances of behavior problems, such as alcoholism, weekly performance checks are advisable.

FORMAL AND INFORMAL REVIEWS. A re-evaluation of performance can be formal or informal. A formal progress review takes the form of a performance-appraisal session. It might include written documentation of the employee's progress and samples of his or her work. Formal reviews are particularly important when the employee has been advised that dismissal is pending unless improvements are made. Reviews are critical to avoid lawsuits over a dismissal.

The first level of informal review consists of checking on whether the employee has started the action plan. For example, suppose the reserved sales representative we mentioned agreed to attend an assertiveness training program. One week later, the manager could ask the rep, "Have you signed up for or started the training program yet?"

The next level of informal review is a discussion of the employee's progress. The manager can ask casual questions such as, "How much progress have you made in accounting for the missing inventory?" Or the manager might ask, "Have you learned how to use the new diagnostic equipment yet?"

POSITIVE REINFORCEMENT AND PUNISHMENT. If the employee has made progress toward reaching the improvement goal, positive reinforcement is appropriate. Rewarding an employee for progress is the most effective way of sustaining that progress. The reward might be praise, encouragement, or longer intervals between review sessions. The longer time between reviews may be rewarding because the employee will feel that he or she is "back to normal."

Giving rewards for making improvement is generally more effective than giving punishments for not making improvement. Yet if the problem employee does not respond to positive motivators, some form of organizational punishment is necessary. More will be said about punishment in the discussion about employee discipline.

CONTINUE OR DISCONTINUE THE ACTION PLAN FOR IMPROVEMENT

Step 8 in the controlling process for managing ineffective performers is making the decision whether to continue or discontinue the action plan. This step can be considered the feedback component of the control process. If the performance review indicates that improvement goals have not been met, the action plan is continued. If the review indicates that goals have been met, the action plan is discontinued.

An important part of using the controlling process to manage ineffective performers is realizing that positive changes may not be permanent. Performance is most likely to revert to an unacceptable level when the employee is faced with heavy job pressures. For instance, suppose an employee and a manager formulated an action plan to improve the employee's work habits. The employee's performance improved as a result. When the employee is under pressure, however, his or her work may once again become badly disorganized. The manager should then repeat the last five steps of the process, beginning with confrontation.

COACHING AND CONSTRUCTIVE CRITICISM

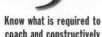

LEARNING OBJECTIVE

Know what is required to coach and constructively criticize employees.

---

coaching
A method for helping employees perform better that usually occurs on the spot and involves informal discussion and suggestions.

---

constructive criticism
A form of criticism designed to help improve performance or behavior.

Most performance improvement takes place as a result of a manager dealing directly with the worker not meeting standards. The usual vehicle for bringing about this improvement is **coaching**. It is a method for helping employees perform better that usually occurs on the spot and involves informal discussion and suggestions. Workplace coaching is much like coaching on the athletic field or in the performing arts. Coaching involves considerable **constructive criticism**, a form of criticism designed to help people improve. To be a good coach, and to criticize constructively, requires considerable skill. The following suggestions will help you improve your skill if practiced carefully.

1. *Focus on what is wrong with the work.* A major principle of employee coaching is to focus on the substandard behavior itself, not the person. When a person's self-image is attacked, he or she is likely to become hostile. Then the person's energy will be focused on getting even, not getting better.

2. *Listen actively.* An essential component of counseling employees is listening carefully to both their presentation of facts and their feelings. Your listening will encourage the employee to talk. As the employee talks about his or her problem, you may develop a better understanding of how to help improve performance.

3. *Ask good questions.* An effective workplace coach asks questions that help people understand their needs for improvement. Consultant Marilyn J. Darling says that effective coaching is based on asking good questions. She notes that the simpler the question the better:

- What are you trying to accomplish?
- How will you know if you've succeeded?
- What obstacles do you believe are stopping you?
- How can I help you succeed?[8]

All the above questions are part of active listening because they are open-ended. An open-ended question requests that the person provides details rather than a "yes" or "no" response. "What obstacles do you believe are stopping you?" is open ended because the worker must point to obstacles to answer the question. A closed question on the same topic would be "Are there any obstacles stopping you?" Such a question fails to promote dialogue.

4. *Engage in joint problem solving.* Work together to resolve the performance problem. One reason joint problem solving is effective is that it conveys a helpful and constructive attitude on the part of the manager. Another is that the employee often needs the superior's assistance in overcoming work problems. The manager is in a better position to get problems of this type resolved than is the employee.

5. *Offer constructive advice.* Constructive advice can be useful to the employee with performance problems. A recommended way of giving advice is first to ask an insightful question. You might ask the employee, "Could the real cause of your problem be poor work habits?" If the employee agrees, you can then offer some specific advice about improving work habits.

6. *Give the poor performer an opportunity to observe and model someone who exhibits acceptable performance.* A simple example of modeling would be for the manager to show the employee how to operate a piece of equipment properly. A more complex example of modeling would be to have the poor performer observe an effective employee making a sale or conducting a job interview. In each case the ineffective performer should be given opportunities to repeat the activity.

7. *Obtain a commitment to change.* Ineffective performers frequently agree to make improvements but are not really committed to change. At the end of a session, discuss the employee's true interest in changing. One clue that commitment may be lacking is when the employee too readily accepts everything you say about the need for change. Another clue is agreement about the need for change but with no display of emotion. In either case, further discussion is warranted.

LEARNING OBJECTIVE

4

Understand how to discipline employees.

discipline
Punishment used to correct or train.

EMPLOYEE DISCIPLINE

So far, this chapter has emphasized the positive approaches to improving substandard performance. There are times, however, when the controlling process requires a manager to discipline employees in an attempt to keep performance at an acceptable level. **Discipline,** in a general sense, is punishment used to correct or to train. In organizations, discipline is divided into two types, summary and corrective.

Summary discipline is the immediate discharge of an employee because of a serious offense. The employee is fired on the spot for rule violations such as stealing, fighting, or selling illegal drugs on company premises. In unionized firms, the company and the union have a written agreement specifying which offenses are subject to summary discipline.

Corrective discipline allows employees to correct their behavior before punishment is applied. Employees are told that their behavior is unacceptable and that they must make corrections if they want to remain with the firm. The manager and

summary discipline
The immediate discharge of an employee because of a serious offense.

corrective discipline
A type of discipline that allows employees to correct their behavior before punishment is applied.

the employee share the responsibility for solving the performance problem. The controlling process for managing ineffective performers includes corrective discipline. Steps 4 through 7 in Exhibit 16-2 are based on corrective discipline.

Taking disciplinary action is often thought of in relation to lower-ranking employees. Managers, professionals, and other salaried employees, however, may also need to be disciplined. Textron, Inc. is an example of a company that has seen the need to state explicitly a discipline policy for salaried employees. The discipline procedure follows quite closely the approach to progressive discipline described here.

The paragraphs that follow will describe three other aspects of discipline. First, we describe the most widely used type of corrective discipline, progressive discipline. Second, we explain the rules for applying discipline. Third, we examine the positive consequences of discipline to the organization.

PROGRESSIVE DISCIPLINE

progressive discipline
The step-by-step application of corrective discipline.

Progressive discipline is the step-by-step application of corrective discipline, as shown in Exhibit 16-4. The manager confronts and then coaches the poor performer about the performance problem. If the employee's performance does not improve, the employee is informed in writing that improvements must be made. The written notice often includes a clear statement of what will happen if performance does not improve. The "or else" could be a disciplinary layoff or suspension. If the notice is ignored and the disciplinary action does not lead to improvement, the employee may be discharged.

RULES FOR APPLYING DISCIPLINE

This chapter has discussed discipline as it relates to the correction of ineffective performance. However, discipline is more frequently used to deal with infractions of policy and rules. The employee in these situations may not necessarily be a poor performer. The administration of discipline, whether for poor performance or infractions, should adhere to certain time-tested rules. Before applying these rules, a manager in a unionized firm must make sure they are compatible with the employee discipline clauses in the written union agreement.

The red-hot-stove rule is an old-fashioned but still valid principle in administering discipline. According to the *red-hot-stove rule,* employee discipline should be the immediate result of inappropriate behavior, just as a burn is the result of touching a very hot stove. The employee should receive a warning (the red metal), and the punishment should be immediate, consistent, and impersonal. A manager should keep this rule and those that follow in mind when disciplining employees. Several of these suggestions incorporate the red-hot-stove rule.

1. *All employees should be notified of what punishments will be applied for what infractions.* For example, paralegal assistants might be told that discussing the details of client cases with outsiders, a violation of company policy, will result in discharge.
2. *Discipline should be applied immediately after the infraction is committed.* As soon as is practical after learning of a rule violation, the manager should confront the employee and apply discipline.
3. *The punishment should fit the undesirable behavior.* If the punishment is too light, the offender will not take it seriously. If, on the other hand, it is too severe, it may create anxiety and actually diminish performance.
4. *The manager should focus attention on the unsatisfactory behavior or performance, not on the person's attitudes or traits.* A core principle of discipline and punishment is for the person administering the discipline to point out what results are unaccept-

Exhibit 16-4
Steps in Progressive
Discipline

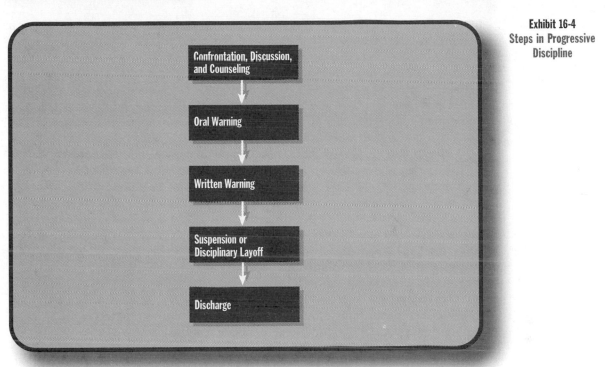

able rather than insulting or diagnosing the group member's personality. Thus the manager would say, "Your store received five consecutive below-average customer service ratings." The same manager should not say, "You couldn't care less about customer service."

5. *Managers should be consistent in the application of discipline for each infraction.* Every employee who violates a certain rule should receive the same punishment. Furthermore, managers throughout the organization should impose the same punishment for the same rule violation.

6. *Disciplinary remedies should be applied impersonally to offenders.* "Impersonal," in this context, implies that everybody who is a known rule violator should be punished. Managers should not play favorites.

7. *There must be documentation of the performance or behavior that led to punishment.* Justification for the discipline must be documented in substantial detail. Documentation is essential for defending the company's action in the event of an appeal by the employee or the union or in the case of a lawsuit.

8. *When the discipline is over, return to usual work relations.* The manager should not hold a grudge or treat the rule violator as an outcast. How the person who violated the rule is treated could become a self-fulfilling prophecy. Treating the person who was disciplined as an outcast may make that person feel alienated, causing his or her performance to deteriorate. If the person is treated as someone who is expected not to commit mistakes, he or she will most likely try to live up to that expectation.

POSITIVE CONSEQUENCES OF PUNISHMENT FOR THE ORGANIZATION

Conventional wisdom is that punishment should be avoided in the workplace or used only as a last resort because of its negative side effects. Workers who are punished may become anxious, fearful, revengeful, and even violent. More recent evidence, however, suggests that if punishment is perceived in certain ways, it can benefit the organization.[9]

A key factor in whether punishment is beneficial is the employee's *belief in a just world*, or that people get the rewards and punishments thcy deserve. Employees who believe in a just world are likely to accept punishment when they violate rules or perform poorly. The reason is that they believe they deserve to be punished. As a consequence, they do not complain about punishment, and might even spread the word that the organization is fair.

When employees observe that another employee has been punished justly (fairly), they will often rally on the side of management. The employee may think that the offending employee deserved the punishment. In some instances, other employees may desire that a rule violator be punished because it fits their sense of justice.

Another contribution of punishment is that it sends the message to most employees that they should take performance standards and rules seriously. At one company, the CEO was dismissed because he was accused of sexual harassment by 12 women employees. Many employees were happy to know that the company took sexual harassment seriously.

This section has described the many causes of ineffective performance and the manager's role in helping employees directly. The next section will consider comprehensive programs designed to rehabilitate troubled employees.

EMPLOYEE ASSISTANCE PROGRAMS

LEARNING OBJECTIVE 5

Explain the purpose and operation of an employee assistance program.

employee assistance program (EAP)
An activity to help employees deal with personal and job-related problems that interfere with their job performance.

An **employee assistance program (EAP)** is an activity to help employees deal with personal and job-related problems that interfere with their job performance. In many instances, job stress contributes to personal problems. Employees and their families use assistance programs to cope with a variety of personal problems and illnesses. Among them are alcoholism and other substance abuse, financial and legal difficulties, emotional problems, chronic illness such as AIDS or cancer, compulsive gambling, and weight control. Employees also use EAPs to deal with job-related concerns such as work stress, job dissatisfaction, and sexual harassment.

Marital and family relationship problems have become the most frequent reason for employees to visit an assistance program. Domestic problems account for 40 to 50 percent of EAP referrals. Nevertheless, substance abuse continues to have a greater negative effect on job performance and is more costly to treat.[10] Be aware that many seeking help for one problem have in reality a mixture of related problems. For example, an alcoholic worker might become financially troubled and then become an abusive partner.

All employee assistance programs offer confidential, professional help to employees seeking assistance with personal problems. Assistance programs are aimed at helping employees get job performance back to standard. A company EAP usually refers troubled workers to an outside agency, though some larger employers operate a comprehensive facility of their own. Members of the program are all company employees. Close to 40 percent of U.S. and Canadian workers have access to an assistance program. The paragraphs that follow summarize common characteristics of these programs.

- *Overall philosophy emphasizes rehabilitation.* EAPs are usually committed to rehabilitating employees. Use of an EAP is based on the assumption that personal problems spill over to the job, adversely affecting individual and organizational

ORGANIZATION IN ACTION: HELP FOR GAMBLERS

Drug and alcohol addictions have long been recognized and understood. But there is another addiction, equally strong, equally compelling, and equally destructive, that has only recently been recognized as a major emotional problem. It is the addiction to gambling.

Like those addicted to alcohol and drugs, the compulsive gambler soon loses sight of everything but his or her addiction. Home, family, friends, employment, respect, and self-esteem all become secondary to the next big bet, the next big chance, the next surge of excitement.

For compulsive gamblers caught in the vice of obsession, life is out of control. To regain that loss of control and return their lives to normalcy, they need the kind of specialized help available from the Taylor Manor Hospital Gambling Treatment Center. This unique program offers an intensive, highly individualized approach to the thorough rehabilitation of the compulsive gambler, with special focus on the needs of both the patient and the family.

The program's aim is to break the addiction's hold and to restore the patient to the normal worlds of family, work, and community.

Source: Brochure from Taylor Manor Hospital, Ellicott City, Maryland 21043.

productivity. Therefore, when the organization can provide help in problem resolution, it is helping itself.

- *Managers are the major source of referral.* Written records of employee performance are kept by supervisors and are ordinarily part of the performance-appraisal system. Employees are notified promptly of performance problems. The majority of referrals to EAPs are from managers who identify performance problems and then strongly suggest that the employee seek help. However, employees are responsible for using the EAP. As EAPs have gained in acceptance, more employees go to EAPs on their own. Family members who visit an EAP are typically referred by the employee.

- *Programs address specific problems.* Most EAPs offer formalized approaches for dealing with specific problems, such as the financial-counseling program for people with money problems. The accompanying Organization in Action feature illustrates the diversity of help available to troubled employees.

- *Time span of treatment is relatively short.* The time framework for EAP programs tends to be short, from one hour to one year. During this period, the employee can obtain professional assistance, become rehabilitated, and improve job performance. Some EAP professional have achieved good results through telephone consultations with troubled employees. Telephone treatments are often as short as 5 minutes. For example, the counselor may give an employee quick advice on dealing with a creditor.

- *The program is confidential.* An essential feature of EAPs is that they are confidential, and publicity about the programs emphasizes this characteristic. Brochures, notices, and articles in company newspapers all mention confidentiality and that records remain in EAP files only. To maintain confidentiality, record keeping should be beyond reproach. Employee assistance records should be kept separate from personnel files *and* medical records. Managers must comply with state and provincial laws regarding privacy of employee records.

Confidentiality can be broken if the EAP specialist believes the employee is homicidal, suicidal, or a potential saboteur. Despite the confidentiality of EAPs, organizations have a record of which people they refer to the EAP. Most EAPs do not reveal the names of self-referrals.

The balance of evidence suggests that EAPs are a good financial investment. When an employee's performance is brought back to acceptable levels, his or her productivity increases. An EAP can also reduce certain costs. The assistance plan at McDonnell Douglas Corp. yielded specific savings associated with employees who received counseling for drug abuse and mental illness. Among the savings were less absenteeism, fewer terminations, and less medical costs for the employees and their dependents. A company representative commented, "The greatest impact of the EAP has been to show that you can care about people and still save money. It's the caring way."[11]

DEALING WITH DIFFICULT PEOPLE

LEARNING OBJECTIVE

6

Develop an approach to dealing with difficult people.

---

difficult person
An individual whose personal characteristics disturb other people.

The focus of this chapter has been on dealing with substandard performers. Another group of employees may perform adequately, yet they are annoying and they waste managers' time. At times their performance slips below standard because they divert their energy from getting work accomplished. A person in this category is often referred to as a **difficult person**, an individual whose personal characteristics disturb other people. Among such people are whiners and complainers, know-it-alls, dictators, pessimists, and poor team players. The list that follows describes seven tactics for dealing with a variety of difficult people.

- *Stay focused on the issues at hand.* A general strategy for dealing with difficult people is to not react specifically to the problem-makers' antics and instead to stay focused on work issues. Describe the behavior you want changed, and explain why the behavior is disruptive. Pause for a moment, then wait for a response. Acknowledge what the person says, then state what needs to be changed, such as: "Please stop giving customers an exasperated look and a loud exhale when they make a special request." Ask how the difficult person will make the change, and then get a commitment to change.[12] (Notice the good coaching technique.)

- *Take the problem person professionally, not personally.* A key principle in dealing with difficult people is to not take what they do personally. Difficult people are not necessarily out to "get" the manager or coworker. You or somebody else might just represent an obstacle, or a stepping stone for them to get their way.[13] Remind yourself that you are paid to do your job, and dealing with difficult people is part of it. As you learn to take insults, slights, and backstabbing professionally rather than personally you will experience less stress and harassment.

- *Use tact and diplomacy.* Team members who irritate you rarely do annoying things on purpose. Tactful actions on your part can sometimes take care of these problems without your having to go through the controlling process. For example, close your door if a team member is busily engaged in conversation outside your office. When subtlety does not work, you may have to confront the person. Incorporate tact and diplomacy into the confrontation. For example, as you confront a team member, point out one of his or her strengths.

- *Use humor.* Nonhostile humor can often be used to help a difficult person understand how his or her behavior annoys or blocks others. The humor should point to the person's unacceptable behavior but not belittle him or her. You might say to a subordinate who is overdue on a report: "I know we are striving for zero defects in our company. But if you wait until your report is perfect before submitting it, we may not need it any more." Your humor may help the team member realize that timeliness is an important factor in the quality of a report.

- *Give recognition and attention.* Difficult people, like misbehaving children, are sometimes crying out for attention. Give them recognition and attention, and their difficult behavior will sometimes cease. For example, in a staff meeting, mention the person's recent contributions to the department. If the negative behavior is a product of a deeper-rooted problem, recognition and attention by themselves will not work. The employee may have to be referred for professional counseling.

- *Listen and respond.* When discussing the problem with the difficult person, allow the individual a full expression of feelings. Next, acknowledge your awareness of the situation, and describe how you size up the situation. Finally, specify what you would like changed, such as: "Please stop complaining so much about factors beyond our control." Avoid judging the person ("You *shouldn't* be like that") or generalizing ("You always act this way").[14]

- *Explain the importance of teamwork.* One way of looking at the behavior of difficult people is that they are poor team players. For example, it is poor team play to give others a hard time. The manager might therefore coach the difficult person about the importance of making a better contribution to the team by being more pleasant and cooperative. With such an emphasis on teamwork today, the difficult person *might* get the point.

TERMINATION

When corrective actions fail to improve ineffective performance, an employee is likely to be terminated. The company may also assist the person in finding new employment. Termination is considered part of the control process because it is a corrective action. It can also be considered part of the organizing function because it involves placing people.

Termination is the process of firing an employee because of poor job performance, unacceptable behavior, or interpersonal problems. Termination is regarded as the last alternative. It represents a failure in staffing and in managing ineffective performers. Nevertheless, to maintain discipline and control costs, a firm is often forced to terminate nonproductive employees. When substandard performers are discharged, it communicates the message that adequate performance must be maintained. Thus, a firing can also be valuable because it may increase the productivity of employees who are not fired.

Termination usually takes place only after the substandard performer has been offered the types of help described throughout this chapter. In general, every feasible alternative—such as retraining and counseling—should be attempted before termination. A manager must also accumulate substantial written documentation of substandard performance. Appropriate documentation includes performance appraisals, special memos to the file about performance problems, and statements describing the help offered the employee. Exhibit 16-5 summarizes the steps in making a termination decision.

If these steps are not documented, the employer can be accused of wrongful discharge. **Wrongful discharge** is the firing of an employee for arbitrary or unfair reasons. Many employers have been sued for wrongfully discharging employees. Court rulings in the last decade have increasingly prohibited the termination of employees when good faith, fair dealing, and implied contracts have been at issue. In a noteworthy case, the Michigan Supreme Court held that the organization's personnel manual represented an implied contract with the employee. The handbook distributed to employees stated that discharge would only be "for cause."[15]

LEARNING OBJECTIVE 7

Explain the recommended approach to terminating employees.

termination
The process of firing an employee because of poor job performance, unacceptable behavior, or interpersonal problems.

wrongful discharge
The firing of an employee for arbitrary or unfair reasons.

Exhibit 16-5
Framework for Deciding
Whether to Terminate
or Provide Additional
Counseling to an
Employee

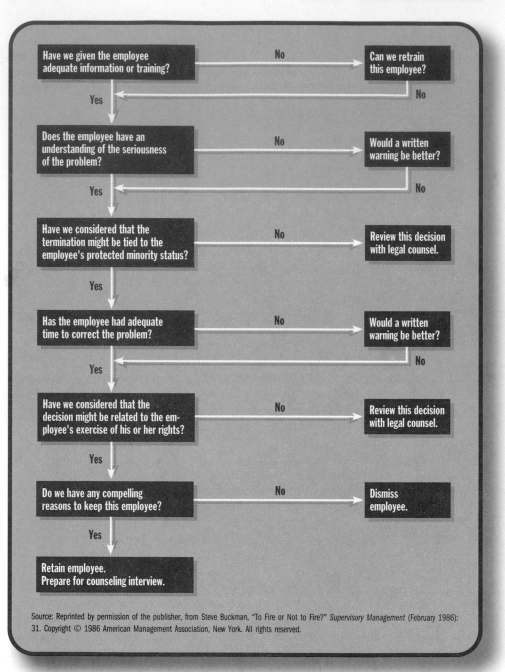

Have we given the employee adequate information or training? — No → Can we retrain this employee?

Yes

Does the employee have an understanding of the seriousness of the problem? — No → Would a written warning be better?

Yes

Have we considered that the termination might be tied to the employee's protected minority status? — No → Review this decision with legal counsel.

Yes

Has the employee had adequate time to correct the problem? — No → Would a written warning be better?

Yes

Have we considered that the decision might be related to the employee's exercise of his or her rights? — No → Review this decision with legal counsel.

Yes

Do we have any compelling reasons to keep this employee? — No → Dismiss employee.

Yes

Retain employee.
Prepare for counseling interview.

due process
In relation to employee rights, giving a worker a fair hearing before he or she is dismissed.

Another way of looking at wrongful discharge is to consider the idea that employees have certain rights in relation to preserving their jobs. According to **due process,** employees must be given a fair hearing before being dismissed. This includes the right to progressive discipline and the right to present one's side of the story to management.

After an employee is fired, the manager must deal with the questions and feelings of the group members within the unit. Often these people were close friends of the terminated employee. Be honest with the other employees, but do not bad-mouth the terminated worker. Avoid being too specific to avoid a lawsuit about defamation of character. Emphasize how performance factors led to the discharge. Allow coworkers to express their feelings and concerns in a group setting or one-on-one with you, the manager.[16]

SUMMARY OF KEY POINTS

1
Identify factors contributing to poor performance.

Job performance is ineffective when productivity is below a standard considered acceptable at a given time. Ineffective performers consume considerable managerial time. The causes of poor job performance can be rooted in the person, the job, the manager, or the company. Usually, ineffective performance is caused by a combination of several factors.

2
Describe in detail the control process for managing ineffective performers.

The approach to improving ineffective performance presented in this chapter is a controlling process. It consists of eight steps that should be followed in sequence: (1) define performance standards, (2) detect deviation from acceptable performance, (3) define and assess the cause, (4) confront the substandard performer, (5) set improvement goals, (6) select and implement an action plan for improvement, (7) re-evaluate performance after a time interval, and (8) continue or discontinue the action plan.

Corrective actions for ineffective performers are divided into managerial actions and techniques, and organizational programs. Managerial actions include close supervision and corrective discipline. Organizational programs include career counseling, outplacement, and job re-design.

3
Know what is required to coach and constructively criticize employees.

Coaching and constructive criticism are useful approaches to managing poor performers. Coaching consists of giving advice and encouragement. Most coaching includes constructive criticism. Skill is required to coach ineffective performers and criticize them constructively.

4
Understand how to discipline employees.

The controlling process may also call for discipline. Summary discipline is the immediate discharge of an employee who commits a serious offense. Corrective discipline gives employees a chance to correct their behavior before punishment is applied. Both the manager and the employee share the responsibility for solving the performance problem. Corrective discipline involves counseling.

The major type of corrective discipline is called progressive discipline. It represents a step-by-step application of corrective discipline. The manager confronts the ineffective performer about the problem and then coaches him or her. If the employee's performance does not improve, the employee is given a written warning. If this fails, the employee is suspended or given a disciplinary layoff. The next step is discharge.

The red-hot-stove rule refers to administering discipline right away. The situation should include a warning; consistent, impersonal punishment should be administered immediately after the infraction is committed.

5
Explain the purpose and operation of an employee assistance program.

An employee assistance program (EAP) is an organizational unit or separate firm that helps employees deal with personal and job-related problems that interfere with their job performance. These problems include marital and family problems, alcoholism or drug addiction, and financial problems. EAPs are committed to rehabilitation and improving job performance, and they offer specific programs and professional assistance for each type of problem. When substandard performance is improved, productivity is increased. EAPs are usually cost-effective because of the money saved on absenteeism and health-care claims.

6
Develop an approach to dealing with difficult people.

When dealing with difficult people, stay focused on the issue at hand, and take the problem professionally, not personally. Also use tact and diplomacy, and humor, while also giving recognition and attention. Listen to the difficult person and respond, and explain the importance of teamwork.

7
Explain the recommended approach to terminating employees.

Termination should take place only after the substandard performer has been offered the type of help built into the control model. Documentation of poor performance is required. Coworkers should be offered a performance-based explanation of why the substandard performer was terminated.

KEY TERMS AND PHRASES

Ineffective Job Performance *pg. 370*
Behavior Mismatch *pg. 373*
Confrontation *pg. 375*
Improvement Goal *pg. 376*
Coaching *pg. 378*
Constructive Criticism *pg. 378*
Discipline *pg. 379*
Summary Discipline *pg. 379*

Corrective Discipline *pg. 379*
Progressive Discipline *pg. 380*
Employee Assistance Program (EAP) *pg. 382*
Difficult Person *pg. 384*
Termination *pg. 385*
Wrongful Discharge *pg. 385*
Due Process *pg. 386*

QUESTIONS

1. What is the link between managing ineffective performers and organizational productivity?
2. Why does chronic complaining contribute to poor performance?
3. How can a person prevent himself or herself from becoming a substandard performer?
4. What responsibility should management take for violent behavior in the workplace?
5. Why is coaching such an important part of performance improvement?
6. How can a manager use employees' belief in a just world to help maintain discipline in the organization?
7. Why should management be willing to rehabilitate employees through an employee assistance program when so many workers have been downsized in recent years?

SKILL-BUILDING EXERCISE 16-A: THE SELF-SABOTAGE QUESTIONNAIRE

Directions: Indicate how accurately each of the statements below describes or characterizes you, using a five-point scale: (0) very inaccurately, (1) inaccurately, (2) midway between inaccurately and accurately, (3) accurately, (4) very accurately. Consider discussing some of the questions with a family member, close friend, or work associate. Another person's feedback may prove helpful in providing accurate answers to some of the questions.

Answer

1. Other people have said that I am my worst enemy. _____
2. If I don't do a perfect job, I feel worthless. _____
3. I am my own harshest critic. _____
4. When engaged in a sport or other competitive activity, I find a way to blow a substantial lead right near the end. _____
5. When I make a mistake, I can usually identify another person to blame. _____
6. I have a sincere tendency to procrastinate. _____
7. I have trouble focusing on what is really important to me. _____
8. I have trouble taking criticism, even from friends. _____
9. My fear of seeming stupid often prevents me from asking questions or offering my opinion. _____
10. I tend to expect the worst in most situations. _____
11. Many times I have rejected people who treat me well. _____
12. When I have an important project to complete, I usually get sidetracked, and then miss the deadline. _____

13. I choose work assignments that lead to disappointments even when better options are clearly available.   _____

14. I frequently misplace things such as my keys, then get very angry at myself.   _____

15. I am concerned that if I take on much more responsibility people will expect too much from me.   _____

16. I avoid situations, such as competitive sports, where people can find out how good or bad I really am.   _____

17. People describe me as the "office clown."   _____

18. I have an insatiable demand for money and power.   _____

19. When negotiating with others, I hate to grant any concessions.   _____

20. I seek revenge for even the smallest hurts.   _____

21. I have a blinding ego.   _____

22. When I receive a compliment or other form of recognition, I usually feel I don't deserve it.   _____

23. To be honest, I choose to suffer.   _____

24. I regularly enter into conflict with people who try to help me.   _____

25. I'm a loser.   _____

Total score _____

Scoring and interpretation: Add your answers to all the questions to obtain your total score. Your total score provides an approximate index of your tendencies toward being self-sabotaging or self-defeating. The higher your score, the more probable it is that you create conditions to bring about your own setbacks, disappointments, and failures. The lower your score, the less likely it is that you are a self-saboteur.

0–25: You appear to have very few tendencies toward self-sabotage. If this interpretation is supported by your own positive feelings toward your life and yourself, you are in good shape with respect to self-defeating behavior tendencies. However, stay alert to potential self-sabotaging tendencies that could develop at later stages in your career.

26–50: You may have some mild tendencies toward self-sabotage. It could be that you do things occasionally that defeat your own purposes. A person in this category, for example, might write an angry memo to an executive expressing disagreement with a decision that adversely affects his or her operation. Review actions you have taken during the past six months to decide if any of them have been self-sabotaging.

51–75: You show signs of engaging in self-sabotage. You probably have thoughts, and carry out actions, that could be blocking you from achieving important work and personal goals. People whose scores place in this category characteristically engage in negative self-talk that lowers their self-confidence and makes them appear weak and indecisive to others. For example, "I'm usually not good at learning new things." People in this range frequently experience another problem. They sometimes sabotage their changes of succeeding on a project just to prove that their negative self-assessment is correct.

76–100: You most likely have a strong tendency toward self-sabotage. (Sometimes it is possible to obtain a high score on a test like this because you are going through an unusually stressful period in your life.) You might discuss your tendencies toward undermining your own achievements with a mental health professional.

SKILL-BUILDING EXERCISE 16-B: DATA ON INEFFECTIVE PERFORMANCE

Each student asks an experienced manager what he or she thinks is the most frequent cause of ineffective performance. Relate the manager's answer to Exhibit 16-1. During class, students later make about a one-minute presentation of their findings. Look for trends, especially the most frequent cause of ineffective performance revealed by the research.

VIDEO DISCUSSION QUESTIONS

1. Was the water being inserted into the tank at Bhopal a management error, an employee error, or both? **[Bhopal]**
2. How might the survivor syndrome contribute to ineffective performance? **[Morale Crisis]**
3. What factors contribute to the below-standard performance of many employees who work in a downsized organization? **[Morale Crisis]**

CASE PROBLEM 16-A: THE DISTRACTED CLAIMS EXAMINER

Rodney Perry works as a claims examiner at a drive-through claims office for a major insurance company. A drive-through claims office is an alternative to a claims examiner doing on-site inspections of damaged vehicles. If the vehicle (car, small truck, van, or motorcycle) is drivable, the person with a claim against the company visits the drive-through office. The vehicles assessed for damages are either owned by company policyholders, or were damaged by company policyholders. Each drive-through office is staffed by one claims examiner and one office assistant.

Rod has worked three years at the same drive-through location as a claims examiner. Based upon two years of excellent productivity and a positive attitude, he has been under consideration for promotion to claims manager. Based on his presumed promotability, Rod was asked to prepare a 30-page report analyzing the nature of claims at his branch. To prepare the report, Rod needs to regularly consult the computerized records available on the PC at his office.

Rod works on the company report whenever he can grab a few moments between claim inspections, telephone calls, preparing the computerized claim evaluations, and consulting with the office assistant. During extra-busy periods, such as the week following a snow or sleet storm, he can find no time to work on the report. Rod's manager, Keith Piotrowski, telephoned him recently to discuss the report.

"Rod, I think we have a problem," said Piotrowski. "I asked you five months ago to prepare that claims analysis. You tell me you've made some progress, yet you still haven't delivered. When we considered you for promotion to claims manager, we didn't know you were a procrastinator."

"Keith, I don't consider myself to be a procrastinator. It's just that I'm in a very difficult position to write a report. Doing the claims work alone has me working about 50 hours a week. I thought claims examinations took priority over this report. I don't think you know how difficult it is to write a special report when I'm already overloaded with claims work.

"I would like to write the report at home, but all the records I need are at the office. Besides, I'm already putting in enough hours of unpaid overtime."

Piotrowski replied, "I hope I'm not hearing excuses from a man we thought had excellent potential for promotion. I want to see the report on my desk in two weeks, and I don't expect you to fall behind on claims work."

CASE QUESTIONS

1. What responsibility should Rod take for not producing the report on time?
2. What responsibility should the company take for the report not being produced on time?
3. If you were Rod, how would you handle the ultimatum from Keith Piotrowski?

CASE PROBLEM 16-B: THE DISTURBING MESSAGE

Jerry Randall, a human resources manager, opened his mailbox, as he does every workday. On this day he found a note made up of words cut from magazines: "I KNOW WHAT YOU DID. YOU WILL NOT GET AWAY WITH IT."

A survey of the unit's four supervisors, 24 employees, and three support staff members revealed nothing. Nobody claimed it had been a joke, nobody could explain it, and nobody else had access to the mailbox. The

human resources unit was experiencing heavy pressure. The pressure was triggered by an unexpected organizationwide downsizing ordered by the CEO that had been linked to human resources recommendations.

Randall's immediate boss, human resource vice-president Sara Sanchez, at first thought of dismissing the incident as a gag. Yet two thoughts stopped her. First, Sanchez pondered how it would look if violence did erupt and the note had not been investigated. Second, she was concerned about additional information Randall had volunteered about incidents that might have been significant. These included a brief pushing and shoving incident over the use of the photocopier, and open hostility at an cross-departmental meeting.

Randolph and Sanchez agreed they should take immediate action to deal with the note. They decided not to leave the office until a solid plan was formulated.

CASE QUESTIONS

1. What strategy do you recommend for dealing with the threatening letter?
2. Or do you think Randall and Sanchez should regard the letter as a harmless prank?

Source: Based on facts reported in Dennis L. Johnson, John G. Kurutz, and John B. Kiehlbauch, "Scenario for Supervisors," *HRMagazine* (February 1995): 63–67.

CASE PROBLEM 16-C: PURGING THE OLD GUARD

Hitech Corporation is a telecommunications company offering a variety of services and products throughout the United States. The company provides local and long-distance telephone service, cellular telephone service, wireless transmission of electronic data, and cable television. Hitech also sells hardware including wired and cellular telephones, and personal digital assistants. The company has been a regulated, local telephone company for 75 years. Ten years ago Hitech made the transition to starting and acquiring nonregulated businesses such as cellular telephone services and teleconferencing.

Diane Preston, the Hitech CEO, was a key factor in moving Hitech from a traditional telephone company to a modern telecommunications corporation. Hitech has shown improved earnings for 20 consecutive quarters. Yet Preston and the executive vice-president, Rich Roncone, were not satisfied with the company's progress. As Preston explained during a meeting with her top-management team, "The stockholders are moderately satisfied with our earnings, and the media has been appreciative. But I'm not happy about our return on investment. And I'm outright annoyed with our level of customer service.

"Too many company veterans still think we are a regulated monopoly that doesn't have to please the customer. They have the attitude that if the customers don't like the telephone service, let them create their own telephone system. Unfortunately, there are now four competitive telephone companies in our market from which the customer can choose."

Roncone then volunteered a comment: "Diane, I think the problem runs even deeper with some of the old guard. They are just not buying into our new vision of a world-class telecommunications company. They still think of us as 'the local telephone company.' Unfortunately, their perception is about 10 years behind the times."

Preston told the group, "I agree with Rich's analysis of employees who are not buying into our vision. The same employees are precisely those who don't get the point about competition. My job is to move the company forward. I'm losing my patience.

"Any manager, supervisor, or technician who keeps thinking like the old guard shouldn't have a job with us. I want all the people who are holding the company back to be out of here in three months. Put them at the top of the list in the next downsizing."

Another member at the meeting said, "Diane, you mean you want us to lay off people just because their thinking is behind the times?"

Preston responded, "The alternatives you have are to get people to update their attitudes or to get them out of the company."

CASE QUESTIONS

1. Should the employees who still look upon Hitech as a regulated monopoly be considered ineffective performers? Explain.
2. What can the Hitech top-management team do to change the attitudes of those who still think of the company as a regulated monopoly?
3. Would dismissing people as Preston suggests be an act of wrongful discharge?

CASE PROBLEM 16-D: THE DELINQUENT EXPENSE REPORT

Larry Packard is a sales representative for a manufacturer of earth-moving equipment. Most of his customers are private construction companies for the engineering divisions of state, provincial, or local governments. Sales take a long time to develop, including multiple trips to a prospective customer's location. Larry is out of town on business trips about three nights each week. He has a wife, Linda, and two children, Phyllis and Roger. Linda works full-time as an accountant at a food wholesaler. The Packards spend close to $700 per month for child-care services, before and after school. Despite a well-above-average family income, the Packards are just meeting expenses.

Larry's company reimburses him fully for travel and entertainment expenses, which amount to about $3,500 per month. Sales representatives are required to submit monthly expense reports. Larry regards preparing expense reports as the most distasteful part of his job. He received an E-mail message recently from the accounting department informing him that he was three months behind with his expense reports. Larry was also reminded that reports submitted more than 30 days beyond the end of a fiscal year might not be reimbursed.

Linda is also concerned about him being behind on expense reports. "As I see it," said Linda, "we're giving your employer an interest-free loan of about $7,000. Meanwhile we're borrowing money at 18 percent on our credit card to pay for your travel expenses. Our budget just can't support your shoddy approach to submitting expenses."

The next day Larry informed the accounting department and Linda that he would get his delinquent expense reports submitted within a week. He also stated that he would stay current on future reports.

Late that afternoon, Larry began searching his desk and attaché case for the appropriate receipts. Forty-five minutes into the task, Larry found about one-half the receipts he needed. "Maybe I stuffed some of these receipts in my desk drawer at home," he thought to himself. As Larry was making a note to search at home for the receipts, the phone on his desk rang. The caller, a construction-company owner, asked Larry if he could be in Minneapolis tomorrow afternoon to bid on a $350,000 piece of equipment. Larry assured the caller he would be there tomorrow, no matter how difficult the flight arrangements.

Larry decided to put aside the expense report project until he returned from the Minneapolis trip. He reasoned that making a big sale was a much higher priority than preparing an overdue expense report. He thought that he would ask the accounting department for an extension, and plea with Linda for patience and compassion.

CASE QUESTIONS

1. In what way is Larry Packard exhibiting ineffective performance?
2. What is your diagnosis of the cause of Larry's problem?
3. What steps should the company take to get Larry to submit his expense reports more promptly? Or should they be concerned about the problem?

REFERENCES

1. Bill Oliver, "How to Prevent Drug Abuse in Your Workplace," *HRMagazine* (December 1993): 78.
2. Sandra L. Robinson and Rebecca J. Bennett, "A Typology of Deviant Workplace Behaviors: A Multidimensional Scaling Study," *The Academy of Management Journal* (April 1995): 555.
3. Phil Ebersole, "American System Abandons Workers, Needs Overhaul," Rochester, New York, *Democrat and Chronicle* (1 July 1990): F1.
4. Michael R. Manning, Joyce S. Osland, and Asbjorn Osland, "Work-Related Consequences of Smoking Cessation," *Academy of Management Journal* (September 1989): 606.
5. John R. Hollembeck, Daniel R. Iglen, and Suzanne M. Crampton, "Lower Back Disability in Occupational Settings: A Review of the Literature from a Human Resource Management Perspective View," *Personnel Psychology* (Summer 1992): 247
6. Rebecca Mann, *Behavior Mismatch: How to Manage "Problem" Employees Whose Actions Don't Match Your Expectations* (New York: AMACOM, 1993).
7. Kenneth H. Blanchard, "How to Turn Around Department Performance," *Supervisory Management* (March 1992): 3.
8. Marilyn J. Darling, "Coaching People through Difficult Times," *HRMagazine* (November 1994): 72.
9. Gail A. Ball, Linda Klebe Trevino, and Henry P. Sims, Jr., "Just and Unjust Punishment: Influence on Subordinate Performance and Citizenship," *Academy of Management Journal* (April 1994): 300–301; Trevino, "The Social Effects of Punishment in Organizations: A Justice Perspective," *Academy of Management Review* (October 1992): 647.
10. Stuart Feldman, "Today's EAPs Make the Grade," *HRFocus* (February 1991): 3.
11. Peggy Stuart, "Investments in EAPs Pay Off," *Personnel Journal* (February 1993): 48, 54.
12. Marilyn Wheeler, *Problem People at Work* (New York: St. Martin's-Griffin).
13. "Help! I'm Surrounded by Difficult People," *Working Smart* (25 March 1991): 2.
14. Sam Deep and Lyle Sussman, *What to Say to Get What You Want* (Reading, MA: Addison-Wesley, 1991).
15. Catherine Schwoerer and Benson Rosen, "Effects of Employment-at-Will Policies and Compensation Policies on Corporate Image and Job Pursuit Intentions," *Journal of Applied Psychology* (August 1989): 653.
16. Robert McGarvey, "After the Fire," *Entrepreneur* (September 1995): 80.

CHAPTER 17

Managing Change, Personal Productivity, and Stress

LEARNING OBJECTIVES
After studying this chapter and doing the exercises, you should be able to:

1
Explain why people resist change and know how to gain support for change.

2
Identify techniques for improving your personal productivity, including reducing procrastination.

3
Be prepared to manage stress and burnout.

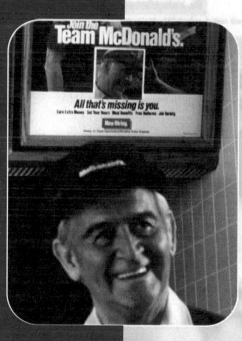

McDonald's Corporation has a program of offering sabbatical leaves to full-time employees who have completed at least 10 years of service. Employees are then eligible for an 8-week paid leave. After 20 years of service, a 20-week leave is possible. • Company spokesperson Mark Walker says, "Our definition of a sabbatical is a program that offers employees an opportunity to reflect on their jobs and careers, as well as the overall operation of the business. We also believe they should do it away from the daily pressures of work. We feel this time should be spent any way the employee feels will contribute to his or her personal growth and professional growth with McDonald's." • "The leave must be taken all at once," Walker says. "That's because it isn't a reward for past performance, but an investment in the employee's future. It isn't seen as a fringe benefit."[1] Yet a distinct benefit of the program is that many employees who take a sabbatical see it as an opportunity to reduce job stress and prevent burnout.

The sabbatical program at McDonald's Corp. illustrates that organizations take seriously the need for employees to reinvigorate and renew themselves. Individuals also have a responsibility for finding ways to enhance their productivity and properly manage stress and burnout. Two of the major topics of this chapter are improving individual productivity and managing stress. First, however, we look at the challenge of managing change. Unless change is managed effectively, it can lower productivity and create stress.

In previous chapters, the major emphasis was managing others. The discussion of change generally follows this perspective. However, the information about personal productivity and stress pertains to managing oneself.

MANAGING CHANGE

LEARNING OBJECTIVE 1

Explain why people resist change and know how to gain support for change.

"The only constant is change" is a cliché frequently repeated in the workplace. To meet their objectives, managers must handle change effectively on an almost daily basis. Changes in the workplace can be grouped into four major categories. The first category is changes in organizational structure such as mergers, acquisitions, and downsizings. Structural changes include changes in administrative practices and procedures. The second category is changes in technology—the way work is done stemming from information and manufacturing technology. The third category is changes stemming from worldwide competition. The fourth category is changes in the workplace profile. The new mix includes an increase in older people, minorities, and women. Also, many functionally illiterate people are now found in entry-level positions.[2]

The following description of managing change has four components: a model of the change process, reactions to change, why people resist change, and how to gain support for change. Knowledge of all four components is helpful in managing change that affects others or oneself.

THE UNFREEZING–CHANGING–REFREEZING MODEL OF CHANGE

Psychologist Kurt Lewin developed a three-step analysis of the change process.[3] His unfreezing–changing–refreezing model is widely used by managers to help bring about constructive change. Many other approaches to initiating change stem from this simple model, which is illustrated in Exhibit 17-1. *Unfreezing* involves reducing or eliminating resistance to change. As long as employees oppose a change, it will not be implemented effectively. To accept change, employees must first deal with and resolve their feelings about letting go of the old. Only after people have dealt effectively with endings are they ready to make transitions.[4]

Changing or moving on to a new level usually involves considerable two-way communication, including group discussion. According to Lewin, "Rather than a one-way flow of commands or recommendations, the person implementing the change should make suggestions. The changees should be encouraged to contribute and participate." Refreezing includes pointing out the success of the change and looking for ways to reward people involved in implementing the change.

RESPONSES TO CHANGE

When significant change is introduced to a firm, employees react in various ways. Some view major change so negatively that they experience job stress. At the other extreme, some employees react positively to change. They welcome the excitement

Exhibit 17-1
The Change Process

and challenge of a major disruption to the system. The various employee reactions to change have been placed on a continuum with the following seven anchor points:

1. The most upset employees will *leave.*
2. Another group will show *active resistance* (e.g., a manager refusing to use electronic mail).
3. Some employees will show *opposition,* or foot dragging.
4. Another group will show *acquiescence* and comply with an unwanted change.
5. To the right of center on the continuum, some employees will show *acceptance/ modification.* They will go along with the change but will attempt to negotiate details.
6. Another group of employees will show *acceptance,* even if their attitude is neutral.
7. The most positive group includes those who show *active support.* Active supporters attempt to increase a change's chance for success by, for example, encouraging others to accept the change.[5]

WHY PEOPLE RESIST CHANGE

Before a company's managers can gain support for change, they must understand why people resist change. People resist change for reasons they think are important, the most common being the fear of an unfavorable outcome, such as less money or personal inconvenience. People also resist change for such varied reasons as not wanting to disrupt social relationships and not wanting to break well-established habits.

Even when people do not view a change as potentially damaging, they may sometimes cling to a system they dislike rather than change. According to folk wisdom, "People would rather deal with the devil they know." Workers may also resist change because they are aware of weaknesses in the proposed changes that may have been overlooked or disregarded by management.[6]

A sales manager resisted her company's proposal to shift a key product to dealer distribution. She explained that dealers would give so little attention to the product that sales would plunge. Despite her protests, the firm shifted to dealer distribution. Sales of the product did plunge, and the company returned to selling through sales representatives.

GAINING SUPPORT FOR CHANGE

Gaining support for change, and therefore overcoming resistance, is an important managerial responsibility. Let us look at seven techniques for gaining support for change.

1. *Invest time in planning the change.* A hard-hitting change strategy is to invest time in planning a change before implementation begins. If possible, the people to be involved in the change should help in the planning. A change consultant advises, "One of the biggest mistakes American organizations make is that

they do not take the time required to develop a comprehensive change plan and to get buy-in from the people who will be affected by the change."[7]

2. *Allow for discussion and negotiation.* Support for change can be increased by discussing and negotiating the more sensitive aspects of the change. It is important to acknowledge the potential hardships associated with the change, such as longer working hours or higher output to earn the same compensation. The two-way communication incorporated into the discussion helps reduce some employee concerns. Discussion often leads to negotiation, which further involves employees in the change process. The accompanying Manager in Action illustrates a skillful use of discussion to implement important change.

3. *Allow for participation.* The best-documented way of overcoming resistance to change is to allow people to participate in the changes that will affect them. An application of this concept is allowing employees to set their own rules to increase compliance. A powerful participation technique is to encourage people who already favor the change to help in planning and implementation. These active supporters of the change will be even more strongly motivated to enlist the support of others.

4. *Point out the financial benefits.* Given that so many employees are concerned about the financial effects of work changes, it is helpful to discuss these efforts openly. If employees will earn more money as a result of the change, this fact can be used as a selling point. For example, a company owner told his employees, "I know you are inconvenienced and upset because we have cut way back on secretarial support. But some of the savings will be invested in bigger bonuses for you." Much of the grumbling subsided.

5. *Avoid change overload.* Too much change too soon leads to negative stress. So it is helpful to avoid overloading employees with too many sweeping changes in a brief period of time. Too much simultaneous change also causes confusion, and it leads to foot dragging about the workplace innovation. The more far-reaching the innovation, such as restructuring a firm, the greater the reason for not attempting other innovations simultaneously.

6. *Gain political support for change.* Few changes get through organizations without the change agent's forming alliances with people who will support his or her proposals. Often this means selling the proposed changes to members of top-level management before proceeding down the hierarchy. It is much more difficult to create change from the bottom up.

7. *Ask effective questions to involve workers in the change.* An *effective question* aims to move people toward a goal or objective instead of dwelling on what might have gone wrong. The effective question focuses on what is right rather than wrong, thereby offering encouragement. As in active listening, effective questions are open-ended. They also ask *what* or *how* rather than *why*, thereby decreasing defensiveness. (E.g., "How is the software installation coming along?" rather than "Why hasn't the new software been installed?") Effective questions are also you-oriented; they focus on the person who is supposed to implement the change. Two examples of effective questions are:

"How would you describe your progress so far?"

"What kind of support do you need to ensure your success?"[8]

LEARNING OBJECTIVE 2

Identify techniques for improving your personal productivity, including reducing procrastination.

INCREASING YOUR PERSONAL PRODUCTIVITY

High personal work productivity leads to positive outcomes such as higher income, more responsibility, and recognition. Furthermore, in an era of work streamlining

MANAGER IN ACTION: HOSPITAL CEO INITIATES CHANGE

The following conversation took place between a hospital CEO and his staff.

CEO: I want to implement a quality-improvement program.

Director of Administration: What's this all about?

CEO: Several things. First, we are getting too many complaints from our patients. Second, the current climate for reform makes quality essential. Third, I am convinced we can deliver better care.

Director of Nursing: I'm not sure we need to improve quality. We have a well-trained staff, and they do a good job. The average performance ratings of the nurses are up, and many changes would just give them more work to do.

CEO: The staff may be doing a better job as individual workers, but not as a team. There must be some reasons for the complaints.

CEO (after more discussion): Okay, so we are all agreed that we should undertake a quality-improvement program. Now, how will we know whether the program works?

Director of Administration: What if we used the number of formal complaints received to tell? We received over 100 complaints last month, both written and verbal. That translates into about three complaints per thousand patients.

Director of Nursing: OK, so if the number of complaints is less than one per thousand per month by the end of this calendar year, we will say the program worked.

CEO (speaking to Director of Administration): Will you contact all of the department heads and ask them to generate lists of things they think they could contribute to our getting fewer complaints? Also, can you get them to bring their lists with them to a meeting on the sixth of this month at 1:00 P.M.?

Director of Administration: Yes. Do you want us to make a list also?

CEO: No.

Director of Nursing: I will meet with my supervisors and ask them to generate a similar list and bring it to a meeting on the eighth of this month starting at 3:00 P.M.

CEO: Great. At the meetings, we will identify things that can be done and assign them to some project teams. I want to thank each of you for the work you did here today. Your willingness to press in on the issue made it possible for use to see what is needed to get our quality program well defined. Does anyone have anything to say about the meeting or what happened here?

Source: Adapted from Jeffrey D. Ford and Laurie W. Ford, "The Role of Conversations in Producing Intentional Change in Organizations," *Academy of Management Review* (July 1995): 547.

and reengineering, the demand for high productivity among managerial workers has never been higher. Productivity enhancers, such as desk planners, are selling at a record rate. High job productivity is also important because it allows you to devote more worry-free time to your personal life. In addition, high productivity helps reduce the stress experienced when a person's job is out of control. The following discussion of personal productivity focuses on two related topics: (1) improving work habits and time management and (2) reducing procrastination.

IMPROVE WORK HABITS AND TIME MANAGEMENT

A direct method of improving personal productivity on the job is to improve your work habits and management of time.[9] These techniques can also be helpful to a student who wishes to increase productivity. Here we will describe both well-accepted and novel techniques of developing and maintaining good work habits and effective time management practices.

CLEAN UP YOUR WORK AREA AND SORT OUT YOUR TASKS. People sometimes become inefficient because their work area is messy. They waste time looking for things and neglect important papers. So, to get started at improving personal productivity, clean up your work area and sort out what tasks you need to accomplish. Cleaning up your work area includes your briefcase, your file of telephone numbers, and your computer files. Weeding out your mailing list is also important. Ask to be removed from the distribution of paper and electronic mail that is of no value to you.

PREPARE A "TO DO" LIST AND ASSIGN PRIORITIES. A "to do" list lies at the heart of every time management system. In addition to writing down tasks you need to do, assign priorities to them. A simple categorization, such as top priority versus low priority, works well for most people. In general, take care of top-priority tasks before low-priority ones. There are so many things to do on any job that some very low-priority items may never get done. Keep your "to do" list on a desk calendar or a large tablet or in your computer. A word processing file may suffice, but more advanced software for work scheduling is also available. Small slips of paper in various locations are distracting and tend to get misplaced.

Taking care of a small, easy-to-do task first—such as getting a new red ballpoint pen—has a hidden value. It tends to be relaxing because it gives you the psychological lift of having crossed at least one item off your list. A representative "to do" list for a manager is shown in Exhibit 17-2. This particular manager sorts priorities according to when they need doing: today, this week, or this month. Skill-Building Exercise 17-B at the end of the chapter provides a more advanced tool for list making and priority setting.

STREAMLINE YOUR WORK. The most important new work habit and management principle is **work streamlining**—eliminating as much low-value work as possible and concentrating on activities that add value for customers or clients. To streamline work, justify whether every work procedure, memo, report, meeting, or ceremonial activity is contributing value to the firm. Group luncheon meetings away from the office might be cut in half, giving staff members more time during the day to conduct urgent work. Another example of work streamlining would be to decrease the number of holiday cards sent to work associates. What can you do to streamline schoolwork?

> **work streamlining**
> *Eliminating as much low-value work as possible and concentrating on activities that add value for customers or clients.*

WORK AT A STEADY PACE. Although a dramatic show of energy (as in "pulling an all-nighter") is impressive, the steady worker tends to be more productive in the long run. The spurt employee creates many problems for management; the spurt student is in turmoil at examination time or when papers are due. Managers who expend the same amount of effort day by day tend to stay in control of their jobs. When a sudden problem or a good opportunity comes to their attention, they can fit it into their schedule.

MINIMIZE TIME WASTERS. An important strategy for improving personal productivity is to minimize time wasters. Each minute diverted from unproductive activity can be invested in productive work and can save you from working extra long hours. For example, if you decrease lengthy social lunches on work days, you can leave the office on time. Exhibit 17-3 presents a list of significant ways to reduce wasted time. Many of the other suggestions in this chapter can also help you save time directly or indirectly.

CONCENTRATE ON ONE TASK AT A TIME. Productive managers have a well-developed capacity to concentrate on the problem facing them at the moment, however engulfed they are with other obligations. Intense concentration leads to sharpened judgment and analysis and also decreases the chances of making major errors. Another useful

**Exhibit 17-2
A Sample "To Do"
List**

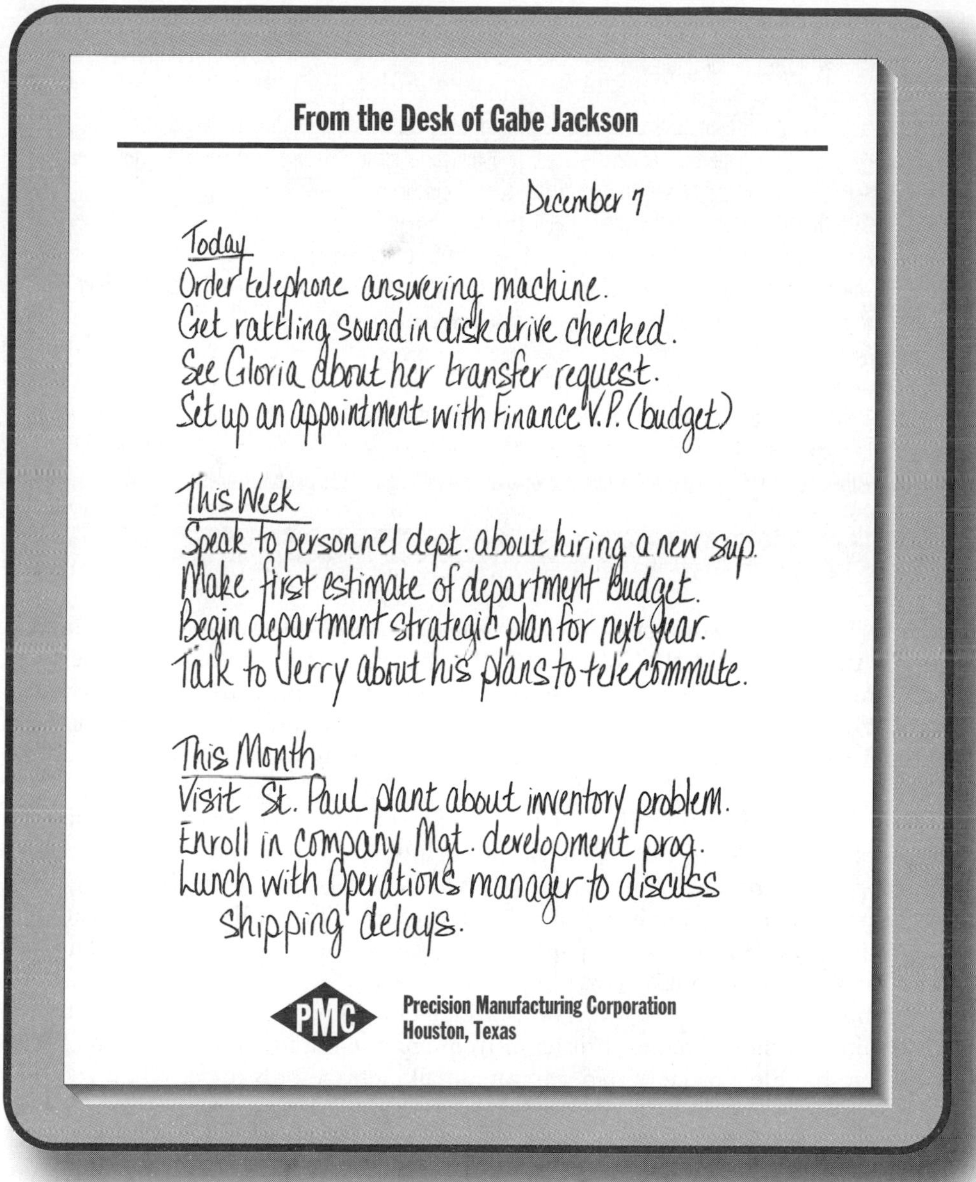

From the Desk of Gabe Jackson

December 7

Today
Order telephone answering machine.
Get rattling sound in disk drive checked.
See Gloria about her transfer request.
Set up an appointment with Finance V.P. (budget)

This Week
Speak to personnel dept. about hiring a new sup.
Make first estimate of department budget.
Begin department strategic plan for next year.
Talk to Jerry about his plans to telecommute.

This Month
Visit St. Paul plant about inventory problem.
Enroll in company Mgt. development prog.
Lunch with Operations manager to discuss
    shipping delays.

PMC Precision Manufacturing Corporation
Houston, Texas

by-product of concentration is reduced absentmindedness. The person who concentrates on the task at hand has less chance of forgetting what he or she intended.

CONCENTRATE ON HIGH-OUTPUT TASKS. To become more productive on the job or in school, concentrate on tasks in which superior performance could have a large payoff. For a manager, a high-output task would be to develop a strategic plan for the department. For a student, a high-output task would be to think of a creative idea for an independent study project. Expending your work effort on high-output items is analogous to looking for a good return on investment for your money. The high-output strategy also follows the Pareto Principle, described in Chapter 7.

DO CREATIVE AND ROUTINE TASKS AT DIFFERENT TIMES. To improve productivity, organize your work so you do not shift between creative and routine tasks. For many

**Exhibit 17-3
Ways to Prevent and
Overcome Time Wasting**

1. Minimize daydreaming on the job.
2. Use a time log to track time wasters.
3. Avoid using the computer as a diversion from work, such as for playing video games.
4. Keep track of important names, places, and things to avoid wasting time searching for them.
5. Set a time limit for tasks after you have done them once or twice.
6. Set strict limits on nonwork-related conversations during working hours.
7. Make good use of office technology, such as electronic mail, to reduce memo-preparation time.
8. When only routine messages need to be communicated, call people before and after normal working hours and use voice mail. (This saves conversation time.)
9. Avoid perfectionism, which leads you to keep redoing a project. Let go and move on to another project.
10. Make use of bits of time, for instance, 5 minutes between appointments. Invest those 5 minutes in a business phone call, or revise your "to do" list.
11. Minimize procrastination, the number one time waster for most people.

people it is best to work first on creative tasks because they require more mental energy than routine tasks. A minority of people prefer to get minor paperwork and E-mail chores out of the way so they can get to the pleasure of doing creative tasks. Whichever order you choose, it is important not to interrupt creative (or high-output) tasks with routine activities such as sorting mail or rearranging the desk.

STAY IN CONTROL OF PAPERWORK AND ELECTRONIC MAIL. No organization today can accomplish its mission unless paperwork, including the electronic variety, receives appropriate attention. If you handle paperwork improperly, your job may get out of control. Once your job is out of control, the stress level will increase greatly. Invest a small amount of time in paperwork and electronic mail every day. The best time to take care of routine correspondence is when you are at less than peak efficiency but not overfatigued. Reserve your high-energy periods for high-output tasks.

Avoid becoming a paper shuffler or frequently re-reading E-mail messages. The ideal is to handle a piece of paper or an E-mail message only once. When you pick up a hard copy memo or read an electronic one, take some action: throw it away or delete it, route it to someone else, write a short response to the sender, or flag it for action later. Loose ends of time can be used to take care of the flagged memos.

PRACTICE THE MENTAL STATE OF PEAK PERFORMANCE. To achieve maximum potential producivity one must transcend ordinary levels of concentration and devotion to duty. That occurs in **peak performance**, a mental state in which maximum results are achieved with mimum effort. Peak performers are mentally calm and physically at ease when challenged by difficult problems. They are intensely focused and involved, much like they would be in playing the best tennis games of their lives. You may have experienced the state of peak performance when totally involved with a problem or task. At that moment, nothing else seems to exist.

To achieve peak performance, you must continually work toward being mentally calm and physically at ease. Concentrate intensely, but not so much that you choke. In addition to frequent practice, peak performance can be achieved through visualization. In *visualization* you develop a mental image of how you would act and feel at the point of peak performance. For example, imagine yourself making a flawless

peak performance
A mental state in which maximum results are achieved with minimum effort.

presentation to top-level management about the contributions of your department. Psychologist Charles Garfield observed that people who achieve peak performance typically have an important mission in life—such as building a top-quality company.[10]

TAKE POWER NAPS. A fast-growing trend for increasing personal productivity is to take a **power nap**, a brief period of sleep of about 15 to 30 minutes designed to recharge the individual. Well-placed naps actually enhance rather than diminish productivity, and they are also an excellent stress reducer. You can combat procrastination by taking a brief nap before beginning an uncomfortable task.

According to one researcher, "The remarkable aspect of prophylactic napping, or napping in advance of an extended period of work, is that the benefits of the nap, even one of only 25 minutes duration, can be evident in performance hours afterward."[11] Naps can also prevent industrial disasters by overcoming grogginess before it leads to an accident such as the *Exxon Valdez* oil spill.

Among the famous nappers are Thomas Edison, Winston Churchill, Ronald Reagan, Bill Clinton, and Martha Stewart. A caveat: The organizational napper must use discretion in napping so as not to be perceived as sleeping on the job. Toward this end, some workers nap in their cars or in a store room during lunch break.

> **power nap**
> *A brief period of sleep of about 15 to 30 minutes designed to recharge the individual.*

BUILD FLEXIBILITY INTO YOUR SYSTEM. A time management system must allow some room for flexibility. How else could you handle unanticipated problems? If you work 50 hours per week, build in a few hours for taking care of emergencies. If your plan is too tight, delegate some tasks to others or work more hours. Perhaps you can find a quicker way to accomplish several of your tasks. Finally, to avoid staleness and stress, your schedule must allow sufficient time for rest and relaxation.

REDUCE PROCRASTINATION

Procrastination is the number one time waster for most people. Therefore, reducing it pays substantial dividends in increased productivity. Reducing procrastination shortens cycle times, which is an important goal of total quality management. Before describing remedial tactics, we will consider five leading reasons why people procrastinate.[12]

First, some people fear failure or other negative consequences. As long as a person delays doing something of significance, he or she cannot be regarded as having performed poorly on the project. Other negative consequences include looking foolish in the eyes of others or developing a bad reputation. For instance, if a manager delays making an oral presentation, nobody will know whether he or she is an ineffective speaker.

Second, procrastination may stem from a desire to avoid uncomfortable, overwhelming, or tedious tasks. Third, people frequently put off tasks that do not appear to offer a meaningful reward. Suppose you decide that your computer files need a thorough updating. Even though you know it should be done, having a completely updated directory might not be a particularly meaningful reward to you.

Fourth, some people dislike being controlled. When a procrastinator does not do things on time, he or she has successfully rebelled against being controlled by another person's time schedule.

Fifth, people sometimes are assigned tasks they perceive to be useless or needless, such as rechecking someone else's work. Rather than proceed with the trivial task, the individual procrastinates.

Procrastination often becomes a strong habit that is difficult to change. Nevertheless, the following strategies and tactics can be helpful in overcoming procrastination:

1. *Break the task down into smaller units.* By splitting a large task into smaller units, you can make a job appear less overwhelming. Subdividing the task is referred to as the "Swiss-cheese method" because you keep putting little holes into the overall task. This approach is useful, of course, only if the task can be done in small pieces.

2. *Make a commitment to others.* Your tendency to procrastinate on an important assignment may be reduced if you publicly state that you will get the job done by a certain time. You might feel embarrassed if you fail to meet your deadline.

3. *Reward yourself for achieving milestones.* A potent technique for overcoming any counterproductive behavior pattern is to give yourself a reward for progress toward overcoming the problem. Make your reward commensurate with the magnitude of the accomplishment.

4. *Calculate the cost of procrastination.* You can sometimes reduce procrastination by calculating its cost. Remind yourself, for example, that you might lose out on obtaining a high-paying job you really want if your résumé and cover letter are not ready on time. The cost of procrastination would include the difference in the salary between the job you do find and the one you really wanted. Another cost would be the loss of potential job satisfaction.

5. *Use subliminal messages about overcoming procrastination.* For example, software called *MindSet* flashes positive, reinforcing messages across your computer screen. The user can adjust the frequency and duration of the suggestions. The message can flash by subliminally (below the level of conscious awareness) or remain on screen for a few seconds. The antiprocrastination message reads: "My goals are obtainable. I am confident in my abilities. I make and keep deadlines."[13]

6. *Counterattack.* Another way of combatting procrastination is to force yourself to do something uncomfortable or frightening. After you begin, you are likely to find that the task is not as onerous as you thought. Assume you have been delaying learning a foreign language even though you know it will help your career. You remember how burdensome it was studying another language in school. You grit your teeth and remove the cellophane from the audiocasette for the target language. After listening for five minutes, you discover that beginning to study a foreign language again is not nearly as bad as you imagined.

MANAGING STRESS AND BURNOUT

LEARNING OBJECTIVE

Be prepared to manage stress and burnout.

Job stress and its related condition, job burnout, have always been potential sources of discomfort and poor physical and mental health. This discussion will focus on a number of steps you can take to prevent and control these problems. However, let us first look at the nature and causes of these conditions.

THE NATURE OF STRESS AND BURNOUT

stress
The mental and physical condition that results from a perceived threat that cannot be dealt with readily.

As used here, **stress** is the mental and physical condition that results from a perceived threat that cannot be dealt with readily. Stress is therefore an internal response to a state of activation. The stressed person is physically and mentally aroused. Stress will ordinarily occur in a threatening or negative situation, such as being fired. However, stress can also be caused by a positive situation, such as receiving a large cash bonus.

A person experiencing stress displays certain symptoms indicating that he or she is trying to cope with a stressor (any force creating the stress reaction). These symptoms can include a host of physiological, emotional, and behavioral reactions.

Physiological symptoms of stress include increased heart rate, blood pressure, breathing rate, pupil size, and perspiration. If these physiological symptoms are severe or persist over a prolonged period, the result can be a stress-related disorder, such as a heart attack, hypertension, migraine headache, ulcer, colitis, or allergy. Stress also leads to a chemical imbalance that adversely affects the body's immune system. Thus, the overly stressed person becomes more susceptible to disease and suffers more intensely from existing health problems.

Emotional symptoms of stress include anxiety, tension, depression, discouragement, boredom, prolonged fatigue, feelings of hopelessness, and various kinds of defensive thinking. Behavioral symptoms include nervous habits such as facial twitching, and sudden decreases in job performance due to forgetfulness and errors in concentration or judgment. Increased use of alcohol and other drugs may also occur.

Not all stress is bad. People require the right amount of stress to keep them mentally and physically alert. If the stress is particularly uncomfortable or distasteful, however, it will lower job performance—particularly on complex, demanding jobs. An example of a stressor that will lower job performance for most people is a bullying, abrasive boss who wants to see the employee fail. It is a person's perception of something (or somebody) that usually determines whether it will be a positive or negative stressor. For example, one person might perceive an inspection by top-level managers to be so frightening that he is irritable toward team members. Another manager might welcome the visit as a chance to proudly display her department's high-quality performance.

After prolonged exposure to job stress, a person runs the risk of feeling burned out—a drained, used-up feeling. **Job burnout** is a pattern of emotional, physical, and mental exhaustion in response to chronic job stressors. Cynicism, apathy, and indifference are the major behavioral symptoms of the burned-out worker. Research evidence suggests that supervisors are more at risk for burnout than other workers because they deal so heavily with the demands of other people.[14]

> **job burnout**
> *A pattern of emotional, physical, and mental exhaustion in response to chronic job stressors.*

FACTORS CONTRIBUTING TO STRESS AND BURNOUT

Factors within a person, as well as adverse organizational conditions, can cause or contribute to stress and burnout. Personal life stress and work stress also influence each other. Work stress can create problems—and therefore stress—at home. And stress stemming from personal problems can lead to problems—and therefore stress—at work.

FACTORS WITHIN THE INDIVIDUAL. Hostile, aggressive, and impatient people find ways of turning almost any job into a stressful experience. Such individuals are labeled Type A, in contrast to their more easygoing Type B counterparts. In addition to being angry, the outstanding trait of Type A people is their strong sense of time urgency, known as "hurry sickness." This sense of urgency compels them to achieve more and more in less and less time. Angry, aggressive (usually male) Type A people are more likely than Type Bs to experience cardiovascular disorders. In one study, Type A behavior was measured among 250 police workers and firefighters. A seven-year follow-up indicated that Type A people were more likely to have experienced cardiovascular disorders, including a fatal heart attack.[15]

Recognize, however, that not every hard-driving, impatient person is correctly classified as Type A. Managers who love their work and enjoy other people are not particularly prone to heart disease.

People who have high expectations are likely to experience job burnout at some point in their careers, because there will be times when they do not receive as many rewards as they are seeking. People who need constant excitement are also at high risk of job burnout, because they bore easily and quickly.

ADVERSE ORGANIZATIONAL CONDITIONS. Under ideal conditions, workers experience just enough stress to prompt them to respond creatively and energetically to their jobs. Unfortunately, high stress levels created by adverse organizational conditions lead to many negative symptoms. A major contributor to job stress is work overload. Demands on white-collar workers appear to be at an all-time high, as companies attempt to increase work output and decrease staffing at the same time.

Job frustrations caused by such factors as part shortages, excessive politics, or insufficient funds can create job stress. Extreme conflict with other workers or with management is also a stressor. Having heavy responsibility without the right amount of formal authority upsets many employees. Another annoyance is short lead times—too little notice to get complex assignments accomplished. A powerful stressor today is job insecurity due to the many mergers and downsizings. Worrying about having one's job outsourced to another region, country, or a subcontractor is also a stressor.

> **job demand–job control model**
>
> *A model demonstrating the relationship between high or low job demands and high or low job control. It shows that workers experience the most stress when the demands of the job are high yet they have little control over the activity.*

According to the **job demand–job control model**, workers experience the most stress when the demands of the job are high, yet they have little control over the activity.[16] (See Exhibit 17-4.) A customer service representative with limited authority who has to deal with a major error by the firm would fit this category. In contrast, when job demands are high and the worker has high control, the worker will be energized, motivated, and creative. A branch manager in a successful business might fit this scenario.

Absence of ample positive feedback and other rewards is strongly associated with job burnout. As a consequence of not knowing how well they are doing and not receiving recognition, employees often become discouraged and emotionally exhausted. The result is often—but certainly not always—job burnout.

METHODS OF CONTROL AND ESCAPE

Organizations can play a major role in preventing and remedying stress by correcting the kinds of conditions we have discussed and by offering wellness programs. This chapter, however, emphasizes what individuals can do to deal with stress and burnout. Techniques for managing job stress can be divided into three categories: control, symptom management, and escape.[17]

CONTROL AND REDUCTION OF STRESS. The control techniques described next consist of both actions and mental evaluations that help people "take charge" in stressful situations.

1. *Get social support.* Few people can go it alone when experiencing prolonged stress. Receiving social support—encouragement, understanding, and friendship—from other people is an important strategy for coping successfully with job stress.
2. *Improve your work habits.* You can use the techniques described for improving your personal productivity to reduce stress. People typically experience stress when they feel they are losing or have lost control of their work assignments. Conscientious employees are especially prone to negative stress when they cannot get their work under control.
3. *Develop positive self-talk.* Stress-resistant people are basically optimistic and cheerful. This kind of positivism can be learned by switching to positive self-talk instead of thinking many negative thoughts. (Refer back to the discussion of SuperLeadership in Chapter 11.)

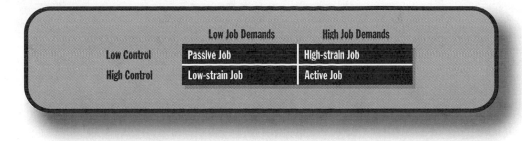

Exhibit 17-4
The Job
Demand–Job
Control Model

4. *Hug the right people.* Hugging is now being seriously regarded as vital for physical and mental well-being. People who do not receive enough quality touching may suffer from low self-esteem, ill health, depression, and loneliness. Conversely, quality touching may help people cope better with job stress. The hugging, however, has to represent loving and caring.

5. *Demand less than perfection from yourself.* By demanding less than 100-percent performance from yourself, you will fail less frequently in your own perceptions. Not measuring up to one's own unrealistically high standards creates a considerable amount of stress. Few humans can operate with zero defects or ever achieve six-sigma perfection!

SYMPTOM MANAGEMENT. This category of stress management refers to tactics that address the symptoms related to job stress. Dozens of symptom-management techniques have been developed, including the following:

1. *Make frequent use of relaxation techniques.* Learning to relax reduces the adverse effects of stress. The **relaxation response** is a general-purpose method of learning to relax by yourself. The key ingredient of this technique is to make yourself quiet and comfortable. At the same time, think of the word *one* (or any simple chant or prayer) with every breath for about 10 minutes. The technique slows you down both physiologically and emotionally. An extremely easy relaxation method is to visualize yourself in an unusually pleasant situation, such as floating on a cloud, walking by a lake, or lying on a comfortable beach. Pick any fantasy that you find relaxing.

2. *Get appropriate physical exercise.* Physical exercise helps dissipate some of the tension created by job stress, and it also helps the body ward off future stress-related disorders. A physically fit, well-rested person can usually tolerate more frustration than can a physically run-down, tired person. One way in which exercise helps combat stress is that it releases endorphins. These are morphine-like chemicals produced in the brain that act as painkillers and antidepressants.

3. *Try to cure hurry sickness.* People with hurry sickness should learn how to relax and enjoy the present for its own sake. Specific tactics include having at least one idle period every day; eating nutritious, not overly seasoned foods to help decrease nervousness; and finding enrichment in an area of life not related to work.

ESCAPE METHODS OF STRESS MANAGEMENT. Escape methods are actions and reappraisals of situations that provide the stressed individual some escape from the stressor. Eliminating the stressor is the most effective escape technique. For example, if a manager is experiencing stress because of serious understaffing in his or her department, that manager should negotiate to receive authorization to hire additional help. Mentally blocking out a stressful thought is another escape technique, but it may not work in the long run.

relaxation response
A general-purpose method of learning to relax by yourself.

SUMMARY OF KEY POINTS

1
Explain why people resist change and know how to gain support for change.

A model of change suggests that the process has three stages: unfreezing attitudes, followed by attitude change, then refreezing by pointing to the success of the change. Employees react to change in various ways, from being very upset to showing active support for the change. People resist change for reasons they think are important, the most common being the fear of an unfavorable outcome.

Seven techniques for gaining support for change are as follows: invest time in planning the change; allow for discussion and negotiation; allow for participation; point out the financial benefits; avoid change overload; gain political support for change; and ask effective questions to involve workers.

2
Identify techniques for improving your personal productivity, including reducing procrastination.

One way of increasing your personal productivity is to improve your work habits and time management skills. To do this, clean up your work area and sort out your tasks, and prepare a "to do" list and assign priorities. Work streamlining, or getting rid of low-value work, is exceptionally important. Also, work at a steady pace, minimize time wasters such as hunting for misplaced files, and concentrate on one task at a time. Do creative and routine tasks at different times, stay in control of paperwork and electronic mail, strive to achieve peak performance, and take power naps. Despite these suggestions, remember to build flexibility into your system.

Avoid procrastinating by understanding why you procrastinate and taking remedial action, such as the following: break the task down into smaller units, make a commitment to others, and counterattack by charging into a distasteful task.

3
Be prepared to manage stress and burnout.

Learn to manage stress and burnout. Stress is the mental and physical condition that results from a perceived threat that cannot be dealt with readily. Job burnout is a pattern of emotional, physical, and mental exhaustion in response to chronic job stressors. Key stress symptoms include tension, anxiety, and poor concentration and judgment. Job stress is caused by factors within the individual, such as Type A behavior, and by adverse organizational conditions. People with high expectations are candidates for burnout. Limited rewards and lack of feedback from the organization contribute to burnout.

Methods of preventing and controlling stress and burnout can be subdivided into three categories: attempts to control stressful situations, symptom management, and escapes from the stressful situation. Specific tactics include eliminating stressors, getting sufficient physical exercise, using relaxation techniques, curing hurry sickness, getting emotional support from others, and improving work habits.

KEY TERMS AND PHRASES

Work Streamlining *pg. 398*
Peak Performance *pg. 400*
Power Nap *pg. 401*
Stress *pg. 402*

Job Burnout *pg. 403*
Job Demand–Job Control Model *pg. 404*
Relaxation Response *pg. 405*

QUESTIONS

1. Can you give an example of how the unfreezing–changing–refreezing model of change has applied to you?
2. How can a manager tell whether an employee is resisting change?
3. Why should a manager bother discussing a change that he or she knows must be implemented no matter what employees think?
4. How can a person be well organized yet unproductive?
5. What can managerial workers do when their time is being drained by dozens of E-mail messages of no importance or interest to them?
6. How can a person use achieving a state of peak performance to reduce stress?
7. How can you apply the job demand–job control model to help you do a better job of managing stress?

SKILL-BUILDING EXERCISE 17-A: THE STRESS QUESTIONNAIRE

Here is a brief questionnaire to give a rough estimate of whether you are facing too much stress. Apply each ques- tion to the last six months of your life. Check the appropriate column.

Mostly Yes	Mostly No	
☐	☐	1. Have you been feeling uncomfortably tense lately?
☐	☐	2. Do you frequently argue with people close to you?
☐	☐	3. Is your romantic life very unsatisfactory?
☐	☐	4. Do you have trouble sleeping?
☐	☐	5. Do you feel lethargic about life?
☐	☐	6. Do many people annoy or irritate you?
☐	☐	7. Do you have constant cravings for candy and other sweets?
☐	☐	8. Is your cigarette consumption way up?
☐	☐	9. Are you becoming addicted to soft drinks, coffee, or tea?
☐	☐	10. Do you find it difficult to concentrate on your work?
☐	☐	11. Do you frequently grind your teeth?
☐	☐	12. Are you increasingly forgetful about little things, such as mailing a letter?
☐	☐	13. Are you increasingly forgetful about big things, such as appointment and major errands?
☐	☐	14. Are you making far too many trips to the lavatory?
☐	☐	15. Have people commented lately that you do not look well?
☐	☐	16. Do you get into verbal fights with others too frequently?
☐	☐	17. Have you been involved in more than one break-up with a friend lately?
☐	☐	18. Do you have more than your share of tension headaches?
☐	☐	19. Do you feel nauseated much too often?
☐	☐	20. Do you feel light-headed or dizzy almost every day?
☐	☐	21. Do you have churning sensations in your stomach far too often?
☐	☐	22. Are you in a big hurry all the time?
☐	☐	23. Are far too many things bothering you these days?

Scoring

0–5 Mostly Yes answers: You seem to be experiencing a normal amount of stress.

6–15 Mostly Yes answers: Your stress level seems high. Become involved in some kind of stress management activity, such as the activities described in this chapter.

16–23 Mostly Yes answers: Your stress level appears to be much too high. Seek the help of a mental health professional or visit your family doctor (or do both).

Source: Andrew J. DuBrin, *Human Relations for Career and Personal Success*, 4e (Englewood Cliffs, NJ: Prentice Hall, 1995) 91. Reprinted by permission of Prentice Hall.

SKILL-BUILDING EXERCISE 17-B: MANAGING MULTIPLE PRIORITIES

Most higher-level workers (and students) often face the challenge of having a "to do" list that is so long that they have difficulty deciding which tasks to tackle first. When this situation occurs, it is easy to become distracted and to neglect important activities or fail to take care of a crisis properly. Learning to manage competing priorities is an essential managerial skill. The five-step system described here will help you assess your priorities and delegate to others where feasible. The system will also help you reorganize your "to do" list and make it a more powerful action tool.

Step 1: Make a complete list of every task facing you. Forget about the order of importance for now, just write down everything you are supposed to do. Include recurring items as well as special projects. Allow space beside each item for notes.

Step 2: Rate each activity according to importance using the scale below. For each task, ask yourself, "What would be the consequences if I didn't do this?" Recognize that not everything on your list is critical to your success or that of the company.

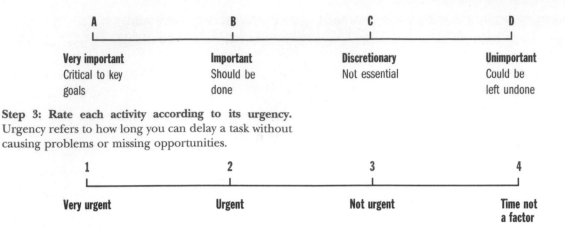

Step 3: Rate each activity according to its urgency. Urgency refers to how long you can delay a task without causing problems or missing opportunities.

Step 4: Evaluate the delegation potential of each activity. If you are a manager with subordinates, figure out which tasks can be delegated. If you are not a manager, you can still inquire about having some of your tasks assigned to someone else in the department with more discretionary time. Off the job, it may be possible for you to hand over a few tasks to family members or friends.

Step 5: Prioritize your activities. Each task on your list has an importance letter and an urgency number. You have also identified items that can be or have been assigned to somebody else. Move the delegated or as-

signed tasks to a separate follow-up list. Now rearrange your list in alphanumeric order such as A1, A2, B1, B2, B3, C3, C4, and so forth. Important items should be taken care of before less important or less urgent tasks. Several items may have the same designation, such as three B2s. In this case, reevaluate those items to determined their respective priorities. You now have a weighted "to do" list that will help keep you focused on your most important and urgent tasks.

Source: Modified from Lester Bittel, *Right on Time! The Complete Guide for Time Pressured Managers* (New York: McGraw-Hill, 1991).

REFERENCES

1. Christoper J. Bachler, "Workers Take Leave of Job Stress," *Personnel Journal* (January 1995): 40.
2. Marcia Kleinman, "Ease the Stress of Change," *Personnel Journal* (September 1989): 107.
3. Kurt Lewin, *Field Theory and Social Science* (New York: Harper & Brothers, 1951).
4. Harry Woodward and Steve Bucholtz, *Aftershock: Helping People Through Corporate Change* (New York: Wiley, 1987).
5. Jon L. Pierce and Randall B. Dunham, *Managing* (Glenview, IL: Scott, Foresman/Little Brown, 1990): 428.
6. James A. F. Stoner and R. Edward Freeman, *Management*, 4th ed. (Englewood Cliffs, NJ: Prentice Hall, 1989): 369.
7. H. James Harrington, *Business Process Improvement: The Breakthrough Strategy for Total Quality, Productivity, and Competitiveness* (New York: McGraw-Hill, 1991).
8. Ed Oakley and Doug Krug, *Enlightened Leadership* (New York: Simon & Schuster, 1993).
9. "How to Control Your Time," *Supervisory Management* (July 1994): 7.
10. Ingrid Lorch-Bacci, "Achieving Peak Performance: The Hidden Dimension," *Executive Management Forum* (January 1991): 1–4.
11. Donald J. McNerney, "Napping at Work: You Snooze, You Win!" *HRfocus* (March 1995): 3.
12. Kenneth Labic, "Take Control of Your Career," *Fortune* (18 November 1991).
13. Michael Maren, "Program Yourself: Software for the Right Side of Your Brain," *Success* (October 1991): 58.
14. Cynthia L. Cordes and Thomas W. Dougherty, "A Review and an Intergration of Research on Job Burnout," *Academy of Management Review* (October 1993): 644.
15. John Schaubroeck, Daniel C. Ganster, and Barbara E. Kemmer, "Job Complexity, 'Type A' Behavior, and Cardiovascular Disorder: A Prospective Study," *Academy of Management Journal* (April 1994): 426–439.
16. Marilyn L. Fox, Deborah J. Dwyer, and Daniel C. Ganster, "Effects of Stressful Job Demands and Control on Physiological and Attitudinal Outcomes in a Hospital Setting," *Academy of Management Journal* (April 1993): 290–292.
17. Janina C. Latack, "Coping with Job Stress: Measures and Future Directions for Scale Development," *Journal of Applied Psychology* (August 1986): 522–526.

Achievement motivation Finding joy in accomplishment for its own sake.

Action plan The specific steps necessary to achieve a goal or objective.

Active listening Listening for full meaning, without making premature judgments or interpretations.

Activity In the PERT method, the physical and mental effort required to complete an event.

Affiliation need A desire to have close relationships with others and be a loyal employee or friend.

Affinity group An employee-involvement group composed of professional-level workers who meet regularly to share information, capture opportunities, and solve problems affecting the work group and the larger organization.

Affirmative action An employment practice that complies with anti-discrimination law *and* correcting past discriminatory practices.

Authority The formal right to get people to do things or the formal right to control resources.

Autocratic leader A task-oriented leader who retains most of the authority for himself or herself and is not generally concerned with group members' attitudes toward decisions.

Balance of trade The difference between exports and imports in both goods and services.

Behavior In performance appraisal, what people actually do on the job.

Behavior mismatch A condition that occurs when one person's actions do not meet another's expectations.

Behavior modification A way of changing behavior by rewarding the right responses and punishing or ignoring the wrong responses.

Behavioral school of management The approach to studying management that emphasizes improving management through understanding the psychological makeup of people.

Benchmarking The process of comparing a firm's quality performance to that achieved by a competing firm.

Bounded rationality The observation that people's limited mental abilities, combined with external influences over which they have little or no control, prevent them from making entirely rational decisions.

GLOSSARY

Brainstorming A group method of solving problems, gathering information, and stimulating creative thinking. The basic technique is to generate numerous ideas through unrestrained and spontaneous participation by group members.

Break-even analysis A method of determining the relationship between total costs and total revenues at various levels of production or sales activity.

Broadbanding In salary administration, basing pay more on the person than the position, thus reducing the number of pay grades.

Budget A spending plan expressed in numerical terms for a future period of time.

Bureaucracy A rational, systematic, and precise form of organization in which rules, regulations, and techniques of control are precisely defined.

Capital-expenditure budget A plan for spending money on assets used to produce goods or services.

Cash budget A forecast of cash receipts and payments.

Cause-and-effect analysis A graphical technique for analyzing the factors that contribute to a problem. It relies on an Ishikawa, or fishbone, diagram.

Centralization The extent to which authority is retained at the top of the organization.

Classical school of management The original formal approach to studying management. This school of thought searches for solid principles and concepts that can be used to manage people and work productively.

Coaching   A method for helping employees perform better that usually occurs on the spot and involves informal discussion and suggestions.

Coalition   A specific arrangement of parties working together to combine their power, thus exerting influence on another individual or group.

Coercive power   A leader's control over punishments.

Communication   The process of exchanging information by the use of words, letters, symbols, or nonverbal behavior.

Communication network   A pattern or flow of messages that traces the communication from start to finish.

Compressed work week   A full-time work schedule that allows 40 hours in less than five days.

Computer-based training   A learning experience based on the interaction between the trainee and a computer.

Computer goof-off   A person who spends so much time attempting new computer routines and accessing information of questionable value that he or she neglects key aspects of the job.

Concurrent control   A type of control that monitors activities while they are being carried out.

Conditional value   In a payoff matrix, the possible payoff of pursuing an alternative solution to a problem under a particular level of demand.

Conflict   The simultaneous arousal of two or more incompatible motives.

Conflict of interest   A situation that occurs when one's judgment or objectivity is compromised.

Confrontation   Dealing with a controversial or emotional topic directly.

Constructive criticism   A form of criticism designed to help improve performance or behavior.

Contingency approach to management   A perspective on management that emphasizes that there is no one best way to manage people or work. It encourages managers to study individual and situational differences before deciding on a course of action.

Contingency plan   An alternative plan to be used if the original plan cannot be implemented or a crisis develops.

Contingent workers   Part-time or temporary employees who are not members of the employer's permanent work force.

Corporate social performance   The extent to which a firm responds to the demands of its stakeholders for behaving in a socially responsible manner.

Corrective discipline   A type of discipline that allows employees to correct their behavior before punishment is applied.

Creativity   The process of developing novel ideas that can be put into action.

Critical path   The path through the PERT network that includes the most time-consuming sequence of events and activities.

Cultural sensitivity   Awareness of local and national customs and their importance in effective interpersonal relationships.

Culture shock   A group of physical and psychological symptoms that can develop when a person is abruptly placed in a foreign culture.

Cumulative trauma disorder   Injuries caused by repetitive motions over prolonged periods of time.

Customer departmentalization   An organization structure based on customer needs.

Cycle time   The interval between the ordering and delivery of a product or service.

Decentralization   The extent to which authority is passed down to lower levels in an organization.

Decision   A choice among alternatives.

Decision-making software   Any computer program that helps a decision maker work through problem-solving and decision-making steps.

Decision tree   A graphic illustration of the alternative solutions available to solve a problem.

Decisiveness   The extent to which a person makes up his or her mind promptly and prudently.

Decoding   The communication stage in which the receiver interprets the message and translates it into meaningful information.

Defensive communication The tendency to receive messages in a way that protects self esteem.

Deficiency needs Lower-order needs that must be satisfied to ensure a person's existence, security, and requirements for human contact.

Delegation Assigning formal authority and responsibility for accomplishing a specific task to another person.

Departmentalization The process of subdividing work into departments.

Development A form of personal improvement that usually consists of enhancing knowledge and skills of a complex and unstructured nature.

Deviation In a control system, the size of the discrepancy between performance standards and actual results.

Difficult person An individual whose personal characteristics disturb other people.

Disability A physical or mental condition that substantially limits an individual's major life activities.

Discipline Punishment used to correct or train.

Downsizing The slimming down of operations to focus resources and boost profits or decrease expenses.

Due process In relation to employee rights, giving a worker a fair hearing before he or she is dismissed.

Economic-order quantity (EOQ) The inventory level that minimizes both administrative costs and carrying costs.

Employee assistance program (EAP) An activity to help employees deal with personal and job-related problems that interfere with their job performance.

Employee benefit Any noncash payment given to workers as a condition of their employment.

Employee orientation program A formal activity designed to acquaint new employees with the organization.

Empowerment The process by which managers share power with group members thereby enhancing the employee's feelings of personal effectiveness.

Encoding The process of organizing ideas into a series of symbols designed to communicate with the receiver.

Entrepreneur A person who founds and operates an innovative business.

Ethically centered management An approach to management that emphasizes that the high quality of an end product takes precedence over its scheduled completion.

Ethics The study of moral obligation, or separating right from wrong.

Event In the PERT method, a point of decision or the accomplishment of a task.

Expectancy theory of motivation An explanation of motivation that states that people will expend effort if they expect the effort to lead to performance and the performance to lead to a reward.

Expected value The average value incurred if a particular decision is made a large number of times.

Expected time The time that will be used on the PERT diagram as the needed period for the completion of an activity.

Expert power The ability to influence others derived from a leader's job-related knowledge as perceived by group members.

External control strategy An approach to control based on the belief that employees are motivated primarily by external rewards and need to be controlled by their managers.

Feedback control A control that evaluates an activity after it has been performed.

Feedforward control A control that takes place prior to the performance of an activity.

Filtering Coloring and altering information to make it more acceptable to the receiver.

First-level managers Managers who supervise operatives (also known as first-line managers or supervisors).

Flat organization structure A form of organization with relatively few layers.

Flexible benefit package A benefit plan that allows employees to select a group of benefits tailored to their preferences.

Flexible working hours A system of working hours wherein employees must work certain core hours but can choose their arrival and departure times.

Formal communication channels The official pathways for sending information inside and outside an organization.

Formal group A group deliberately formed by the organization to accomplish specific tasks and achieve goals.

Free-rein leader A leader who turns over virtually all authority and control to the group.

Functional departmentalization An arrangement in which departments are defined by the function each one performs, such as accounting or purchasing.

Gainsharing A formal program allowing employees to participate financially in the productivity gains they have achieved.

Gantt chart A chart that depicts the planned and actual progress of work during the life of a project.

General environmental force A force that influences the organization's goals, strategies, and tasks in a general way.

Global startup A small firm that comes into existence by serving an international market.

Grapevine The informal means by which information is transmitted in organizations.

Gross profit margin A financial ratio expressed as the difference between sales and the cost of goods sold, divided by sales.

Group A collection of people who interact with each other, are working toward some common purpose, and perceive themselves to be a group.

Group decision The process of several people contributing to a final decision.

Group polarization A situation in which post-discussion attitudes tend to be more extreme than pre-discussion attitudes.

Groupthink A psychological drive for consensus at any cost.

Growth needs Higher-order needs that are concerned with personal development and reaching one's potential.

Horizontal organization The arrangement of work by teams that are responsible for accomplishing a process.

Hoshin planning A disciplined management system to accomplish strategic priorities.

Human resources budget A schedule that identifies the human resource needs for a future period and the labor costs to meet those needs.

Improvement goal A goal, that if attained, will correct unacceptable deviation from a performance standard.

Ineffective job performance Job performance that lowers productivity below an acceptable standard.

Informal communication channel An unofficial network that supplements the formal channels in an organization.

Informal group A group that emerges over time through the interaction of workers.

Information overload (or **Communication overload**) A condition in which an individual receives so much information that he or she becomes overwhelmed.

Information superhighway The combination of computer, telecommunications, and video technologies for the purpose of disseminating and acquiring information.

Information system (or **Management information system**) A formal system for providing management with information useful or necessary for making decisions.

Informative confrontation A technique of inquiring about discrepancies, conflicts, and mixed messages.

Internal control strategy An approach to control based on the belief that employees can be motivated by building their commitment to organizational goals.

Intuition An experience-based way of knowing or reasoning in which weighing and balancing evidence are done unconsciously and automatically.

ISO 9000 A series of management and quality-assurance standards developed for firms competing in international markets.

Job burnout A pattern of emotional, physical, and mental exhaustion in response to chronic job stressors.

Job characteristics model A method of job enrichment that focuses on the task and personal dimensions of a job.

Job demand–job control model A model demonstrating the relationship between high or low job demands and high or low job control. It shows that workers experience the most stress when the demands of the job are high yet they have little control over the activity.

Job description A written statement of the key features of a job, along with the activities required to perform it effectively.

Job design The process of laying out job responsibilities and duties and describing how they are to be performed.

Job enlargement Increasing the number and variety of tasks within a job.

Job enrichment An approach to making jobs involve more challenge and responsibility, so they will be more appealing to most employees.

Job involvement The degree to which individuals are identified psychologically with their work.

Job rotation A temporary switching of job assignments.

Job sharing A work arrangement in which two people who work part-time share one job.

Job specialization The degree to which a job holder performs only a limited number of tasks.

Job specification A statement of the personal characteristics needed to perform the job.

Judgmental forecast A qualitative forecasting method based on a collection of subjective opinions.

Just-in-time (JIT) inventory control A system to minimize inventory and move it into the plant exactly when needed.

Lateral thinking A thinking process that spreads out to find many different alternative solutions to a problem.

Law of effect The underlying principle of behavior modification stating that behavior leading to positive consequences tends to be repeated and that behavior leading to negative consequences tends not to be repeated.

Leadership The ability to inspire confidence and support among the people who are needed to achieve organizational goals.

Leadership Grid® A visual representation of different combinations of a leader's degree of concern for task-related issues.

Leadership style The typical pattern of behavior that a leader uses to influence his or her employees to achieve organizational goals.

Learning organization An organization that is skilled at creating, acquiring, and transferring knowledge.

Legitimate power The authentic right of a leader to make certain types of requests.

Linear regression A quantitative method of predicting the relationship of changes in one variable to changes in another.

Management The process of using organizational resources to achieve organizational objectives through planning, organizing and staffing, leading, and controlling.

Management by objectives (MBO) A systematic application of goal setting and planning to help individuals and firms be more productive.

Management science (or Decision sciences) The field of study dealing with quantified planning and decision making.

Management-science school The school of management thought that concentrates on providing management with a scientific basis for solving problems and making decisions.

Manager A person responsible for the work performance of group members.

Maquiladora A manufacturing plant close to the U.S. border that is established specifically to assemble American products.

Maslow's need hierarchy The motivation theory that arranges human needs into a pyramid-shaped model with basic physiological needs at the bottom and self-actualizing needs at the top.

Master budget A budget consolidated from the budgets of various units.

Materials purchase/usage budget A plan that identifies the raw materials and parts that must be purchased to meet production demands.

Materials-requirement planning (MRP) A computerized manufacturing and inventory-control system designed to ensure that materials handling and inventory control are efficient.

Matrix organization A project structure superimposed on top of a functional structure.

Micromanagement Supervising group members too closely and second-guessing their decisions.

Middle-level managers Managers who are neither executives nor first-level supervisors, but who serve as a link between the two groups.

Milestone chart An extension of the Gantt chart that provides a listing of the subactivities that must be completed to accomplish the major activities listed on the vertical axis.

Mission A statement of the firms's purpose and where it fits into the world.

Modified work schedule Any formal departure from the traditional hours of work, excluding shift work and staggered work hours.

Moment of truth A situation in which a customer comes in contact with the company and forms an impression of its service.

Moral intensity The magnitude of an unethical act.

Moral laxity A slippage in moral behavior because other issues seem more important at the time.

Motivation The expenditure of effort to accomplish results.

Multiculturalism The ability to work effectively and conduct business with people from different cultures.

Multinational corporation (MNC) A firm with units in two or more countries in addition to its own.

Need A deficit within an individual, such as a craving for water or affection.

Network The linking by computer of workers throughout the organization with each other.

Network structure (or **Virtual corporation**) A temporary association of otherwise independent firms linked by technology to share expenses, employee talents, and access to each other's markets.

Noise In communication, unwanted interference that can distort or block a message.

Nominal-group technique (NGT) A group decision-making technique that follows a highly structured format.

Nonprogrammed decision A decision that is difficult because of its complexity and the fact that the person faces it infrequently.

Nonverbal communication The transmission of messages by means other than words.

Operating plans The means through which strategic plans alter the destiny of the firm.

Operational planning Establishing plans that relate to running the firm on a day-to-day, short-term basis.

Organizational culture (or **Corporate culture**) The system of shared values and beliefs that actively influence the behavior of organization members.

Organizational design The process of creating a structure that best fits a purpose, strategy, and environment.

Organization structure The arrangement of people and tasks to accomplish organizational goals.

$P = M \times A$ An expression of the relationship between motivation and performance, where P refers to performance, M to motivation, and A to ability.

Paradigm The perspectives and ways of doing things that are typical of a given context.

Pareto diagram A bar graph that ranks types of output variations by frequency of occurrence.

Participative leader A leader who shares decision making with group members.

Payoff matrix A technique for indicating possible payoffs, or returns, from pursuing different alternatives.

Peak performance A mental state in which maximum results are achieved with minimum effort.

Performance appraisal A formal system for measuring, evaluating, and reviewing performance.

Pet-peeve technique A creativity-training (or problem-solving) exercise in which the group thinks up as many complaints as possible about every facet of the department.

Polarized workplace A workplace in which there are more high-paying and low-paying than moderate-paying jobs.

Policies General guidelines to follow in making decisions and taking action.

Power The ability or potential to influence decisions and control resources.

Power motivation A strong desire to control others or get them to do things on your behalf.

Power nap A brief period of sleep of about 15 to 30 minutes designed to recharge the individual.

Problem A discrepancy between ideal and actual conditions.

Procedures A customary method for handling an activity. It guides action rather than thinking.

Procrastinate To delay in taking action without a valid reason.

Production budget A detailed plan that identifies the products or services that must be produced to match the sales forecast and inventory requirements.

Product-service departmentalization The arrangement of departments according to the products or services they provide.

Profit margin A financial ratio measuring return on sales, or net income divided by sales.

Program and review technique (PERT) A network model used to track the planning activities required to complete a large-scale, nonrepetitive project. It depicts all the interrelated events that must take place.

Programmed decision A decision that is repetitive, or routine, and made according to a specific procedure.

Progressive discipline The step-by-step application of corrective discipline.

Project organization A temporary group of specialists working under one manager to accomplish a fixed objective.

Qualitative control technique A method of controlling based on human judgments about performance that result in a verbal rather than numerical evaluation.

Quality The totality of features and characteristics of a product or service that bears on its ability to satisfy given needs.

Quality circle A small group of employees who perform similar work and who meet regularly to identify, solve, and sometimes implement solutions to work-related problems.

Quality control Any method of determining the extent to which goods or services match some specified quality standard.

Quantitative control technique A method of controlling based on numerical measures of performance.

Readiness In situational leadership, the extent to which a group member has the ability and willingness or confidence to accomplish a specific task.

Recognition need The desire to be acknowledged for one's contributions and efforts and to feel important.

Recruitment The process of attracting job candidates with the right characteristics and skills to fill job openings.

Reengineering The radical redesign of business processes to achieve substantial improvements in performance.

Reference check An inquiry to a second party about a job candidate's suitability for employment.

Referent power The ability to influence others derived from followers' desire to identify with their leaders and be accepted by them.

Relationship behavior The extent to which the leader engages in two-way or multi-way communication.

Relaxation response A general-purpose method of learning to relax by yourself.

Results In performance appraisal, what people accomplish, or the objectives they attain.

Return on equity A financial ratio of how much a firm is earning on its investment expressed as net income divided by owner's equity.

Revenue-and-expense budget A document that describes plans for revenues and operating expenses in dollar amounts.

Reverse discrimination The situation in which members of a majority group are denied access to jobs or promotion.

Reward power A leader's control over rewards of value to the group members.

Robust quality The concept of designing a part or process so well that it can withstand fluctuations on the production line without a loss of quality.

Role An expected set of activities or behaviors stemming from a job.

Rule A specific course of action or conduct that must be followed. It is the simplest type of plan.

Satisficing decision A decision that meets the minimum standards of satisfaction.

Situational leadership model An explanation of leadership that explains how to match leadership style to the readiness of group members.

Small-business owner An individual who owns and operates a small business.

Social leave of absence An employee benefit that gives select employees time away from the job to perform a significant public service.

Social loafing Freeloading or shirking individual responsibility, when a person is placed in a group setting and removed from individual accountability.

Social responsibility The idea that firms have obligations to society beyond their obligations to owners or stockholders and also beyond those prescribed by law or contract.

Span of control The number of workers reporting directly to a manager.

Specific environmental force A force that influences the firm in a regular and specific way.

Stakeholder viewpoint The viewpoint on social responsibility contending that firms must hold themselves responsible for the quality of life of the many groups affected by the firm's actions.

Standard A unit of measurement used to evaluate results.

States of nature Circumstances beyond the control of the decision maker.

Statistical process control A technique for spotting defects during production that utilizes graphical displays for analyzing deviations.

Stockholder viewpoint The traditional perspective on social responsibility that a business organization is responsible only to its owners and stockholders.

Strategic human resources planning The process of anticipating and providing for the movement of people into, within, and out of an organization to support the firm's business strategy.

Strategic planning Establishing master plans that shape the destiny of the firm.

Strategy The organization's plan, or comprehensive program, for achieving its mission and goals in its environment.

Stress The mental and physical condition that results from a perceived threat that cannot be dealt with readily.

Subordinate power Any type of power that employees can exert upward in an organization.

Suggestion program A formal method for collecting and analyzing employees' suggestions about processes, policies, products, and services.

Summary discipline The immediate discharge of an employee because of a serious offense.

SuperLeader A person who leads others to lead themselves.

SWOT analysis A method of considering the strengths, weaknesses, opportunities, and threats in a given situation.

Systems approach A perspective on management problems based on the concept that the organization is a system, or an entity of interrelated parts.

Task behavior The extent to which the leader spells out the duties and responsibilities of an individual or group.

Team A special type of group in which members have complementary skills and are committed to a common purpose, a set of performance goals, and an approach to the task.

Team leader A manager who coordinates the work of a small group of people, while acting as a facilitator and catalyst.

Teamwork The situation in which there is understanding and commitment to group goals on the part of all team members.

Technology The systematic application of scientific or other organized knowledge to practical tasks.

Telecommuting An arrangement in which employees use computers to perform their regular work duties at home or in a satellite location.

Termination The process of firing an employee because of poor job performance, unacceptable behavior, or interpersonal problems.

Territorial departmentalization An arrangement of departments according to the geographic area served.

360-degree appraisal A performance appraisal in which a person is evaluated by a sampling of all the people with whom he or she interacts.

Time-series analysis An analysis of a sequence of observations that have taken place at regular intervals over a period of time (hourly, weekly, monthly, and so forth).

Top-level managers Managers at the top one or two levels in the organization.

Total quality management A management system for improving performance throughout a firm by maximizing customer satisfaction and making continuous improvements.

Tough question A question that helps the group achieve insight into the nature of a problem, what it might be doing better, and whether progress is sufficient.

Training Any procedure intended to foster and enhance learning among employees, particularly directed at acquiring job skills.

Traits Stable aspects of people, closely related to personality.

Transformational leader A leader who helps organizations and people make positive changes in the way they do things.

Two-factor theory of work motivation The theory contending that there are two different sets of job factors. One set can satisfy and motivate people, and the other set can only prevent dissatisfaction.

Unity of command The classical management principle stating that each subordinate receives assigned duties from one superior only and is accountable to that superior.

Valuing-differences training A form of training that attempts to bring about workplace harmony by teaching people how to get along better with diverse work associates.

Vertical thinking An analytical, logical process that results in few answers.

Virtual office An arrangement whereby employees work together as if they were part of a single office despite being physically separated.

Whistle blower An employee who discloses organizational wrongdoing to parties who can take action.

Work streamlining Eliminating as much low-value work as possible and concentrating on activities that add value for customers or clients.

Work team A group of employees responsible for an entire work process or segment that delivers a product or service to an internal or external customer.

Wrongful discharge The firing of an employee for arbitrary or unfair reasons.

Zero defections Keeping every customer a company can profitably serve.

Zero defects The absence of any detectable quality flaws in a product or service.

Zone of indifference The psychological zone that encompasses acceptable behaviors toward which employees feel indifferent (do not mind following).

INDEX